RED ELLEN

Red Ellen

THE LIFE OF ELLEN WILKINSON, SOCIALIST, FEMINIST, INTERNATIONALIST

Laura Beers

Harvard University Press   Cambridge, Massachusetts · London, England   2016

Second printing

Library of Congress Cataloging-in-Publication Data

Names: Beers, Laura, 1978– author.

Title: Red Ellen : the life of Ellen Wilkinson, socialist, feminist,
    internationalist / Laura Beers.

Description: Cambridge, Massachusetts : Harvard University Press,
    2016. |

Includes bibliographical references and index.

Identifiers: LCCN 2016012438 | ISBN 9780674971523 (alk. paper)

Subjects: LCSH: Wilkinson, Ellen Cicely, 1891-1947. |
    Stateswomen—Great Britain—Biography. | Statesmen—Great
    Britain—Biography. | Feminism—Great Britain—History—20th
    century. | Internationalists—Great Britain—Biography. |
    Communist Party of Great Britain—History. | Labour Party
    (Great Britain)—History.

Classification: LCC DA566.9.W459 B44 2016 | DDC 328.41092—dc23
    LC record available at http://lccn.loc.gov/2016012438

For Gabriel, my angel

CONTENTS

RED ELLEN

INTRODUCTION

Born to a working-class family in south Manchester, Ellen Wilkinson had not left the northwest of England by the time she won a scholarship to the University of Manchester in 1910. In the thirty-five years that followed, she helped found the British Communist Party and met Russian revolutionaries Vladimir Lenin and Leon Trotsky in Moscow. She was the tenth woman to gain a seat in parliament and became a renowned advocate for the poor and dispossessed at home and abroad. She travelled across Europe, America, and Asia in pursuit of international peace; went to San Francisco as one of the few female delegates to the inaugural meeting of the United Nations; and returned to Britain to play a central role in the postwar government. Along the way, she forged a remarkable series of friendships—she was on intimate terms with the leaders of the Indian Congress Party, the German anti-fascist resistance, and the Spanish Republican government; spent a Christmas with Nobel Peace Prize winner Jane Addams; and had a tempestuous, if mutually admiring, relationship with Winston Churchill. In an era when several of her female parliamentary colleagues—including Lady Nancy Astor and Lady Cynthia Mosley—entered parliament on their husbands' coattails, Wilkinson was a self-made woman, although her repeated affairs with male colleagues inspired rumours of favouritism.

Red Ellen tells the story of Ellen Wilkinson's remarkable life, but it also offers a portrait of a period in British and international history when men and women from an unprecedented range of backgrounds were lured onto the political stage by the desire to reshape domestic, imperial, and international affairs. Ellen's younger brother Harold destroyed her personal papers in a huge bonfire following his sister's death, a decision likely provoked by the desire to protect her unorthodox personal life from public scrutiny.[1] The following history thus relies heavily on the records of Ellen's involvement in a wide range of party political, industrial, and activist organizations, as well as on her surviving correspondence and prolific journalistic record. Although the absence of her papers necessarily leaves aspects of her life shrouded in mystery, the limitation forced me to look outward and write a book that became as much a story of the networks through which Ellen moved during her brief but intense career as a story of the woman herself.

The first decades of the twentieth century witnessed almost limitless optimism about the potential to remake a brave new world. Feminist reformers brought a new set of (often conflicting) ideas about the relationship between men and women in the social and political spheres. Communists, Socialists, Nazis, and Fascists sought to reshape their countries' domestic and foreign policies. And committed democrats and pacifists found themselves forced to grapple with the question of political violence in an increasingly polarized world. In recent years, scholars have shed substantial light on the transnational communities of men and women committed to creating a new and better future in the decades after the First World War.[2] Yet there is still much we do not know, especially about the work of the non-Communist, radical left.

Ellen Wilkinson was more active in her pursuit of social change than were most men and women of her era, but she was only one of many radical Britons who sought to transform not only British but also international society. Amongst this generation of activists, Wilkinson is exceptional for the sheer breadth of her participation in both domestic and international affairs. Short of the League of Nations Union, which she dismissed as misguided and bourgeois, there seems to have been no major progressive organization with which she was not involved in the interwar decades. She was an inveterate leaguer—from the Plebs League to the Women's International League for Peace and Freedom to the League Against Imperialism to the India League. Like Zelig, she pops up everywhere. Her sheer ubiquity marks her out from her peers, as does her later promotion to the rank of cabinet minister in the postwar Labour government. But her exceptionalism serves to highlight the scope of opportunity within the interwar radical left.

No two activists follow an identical path to political consciousness, and the pursuit of social justice means different things to different people. Still, by focusing on one woman's political work, *Red Ellen* seeks to shed broader light on the culture of interwar radicalism in Britain and internationally. In so doing, it reframes our understanding of the British left in this period, highlighting the extent to which many British radicals viewed themselves as members of an international socialist community, despite the exceptionalism of British Labour's political development. The international networks forged by radical men and women are crucial for understanding their approach to colonial and foreign policy. Their analysis of international affairs, in turn, impacted how they approached their own domestic political challenges. As today's Labour Party struggles to come to terms with its relationship to political radicalism, *Red Ellen* raises important questions about both the history and the future direction of the British left.

For many readers, the emphasis on Wilkinson's international activism will come as a surprise. Nearly seventy years after her death, Ellen Wilkinson is best remembered not for her fight against war and fascism, but for her role as a leader of the 1936 Jarrow Crusade, the 300-mile march of 200 unemployed shipwrights and steelworkers from the Tyneside to London to petition the government for assistance for their blighted community. Ellen was the town's MP; and although the march was not her brainchild, she gave her time and energy to planning and publicizing the event and marched alongside the men for much of the route. She famously burst into tears as she presented the men's case at the bar of the House of Commons, overwhelmed by her colleagues' indifference to Jarrow's plight. At the time, the Labour Party and the Trade Union Congress sought to distance themselves from the Crusade and the rebellious, redheaded MP who made the men's cause her own, afraid the Crusaders were under Communist influence. Yet less than fifteen years later, the Labour Party had embraced the Jarrow Crusade as its own. Had she lived to see the 1950 general election campaign, Ellen would have appreciated the irony that many of the same men and women who refused to support the Crusaders in 1936 now campaigned beneath posters of the Crusade emblazoned with the caption "Remember Unemployment? Don't give the Tories another chance. Vote Labour." It was a lesson better learned late than never.

The Jarrow Crusade was a crucial moment in Ellen's political career, but it was only one piece of her larger project to remake both British and international society in a more just image. At the same time she was helping to plan the march, she was deeply involved in the campaign to gain official recognition for the Spanish Republican government in its war against Franco's insurgents. She was also coordinating Jawaharlal Nehru's visit to Britain to plead the case for Indian self-government, and working with Jewish refugee organizations to raise funds to smuggle men and women out of Germany. Between days spent marching with the Crusaders, she argued the case against fascism on the floor of the House of Commons and on public platforms before both general audiences and the feminist groups to whom she had for years championed the cause of women's rights.

For Ellen, as for others of her generation and outlook, the ways in which she understood both domestic and international affairs were intimately interwoven. She brought a Marxist economic analysis into her understanding of both continental fascism and British imperialism; and, in turn, her appreciation of Britain's role in international affairs affected her analysis of domestic politics. Her feminism was imbricated by class analysis that affected the way she perceived the status of women both at home and abroad. To Ellen, the campaign against mass unemployment in Britain was linked to the movements against fascism and colonialism and the campaign for women's rights in that each was a crucial front in the war against injustice and human suffering.

In 1940, when Ellen was appointed parliamentary secretary to the minister of pensions in Churchill's wartime coalition government, *Picture Post* ran a three-page profile by her longtime friend the *New Statesman* editor Kingsley Martin. One photo caption read: "She has always been open to new ideas, persistent in promoting those in which she believes. Her new job gives scope to her passionate desire for social justice." After Ellen's death on February 6, 1947, the *Manchester Guardian* noted that the woman who ended her career as Minister of Education had "brought to public affairs an acute mind, an ebullient spirit, and—the dominant thing in her—a passion for social justice, an intuitive and devoted partisanship for the poor and the weak." Looking back on Ellen's career, historian Kenneth O. Morgan would write, "She remained unique as a voice for social justice in her generation."[3]

What follows is a portrait of how Ellen Wilkinson developed her understanding of what social justice meant in the first half of the twentieth century and how she devoted her life to achieving a more socially just world. The defeat of European fascism, the formal end of colonialism, and the introduction of state welfare programs across the Western world brought an end to many of the evils she fought against. Yet, a century after Ellen began her political career, we are still confronted with a world beset by poverty, economic inequality, and human suffering and tyrannized by dictatorial political regimes. Red Ellen's life story is as much an inspiration for activism today as it is a history of an increasingly distant radical past.

1

THE ONLY GIRL WHO TALKS IN SCHOOL DEBATES

As a child, Ellen Wilkinson had a knack for winning at neighbourhood games. Her quick wit was especially suited to the card game Proverbs, in which one assembled words on individual cards into a proverb, such as "The early bird gets the worm" or "God helps those who help themselves." Proverbs was considered an acceptable game for the children of staunch Methodists, as the focus was not on gambling but on recalling character-building catchphrases. The Wilkinsons were not "ravening nonconformists"; but they did their best to bring the children up in a quiet Wesleyan atmosphere, an effort Ellen, in retrospect, "count[ed] not least among the advantages life has given me."[1]

On October 8, 1891, Ellen Cicely, the third of four Wilkinson children, was born at home to Richard and Ellen. Baby Nellie, with her "enormous, arresting, vivid" brown eyes, wasn't a notably small infant.[2] It was only later that she was overtaken by her peers, topping out at less than five feet tall. Her older sister, Anne, was ten when Ellen was born and from the beginning helped to look after her. Her older brother, Richard Arthur, was eight. Ellen's father was temporarily unemployed at her birth, and her mother could not afford proper attendance by a midwife.[3] She suffered complications from the labour that left her in considerable pain for the rest of her life but nonetheless went on to bear one more child, Harold, who arrived when Ellen was nearly eight.

Ellen was a native Mancunian; and Manchester, in the final years of Queen Victoria's reign, had become one of the great cities of the British Empire. The city's grand gothic town hall, facing Albert Square, was completed in 1877. Its imposing edifice served as a testament to the power of the Manchester City Council. Amongst the largest monuments to Manchester's social and cultural significance was the Free Trade Hall, completed in 1856 and named in honour of the free-trade campaign of the 1830s and 1840s, in which Mancunian manufacturer and Liberal statesman Richard Cobden played a leading role. The building, with its ornate Italianate façade, quickly became a popular site for mass political meetings as Lancashire became a focal point in the Liberals' campaign to regain control of parliament from the Conservatives. By Ellen's adolescence, the hall played regular host not only to leaders of the Conservative and Liberal parties but to socialist politicians and feminist activists, in a city that was to become a centre of national campaigns for political reform.

The Wilkinson clan doubtless felt pride in their city's national and international stature, but their own life was worlds away from the majesty of Albert Square and Peter Street. Ellen's family lived a cramped, unexceptional existence in a series of terraced houses in Chorlton-on-Medlock, Ardwick, a working-class neighbourhood south of the river Medlock. The area just north of the river had been memorialized by Friedrich Engels in 1845 as the site of Little Ireland. In that wretched immigrant community, men, women, children, and old folk lived in overly close quarters in "ruinous cottages" surrounded by "measureless filth and stench." At the time of Engels's writing, the area south of the Medlock was more socially mixed.[4] Yet the proximity to such desperate poverty quickly pushed the middle classes out of Chorlton. By the time of

Ellen's birth, Chorlton was predominantly working-class and contained large sections of slum housing. A 1904 survey pronounced, "In no part of town have we found worse conditions prevailing among the homes of the people."[5] Ellen's own circumstances were not so bleak, but she early on became conscious both of her own comparative good fortune and of the desperate poverty of too many working-class families.

Ellen was born at 41 Coral Street in a Victorian terrace down the road from an identical home where her widowed maternal grandmother, Eliza Wood, lived with two sons, Ellen's uncles Charles and Alfred, who had moved back in with their mother after their father's death. Before she was ten years old, the family moved to a slightly larger home on nearby Everton Road and a few years later into another house a few doors down with space to accommodate Eliza. A neighbour described the houses on Everton Road as classic two-up two-downs, with a privy in the back yard.[6] Chorlton has changed significantly as the result of slum clearance and the expansion of the University of Manchester; and each of Ellen's childhood homes has since been demolished, as was the building on Plymouth Grove where she rented a room after graduation from university.[7]

To the urban planners who began the decades-long process of clearing Manchester's slums in the 1930s, the conditions were such that the only solution was to raze whole streets and start from scratch.[8] Yet to the men and women who lived there, some houses were viewed as significantly better than others. While back-to-back properties with only a single window on each level and no access to a backyard privy were least desirable, the two-up two-downs were comparatively coveted.[9] In *The Classic Slum,* Robert Roberts, who grew up in a similar working-class community in neighbouring Salford, described the pride his family and most of his neighbours took in maintaining their modest dwellings: "Most people kept what they possessed clean in spite of squalor and ever-invading dirt. Some houses sparkled." He described the hard lot of working-class housewives who devoted their lives "to cleaning and re-cleaning the same objects so that their family, drilled into slavish tidiness, could sit in state, newspaper covers removed, for a few hours each Sunday evening."[10] In the Wilkinson household this Sunday night ritual would have taken place in the parlour, which Ellen later recalled as a depressingly dark room: "In Lancashire the favourite decoration for the walls was brown paint and a darkish red or green paper. We always had that, because it did not show the dirt." The dark walls were made gloomier by red baize curtains over the windows. The parlour, in Ellen's view, was "no use to anyone except for my father and elder brother to hang their Sunday coats over the chair-backs when they came in from chapel."[11] Regular socializing took place in the kitchen, the larger room and the centre of family activity.

In the kitchen her mother did sewing she took in to help augment the family income, as well as making clothes for the family. In the kitchen the Wilkinson children studied their lessons, and friends came over to talk religion and parish gossip. Ellen's parents were native Mancunians. Her mother grew up in Chorlton, while her father's family lived in a series of homes north of the city centre in the old municipal ward of St. Michael's, not far from Queens Park. Ellen's paternal grandmother, an Irish woman from whom she inherited her auburn hair and her fiery temper, died before she was born.[12] Although Ellen, in later life, liked to exaggerate her Irish blood, it was her English maternal family that played the larger role in her upbringing.[13] Eliza Wood had six sons in addition to her only daughter, and Ellen's uncles were regular features in her childhood, joining the family at church and often stopping by the house to discuss scripture with her father. Eliza Wood helped look after Ellen and her siblings, although her advanced age and her own ill health limited her ability to assist her often ailing daughter.

Ross Waller, a childhood neighbour of the Wilkinsons, remembered Chorlton as "lower middle class respectable." The Wilkinsons' home, in his recollection, was "certainly not opulent just as certainly it was not deprived. I should say just over the margin of lower middle." It was a mark of the family's respectability that once Richard found permanent employment as an insurance collector, they were able to afford a weekly washerwoman.[14] Ellen's own recollections were much grimmer. "How can Lancashire folk continue to put up with their ugly houses, and not merely endure them but even get fond of acres of narrow streets and brick boxes with slate roofs?," she wondered. "Every time I go back home and take a tram up Oldham Road or Ashton New Road I find myself asking, how can anyone endure this soul-destroying ugliness?"[15] Her later love of colour—her Bloomsbury flat in the 1920s was decorated in bright blues and orange—was her rebellion against a childhood of drabness. Even the leaves in Ardwick Green Park, at the end of the Wilkinsons' street, were grey with soot.[16] The omnipresence of soot likely contributed to Ellen's and Annie's asthma, which plagued both sisters throughout their lives.

Lack of colour notwithstanding, the Wilkinson children had a happy childhood. The Wilkinsons got on with their neighbours, and the families had regular get-togethers at which the children played Proverbs and other games suitable for devout Methodist children. Methodism was a central part of family life. Unlike many Irish emigrants to Manchester in the nineteenth century, Richard Wilkinson's mother was not Catholic, or if she was she was not religious. Richard and his eight younger siblings were raised as Methodists, and Ellen's father's sole formal education came from the Methodist Sunday School. Between his temperamental mother and his "feckless" father, the chapel provided a rare source of stability in Richard's life.[17] Chorlton was a neighbourhood well served with pubs—there were local pubs near Ellen's homes on both Coral Street and Everton Road—but the chapel, not the pub, was the centre of Richard's social world. Religion offered a balm to working men whose lives had failed to live up to their expectations, but it also provided a connection to the world beyond south Manchester. Despite his lack of formal education, Richard took a strong interest in the world around him, and the chapel was a place to learn about and discuss not only scripture but domestic and foreign affairs. In Ellen's childhood her father served as a lay preacher, and he sought to instil in his children the moral rectitude and respect for their fellow man that Methodism emphasized.

It was likely through the chapel that Richard met his wife, although the pair may have been introduced by one of Ellen's uncles, as George Wood was also an insurance collector. Various census records put Ellen Wood at either two or three years older than her husband; and Annie, their first child, was not born until Ellen was twenty-six. She wore her hair long, and when it was not braided and put up, it reached down past her waist. She was a chubby woman, but slight in comparison to her "rather grossly fat" husband. A neighbour recalls her having been a quiet counterpoint to Richard's boisterous personality.[18] From the little evidence that remains, Mrs. Wilkinson appears to have been the calm centre of family life. Unlike many Mancunian women, she did not work outside the home after her children's birth and instead devoted herself to housekeeping and her children's upbringing. She was particularly attentive to Ellen, who fell victim to scarlet fever when she was five years old.[19] She nursed her daughter through the illness and even after Ellen regained her strength continued to homeschool her little girl until Harold's arrival meant she could not give Ellen's education the attention it deserved. Whether she kept her daughter at home for fear of her falling victim to another ailment or because she simply could not bear to part with her, their exceptional time together forged a deep bond. Ellen looked up to her mother, and when she finally finished university and got a paying job, she used to take pride in buying her "little luxuries."[20] But if she respected and admired her namesake, she had more in common with her outspoken and intellectually curious father.

To his credit, Richard Wilkinson took an active interest in all his children. He encouraged his eldest son Arthur to pursue the career he had not had the opportunity to consider; and in July 1905, when Ellen was thirteen, her elder brother was accredited to the ministry at the Wesleyan conference in Bristol.[21] Harold, whom Waller remembers as a "good natured rough diamond with slightly protruding teeth" was allowed to nurse his passion for maths (at which Ellen was incorrigible) and went on to get an engineering degree and work for the BBC.[22] Ellen allegedly resented him for taking her place as the family pet and once bundled baby Harold up in his blankets, pushed his pram down the street, and left him to his fate.[23] But Harold's arrival did not eclipse Ellen in the family firmament—a feat well-nigh impossible.

Richard's eldest daughter was the only one who does not seem to have been a particular recipient of his attentions. As the oldest child and a girl, Annie was expected to help her mother. She was the only one of the Wilkinson children to stop her education after elementary school, and though she taught dressmaking and later did secretarial work for the Women's International League (WIL) during and after World War I, she was the only one not to have a career. Friends rued her wasted potential. Stella Davies recalled that she "had a genius for organization, was good with people and combined a strong sense of rectitude with tact." Her personality was "at once attractive and stimulating."[24] Yet, to another neighbour, Annie's charms were largely wasted. She was essentially a "beast of burden to Ellen and Harold. Annie gave up all idea of marriage and employment because she had to look after the young 'uns."[25]

Mabel Tylecote, her colleague on the WIL, believed that Annie was resentful of the sacrifices she had made so that Ellen could have the opportunities she did. But while others concurred with the view that Annie had "sacrificed herself" for Ellen, they did not see the same resentment, merely the pride the older sister felt in the younger.[26] Certainly, Ellen both loved and depended upon Annie.

Annie's pride in Ellen was shared by their father, who recognized his younger daughter's potential from early on. Ellen was not an easy child. Working-class children were drilled in manners and "humble politeness" from a young age, and honesty and truthfulness arguably ranked well below deference as desirable traits.[27] If Ellen was not wilfully rude, she could be impertinent. She was bright and curious and did not shrink from posing awkward questions or generally speaking her mind, tendencies that appeared to have been indulged by her parents and elder siblings. One neighbour a few years younger than Ellen recalled her as lively and combative. She had opinions on everything and was not afraid to speak her mind to grownups.[28] Her personality comes through clearly in the few photographs that survive from her childhood. In one, taken at age eight or nine, Ellen is staring straight at the camera with a confident gaze and a thin but unmistakable smile that contrasts sharply with the solemnity of most Victorian portraits. In a school photo taken a few years later, she stands with her head thrown back and one shoulder poised provocatively forward. While many of her classmates stare solemnly at the cameraman, Ellen is smiling broadly, clearly enjoying the attention.

Her playful presumption would get her into no end of trouble at school and would occasionally exasperate her mother, but her father seems to have taken his youngest daughter's outspokenness and high spirits in stride. If her mother was "thoroughly shocked" to find her one Sunday evening, at a young age, standing on a chair and imitating the sermons she had heard that morning for the benefit of her infirm grandmother, Richard doubtless appreciated this for the sincere flattery it was. As Ellen recalled later, "Because my father and my mother's favourite brother were local preachers, and many of the men who came into the house were also, 'preaching' and sermons were as much the current 'shop,' as golf or cricket in households where the father and brothers are enthusiasts in those games." Although she "thoroughly enjoyed" the singing and the "cheerful services," young Ellen was bored by the long sermons; but she was able to recognize that "to my father . . . chapel meant everything." As she later recalled, "There he was taught to read, was lent books. It was his only contact with education, its pulpit his only means of self-expression. To a proud and sensitive man, its doctrine of the Fatherhood of God and the Brotherhood of man was the assertion of an equality which the next generation were to find in the socialist movement."[29] As a young girl, she could not have appreciated the full extent of the church's meaning for her father, but she could recognize how important religion was to him. And although she was not a regularly practicing Wesleyan as an adult, she continued to identify with Methodism—excepting for a brief flirtation with atheism in her early twenties—and credited the chapel for teaching her and thousands like her that "the real thing in life, and the real happiness in life, came from character, from trying to do one's job and sticking to it whatever the difficulties were."[30]

Ellen's parents had come of age before the passage of the 1870 Education Act, which first provided state funding for elementary schooling. By the 1890s, however, elementary school until the age of thirteen had become mandatory for all boys and girls—although the requirement was occasionally observed in the breach. Thus, Ellen was enrolled in the local infant school just before her sixth birthday. Since her brother and sister were significantly older, little red-haired Ellen did not have anyone to look after her at school, which perhaps explains why her mother kept her out for so long after she contracted scarlet fever.

The scarlet fever likely contributed to Ellen's diminutive stature as an adult. Once she entered parliament, the press christened her the "elfin fury" and the "mighty atom." Her height was variously recorded as anywhere from 4'9" to five feet." She owned to being 4'10".[31] At one point she joked that while her height made her feel "specially short" in London, in Manchester a five-foot woman seemed a positive giant—a reference to the impact of generations of malnutrition and hard labour on the Manchester working classes. But even by Mancunian standards, or those of her own family, Ellen was "small, even tiny," as her friend Stella Davies recalled.[32]

Her extended stay at home with her mother likely contributed to the wilfulness and lack of respect for authority that characterized young Ellen. The principal aim of Victorian elementary schools was to socialize children to their future role within British society; and obedience to authority was privileged as highly as literacy, if not more so. Students were not encouraged to question the teacher, and clever students were not challenged. At home, Ellen's mother did not hold her to the same strict rules a classroom teacher would have done. She could progress at her own pace, asking her mother questions when she did not understand and focusing her attention on what most interested her. When she returned to school, she was disappointed to find she was just "a little sausage in the vast educational sausage factory in the eyes of the makers of the state scheme. That I, and others like me, were keen, intelligent, could mop up facts like blotting paper, wanted to stretch our minds in every direction, was merely a nuisance. We must fit into the mold, or be pressed into it."[33] Boredom breeds mischievousness in young boys and girls, and Ellen, by her own admission, was a "naughty" little pupil.

In later years, she was better able to appreciate the constraints under which her elementary school teachers operated. The school housed five classes of boys and girls crammed into one dingy room, and the teachers had neither the time nor the resources to prepare extra lessons for those who found the regular curriculum insufficiently stimulating. Nor did they possess the willpower to tame a recalcitrant little girl into performing well at subjects in which she had no interest. She enjoyed reading, history, and languages and did well in these; but she was frustrated and bored with maths, art, and home economics and so simply refused to apply herself. The teachers knew her strength in the former would offset her weakness in the latter when it came to the grammar school exam and so let her coast through subjects she did not like. "What ought to have happened to me was that someone who had time to take a personal interest in my affairs ought to have made me do the things I hated," she later opined. But no such volunteer was forthcoming, and so, "The strike that started in standard three when I decided I didn't like sums, and wasn't going to do any, that I loathed sewing, so teacher had better let me read to the class to keep me quiet, simply went on unchecked."

The result was that, as a grown woman, Ellen still had "to add up on my fingers and [could not] do the simplest sum in percentages."[34] Nor could she sew, though fortunately, "Annie had considerable clothes sense and . . . made most of her own and Ellen's dresses."[35]

If elementary school for Ellen was a "hateful" experience that left her so resentful she could barely set foot in a primary school until after becoming education secretary in 1945, Sunday School provided a different, more entertaining form of education. Ellen's family and most of their neighbours rarely, if ever, strayed far from Manchester, but the Wesleyan chapel offered them a bridge to the wider world. Years later, at the fifty-fifth anniversary of the Manchester and Salford Mission in 1941, Ellen recalled the many meetings she attended growing up that "were neither narrowly religious nor narrowly political," including "protests against the Congo atrocities"—the Belgian exploitation of forced labour in the Congo Free State in the decades before the First World War—or against the British government's "repression in India."[36] In the first decades of the twentieth century, the international socialist and feminist movements would open up many young men's and women's horizons to events beyond Britain's borders, creating a new cosmopolitan generation of activists. In the late nineteenth century, particularly but not exclusively for women, nonconformity was one of the principal conduits by which ordinary Britons were introduced to international affairs.[37] It is not coincidental that many of the men and women from the generation before Ellen with whom she would work on international issues in the 1920s and 1930s came up through the Methodist church, including most notably Labour Foreign Secretary Arthur Henderson.[38]

The Methodist emphasis on missionary work and on teaching tolerance and understanding of foreign cultures extended into its youth education. One of Ellen's earliest ventures into public speaking came at a Sunday School foreign missionary festival, at which she recalled "dressing up in a Chinese gown and having to speak on behalf of China. I would not have one word written for me and insisted on making the speech myself." On another occasion, she dressed up as an Indian girl to speak on behalf of the subjects of the Raj.[39] The idea of dressing children up in costume to learn about foreign cultures, which remained a popular educational practice amongst pacifists through the interwar years, has more than a flavour of fetishizing and Orientalising; and it seems more likely to have emphasized the exotic difference of Asian peoples than to have underscored their common humanity.[40] Nonetheless, it did expose young Ellen to the existence of foreign cultures, and, to her credit, she remained remarkably immune from tendencies to stereotype or idealize foreigners.

These Sunday School performances gave her a taste of public speaking, to which she was exceptionally well suited. Ellen may have been small, but she had an outsized personality. She loved to show off and perform, whether it was reciting sermons for her grandmother or poems at the Band of Hope (a temperance organization), or later performing in the drama club at secondary school or debating in the University of Manchester Women's Union. A childhood neighbour recalled, "She projected the image she wanted—pure magic . . . a magical magnetic quality." Her size belied the power of her voice, which was piercing and filled with genuine emotion. She would often begin a speech quietly then build up to a feverish intensity "like an electric live wire."[41] By the time she left university, she already possessed "a complete unselfconsciousness on a public platform"[42] that helped her gain a position as a suffrage organizer at age twenty-two and led one observer to recall of her first career in Manchester politics: "she was an exceedingly able speaker even in these early days and was particularly good at open air meetings."[43]

Although Ellen felt oppressed by the monotony and stricture of primary school, she was not one to fail at her lessons to spite her teachers. Failure, for any reason, was anathema to her. Thus, at age eleven, Ellen earned a scholarship to Ardwick Higher Elementary Grade School on Devonshire street, where she stayed for three years before earning another scholarship to attend the Stretford Road girls' secondary school.[44] Her sister Annie taught dressmaking at Ardwick. Unlike the elementary, these were clean, well-lit, modern institutions, but neither was more to Ellen's liking than elementary school had been. Years later, she recalled that at age nine she had acted up so terribly that the exasperated teacher of the girls' class had banished her to the boys' room as a punishment. "That suited me quite well," she joked, "but unfortunately it only lasted for three days."[45] Her mother recognized her unhappiness and would give her an occasional reprieve at lunchtime, springing her from school to attend the Manchester and Salford Mission's midday services. She would "race off" from school to meet her mother in the city centre. "While her mother remained at the mission, Ellen was given a penny to go on the tram so that she could be back for two o'clock."[46]

At Ardwick, for the first time, Ellen encountered the sexual double standard she would fight against for the rest of her career. Like the cleverest boys at the school, she could have benefited from mentoring and encouragement. But while "the masters would often give extra time, lend books and so on to a bright lad[,] I never remember such encouragement. I was only a girl anyway." At secondary school, she did not have to compete with the boys for attention, but the experience was no less "horrid" for it. One of her principal memories of that school came from her final year, when their "prim and ultra-proper" Victorian headmistress set out to instruct them on plant fertilization, and the classroom full of girls seized the opportunity to discomfort her by pretending to an overly keen interest in the sex life of flowers. The unfortunate woman ultimately fled the room in embarrassment at the suggestive questions about stamens and carpals.[47]

Fortunately, her father ensured she had ample opportunities for intellectual expansion outside the classroom. When Richard Wilkinson arrived at the Free Trade Hall with Ellen for the first of a series of lectures on Darwin and evolution, they must have turned a few heads. Richard, clad in his Sunday best, formed a stark contrast to his adolescent daughter. Young women were an increasingly common sight at public meetings in the Edwardian era. But Ellen, barely twelve, with her tumbling pile of auburn hair, and standing well below five feet tall, was by no means a typical audience member. Richard, whose job brought him into constant contact with other people, "hated going out by himself," however, and his favourite daughter's insatiable intellectual curiosity made her a ready, if unusual, companion for these outings. Keen to follow up on the debates they heard in town, the duo took to reading up on evolution. "By the time I was fourteen I was reading Haeckel, and Huxley and Darwin with my father," she recalled. "This never upset my cheerful faith in my friend God: that was the result of my Methodist mother's training, but it produced a queer philosophical mix-up, when my father added *Bergson's Creative Evolution* on my sixteenth birthday. I didn't get this fuzzy mess sorted out until I discovered Karl Marx in my early twenties."[48] Much later in life, she would befriend the evolutionary biologist Julian Huxley, the grandson of Thomas Henry Huxley, whose treatises in support of Darwin's theories she and her father had reverently consumed.

Ellen was a precocious adolescent, possessed of boundless intellectual energy but with no avenue to direct it towards. Bored by her classes, she took to reading novels from the library and despite her parents' disapprobation developed a lifelong fondness for Charles Dickens.[49] Her salvation came at age sixteen with her acceptance at the Manchester Day Training College Pupil Teachers' Centre on Princess Street. The centre was only a short ride on the electric tramway from her home in Chorlton but was in many respects a world away. For two years, she spent half the week in classes at the centre and the other half as a trainee teacher at Mansfield Street Elementary School. Her experience at the centre did not inspire her to a love for teaching—far from it. Ellen was born to impassion and convert her fellow men, not simply educate them by rote. One of the few times she did manage to inspire her final-year elementary students—deviating from the curriculum to teach them about the Renaissance—she was told off by her supervisors and advised, "Don't do any more teaching when you have finished your two years here. Take my advice. Go and be a missionary to China."[50] Her dislike of teaching motivated her to study for a scholarship to university. A friend recalls Ellen at age seventeen vehemently declaring to her father her unwillingness to become a teacher, to which Richard replied in laconic Lancashirese, "Well dinna teach, lass, if thou doesn't want to."[51] But without a scholarship, teaching seemed the inevitable price to pay for a shot at a university education. There were few possibilities for working-class students to obtain educational loans, and, at any event, her proud and self-reliant parents "would have had a fit if I had suggested borrowing money."[52] If she could not win a scholarship, she would be forced to take a government grant for teacher training and in turn to commit to five years as a teacher after graduation.

If the Pupil Teachers' Centre put Ellen off a career in education, it finally offered her the intellectual challenge she had been craving, and, more importantly, introduced her to the world of politics. She remembered her time there as amongst the "happy days" of her childhood.[53] Students were allowed to study French as literature, not as grammar and vocabulary to be memorized and recited. (Young Ellen used to combine chores and homework by reciting French verb conjugation as she scrubbed the kitchen floors.[54]) At college, she finally had the experience she had envied while in grade school: a teacher took a special interest in the young bright-eyed student "starving for some intelligent direction in study." W. E. Elliott encouraged Ellen to write for the school magazine and to try to get herself published elsewhere. His encouragement launched her on what would become an extraordinary extracurricular career in print journalism. A journalist friend later claimed that "letters or journalism had lost a craftsman to politics" in Ellen, although he added that "it is hard to think of her making her career in anything but the Labour movement."[55] For this too she had Elliott to thank, as it was he who first suggested she turn her obvious oratory talent towards school politics.

Almost every successful politician has an origin story. For most, the recognition that they want to devote their lives to politics comes through an awareness of what they want to achieve through political action. Ellen's origin story puts the chicken before the egg. In her recollection, the school's staff wanted the students to run a female candidate in the upcoming elections, and as she was "the only girl who talks in school debates," Ellen was the natural choice. The election was not run on "school issues" but as a mock version of a general election, with the candidates debating party political positions before the full student body. Two boys had already claimed the mantels of Liberalism and Conservatism. This was in 1908; Keir Hardie's Independent Labour Party had won twenty-nine seats at the general election two years earlier, and though the school had never had one before, they decided it was time to include an ILP or "Socialist" candidate on the platform. And so Ellen was nominated as the Socialist.

Ellen's father may have been a trade unionist, but he was no socialist. He felt sympathy for his fellow man, but his general view was that each should pull himself up by his own bootstraps. Methodism had a long history with the Liberal party, and Ellen's mother was a "staunch Liberal." Ellen later recalled a childhood memory of her mother returning home from a meeting at the Free Trade Hall at which John

Morley, the Lord President of the Council, had spoken, "softly weeping her gratitude that there were such good men in the world."[56] Richard Wilkinson did not share his wife's admiration for the party. He considered himself a Conservative and worked on behalf of Arthur Balfour at election times when he was MP for Manchester East.[57] He once took Ellen with him, tightly gripping her hand in the bustle of a large open-air crowd, to hear the prime minister speak. At the last minute Balfour cancelled his appearance, but Richard's young daughter was left with a strong impression of the reverence in which her father held the country's leader.[58]

His appreciation for Balfour notwithstanding, Richard was not overly interested in party politics. It was religion and science he and his friends discussed around the kitchen table, not political issues such as tax reform or Irish Home Rule. Even before the school election, Ellen recalled having grown bored of all the talk of "what this or the other [scriptural] text meant," and yearned to expand her horizons beyond the chapel. As a sixteen-year-old, she once gazed wistfully out the window of the family's Everton Road terrace as cars took voters to the poll in a by-election. This was most likely the dramatic contest between William Joynson-Hicks and Winston Churchill for Manchester North West in April 1908—two men whose names then meant little to Ellen but whom she would come to view as her principal opponents during the clashes over the general strike and the trade disputes and trade unions bill two decades later. To the bored adolescent idly dusting the front room, "those motor cars gave a hint of another and wider world."[59]

Inspired in part by her memories of the by-election drama the previous spring and in part yearning for something to focus her restless intellectual energy, Ellen accepted the challenge to become the school's Socialist candidate the autumn of 1908. As she remembers it, her education in socialism began with Robert Blatchford's two books, *Britain for the British* and *Merrie England,* lent to her by an older schoolmate to help her prepare for the debate. Blatchford was no Karl Marx. *Merrie England,* which billed itself as "a plain exposition of socialism, what it is and what it is not," did not preach the language of class warfare, which Ellen would later briefly embrace in the 1920s. Rather, Blatchford critiqued the current system in which "the land, the factories, the railways, ships and machinery are not used for the general good of the people, but are used to make wealth for a few rich men who own them" as "unjust and unwise," but instead of focusing on the wickedness of the "few rich idlers" who controlled the majority of English land and industry, he emphasized the benefits of the socialist alternative. For Ellen, who had witnessed her mother's prolonged physical suffering as a result of her inability to afford proper medical attendance at her younger daughter's birth, and who had seen her father yearn for the educational opportunities from which his material circumstances had excluded him, the argument that socialism could raise the welfare of the entire country by replacing an inefficient system of class ownership had the forceful logic of a moral imperative. "Here was the stuff I was looking for," she later wrote. "The answer to the chaotic rebellion of my school years. My mother's illness fitted into this protest against the treatment of the sick who could not pay, the inefficiencies of commercialism, the waste and extravagance and the poverty.... Blatchford made socialists in those days by the sheer simplicity of his argument. I went into that election an ardent, in fact a flaming socialist."[60]

Not everyone in the audience of around five hundred students and faculty in the school auditorium took the same view. Few of her peers had read Blatchford, but most were well versed in the scathing critiques of socialism that appeared in the popular press. After the three candidates made their speeches, the floor was opened to questions, and the majority were directed at Ellen. Asked for details on how the socialist utopia would be implemented, how, or even if, current property owners would be compensated by the state, and how the state would find the expertise to run the economy more efficiently than private enterprise, Ellen was on unsure footing. But she brazened it out, answering the questions as best she could and deflecting those that she could not with her signature caustic humour. "I learned all too early that a clear decisive voice and a confident manner could get one through 90 per cent of the difficulties of life." In the end, the Socialist candidate edged out her opponents by a narrow four-point margin—after a recount.[61]

Her victory may have been slender, but her newfound commitment to socialism took deep root. At home on the weekends, she would argue politics with the neighbourhood grownups. One neighbour, several years her junior, remembers her "often engaged in lively arguments with my conservative father. He liked her because she was lively and combative! He used to say she would live to know better!"[62] How wrong that prophecy proved. The passionate desire to upend the capitalist system that Ellen felt at sixteen continued to fuel her political career until her death.

At sixteen, however, she had not yet encountered Marx's dialectics and as likely as not had not yet encountered the word proletariat. She had learned enough to know she wanted to learn more and she wanted to get involved. Ellen had run for election shortly after joining the centre, before she had really had time to get to know her classmates well or to build any close friendships. Her campaign performance put her on everyone's radar, and she soon fell in with a crowd of mostly older boys, all of whom were excited about radical ideas, and a few of whom were actually active in socialist politics. After the school election, Ellen asked one of her new friends how to go about joining the Independent Labour Party (ILP), the political party founded in nearby Bradford in 1893 by Keir Hardie, Robert Blatchford, and several others.

The party's principal platform was the necessity of independent working-class representation in parliament: working-class MPs elected by working men to defend the interests of working men. The party embraced socialist rhetoric, although it emphasized social welfare and redistribution, not class conflict. And while some of its leaders were sceptical of the women's suffrage movement, the party was unique in calling for female enfranchisement. By 1908, the growing party had seventeen branches in Manchester and Salford.[63] A friend gave Ellen the address for the Longsight branch, just a few miles down the road from the Wilkinsons' home. On the appointed evening, Ellen dressed up in her Sunday best and made up an excuse to her suspicious parents, who would not have taken well to their youngest daughter going off on her own at night to a fringe political meeting. She was only able to get out of the house by promising she would be home no later than nine-thirty. Ellen arrived at the rooms at the appointed time only to find the place completely empty. She was crestfallen and worried she had the wrong night. A charwoman, the only person there, reassured her. This was the right place, but the local socialists were not known for their punctuality. Things were unlikely to get started before nine o'clock. This was bad news for Ellen, but she decided to hang around as long as she could. After a while, a "few men strolled in. Someone read some minutes. There were a lot of incomprehensible initials. They talked in a kind of short-hand. ASRS, ASLE&F, TWF, ASE, SDF, BSP. I did not know then these initials represented trade unions and movements which have since become part of my own daily speech. I had to slip away before any other business could be taken, feeling that if this were politics there seemed to be little room for me."[64]

It was not quite the glamorous introduction to "that magical sphere of politics" Ellen had imagined. But she would not be put off easily. One of the members of her new set, a thin Jewish boy and a fellow redhead, was a practicing socialist in that he spoke from socialist platforms at street corner meetings. He offered to take her along with a few friends to a meeting of the Church Socialist League (CSL), a radical group of reformist Anglicans who embraced Christian Socialism and encouraged the cultivation of an independent working-class culture. Although its leaders occasionally struck an independent note, there was significant overlap between membership in the CSL and membership in the ILP, and the League was dismissed by critics as "a sort of ecclesiastical racket, run in the interests of the Labour Party."[65] It took serious negotiating with her father to get permission to go. The meeting was being held on a Sunday evening, and Richard could not see why a political meeting, even a meeting of the so-called Church Socialist League, should be held during church time. But Richard had a soft spot where Ellen was concerned, and it must have proved impossible to deny her in the face of her obvious eagerness and enthusiasm. So that Sunday, February 3, 1909, Ellen headed across the river to the Pankhurst Memorial Hall in Salford to her first big political meeting.

It was a dull evening, damp and blustery, but unseasonably warm for February, and Ellen must have been tempted to make the journey on foot. Such was her excitement that she got there early, and, rather than wait for her friends, she laid claim to a coveted seat in the first row of the gallery where she would not have to worry about an obstructed view. The meeting was chaired by Conrad Noel, the CSL's former organizing secretary, who was soon to be appointed to the vicarage in Thaxted, Essex, where he became known as the "Red Vicar" for his support of Christian Socialism, his championship of the ideas of the Marxist utopian socialist William Morris, and his opposition to imperialism.[66] The principal speaker was Fred Jowett, MP, a short, fiery-tempered Lancashire native and a founding member of the ILP. His topic was "the organization of labour into a political fighting force."[67] In later years, Ellen would become close friends with both Noel and Jowett, as all three found a home in the left wing of the postwar Labour Party. But, looking back on the event from thirty years hindsight, Ellen recalled neither man. Rather, her whole attention was caught by the final speech of the night, delivered by Katharine Bruce Glasier.

Glasier's topic, appropriately for the occasion, was "Socialism as Religion." She was unlike anyone Ellen had met. A prepossessing woman in her late thirties, she was the daughter of a Congregationalist minister, had grown up in comfortable circumstances in North London, and held a classics degree from Newnham College, Cambridge. After graduation she moved to Bristol to teach and for the first time came face to face with real poverty and social injustice. The experience radicalized Glasier, who became an early member of the Fabian Society, Britain's oldest think tank, formed in 1884 to study methods of social reform. As the only woman on the ILP's original fifteen-member executive committee and a renowned platform speaker, she might have been assumed to have become active in the suffrage movement. However, socialism, not suffrage, always remained Glasier's burning political issue.

Glasier's speech mesmerized young Ellen. Years later, she could still recall the older woman's appearance, clad in "a plain woolen frock of soft blue, her hair simply coiled into her neck." From her seat in the gallery, Ellen saw in Glasier the future she hoped for herself, "to be able to sway a great crowd as she swayed it, to be able to make people work to make life better, to remove slums and underfeeding and misery just because one came and spoke to them about it . . . that seemed the highest destiny any woman could ever hope for." After the talk, she introduced herself to Glasier, who said to her, "Now you must come out and speak at our meetings. We need young women for Socialism. They are all going off asking for votes and forgetting the bigger thing." Later, walking home from the meeting with two male companions, Ellen complained, "Only you fellows will be able to go to Parliament and do the job, and they won't even let me vote for it." In response, one of her companions chided her: "Oh cheer up . . . perhaps you will get a vote before you die, and anyway you can come and help to get us in." In Ellen's recollection, "that truly seemed the highest good in life at that moment."[68]

Her reminiscence contains many of the standard features of socialist autobiography, in which a definable moment of conversion leads the subject onto the path towards Socialism. What it does not reveal is the complex interaction between socialist and feminist activism that shaped Wilkinson's early political development and how her initiation into both socialist and feminist politics awakened in her a lifelong commitment to internationalism.

But all of that still lay in the future. In 1909, Ellen had not yet discovered feminism, although her membership in the ILP did bring her into contact with many women with whom she would later work in the suffrage and women's peace movements. These included ILP leader Dick Wallhead's daughter Muriel, who was two years younger than Ellen and joined her in the Clarion Rambling Club, a recreational group for young socialists.[69] Muriel, like Ellen, would go on to become a Labour MP. She and her family lived a few miles south of the Wilkinsons in the newly built garden suburb of Burnage, a model community for the respectable working classes filled with journalists, artists, teachers, and skilled craftsmen. Although only four miles away, Burnage was a different world from the quiet nonconformist community in which Ellen had been raised. Although not all of the tenants shared the Wallheads' politics, the garden village had its share of "quacks" and eccentrics.[70] George Orwell famously sent up the socialist quack denizen of Letworth Garden City in his *Road to Wigan Pier*, saving special scorn for the "food crank," more commonly known as a vegetarian: "This kind of thing is by itself sufficient to alienate plenty of decent people. And their instinct is perfectly sound, for the food-crank is by definition a person willing to cut himself off from human society in hopes of adding five years on to the life of his carcass; that is, a person out of touch with common humanity."[71] It was perhaps as a result of time spent in Wallheads' company that Ellen, in her early twenties, embraced vegetarianism.

In 1913, Ellen and Muriel would become organizers for the National Union of Women's Suffrage Societies (NUWSS), as part of the Election Fighting Fund Committee.[72] By then, they were more aware of the institutional barriers that kept women out of public life; but as teenagers, supported and privileged by their parents, neither had yet fully felt the impact of gendered double standards on their own lives (the slights of close-minded teachers notwithstanding). They were two clever and restless girls, who had just discovered a passion for socialism and who threw themselves into their new religion with the engrossed enthusiasm of the very young. Years later, Ellen wrote an essay for a volume edited by her friend Margaret Cole entitled *The Road to Success*. Margaret had asked her to describe the attributes that best suited a modern young woman to a career in organising and political work. It is characteristic of Ellen's unintentional but unmistakable self-regard that she described a hypothetical young woman exactly like her teenaged self.

> A really good organizer must have supreme self-confidence. That, I think, is an absolute essential.... The type of girl I should chose for a political career (actually, as I have said, she can only choose herself) is the type who does brilliantly in some subjects, and abysmally badly in others. She will have quarrelled violently with half the staff and adored and been adored by a discriminating few. She will have led her classmates in revolt, neglected her schoolwork to run all kinds of sideshows from the school magazine to the debating society. Her school career will have ended with the wails of teachers and parents—'How many more prizes she would have won if only she had not tried to do so many things!' Such a girl will make a good organizer, and if her tastes lie that way, a successful politician.[73]

In one respect, Ellen's thinly veiled self-portrait of a dyed-in-the-wool activist hit slightly wide of the mark. She piled her plate high while at the Pupil Teachers' Centre, to be sure, but she did not neglect her schoolwork. She was determined to win a scholarship to university. She applied to study history in 1910 and was awarded the Jones Open History Scholarship to the University of Manchester, which paid her £35 per annum for two years. It was one of only six scholarships the university awarded, and the second largest in terms of monetary value. The contest was open to students from across the British Isles, making her achievement all the more impressive. Decades later, Ellen would claim that, days before the results were announced, she was struck with a premonition and knew with utter certainty she had been awarded the scholarship. "I was cleaning taps in the bathroom, I remember, when suddenly there came, not so much into my mind, as over my whole body the complete certainty that I had won that scholarship. I stood perfectly still . . . and I *knew*." Five days later, the awards were announced. "Never before or since have I had such an experience which is as vivid in my memory as though it happened yesterday. . . . I am the last person likely 'to go psychic'. But I keep an open mind about telepathy after that."[74] It was perhaps her recollection of her episode of teenage clairvoyance that persuaded her to attend a séance years later.[75]

The scholarship was announced in late May. Over the summer, she helped her mother and sister around the house, looked after her younger brother, attended political meetings when she could, and, as likely as not, enjoyed some late summer evenings with male admirers. She had embarked on her first "love affair" shortly after starting at the Pupil Teachers' Centre with a boy who did not share her interest in politics, and unsurprisingly it did not last.[76] Ellen was an exceptionally pretty young woman, slender, with bright brown eyes and an attention-grabbing mane of auburn hair. Combine her appearance with her outspoken, vivacious personality, and she could not have been without her share of admirers. In her recollection, however, these early romances carry little weight. "Nothing could ever convince my mother," she recalled, "that while I had plenty of boyfriends . . . I was honestly more interested in politics than in love affairs."[77] Unsurprisingly, when she did find a serious boyfriend at university, he—like every man she would later become involved with—shared her passion for politics.

Not that she spent her undergraduate days entertaining gentlemen suitors. She continued to live at home while at university, sharing a room with her sister and younger brother and likely also with her grandmother, who was at that point living with the Wilkinsons. Nonetheless, university life offered her more freedom than she had ever known. Women were first admitted to the University of Manchester, or Owens' College as it was then known, in 1877. Their numbers started off small, but the female ranks swelled quickly and by the time Ellen matriculated more women than men read for history degrees.[78] The female students were not admitted to the general student union but had their own Women's Union in a large house on the Oxford Road, with a refectory, reading room, library, drawing room, and committee room. Although the 10s. annual subscription would have cost her dearly, Ellen joined for the private space the union provided to pursue her studies outside of her crowded family home and because membership was a requirement for participation in the university debating society.[79]

Ellen's involvement with the debating society further honed her skills at public speaking and helped awaken her to the many ways in which the gendered division of Edwardian society disadvantaged women and limited their choices. The women's debating society was absorbed into the existing political union in 1904, but women and men continued to compete in separate debates until well after the war. Ellen, who had begun her political career successfully debating boys at the Pupil Teachers' Centre, must have chafed at being consigned to the girls' table, especially as most of the women lacked her interest in passionate political jousting. The women took on serious issues, including the desirability of strikes, women's suffrage, and the naval arms race, and Ellen was pleased to find that most of them took a progressive view on such issues. But she wished they would sound their views with more fervour! In her second year, she became the women's secretary of the debating society and noted in the *Manchester University Magazine* that the women's debates "form a striking contrast, from a political standpoint, to those in the other Hall. With the exception of one or two known Socialists it would be difficult to tell to which political party the speakers belonged. . . . oh, for some red-hot Revolutionists to raise our severely-proper and conventional debates into life!" Not only did the women not speak as passionately as the men, many did not speak at all, presumably due to "nervousness on the part of many." Too often, "after the principals have had their say, the same four or five people speak, after which there is a dead silence till the chairman declares the meeting closed." Other than Ellen, who modestly described herself in the school magazine as "undoubtedly one of the speakers we trust in for next year; she is one of the most energetic debaters and generally can be relied on," the small group of talkers included Susie Fairhurst, whom Ellen characterized as having "brought tact to a fine art" (a skill Ellen never mastered); Miss Hewitt, a self-confident and practiced orator able to speak eloquently even in defence of positions with which she disagreed; Miss Browne, "a quiet, but very effective speaker"; and Miss Lodge, to whom Ellen was grateful for providing "the humour generally lacking in our grimly earnest debates." This group of confident young women did their best to mentor their shyer sisters, inaugurating, at Ellen's instigation, a regular series of "sharp practice debates" to coach prospective orators. In this way, they provided training for the likes of Miss Williamson, who, "though distinctly nervous, . . . always says something worth hearing" and Miss Henderson, a young woman with "the courage of her convictions" whose speeches were often hampered by a tendency to mumble and wander from her point.[80]

The young women did not debate only each other. They held occasional debates with the men's union and travelled to Liverpool, Sheffield, and Leeds for inter-university debates. In Ellen's freshman year, the girls made their first visit to Cambridge to debate the Newnham and Girton women.[81] All of this travelling was exciting for Ellen, whose life had hitherto been confined to Lancashire. Involvement with the debating society also brought the issue of women's suffrage more firmly onto young Ellen's radar. If Katharine Glasier's speech the year before had convinced her that the fight for socialism was more pressing than the cause of women's votes, her experience coaching nervous young women in the society impressed upon her the reality that women's position as unequal political citizens and their marginalization and exclusion from many public spheres was not conducive to their becoming successful foot soldiers in the socialist revolution. If women were to fight equally alongside men for socialism, they must be regarded—by those men and by society at large—as equals.

It is unknown whether Ellen attended a meeting of the Women's Freedom League (WFL) advertised during a Freshers' Social held in her first month at the university.[82] The WFL was a comparatively small offshoot of Emmeline Pankhurst's militant Women's Social and Political Union. The group eschewed political violence but encouraged civil disobedience such as tax resistance to make its voice heard. Ellen must have found the passionate commitment of women such as Charlotte Despard—with whom she would later work in the women's peace movement—inspiring, but at this point the nineteen-year-old student was not ready to commit herself to such a militant agenda.

When Ellen did become involved in the women's movement it was through the Manchester Society for Women's Suffrage (MSWS), an affiliate to the "constitutionalist" NUWSS led by Millicent Garrett Fawcett. The MSWS was run by Margaret Ashton, a formidable woman who paved the way for Ellen's later entrance into Manchester politics by being the first woman to win a seat on the city council in 1908. Although she started her career as a Liberal, Ashton became increasingly frustrated with the party's prevarications over women's suffrage and in 1912 endorsed the NUWSS decision to support only Labour candidates at elections. (The Labour Party's own history in terms of women's suffrage is at best complicated. The ILP was the only branch of the Labour movement formally committed to women's suffrage; though as Glasier's comments to Ellen attest, the class struggle was still viewed by the majority as more important than women's rights. It was not until 1912 that the Labour Party conference passed a resolution not to support a bill for manhood suffrage unless it also included votes for women.[83]) Ellen's decision to join the MSWS may have been influenced by her sister, who became a paid subscriber in 1911.[84] Intelligent and vivacious, Annie Wilkinson, with her prematurely grey hair and comparative lack of formal education, had more reason than Ellen to resent the gender disabilities that circumscribed women's lives. Ellen joined her sister in subscribing to the organization the following year and gave her time volunteering alongside the ILP and suffrage activist Annot Robinson in support of the by-election campaigns of Labour candidates J. R. Clynes and John Hodge. (Both were successfully reelected.) Suffrage campaigning was no easy task. "On one occasion at an election in Salford in 1912 she was showered with stones by angry men as she stood on a lorry which bore a huge banner proclaiming VOTES FOR WOMEN. They called her 'Carrots' and advised her to go home and darn the stockings." Carrots was undaunted. "She stayed, quelled the noisy hecklers and delivered her speech."[85]

Once Ellen graduated from university, Ashton would hire her, alongside Annot and Mabel, as a paid organizer for what became known as the Election Fighting Fund campaign. Her involvement with the MSWS was the beginning of a lifelong commitment to the women's movement. Yet, unlike other "equal rights feminists," Ellen never saw suffrage or the removal of political and legal disabilities as ends in and of themselves. Civil rights were only a prerequisite for women to improve their social and economic standing in British society.

Ellen's involvement with the ILP during her time at the Pupil Teachers' Centre had exposed her to many of the major socialist thinkers of the early twentieth century, and cemented her commitment to the fight for social justice. The ILP at this point was still a small organization, more an archipelago of local strongholds than a truly national movement.[86] It is likely therefore that she had made the acquaintance of J. T. Walton Newbold, an economics master's student three years her senior and active member of the ILP, even before she started university. The two would become much closer working together as members of the University Fabian Society, ultimately becoming briefly engaged in Ellen's final year.

Walton Newbold was not an attractive person. The papers of Ellen's first biographer include a note compiled after she read Newbold's vain and deluded draft autobiography at the John Rylands Library: "Walton N was a man of arrogance and duplicity. He was conceited, selfish, disloyal, without feeling and ruthlessly used people. He appears to have insinuated himself into organizations and resigned, recoiled and redirected his activities with regularity . . . Tho he dug out facts and information travelled and enquired . . . his dreams of directing the Labour Movement appear to have been wholly insubstantial . . . a thoroughly dishonest opportunist with precious little concern, let alone affection, for anyone but himself. Without doubt he *USED* Ellen." It is a damning indictment and gives short shrift to the traits Ellen doubtless found most attractive in the adenoidal young man from south Lancashire. Newbold was intelligent, impressively knowledgeable about economics, and passionately committed to the socialist struggle. For Ellen, particularly before she became better acquainted with leaders of the national movement, Newbold must have personified the socialist cause to which she was so eager to commit herself. Fifteen years later, Ellen wrote her first novel, *Clash,* in which the heroine chooses a companionate marriage over a passionate love affair. Rationalizing her choice, the heroine tells herself, "With Gerry one would be on the stretch all the time, working at top speed. Gerry never spared himself. Pain and utter fatigue might pull him down, but somehow he went on. There would be no possibility of Gerry's wife watching things as an interested spectator in the stalls. She would be expected to do her job and anyone else's that needed doing."[87] For a brief moment before the First World War, Newbold appeared to offer Ellen the same opportunity to marry herself simultaneously to a man and a cause.

It was likely Walton's influence that persuaded Ellen to read for the intermediate B. A. examination in political economy during her first year. (She also read for the French examination, earning a second.) Either as official course reading or at Walton's instigation, she almost certainly came into contact with the work of J. A. Hobson at university. His ideas on empire, elaborated in his magisterial *Imperialism* (1902), clearly informed Ellen's own understanding of international affairs (as well as influencing the writings of Lenin and Trotsky). Briefly, Hobson argued that the expansive nature of capitalism would cause a nation's industrialists to look outside their own borders for markets and ultimately to push their government to annex territories to secure those markets. The struggle between competing industrial nations would in turn lead, inevitably, to war. Ellen continued to espouse this economically deterministic understanding of international politics well into the 1930s, even as it became increasingly apparent that Hitler's foreign policy was driven more by racial than economic imperative. Shortly before she entered university, Hobson published his second most influential work, *The Industrial System* (1909). Here, he elaborated the theory of underconsumption, arguing it was not absolute scarcity but the maldistribution of income that caused economic stagnation and want. Redistribution of the idle surplus could best be achieved by government action, through taxation and nationalization. Hobson's analysis of both international and domestic political economy would have a profound and lasting influence on Britain's radical left, Ellen included.

When Ellen entered university, Newbold was running the small Manchester University Fabian Society, an offshoot of the London-based progressive think tank. Fabian societies existed at several other universities, with two of the most vibrant being the Glasgow University society, headed by the fiery socialist Robin Page Arnot, and the two Oxbridge societies. The Cambridge group was run by the pacifist Clifford Allen, while the Oxford society was headed by the dynamic polymath G D H Cole. Rajani ("Johnnie") Palme Dutt, the half-Swedish/half-Indian future communist, had not yet matriculated to Balliol when Ellen joined the Manchester society; but before she graduated the two had begun what would become a lifelong friendship. While the university groups were technically affiliated to the London organization, there was initially little coordination between them. In Manchester, Newbold focused his energies on bridging connections between the university society and the wider community of trade unionists, co-operators, and socialists. He was a remarkably successful networker. In 1910, he had secured Ramsay MacDonald, MP, the rising star of the ILP, as the society's honorary president.

Ellen and Newbold's fellow Fabians included Ellen's friend from the debating society Susie Fairhurst, a Methodist-turned-atheist philosophy student a few years her senior who went onto fame as a child psychologist in the 1930s, and Arthur Doyle, Newbold's co-secretary and partner in crime.[88] Membership in the society offered Ellen an entrée to the wider community of Mancunian and ultimately national socialist and labour politics. Through the university Fabians, she would meet not only MacDonald, but also local men and women such as Mary Quaile, one of the few female members of the Manchester and Salford Trades Council, for whom she volunteered as an organizer during her final year. Quaile was only four years older than Ellen, but she already had substantial experience as a union organizer. In addition to working as a waitress in the Clarion Café, a centre of ILP life in the city, Quaile was a representative for the Home Workers Association and committed substantial time and energy to the uphill battle of organizing women working from their homes as seamstresses and laundry workers. Working alongside Mary, organizing a strike to secure higher rates for such women in the spring of 1913, Ellen learned many of the tactics that would come in useful in her later career as a national trade union organizer. Mary would also graduate from local to national organizing, becoming in 1919 the women's organizer for what became the Transport and General Workers' Union.[89]

Ellen's second year was Newbold's final year of study for his MA in economics and Fairhurst's and Doyle's final year of their bachelor's studies. That spring, the Manchester Fabians hosted a conference of representatives from the Oxford, Cambridge, Birmingham, Edinburgh, Liverpool, London, and Glasgow University Socialist Societies. Together, the students formed the University Socialist Federation (USF), with the aim of increasing communication and cooperation among the existing university societies, creating new societies, and bridging a "closer relationship between University Socialism and the general Socialist Movement."[90] An executive was elected from recent graduates based in London, including Fairhurst. Newbold remained in Manchester as treasurer of what was thenceforth known as the Manchester University Socialist Society. As he recalls, he and Doyle put considerable thought into who should replace Susie in the "key position" of woman secretary, who would serve alongside the male secretary Lawrence Redfern. The pair identified Ellen as a possible candidate. In his rambling memoirs, Newbold insinuates they really chose Ellen because of his romantic interest in her, as opposed to her merits, concluding with the disparaging remark that "at least she knows that we were the two who introduced her to the Labour Movement."[91]

If Newbold asked Ellen to serve as women's secretary in an attempt to win her heart, the least that could be said is that he knew his mark. Already secretary of the debating society, Ellen took up her second post with relish. It could only have increased her enthusiasm for her new role that Doyle and Newbold had secured Katharine Bruce Glasier to replace MacDonald as honorary president. Ellen exhorted the USF members to think of themselves as socialist propagandists and encouraged speaking engagements outside of the university. She also followed in Walton's footsteps in terms of forging connections with the local community. It was through her initiative that the USF became involved with the strike of female sweated labourers led by Mary Quaile. As well as sending their members out into the community, Ellen and Redfern brought in an illustrious series of speakers to address the society, including, almost certainly at Ellen's instigation, several prominent Labour women such as Charlotte Despard, Beatrice Webb, and, of course, Glasier.[92]

Ellen was extremely fortunate to study history at Manchester under the tutelage of Thomas Frederick Tout, a renowned scholar of medieval England who sought to introduce undergraduates to historical method and the use of primary sources. It was an exciting departure from the "machine-made education" of her early school days,[93] but Ellen increasingly found herself distracted from her studies by her deepening engagement with political activism. Her course work and her extracurricular reading had given her a stronger analytical underpinning for her politics. It was at university that she first read Marx's analysis of the dialectical nature of history and the determinant role of the economic superstructure in social relations. Ellen was by nature a doer and a problem-solver rather than a theorist; but she did her best with Marxist theory, continuing her education well past university—years later, she was still asking friends to recommend further reading on Marxism.[94]

She remained a self-professed Marxist throughout her political career: on an icy morning in March 1933, it was Ellen who laid the National Council of Labour Colleges's wreath on Marx's grave in Highgate cemetery to commemorate the fiftieth anniversary of his death.[95] Her ideas on how best to change British society evolved and reshaped themselves over time, but she never abandoned her fundamentally materialist analysis of Britain's social ills.

Ellen later put her failure to win a first-class degree down to the amount of time she devoted to extracurricular activities, particularly strike organizing in the spring of 1913. In the event, when the exam results were released in June, she received a 2:1. Although she may have yearned for a first, hers was the highest degree given to a female history student that year; of the thirteen history graduates in 1913, only two students achieved top honours. She would later console herself that although it frequently proved useful to have a degree, no one ever asked her about its class.

Ellen's graduation photo depicts a serious young woman staring straight into the camera with enormous, slightly nervous eyes. Clad in a black undergraduate gown with a matching black mortarboard perched atop her voluminous pile of neatly pinned-up hair, she is wearing the comparatively masculine costume of a modern woman: straight broadcloth skirt, buttoned-down shirt, and necktie. She looks like a bit like a child playing grown-up, eager to tackle the future but perhaps unsure of what, precisely, it would bring.

2

ELLEN'S GREAT WAR

Ellen received her final year examination results from the University of Manchester at the end of June 1913. A few weeks later, she was appointed assistant organizer in training to the Manchester Society for Women's Suffrage (MSWS). She later recalled, "Never in life will I again be so rich as the first week I earned my first wage, two gold sovereigns, as an organizer for the National Union of Women's Suffrage Societies."[1] Now that she had a regular salary, Ellen was determined to move out of her parents' home. Not long after graduation, she was living in rented rooms in Chorlton—less than a mile from Everton Road but a world away from her childhood bedroom.[2] During her final year, she and Newbold had become engaged, and he later claimed the two had lived together in the months after her graduation.[3] Although there is no concrete evidence that this was the case, they probably were briefly intimate. Despite her religious upbringing, the young university graduate saw herself as an advanced young woman or, in the vernacular of the day, a "modern girl." She was deeply immersed in radical politics, flirted with atheism and had a more sustained relationship with vegetarianism, dressed unconventionally, and, as likely as not, saw herself as sexually liberated. Certainly, her later sexual politics were less than conventional. She had multiple affairs with married men and took a permissive attitude toward homosexual activity.[4] Her enemies' criticism of her as a bitter virgin were wide of the mark.[5] But if she and Newbold did have a sexual relationship, it was short-lived. Her first taste of life as an independent working girl proved too sweet to sacrifice, and their relationship did not last.

The MSWS offices were on Deansgate, and the Society operated a "suffrage shop" in St. Ann's Square, but much of Ellen's work took place outside the city centre, organizing women in Manchester's outlying wards. She organized countless "at homes," lectures, and public meetings in an effort to raise funds and recruit members. By 1913, the National Union of Women's Suffrage Societies (NUWSS) tactics had shifted from publicity stunts to electoral organization. Ellen could appreciate the wisdom of the shift, but a part of her must have longed for the vivid tableaux of flags, sashes, and banners that had defined past suffrage events. Friends from their Manchester days recall Ellen and Annie as having a penchant for wearing unusual and striking modern dresses in the suffrage colours of purple and dark green, accompanied by vivid costume jewellery. Both women's dresses were sewn by Annie, who took her sartorial inspiration in equal measure from the art nouveau and women's movements.[6]

Ellen's eccentric fashion sense must have made her an even more arresting figure as a suffrage activist. She personally spoke at many events, and one of the movement's senior leaders recalled that from a young age, she possessed both "courage in facing hostile audiences and wit to deter hecklers."[7] Many of the women in the MSWS, including most notably the Scottish activist Annot Robinson, shared Ellen's commitment to Labour politics. In addition to her paid organizational work for the MSWS, Robinson volunteered her time to the Women's Labour League, to "work for independent Labour representation for women in connection with the Labour Party, and to obtain direct Labour representation for women in parliament and on all local bodies."[8] When a new branch was established in Tyldesley, near Chorlton, Ellen became its branch secretary.[9] Her connections with the local labour movement facilitated her efforts to set up a Suffrage and Labour Club in Ancoats under the auspices of the MSWS, which quickly recruited seventy members who raised funds through jumble sales and whist drives. Impressed by her initiative, the local party asked Ellen to sit on a committee established to get Labour candidates into parliament—a connection that would serve her well a decade later when she became a Labour candidate for the Manchester constituency of Ashton-under-Lyne.[10]

Ellen's traineeship did not last long. In May 1914, she was promoted to Election Fighting Fund (EFF) organizer, working alongside Annot. The EFF was the result of a controversial policy adopted by the National Union in 1912, after the failure of the "Conciliation Bill" to pass its second reading in the House of Commons. So called because of its intent to "conciliate" the anxieties of antisuffragists by limiting female enfranchisement to around one million propertied women and foregoing more radical calls for equal suffrage, the bill went down to a narrow defeat of 222 to 208. In the wake of the defeat, the executive of the National Union of Women's Suffrage Societies decided on a policy of punishing the Liberal government by working on behalf of pro-suffrage Labour candidates facing Liberal opponents. Some members of the NUWSS executive, such as Eleanor Rathbone, supported the policy with great reluctance in the hopes that it would frighten the Liberal party into a more solid support for women's suffrage. For others, such as Catherine Marshall, who became the national secretary of EFF, the policy was the first step toward a closer collaboration between the NUWSS and Labour. Under Marshall's direction, the suffragists funnelled much-needed funds and manpower to the Labour Party between 1912 and the outbreak of the First World War. Although none of the Labour candidates supported by the EFF won election, it was widely believed suffragist intervention was responsible for the defeat of several Liberal candidates. By 1914, when Ellen was appointed an EFF organizer, the fund had expanded from direct by-election work to the establishment of and support for Labour organizations in several constituencies in anticipation of the upcoming general election. Ellen's job was to organize disenfranchised women to work for Labour.

The working agreement between the NUWSS and the Labour Party meant Ellen did not have to choose between the women's and the labour and socialist movements. Yet, even if the establishment of the EFF had not turned suffrage workers into active Labour party propagandists, she would likely still have supported the suffrage campaign. In this respect, she differed from Glasier and others who saw women's suffrage as a distraction from the class struggle. Ellen firmly believed that the enfranchisement of working women was a crucial step toward their economic emancipation. It is unclear whether she read reports of the German Social Democrat Rosa Luxembourg's speech on suffrage in Stuttgart in May 1912, but she would doubtless have agreed with its sentiments: "The current mass struggle for women's political rights is only an expression and a part of the proletariat's general struggle for liberation. In this lies its strength and its future. Because of the female proletariat, general, equal, direct suffrage for women would immensely advance and intensify the proletarian class struggle." Yet, above and beyond the implications of women's suffrage for socialism, Ellen was a committed believer in gender equality.

Given Ellen's fiery temperament, it may be surprising that she did not join the militant suffragist movement led by Emmeline and Christabel Pankhurst. Several of Ellen's colleagues in the Manchester socialist movement supported militancy. Annot Robinson had initially been active in the Women's Social and Political Union (WSPU) and had been imprisoned in 1908 before joining the MSWS.[11] Yet Ellen, for all of her love for publicity and theatrics, kept her political activism within the bounds of the law. Perhaps it was political ambition that drew her to the constitutional movement; she had too much to accomplish to risk wasting away in prison as a martyr to the suffrage cause. More likely it was her background in debate and public speaking. She believed that thinking men and women could be persuaded of the logic of women's suffrage without resort to violence and intimidation.

The outbreak of war on August 4, 1914, however, displaced suffrage from the political agenda. As a socialist, Ellen objected to Britain's entry in the war, which she saw as an imperialist struggle over colonies and capital. She also professed to reject war on feminist grounds—a sentiment shared by many of her NUWSS colleagues who simultaneously supported gender equality and believed that, as nurturers, women had a special investment in promoting peace. Some members of the NUWSS leadership, including the Fighting Fund's guiding light Catherine Marshall, as well as rank-and-file suffragists such as Ellen's good friend Muriel Wallhead, supported the No Conscription Fellowship, a group founded by Ellen's University Socialist Federation (USF) colleague Clifford Allen that advocated conscientious objection to the war.[12] Ellen, however, was not actively involved in the pacifist protest movement. As her friend Robin Page Arnot recalled of their clique at the time: "Their attitude was expressed mainly as a sort of personal boycott of war, not as an active participation in anti-war propaganda."[13] If one is to believe Walton Newbold (never the most reliable source where Ellen was concerned), Ellen was in fact rudely dismissive of conscientious objectors.[14] In the end, her need for paid employment trumped her reservations about the conflict; and she briefly worked as organizing secretary of the Women's Emergency Corps, a group founded by the pro-war suffragette Eveline Haverfield that organized women to help the war effort as doctors, nurses, and motorcycle messengers.[15]

If Ellen did not agree with Catherine Marshall over the wisdom of conscientious objection, she shared her concerns for the impact of the war on the working women who were already being asked to step in and fill their menfolk's shoes in munitions factories. These women were being asked to do men's work, under often-hazardous conditions, but were not being offered the same wages or perquisites. When the Manchester and Salford branch of the NUWSS decided to redirect its funds and organizational apparatus toward the establishment of a "Women's War Interest Committee (WWIC)," with the express purpose of lobbying for equal pay for women war workers, Ellen and Annot Robinson became joint secretaries of the new organization.[16] In addition to her work for the WWIC, Ellen also found temporary employment with a series of agencies to promote the welfare of women workers that sprang up in Manchester during the war, including as secretary of the Women's Registration Office in Manchester, which enrolled women for war work.[17]

Ellen, Annot, and the other members of the Manchester and Salford WWIC fought hard to keep the issue of women's wages at the forefront of Mancunian and national politics. As Ellen wrote to the *Manchester Guardian,* "With food at its present price it is not possible for women to maintain the physical efficiency necessary for using heavy machinery on 15s. a week [the average wage for female munitions workers in Manchester], especially when travelling expenses and insurance have to be deducted from this."[18] Her experience with the WWIC proved a turning point in Ellen's life, awakening in her a lifelong interest in the defence of female labourers and leading directly to her appointment as women's organizer for the Amalgamated Union of Cooperative Employees (AUCE), with which she would remain associated for the remainder of her political career.

Munitions was not the only industry to see an influx of female labour during the war. As men headed for the front, they left behind jobs as clerks, shopworkers, and countless other occupations, and the country looked to women to take their place. The AUCE, which represented not only shopworkers but also those who worked in the production and distribution of goods for sale in cooperative shops, had long recognized the potential value of organizing women workers. The union had already once tried to recruit a women's organizer but had failed to find a woman with suitable energy and dynamism. In March 1915, they decided to readvertise the post, this time expanding the scope of the search from union members to all qualified female candidates. In addition to posting in cooperative publications, they also took out an advertisement in the Independent Labour Party (ILP) journal, *Labour Leader,* and it is likely Ellen spotted the job in that paper. In June 1915, she was interviewed alongside three other candidates brought in from around England and Scotland.

Ellen Wilkinson M. A. was not a typical candidate for a trade union post. (In June 1914, Ellen had been awarded an honorary master's from Manchester University without writing a thesis, a once-common custom since discontinued at all British universities save Oxford and Cambridge). Her competitors, in contrast, had all come up through the cooperative or union ranks. These included Nellie Barton of Sheffield, a member of the ILP and the Women's Cooperative Guild (WCG) of long standing who had given evidence to the 1910 Royal Commission on Divorce on behalf of the WCG and whose politics were at least as radical as Ellen's. At age twenty-three, Ellen was considerably younger and less experienced than her rivals. Nonetheless, her passion and enthusiasm must have weighed heavily in her favour. She was the interviewing committee's first choice and started the job the first week of September.[19] Her salary of £2 5s per week plus travelling expenses was little more than she had made as a suffrage organizer. However, rapid promotion and wartime inflation quickly boosted her salary—by the time of the armistice in November 1918, she was earning £300 a year.[20]

Ellen was tasked both with organizing new branches and recruiting members and with coordinating negotiations and industrial action. It was a job that required near-constant travel from one end of the country to the other. She began the summer of 1916 mediating negotiations in a dispute over piece rates between female garment workers and the Scottish Co-operative Wholesale Society in Glasgow and ended it in Plymouth leading a joint strike of the AUCE and the dockworkers' union for higher rates for shop and distributive workers at the Plymouth Society.[21] In Plymouth, Ellen first met Nancy Astor, the eccentric American wife of Waldorf Astor who would go on to become the first woman MP in 1919 (elected as a Conservative for her husband's former seat of Plymouth Sutton) and ultimately Ellen's close friend in Parliament. In between the two great conflicts, Ellen travelled south to Woolwich and east to Leeds organizing women workers.[22] It was exhausting work, but it quickly became a labour of love. As she would later write, "public work—a general title for haranguing and organizing and sympathizing with one's fellow-humans—is definitely one of the hobby careers," only suitable to those who, were they to win "a sweepstake fortune, would be found at their posts next day."[23] Ellen's resonant voice and platform experience recruiting members and raising money for the NUWSS proved invaluable assets. In the year after she was brought on board, the comparatively small union for the first time enrolled more women than men—563 new male and 665 new female members.[24] This was no mean feat, although it took its toll on the young university graduate. "The life of an organizer, with its continual travelling, food at any time, late nights and rushed mornings, wears any woman out by middle age," she lamented.[25]

Ellen's work for the AUCE was not limited to organizing shop assistants, laundry workers, seamstresses, food servers, kitchen workers, bootmakers, and other industry employees to "bring pressure to bear on the prejudice-clogged minds of many co-operative committees" either through negotiation or strike action.[26] Unexpectedly and dispiritingly, she found that much of her time during the war and afterwards was spent in pitched battle with other trade unions. Traditionally, British trade unions had been organized by craft and limited to skilled workers (bookmakers, tailors, carpenters, etc.) In the last decades of the nineteenth century, the emergence of "new unionism" saw a shift in which larger unions sought to organize all workers involved in a single industry, such as dockworkers or railwaymen, including unskilled labourers. As the would-be representative of all cooperative employees regardless of craft or industry, the AUCE fell into this category, and in doing so stepped on the toes of many rival unions, including, most frequently, the National Union of Clerks and the National Amalgamated Union of Shop Assistants. These unions accused the AUCE of being "piratical" in their efforts to "poach" members, or potential members, from the existing craft unions. The Trades Union Congress, eager to preserve the existing order, sided with the craft unions, with the result that, just as Ellen came on board, her union temporarily withdrew its affiliation. The cooperative associations were not blind to the conflict between the AUCE and its self-professed rivals and sought to widen the cleavages between what Ellen termed her own proud "fighting union" and the "nice, safe, manageable [craft] unions."[27] Over and over, regional Co-operative Associations offered separate agreements to the local craft unions if their members agreed not to cooperate with the AUCE. Once they had split the unions, several Co-ops announced their unwillingness to recognize the AUCE in their shops, plants, or warehouses. On several occasions, Ellen and her union found themselves embarking on a battle over wages and ending up in a fight over union recognition, with their opponents abetted by "treacherous" fellow workers who had "gone over to the side of the enemy."[28]

Opposition to the AUCE became even fiercer from 1917, when the union decided to expand its remit to recruit workers from noncooperative-owned industries, including a large number of female laundry workers, shop assistants and food servers organized under Ellen's direction. The AUCE's success in recruiting female workers, both inside and outside the Co-operatives, was fuelled by its strong tradition—in stark contrast to its rivals—of advocacy on behalf of women workers. The question of equal pay came to the fore during the war as women were brought in to jobs previously dominated by male workers. In theory, the union advocated for "the rate for the job" regardless of sex. In industries where this proved unobtainable, the AUCE pushed more strenuously than other unions for an adequate living wage for women workers.[29] Most of the time, the AUCE was able to defeat employer attempts to sideline the union, in no small part due to Ellen's tireless activism organizing workers on the shop floor, holding public meetings, and coordinating publicity campaigns that shouted the union's case from huge posters and placards hung around the towns.[30]

In mastering the art of union organizing, Ellen took her cues in part from veteran women's organizer Mary Macarthur and in part from John Jagger, the AUCE's president and Ellen's close friend and mentor. Macarthur was one of the pioneers of women's trade unionism, crafting a women's organization from almost sheer force of will. Born into a Conservative Scottish family, she was only eleven years older than Ellen; but by the time Ellen started university, Mary had already cofounded the National Federation of Women Workers, established and taken on the editorship of the widely read *Woman Worker,* and been elected to the National Administrative Committee of the ILP. Years after her premature death from cancer in 1921, her colleague Margaret Bondfield remembered her first impression: "Here was genius, allied to boundless enthusiasm and leadership of a high order."[31] Ellen first met Macarthur the summer after she graduated from university, when she helped organize a meeting for women workers in conjunction with the annual Trades Union Congress, which met in Manchester in September 1913. As she remembered the event, "The amiable solid Labour leaders talked common sense a la Samuel Smiles, and the girls were frankly bored. Miss Macarthur demanded a wage which would provide pretty frocks, holidays, chocolates, and the girls woke up and began to realize that there was something in Trade Unionism after all."[32] Ellen claimed the older woman's tactics had offended her "priggish" sensibilities, yet in years to come she was not above championing "the desire of [a] girl to look as nice as possible" as a legitimate "part of her self-respect" and her right as a worker.[33] After Ellen joined the AUCE, Macarthur became a mentor for the young organizer. Even when the two disagreed—as when Mary, then chair of the Standing Joint Committee of Industrial Women's Organizations, mooted replacing the Committee's long-standing commitment to "equal work for equal pay" with the much less rigid alternative that "the wages paid to women must not cheapen production"—Ellen retained her admiration for the pioneering women's organizer.[34] Bondfield recalled that the two were temperamentally very similar: "The emotional strain in both had to have an outlet in tears, or in some wild excess of work." Ellen, Bondfield conceded, ultimately developed stronger self-control than her volatile mentor.[35] In a moving memorial penned after Macarthur's early death in 1921, Ellen recalled that Mary had been "loved and admired intensely" by herself and the other young women she had tirelessly trained in the tactics of women's organizing. Although Ellen recognized Macarthur's capacity for "hat[ing] hard" and her dedication to social revolution, she praised her generous heart and her sympathy with the younger generation, which aided her efforts both as a teacher and as an organizer.[36] Macarthur entered the scene shortly after Ellen's mother's death and helped fill a maternal void for the young feminist radical.

If Mary briefly played a maternal role in Ellen's life, John Jagger was a surrogate father. Scholars have noted that successful female politicians—including Ellen—have more often than not benefited from paternal backing and support.[37] But it was Jagger's unstinting promotion and protection that allowed Ellen to launch successfully a parliamentary and later an international political career while maintaining a secure trade union base. Looking back, Ellen recalled, "the only reason I did not go under was the wonderful patience and kindness of the men I had to work with. They were considerably older than I, at least the leaders were, but they somehow managed to combine treating me as a daughter and an equal."[38] That was undeniably true of Jagger. Nearly twenty years Ellen's senior, and as broad as she was petite, "J. J.," an Oldham native, was "burly, humourous and drawling," a "wise and fatherly guide," and a trusted leader of his union for more than twenty years—rising to the presidency of the AUCE in 1919 and remaining as president of the National Union of Distributive and Allied Workers (NUDAW) after the AUCE merged with the warehouse workers' union in 1921.[39] He had been a founding member of the AUCE before travelling overseas to work for the Burma Co-operative Society in Rangoon. In his capacity as union president, Jagger travelled regularly to speak to regional organizations; and Ellen, who in autumn 1917 was made the head of the union's new Women's Department, was his frequent side-kick. Jagger's open good-natured sense of humour helped temper Ellen's more biting wit. The two worked together on countless negotiations and strikes, but their mutual sympathy and understanding went beyond union issues. Both were left radicals—although Jagger did not follow Ellen into the Communist party, he frequently supported the Communists and was an unhesitating admirer of the Soviet Union. Both understood social justice in global as opposed to national terms. It was doubtless partly as a result of Jagger's influence that Ellen began to take a greater interest in international affairs after leaving university. Together, they promoted pacifism, anti-imperialism, and anti-fascism throughout the interwar period.

The two were so close that many suspected they were romantically involved.[40] Wilkinson was not above entering into a romance with a married man, but it is more likely their relationship developed along the lines of their two analogues in Wilkinson's novel *Clash*—occasionally sexually charged, but respectfully platonic. That such rumours existed highlights the anomaly and attendant difficulties of Ellen's position. Her aptitude for her job led to her swift ascent to the top rung of her union's national organizing and negotiating team. But although she felt herself to be—and although Jagger treated her as—one among equals, it was occasionally difficult for others to look beyond her sex. Her friend Margaret Cole recalled one occasion in the 1910s when Ellen, "tiny and young and fiery as her hair," stormed into the offices of the Fabian Research Department "flaming with rage because the wife of the secretary of another Trade Union had insisted on 'sitting-in' on his (purely professional) discussions with Ellen."[41]

Guided by her two mentors, Ellen grew comfortable and confident in her role as union organizer. Her belief that she had the measure of her job is evident from the monthly reports she sent to the union's journal. Here she described "girl strikers . . . learning that in the strength of organization lies their only hope for a fair share of the products of their labour," and denounced cooperative societies that took the position that "ideals must not be allowed to interfere with business—they must apparently be kept for platform and conference use!" She felt equally comfortable taking her own colleagues to task, urging in one column, "A canvass at Bury shows the necessity . . . of the Union framing a policy for seasonal workers, to whom certain seasons mean long weeks of unemployment."[42] However, her experience on the Women's War Interest Committee had impressed upon her the discrimination female replacement workers faced in the workforce, and she was grateful to her union for its commitment to advocating for equal pay for equal work. As she wrote in *The Cooperative Employee:* "The employer and the press tell [women workers] that 'the man has a wife and family to keep.' The under-payment of women will never improve the amount the wife has to spend on housekeeping. The rate for the job, not the sex or supposed needs of the worker, appears to be the only safe basis while the wage system lasts."[43] In the decades to come, she would maintain her commitment to equal pay.

The language Ellen used to discuss her work suggested a militant commitment to her cause. During the Plymouth strike, she wrote that "a good deal of hard work will have to be done at Plymouth before the war against poverty among the employees can be won, but one has the satisfaction of knowing that one will be fighting a society that well deserves a licking."[44] Of a strike in Keighley, she crowed, "If the members continue the stand they are making at present, another scalp will be added to the belt of the Yorkshire District, which is getting pretty heavy."[45] Although frequently an asset, Ellen's aggression almost cost her the job in December 1918. During the summer, she had been involved in organizing a strike at a print works in Longsight, Manchester, held in response to the Longsight Co-operative's notice that it would only recognize members of the print operatives union. On the eve of the strike, the Trades Union Congress condemned the AUCE and sided with the Co-op, albeit not without protest from a significant minority.[46] The Ministry of Labour and the Board of Trade were brought in to mediate the conflict, without success; and ultimately the dispute was taken to arbitration before a board comprising industry, union, and government representatives. The tribunal decided unanimously for the Co-op, censuring the union for "withdrawing essential employment . . . during a time of war."[47] Ellen was not the sole architect of the strike, and in fact her name never even appeared in the local coverage of the conflict. Nonetheless, her outspoken radicalism made her an attractive scapegoat, and the union announced her dismissal effective February 1919. But the rank and file came to her rescue. AUCE members around the country wrote to headquarters in protest, a special delegate meeting was called to challenge the right of the executive to fire "Red Ellen," and ultimately the union reinstated her after she issued a formal apology for her conduct.[48] The union executive may have hoped the incident would serve to tame the young firebrand. If anything, it cemented her conviction of the power of grassroots action to influence authority.

Such was Ellen's insatiable energy that it was never possible for any one cause or job to absorb her full capacity. Ellen's peripatetic remit gave her frequent occasion to travel down to London, whether to organize workers in Woolwich or to attend the annual congress of the Women's Cooperative Guild. Often, after her work was done, she managed to stay another night, either with friends or in a hotel paid for by the union. In a few stolen hours in London, she would volunteer her time to the Fabian Research Department (FRD), the quixotic collective of stalwart Fabians and young idealistic researchers with which Ellen remained closely associated throughout the 1920s.

Ellen's association with Douglas Cole, Robin Page Arnot, William Mellor, and the other young men and women she had met through the University Socialist Federation (USF) did not end with her graduation from Manchester. The USF discouraged its alumni from remaining active members of their alma mater's organization, arguing that such a policy would be "disastrous" for the local societies, which, to be kept alive, "must secure each year the introduction of new blood."[49] But if the individual branches were to be run by undergraduates, the executive committee remained dominated by the USF's founders. Ellen had been co-opted onto the USF executive during her finals year at Manchester. In 1915, she served as vice-chairman under Cole's leadership.

The University Socialists remained scattered around the country. Cole briefly lived in Newcastle before settling in Oxford. Ellen and Newbold remained in Manchester, while Mellor and Arnot moved to London, the former to work as a journalist for George Lansbury's *Daily Herald* and the latter to become, in 1914, secretary of the newly formed Fabian Research Department (FRD). But the group continued to meet, as speakers on platforms around the country, at Fabian summer schools at Barrow House in Keswick, and, increasingly, from 1914, in the offices of the FRD in the Fabian Society headquarters in Westminster.

The Fabian Society rented the house near St. James Park in 1914, moving from a dismal basement in Clement's Inn.[50] By then, the society, founded in Edward Pease's drawing room by a small group of associates in 1884, had expanded into an international (in that there were a few members in France, Australia, and the United States) organization of over 2,000 members. It held lectures, published "Fabian Tracts" on various social and political issues, and generally defined what it meant to be a modern political think tank. In the early decades of its existence, an implausible number of Britain's progressive thinkers claimed an affiliation to the group, including playwright and essayist George Bernard Shaw, future Labour prime minister Ramsay MacDonald, and Ellen's first socialist heroine, Katharine Bruce Glasier. Although Shaw is better known for his popular writing, and MacDonald and Glasier for their work in the ILP, the careers of Beatrice and Sidney Webb are inseparably linked to the Fabians.

Sidney was one of the first members of the society, joining with Shaw in 1884. Beatrice Webb, née Potter, met Sidney in 1890. She joined the Fabians shortly thereafter, and the pair married two years later. Physically, they were not well suited. Beatrice was tall and slender with the self-possessed comportment of a young woman born into comfortable circumstances. Sidney, then a young lawyer from a lower-middle-class background working as a clerk in the Colonial Office, was a small, slightly chubby man with a monocle and a Mephistophelian goatee. Other than the monocle, he bore no resemblance to Beatrice's previous suitor, Joseph Chamberlain, the renegade Conservative politician from Birmingham whose son would go on to serve as prime minister during the Munich Crisis. But if the couple were physically mismatched, they were intellectually perfectly mated. Jointly, they published hundreds of books and articles, including the monumental *History of British Trade Unionism* (1894) and *Soviet Communism: A New Civilization* (1935), an optimistic, if ultimately misguided, endorsement of the Soviet experiment. In between they established two pillars of British intellectual life, the London School of Economics and the *New Statesman* magazine. The pair was so closely linked that one was rarely mentioned without the other—a young secretary recalled spending her first several weeks under the impression that "Beatriceandsidney Webb" was one person.[51]

The FRD was one of Beatrice's many brainchildren, but one that quickly grew into an enfant terrible. In late 1912, the Webbs established a new Control of Industry Committee, tasked with investigating the feasibility of different methods of industrial control, from consumers' cooperatives to state ownership to industrial syndicalism. By early 1913, the committee already had a membership of over eighty Fabians and more than sixty outside "consultants"—"a few paid (or, in the Fabian tradition, underpaid), but for the most part not paid at all but working in their spare time for the love of it."[52] This group, which soon started calling itself the Fabian Research Department, was staffed primarily by young Turks—at forty years old, the socialist barrister and future solicitor general Henry Slesser was one of the oldest members.[53] Most members of the group, including Ellen, were inclined to the view that the answer to industrial control lay not in state ownership and direction of the economy but in a utopian form of industrial syndicalism that became known as Guild Socialism.

Under the direction of the Webbs, and of Bernard Shaw, who "ha[d] taken a sudden fancy to research as the primary purpose of the Fabian Society,"[54] the FRD staff combed through local union branch minutes, annual conference reports, and union journals in an effort to compile a comprehensive database of British trade unionism. Although their initial remit was to investigate alternative models for reorganizing industry, they quickly became bogged down in understanding the current organization of industry, and the department began producing a series of monthly circulars and annual yearbooks on the state of British trade unionism. Their aim, as Ellen later recalled, was to determine the boundaries of each industry in Britain: "We wished to define a trade or industry because we were anxious to get some kind of water-tight definition on which we could proceed, as we thought in our youthful enthusiasm, to reorganise the entire trade union movement."[55] If Beatrice had thought this close investigation into the practicalities of industrial organization would disabuse the recent university graduates of their revolutionary enthusiasms, she was sorely mistaken. Rather, the young rebels "neatly turned the tables on the Webbs," and captured the FRD for their cause.[56]

At a meeting in London in April 1915, some forty representatives of the FRD came together to form the National Guilds League (NGL). Ellen was right at the centre of the rebellion and went on to cofound a Manchester branch of the organization. When, five years later, she attended the inaugural meeting of the Communist Party of Great Britain, it was as an NGL representative. From the hindsight of a century, Guild Socialism seems hopelessly utopian—as indeed it did even to the majority of Fabians at the time.[57] But to the young men and women who coalesced around the FRD and the NGL—the group Margaret Cole in her memoirs referred to as "The Movement"—it appealed as a sensible and just answer to the question of what socialism should look like in practice. Although the Guild Socialist movement rapidly crumbled in the years after the war, it left a permanent imprint on many of its members, including Ellen, particularly in regard to the importance of consultation and cooperation with the trade unions to the future of British socialism.

Briefly, the Guild Socialists, led by Cole and Mellor, who authored most of the group's prolific pamphlets, advocated for the cooperative ownership and operation of the means of production by a group of industrial guilds. The guilds would produce not for profit, but for the good of the community. Workplace practices, organization, hours of labour, and admittance into the guild would be determined by the guilds themselves. Prices would be set not by the market but in consultation between the guilds and the state, which would represent the interests of the consumer. All workers, manual or professional, would be paid a similar living wage, determined by their guild; wages would be paid regardless of demand for labour, so a worker would not have to fear loss of livelihood during unemployment. Goods would be sold by a producers' guild, which again would not be driven by the profit motive but by determinations of social welfare. Women working in the home would be provided for by state revenue. Knowing they would be provided for by the guilds and the state from the cradle to the grave, individuals would not have the same urge for acquisitiveness that currently drove men and women to shore themselves up against future calamity; and ultimately the profit motive would die a natural death and be replaced by collective conscience.

The Guild Socialists were inspired by the work of A. J. Penty, S. J. Hobson, and A. R. Orage, the editor of the journal *New Age,* which became required reading for The Movement, as well as by their under-standing of developments in wartime trade unionism.[58] The unwilling-ness of union leaders to disrupt the war effort shifted the initiative in strike action from headquarters to the shop floor.[59] (Even Ellen fre-quently found herself rushing in to take control of conflicts initiated at the local level.) Such factory-level protests inspired Guild Socialists' optimism that workers within industries could organize themselves collectively not only to protest mistreatment but also to displace the capitalist class and run the industries themselves.

Another development that may have influenced Ellen's enthusiasm for Guild Socialism was the expansion of trade boards during the war. Under the 1909 Trade Boards Act, nationally elected boards could es-tablish minimum rates of pay in industry, particularly in the sweated industries dominated by women and child workers. The boards, many of which Ellen would serve on during and after the war, were comprised of an equal number of representatives from workers and employers in addi-tion to three independent members.[60] The expansion of trade boards was part of the corporatist trend in Lloyd George's wartime and postwar administration. Despite the boards' frequent capture by employers' in-terests, they represented a first, albeit woefully inadequate, step toward the rationalization of industry and the shift from market-determined wages to wage scales set with input from workers and experts.

To the older generation of Fabians, whose own inclinations tended toward gradual nationalization of industry under a model similar to that which emerged after 1945, Guild Socialist schemes seemed so much pie-in-the-sky nonsense. But to Douglas Cole in particular, Guild So-cialism became a crusade. When the older Fabians would not come around to his ideas, he took to hurling verbal abuse at them, a response he kept up throughout the war, even as he continued to accept money from the society. (In 1917, he declared in a letter to Beatrice "If I find myself secretary of a 'group of the Fabian Society' it is from the basest financial motive and without any feeling of obligation to or friendship for the Fabian Society, which to be candid I detest."[61])

In early 1915, recognizing that the FRD was a Guild Socialist stronghold, Cole embarked on a quixotic attempt to "capture" the Fa-bian Society for research—a doomed effort in which he had Ellen's full support. In April, the *Fabian News* published a formal proposal by Cole and the other Guild Socialists to alter the society's basis. Essentially, the proposal sought to eliminate the propaganda work of the society, allowing it to focus solely on research and particularly research conducted in consultation and alliance with the unions. "The Research Department, in which the remaining life of the Society is centred, has already gone far in the direction of such an alliance," the rebels claimed, "and the Research Department, with all its imperfections, is the model of what the whole Society ought to be."[62] In place of the old Basis, the rebels sought to put that "the Fabian Society consists of Socialists and forms part of the national and international movement for the emancipation of the community from the capitalist system." Ellen attended the May 1915 annual meeting of the society at which the proposal was put to a vote but was unable to prevent it sinking like a stone. Beatrice Webb's description of the rebels' "great attack" reveals a considerable degree of indulgence of the young men and women seeking to torpedo her life's work:

> Clifford Allen made a dignified speech, Mellor was frank and good-humoured, half-buffoon, half-bully. Cole disgraced himself and ruined his cause: first by an ill-tempered and tactless argument and then, when the vote went against him, by a silly display of temper. When the show of hands was decisively against the rebel resolution, someone suggested that there was no need for a count. "Let us know how many fools there are in the world," he spitted out. When called to order he sprang to his feet: "I withdraw the word fools, I say "bloody fools." Then white with rage he sprang from his platform and marched dramatically out of the hall, a few minutes later sending in a letter to Sanders, resigning his membership of the society in terms which were meant to be insolent but were merely childish."[63]

Cole's over-the-top behaviour can perhaps be excused by the fact that he was only twenty-five, and Ellen's support for his antics, both before and after his resignation from the society, excused by the fact that she was a mere twenty-three. As one Guild Socialist later recalled, "We were very young; and we were as arrogant as we were young, and contemptuous of anyone with whom we disagreed even on the smallest points. . . . But I should in justice add that we were arrogant because we were public-spirited, deeply convinced that we were right and upholding a righteous cause against embattled might."[64] Over time, the FRD evolved into an effective research and lobbying firm that trade unions, cooperative societies, trades councils, and local Labour parties could hire to produce books, reports, and pamphlets on their behalf. Its ties with the trade unions grew closer; and in 1919, it would change its name to the Labour Research Department (LRD). However, it never lost its deserved reputation as a radical incubator and shelter for Communists and fellow travellers. Ellen was elected to the LRD executive in 1920 and remained on the committee for the next two decades. It was her longest-lasting institutional relationship to an unorthodox fringe group of the Labour left.

Her youth notwithstanding, Ellen's initial attraction and sustained relationship to this rebel cabal has puzzled scholars, including her first biographer, who explained her involvement in terms of her lifelong tendency to "grasp onto ideas of the moment . . . because warm, impulsive and angry with any form of injustice she frequently saw solutions implicit in new theories."[65] Yet, such an explanation remains unsatisfactory. After all, unlike Mellor and Cole, who could be described as "middle-class and highly intellectualized" young "romantics," Ellen had actual real-life experience of industrial organization.[66] Even if she recognized the impracticality of the guild scheme, the Guild Socialists correctly identified and sought to address many of the injustices of modern capitalist society with which she was particularly concerned. Her work naturally brought her into close contact with cooperative societies, and she was frequently less than impressed with the capitalist ethos of the cooperative management. The Guild Socialists' schemes for a distributive guild appeared to build on what was best about the coops—workers' control and passing on wholesale savings to the consumer—while addressing the persistent pestilence of the profit motive within cooperative production and distribution.

The Guild Socialists, too, were avowed feminists, despite the comparative minority of women within their ranks. Although they disagreed over the practicability of rapidly doing away with the traditional family structure that kept many women tending house and raising a family, they accepted women's equal rights as citizens. As they wrote in the so-called Storrington Document, the unofficial NGL constitution named after the Sussex village where it was drafted, "In a democratic system, there must be complete equality of rights between men and women."[67] Finally, the Guild Socialists' schemes were based on a faith in the working-class's ability to govern itself, a faith Ellen fully shared. After the October revolution, those members of the NGL who did not support the Communist Party would argue the Bolsheviks had sacrificed the ideal of workers' control on the altar of state socialism; and in retrospect this was clearly the case. But for Ellen and Arnot, Mellor, and the other Guild Socialists who attended the July 1920 conference that founded the Communist Party of Great Britain as NGL delegates, the concept of the "dictatorship of the proletariat" initially did not seem incompatible with workers' control of industry.

So, arguably, membership in The Movement wasn't as out of sync with Ellen's politics as it might initially seem. And then, also, it was fun. Ellen was passionate, she was witty, and she was up for adventure, but she was also intensely focused. Her friend Stella Davies described her as having "an infinite capacity for work or play," but rarely at the same time.[68] She took everything too seriously; Robin Page Arnot recalled the young Ellen as having an "eager face—intense concentration in which she registered approval or disapproval."[69] It is perhaps for this reason— as well as for her hair—that Gertrude Hutchinson, when she worked as an office girl for the organization in the late 1910s, anointed Ellen as the Red Queen alongside Beatrice's White Queen in the FRD Wonderland.[70] But if Ellen was too naturally focused for goofing around, many of her fellow Fabian researchers were not; and their screwball antics entertained Ellen even if she could not bring herself to give as well as she got. One of Gertie Hutchinson's most vivid memories of her days with the Fabians was the comic songs of Maurice Reckitt, the older brother of Eva Reckitt, who later ran Collett's, the radical bookshop on Charing Cross Road. Eva's diligently compiled press clippings provided fodder for her brother's tunes: "I remember one distinctly that he wrote to the tune of Ka-Ka-Ka-Katie. 'Tr-tr-tr-Trotsky, beautiful Trotsky, you're the only commissar that I adore. When the ma-moon shines, on the Ka-Kremlin, I'll be waiting at the Sa-Sa-Sa-Soviet door.'"[71] Trade Union journals— Reckitt's area of expertise in the department—provided further comic material, inspiring lyrics such as "The *Shop Assistant* / Is over-persistent /

I cannot trust myself to speak / Of a paper that comes out once a week."[72] Gertrude thought the FRD regulars "quite mad and perfectly delightful." She remembers coming along to summer schools, replete with "games of cricket, and long walks over the Yorkshire moors, led by the tireless [C. E. M.] Joad, whether the weather permitted or not. . . . In the evening, they would sometimes put on one of Shaw's plays, or a revue written and performed by themselves. The lyrics were put to popular tunes."[73] Margaret Cole too remembered the place as full of song: "we closed all of our meetings by singing the songs out of Chesterton's *Flying Inn,* satiric chants written by Cole or Reckitt, and the *Red Flag* to end up."[74] The playful atmosphere of the department perfectly suited Frank Horrabin, the cartographer, cartoonist, and sometime LRD volunteer who would become Ellen's lover a few years later. His sense of humour was one of many things that separated Horrabin from Walton Newbold, who, unlike so many University Fabians, never became an enthusiast for the guild movement. As a self-identified "Neo-Marxian," Newbold denounced Ellen and her collaborators' schemes as a "bureaucratic variation of Collectivism intended to perpetuate the authority of the middle class."[75]

Ellen's immersion in The Movement during the war helped her move on from Newbold, with whom she broke off her engagement in August 1913, at the second Fabian summer school held at Barrow House in Keswick. Beatrice Webb thought Barrow House "large, ugly bare and somewhat dirty" and the food served during the exhausting two weeks of the summer school "scrimagy," but Edward Pease more optimistically characterized it as "a beautiful place with the Barrow Falls in the garden on one side, and grounds sloping down to the lake on the other, with its own boating pier and bathing-place."[76] Ellen was an enthusiastic if not overly athletic swimmer, and years later, Fenner Brockway recalled seeing "Ellen standing by the lake, drying her hair after a swim, very calm . . . Walton was in an uncontrollable state. He dashed up the sloping lawn in front of the House, where tea was being served and threw crockery around," before declaring to the assembled group that Ellen had thrown him over.[77] It is tempting to think she broke off their year-long engagement because she realized Newbold was a horrible person; but, in light of their continued working friendship, it is hard to justify such a conclusion. It is more likely that Ellen, newly graduated from university, with an exciting job as a suffrage organizer and heady with the possibilities for the future stoked by the lectures she attended that week and the "exceptionally fine" August weather, simply decided she was not ready to settle down.[78] Newbold recovered from the heartbreak quickly enough. In December he met Marjory Neilson at a lecture in Scotland, and the two were engaged by the following April.

If Ellen's parting from Newbold was only lightly mourned, the death of her mother three years later was a much harder blow. By early 1915, Ellen had moved out of her parents' house and gave her address to the Labour Party as 107 Plymouth Grove. It was a liberating experience. Years later, she would claim there was nothing "comparable to utter privacy at the end of a strenuous day. . . . To be able to be alone when one wants to be, without permission or explanations, is one of the deep-seated needs of any intelligent human being."[79] It was a deep-seated need her older sister was not offered the same opportunity to meet. Now in her mid-thirties, Annie was left at home to care for her mother and fourteen-year-old brother. Their mother finally lost a long fight with cancer in 1916, shortly after turning sixty. If Annie had devoted the first half of her life to taking care of her mother and siblings, she was not willing to give the rest of it to looking after her father. The three youngest Wilkinson children moved into a shared flat off of Platt Fields, which a friend described as "Bloomsbury-like" in its arrangement in that each sibling had a private bedroom while they shared a common room.[80] Harold was by then well on his way to becoming a young man (before the war was over, he would be drafted and sent to Ireland), and Annie turned her energy from child-minding to peace work, taking a job as office secretary for the newly formed Women's International League (WIL).

In April 1915, an International Committee for Women for Permanent Peace (ICWPP) had met in The Hague. The ICWPP brought together over 1,000 women representing more than 150 women's organizations from the United States and eleven European countries. Nearly all were members of the International Women's Suffrage Alliance, an umbrella group to which the NUWSS was affiliated. The conference elected American social worker Jane Addams as its president and drew up a list of resolutions concerning Women and War; Action toward Peace; Principles of a Permanent Peace; International Cooperation; Education of Children; and Actions to be taken. When the women returned to their home countries, they set about establishing national peace societies, including the British WIL. Both Ellen and Annie were early members of the Manchester branch, as was Annot Robinson and several of the Wilkinsons' friends. The group hired Annie as its office secretary in 1917, and, barring absences due to illness, she remained in the post until 1931, when she moved south to be nearer to her sister.

Stella Davies remembered the Manchester branch of the WIL as "large and active, holding monthly meetings with lectures on an informative and educational nature about international problems" and hosting weekend schools in the country attended mostly by "housewives with little previous knowledge of countries which had so vitally affected our lives."[81] Ellen's energies were initially directed elsewhere, although she occasionally lectured at WIL meetings on industrial issues such as "armament makers and the war" or women's wages and unionization. Toward the end of the war, Ellen began to take a greater interest in her sister's employer, joining the executive committee of the Manchester branch just before the armistice.[82] The WIL would be only one of many internationally oriented ventures with which she began to engage in the 1920s, and, increasingly, she would come to see national and international politics as inextricably linked. During the war, however, her attention remained principally focused on finding her foothold within the national Labour movement.

3

ON THE ROAD TO RADICALIZATION

On the morning of October 15, 1918, Ellen Wilkinson and Annot Robinson walked through the doors of London's Caxton Hall to take their seats at the first of what would become an annual meeting of women Labour Party members. Ellen was by now a veteran traveller, her ABC railway guide already well-worn. Her friend, in contrast, was a single mother with two girls under the age of ten, and the trip south meant leaving her daughters in the care of Annie Wilkinson or another friend.[1] That Annot undertook the journey reflects the significance of the occasion. Eight months earlier, Parliament had granted the vote to the vast majority of women over the age of thirty. Lawmakers at the time presented the reform as a reward for women's war work, although it was principally women between the ages of twenty-one and thirty—those excluded from the franchise—who had served the country most directly as nurses and munitions workers. Nonetheless, Ellen, Annot, and the other former suffrage activists at the conference, such as Charlotte Despard and Sylvia Pankhurst, could confidently feel their prewar work educating public opinion on women's suffrage had laid the groundwork for the reform.

There were close to 300 delegates in attendance. Most, like Annot, represented local Labour parties, with a large contingent, including Ellen's future mentor Susan Lawrence, coming from the well-organized Women's Advisory Committee of the London Labour Party, which had met separately before the conference. Ellen attended in her capacity as the Amalgamated Union of Cooperative Employees (AUCE) women's organizer and was disappointed to find fewer than forty trade union delegates present. The architect of the conference was Dr. Marion Phillips, the secretary of the recently established Standing Joint Committee of Industrial Women's Organizations, on which Ellen would serve for most of the 1920s. A stout, bespectacled Australian, Phillips was emerging as one of the leading women within the Labour movement. In response to the franchise expansion, the Labour Party had created a new position of Chief Woman Officer and appointed Phillips, who would remain in the post until her death in 1932. Ellen had known Marion since before the war when, as a member of the Fabian Society, she had supported the guild faction in its failed takeover bid. The two worked well together, although, according to Beatrice Webb, Marion was not universally admired by other women in the movement. In a typically uncharitable assessment, Beatrice—who claimed her as a friend—wrote that Marion was "a big and blatant woman—handsome in a coarse and sumptuous way, with plenty of brains of a common sort and sharp satirical tongue. . . . Her keen rationalist intellect is refreshing, and she has virility and persistency of purpose. Her worst defect is her insolently critical attitude towards all persons and all institutions."[2]

Phillips's principal concern at the conference was the question of how best to organize the new women voters, who hitherto had likely "never had a thought at all about politics."[3] She had not been active in the suffrage movement and had little sympathy with so-called women's issues. Her own view, put forward in a resolution on the second morning of the conference, was that progressive women should join the Labour

Party, "throwing their whole strength into the labour organizations and working for their common aims." Ellen seconded the resolution, arguing that political parties were the key vehicles for educating the woman voter. However, she doubtless felt more sympathy than Phillips with the delegates who argued that women's issues were not always prioritized by the labour movement and that certain reforms—such as the repeal of the invasive regulations permitting prison doctors to inspect for venereal disease those women arrested for prostitution—would never be prioritized unless women formed "strong *ad hoc* organizations, which might find it greatly to their interest to cooperate with the friends of reform in all parties." As a conference delegate, Ellen endorsed Annot's view that, too often, ostensibly apolitical women's organizations functioned as fronts for the Conservative and Liberal parties.[4] Nonetheless, in the decades to come, she would prove more willing than many Labour women to cooperate with such ad hoc organizations in pursuit of feminist aims.

Although Ellen applauded the passage of Phillips's resolution on women's organization, she was ultimately disappointed in the "timid and conservative" debate at the conference. Her colleagues, she felt, were not paying enough attention to the women on whose behalf she had been working for the past four years. The franchise reform had given older women a voice in politics, but who would speak for "the industrial women who, although they might not yet have votes, were the enthusiasts of today and the voters of tomorrow, and whose interests were being neglected by all parties."[5] These women, she rightly anticipated, would face a difficult struggle once the war was won. (Everyone at the conference was confident the war would ultimately be won. With the entrance of the Americans into the conflict, victory seemed inevitable.) When men returned home from the front, the priority would be on reabsorbing them into the labour market, not on protecting the women who had stepped into the jobs in their absence.

Ellen's sense of frustration only magnified in the months and years to come as the high hopes held by so many that the end of the war would usher in a new age of international and industrial reform were seemingly shattered by what she dubbed the "sickening greed of the peace conference."[6] In the immediate aftermath of the war, millions had turned their sights to Versailles in the hopes that "the international order [would] be recreated, perhaps on a different basis. . . . After such a great catastrophe the expectations were enormous."[7] American president Woodrow Wilson, with his talk of a war to end all wars, appeared as "the incarnation of the hope of the future."[8] Ellen was not immune to such hopes. She was optimistic that the peace settlement could pave the way not only for the end of war but for a new era in international labour relations. However, the punitive economic provisions of the Versailles settlement, the weakness of the newly created International Labour Organization, the onset of deflationary policies in many countries, and the seeming unwillingness of workers to support their comrades in the international struggle against capitalist exploitation all contributed to Ellen's conviction that the international system could not change while capitalism remained in place. Although she remained publicly hopeful about the potential of the League of Nations to end war through a policy of collective security, the unwillingness of the new organization to take a stand against the invasion of the Soviet Union by foreign powers, including Britain, served as an early warning that the League might not be able to deliver on all of its promises. "Scandalous" became one of Ellen's favourite words in describing both domestic economic policies and international affairs in the early 1920s. Domestic and international developments in this period radicalized her politically and drove her, despite reservations, to support the creation of the Communist Party of Great Britain on July 31, 1920.

The war's end had a disastrous effect on the women workers Ellen was tasked with organizing. The British economy witnessed a brief boom in the wake of the armistice declared on November 11, 1918. David Lloyd George, prime minister of the wartime coalition government, called a snap general election in hopes of capitalizing on the victory to gain a renewed mandate. The Labour Party had been split between pacifists and supporters of the conflict, with the party's secretary Arthur Henderson serving as a member of the war cabinet while its chairman and treasurer, future prime minister Ramsay MacDonald, took an antiwar stand. The schism did not, however, destroy the party. The Labour ministers withdrew support from the government after the armistice and ran on an independent platform, hoping to secure support from the newly enfranchised working men and women in an electorate whose size had trebled since the last general election in December 1910. The party fielded over 350 candidates, many running in three-cornered contests against government candidates and independent Liberals, and secured a respectable, if disappointing, 57 seats in parliament.

Labour's modest parliamentary showing masked considerable support in the country. The party won a fifth of the vote nationally. Lloyd George read the results as an indication of the growing strength of organized labour, and his economic policy in the immediate postwar period was premised in large part on the desire to minimize industrial conflict. The government initially pursued a policy of "stabilization" intended to smooth the economic effects of demobilization. Cheap credit was prioritized over stabilizing the currency. The wartime Temporary Regulation of Wages Act was extended until November 1919 to ensure that the influx of demobilized soldiers back into the workforce did not depress wages. Perhaps inevitably, the resultant economic boom quickly led to inflation, eating away at real wages. Workers in powerful unions, such as the National Union of Railwaymen, were able to secure cost-of-living adjustments through strike action. The Labour Research Department, with which Ellen remained intimately involved, played a crucial role in publicizing the men's case for higher wages during their national railway strike in autumn 1919 and bringing public opinion behind their cause.[9] But if the well-organized railwaymen could defend their wartime gains, at least temporarily, the shop workers and garment makers Ellen represented were hit hard by postwar inflation.

Despite Ellen and her colleagues' valiant efforts, the retail and garment industries were in an even worse position to defend themselves once the government changed tack and began to implement a deflationary policy in the autumn of 1919. The 1920 budget saw sharp decreases in government spending; and the bank rate was raised to seven percent, discouraging private investment. The result was a sharp rise in unemployment, with 15 percent of the workforce out of work by 1921. Competition from the unemployed created a downward pressure on wages felt most keenly in the unskilled and semiskilled trades Ellen's union represented. Although falling prices took some of the sting out of wage cuts, Ellen was enraged and disheartened, if not surprised, to see employers—both the capitalists and the directors of the so-called Working Man's Co-operative Society—taking advantage of the economic slump to slash real wages below prewar levels.

During the inflationary boom, Ellen's union did attempt strike action to defend its members against real wage cuts. The largest was the Lisburn shopworkers' strike, which lasted from June 28 to July 7, 1920. The AUCE had a strong organization amongst the grocery, boots, hardware, and drapery shop assistants; the dressmakers and milliners; and many of the carters, van men, and bread servers. In Lisburn, the whole of these, excepting those employed in the better-paid cooperative shops, were called out on strike in support of demands for a shorter work week, higher wages, and union recognition. Women were out alongside men, compelling the *Lisburn Standard* to declare it "pitiable to think of pretty little girls distributing handbills on the public streets," and to demand that workers return to their posts while "say, three or more level-headed, fair-minded men" sit down and sort things out. The strikers did no such thing, and the Irish edition of the *Co-operative News* noted, "Splendid meetings have been held, and the stirring addresses of Miss E. C. Wilkinson . . . and the friends who rallied to her assistance have set Lisburn workers thinking along new lines." Ultimately, the local canon interceded; and negotiations were opened between the employers and the strikers, resulting in a near-total victory for the latter.[10] The one stipulation was that future wage disputes should first be dealt with by a designated committee of employers and members of the local union—a condition perhaps insisted upon to keep "Miss E. C. Wilkinson" from returning to town with her stirring platform oratory.[11]

Lisburn was a market town eight miles south of Belfast, and the strike was Ellen's first major engagement in Ireland. She was sent across the Irish Sea to handle the negotiations with Mr. Kirk, the AUCE's regional organizer, and Messieurs Warnock and Bryans, the president and secretary of the local branch. While there on union business, she could not help but appreciate how partisan conflict between nationalists and loyalists permeated all aspects of Lisburn life. Writing in her union journal, she told her British colleagues how the employers had sought to brand the local union leaders as Sinn Feiners, although Warnock was the president of the local Orange Lodge, and Bryans a member of the Orange Order. She noted that many of the men were members of the anti–Home Rule Ulster Volunteer Force and that the strict order of their picket lines owed much to these men's paramilitary training. Although the strikers were predominantly loyalists, the culture of violence that had infected northern Irish life was felt in the conduct of the strike. At least one member of shop management had to be evacuated from the town for his safety. Strike-breakers were hospitalized, and the Royal Irish Constabulary was called in to keep order. Ellen may well have been at least partially serious when she joked that "Mr. Kirk and I began to calculate our chances of being gaoled for vicarious manslaughter." The episode must have made her anxious for Harold, her youngest brother, who had been drafted into the army and sent to Ireland at the end of the war. It likely also fuelled her interest in Irish politics and her willingness, the following year, to volunteer for a fact-finding expedition to Ireland with the Women's International League.

The Lisburn strike was anomalous in that the AUCE was able to unify the town, a reflection of the high percentage of local business controlled by the Co-operative Society and the unity of grievances among workers across the distributive sector. Localized single-industry conflicts were less successful, as when the downtrodden waitresses at the County Arcade Café, the largest branch of the Lyons' Café chain in Leeds, came out on strike against what Ellen characterized as "simply unendurable" conditions. The union did their best by the women. In addition to Ellen, John Jagger (a native Yorkshireman) was sent by the head office to speak at the regular public meetings held in Victoria Square. Ellen's old friend Muriel Wallhead also loaned her services to the women's cause. The union sought to organize boycotts by the local workers' associations, printing leaflets in both English and Yiddish, in recognition of the large working-class Jewish population in the city. Solicitations were made for a "Food Fund" to provide the picketing women with buns in the union office—for many, their only midday meal. Yet the union faced an impossible task. The women fought hard and showed an "indomitable will" but quickly found out "how easily replaced by scab labour they are." And although the Leeds women were driven to desperation trying to live on wages of 25s a week, less deductions for uniform and laundry costs and a further 1.5 shillings for "food of a very inferior quality . . . [t]eas boiled up on the stoves and crusts of bread with rancid margarine, eaten in a rat-infested cellar," they were better off than many.

As Ellen would later report, "The private trade cafes simply do not pretend to pay a living wage. Working among them recently, I found that Lyons' pays the highest wage . . . about 25s per week. The various picture-house cafes pay from 11s to 17s, and the average of certain smart Manchester tea shops is about 10s." Although the cafes claimed that the low nominal wages did not account for tips, Ellen reported some girls made only 3s. a week in tips, "on a good week." An exceptional waitress may do considerably better, but it was impossible to justify a system that "pits one woman against another, and separates the smart girl from her less wide-awake colleagues."[12] To Ellen, the obvious conclusion was that strikes by such women could succeed only if they were supported by sympathetic action by their fellow workers—a highly unlikely outcome in an economy where unemployment levels remained high and out-of-work relief was both scandalously low and frequently denied to female labourers.

The increasingly futility of all but the best organized strike action in a depressed economy led Ellen and her colleagues at the AUCE to pursue new strategies to improve their leverage with employers. In the summer of 1919, the union initiated talks with the National Warehouse and General Workers Union and with the National Amalgamated Union of Shop Assistants and Clerks (NAUSA). More than a year later, the AUCE merged with the first of these unions to become the National Union of Distributive and Allied Workers (NUDAW). The organization established new headquarters at Wilmslow Road in the leafy district of Fallowfield in south Manchester, and Ellen and Annie rented a flat in a new block of apartments with a communal garden nearby.[13] The new union was nearly 80,000 strong, and the combination of forces meant that the amalgamated organization had a stronger claim in negotiating with employers.

The amalgamation brought more women into the union's fold, and Ellen, who had begun her career as the lone woman officer, soon had a growing staff of women working under and alongside her. Mary Bamber, who became her co-national organizer, was a fiery platform speaker from Liverpool, actively involved in the socialist movement. Mary would visit the Soviet Union a year before Ellen made her own trip in 1921 and would join Ellen as an early member of the British Communist Party. NUDAW also took on several regional women's officers, including

Ellen's friend Mary Welch, who became the Lancashire organizer and who would serve with Ellen on the Manchester City Council.

Although Ellen was no longer the only woman in the office, NU-DAW's executive remained a male-dominated preserve. She didn't mind the testosterone-filled work environment. In 1929, she published *Clash*, a novel about a young female trade union organizer who is caught in love triangle that unfolds against the backdrop of the 1926 general strike. The novel's heroine, a young, unmarried union organizer named Joan Craig, is rather obviously modelled on the author. In a notably self-aware moment, Ellen has Joan reflect that, while she "'would have protested hotly if she had been told that she liked being the only woman to be doing any particular job," she in fact did like the special attention that her feminine exceptionalism won her. Amongst the men with whom she worked most closely, Joe Hallsworth, a native Mancunian not much older than Ellen, had been the AUCE's assistant secretary when she joined the union and took over as general secretary of NUDAW after the merger. He shared Ellen's radical impulses and was a key ally in her early career. Ellen described him as handicapped by his appearance as a "dreaded" intellectual. He would be more clubbable with the old guard of trade unionists if he grew a beard and added at least twelve inches to his waistline, she mused.[14] J. J. Jagger, of course, began as and remained her stalwart backer. Others, however, were less fond of their diminutive colleague. Rhys Davies, for one, was no fan of Ellen's. Although a former coalminer who moved to AUCE head office from the Rhondda Valley, he did not share the revolutionary spirit of many Welsh pitmen. Over and over again at the union's delegate meetings, he tore into Ellen for ill-conceived support for revolutionary schemes such as Guild Socialism. When both served as MPs in the 1920s, he declined to invite her to join the Labour members' glee club he formed. (Ellen pretended not to mind the snub and claimed that, even had she been invited, she would not have joined, "Firstly, because I, like the other women members of my party, am too busy to sing. Secondly, because I can't sing."[15])

Ellen's other prominent detractor in the head office was Wright Robinson, from 1923 the union's political secretary, with whom she worked not only in headquarters but later as a Manchester City Councillor. (Robinson remained on the council throughout his career and served as Lord Mayor in 1941–1942.) Unlike Davies, Robinson was not wholly unsympathetic with Ellen's politics, although he had no interest in the Communist Party. He was, however, unsympathetic to Ellen. He wrote in his diary that she was "a little vulgar, clever and unscrupulous woman." When Ellen was sent to Bishop Auckland on union work in 1922, she overrode Robinson's wishes and got Jagger to allow her to take Mary Welch along for assistance, spurring Robinson to gripe, "It was like Ellen to arrange a crisis to get her own way without regard to the welfare of the Union or anybody except herself."

Mary and Ellen's time together in County Durham led to a further rift in relations between the two. Robinson had confided in his diary that "divorce reform or no divorce reform," times were changing, as evidenced by the "strange undefined relationship of Ellen and Jagger, George Burke and Mary Welch." Although he did not come out and say he thought that either couple was having an office romance, he clearly believed something inappropriate was afoot. The following year, when Ellen ran for the council, he gleefully recorded a fellow councillor's inquiry whether Jagger was "a bit soft," and his subsequent explanation that "Jagger had haunted [Ellen] at campaign meetings, buying sweets for her, running for tea, and waiting upon her like a lackey"—"moonstruck and undignified" behaviour. Unwilling to confront Ellen about Jagger directly, he "asked Ellen as a lifelong friend of Mary Welch to warn her of the pitfalls of her relationship with Burke." Instead of taking the hint, Ellen turned around and told Mary that Robinson thought she was Burke's mistress. Either Mary herself or Burke must have set Robinson straight, as he was soon complaining to his diary, "Such a betrayal of my confidence in her, and such a wanton approach to the subject as the culminating point in a record of mendacity, settled Ellen as far as I am concerned for good." For Ellen's part, she doubtless resented Robinson's thinly veiled insinuations about her relationship with Jagger. Although the two continued to work alongside each other, there was no love lost between them.[16]

Office politics were only a sideshow from the larger problems facing NUDAW's chief women's organizer. The economic downturn and the resultant inability of unions to secure significant gains made many workers cynical and apathetic about the value of trade unionism. The falloff in membership numbers, in turn, further weakened the bargaining position of the unions. In July 1922 Ellen recalled how, having already held three organizing meetings, she arrived at the gates of a laundry house just before six o'clock. She was "half dead with fatigue" but committed to organizing the women, who had seen wages fall due to a recent adverse decision by the laundry trade board. As she opened her mouth to speak, the women "proceeded to vent their wrath on her. Trade Unions indeed! What were Trade Unions doing but reducing wages. Paying to keep a lot of lazy officials like her, that's all it was." In vain Ellen tried to persuade them that if they unionized they would have the strength to collectively push employers to offer rates above the threshold laid down by the trade boards. For a moment, she thought she had them, until the older women sighed and said, "What's the use?" and the younger girls followed their lead from the factory gates.[17]

If laundry workers were too downtrodden to be easily organized, shopgirls in the big London department stores were too cowed by their employers to trust the union reps, like Ellen, who approached them at counters or outside the revolving glass doors of the shops. Scholars have emphasized the glamour of working in shops such as Harrods, Whiteleys, or Selfridges.[18] Less well recorded is the constant supervision these women were under, with "shopwalkers" pacing the floors in search of gossiping, slouching, or pilfering. Ellen was reduced to petty subterfuge in her efforts to speak to some of the "underpaid, underfed worker[s], serving amid luxuries the seller would never enjoy, yet afraid to take the first step that would mean emancipation, for fear of the greatest evil of all—unemployment." As the shop workers were not allowed to converse with customers other than over purchases, Ellen, on one visit, disguised herself as a shopper. She bought a hair barrette from a young woman "pathetically incredulous" to hear the wages NUDAW had won for fellow shopgirls; a nailbrush from a widowed mother trying to care for two children and "frightened to death" of losing her job; a writing pad from "a handsome girl who believed that trade unions will ruin the country, and is quite satisfied, thank you"; a box of furniture nails from "an embittered discharged solider who willingly took the Union bills for his department, but hoped to be emigrating from an ungrateful country as soon as possible"; as well as several other odds and ends that bought her precious seconds of conversation.[19]

Given Ellen's skills at persuasion—one colleague joked that she would organize the angels when she got to heaven—at least some of these small purchases probably paid off in union dues. However, Ellen was keenly aware that her hard work would as likely as not be undone in a few weeks' time by a NAUSA organizer coming round to argue his union alone "could produce the goods." After the failed steps toward a merger in 1919, NAUSA and Ellen's union had resumed their tradition of back-biting and member-poaching, a self-defeating and childish game that proved "simply fatal" in the cause of organizing department store employees and others "who need so much coaxing to take even the first step."[20]

As the embittered home furnishings salesman's story attests, the wages crisis in the retail industry was not exclusively a women's issue. However, Ellen could not fail to see that the postwar downturn was affecting women particularly cruelly. As early as February 1916, Ellen had spoken to a meeting of the Manchester Branch of the Women's International League—which concerned itself with domestic as well as international issues—of the risk of women who had learnt new trades "being thrown after the war on the scrap-heap of sweated industries, to lose the valuable experience they had gained, and to work for wages infinitely lower than those of men."[21] By 1920, she was confronted by a new anxiety: Women's real wages in organized industries were being pushed below those of workers in sweated industries in the prewar period. In a period of high unemployment and weak trade union bargaining power, unskilled and semiskilled workers were increasingly reliant on the trade boards to secure decent wages. In 1920 these boards set minimum wages for over two million workers, the vast majority of them women. As a union representative on trade boards for milliners, dressmakers, café workers, laundry workers, and other industries, Ellen did her best to plead the case that higher thresholds were needed to guarantee women a living wage. However, she too often found that the votes of the three union members of the trade board were cancelled out by the votes of the three employers, and decisions were left to the appointed members. Occasionally, these men and women, appointed to represent the public, took a sympathetic view to the case put by the union representatives. Most of the time, they were swayed by the employers' associations, which more consistently and effectively lobbied their case before the boards.

At the 1920 AUCE annual delegate meeting held over Easter weekend in what *The AUCE Journal*'s reporter ironically referred to as "sunny Manchester" (it was a rainy, dismal weekend), Ellen took the floor to highlight the "perfectly scandalous" position of women workers represented by the union whose wages, determined by the trade boards, were set "far below subsistence level." She exhorted the branch secretaries amongst the delegates to introduce resolutions protesting the inadequacy of the rates set by the trade boards and send them on to the board members. "If we had a thousand workers' objections, I'm sure that it would do a great deal in the direction of raising the rates." It is noteworthy that Ellen focused her attention on the trade boards as the realistic arbiters of women's wages. The union president Joe Hallsworth made the case to the delegates that "the argument that will give you the best wages on the Trade Boards is for you to have won in the country by industrial action".[22] Ellen, by this point, was not so optimistic about the chances of industrial action. Until the fear and apathy that kept women out of the unions could be overcome, there was little hope of strike action leading to anything other than poverty and unemployment.

Ellen's experience of the uphill process of industrial organization in Britain combined with her observation of the lack of workers' solidarity internationally and the weakness of the international institutions created by the peace treaties to convince Ellen that a more revolutionary course was needed. Her support for the British Communist Party was as much a product of her disappointment and discouragement at current developments in Britain and the capitalist West as it was a show of solidarity with the Soviet "experiment" in Russia. Although it might seem paradoxical, in light of the middle-class origins of many of the organization's founders, Ellen's commitment to the Women's International League (WIL) was another manifestation of her desire to revolutionize the current international order.

Although the WIL would become increasingly influential in the interwar period, it remained a small organization. Its strength lay not in its numbers but in the talent and influence of its leadership. The League had attracted 2,458 members in 34 branches across Britain by the end of its first year—figures that rose to 4,000 members and 50 branches by the end of the war. After London, Manchester was its largest branch, which had around 700 members by 1918.[23] At their offices on Princess Street in Albert Square, the executive committee, which included representatives from Bolton, Stockport, and Oldham as well as Manchester city, met biweekly to coordinate policy and plan public education and propaganda campaigns, many of which were developed in concert with other pacifist internationalist groups.

Many of Ellen's friends and colleagues from the Labour and trade union movements were involved with the WIL in its early years, including Annot Robinson, Isabella Ford, and Margaret Bondfield. The political tone of WIL branches, particularly in the northwest of England, was reliably leftwing, most notably in regards to their support for the Russian revolution. In early 1919, the Manchester branch held a series of talks on Russia. That spring they produced leaflets contradicting what they claimed to be false rumours about the Russian treatment of women and protested to the government about the proposed blockade of Russian ports. When in July 1919 the WIL's London headquarters sent a suggestion to its branches that they consider arranging demonstrations against intervention in Russia in conjunction with local Labour parties, the Manchester branch replied they had already done so and were participating in such a demonstration on July 21 in Stevenson Square.[24] The following year, when Poland invaded Russia, ostensibly to liberate Polish subjects in those territories from mistreatment by the Soviet government, the Manchester WIL wrote to the fledging League of Nations directly to protest Polish action.[25] The WIL worked with the Blackley Labour Party to hold an open-air demonstration on May 16, 1920, against allied support of the Polish invasion, with Annot Robinson, Ellen, and John Jagger as speakers.[26] Over the next two decades, the WIL would serve as a crucial bridge between Ellen and international communities of radical reformers.

During the war, with travel between belligerent countries difficult if not impossible, the various national organizations that formed in the wake of the 1915 meeting in The Hague had concentrated on propaganda and education work within their own countries.[27] Once the war ended, the women moved quickly to organize a meeting of representatives from across Europe and the United States to put forth a "minimum feminist programme" for peace. They would have liked to have met in Paris, to underscore the link between their own congress and the congress of international powers meeting at Versailles to hammer out the peace treaty. Unfortunately, the armistice negotiations had placed restrictions on travel between the former belligerent nations, and

German and Austrian delegates were not permitted to attend a congress held in Paris. They decided, therefore, to hold their meeting in neutral Switzerland.

Jane Addams worked in concert with Dutch doctor Aletta Jacobs and Scottish lawyer Chrystal Macmillan to organize the congress, held in the centre of Zurich from May 12 through 16. One hundred and fifty-two women from fifteen countries attended, including twenty-five delegates from the British WIL and three from the Irish WIL. The Manchester branch sent five delegates, of whom the youngest was Miss Ellen Wilkinson, making her first journey across the Channel at age twenty-seven. She set off from Manchester with Margaret Ashton, the venerable feminist and local government activist who served as chairman of the Manchester branch, Mrs. Anderson Fenn, Mrs. Giles, and Annot Robinson.

Their fellow British delegates included several women with whom Ellen would find herself collaborating on various causes over the next two decades, including Chrystal Macmillan, with whom she worked on the campaign to change Britain's citizenship laws; Margaret Bondfield; and suffragette Helen Crawfurd, who like Ellen was an early member of the Communist Party of Great Britain, and who worked with her on various anti-fascist committees in the 1930s. Several members of the British delegation took the ferry together across the Channel and travelled by train to Paris and then on to Zurich. In Paris, Ellen and Crawfurd split off to visit the Bastille and the graves of the Communards in Père Lachaise Cemetery. Crawfurd recalled Ellen was "filled with revolutionary fervour" by the memorial to the 1871 martyrs to the second Paris commune, a fervour she took with her to the debating halls in Zurich.[28]

By 1919, Ellen would have been used to speaking before audiences larger and more intimidating than that assembled in Zurich. In the autobiography she submitted to the conference organizers, she described herself as a "Lecturer for Trade Union, Labour and Socialist organizations"; over the past four years, she had spoken to groups of sceptical women outside factory gates and testified before government officials on trade boards representing the laundry, clothing, and corset trades. But Ellen could not have felt entirely comfortable in her surroundings. Most of the women at the Congress were older and more accomplished.

Further, the cosmopolitan women who attended the conference were for the most part middle-class, well-educated, and well-travelled, comfortable moving in a society where conversation shifted easily from English to German to French. Ellen had studied French at school and university, but her exposure to native-spoken French had hitherto been limited. Outside of the conference, she was reliant on her colleagues' knowledge of German or her own poorly accented French and, less frequently, the locals' knowledge of English. Whereas Jane Addams had thrown herself into social work in part out of a sense of guilt at not being able to relate to the working classes, Ellen's working-class origins must have made her feel out of place in such predominantly middle-class company.[29]

Yet, although Ellen might have felt a social disadvantage compared to many of the women in Zurich, she was also aware of her comparative good fortune as a British citizen. At home, her union struggled to deal with the challenges of demobilization and postwar inflation. In continental Europe, and particularly in the defeated countries, men and women struggled with starvation. The effects of the blockade on the peoples of Central and Eastern Europe, kept in place by the victorious Allied powers during the Versailles negotiations, were evident in the gaunt and exhausted delegates from Germany, Austria, and Hungary. To the American delegates in particular, who had been buffeted from the full effects of the war, the stories of hunger and privation were a shock. One of the first acts of the congress was to debate a resolution demanding that the peace conference immediately raise the blockade and initiate relief measures, "that the lives of millions of starving children shall be saved, regardless of the financial cost. That . . . luxuries shall not be allowed transport from one country to another, until the necessaries of life are supplied to all: and the people of every country shall be rationed, in order that all the starving shall be fed."[30] Although the final clause was ultimately removed from the resolution sent to the leaders of the Paris Peace Conference, the belief of the women that human rights transcended national prerogative and that those who were better off had a moral obligation to help those in need pervaded both the congress proceedings and the later work of the Women's International League for Peace and Freedom (WILPF)—the new name the international committee adopted at Zurich. (The international organization's name would cause some confusion in the British and international press, as the British and Irish branches had already taken the name Women's International League.)

Over the next several days, the women debated the best response to the peace terms proposed at Versailles, and particularly the attitude they should take toward the proposed League of Nations. Although all were heartened by the inclusion in the draft Covenant of the League of Nations the proviso "that women should be admitted to all positions in connection with the League," their agreement ended there. Some felt the League as proposed was an important step toward world peace and should be encouraged. Others felt it did not go far enough, and the women ought to call for the revision of the Covenant to include universal disarmament and the abolition of conscription, the immediate reinstitution of free trade in raw materials, and, in the view of some, international regulation of labour standards and of the education of youth. Although agreement could not be reached on the more progressive proposals put forth at the congress, the women concurred on the danger posed by the deviation of the peace terms being developed at Versailles from the proposals originally put forth by Woodrow Wilson. After the close of the congress, they sent a delegation composed of Addams, Macmillan, Charlotte Despard of Ireland, Gabrielle Duchêne of France, Rosa Genoni of Italy, and Clara Ragaz of Switzerland to Versailles to articulate their concerns. The statesmen gave the women a hearing but ultimately ignored their counsel.[31]

Ellen spoke comparatively little at Zurich, but her contributions reveal her radicalism, even compared to the progressive women who filled the congress halls. In the debate on the proposed League of Nations, she allied herself with the faction arguing for a tougher stance vis-à-vis the current draft covenant. She "spoke of the two different tendencies everywhere—liberals always very mild and moderate in what they ask, and ready to compromise, and on the other hand young democrats afraid of nothing when it is a question of taking a stand for the new time. We women propose to take a stand for the new times, and shall not let ourselves be frightened by the old story that what is ideal is unpractical. We maintain that we shall be able to find the practical way to realize our ideal." Helen Crawfurd, who shared a hotel room with Ellen in Zurich, recalled that Ellen's radical speeches got considerable publicity and drew censure from the moderate British Labourite Ethel Snowden, who feared they would alarm the Swiss authorities.[32]

In the debate over the resolution to be sent to Versailles, Ellen's continued commitment to syndicalism, not yet abandoned from her Guild Socialist days, showed through. One of the German delegates had proposed an amendment committing the women to collectivism. In Ellen's view, such a declaration would limit the women unnecessarily. "Many ardent socialists," she contended, objected to collectivism. Could they not, she suggested, "include a clause affirming self-government in industry, then all forms of socialism are included." Although Ellen was an ardent supporter of the Russian revolutionaries, she was not yet willing to abandon her commitment to a bottom-up revolution in favour of one-party dictatorship.

Her final contribution came in the debate over proposals to create a permanent international educational council to promote the idea of world organization and international ethics and citizenship. She called for children to have more say in school curricula and teaching, arguing that "if children were led to feel a responsibility for school conditions they would feel a responsibility for what was done in their country." Her belief in the link between the education of children and the foreign policy of nations would fuel her commitment as an architect of the United Nations Educational, Scientific and Cultural Organization after the next war.[33]

Ellen's journey to Zurich inspired her about the potential for international collaboration in pursuit of peace and social reform. Hitherto, her career had been centred around national propaganda and organization. From 1919 on, she was increasingly drawn into an international sphere of activism and cooperation in pursuit of the dual aims of peace and socialism. If her longstanding links with the women's movement offered one entrée into international activism, the British socialist movement provided the other key ticket to a political wider world.

In the heady environment of postwar Europe, it was not only women who were seeking to organize themselves internationally, and Ellen found herself back in Switzerland only months after returning from the

WILPF conference. In December 1919, she crossed the Channel again, this time bound for Geneva with her colleague from the Labour Research Department, Rajani Palme Dutt and two other members of the University Socialist Federation to attend an international conference of socialist students.[34] The USF sponsored the delegation, and it is perhaps a testament to her experience meeting with international women in Zurich seven months earlier that Ellen volunteered to go. Taking a decision that put socialist comradeship before family companionship, the International Committee of Socialist Undergraduates scheduled the conference for December 26–29; so Ellen spent Christmas travelling with her comrades, not celebrating with her father and siblings.

When the students—nearly one hundred young men and women from France, Britain, Germany, Switzerland, Yugoslavia, and the United States—assembled in Geneva, the ensuing debate exposed the gulf between the radicalism of many supporters of the Bolshevik revolution and the more moderate approach favoured by, amongst others, the British Labour Party. The continental students were committed supporters of the Moscow-dominated Third International (later better known as the Comintern), a revolutionary socialist body devoted to the overthrow of bourgeois society, if necessary by force. The British delegates were divided between supporters of the Third International, including Dutt, and those, like Ellen, who followed the Labour Party in maintaining their commitment to constitutional reform. Given their difference, the British delegation determined to remain neutral between the two factions, to the frustration of their comrades. In Dutt's recollection:

> Accordingly that night a fraction meeting was called of the communist representatives . . . to decide what to do with the English: we were allowed to be present as silent spectators. The discussion was held in an attic and continued into the small hours: at one point the police arrived in the house in search of the Spartakus students: we adjourned through the attic window into a neighbouring attic, and the discussion continued. The pros and cons were weighed; our organization and line was analysed relentlessly like a body being dis-

sected on a mortuary slab; at the end the decision went against us. As we came away in the cold air of that December night (it was Christmas), Ellen Wilkinson said to me (and she had had plenty of experience of trade union, Fabian and Labour infighting): "This is the most ghastly, callous, inhuman machine I have ever witnessed." I said to her: "'At last I have found what I have been looking for: socialists who mean business."

As the English delegates journeyed back home, Dutt sought to bring Ellen around to support for revolutionary Bolshevism. The two argued on trains, in taxis, and in hotel rooms until, as "they stood on their hotel balcony in Paris on New Year's Eve—'while the crowd danced below in the square'—the romance of the revolution temporarily overcame her initial revulsion and by the morning she had promised to join the future Communist Party when it would be formed in Britain."[35]

Dutt's story of Ellen's "conversion" to support for the Third International, and her subsequent decision to attend the founding meeting of the Communist Party of Great Britain, is full of romance and excitement; but it almost certainly elides a much longer process of soul-searching and internal debate. Ellen, and nearly all her young friends from The Movement, initially supported the Russian revolution. As Maurice Reckitt riffed, Trotsky was "the only commissar that they adored." In a world ruled by capitalist plutocrats, here were a group of self-professed Marxists seizing control of one of the major world powers in the name of the dictatorship of the proletariat. The revolution was a cause worth dying for, and those that gave their lives to the cause were as much martyrs as the communards whose graves Ellen and Helen Crawfurd visited in Paris. American journalist John Reed captured the enthusiasm and the hopefulness of the early days of the revolution when he described the funeral procession of Bolshevik fighters slain in the battle of Moscow in October 1917:

All the long day the funeral procession passed, coming in by the Iberian Gate and leaving the Square by way of the Nikolskaya, a river of red banners, bearing words of hope and brotherhood and stupendous prophecies, against a background of fifty thousand people,—under the eyes of the world's workers and their descendants forever. . . .

I suddenly realised that the devout Russian people no longer needed priests to pray them into heaven. On earth they were building a kingdom more bright than any heaven had to offer, and for which it was a glory to die.[36]

The initial promise of the revolution led men and women from the centre to the left of the political spectrum to support Lenin and Trotsky's cause in the early days of 1917–1918. The schisms between the left began to surface only later, as the Bolshevik regime took shape, and the brutality and centralization of Marxism in power revealed itself. For some, the violence perpetrated by the Red Army was reason enough to condemn the revolution, although a surprising number of the "constitutional" and pacifist left proved willing to condone the excesses of the Bolsheviks as necessary in the cause of revolution. The sympathy shown for the Bolshevik regime at the 1919 WILPF conference in Zurich is testament to the lengths some pacifists were willing to go to rationalize revolutionary violence as a necessary price to create a future free from capitalist war.

Further divisions surfaced once the revolution had been secured and the nature of Bolshevik rule revealed itself. By the mid-twentieth century, most had come to accept that socialism in practice meant state control and direction of industry and resources. In the 1910s, it had not been clear this would be the case. Guild Socialism, for example, had been premised upon a very different model of industrial democracy. Douglas Cole refused to join the British Communist Party because he objected to the Bolshevik scheme of state socialism. It is clear from Ellen's speech at the WILPF conference in Zurich that she too aspired to a more participatory model of industrial reform.

Why then did Ellen join ranks with those who founded the Communist Party of Great Britain? Her decision cannot be explained solely by Dutt's persuasive force, or her weariness with arguing with him. Rather it lies in Ellen's impatience with inaction and gradualism and her optimistic belief in building a brave new world on the ashes left over from the war. For the past year and a half, she had witnessed the failures of incremental reform, from the weakness of the trade boards to the timidity of the trade union leadership. Ellen was a doer, not a talker. The Communists were "taking a stand for the new time," and she was determined to take a stand alongside them.

In that spirit, Ellen attended the Communist Unity Convention at the Cannon Street Hotel in the City of London the following summer. She went as a representative of the Manchester Guilds League, alongside Mary Moorhouse, who had travelled with her and Dutt to Geneva that winter. She and Mary were amongst only 19 women present, out of a total of 152 delegates, an early sign that the CPGB would not concern itself overly with women's issues. The atmosphere inside the conference hall was "intense, with the earnestness and determination of the delegates."[37] After a silent tribute to the men and women who had died in the cause of revolution, including German Communist leaders Rosa Luxemburg and Karl Liebknecht, the delegates set about defining the policy and constitution of the party.[38] In her sole contribution to the debate, Ellen made an uncharacteristic statement that revealed how deeply her decision to join the new party was rooted in her desire to revolutionize British society. The fiery young woman, never known for her obedience to anyone, insisted that "if we were going in for a revolutionary party, we must have a general staff and be willing to obey it. . . . A revolution meant discipline and obedience."[39]

Just a few years later, the formation of the first Labour government would lead Ellen to rethink where her loyalties ought to lie. After 1924, it became clear to her that revolutionary change, if it were to come, would arrive on the heels of a Labour government. Yet her conviction that revolution could only be achieved through unified ranks carried over into her relationship with the Labour Party. Although she would always remain on Labour's left wing, she repeatedly trimmed her politics to the party's course rather than resign on principle and leave herself politically isolated. In 1920, however, with Labour holding less than ten percent of the seats in parliament, it was less than clear that the party could deliver real change. Communism, at least, offered action. It also offered a way of understanding the struggle for reform in Britain within a larger geopolitical framework.

4

FROM IRELAND TO RUSSIA

After three long years of war, 1918 had appeared as a watershed political moment. The Russian Revolution was initially widely perceived as a herald of reform on Europe's eastern periphery. Not only radicals like Ellen but more centrist figures like American President Woodrow Wilson met the news of the revolution with optimism. Those who saw the war not in nationalist terms but as a tragedy never to be repeated welcomed Wilson's rhetorical commitment to a peace without victors and a new world order based on national self-determination and peaceful arbitration of international disputes. Two interlinking networks in which Ellen was increasingly enmeshed—the women's peace movement and international Communism—responded to events in Europe with a commitment to work with "sisters" and "comrades" across national borders in pursuit of a new world order. Ellen found herself travelling across Europe and as far afield as Russia and the United States in furtherance of international peace and progress.

Ellen was initially optimistic about the possibilities for cooperation between the women's peace movement and the Communists. Shortly after returning from the conference of university socialists in Geneva, Ellen had brought Dutt to speak to the Women's International League (WIL) women on the "course of revolutionary movements in Europe arising from the war."[1] Yet, in the face of the Communist Party of Great Britain's (CPGB) determined vilification of "work in purely women's organizations [as] at best a diversion and at worst dangerously reactionary," the names of other Communist women—including Helen Crawfurd and Marjory Newbold—quickly disappeared from the records of the Manchester WIL after August 1920.[2]

Historians have repeatedly emphasized the incompatibility of feminist and socialist internationalism. After the initial burst of enthusiasm for reforming the international system in 1918–1919, many women who considered themselves both radical leftists and feminists felt pressured to choose between commitment to social revolution and commitment to the transformation of international relations through women's networks. The Comintern aggressively discouraged Communist women from collaborating with "bourgeois" women's organizations of any sort. The British Labour Party similarly, albeit less adamantly, disapproved of Labour women's participation in non-party women's groups on the grounds that such involvement split women's energies and allegiances. After initially attempting to keep a foot in both camps, many high-profile socialists, such as the Communist Dora Montefiore and Labour leaders Ethel Snowden and Margaret Bondfield, abandoned the women's international movement.[3] Ellen did not. Driven in part by her youthful optimism and in part by an iconoclastic stubbornness, Ellen remained a member of the Women's International League for Peace and Freedom (WILPF) throughout her career in the Communist and Labour parties. The war had impressed upon her the evils of nationalism, and her travels in the years immediately following crystallized a cosmopolitan consciousness that would inform her politics for the rest of her career. Only when men and women accepted their shared humanity as world citizens could the roots of war be torn up. The WILPF might be a "bourgeois" organization, but it was one that truly believed in the equality of all men and women.

Ellen continued to attend meetings of the Manchester WIL's executive only sporadically and, unlike many of her fellow executive committee members, rarely bothered to send excuses for her absences. But she became a more regular platform speaker in the early 1920s—an activity more to her liking than committee work—and when the women decided to send a mission to Ireland to report on the conditions resulting from the British presence, she volunteered to make the journey. The Irish mission was first mooted at the Manchester executive committee meeting on September 28, 1920. The executive endorsed the idea and within a week Agatha Watts was in Ireland with Helena Swanwick. In addition to being chair of the British WIL, Swanwick had been appointed one of two vice-presidents of the WILPF at the Zurich conference and thus was well poised to give the Manchester venture international publicity. A few days later, they were joined by five more members of the Manchester branch, including Annot Robinson and Ellen, and by two Scottish women, M. Mewhort of Edinburgh and Agnes Dollan of Glasgow. Their cooperation was likely orchestrated by Annot, who maintained connections in her native Scotland—an example of the informal networks that bound these women together.

The party divided itself into three groups, with three women going north to Belfast, Derry, and Lisburn, and the remaining seven covering the south. Ellen and two of the women visited Dublin, Limerick, Galway, and Tuam and then turned north, driving up the west coast of County Clare to Ennistymon and from there on to Cork and Mallow. After travelling by train from Dublin to Limerick, the women hired a car and for two weeks drove around the Irish countryside, a breathtaking journey that likely stoked Ellen's future love of motoring holidays.

The Irish mission, however, was no holiday. In planning their trip, the British women received advice on their itinerary from Louie Bennett, a prominent Irish feminist trade unionist and head of the Irish WIL. In a densely packed itinerary, the women met with unionists, nationalists, Sinn Feiners, trade unionists, town councillors, co-operators, women of the working and middle classes, and Roman Catholic and Protestant clergy. Ellen later recalled that she had first met one of the members of the post-independence Irish government when he was a "gaunt and hunted young IRA officer . . . on the run in Ennis with a price on his head."[4] The women paid particular attention to the agricultural situation and visited several cooperative creameries, many of which had been vandalized by the Black and Tans, the notorious paramilitary forces sent in to stabilize the area. On her return to Manchester, Ellen recalled to a WIL audience a farm she had visited, run by a mother, her daughter, and a young farmhand: "That farm was raided in the night, the women forced up the mountain road in bare feet and night attire, and the girl was beaten with the butt-end of rifles by soldiers in order to make her tell where her brothers, who were Sinn Feiners, were." In another village, Ellen had heard reports of a member of the nationalist Irish Volunteers penned within a ring of bayonets and shot at. The man's house was set on fire and the "British soldiers flung that man, still shrieking, into the middle of the fire." Such recrimination was not directed solely at the Catholic population. Protestant clergy had also told her of cases of parishioners' homes set on fire by government forces.[5]

The report of their visit, penned by Swanwick and tellingly titled *A "Sort of War" in Ireland,* began with a confession of the women's biases. "We feel," she wrote, "a special international responsibility to inform ourselves as to how the nations within the British Empire are being treated by our Government, and although we endeavoured to discover the truth in all cases, we do not pretend to have gone to Ireland with minds bare of principles." She noted, "We are women organized for constructive peace and, as such, we hold that freedom is the first condition of peace. We are against violence in all forms; we should welcome the disarming of all men; we regard killing and maiming, and terrorism, *by whomsoever it is practised,* as barbarous and politically vicious." Although the women strove to maintain an open mind and to interview men and women from all sides of the conflict, their findings were perhaps inevitably influenced by the Labour and trade union sympathies of a majority of the party. Their analysis of the troubles placed very little blame on insurmountable religious differences and much on the incendiary actions of business interests and the British state. Of the tense situation in the Belfast shipyards, the women wrote: "It was felt that this was not in the interest of a separate race or a separate religion, but that it was the *business interest* that were being conserved and political differences perpetuated." Of the economic circumstances in the South, they recorded that "we found a conviction among the Irish people that it is the purpose of the British Government to ruin Irish trade and industry in order to drive the young men to emigrate."

The pamphlet concluded with a damning indictment of the British presence in Ireland. Noting that the 1918 general election had seen a majority of 70 percent for Sinn Féin and that the newly created legislative chamber, Dáil Éireann, ruled by "the overwhelming consent of the people," the women called for an immediate truce "during which all armed forces shall be withdrawn and the keeping of order be placed in the hands of Irish local elected bodies, thus creating conditions under which the Irish people may determine their own form of government." This, they felt, was the only viable option, as

> the British Government, attempting to rule against the will of 70 per cent of the people, can do so only by force complicated by fraud. Spies and informers are an essential part of the Government where the mass of people are hostile. There is no co-operation between governors and governed, and the army of occupation (whether military or armed police) is demoralized by perpetual and agonizing fear and the constant use of debasing methods of espionage and lawless intimidation and revenge.... This state of affairs can lead only to the economic ruin of Ireland and great economic injury to Great Britain; to a still more disastrous moral injury to Great Britain and to her reputation in all the world.[6]

The report was published almost immediately after the mission returned to Britain; and the women, individually and collectively, embarked on a national publicity campaign, acting frequently in cooperation with other progressive organizations. Their remit was to educate the public, not to broker a peace between the warring factions. As Helena Swanwick wrote to Jane Addams, "We are not attempting to originate or cooperate with any movement for compromise and I think we shall probably keep out of such entanglements. We have no power but that of reason, so we have nothing to bargain with."[7] Their campaign kicked off with a meeting at the Free Trade Hall on Monday, October 18, to welcome back the delegates. They went on to address meetings throughout the country in cooperation with the "Peace with Ireland Council." Ellen, although preoccupied with both trade union work and Communist Party organization, continued her involvement with the campaign through 1921, speaking alongside Fenner Brockway and Agatha Watts at the Milton Hall in March. In early December, the WIL and the Labour Party discussed the possibility of coordinated action over Ireland. Swanwick attended a national Labour conference on Ireland just before New Year; and, although the two groups did not ultimately merge their campaigns, Annot and Ellen both spoke on Ireland to the National Conference of Labour Women held in Manchester in 1921.[8]

The women followed up on their initial visit with several more trips to the region to document the mistreatment of female prisoners in Irish gaols and "to get sworn evidence of outrages" against the Irish populace by representatives of the British state. In addition to (unsuccessfully) lobbying members of their own government, the British women worked with members of the WILPF in other countries to amplify their pacifist message.[9] The connections forged through the WILPF also brought them into new arenas of political activism. Upon learning of the British women's work, Jane Addams, the president of the WILPF, arranged for Louie Bennett, Annot Robinson, and Ellen to testify before the American Commission on Conditions in Ireland.

The commission was put together under the auspices of the New York-based progressive journal *The Nation* with the remit "to perform the service of ascertaining for the American people the truth about conditions in Ireland, which increasingly menace the friendly relations that have existed between Great Britain and the United States." The 150 commissioners included 5 state governors, 11 senators, and 13 congressmen, as well as several religious leaders and other prominent men and women. However, the actual work of interviewing witnesses was done by a much smaller group—including Addams—which held six hearings in Washington, DC, between November 1920 and January 1921. "Because the Commission had great difficulty in finding anyone willing to testify representing the [official] British point of view (in large part because many saw the Commission's actions as interference in an internal matter), the report and activities of the Commission were considered biased and controversial in many quarters."[10]

Concerns about the committee's bias almost prevented the British women from sending delegates to Washington; but ultimately Swanwick's faith in Addams's judgment overcame any reservations, and the British WIL agreed to send Ellen and Annot to the United States at the Commission's expense.[11] The U.S. government did not share Swanwick's optimism, and the two women nearly were not granted visas. Annot's letters to her sister record the tense negotiations the women went through in the run-up to their departure. The day before they were scheduled to sail from Liverpool, Annot wrote from London: "Trouble has arisen over the USA visa for our passports and this morning I have been to Lord Bryce [the former British ambassador to the United States], have been to the American Embassy and to the USA Consul General and am now awaiting the decision as to whether Ellen Wilkinson and I can sail on Wednesday. I have had no time to get my things together and had to come here by the midnight train and feel sick of officials and diplomats."[12] When Annot returned to Manchester that night, she was still unsure whether they would receive their visas in time to depart on the S. S. Baltic. "I left home this morning not knowing whether we should go or not having flung something together and doing some shopping at Lewis's afterwards and feeling that I was leaving chaos behind me," Annot wrote to Nellie.[13]

Ultimately the U.S. consulate in Manchester issued their visas at noon, "after extracting from us a definite promise that we would not address meetings, engage in any propaganda, or grant any interviews while we were in America."[14] The two women caught an afternoon train to Liverpool. When they made it onboard the S. S. Baltic, they found that the ship had been overbooked and they were upgraded to first-class cabins, although their excitement at the unexpected "luxury and comfort" was offset by the poor weather—the fog was so dense they could not leave port for two days. Annot wrote to Nellie, "We are all overeating ourselves and Ellen Wilkinson is already bored. I'm not. I'm enjoying the rest after the last few hectic days. But we ought to give evidence on the 17th and at this rate we won't reach Washington by then."[15]

Once they got moving, they crossed the Atlantic in less than four days, arriving in New York on Sunday and disembarking the following morning. Annot's letters to her sister suggest the White Star Line was either ultimately able to find them second-class accommodation or did not extend them the courtesy of allowing them to dine with the first-class passengers, as she reports that the feminist preacher Maude Royden was on board, but "she is travelling first class, and so I have not seen her." Annot nonetheless had an entertaining voyage, with "days filled with sunshine and gossip and social life" and whist drives and dances in the evenings.[16] Although they could have made the journey to Washington in time for their originally scheduled date, the commission pushed their testimony back until the following Tuesday, giving the women time to relax and do some sightseeing in the capital.

The Commission had established itself in the Hotel Lafayette, directly across the street from the White House. (The grand hotel would, ironically, later be bought by the American Federation of Labour.) Now, two representatives of the British Labour movement gave their impression of events in Ireland to a commission that included not only Addams but also Quaker pacifist and civil rights advocate L. Hollingsworth Wood, who served as chairman; economist Frederic Howe; the Socialist trade unionist Jim Maurer; Massachusetts senator David Walsh; journalist and sociologist Oliver P. Newman; Nebraska senator George W. Norris; and the Reverend Norman Thomas.

Annot testified first, speaking of her experiences touring Ulster. She emphasized that disputes between Ulster dockworkers and their employers were caused not by religious hatred but by class conflict. "I was surprised to find that it was much more an economic question than the question of religious domination," she stated. "The point I wish to make is that Carsonism and Unionism are becoming the stronghold of capitalism and aristocratic feeling."[17] In her assessment, the capitalist class wanted to remain united with Britain for fear of tax hikes by the Irish Republican government.

The Commission broke for lunch and returned with Jane Addams in the chair to question Ellen on her experiences in southern Ireland. Despite her bravado, Ellen's testimony hints at her nervousness giving evidence before such company. In speaking of the Industrial Development Commission of the Dáil Éireann, for example, she told the commission "Darrell Figgis was head of this commission; and he was arrested, of course, and the documents of the commission confiscated, and the movement crushed. Then, of course, there was in Ireland the general cooperative movement along the English lines. The terrible thing is that a great many of the Irish people feel that this crushing of the new industrial movement and the burning of creameries and factories is part of England's policy toward Ireland. And, of course, everyone who knows history knows that during the time of Mercantilism, England did ruin the wood industry of Ireland."[18]

She appears to have relaxed as she went on, and her later responses are less rambling, with fewer verbal tics. The most moving part of her testimony was when she attempted to defend the young Englishmen— like her brother Harold—who had been swept up in the cycle of political violence in Ireland. Although she attributed the atrocities to the Black and Tans, she did not blame the men themselves so much as the militaristic policies of the government:

> After all, the armed forces of the Crown in Ireland are our own men. And any English audience to which you talk will say, "Well, my husband is there." And as far as that is concerned, my own brother, a boy of eighteen, was stationed at Ennis during the latter part of the war. Therefore, I want to be fair in dealing with this question. It is difficult to make English people understand it. And it is also important for people who are looking at matters not from the standpoint of any country or any government, but from the human point of view, to realize that the military authorities in Ireland are concentrating on propaganda amongst these men, which is producing a mentality that makes them believe that every Irishman is a murderer. If you are going to consider the Irish problem, it seems to me that you cannot get away from the mentality of the English soldiers who are over there.[19]

Her ability to see both sides of an issue and to recognize the humanity even of those whom she was most critical of would make her an effective parliamentary politician in later years. The same traits would serve her less well as a member of the Communist Party, which, as time went on, increasingly privileged sectarianism and left little space for human sympathy.

The commission held two more hearings before breaking for the holidays. Annot and Ellen journeyed to Chicago with Addams and spent Christmas with her in Cedarville, Illinois. Addams showed them around Hull House, the settlement home she had cofounded with Ellen Starr thirty years earlier, and took them around the city. Both women enjoyed the trip immensely, although Annot found that "speaking to people who are cleverer than yourself and discussing movements was very exhausting." On their return east, "We stopped and saw Niagara on our way from Chicago to New York, on the principle that 'you couldn't be in Kent and not go to see Canterbury.' The spray and mist had frozen overnight and the spectacle was a wonderful one." The sightseeing, whilst exciting, took its toll on Ellen, who "slept poorly, and suffered from an upset stomach," which was not helped by the rough crossing on their journey home.[20] Ellen later recalled the crossing as "three days tossing about with the hatches battened down, or whatever they do to hatches, and water swishing round the cabin floor."[21]

Ellen had little chance to recuperate from her illness when she got home to Manchester. As she wrote to Addams nearly three weeks after landing, "I was rushed away to a strike almost as soon as I landed in England and have only just finished it."[22] The rapid shift from international work to domestic labour activism would characterize her career. For Ellen, British working-class politics were not merely a domestic struggle for higher wages and better hours. Rather, she saw domestic and international politics as inextricably linked. In the 1930s, this would manifest itself in her campaigns to raise British awareness about the threat posed by anti-socialist terror in Germany and Spain. In the early 1920s, it took the form of involvement in the Red International of Labour Unions, which sought the international overthrow of the capitalist system of industrial ownership and control.

For those Communists, like Ellen, who were intimately concerned with the industrial side of the British labour movement, reform of trade union organization appeared a crucial first step in the spread of world revolution to Britain. The British Trade Union Congress was already in conversation with trade unionists from across Europe through the International Federation of Trade Unions, based throughout the 1920s in Amsterdam. The so-called Amsterdam International sought to mass the strength of trade unionism across Europe and the United States, but its leaders had no desire to see the trade union movement transformed into a revolutionary vehicle that would use its power to effect political change through "direct action"—or coordinated strikes over organizational and political issues, as opposed to simply over wages, hours, and conditions of labour.

To radical internationalists, the Amsterdam International was an overly cautious, arguably even a reactionary, body. Nationally, Communists in Britain, France, Czechoslovakia, and other countries were already working to "infiltrate" national unions and turn their members toward the need for industrial revolution. Yet the leaders of the international Communist movement feared this gradual process would move too slowly to convert the "yellow" Amsterdam International into a truly "red" body in time to take advantage of the revolutionary fever gripping the West in the wake of the Great War. Thus, after the second meeting of the Third International in Moscow in 1920, a group of radical trade unionists determined to establish a rival Red International of Labour Unions (RILU)—a body prepared to capitalize on the transformation of approach within individual national unions.

In April 1921, a small group of around twenty Communists from the guild movement and the Labour Research Department began meeting at a rickety old building on the Strand end of Waterloo Bridge, under the leadership of the shop steward Jack Murphy, who had attended the Moscow meeting at which the decision to establish the RILU had been taken. Robin Page Arnot, whom Ellen had known since university, suggested her name to Murphy, and Ellen eagerly joined the group, which focused its energies on converting the British trade unions to a revolutionary platform.[23]

Ellen described their goal and methods in the journal the *Communist*. Although her trademark colloquialisms filled the columns—she refers to ideas of workers' control and amalgamation being "in the air" and the feeling that trade unionism "on the old lines" had "met its match"—the article lacked her usual humour, its earnestness revealing how fully she had thrown herself into the RILU project. "The Red Trade Union propaganda," she argued, "brings the trade unionist to realise the only way out of the present deadlock"—namely the radical reconstruction of international industry along Communist lines. She went on to outline the work she and her colleagues had been engaged in: "Taking industry by industry, special leaflets and circulars have been prepared suitable to the different unions, committees, consisting not of ornaments but of the people doing the spade work in the unions, have been formed, and these are preparing the grounds within the lines."[24] Unsurprisingly, the majority of the trade union leadership was not enthusiastic about this attempt to co-opt the British labour movement to the international revolution. Here again, Ellen was fortunate to have the support of John Jagger. Although not at the Cannon Street conference, Jagger was sympathetic to the Communists and encouraged Ellen in her revolutionary work.

The British government, however, was not so indulgent. The British branch of the RILU quickly attracted the attention of Scotland Yard, which kept a disapproving eye on the group's preparations to send Murphy, Ellen, Tom Mann, Harry Pollitt, Olive Budden, and several others on a five-week expedition to Russia to attend the Third International and the RILU's inaugural meeting that June. The activities of the group feature regularly in the monthly review of revolutionary movements prepared for the secretary of state. The Home Office was particularly concerned about the group's finances, arguing Moscow's subventions of the RILU constituted "if not a technical, an actual breach of the conditions of the Trading Agreement" between the two countries.[25]

The government did not, however, prevent their departure. Ellen received a visa from the Russian trade delegation in London and in June set off on a winding journey to Moscow with Arnot and Olive Budden, who would later marry. The group travelled first-class across the North Sea, down the east coast of Denmark, through the Kiel Canal and the Baltic Sea, to Tallinn in Estonia.[26] The steamer stopped only once, in Liepāja, which had briefly served as the capital of the Latvian provisional government during the recent fighting between the Bolshevik and White armies. The trio took the chance to stretch their legs for a couple of hours in a seaside park. They were shocked to discover how the conflict had taken its toll on the town. The group "found it completely deserted: the very blades of grass seemed lonely."[27] The few children they saw out and about looked heartbreakingly listless and ill-fed.[28]

From Tallinn, they made their way by train to Petrograd and then south to Moscow. Their international wagon-lit carriage found them in cosmopolitan company—Arnot suspected two fellow passengers of being Turkish diplomats. The train stopped to reprovision in the medieval town of Yamburg (now Kingisepp), which had seen heavy fighting during the Russian Civil War. While Olive stayed on board, Robin and the ever-curious Ellen went out on the town, where, not far from the baroque cathedral, they saw a statue of Marx that had been defaced by the White Army.[29]

The desolate, war-scarred towns on the Baltic Coast did not prepare Ellen for the experience of visiting Russia's two greatest cities. As H. G. Wells wrote after his visit to Russia in 1920, "the harsh and terrible realities of the situation in Russia cannot be camouflaged . . . it is hardly possible to dress up two large cities for the benefit of . . . stray visitors." Although the Soviet government had attempted to restore order to the city, the sights Ellen witnessed in Petrograd would not have been far removed from those described by Wells. "Its palaces are still and empty," he recorded. "Its streets were [before the war] streets of busy shops. . . . All these shops have ceased. There are perhaps half a dozen shops still open in Petersburg." Wells recognized that such desolation would be hard for a Western reader to imagine. He went on to emphasize, "It is not like Bond Street or Piccadilly on a Sunday, with the blinds neatly drawn down in a decorous sleep, and ready to wake up and begin again on Monday. The shops have an utterly wretched and abandoned look: paint is peeling off, windows are cracked, some are broke and boarded up, some still display a few fly-blown relics of stock in the window, some have their windows covered with notices; the windows are growing dim, the fixtures have gathered two years' dust." The population of Petersburg he described as "nearly starving, and hardly anyone possesses a second suit of clothes or more than a single change of worn linen. . . . Everyone is shabby; everyone seems to be carrying bundles in both Petersburg and Moscow." "Drugs and any medicines are equally unobtainable," Wells noted—a truth that came home to Ellen and her companions when one of them fell ill and needed an injection only to find hypodermic syringes unobtainable in the city. (Ellen, with characteristic hyperbole, claimed in the columns of the *Manchester Guardian* that there was only one hypodermic syringe in all of Moscow.[30])

In placing blame for the spectacular collapse, Wells pointed his finger not at the Bolsheviks, but at the indifference of the capitalists and imperialists who had driven the Russian people to the point of desperation. The Bolsheviks, he admitted, were naïve and conspiracy obsessed; but they also possessed a "youth and energy" and an essential hopefulness and honesty that made it difficult for him to condemn them outright, his scepticism about the Communist experiment notwithstanding. In this respect, Wells stood in the middle of a spectrum of progressive British opinion on the Bolsheviks. Since the revolution, several members of the British left had been to Russia on official delegations and unofficial pilgrimages. In May 1920, the ILP, the Labour Party, and the Trades Union Congress had sent a group of eleven men and women to the country. These included Clifford Allen, Ellen's colleague from her University Socialist Federation days, and Ethel Snowden, wife of the future Labour chancellor of the exchequer and a fellow delegate to the Zurich conference, who were both in their own way disappointed by what they saw. Others members of the delegation, including Welsh miners' leader Robert Williams and ex-Liberal MP Charles Buxton, were more enthusiastic, as had been George Lansbury, the Christian Socialist editor of the radical *Daily Herald* newspaper, who made his own journey to Russia in February 1920.

These latter men were not oblivious to the destruction and deprivation in modern Russia. Like Wells, Buxton wrote of the collapse of the retail sector, describing the boarded-up shops in Russia's principal cities and concluding, "something has been destroyed in Moscow and Petrograd which made a part of all our lives in the Western States of Europe. . . . We might call this something 'Regent Street.'" But this loss was to him offset by what the revolution had gained. "A short detour behind these once opulent facades would reveal former slum dwellers rehoused in flats that had previously been the exclusive domain of the middle class." "When I think of the colossal effort that is being made, the tragic conditions of the experiment, the feverish atmosphere of excitement, of elation, of depression, now one and now the other, which has surrounded it, I feel that I cannot isolate the machinery of the Revolution from the human elements that play around it and make, mar, or modify it. . . . We have forced them to employ many odious means to maintain their footing—and then abused them for employing these means."[31]

Buxton owned to what had been lost in the revolution but argued that present and future gains of the Communist experiment outweighed the "odious" costs. Ellen reached a similar conclusion, although she was less inclined to admit the revolution had had its victims. She returned to Britain determined to silence Russia's critics. Although she accepted that Russia still had far to go, she was impressed by how far the country had come, even in the face of the Western blockade, and saved particular praise for their advanced approach to questions of gender, sexuality, and family life. Women, she noted, were given the "rate for the job," both in terms of cash payments and rations—even down to their tobacco ration, a detail of particular interest to the young cigarette smoker. She praised the government's attitude toward unwed mothers, noting, "Illegitimate children carry no social or legal stigma, the supply of extra rations taking away that horror of destitution that faces the western unmarried mother of the working class." She defended the legalization of abortion as providing an invaluable safety valve for desperate women. (She would be disappointed fifteen years later when Stalin's government reversed this policy, making abortion illegal except to save the life of the mother.) The Soviet Ministry of Health also worked to educate women about sexual health above and beyond conception. Of a pictorial poster campaign on the symptoms and effects of syphilis, Ellen noted that while "the entire British Press would have raged had these been exhibited in England; . . . as I observed the quiet, decent interest of the men and women round the window, I wondered whether this sanitary removal of facts from romance to reality was not infinitely more decent and effective than the veiled, shamed advertisements of the British Council for Combating Venereal Diseases."[32]

When colleagues "bombarded" her with questions about the availability of food in Moscow, Ellen emphasized the spiritual sustenance Communism gave the Russian people: "the spirit of things in Russia was so entirely different from anything in this country. The people in Russia were able to look forward with hope." When people asked about rumours of infighting among the Bolshevik leadership, she protested that "the stories of fundamental differences between Lenin and Trotsky were nonsense," and she said they "worked with one another on the affectionate terms of men who had been through a lot together." And when people asked, "Is Communism a success in Russia?" she emphasized the role she and her comrades in Britain must play in bringing about the success of the revolution. "Communism in Russia has only begun as yet," she wrote. "It cannot succeed until the Communists in other countries have done their part. It is no more possible to have a Communist Russia in a capitalist world than to have a Communist Manchester in a Capitalist Britain."[33]

Ellen's greatest rationalizations dealt with the ongoing famine in the Volga, which would ultimately cause the deaths of an estimated five million people. In an interview with the *Manchester Guardian* on her return, she said of the famine: "While not wishing to minimize the gravity of the situation, . . . much that had been written about it could not be relied upon. The Soviet Government . . . was not, as has been asserted, panic-stricken by the crisis, but had set up adequate machinery for distributing relief when it arrived and for getting food from other parts of Russia to the famine area." She claimed, "The reason for the incorrect newspaper stories is that most of the journalists who are writing about Russia are outside Russia. They are not allowed to come into it, and so they write fanciful yarns from the frontier towns—Riga, Warsaw or Reval [Tallinn]."[34] Yet from her perch in Moscow, 1,000 kilometres from the Volga basin, Ellen was no better informed than the Western journalists. Her only source of information was the reports of Bolshevik officials, which in her eagerness to believe she accepted as truth.

Ellen's descriptions of both the Comintern conference and the inaugural meeting of the Red International of Labour Unions were similarly optimistic, as was her report of the Women's International, which she and Olive attended immediately before the opening of the main conference. Her writing reveals both her respect for the Bolshevik leaders and for the project of world revolution and her thrill at belonging to an international community of revolutionaries. The third Comintern congress was noteworthy in its retreat from the optimism that had characterized the first two meetings. The world revolution no longer seemed as imminent as it had in 1919 or even in 1920. Beleaguered by civil war and faced with massive famine in the Volga region, the Bolsheviks had agreed to accept humanitarian aid from the West and had reinstituted modified capitalism in the form of the New Economic Policy. Arnot described the changed mood thus: "Facing the fact that there had been very serious setbacks in every sector of the World, . . . all Lenin's speeches and everything concerned with it were based on teaching people somehow to retreat in order and not to be routed." Yet even in retreat, the Bolsheviks were not lacking in revolutionary bravado. The Russians spent much of the conference reiterating the need for discipline within the international movement and emphasizing their mastery of the situation at home. And Ellen, who felt a keen "desire for a plan and a direction, of wanting to feel part of a society which was going somewhere," was—like so many others who journeyed to Moscow between the wars—naïve in her eagerness to believe the best and discount the worst of her Soviet allies.[35]

In the packed hall of the Kremlin, Leon Trotsky gave a three-and-a-half-hour speech in German on the future of the world struggle. Although Ellen would need to read the transcript to make out the details, she could appreciate its gist; and hearing Trotsky's impassioned oratory was for her the highlight of the conference. On her return to Britain, she praised his "brilliant analysis" of the dangerous work of the bourgeois reactionaries throughout the West and insisted his speech should be "carefully mastered by every Communist." Lenin chaired the debate on the situation within Russia and the introduction of the New Economic Policy. Although the leader was greeted with "a storm of applause," Ellen "thought his humourous smile grew somewhat bitter as certain delegates from countries that had thrown away priceless opportunities for revolution, complained that Russia's attempt to save her people from starvation might make their struggle a little harder." She briefly had a chance to speak with Lenin and noticed that while he projected an aura of humour and alertness, up close he "looked very tired. It was obvious he was overworked." Hearing the two Bolshevik leaders was formative for Ellen, and she would later describe it as one of the great moments of her political career, alongside meeting Gandhi in 1931.[36]

Although Ellen shared Lenin's frustration with outsiders who sought to criticize the Russian leader, she was nonetheless moved by Alexandra Kollantai's "magnificent reply to Lenin," in which she asked him, "Are you not putting too much faith in locomotives and machinery, and too little in the creative impulses of the people that made the revolution possible?" A striking woman twenty years Ellen's senior, Kollantai was a feminist role model for Ellen—a Communist answer to many of the bourgeois women Ellen had met in Zurich two years earlier. Kollontai was a Russian aristocrat by birth, who, Ellen thought enviously, "would look distinguished if wrapped in a blanket."[37] Wealthy and well-educated—she was fluent in eleven languages—Kollontai had spent much of her life abroad, studying Marxism and developing a Communist critique of women's social subjugation in Russian society. She had returned to Russia on the eve of the revolution, and was appointed People's Commissar for Social Welfare, becoming the first female government minister in Europe. She advocated for the introduction of state-sponsored maternity services and childcare, on the grounds that women could not play their full role as revolutionaries if society continued to confine them to the home. In 1919 she founded the women's department of the Russian Communist Party with the aim of educating women for equal citizenship.[38] Kollontai's belief in the reciprocal obligations of the state to its female citizens would find an echo in Ellen's own arguments in the House of Commons a few years later for state provision for widows.

Even before Kollontai's speech at the general Comintern conference, Ellen had had a chance to meet the minister for social welfare at the women's conference, where she had first been impressed by her "common-sense and humourous toleration." Ellen was frustrated by her inability to communicate with the women whose only language was Russian, but Kollontai's fluency is so many languages made her an ideal ambassador for the Russian position to the foreign women in attendance. Ellen also had a brief opportunity to converse, most likely in French, with Lenin's wife, Nadezhda Krupskaya, an experience she described as "the great event" of the conference. Krupskaya, unlike Lenin, was reserved and composed, although her "vivid blue eyes" gave away her interest in her interlocutor.[39]

At the women's conference, Ellen met several "Mohammedan women, and the enclosed women of the various Eastern races." This was her first encounter with a group of non-Western women, and the language she used in describing the encounter—"women with minds as veiled as their faces"—suggests a tendency to exoticize them. In later years, when she became more closely involved with the Indian women's movement, she would show a real desire to understand non-Christian cultures on their own terms. In 1921, however, she viewed these women through a Western lens and spoke of the Russian women's efforts to rouse a desire for "emancipation" in the hearts of their Eastern comrades within the Soviet Union.[40]

At the same time that the great leaders of the Bolshevik revolution were speaking in the Kremlin, the RILU, also known as the Profintern, held its inaugural meeting in the Hall of Columns, in what was now known as the House of Trade Unions. Jack Murphy described the meeting as a coming together of "hundreds of keen, alert minds, determined on the task of mobilising and leading the rest of the international working-class army towards the conquest of power."[41] To Ellen, it was "a less imposing" event than the Third International, but one no less important to the future of the international revolution. Syndicalists arguing for an autonomous trade union organization made their case against Communists, who sought to see the RILU fully integrated into the Comintern, and centrists——including most of the British delegates—who wanted close cooperation between the two organizations but knew that an explicit affiliation with the Comintern was more likely to alienate than to attract workers to their cause. The moderate position ultimately won out, although the links between the Comintern and the RILU were so close as to undermine any claims to autonomy. Ellen wrote of the two, "there is but one aim for us—the overthrow of world capitalism. To secure this there can only be one army, the International of the Revolutionary Proletariat. This may for convenience be divided into regiments and corps, but they are all part of the one movement, imbued with the same ideas."[42]

The martial rhetoric Ellen used to describe the joint mission of the RILU and the Comintern had echoes in her description of the Comintern conference. Ellen described it as "not a gathering of representatives to learn how things are done under Communism but a Council of War, a congress of deputies from the various fronts to consider the world revolutionary conflict, to take stock of gains and losses since the last Congress, and to make plans for the struggle in the immediate future." Her warlike words found echoes throughout the conference sessions. After conference chairman Grigory Zinoviev gave the closing address, the Red Army band burst into a rendition of the Internationale, "and through the great Palace of the Kremlin, monument of the luxury and tyranny of a thousand years rang the Revolutionary Anthem." The Internationale was followed by other "war songs," including the Russian Hymn to Freedom; the French Carmagnole; and Spanish, German, and Yugoslav revolutionary anthems. Just as the crowd finally began to disperse, once more "the International pealed forth over Moscow, silent under the stars. And as the groups of comrades, who, in spite of the barriers of custom and language, had got to know each other so well in these fateful days broke from the crowd to say good-bye, we knew that divided by hostile governments, with little news of what each other was doing, we were not going back to work in separate parties, but in one all-embracing International, to which we were personally dedicated, for the World Revolution."[43]

How Ellen squared this martial enthusiasm with her professed pacifism remains a difficult question. Given her later condemnation of political violence both in Britain and in continental Europe, it is hard to resist the conclusion that her own use of military rhetoric in the early 1920s was simply rhetorical. Harry Pollitt's biographer has argued that, having neither fought nor lost a loved one in the war, "Pollitt's blithe acceptance of political violence was that of a man for whom . . . these things were always at one step removed." For Ellen, who unlike Pollitt distanced herself from Communist extremism after only a few years, the gulf between her rhetoric and her convictions was even wider. She certainly did not envisage a bloody battle between workers and capital in the cities and factories of Britain, nor would she have wished for one. She was even capable of mocking her own rhetoric, as when she starred in a revue at the Fabian summer school only a few weeks after returning from Russia in which a guillotine decapitated all of her comrades until "Ellen, with flaming red hair down to her waist and a vast red bow over her chest, stood on a monstrous pile of corpses, exulting that 'at last we have got rid of all the people with middle-class ideas.'"[44] The scene was part of a three-act comic review written by her friends Douglas Cole and Maurice Reckitt. The play was performed alongside "a brilliant Russian ballet and an efficient beauty chorus" organized by another young Communist, Rose Cohen, and the "riot of executions" was mocking rather than censorious.[45] Given the international situation, Ellen's cavalier attitude toward such inflammatory rhetoric and actual violent practice is at best callous and irresponsible. Yet the war had introduced a militarized language of comradeship that would prove impossible to expunge from the interwar vocabulary, and in this context Ellen's use of such language likely illustrates her deep feelings of kinship for her fellow Communists in Europe and abroad rather than an enthusiastic endorsement of political violence.

After the 1921 Comintern conference, Ellen remained in Russia for the month of July. The members of the British delegation to the RILU travelled around the country to study trade union conditions there.[46] Afterwards, she departed Russia with Harry Pollitt, the future general secretary of the Communist Party. The two travelled by train to St. Petersburg, then took a more leisurely boat journey along the Baltic, stopping at Tallinn, Riga, and Danzig, before heading inland and completing their journey by train. From Danzig, they travelled to Berlin, where they "spent a very pleasant evening" with the *Daily Herald* journalist Morgan Philips Price. Price had been in Moscow during the revolution as a correspondent for the *Manchester Guardian*. He had just published *My Reminiscences of the Russian Revolution,* in which he owned to a much greater scepticism about the dictatorial methods of the Bolsheviks than did Ellen or Pollitt. Yet Price's sympathies remained with the revolutionary left. The British government was convinced he was an intermediary between British extremists and the German Communist Party and a courier for Trotsky.[47] In describing the current situation in Weimar Germany to his guests, he emphasized the "brutal, uncivilised terror carried out with design and efficiency by the military against the left-wing revolutionaries."[48] Price's harrowing stories of the repression of the German Communist revolution by the Social Democratic Weimar leadership further convinced Ellen that even allegedly liberal parliamentarians could not be trusted to transform society. What was needed was an influx of Communist politicians committed to the radical overthrow of the existing order.

5

A WOMAN CANDIDATE WITH COMMUNISTIC VIEWS

On October 8, 1921, Ellen Cicely Wilkinson turned thirty. She was not married and had come to accept she would likely remain single. As she later reflected, if a woman is to marry and have children, "her peak period is between eighteen and twenty-five. But if her ambition is to be . . . a politician, she inevitably kicks her colt-feet around till well in the thirties, as a man does, suffering and learning from her mistakes, building the personality that can do things in the forties." When she cast off Walton Newbold's proposals seven years earlier, Ellen had chosen to marry herself to politics, but by 1921 she still wasn't clear what kind of political career she wanted to have. Would she make her name as a Communist firebrand? A feminist crusader? A radical Labour backbencher? Or something else entirely?

In the four years between her participation in the founding conference of the Communist Party of Great Britain (CPGB) in 1920 and her election as Labour member of parliament for Middlesbrough East in 1924, Ellen's political priorities shifted. Politics increasingly appealed to her as a venue to effect immediate change, as opposed to a platform to debate policies for a distant revolution. Without abandoning her commitment to activism, she decided she wanted to become a legislator. But her rapid turn towards electoral politics could not necessarily have been predicted in 1920. In the first years of the decade, she poured an unprecedented amount of energy into radical propagandizing. She returned from Moscow in the summer of 1921 ready to double down on her commitment to the Red International of Labour Unions and give her support to the newly formed Communist Women's Committee. She also became increasingly involved with two Marxist educational organizations, the National Council of Labour Colleges (NCLC) and the Labour Research Department (LRD).

The NCLC was established in autumn 1921 to provide coordination between the Central Labour College (CLC) in London and the grassroots working-class education groups that had sprung up around the country, principally but not exclusively in the northeast and in the Welsh mining country. The college had opened its doors in Earl's Court in 1911, after a group of Marxist students fell out with the leadership of Ruskin College, the adult education college established in Oxford in 1899. The CLC predated the formation of the Communist Party, and the National Council retained its independence from the CPGB, although the party had close ties to the new organization in its early years.[1] The NCLC's focus was ostensibly education, not propaganda. Yet, unlike Ruskin College and the Workers' Education Association (WEA), which focused on providing workers' access to educational courses in traditional subject matter, the labour colleges saw themselves as educating workers for the revolution. Whereas the WEA paid its lecturers, the NCLC lecturers volunteered their time. Lecturers' interpretation of history stressed the narrative of class struggle. The colleges had a close, if often fractious, relationship with the *Plebs* journal. The journal, for which Ellen wrote frequently in the 1920s, sought to report on politics and international affairs through a class-conscious lens. In 1924, Ellen jestingly told her colleagues at the NCLC annual meeting, "I was astonished to discover when I came into contact with the National Council of Labour Colleges how little real history I had been taught."[2] Yet although NCLC courses may have foregrounded episodes like the 1834 prosecution of the Tolpuddle Martyrs for their attempts to form an illegal trade union or the Paris Commune of 1871, as Ellen willingly conceded, "The value of IWCE [independent working-class education] is not the actual amount of facts of history or economics imparted, but that, by making the class struggle the basis of all its teaching, its members can be trusted to take the right *attitude* at the moment of crisis."[3]

Ellen's advocacy on behalf of the NCLC within her union underscores the importance she placed on political education as a prerequisite to revolutionary change. In 1923, she threw her support behind a controversial proposal by members of her union to engage the NCLC to provide courses for union members. In the past, she argued, "the great movements for working-class liberty, led by Wat Tyler or Jack Cade, had been made to appear as the riotings of ignorant rebels." In Russia, once the Bolsheviks had come to power, they were faced with a shortage of teachers equipped to educate students in class-conscious history. The National Union of Distributive and Allied Workers (NUDAW) should do its best to educate members to take their place as leaders in the revolutionary struggle.[4] Plans for the scheme were ultimately passed, although dissent continued. At the following year's conference, Ellen again came to the defence of the scheme, which had gotten off to a rocky start and which continued to face criticism in the letters columns of the union's journal, the *New Dawn,* for its failure to cover key historical episodes and economic theories deemed "bourgeois" by NCLC instructors.[5]

The leaders of the NCLC movement alongside whom Ellen worked closely in the early 1920s had committed their careers to political education and had little interest in electoral politics. Jim and Christine Millar devoted their lives to the NCLC movement, with Jim serving as general secretary of NCLC for four decades. Bill Craik stayed on as principal of the Central Labour College for the entirety of his career. Mark Starr fell out with the NCLC crowd in the mid-1920s and moved to America but remained active in the field of working-class education. Personally, Ellen must have enjoyed the courses and lectures she taught for the NCLC, which focused on economic history. If she had hated her brief stint as a pupil teacher in Manchester because the curriculum was staid and uninspiring, the NCLC offered an opportunity to teach a different kind of history. But, although Christine Millar would eulogize Ellen after her death for her commitment to IWCE in the 1920s, Ellen's political career was not destined to reside exclusively in education.[6]

Ellen's colleagues in another educational venture, the Labour Publishing Company (LPC), shared her broader conception of political engagement. The LPC began life in February 1921 as an offshoot of the Labour Research Department (LRD), on whose executive Ellen served until the Second World War. Its initial board of directors was made up primarily of journalists and authors, not educators. In addition to LRD stalwarts Douglas Cole and Robin Page Arnot, these included pacifist author Norman Angell and Christian Socialist MP and editor of the *Daily Herald* George Lansbury. Ellen, who had become one of the most prolific journalists amongst the core members of The Movement, was a natural addition. The company's professed mission was first to act as a publisher for LRD publications but also to commission new work of interest to The Movement and to publish, as Ellen put it, reprints of "Labour Classics"—"writings that are landmarks in the workers' struggle, but which have been allowed to fall out of print by ordinary publishers not too anxious that their influence should remain to hearten the rebellious spirit of our times."[7]

As a member of the LRD executive, Ellen did her best to promote the new company in her union journal. In May 1921, she advertised the publication of a new translation of Karl Marx's 1871 pamphlet *The Civil War in France* and the reprint of speeches by the leaders of the 1st Internationale on the eve of the Franco-Prussian War. "Would that their like could have been produced by the Amsterdam International in 1914," she lamented—a reference to the comparative pusillanimity of the modern-day socialists who had failed to take a principled stand against the capitalist-imperialist World War.[8] Four months later, she touted the publication of a translation of Leon Trotsky's "Defense of Terrorism," arguing, "It gives to the Communist and the anti-Communist alike a brilliant explanation and defense of those policies of the Bolsheviks which have been most seriously and most severely criticized in this country."[9]

The Labour Research Department had emerged out of the Guild Socialist movement. However, the pull of the Communist Party tore

many, including Ellen, away from earlier revolutionary syndicalist allegiances. The National Guilds League was wound up after its last, poorly
attended, annual conference in 1923; but guildsmen and Communists
continued to work together on the LRD executive.[10] As an LRD Communist, Ellen likely had a hand in the selection of *Defense of Terrorism*
for the LPC list. If the Guild Socialist members of the executive had any
reservations about publishing *Defense of Terrorism,* they got their own
back with the publication of the *Bolo Book,* a compendium of the spoof
songs sung in the LRD offices, which included both "T-T-T-Trotsky"
and "Proscription Carol" sung to the tune of "Widdicome Fair," which
gently deflated the doctrinaire pomposity of the Communists:

> *Friend Lenin has warned us we first must proscribe*
> *Peace upon earth and goodwill towards men*
> *All renegades of the Socialist tribe*
> *Such as Henderson, Clynes, Will Thorne,*
> *Philip Snowden, Ethel Snowden, Jimmy*
> *Thomas, and Ramsay MacDonald and all—*
> *James Ramsay MacDonald and all*
>
> *Ned Pease, Ned Pease, shall lend us his list;*
> *Peace upon earth and goodwill towards men.*
> *We need to make sure that no Fabian is missed,*
> *Such as Mallon, Emil Davies, Lawson Dodd,*
> *Haden Guest, Susan Lawrence, Bernard*
> *Shaw, and Beatrice and Sidney and all—*
> *Dear Beatrice and Sidney and all.*
>
> *Then most of the Guildsmen deserve to be dead;*
> *Peace upon earth and goodwill towards men.*
> *So let armies of Communists cut off the head*
> *Of Sam Hobson, Mrs. Ewer, Maurice Reckitt,*
> *Page Arnot, Douglas Cole, Margaret Cole,*
> *Orage, Major Douglas and all—*
> *O God, Major Douglas and all.*[11]

The tune had been used in the Fabian Summer School revue at
Goldalming in 1920, when "flaming-haired" Ellen had emerged as the

sole survivor of an imagined Red Revolution in London.[12] The cover art for the *Bolo Book* was prepared by cartoonist Frank Horrabin, who briefly sat on the LRD executive in 1921–1922. Horrabin's irrepressible sense of humour made him the perfect artist to commission for the task. It also endeared him to Ellen, as a welcome leaven to her own more caustic wit.

The Labour College courses and the books and pamphlets produced by the LRD's new publishing company were intended to educate men and women in the fundamentals of Marxist ideology and the history of the class struggle. They were both relatively blind to the gendered aspect of the class struggle, taking the proletariat as an undifferentiated whole. Yet over and over, Ellen had been confronted with the reality that capitalist exploitation was heavily gendered. She had been impressed on her visit to Russia by the political and social advancement of women under Bolshevism.[13] Unfortunately, the British Communist Party did not appear to place the same emphasis on women's emancipation as their Russian comrades. The German Clara Zetkin, who became secretary of the Moscow-based Women's Secretariat of the Comintern Executive in 1920, complained that many national Communist parties, including Britain's, did not have women's organizations. In January 1921, Ellen and her NUDAW colleague Mary Bamber were put in charge of drafting a "women's manifesto" for the British branch of the RILU; however, the branch did not follow up with an ongoing agenda of activism amongst women workers.[14] A year later, *All Power,* the RILU's monthly newssheet, inaugurated a new series of "Notes for Women Workers," written by Ellen. In announcing the venture, the journal conceded, "Too long has the idea been prevalent that that [*sic*] the Revolutionary Movement is the special preserve of men." In yet another instance of the martial rhetoric that pervaded the CPGB, Ellen's remit in her new column would be to "destroy" this misconception by highlighting the struggles of women workers and the need for them to organize internationally.[15]

Ellen's methods of destruction proved less straightforward than her male colleagues might have hoped. She clearly hoped her column would be passed to non-Communist female factory workers by their male Communist colleagues. Her columns were written as conversations, full of illustrative stories and anecdotes meant to humanize the argument about the exploitation of workers under capitalism, from her depiction of wearied laundresses too ground down and cynical to improve their lot by striking over low wages to her story of the struggle of Rebecca Cohen, a garment worker at the fictional Samuel and Marks Wholesale Clothing Manufacturers, to organize colleagues to strike. In the latter story, Rebecca manages to convince her fellow workers to organize against their employer only for the devious Mr. Marks to undermine her support by orchestrating a visit to the factory by the Prince of Wales. Rebecca's republican sidekick tries to keep up hope, "What does a prince matter, anyway?" she asks. "Rebecca knew better. To these East End Girls, with their drab lives, starved of all excitement, he meant a great deal."[16] The messages weren't exactly subtle, and the short stories were more than a bit mawkish and overblown, but they demonstrated an effort on Ellen's part to craft her journalistic style to the perceived interests of her audience.

At the Fourth Comintern Congress in Moscow in 1922, Zetkin held a meeting with the British delegates, including Minnie Birch, Jack Leckie, and John Murphy, and impressed upon them Moscow's view that the British could be doing more to recruit women. The British representatives pled poverty and suggested any such efforts would require a subvention from Moscow. Zetkin, however, would not be put off. She concluded the meeting by noting she "had written to England many times but had received no reply. She had almost come to feel that the Party in England was indifferent so far as the Women's Question was concerned. . . . A real and sympathetic attempt must be made by the Party to understand this question in all its aspects and the best assistance possible much be afforded to the Women's Sections." She ended by assuring the British delegates "with all her sincerity that she would do her best to have the Party assisted over its [financial] difficulties." Although she was not able to make them any material promises, "as far as her influence was concerned she would do what she could."[17]

Zetkin followed up with a surprise speaking tour of Britain the following February.[18] Minnie Birch, in turn, ensured the CPGB followed through on its own promises to improve the British party's women's organization. In, March 1922, she reported, "It is definitely laid down in the Theses that a Women's Movement must exist within every Communist Party for the purpose of extending Communist work among proletarian and semi-proletarian women. Women's groups must be formed and there must be national and international committees."[19] Birch's dictatorial pronouncement was an indication of the CPGB's tendency to take its orders directly from Moscow, a tendency that would increasingly alienate Ellen from the party.

In February 1922, a national women's executive had been established.[20] Two months later, the Home Office, which kept close tabs on "revolutionary activities" within the British Isles and Empire, reported that a group of women including Helen Crawfurd, Mary Morehouse, Minnie Birch, Winifred Horrabin, Cedar Paul, and Ellen were actively trying to organize Communist women in the country.[21] However, the evidence suggests that this organization was not particularly active. All the women involved had other demands on their time. Ellen was working full-time as a union organizer and was actively involved with a government commission on the work of the trade boards. Helen Crawfurd had taken on board the administration of the British branch of the Workers International Relief committee, an umbrella relief organization initially established to raise international funds for relief of the victims of the 1921–1922 famine in Russia.

At the sixth CPGB conference in May 1924, the executive called upon the newly inaugurated Communist Women's Conference to "discuss and so avoid the mistakes and neglect that has so far characterized this work."[22] By that time, Ellen had at least one foot out the door of the CPGB. In January 1924, she had written to the party executive expressing her discontent with the increasingly dictatorial bent of the party leadership. The leadership, she felt, were "ruining the Party," with the result that "today there are I believe more communists outside the Party than in it. The Party has a wonderful opportunity now, one that may never recur again, and if it is to be thrown away and the magnificent work of the rank and file frustrated again, as it has been continually since late 1921, then drastic moves will have to be made. . . . Meantime, I am not accepting C. P. engagements until the whole position is cleared up. We must make a stand."[23] Her frustration had been boiling up for some time, although her retrospective dating of the "turn" in the party's direction to late 1921 does not reflect her feelings at that time. At the party's founding conference in 1920, Ellen had spoken of the need for discipline and obedience, and she initially appreciated the strict militancy of the party leadership. But with her natural tendency to question received assumptions and challenge authority, she was not an unquestioning foot soldier in someone else's army. As time went on, she became increasingly disillusioned with what she saw as Albert Inkpin and Jack Murphy's slavish adherence to the Moscow line, even as the political situation on the ground in Britain indicated that her country was, to say the least, not well-suited to a Soviet-style revolution.

Although Ellen did not explicitly address the CPGB's policy—or lack thereof—towards women workers in January 1924, it is likely that this contributed to her frustration with the organization. In March 1922, after the national women's committee was formed, Minnie Birch wrote, "It should be distinctly understood that it is not intended to form a *separate* women's organization. It is the intention to stimulate and encourage any women workers who are at all interested in the Class Struggle, and the work of the Women's Movement comes from *within* the Communist Party, which accepts men and women on equal terms."[24] However, when the CPGB decided to hold its first women's conference, they scheduled it at the same time as the general conference, with the result that "women delegates had to choose between identifying with the woman question or staying in the main conference to discuss major party policy." To Ellen, such an approach would have been anathema, and there is evidence many other Communist women equally resented being pigeonholed in this way.[25]

If the propaganda of the Women's Committee of the CPGB proved to offer little practical appeal to women workers, Ellen's trade union work was increasingly drawing her into the realm of practical politics. In December 1921, she made her first visit to the corridors of Whitehall to give evidence before the Committee of Inquiry into the Working and Effects of the Trade Boards Acts, better known as the Cave Committee, after its chairman Viscount Cave. In a conference room in the ornate Renaissance-styled Montagu House overlooking the Thames, Ellen met with legislators and outside experts convened to reconsider the operation of the trade boards that dictated minimum wages for so many of the women in her union. Many business owners had begun to advocate for scaling back the use of trade boards, which had expanded precipitously during the war years as the government sought to avoid industrial unrest through mediation. As a Communist, Ellen saw the trade boards as a pillar of a decaying capitalist system, but as an advocate for NUDAW's female members, she appreciated that the boards could offer real and immediate improvements to thousands of women and men and fought hard for their maintenance and strengthening. As she wrote in *All Power*, "when (if ever) better times come again, trade unionists may have to reconsider their whole position. But, at present, it is fairly safe to support what the FBI [Federation of British Industries] are out to smash."[26]

Ellen gave evidence before the Cave Committee twice, first as one of three representatives of NUDAW, alongside Alfred Burrows from Leicester, the union's Midlands Divisional Officer, and the political secretary Wright Robinson, and then again as a representative for the workers' side of the Laundry Trade Board. The experience was one of the few times Robinson felt compelled to compliment Ellen, however grudgingly. In advance of their testimony, the NUDAW group presented a memorandum of evidence written by Ellen. In Robinson's retelling, in the week before the memo was submitted, "Miss Wilkinson . . . stoked up an almighty hustle on herself, her colleagues, and on certain office staffs in preparation of our case. . . . On Saturday and Sunday, the 17th and 18th, we were rummaging out evidence as if we were searching for a missing will on which we had based great hopes." (Despite their mutual antipathy, Robinson clearly shared Ellen's penchant for detective novels.) The resulting report was "bristling with fighting facts, supported by schedules that were as full of statistics as a Sinn Feinner is full of fight."[27]

Armed with their pugilistic testimony, the three NUDAW representatives set off for London on Monday, December 19, in advance of their testimony that Thursday. Ellen's brother Harold was home from Ireland and met up with her in the capital. Her nonunion commitments had been bringing her to London more and more regularly, and she was keen to show off her insider knowledge of the city to her colleagues. Robinson would have preferred to dine in their hotel, but Ellen dragged the three men out to a French restaurant in Soho. She was still a vegetarian, and Robinson was unimpressed by the tapas she ordered and insisted they share—dubious "vegetable matter" which included "fish turkey, which looked like flannel." Ellen was then a teetotaller, but her companions were not; and Robinson was scandalized by the extortionate prices trendy London restaurants charged for a bottle of wine and reproached himself for the extravagance. Whether Ellen was trying to win over the political secretary by taking him to a trendy restaurant or simply showing off her mastery of London, she succeeded only in further antagonizing her prickly colleague.[28]

Ellen did better the next day when the group gave evidence. Robinson spoke first, before an assembled panel that included a lord, a few academics, a barrister, three trade union representatives, and two female members. Then came Ellen. She was "piquant" and "quite decided," and Robinson mused, "the Committee were probably amused that such large opinions were to be associated with such small stature." Nonetheless, he conceded that the committee clearly "respected her greatly" and that "she gave her evidence well" in a practiced "University manner"—a comment that perhaps hints at jealousy of his colleague's academic credentials.[29]

During two hours of testimony, Ellen showed a characteristic grasp of detail and a competence in economic theory. She would always say she was terrible with maths, but she understood the principals of capitalist economics well enough to expose their weaknesses. Lord Cave responded to her evidence on the "scandalous" wages paid in the drapery and catering trades by asking whether she did not accept that wages need "have regard to foreign competition and what the trade could bear." Ellen's retort was cutting: "If you followed that argument to its logical issue, you would advocate coolie wages." She concluded with what Robinson deemed her most moving plea: that the trade boards take more care for the welfare of the women in sweated industries "earning a precarious living, and who are too poor to organize."[30] Ellen had propagandized outside of laundry houses and been met with the apathy of women too downtrodden to take steps to join the union. She hoped the trade boards would step in to protect these women.

Theirs was the last sitting before the committee broke for Christmas, but Ellen returned to London again in January to give evidence as a representative of the Laundry Trade Board, on which she served from October 1919.[31] Again she emphasized the value of trade boards in staving off utter destitution in the trades they governed. The committee had been convened under pressure of those who wanted the boards disbanded. Although the official report recommended the power of the

Minister of Labour to appoint a new trade board be limited to instances in which he was satisfied the rate of wages was "unduly low" and there was no adequate extra-governmental mechanism for adjudicating wages, it did not recommend the boards' abolition.[32] If the boards' retention was a pyrrhic victory, it was a victory nonetheless, and it impressed upon Ellen the potential impact of parliament on the lives of the working class.

If Ellen's testimony before the Cave Committee gave her an insight into Westminster politics, her own and her sister's involvement with the Women's International League (WIL) opened her eyes to a form of political activism that combined education and propaganda with efforts to lobby government officials and effect progressive political change through official channels. In early 1920s Manchester, the cause that most regularly brought together her Communist and middle-class feminist colleagues was the peace movement. The WIL offered another forum for Ellen to exercise her skills in both platform politics and political lobbying. Although her involvement in the WIL deepened in this period, the group's issue-based lobbying remained more of a hobby than a full-time occupation.

Ellen's sister, on the other hand, came into her own through her involvement with the Manchester WIL. In the 1911 census, Annie, then thirty, had been classed as a "teacher of dressmaking." Her mother's death would have been a keenly felt loss for a woman who had devoted her life to her family, but it was also a liberation. When she took the post as office secretary in the Princess Street headquarters of the newly formed WIL branch in late summer 1917, Ellen's older sister got her first taste of professional life. Her salary was considerably less than what her baby sister was earning at NUDAW. (In February 1918, she was given a raise to 35/- a week, still less than the two guineas the Manchester Society for Women's Suffrage (MSWS) paid Ellen as an apprentice organizer in 1913.[33]) It was, however, Annie's own money, which allowed her to make an independent financial contribution to the living expenses when she and her siblings set up house in Fallowfield.

Annie's employment with the WIL also brought her into direct touch with the overlapping circles of feminist, pacifist, and radical politics that thrived in postwar Manchester. Annie had been the first Wilkinson sister to subscribe to the MSWS and, as Ellen's lifelong confidant, would have been well-informed about her younger sister's activism on behalf of working women. As the WIL secretary, she was now working directly alongside female activists like the sisters' longtime friend Annot Robinson, and she clearly enjoyed the experience. In November 1922, when the Manchester branch selected their three representatives to attend an international conference of women at The Hague to be held in December, they chose to send both Ellen and Annie, though at the last minute Ellen had to withdraw. At The Hague, the women had decided to launch a new peace campaign, focusing on disarmament and the revision of the Versailles settlement. In February, Annie spoke on the campaign at meetings around Manchester. In April, she was again delegated to represent the WIL outside of the office, attending a preliminary meeting of the Manchester branch of the National Peace Council to discuss arrangements for a forthcoming conference.[34]

Annie also took an increasingly active interest in Ellen's political work. In 1921, she was apparently acting as secretary for the newly established Manchester Labour Women's Advisory Committee.[35] When Ellen ran for parliament in Middlesbrough in 1924, Annie took a nine-day leave of absence to help with the campaign.[36]

Annie's travel was limited by her chronic ill-health, which periodically interfered with her ability even to carry out her office duties. She was away from Princess Street due to illness for over three months in 1920. It is unclear whether she convalesced at home or was sent to a sanatorium overseas. Likely she remained in Manchester, as Ellen was only able to afford her sister's later continental treatment through the intercession of Nancy Astor.[37] Like her sister, Ellen suffered from chronic respiratory infections but was unwilling to devote the time to proper convalescence. Throughout her career, she repeatedly worked herself to the point of collapse, spent a few days in hospital or on bed rest, and then returned to work in contravention of doctor's orders. Ellen's work ethic must have frightened her sister, who moved south to look after her following their father's death in 1929. Annie's concern for her sister was reciprocated. After Annie recuperated from her illness, Ellen used her annual vacation allowance from NUDAW to take her big sister on holiday.[38]

That Ellen's own involvement with the WIL increased in this period is probably as much a testament to her devotion to Annie as to her genuine abhorrence of militarism. As a small organization, the WIL had a tripartite mission. It was, on the one hand, a fact-finding organization—Ellen's mission to Ireland in 1920 was only one example of the group's commitment to obtaining information through firsthand experience. It was also a propaganda organization, aimed at educating the British public on the dangers of militarism and the inequities of imperial rule. Finally, it was fundamentally a lobbying organization, focused on influencing the policy of the British government and the League of Nations towards revising the terms of the Versailles Treaty, bringing Russia into the League of Nations, achieving multilateral disarmament, and reforming international laws relating to the rights and welfare of women and children. The Manchester executive committee dealt with all three aspects of the WIL's work, but although Ellen did a much better job of showing up at EC meetings in 1920 than she had the previous year, she initially showed little interest in the lobbying side of the organization. In 1920, she still saw herself primarily as a political propagandist, and her contribution to the Manchester WIL was largely as a platform speaker. That March she spoke at a WIL conference in Manchester on the position of women in industry and the home, emphasizing the right of married women to remain in work.[39] In May, she brought John Jagger onto the platform at an open-air meeting protesting the Polish invasion of Russia.[40] After the commission of inquiry returned from Ireland on October 16, Ellen and other members did several open-air meetings and events in the Free Trade Hall and other large-scale venues.

In 1921–1922, however, Ellen began to pay closer attention to the policy work of the WIL, proposing resolutions for transmission to His Majesty's Government and volunteering to serve as a delegate to the national council meetings in London. In March 1921, Ellen made her first direct contribution to the lobbying work of the League. She drafted a resolution to be sent to the prime minister and Minister of Health Christopher Addison protesting the government's refusal to carry out their pledges to the League of Nations by failing to ratify the Maternity Protection Convention of the International Labour Organization. This stipulated that a woman should be given at least six weeks leave from her employment commencing at her confinement and that during this period she shall "be paid benefits sufficient for the full and healthy maintenance of herself and her child."[41] The convention, which formed part of the broader set of labour regulations known as the Washington Conventions, also stipulated that a woman should be allowed half an hour twice a day to nurse her child and that she could not be dismissed from employment as a consequence of pregnancy. Its ratification was a priority of the Labour Party's women's sections and was being taken up by the Labour Party in parliament, and Ellen's support for a WIL resolution on the issue indicates her growing interest in Labour's parliamentary agenda.[42] Despite concerted pressure in parliament, the convention was not ratified by Britain or any other Western power until 1927, when the Weimar Republic became the first European nation to endorse it.[43]

From 1921, Ellen also became increasingly involved in the national leadership of the Labour women's movement. Before 1924, membership in the Communist Party was not incompatible with membership in the Labour Party, and Ellen remained active in the Manchester Labour Party in the early 1920s despite her increased involvement with the CPGB. Since the war, she and Annot Robinson had played leading roles in the organization of Labour women in Manchester, with Annot ultimately becoming the vice-chairman of the party.[44] In 1920–1921, the two friends became active in the push for greater women's input into the operation of Labour politics in that city. Following a conference at Heaton Hall in June 1920, the Manchester women established a Labour Women's Advisory Council (MLWAC), modelled on the London council. The aims of the MLWAC were "to coordinate the work of Labour, socialist and trade union women of Manchester and Salford, to promote the candidatures of women to elected bodies and the magisterial bench, to increase the women membership of the party, and to assist in forming women's sections."[45] Annot and Ellen roped in Annie to serve as secretary to the new organization. It would not be the last time Annie would do unpaid secretarial work for one of Ellen's causes.

In 1921, Annot and Ellen attended the Labour Party women's conference as representatives of the Manchester DLP and pushed the

MLWAC's agenda of more direct representation of women within the national leadership. The four female representatives to Labour's National Executive Committee were elected by the full conference on the advice of the Standing Joint Committee of Industrial Women's Organizations (SJCIWO), a body that included both Labour and trade union representatives. At the 1921 women's conference, Annot proposed and Ellen seconded a resolution that the women's conference elect the female representatives to the National Executive Committee (NEC) directly. As Ellen argued, the conference represented "the women who were doing the work of getting at their sisters," and they should have a direct say in their representatives. The proposal was controversial, as the Labour women's conference was run by the SJCIWO, which rightly construed the proposal as intended to shift power from the committee to the broader conference. Marion Phillips, the secretary of the SJCIWO, spoke against the resolution, arguing it would pit women's interests against the interests of the party as a whole, but after a spirited debate the Manchester resolution was adopted on a vote of 201 to 156. Annot's attempts to put forth a similar resolution at the full Labour Party conference that autumn were thwarted on a technicality. In 1922, the Manchester delegation to the Labour Party conference successfully moved the resolution, but it was defeated.[46] The women members of the NEC continued to be elected by the full Labour Party conference, with the SJCIWO having a strong informal influence over the process. (Ellen would later benefit from the process when she was elected to the NEC in 1928.) It was not until 1951 that the Labour Party would constitute a national labour women's advisory committee, made up of members elected directly by the women's sections to advise the NEC "on all matters connected with the organization and work of women in the party."[47]

If the SJCIWO was to remain the locus of decision-making authority for the Labour women's movement, in 1921 Ellen moved closer to that centre of power when her union affiliated to the SJCIWO and she became its representative. She threw herself into the work of the committee, volunteering in her first year to lead the group that set the agenda for the 1922 conference and to present and defend the committee's official resolution on foreign policy. By 1925, she had risen to become chair of the SJCIWO, a position she held for two consecutive years. Her work with the SJCIWO gave her experience with crafting practical political proposals, as the NEC regularly looked to the committee for guidance on policies affecting women. Ellen, however, was not one simply to toe the party line or to keep silent in the interests of consensus. In later years, she would swallow her personal convictions in favour of what the SJCIWO saw as "practical politics," especially when it came to the question of birth control. In the early 1920s, never having served in elected office, she was less accustomed to putting politics before principal. When a delegate from Oxford attempted to amend the SJCIWO's 1922 report on Motherhood and Child Endowment to stipulate that any payments to mothers should be made in cash, not in kind, Ellen spoke for the amendment, arguing "in favour of the educative effect of women having money to spend on their own." Marion Phillips urged the women not to bind the hands of the SJCIWO by supporting the amendment, and ultimately Ellen voted with the majority for its defeat; but she could not resist the impulse to make her personal views known, even if it meant breaking ranks with her fellow members.[48]

Ellen's growing involvement with the SJCIWO helped convince her that her future lay in electoral politics. Although her interests were primarily on the national and international scale, it was extremely difficult for a Labour woman without any elected political experience to secure nomination as a parliamentary candidate. (Early Conservative woman MPs, in contrast, were often the wives of their predecessors.) Increasingly, Ellen's ambitions were focused on London; but, as a stepping stone towards Westminster, she threw her hat in the ring for a seat on the Manchester City Council.

In a sense Margaret Ashton, the woman who had offered Ellen her first paying job as an organizer for the Manchester Women's Suffrage Society, also paved the way for her election to the city council. In 1908, Margaret became Manchester's first woman council member. Although women remained a minority amongst both elected members and candidates (between 1918 and 1929, only 11 percent of Labour candidates for Manchester council seats were women), by the time Ellen contested the Gorton South Ward in 1923, female candidates were no longer an anomaly.[49] That year, not only Ellen but her good friend Mary Welch campaigned successfully to join their colleague Wright Robinson on the council.

Gorton South was a safe Labour seat. Gorton was a poor district, and its parliamentary division and all three of its ward seats on the council were represented by Labour members. The party had a strong organization in the district, including a women's section run by Stella Davies out of her home that was larger and better off than those of most Gorton women. Gorton, Davies recalled, was a district stricken by poverty: "I shopped with women to whom the difference of a penny in price was a vital concern. . . . I saw the struggle these women had to keep their children decently clad and with shoes fit enough to wear to school. For themselves the secondhand stall in the street market or a jumble sale had to suffice. I saw them line up outside Gorton town hall on Friday afternoon when parcels of groceries were distributed, the result of the Lord Mayor's fund raised by public subscription. . . . I had seen poverty before, now I was surrounded by it." It was a stark contrast to Ellen's comparatively comfortable upper-working-class suburb of Fallowfield, and she was moved to tears and deeply impressed with the impact municipal policy could have on the lives of such women. Her compassion was evident, and Stella and the Gorton Labour women gave their hearty support to the young woman running to represent them on the council. So too did John Jagger, who kept her fed and hydrated between her countless platform speeches.[50] Recalling the election years later, Stella noted Ellen's exceptional facility for open-air meetings. It was not just her platform voice but her striking appearance that held voters' attention. "Her small figure generally dressed in green and her flaming hatless hair made a bright spot of colour in the drab Gorton streets."[51] When the votes were counted, Ellen won Gorton South handily, on a majority of 3,341 to 2,501 for her Conservative opponent. Mary Welch had a more difficult time. She had been nominated to contest a seat held by a Conservative councillor. After a hard-fought three-way contest between Mary, the incumbent, and a Liberal candidate, Mary was returned on a majority of 312 in what the *Manchester Guardian* deemed "the most notable Labour gain" in the election.[52] The women joined the small Labour minority on the Council—28 councillors, as opposed to 32 Liberals, 75 Conservatives, and 2 Independents. In an uncharacteristically charitable moment, Wright Robinson admitted in his diary to feeling "prodigiously proud" of Ellen and Mary's success—even if he did put it down largely to his own influence.[53]

Ellen had not attempted to hide her Communist affiliation in the municipal election. The Gorton Trades & Labour Council did not support the CPGB, but, as one of the other Gorton councillors noted, a Communist was "alright as a municipal candidate." Shortly after her election, Ellen spoke on a platform alongside Shapurji Saklatvala, who represented Battersea North as a Labour and Communist MP from 1922 to 1923, at a large open-air meeting in commemoration of the sixth anniversary of the Bolshevik Revolution. Journalist Morgan Philips Price, who had hosted her in Berlin on her way home from Moscow, was back at the editorial offices of the *Guardian* and joined them on the platform. Yet, although CPGB membership had not proved a hurdle to municipal election, Ellen was soon to discover it was not an asset in national politics. Other than Saklatvala, the only Communist in the 1922 parliament was her ex-fiancé Walton Newbold.

The Manchester municipal elections were held on November 1, 1923. Only ten days later, parliament was dissolved as the new prime minister, Stanley Baldwin, sought a mandate for his newly declared policy of tariff protection. The campaign was to be a short one, with less than four weeks between dissolution and polling day. Many divisional Labour parties were unprepared for the second election in a year and found themselves scrambling for a parliamentary candidate. Ellen had assumed that her council election would mean she spent, at the very least, a three- or four-year apprenticeship in local politics before making a bid for a national seat, but she was never one to shy away from an opportunity. Assured by Jagger that the union would give its financial backing—a crucial prerequisite for any would-be Labour candidate without independent resources—Ellen went in search of a seat.

Her first approach, unsurprisingly, was her "local" constituency. Gorton's long-serving Labour MP John Hodge, a moderate trade unionist who had served as minister of labour in Lloyd George's wartime coalition, had made public his intention to resign after the 1922 parliament. Five days after the dissolution, the Gorton Trades and Labour Council met to hear speeches and vote on a new candidate. Councillor John Compton of the Vehicles Builders' Union spoke first. He had local support and considerable campaign experience, having unsuccessfully contested Swindon at the 1918 and 1922 elections and put up "a very good fight."[54] Next came Ellen, who was followed by Mr. Dennison, a representative of Hodge's Iron and Steel Trades Confederation. Everyone had done his and her best to bring in supporters. Although no more than twenty or thirty people showed up at normal Council meetings, Stella Davies estimated there were about one hundred delegates in attendance that evening, many from the men's unions. If Ellen had thought the connections she had recently forged during the municipal campaign would help her cause, she proved mistaken. Many were suspicious of her as a "maverick" (read: Communist), but others simply felt it was inappropriate and not in the interests of the constituency for her to turn her eyes so quickly from the council to parliament. She came in second to Dennison, who won by an "overwhelming" majority.[55]

But Ellen would not be deterred. She had the promise of NUDAW's money and was rightly confident that some constituency would welcome her. Within a week, she secured the candidacy for Ashton-under-Lyne, a largely working-class suburb east of Manchester. As the union's political secretary, Wright Robinson was compelled to help direct her campaign, although he did not relish doing so. In his telling, she showed up in his office "on the verge of tears (real or assumed)" and begged for his aid. He sent his people out to help run the election, alongside the "scores of comrades" she brought in. Harry Ford, of the legal department, who was also secretary of the Ashton Trades Council, became Ellen's election agent. The secretary of the Ashton Labour Party was also a NUDAW man and stepped in as Ford's number two, and the local NUDAW branch "put their backs into the fight from the beginning."[56]

The NUDAW staffers faced an uphill battle during the two-week campaign. "It was impossible" to keep Ellen's Communist friends "off the class war jargon. . . . One would be warming up to the Russian Revolution when he would be pulled up to make room for a speaker with less alarming reasons for voting for a woman! . . . A more disreputable gang it would be impossible to find in any serious political contest," Robinson bemoaned to his diary.[57] In truth, Ellen's Communist affiliations proved a real weakness for the candidate. Ashton was a "three-cornered" contest, and the miners' federation threw its support behind the Liberal candidate, an action Ellen, typically, characterized as "scandalous."

The Labour Party's official position was in favour of the continuance of free trade; but, as a Marxist, Ellen viewed free trade as yet one more vehicle of capitalist oppression. When pressed on the issue of protection versus free trade, she "pour[ed] scorn by the bucketful so impartially over both 'the outworn creeds of the last century'" that it wasn't clear which she thought "more abominable."[58] Her argument that only the socialization of the means of production could ensure employment and growth proved out of tune with a national debate centred around free trade versus protection.

Ellen's politics in the early 1920s put her sharply at odds with the Labour Party leadership, which was keen to emphasize its "constitutionality" and fitness to rule. Although Ellen claimed to "loathe" Labour Party leader Ramsay MacDonald, she nonetheless recognized his personal popularity and was not above basking in some of his reflected light when he came through town to stump for Labour's Manchester candidates. On a cold fog-ridden Sunday evening two weeks before the poll, MacDonald headlined a meeting at the Free Trade Hall, and Ellen stood on the platform alongside current Northwest MPs J. R. Clynes and Ben Tillett. The next day, the *Manchester Guardian* published a photograph of MacDonald and the candidates. In it, Ellen stands front and centre. She, not MacDonald, is the focal point of the photo. The other figures, all male, are without coats, clad either in suits or dinner jackets; while Ellen is already dressed to depart, in a giant shearling-trimmed coat, hat on head, and handbag in hand. The viewer's inevitable impression is that Ellen had attempted to make a quick exit from the event and then been caught out and roped in for the photograph. She is smiling for the cameras, but Robinson ascribed to her an attitude of "derision and petulance."[59]

Nonetheless, the *Manchester Guardian,* which endorsed the Liberal candidate, conceded her meetings were "well attended" and she had proved an "attractive speaker."[60] The paper's coverage emphasized Ellen's appeals to women voters, and, in her summary of the campaign in the *New Dawn,* Ellen underscored the support she received from women in the constituency: "To those who went through the scrap, the women in the little back streets will come back as the warmest memory. We got at women who had never been to a meeting in their lives before, and our great women's meeting two days before the poll was more like a revival service than a political gathering." Ellen worked her connections within the women's peace movement and was invited to speak to the annual meeting of the Ashton branch of the League of Nations Union, a local organization with broad-based working- and middle-class support. According to one observer at the meeting, "A lady in clogs and shawl stood on a chair and leading off with 'three cheers for eaur Ellen,' finished up by adjuring the candidate to 'tak' thi coat off lass, and give it 'um hot."[61]

In the end, "eaur Ellen" polled third, with 6,208 votes to the victorious Conservative's 7,813. Nonetheless, it was seen as a good show and put Ellen on the party leadership's radar. Nationally Labour had fared well, returning 191 MPs, less than the 258 returned by the Conservatives but enough to give the party the balance of power in parliament. Without a clear mandate for tariff protection, Baldwin resigned and allowed MacDonald to form a minority government. In the absence of a working majority, MacDonald's administration could not be expected to achieve much, and most assumed there would be another general election within a year or so. In light of her performance in Ashton, Ellen became a viable candidate for a plum constituency the next time around.

Ellen's two election campaigns in the autumn of 1923 convinced her that her future lay in elected office. She had long recognized her strength as a platform speaker and her ability to inspire listeners. The campaigns gave her a taste of what it might feel like to persuade listeners to vest her with actual power, not only to change their way of thinking but also to change their lives. When Ellen finally entered the House of Commons in December 1924, she would show no intention to sit back and watch how things were done before throwing herself bodily into the ring. The same held true during her brief tenure on the city council. Less than a month after taking her seat, Ellen put forth a motion calling for the Special Committee on Works for the Unemployed to report to the next meeting of council on what relief works could be provided for unemployed women, and for the public health committee to consider and report as to whether some women could be employed as home helps in connection with maternity welfare centres, or otherwise employed by the public health department. The motion was typical of Ellen's approach to legislating. She saw a problem—the growing and neglected mass of unemployed women in Manchester—and sought to find a practical solution. On the stump and at Communist Party meetings, she spoke in terms of the revolution of the economic system. In council, her first priority was to identify practical steps to improve the immediate situation of the working poor. This commitment to achieving small, concrete reforms even as she kept one eye towards a future social revolution was visible throughout her career.

Although Ellen's intentions were good, her method of approach regularly showed a lack of deference to those more experienced, in this case specifically to Councillor Robinson. She was not one to believe that age or experience imparted wisdom, or that youth should wait its turn. For men and women secure in their own position and indulgent of Ellen's enthusiasm, such as John Jagger, such impatience could be endearing. For others, including Robinson, Ellen's lack of respect was evidence that she was selfish, self-promoting, and self-serving. Ellen had already marked her card with Robinson long before she entered the council, but the manner in which she secured passage of her first motion was not designed to raise her stock with her colleague. Robinson had also intended to put a motion of his own at the same meeting on the need to consider further schemes for unemployment relief. In the event, he held over his motion, as fewer than one-third of the council members were in attendance that evening. Ellen, however, "rose with a saucy air and said she was NOT withdrawing hers."[62] She went on to plead the case for the over 6,000 unemployed women in the city who faced a "particularly hard" lot. The government, she opined, regularly denied applications for unemployment assistance to single women between the ages of eighteen and twenty-five on the grounds that their parents or husbands should be taking care of them. It was, Robinson conceded, a "good, temperate speech," which Mary Welch seconded. Alderman Turnbull, the Conservative chairman of the works committee, endorsed the motion; and, after debate, it was passed with an amendment stipulating the committee should consider plans to apply to the Ministry of Labour for a grant to carry out the proposed schemes.

Ellen recognized Labour's minority position on the council and was determined to work with and through her Conservative and Liberal colleagues to achieve her ends. In pleading her case, she praised Turnbull for "doing his very best," while shifting the blame for inaction to the former Conservative government in Westminster. Afterwards, the *Guardian* reported, "In several instances Conservative chairmen of committees blushing under the delicate compliments which came to them with disarming unexpectedness from the Labour benches, surrendered positions which a more truculent and usual method of attack might have induced them to defend obstinately and probably successfully."[63]

Ellen eventually secured backing for a deputation to the Parliamentary Secretary to the Minister of Labour Margaret Bondfield, to include both herself and Mary Welch, to request funds for the proposed schemes to find work for unemployed women. Robinson, ultimately justified in his suspicion the deputation would come to naught, denounced it in his diary as "sheer limelighting . . . An advert for Ellen. Eyewash for the unemployed," and declined an invitation to serve as a member of the party. Although Ellen certainly did not see the deputation in the same terms, it is notable that several of her friends and colleagues from Manchester emphasized her "eye for publicity" in that period.[64] As Fred Meadowcroft, who lived across the street from her family in Everton Road, recalled, she "loved to be making headlines and creating scenes. . . . She would go on doing things for publicity until her dying day."[65]

Ellen, Mary Welch, and Alderman Turnbull's deputation won a guarantee from Bondfield that the Ministry of Labour would provide maintenance grants for women employed by the council on training schemes to learn skills as home helps and seamstresses to make uniforms for schoolchildren.[66] Ten weeks later, however, the Council was still dragging its feet on establishing the training courses.[67] Unable to force her Manchester colleagues to action, Ellen attempted to garner support on a national scale. At the Trades Union Congress (TUC) in Hull that September, she proposed the TUC lobby the government to earmark monies for women's work schemes and for training women as home helps and local public health officials. The Congress agreed to approach the Ministry of Labour to discuss Ellen's proposals, but, before action could be taken, Ramsay MacDonald had resigned from office and the country was faced with its third election in two years.

Ellen was sincere in her commitment to the Manchester unemployed, but she had no intention of remaining a local councillor. Her intellectual development and her political experiences over the decade since leaving university had all, in different ways, impressed upon her that long-term solutions to local problems would not be found on the local level. She was sufficiently steeped in Marxist economic theory to believe that a final cure for unemployment would come only when the world's workers had wrested control of capital and the means of production away from the imperial-monopolists who ran the international economy in the interests of the privileged few. In the interim, however, Westminster was more likely to push through palliative reforms than were Tory-dominated councils. Ellen's collaboration with female internationalists through the WILPF, and with internationally minded Communists, had reinforced her sense of the interconnectedness of the world's nations. The narrow horizons of her childhood and adolescence had expanded immeasurably. If Ellen was determined to change both Britain and the wider world, she needed to be based not in Manchester but in London.

On Thursday, October 9, the prime minister called for the dissolution of parliament. The circumstances highlighted the increasing tension between the Labour Party and the Communists. Earlier that year, Attorney General Patrick Hastings had brought a case against J. R. Campbell, acting editor of the Communist publication *Workers' Weekly*, for publishing an article that urged soldiers, if necessary, to disobey government orders to fire on striking workers. Hastings subsequently withdrew the case at the instigation of the cabinet, as many colleagues feared a public trial would draw unwanted attention to the Communist cause. Ironically, press and parliamentary critics accused the government of squashing the prosecution in response to pressure from influential Communists, and parliament passed a motion calling for a select committee to look into the incident. Parliament had specifically shied away from passing a formal motion of censure on the government, but the prime minister nonetheless determined to resign his office on the principle that his cabinet could not continue to lead with such an imputation of wrongdoing hanging over his head.

In truth, MacDonald was probably happy for an excuse to go back to the country before the government had any major blunders on its balance sheet. In ten brief months in office as a minority government, Labour had acquitted themselves reasonably well. Internationally, they had passed a trade bill with Russia and participated in the successful negotiations culminating in the adoption of the Dawes Plan to withdraw French and Belgian troops from the Ruhr and reorganize the schedule of German reparations repayments. Domestically, they had done comparatively little (much to Ellen's disgust), but at the same time it could not be said that they had attempted anything so radical that it might scare away the more moderate voters whom MacDonald believed his party would need to convert if they ever hoped to win a parliamentary majority.

The fact that MacDonald was content to bide his time while millions of unemployed suffered was one of the many reasons Ellen loathed her party leader. At the same time, she could not help but admire the achievements of the Labour government in forming a cabinet and governing the country for the better part of the year. As much as she claimed to abhor MacDonald's gradualism, her experience on the council had impressed upon her the limitations Labour's minority status placed on effective action, while simultaneously convincing her she wanted to be involved with Labour as it moved forward. In September 1924, shortly after her resignation from the CPGB, the *Daily Herald* reported her view that the Communist party's "exclusive and dictatorial methods made impossible the formation of a real left wing among the progressive elements in the Trade Union and Labour Party."[68]

Contemporary observers and later scholars have suggested Ellen held her ideological convictions lightly and trimmed her radical politics to political ambitions. Her old flame Walton Newold disparagingly credited her decision to leave the Communist Party in 1924 less to a thought-out act of principle than to a pragmatic move to ensure the Labour Party's backing of her candidacy at the next general election. In his view, Ellen's "audacity . . . was more apparent than actual," and her motives were always dictated by "her own self-satisfaction." (In a particularly oedipal reflection, Newbold ascribed the same traits to his mother.)[69] It would be naïve to say Ellen's decision to leave the Communist Party was not motivated, at least in some degree, by political ambition.[70] Labour did not formally ban Communists from party membership or from standing as Labour candidates until its October 1924 conference. However, the writing was on the wall months before. In 1923, Ellen had been endorsed as the Labour candidate for Ashton-under-Lyne while she was a member of the Communist Party. Had she remained in the party, it is much less clear that she would have been endorsed as the candidate for Middlesbrough East in April 1924. But to say that she abandoned the CPGB out of pragmatism is not to discount the sincerity of the convictions that led her to join the party in 1920 and that propelled her campaign to radicalize the Labour Party once she became an MP.

Middlesbrough East was not a promising constituency. Politics in the industrial towns along the Teesside was dominated by the owners' of the large steel mills, and the area had never before returned a Labour member. NUDAW money secured the constituency for Ellen, but it was not clear that even union money could persuade the male trade unionists to support the fiery little interloper who swooped into the constituency five months before the election.

Ellen had seen poverty in Manchester, but even during the slump in the international cotton trade, her hometown remained well-off compared to single-industry cities such as Middlesbrough. Ellen referred to the constituency as "a book of illustrations to Karl Marx" where "capitalism reveals all its hard ugliness, and the struggle for bread is bitter."[71] The working class lived week to week; and, fifty years later, one resident recalled that in the 1920s residents referred to "wheelbarrow Thursday" as the day when, paycheck in hand, wives went to collect the weekly groceries from the local shop.[72] Middlesbrough was not without its civic buildings built during the heyday of the steel industry at the turn of the century. The Dorman Museum, opened in 1904, offered residents a curated tour of the natural sciences and industry. But for Ellen, who, even as a poor girl, had been able to attend lectures by Thomas Henry Huxley and walk the corridors of the venerable Manchester Art Gallery, the industrial town was bereft of the cultural opportunities that could provide uplift to a life of physical drudgery. When asked to characterize Ellen as an MP, one Middlesbrough resident recalled that she "had a real socialist outlook—[she] felt the tragedy of people living and dying without the chance to enjoy and appreciate the pleasant things of life—music, poetry and literature."[73]

More than culture, however, what many of the residents of Middlesbrough needed most was a steady paycheck, and Ellen centred her campaign on the issue of growing unemployment. Whereas the Liberal and Conservative parties did their best to tar Labour with a Communist brush in what infamously became known as the "Red Scare" campaign, Ellen insisted that radical social problems required radical solutions, such as the socialization of the iron and steel industries and state provision of either work or maintenance for the unemployed. NUDAW seconded members from the head office to help with her campaign, as well as giving her local support. She also roped in family and friends. Both her brothers and sister chipped in, as did Walton Newbold—the two were on friendly terms despite his lingering resentment of her rejection.[74] Like Ellen, Newbold left the CPGB in 1924, but both remained on the left wing of the Labour Party. In a more prosperous constituency, where the bite of unemployment was not yet so widely felt, Ellen's radicalism might well have frightened voters, as did the appeals of radical candidates in many constituencies across Britain that autumn. In the event, although Labour lost a net forty seats nationally, including Margaret Bondfield's seat in Northampton, Middlesbrough East returned its first socialist on October 29, 1924, making Ellen Cicely Wilkinson Labour's only woman MP.

Ellen Wilkinson at age eight or nine. Children who suffered from scarlet fever often had their heads shaved. More than a year after Ellen's recovery, her hair still had not fully grown back.
Courtesy People's History Museum

Wilkinson family portrait, c. 1900. Back row: Annie and Richard Arthur; middle: Ellen Sr., Ellen, and Richard Sr.; front: baby Harold. Courtesy People's History Museum

The girls of Ardwick Higher Elementary School, Manchester. Ellen, aged twelve or thirteen years, is in the back row, third from the right, with her head thrown back in a jaunty pose.
Courtesy People's History Museum

At twenty-seven years old, Ellen (front row, second from left) was the youngest member of the British delegation to the founding conference of the Women's International League for Peace and Freedom, held in Zurich in May 1919. Courtesy LSE Library collections, WILPF/22/1

Ellen at her desk in the flat she shared with her sister, Annie, in Fallowfield, Manchester, in 1924. Hulton Archive Courtesy of Getty Images

Britain's only female Labour MP (1925). Courtesy Daily Herald Archive/National Media Museum/
Science & Society Picture Library

After the failure of the 1926 General Strike, Ellen travelled to the United States with a delegation from the Trades Union Congress to raise money for the miners' families. William Green, president of the American Federation of Labour, helped the delegation with fundraising. Courtesy National Photo Company Collection Library of Congress Prints and Photographs Division, LC-DIG-npcc-16146

ELLEN WILKINSON

In the 1920s, Ellen had a long affair with the radical cartoonist Frank Horrabin, who drew this affectionate portrait of the MP. *Peeps at Politicians* by Ellen Wilkinson; with drawings by Low, Matt, Horrabin and others (London: P. Allan, 1930). Reproduced from author's copy.

In 1930, Ellen's old NUDAW nemesis Wright Robinson (centre) unsuccessfully contested the Shipley by-election. Despite their personal animosity, Ellen campaigned on his behalf. Capt. William Hall, Dr. Marion Phillips, and Arthur Henderson (left to right) also came out to support Robinson. Courtesy Daily Herald Archive/National Media Museum/Science & Society Picture Library

Ellen was full of affection and admiration for Susan Lawrence, whom she looked to as a mentor. During the 1929–1931 Labour government, Ellen was Lawrence's parliamentary private secretary at the Ministry of Health. Courtesy Daily Herald Archive/National Media Museum/Science & Society Picture Library

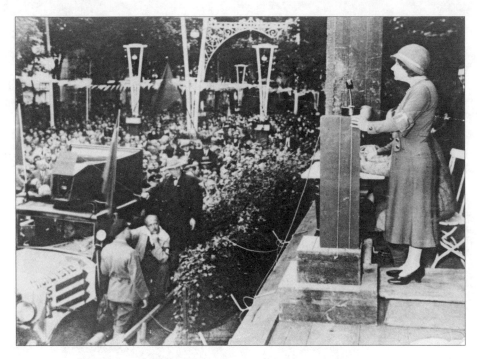

Ellen speaking at a rally in support of the Social Democratic Iron Front in the run-up to the 1932 Reichstag elections in Germany. Courtesy Daily Herald Archive/National Media Museum/ Science & Society Picture Library

Krishna Menon and Ellen posing with a group of six Punjabi men and two young boys who had sought them out to discuss their grievances under British rule during their tour of India in 1932. Courtesy Daily Herald Archive/National Media Museum/Science & Society Picture Library

Margaret Bondfield tries to make Ellen see reason over tea in Edinburgh during the 1936 Labour Party Conference. Ellen was frustrated by the Party's unwillingness to do more to help either the Jarrow crusaders or the Spanish Republicans. Courtesy Daily Herald Archive/National Media Museum/Science & Society Picture Library

It rained hard on October 31, 1936 as the Jarrow crusaders marched the final leg of their journey, through London to Hyde Park. Courtesy Daily Herald Archive/National Media Museum/ Science & Society Picture Library

During her fourth trip to the United States, in February 1937, Ellen climbed through the window of a Ford Motor plant in Flint, Michigan, and expressed her solidarity with a group of strikers who had occupied the plant. Courtesy Daily Herald Archive/National Media Museum/ Science & Society Picture Library

6

THE MIGHTY ATOM BURSTS
INTO PARLIAMENT

After three weeks of campaigning, Ellen and her sister Annie awaited the returns on Wednesday evening with no certainty that her hard work had paid off. Fortunately, they did not have to wait long. The returning officer announced the results for Middlesbrough East before 11 p.m. Ellen had won the constituency by the slender majority of 927 votes. Most of her fellow Labour candidates were not so lucky. The "Red Scare" campaign spearheaded by the *Daily Mail* and encouraged by the Conservative party had worked better than either could have imagined. The betting markets had closed on the eve of the election with "Socialists" selling at 182 seats.[1] When the dust settled on October 30, the parliamentary party had 151 members. Most of these were seasoned MPs, whose constituencies stood by them despite press accusations that the Labour prime minister "salutes Red Flags all day."[2] The party's poor fortunes meant Ellen had few colleagues with whom to share the experience of being a new MP, even if she did benefit from the advice of many more-senior members.

As she stood on the podium in the Middlesbrough town hall, Ellen would not have known she was the first woman to be returned to the new parliament. Not until the next morning did she discover she was to be the only woman amongst the discouragingly small contingent of Labour MPs. She had entered the race "totally unknown outside certain Labour circles"; now she would gain instant celebrity as Labour's sole woman MP.[3] The only other women members were Lady Astor; Mabel Philipson; and Katharine, Duchess of Atholl. Ellen had little in common with the women with whom she would soon share the "ladies' boudoir," alternatively known as "the dungeon"—the small room in the basement of the Palace of Westminster where she, Astor, and Philipson would work (as a minister, the Duchess was given her own office). Nonetheless, she would ultimately become friends with Nancy Astor and forge a productive, if not intimate, relationship with the future "Red Duchess" over their shared support for Republican Spain in the 1930s.

Nancy Astor, the first woman in Parliament, was, ironically, an American. Born in Danville, Virginia, she was the eighth of eleven children born to Nancy and Chiswell Dabney Langhorne, a Civil War veteran and railway mogul. After a disastrous first marriage, the spirited and outspoken—some would say rude—young heiress left Virginia for England and built a new life as the wife of Conservative politician Waldorf Astor. Like Ellen, Nancy was a small woman, but she cut a large figure as a society hostess and political wife. Although herself teetotal, she hosted lavish parties, turning Cliveden, her husband's country house on the Thames, into an elite salon. Ellen, who would later spend several weekends at Cliveden, described Astor as taking "an impish joy in inducing the most extraordinary people to mix together" and the house's guest books read like a who's who of interwar British and American society, from Charlie Chaplin to her good friend George Bernard Shaw to Winston Churchill and Sylvia Pankhurst. Nancy also took a hand in her husband's political career, acting as a leading member of the Conservative social organization the Primrose League in Astor's constituency of Plymouth Sutton. Again to quote Ellen, "For what she feels deeply Lady Astor will fight like a terrier, but she is not a politician in the House of Commons sense. She cares little for party ties and is very aggravating in her outspoken scepticism of those to whom party is a reality." Nonetheless, when her husband moved to the House of Lords in 1919, Nancy stood as the Conservative candidate for Plymouth Sutton in the ensuing by-election, prompting one Tory grandee to bemoan, "the worst of it is, the woman is sure to get in." Astor had served as the sole woman in parliament until the election of Margaret Wintringham in September 1921. She and Margaret became close friends, and the latter's defeat in October 1924 was a personal loss for Nancy that Ellen had neither the personality nor the inclination to make good.[4]

Nor were Nancy and Ellen initially close to the other two female members, Mabel Philipson and Katharine, Duchess of Atholl. One of the less-well-remembered women MPs, Philipson, like Astor and Wintringham, came into parliament at a by-election, assuming her husband's former seat. But, whereas Waldorf Astor had joined the Lords, and Thomas Wintringham had passed away, Mabel's husband Hilton was booted from his parliamentary seat of Berwick-upon-Tweed after an investigation into his election campaign's financial improprieties. Mabel was an odd choice to succeed him. A glamorous woman in her mid-thirties from working-class Surrey, Mabel had married Hilton after a youthful career as an actress in London's West End and had never before shown an interest in politics. Nonetheless, Hilton Philipson wanted to keep the seat in the family, in the hopes of returning to parliament after the seven-year ban imposed on him by the election court, and Mabel agreed to "hold" the seat in readiness. Her biographer notes, "Her theatrical training made her a natural campaigner, answering hecklers with ready wit, blowing kisses to the crowds, signing autographs, and posing for newspaper photographers." Once she arrived at Westminster, however, she took a backseat, literally and metaphorically. Although they spent hours in each other's company, the only recorded interaction between Mabel and Ellen was when the older woman administered first aid to Ellen after one of her many trips and falls in the corridors.[5]

Katharine, the Duchess of Atholl, was the oldest of the four women, celebrating her fortieth birthday the week after the election. Ellen described her as looking more like a high school mistress than the premier Duchess of Scotland. The comment was meant as a backhanded compliment, which she softened by adding, "her fine and sensitive face is one more illustration of how little youth and pink prettiness have to do with real beauty." That said, she had little time for the Duchess's politics. Where Ellen had begun her career in the suffrage movement, Katharine had been an antisuffragist and continued to speak out against the equalization of the franchise. Where Ellen saw government as a vehicle for economic redistribution, Katharine advocated for fiscal restraint. Until the two came together over support for the Republican cause in the Spanish Civil War, they agreed on almost nothing. Nonetheless, Ellen appreciated Katharine's eye for detail. Her efficiency and fastidiousness—in contrast to Astor's irreverence and inconsistency— made her Baldwin's preferred candidate for his first female appointment to ministerial office: Katharine served as parliamentary secretary to the Board of Education from 1924 through 1929.[6]

Ellen's victory meant she had to leave her siblings' flat in Manchester and look for a place in London. The city was by no means *terra nova* for her. She had travelled there countless times on trade union work and as the National Union of Distributive and Allied Workers' (NUDAW) representative on various trade boards, not to mention working at the Fabian Research Department and attending meetings of the Red International of Trade Unions and the Executive Council of the Women's International League. Yet although she knew her way around, could navigate the underground system, and could give directions to a taxi driver, she had never lived in the city she would later come to love and think of as her own. Driven principally by expediency and the recognition that "£400 a year in London is precious little when constituency expenses have to be met and home responsibilities provided for," in November Ellen rented a room in Westminster where she lived for her first several months as an MP.[7]

Shortly after she moved to London, a veteran Labour member took Ellen on her first tour of the Palace of Westminster, during which she characteristically asked to be introduced to the staff. The policemen, "so huge that she only came up to the bottom waistcoat button of their uniforms," joked with her about her "red hair and . . . red views." During her first days in parliament, they repeatedly put her back "on the right track when she got lost in the long corridors of the House." In the years to come, these men would come to know her as one of the most hapless members to ever enter through the palace gates. Their police files record her slipping and falling alighting from her motor car in Commons Court, stumbling and injuring her elbow while running through the members' entrance at Star Chamber Court, mislaying the petrol tin for her car in the same courtyard, and falling and twisting her ankle in the Commons chamber. In 1931, she would repay their kindness in assisting her through her various mishaps by dedicating her second novel, *The Division Bell Mystery,* "with sincere apologies to my good friends among the police and kitchen staff of the House of Commons."[8]

The session officially opened on Tuesday, December 9, with the King's Speech to both houses of parliament. The preceding week Ellen had her formal induction as the member for Middlesbrough East. J. H. Whitley, reconfirmed in his old position as the Speaker of the House, swore in the new members—and Ellen, as Labour's only woman, was specially cheered. Whitley advised those still wet behind the ears to hold themselves in patience and observe the parliamentary process before venturing to contribute to debate—advice Ellen unsurprisingly disregarded.[9] The sartorial conventions of the House of Commons, where government ministers still debated in dinner jackets, posed a challenge for Ellen, who was conscious that as the youngest woman and the only single MP she was likely to come under particular scrutiny. She would later joke in one of her novels that her hero had spent as much time ruminating over what persona he would adopt when he entered parliament "as a newly elected woman M. P. gave to the costume to be worn on her first appearance." Although a sardonic commentary on gender stereotypes, it nonetheless reflected the reality that in 1920s Britain the rare women MPs were treated as veritable celebrities, and their appearance as well as their politics were closely reported on in the domestic and foreign press. After reflection, she came to the House the first day dressed in a dark blue jumper suit and a hat, because "you're always safe in a hat."[10]

Some members of the 1920s Labour Party, including Ramsay MacDonald, Labour's first chancellor of the exchequer Philip Snowden, and Jimmy Thomas, the trade union leader who served as colonial secretary in the 1924 Labour government, were criticized at the time for their susceptibility to the "aristocratic embrace." During the 1922–1923 parliament, a group of radical Scottish MPs tried to induce their colleagues to boycott court social events and "plutocrat dinner parties" on the grounds that to attend such events and to socialize with their class enemies would be a betrayal of their working-class constituents.[11] Had Ellen been in parliament at the time, she would doubtless have voted with the "Red Clydesiders." Although her position on this issue would mellow with time, when she first came to parliament, she was uncompromising in her antagonism toward aristocratic society.

It is no surprise, then, that she was underwhelmed by the pageantry of the King's Speech to open parliament. Following a tradition dating back to the seventeenth century, that morning she and six-hundred-odd fellow MPs assembled in their own chamber to await the ceremonial arrival of Black Rod, whom, after a stern rebuke, they consented to allow to guide them across the hall into the Lords Chamber to attend to the King's Speech. Standing behind the bar of the chamber facing the enthroned King, with the Lords in full regalia seated to either side, the MPs listened to George V read out the speech written for him by Stanley Baldwin's government. The speech was comparatively long—nearly 1,750 words, and focused more on details than on Baldwin's larger vision for the next parliament. The one major statement of policy was made in reference to spending, and its implications riled Ellen's socialist heart. The King pronounced, "Every effort will be made to reduce public expenditure to the lowest possible limit consistent with the security and efficiency of the State. The present heavy burdens of the taxpayer are a hindrance to the revival of enterprise and employment. Economy in every sphere is imperative if we are to regain our industrial and commercial prosperity."[12] After the King finished, the MPs withdrew to their own chamber to discuss the speech.

The experience gave Ellen her first exposure to court culture, and her conclusion was that it was positively "medieval." The elaborate evening dresses of the peeresses admitted as spectators seemed a lurid contrast to the "plain clothes of the women MPs who are here to take their full share of work and responsibility." The jewels and ermine worn by the King and the Lords were, at best, "a little out of keeping . . . with the appeal in the King's Speech for economy, which, under a Conservative

Government, means economy in the great public services." The whole spectacle evoked, if not "medieval mummery" then Victorian farce, a display reminiscent of Gilbert and Sullivan.[13]

The ensuing debate over the speech was much more to her liking. The "rough and tumble" of Commons debate appealed to her pugilistic temper, although she would never fully master "the art of being thoroughly nasty with perfect politeness."[14] The experience furthered her resolution to make her maiden speech early. That night, with the speed and fluidity that would serve her so well in her journalistic career, she prepared to deliver her maiden speech on the next day of debate.

The following morning, Ellen arrived early and took her seat next to George Buchanan, the radical Scottish MP, who, like her, had hair as red as his politics. Buchanan was a charter member of the Red Clydesiders; and Ellen, who shared many of the group's political views, became fast friends with the rebellious Scot. She had staked out her seat next to Buchanan on day one, and her colleagues did not make her enter into a daily struggle for it.[15] She sat impatiently listening to the cut and thrust of debate with her feet dangling above the floor like Alice in Wonderland, until, toward the end of the evening, she finally managed to catch the speaker's eye—a bid perhaps helped by her unmistakable red hair, now unobscured by a hat, and by the sparkle of the gold-embroidered coat worn to keep her warm in the drafty chamber. The house was thinly filled by the time Whitley called on Ellen; but as the news travelled down the corridors into offices, bars, and smoking rooms, the Labour front benchers returned to hear their only woman MP.[16]

Standing at barely five feet in heels, Wee Ellen unleashed a maiden speech that earned her a new epithet: the Mighty Atom. Her speech combined two issues that formed her central preoccupations throughout her political career: the rights of women as citizens and the state's obligations to women workers—issues she argued were inextricably linked. As she rose to speak, Ellen was nervous about getting the right pitch of voice, as speaking from the benches was different than speaking from a dais or platform. Yet her training in debate at school and university came to her aid. Observers noted that her thin, slightly girlish voice was well pitched to the room, and that "she spoke with ease and vigour."[17] Her maiden effort began teasingly, with apologies to the Speaker for disregarding his advice not to address the House too soon. But she quickly moved on to serious affairs, expressing the disappointment of "women as a whole" that there had been no mention of further franchise reform in the King's Speech. As she would numerous times over the following years, Ellen mocked her male colleagues' fears about female voters, eliciting laughter with the jibe that had women actually voted as a bloc at the last election, as some had feared, one would have expected them to have succeeded in returning more than four female MPs to parliament.

Although the disfranchisement of women between the ages of twenty-one and thirty was insupportable on feminist grounds, Ellen went on to argue that the disfranchisement of working women robbed them of more than the vote. Working women were repeatedly overlooked or disadvantaged in legislation impacting British workers, and "I venture to suggest to the House that, had the women been voters, their claims would have received more attention from the Government." She gave her audience several concrete examples. She began with the Unemployment Insurance Act, which offered two types of benefit to workers—covenanted benefit, or benefit to which an employee was entitled as a consequence of having paid into an insurance fund while working, and transitional uncovenanted benefit, or "the dole." Working men were eligible for the dole regardless of family circumstances; but a women under thirty, if she were deemed to have any family who could look after her, was to be denied benefit, "though she may have earned her living since she were 14"—a legislative double standard arguably made easier by the fact that MPs could not be held to account by such women.

Ellen then moved on to the question of "relief work," or the investment by the state in public works projects such as digging reservoirs or paving roads with the aim of providing work for the unemployed. Although women could not be expected to dig ditches, the government could have shown more ingenuity in devising socially useful posts where women could be profitably employed, such as through an expansion of the public health services. Finally, she turned to particularly familiar territory—the implementation of regulations passed by trade boards, which predominantly affected industries dominated by female labour. There was, she contended, "wholesale evasion" of the Trades Board Act. Yet, when unions had requested an expansion of the inspectorate to enforce it, "We are told that it would cost too much money, . . .

but I venture to suggest to this House that if the employers concerned, instead of avoiding payment due to women—and, of course, men too—whom they employ, had been avoiding the payment of Income Tax, there would soon have been a means to bring them to book."

She concluded with a discussion of the proposal to introduce a state scheme of widows' pensions for women whose husbands had been disabled or died prematurely in industrial labour, a move her party had advocated for years. Although she lauded the principle, she implored that these pensions be set up as grants and not as part of a contributory pension scheme, as "at a time when wages of industrial workers are in many cases below the level of any decent subsistence . . . if, in addition to the already heavy burden of insurance, they have to pay for widows' pensions also, although to some of those here it may only seem a matter of coppers, it does mean a very great deal to them." Her closing remarks resonate with modern debates about the privatization and outsourcing of entitlement programs. In response to proposals to bring in private insurance companies to manage the proposed scheme, she protested, "Surely, even in this House, private enterprise is not to be allowed to make a profit out of the necessities of the people."[18]

This was progressive stuff! Right from the start, Red Ellen made clear to the House her belief that government should act as an active agent of economic redistribution. Shortly after her election to parliament, Ellen had described herself as "a keen Socialist strongly of the left-wing," and professed her desire to "see a drastic reorganization of society. . . . I want no millionaires and no paupers."[19] Her maiden speech showed her determination to bring her fight to parliament.

The deft mix of feminism and radical socialism in Ellen's speech was characteristic of her approach to feminist issues throughout the 1920s. Ellen was aware of the hostility toward feminism on the part of many members of the Labour and trade union movement. The prewar demand of feminists for *equal* suffrage between men and women, as opposed to full *adult* suffrage for men and women regardless of economic circumstances, appeared to many an attempt to increase the middle-class franchise at the expense of the working poor. Even after the passage of the 1918 franchise reform, which granted near full suffrage to British men, anxieties persisted that feminism "inasmuch as it fostered sex solidarity among women, threatened the unity of working-class men and women and hence the struggle for socialism."[20] Yet, although she would occasionally trim the sails of her feminism in later years to appease her party, she did not, as some have erroneously suggested, subordinate feminism to socialism.[21] Rather, she construed feminism through a socialist lens, always conscious of how greater political and legal rights for women would further their social and economic emancipation and improve both individual and family life.

Ellen was used to a hectic lifestyle as a national trade union organizer, but becoming a member of parliament took her frenetic schedule to a whole new level. As one interviewer presciently noted at the end of a profile of "The Only Woman M. P. for Labour," she was a member of the Manchester council as well as a NUDAW organizer and an MP, and despite her seemingly "overflowing energies," he feared lest "this appetite for work threaten to undermine her constitutional vigour."[22] If he had considered her numerous speaking engagements for women's organizations and for the party, he would have been even more concerned. She spent a phenomenal amount of her life on trains in this period. Her hours clocked travelling up and down the country allowed her to answer correspondence and keep up a prolific career as a book reviewer for the periodical press. Unfortunately, her tendency to use her train car as a wandering office combined with her absentmindedness once led to her having her handbag stolen en route from London to Manchester.[23]

Ellen's attendance at Manchester City Council meetings became increasingly erratic after her election to parliament, so much so that she declined to stand again in 1926.[24] Early on, however, she did her best to make the meetings and to use her position as an MP to the advantage of the Council. Travelling to Manchester was also an opportunity to visit Annie and to stay involved with the Manchester branch of Women's International League (WIL), of which Annie was still office secretary and Ellen a member of the Executive Committee. Ellen spoke on WIL platforms in Manchester in January and March and in June had top billing at a Women's Peace Demonstration co-organized by the WIL at which a petition was circulated asking the government "to accept forthwith the principle of arbitration in all international disputes."

Given her base in London, she was an obvious choice to serve as one of the Manchester women's ten delegates to the WIL's national council meeting. At the meeting, she was elected to serve on the twenty-eight member council, alongside the former Labour MP Dorothy Jewson and Ellen's future parliamentary colleague Barbara Ayrton Gould. Membership on the Council was principally an honorary appointment—the real organization work was done by the slightly smaller executive committee. Nonetheless, Ellen's election reaffirmed her commitment to the pacifist internationalism she had first espoused in Manchester during the war and foreshadowed an increased engagement in antiwar activism in the 1930s.

Yet, the feminist world of pacifist internationalism had never been Ellen's sole connection to events outside Britain's borders. Although she had left the Communist Party before the 1924 general election, she retained her personal connections to members of the international movement. When the French government took action to deport M. N. Roy, leader of the Indian Communist party in exile, Ellen flew to Paris to attend a protest meeting on his behalf. (It was her first voyage in an airplane, and the first of many flights she would make across the English Channel over the next two decades, the vast majority in conjunction with her human rights activism.)[25] She also maintained close ties with Communists, ex-Communists, and members of the radical left in Britain, principally through her continued involvement with the Plebs League, now merged with the National Council of Labour Colleges and with the Labour Research Department.

Her involvement with both organizations meant she remained in contact with Newbold, whose presence in her life she was unable to shake even as a government minister after the war—her secretary at the ministry of education recalls opening insinuating and sexually inappropriate letters from him seeking favours even then.[26] Yet, although Newbold clearly held a grudge against her, Ellen was better at hating ideas and abstract groups than flesh-and-blood individuals, and she showed no signs of feeling uncomfortable in his presence. Her involvement in the adult education movement also brought her into closer contact with cartoonist Frank Horrabin, who had taken over as editor of the *Plebs* magazine in 1914, with whom she quickly began an affair that lasted for six years.

Seven years her senior, Horrabin had been married for over a decade by the time Ellen moved to London. The presence of his wife, Winifred, however, did not impede him starting a relationship with Ellen in 1925. Tall and lanky, Frank was a committed socialist and internationalist who, unlike Newbold, did not take himself terribly seriously. He did however share Newbold's tendencies toward egocentrism, which helped him rationalize two lengthy extramarital affairs. His joie de vivre and an irrepressible playful streak would have attracted Ellen, as a refreshing contrast to her own more guarded personality. His good friend Margaret Cole recalled him, in their youth, "acting as host at a party of the Marxist Central Labour College in Earl's Court dressed as the Mad Hatter in a tall off-white top hat and looking the part to a 'T.'" Several years later, when he was briefly an MP during MacDonald's second minority government, he brought Margaret and her daughter Jane to tea on the House terrace. When Jane, aged nine, asked him whether "they use all those rooms for thinking in?" Frank replied with typical irreverence, "There's not so much thinking done here as you might fancy."[27]

The differences in temperament between Ellen and Frank hid a similar background. Like Ellen, Frank had grown up in a Methodist household on the margins between the working and the lower-middle class and made his way from Peterborough to London by means of a grammar school education. He had gone to the Sheffield School of Art, where he met Winifred, whom he affectionately referred to in Yorkshire idiom as his "pal." Trained as a cartographer, he soon got a job as a cartoonist for the London-based *Daily News* and *Star* newspapers, creating a series of memorable characters, including Japhet and Happy the Bear. Although his cartoons were gentle apolitical fun, his writing reflected a strongly held commitment to socialism at home and anti-imperialism abroad. He was a member of the Fabian Colonial Bureau, and through him Ellen would, in the 1930s, become involved with the India League. Before that, however, she volunteered to write for his journal, the *Plebs*. It was a rare issue that did not contain an article under her byline or a book review signed "E. C. W."

The Plebs League provided a needed social outlet for Ellen, who once told a journalist that although the armchairs in the House library were notoriously comfortable, she had not yet had a chance to enjoy them due to the "hectic rush" of parliamentary life.[28] In addition to lecturing at the Central Labour College in London, the Plebs Leaguers also held an annual summer school on the continent—an educational holiday for those socialists whose savings or union funds allowed them to partake. Ellen's first year in London, the summer school was held in Wimereux, on the north coast of France. Ellen lectured on Left Wing Problems and Frank on Modern European History, while Winifred's name was conveniently absent from the program.

The adult education movement was one way Ellen kept herself from losing touch with the people she had come to Westminster to represent. Another, of course, was her union work. Although she no longer worked full-time as a union organizer, she, like many of her colleagues on the Labour benches, maintained her position with NUDAW throughout her career. During the parliamentary recess in January 1925, she returned to Manchester to engage in union work, and she still took part in major union actions, such as the lockout of 10,000 shop assistants employed by the Co-op in the northwest that March.[29] She also served as chair of the Standing Joint Committee of Industrial Women's Organizations. In parliament, Ellen claimed she did not only speak for women, but for workers more broadly. Yet, as a NUDAW delegate to the Trades Union Congress (TUC) in Scarborough in 1925, she paid particular attention to women's issues, seconding a motion for equal pay in the civil service and arguing for a special conference to discuss methods for organizing women members. Ironically, it was easier for Ellen to deny that gender mattered in her parliamentary advocacy for the working class than it was surrounded by her working-class compatriots in the masculine environment of Congress.[30]

All of this, of course, was in addition to her political career. The Mighty Atom was a regular attendee in the House during her first few sessions as an MP, with barely a week going by without her participating in debate or asking questions of department heads. She would normally come in early enough for ministerial questions on days when she attended debate. Even when she didn't have a question of her own, she followed the discussion and regularly asked supplementaries. Her sarcasm showed through particularly during question time, and one of her most frequent victims was Home Secretary William Joynson-Hicks, or "Jix" as he was known in parliamentary circles—an impish nickname belied by his serious manner. Ellen and the austere solicitor, more than twenty-five years her senior, saw eye-to-eye on hardly any issue. A member of the diehard conservative wing of the Unionist party, Jix rejected an activist role for government in social policy, opposed home rule in India, occasionally made disparaging remarks about women in politics, took a hardline position against domestic and international Communism, and generally privileged the enforcement of law and order over the defence of civil liberties. When Jix told a Conservative MP that the government had no intention to deport shady American businessmen who had come to Britain to find investors for "bogus companies," Ellen asked the Home Secretary whether such share pushers were not at least as dangerous as Russian violinists—a jab at the recent deportation of a musician accused of Communist agitation.[31]

Although no longer a CP member, Ellen retained her sympathy with the Bolshevik leadership, at least until the show trials in the 1930s. In 1930, she authored the preface to a volume titled *Anti-Soviet Lies Nailed,* published by the Anglo-Russian Parliamentary Committee, and she not infrequently used question time to expose what she deemed as the hypocrisy and viciousness of the government's Russia policy. However, in the aftermath of the Zinoviev Letter affair, when the Tory press had undermined Labour's 1924 reelection campaign by alleging the Soviet ambassador was communicating orders to the Labour leadership, the party was keen to distance itself from the Soviet Union in popular perception, and the opposition steered clear of debates over Russia policy in the late 1920s. Instead, the main issue concerning both parties was how to deal with unemployment, which averaged 1.5 million throughout the decade.

After her maiden speech, Ellen had told reporters she had no intention of becoming an MP for women. Rather "I mean to be in the middle of the fight on industrial questions."[32] Although she did participate in debates over unemployment and industrial policy, Ellen's parliamentary interventions during her first session focused closely on issues of interest to women. In this she differed from Margaret Bondfield, the only other female trade unionist to have been elected to parliament when Ellen won her seat for Middlesbrough East. Bondfield, a small woman with a round face and a freshly scrubbed appearance, was a devout Congregationalist (Beatrice Webb once said of her, "Margaret has her religion as relaxation"[33]), and she had risen up through the Labour movement via the Shop Assistants' Union and the Women's Labour League. Nearly twenty years Ellen's senior, she had gained national prominence before entering parliament. In 1923, Bondfield became the first woman president of the TUC General Council. As one biographer has argued, she "advanced within her union, and therefore within the Party, not because she was a woman, or because of women's votes, but because colleagues valued her combination of dedication, courage, and practical common sense." This is not to say that Bondfield did not support women's rights, but the class struggle was unquestionably her first priority. A tally of Ellen's parliamentary contributions reveals she devoted nearly a tenth of her speeches to issues specific to women (an average figure that masks a greater attention to "women's issues" in her youth, compared to the 1930s and 1940s, when she was preoccupied with the fight against Fascism). Bondfield, in contrast, spent only five percent of her time speaking on women.[34]

To say that Ellen's speeches, particularly during her first parliamentary session, focused on women's issues is not however to say that she served as a mouthpiece for the feminist organization the National Union of Societies for Equal Citizenship (NUSEC). A survey of some of the issues that preoccupied Ellen during the 1924–1925 session sheds light on how she understood the link between politics and gender. Five issues affecting women with which Ellen concerned herself were the amendment of the Representation of the People Act to extend the franchise to women under thirty; equal pay and promotion for women in the civil services; widows' pensions; the taxation of women's luxuries; and the nationality of married women.

The most obviously feminist issue was franchise reform. Between the passage of the 1918 Representation of the People Bill giving the vote to propertied women over thirty and the equalization of the franchise between men and women in 1928, several bills and amendments were put forth to equalize the franchise. They were repeatedly quashed by the government, normally on the grounds that any legislation changing the electoral registers would necessitate the dissolution of parliament, which would mean any legislation still on the table would be stranded. The only franchise reform bill to be allowed into committee was that proposed by the Labour backbencher William Adamson during the first Labour government. But MacDonald, never an enthusiastic fan of women's suffrage, did not give the bill priority in the legislative calendar, and it languished with the government's dissolution in October 1924.[35]

During the ensuing election campaign, the Conservatives had promised that if elected they would form an all-party committee to discuss suffrage reform—not a commitment to reform per se, but a greater concession to the women's movement than at any previous election. In February 1925, Labour member William Whiteley put forth a bill to equalize the franchise, which Ellen seconded. In doing so, she displayed her now-trademark blend of humour and penetrating argument. Opponents of female enfranchisement had suggested that if given the vote women would simply vote for the best-looking candidate. Ellen jestingly sought to dispel her male colleagues' anxieties on this count, disclaiming: "Looking round this House, I cannot see that there is any need for honourable members to be worried." She noted, "It was stated that there were actually women members of the House that were against the extension of the franchise" (a clear reference to the antisuffragist Atholl), which she derided as "an utterly incomprehensible thing" given that women were only in the House owing to the work of the suffrage movement—a jibe that elicited a "hear, hear!" from Nancy Astor on the other side of the aisle. She then turned serious: Young working-class women needed the franchise to ensure that their voices would be heard and their interests protected.[36]

Ellen had made the same point at greater length the day before, in a syndicated press article intended for a popular readership. She was one of many Labour MPs who wrote for the popular press to supplement their income in the 1920s, but her accessible journalistic style separated her from many of her colleagues.[37] She began her article by painting a pen portrait of "a girl of 21." The phrase, she wrote, "conjures up delightful visions of a sweet young thing on the front page of a magazine, simply made for tennis and kisses." But "unfortunately we don't live on magazine wrappers, and most of the girls of today have to think how to earn a living and often how to help to maintain others, taking the joys of youth as an afterthought." She then turned to the oft-repeated arguments about virtual representation—that women over thirty were supposed to act as proxies for their younger "sisters." Such arguments ignored the fact that the unenfranchised were largely a "new class of voters—the industrial and professional women" whose needs were different than those of (largely married) women who currently held the vote. She enumerated the long list of legislation that specifically impacted these women, into which they had no input and for which they could not hold the drafters accountable. She ended with an endorsement of "strengthening the influence of youth on our public life. It is more important to the man or woman whose life is still in front of them what the laws should be than it is to the man whose life is nearly ended."[38] At the Women's International League for Peace and Freedom (WILPF) conference in Zurich, Ellen had spoken up on behalf of the "young democrats afraid of nothing when it is a question of taking a stand for the new time." Even as she left her own youth behind her, she maintained her belief that Britain's (and the world's) future lay with its young people.

The franchise bill was ultimately quashed by Joynson-Hicks. Speaking for the government, he argued that although such a bill would be disruptive if passed at such an early stage of the new parliament, the government would commit to bringing in legislation to equalize the franchise before the parliament had adjourned. Winston Churchill, a staunch opponent of equal franchise, later wrote that Jix "quite unexpectedly, and without the slightest consultation with his colleagues, said that the Conservative Party would enfranchise men and women on the same terms 'at the next election.' Two years later this formidable gesture had to be redeemed. Never was so great a change in our electorate achieved so incontinently."[39] As usual, Churchill's recollections were more than a bit hyperbolic. It is, however, true that the party had not yet reached agreement about either the wisdom of equalizing the franchise or the best methods for so doing. Nonetheless, the feminist societies made repeated reference to Jix's statement in attempting to hold the government to its pledge made during the 1924 election campaign. Equal franchise at age twenty-one would ultimately become law in July 1928. Ellen would be active both in speaking on behalf of the legislation in parliament and in drumming up support for it in the country, speaking on platforms of NUSEC, the Women's Freedom League, and other feminist groups.[40]

Another feminist issue on Ellen's agenda was equal pay. After the passage of the 1918 reform act, the women's movement splintered, with equal rights feminists concerned with removing all of the remaining legal hurdles that separated women from men, and self-proclaimed "new feminists" advocating an approach to politics that recognized the special needs of women as mothers, workers, and homemakers. Divisions over how best to advance women's rights would become increasingly fractious over the course of the 1920s and 1930s, especially in the field of women's employment. Here, equal rights feminists, centred around the Six Point Group and the Open Door Council, opposed protective legislation governing the hours and conditions of women's work, and supported equal pay for men and women based on the "rate for the job." Meanwhile, women such as Eleanor Rathbone, the president of NUSEC and, from 1929, Ellen's colleague in parliament, argued that protective legislation benefitted women workers, and emphasized the provision of family allowances, or payments to the mother, as the best means of undermining wage inequality. Such payments, it was argued, would both prevent women from taking low-paid jobs and undermine male workers' arguments about the need for a "breadwinner's wage" that would allow a man to support a dependent wife and family. On the issue of protective legislation, Ellen, alongside her female colleagues in the Labour movement, sided with the "new feminists." However, although she supported the endowment of motherhood, she remained a vocal advocate for equal pay.

Equal pay campaigners argued that as a first step, the government should lead the way in revising civil service entry requirements and pay scales to treat women and men equally and that, ultimately, there should be legislation to mandate that private employers pay men and women equally. In doing so, they were pushing against a door that would remain stubbornly closed until 1956, when the government finally equalized pay rates in the civil service. Legislation to outlaw discrimination in pay in the private sector was not passed until 1970 and did not come into force until the end of 1975. In 1936, at the behest of the Joint Committee on Women in the Civil Service, Ellen would propose a private member's motion on equal pay in the civil service that would pass a vote in the House only to be overturned on a second vote the government insisted on treating as an issue of confidence in the administration.[41] Well before that, however, she had made herself a gadfly on the issue of female civil service employees, putting down numerous questions about the conditions and rates of pay of women in various branches of government, from doctors to typists.

Historians have frequently contended the incompatibility of allegiance to the Labour and feminist movements for socialist women. Pamela Graves has suggested, "Even the minority of prewar suffragists who argued for equal pay in similar terms to the egalitarian feminists [a group in which she includes Ellen] still placed women's economic equality in the broader context of working-class progress." In support of this contention, she points to Ellen's statement at a National Labour Women's Conference that equal pay "was not a sex question but emphatically it was a class question. It was a question of where women workers should say that they wanted the rate for the job and would not be used to undercut the men."[42] Although Ellen's commitment to raising wages for all working-class men and women cannot be questioned, she was astute at tailoring her sentiments to her audience. Equal pay for clerks in the civil service might be a class question, but it was not a working-class question. Nonetheless, Ellen, a university-educated, self-supporting woman in a male-dominated field, was a steady parliamentary advocate of the rights of professional women.

Ellen's support for franchise reform and equal pay legislation earned her a place alongside Nancy Astor, Commander Kenworthy, Frederick Pethick-Lawrence, and several others on the equalitarian feminist Six Point Group's "white list" of MPs who worked most consistently for women's rights.[43] Her active interventions in the debate over the Widows' and Orphans' Pension Bill reflected a different kind of feminist agenda. Ellen's approach to the bill, to which she proposed several amendments, was closely in tune with "new feminism," and, crucially, if subtly, out of tune with the mainstream of the Labour Party.

The Widows', Orphans' and Old Age Contributory Pensions Act of 1925 established a contributory insurance scheme whereby widows of insured men with children under age fourteen at the time of the husband's death would be paid an amount equal to the (parlously low) sum paid to old-age pensioners for the remainder of their lives. Pressure for state provision for widows had emerged out of the wartime campaign for the state endowment of motherhood, a campaign that would remain at the forefront of the postwar new feminist agenda, largely due to Rathbone. Feminist supporters of "family endowment" argued that "the State wants children, and to give them is a service both dangerous and honourable." As women were doing a service to the state, the state in turn should compensate their labour. "Our object will not be to enable mothers to earn their living, but to ensure that, *since they have earned it,* they should get it."[44]

The wartime call for state support for mothers was taken up and transmuted by the Labour movement after the war. In 1919, 1923, and 1924, trade union MPs proposed resolutions calling for state pensions for mothers with dependent children whose husbands were dead or incapacitated. Yet, although these men agreed with the need for state action to support mothers, their logic in so doing was radically different from that of the feminists. As Ellen's NUDAW colleague Rhys Davies wrote in 1923, "The demand for pensions for mothers . . . springs not from the belief that a woman should be endowed because she is a mother, but rather when and because she is the trustee of her dead husband's family."[45] Labour women, for the most part, got behind this redefinition of family endowment as support for the families of working men. Ellen was the exception.

In Ellen's view the bill should have provided benefit to all mothers, regardless of their marital status. "This money is being paid to the widows for a very definite service," she insisted. "That is, so that she can bring up her children adequately for the State. . . . I wish hon. Members would get into their heads that a non-contributory scheme would not be a dispensing of charity, but a very definite payment for services that the widow had rendered to the State, and that it should enable the women to bring up the children properly."[46] Given the lack of support for this interpretation of widows' pensions on either side of the aisle, Ellen devoted considerable energy to a futile attempt to reform the most egregious provisions of what she deemed to be a terribly flawed bill.

She moved her first amendment at 9:30 p.m. the first night of the debate and spoke passionately in its defence for the next several hours. She first proposed that the pool of eligible women be widened to include not only widows of insured men but also widows of uninsured men who were themselves insured. She made her case through several pointed examples, such as the women "in the County of Lancashire or the County of Yorkshire, where it is the normal custom for the married woman to continue in work after marriage." Most of these women work in insured textile professions; but if such a woman's "husband dies and he is not an insured man, although she is an insured person, and although she has been continually paying her insurance contributions, she is left with the children without a pension. She has then to take part herself as the breadwinner without any of the assistance that is given to other women under the Bill. For instance, there may be a sister of hers who has never paid a penny under the Bill, whose husband may have been insured for a period of two years, and she would draw a pension for life, although she has paid far less in contributions than the woman who is an insured contributor."[47]

Several years later, an observer would say of Ellen, "Nothing is so convincing in Parliament or elsewhere as a 'case' carefully built up and buttressed.... A case-builder of this kind Miss Wilkinson undoubtedly is. She is seldom emotional; ... but sometimes, without employing emotional means, she can produce an emotional effect.... the starkness of the picture produces the appropriate emotional effect."[48] But despite the case she made on behalf of these women workers, the amendment went down on a vote of 178 to 87 at 2 a.m.

Sometime after three in the morning, Ellen and Mabel Philipson disappeared into the women's dungeon for a brief nap.[49] Ellen's doctor had recently ordered her to complete bed rest for nervous exhaustion—a prescription she characteristically ignored. This latest in a series of all-night sittings proved too much for her constitution to bear, however, and she could not resist the lure of sleep. But by 6 a.m., she was back in the chamber, again challenging the convention that a married woman ought to be "kept" by her husband. Under the current pensions legislation, unmarried men and women in an insured trade became eligible to draw a pension at age 65. But no matter how long a woman worked, once she married, if she ceased work she forfeited her right to draw her own pension. The potential injustice in this arrangement was spelled out by Ellen: "Suppose you have an insured woman of 45 who has been paying since she was 16 and marries a man five years younger than herself. She has been paying for 25 years, but she will still not get the pension when she reaches the age of 65." The attorney-general's reply was matter of fact: "The answer to that is quite obviously that, as she will be an uninsured women, she will get her pension when her husband reaches the age of 65, because she is getting it in right of her husband and not in right of any insurance of her own." Ellen's frustration was palpable. "But we are having the continual assumption that, however many years a woman pays in while she is unmarried, all that money is lost when she marries. Surely, when a woman has paid in for many years, she ought to get some benefit." Her entreaties, again, fell on deaf ears.[50]

The house finally adjourned shortly after 7 a.m., only to resume discussion of the bill the next afternoon, when Ellen, exhausted and discouraged, was nonetheless back in the House. She first made the case on behalf of single women, arguing that "the single woman contributing under the Bill is successively penalised; she is penalised at almost every stage of her insured life." By this she meant that a single woman was to be made to pay contributions toward the solvency of the widows' pension scheme. However, if she never married, she would never see the benefit of these contributions. Not only that, if she were to lose her job or to voluntarily leave employment before 65, she would not even receive a pension from the government in her own right. After outlining these injustices, she ended with a plea to the government:

> I ask the Minister to realise the condition of these women. They have paid for unemployment benefit all their lives. Under this scheme they will pay for these widows' pensions also all their lives. They are to help to insure a risk for women who are very much better able to pay than themselves, and then they are to be told that there is nothing for them. I ask, in view of the large amounts which these women have to their credit, whether it is not possible to provide some kind of alternative benefit for them? . . . Do not penalise them at every stage, and after telling them that they must insure and that it is compulsory thrift, reward them for their thrift by turning them off every single fund to which they have contributed.[51]

One of her last rearguard actions concerned the clause debarring a woman who had married a man over the age of 60 from receiving a pension upon his death unless the marriage had resulted in the birth of a child. The stipulation, according to the government, had been put in place to guard against "mercenary marriages" on the part of working-class women, and the debate over the clause brought out Ellen's scathing wit: "Gentleman, may I ask why it should be considered a crime, resulting in a very severe fine, if a working woman marries a man aged 60 or over? Why should it be assumed that she is marrying him, not because she wants to but for the ulterior purpose of sitting at his breakfast table or by his bedside, hoping against hope that he will shortly shuffle off this mortal coil and leave her, not with the money that he is able to provide, but with this magnificent pension of 10s. a week. The whole idea is perfectly ridiculous."[52] The government's insistence on including the clause reflected both a long-standing suspicion about the moral character of the working classes and a strong desire to establish the legislation with the maximum of economy. In arguing for the rights of women who married late in life, Ellen was not making so much a feminist argument as a socialist one. The average working woman earned between 26 and 28 shillings—a wage barely sufficient to keep her properly housed, clothed, and fed. The proposed provision was already so meagre that it seemed especially mean that the government was going out of its way to exclude some women from qualifying. In making such a case, Ellen drew into question the long-standing assumption in British welfare policy that provision should be set so low as to discourage reliance on the state. Although there might be an argument for such an approach in unemployment insurance (one Ellen could recognize but would not have accepted), she could not conceive the rationale for such low payments to women who would have little to no other means of subsistence.

Widows' pensions were the most prominent, if by no means the only, issue where Ellen's feminism and her socialism intersected. In this instance, she had the support of her Labour colleagues in seeking to reform the bill, although their objections rested on class as opposed to gendered grounds. She did not, however, have the backing of one of her more regular supporters on feminist issues: Nancy Astor. The government was treating the pensions bill as a party issue. The whips were called in, and the other three women MPs voted against each amendment put forth by the opposition. Nonetheless, Nancy appreciated the sentiment and conviction behind Ellen's efforts to ensure justice for working women. When the second night of debate finally wound up—at 5:39 a.m.—Nancy rushed amongst the scramble of departing MPs to find the exhausted Ellen and offer to drive her home.[53]

On the issue of women's pensions, Ellen had the new feminists on her side, if not the support of her female colleagues in the House of Commons. In speaking out against the silk tax in Chancellor Winston Churchill's 1925 budget, she was charting a new path in defining what it meant to represent women's interests in the House of Commons. Equal rights feminists focused on legal and political equality. New feminists focused on the recognition of women's social and economic status, focusing principally on their position as mothers and homemakers. The Labour Party focused on the wages of male breadwinners. But what about the single women who did not aspire to have a job outside of the typing pool or the cotton factory, and who were not married but wanted a chance to escape from the bleakness of working-class life and take part in the glamorous consumer culture reflected in shop windows and on the cinema screen? In 1927, Ellen would tell a reporter, "The demand of the modern working girl is for a decent standard of life and dress. . . . The desire of the girl to look as nice as possible is part of her self-respect, and has nothing whatever to do with her moral outlook."[54] Many feminists would bemoan young women's preoccupation with Hollywood films, dresses, and lipstick as a sign that feminism had been abandoned by the postwar generation. Ellen, in contrast, saw the defence of a woman's self-respect as an important part of her job as a feminist MP.

The 1925 budget is best remembered for Britain's return to the gold standard, which one economist later described as "perhaps the most decisively damaging action involving money in modern time."[55] The return to gold was costly, and Churchill sought to offset it by a series of tax increases, including taxes on tea and silk, both real and artificial. The silk duty in particular became a topic of fierce dispute, as the opposition claimed it was a regressive tax that was particularly punitive toward poor women. Ellen took a central part in the debates, attending her first all-night sittings of parliament to defend the rights of young women to their silk stockings, and at one point accusing the government of having "a spite against women."[56] It was a topic close to her heart—she could not pay a visit to the United States without waxing lyrical on the wider and more affordable selection of silk underthings for sale in that country. The final day of Committee debate on the Finance Bill saw Ellen intervene in debate seven times during a sitting that lasted until 6:30 a.m.

Women have argued that such late-night sittings mitigate against the entrance of women into Westminster politics, as they make it extremely difficult for an MP to balance work and home life.[57] Ellen did not have a family waiting for her at home as she sat through the night wrapped in her cloak and munching chocolates from her handbag. The late-night sittings did, however, take their toll. Between the long debates and a punishing schedule of open-air meetings during an exceptionally hot June, she fell ill and was ordered to bed rest. In defiance, she continued to attend parliament. Her determination to ignore the advice of doctors in order to get on with her work would ultimately have tragic consequences. In 1925, however, her defence of young women's interests in parliament—even if ultimately futile—arguably helped Labour to present itself as a party attuned to women's needs.

The final "women's issue" Ellen championed during her first parliamentary session was the nationality of British women married to foreigners. The issue brought together her interest in social justice, her feminist commitment to equality between the sexes, and her pacifist internationalism. It was not resolved until after Wilkinson's death, with the passage of the British Nationality Act of 1948, best known for creating a distinction between British and imperial citizenship. Until 1948, women were assumed to renounce their British citizenship on marriage to a foreigner—even if their husband's country did not automatically grant citizenship to wives of its nationals (a situation that occasionally left some British-born women technically stateless). The 1948 law finally allowed women to maintain their UK citizenship upon marriage, equalizing citizenship rights between the sexes.

The gendered double standard in nationality legislation was uniformly opposed by women's groups. However, compared with equal pay in the civil service, it was not a particularly pressing feminist concern. That the issue received as much attention as it did in the interwar period owes much to Scottish barrister Chrystal Macmillan, who made reform of nationality law a personal crusade.[58] Active in the British suffrage movement and the International Women's Suffrage Alliance, Macmillan had attended the 1915 meeting of women at The Hague and was a charter member of the WILPF. Although she and Ellen moved in different social and professional circles, they would have been known to each other through the WILPF. Like Ellen, Macmillan's concern with nationality law emerged as a consequence of the First World War, when the Aliens Restriction Act and the Defence of the Realm Act led to the persecution of many women married to foreigners. British women married to German men, and hence now German citizens themselves, saw their husbands interned and suffered stigmatization and economic hardship. For Macmillan, this was a human rights issue. For Ellen, it was also a class issue.

Although the law applied equally to women of all classes, as one scholar has written, "The problems faced by middle and upper-class women married to enemy aliens, and the hostility they encountered, paled in significance beside those of their poorer sisters. As soon as internment began in 1914 it became evident that the most serious problem of the families of working-class enemy aliens in Britain during the war would be desperate poverty." The loss of income these families suffered from the internment of the male breadwinner was compounded by the temporary contraction in many industries dominated by women workers in the early months of the war, as well as hostility to hiring "enemy aliens," leaving many families reliant on government relief from the poor law or from societies such as the Destitute Aliens Committee.[59] Through her trade union work, Ellen would likely have encountered women adversely affected by these laws.

The government, however, was not so easily persuaded. Their priority was holding together the ties between the metropole and the empire. Unilateral legislation by the British parliament allowing British-born women to keep their imperial citizenship in the event of marriage was perceived as the thin edge of the wedge in the breakdown of imperial unity. During a three-hour debate over reform of the law in February 1925, Ellen decried the government's policy of making the fate of these women into a "kind of shuttlecock between this parliament and the dominions."[60] The debate ended with the passage of a resolution to amend the nationality law to equalize rights between men and women.

The government, however, took no action on the issue. Over the next decade, Ellen worked with British and international women, both in parliament (where she put forth a private member's bill on the issue) and under the auspices of the International Alliance of Women and the WILPF to push for reform.[61] Although the issue had concrete economic implications for British women, it also served to reinforce national chauvinism and to discourage marriage across national borders. As such, it flew in the face of the pacifist cosmopolitanism to which Ellen remained committed throughout her career. Her work to reform British nationality law was one of the many ways in which her domestic and international politics intersected.

Ellen's engagement with the Women's International League was facilitated from November 1925 when she moved from a rented room in Westminster to a converted apartment in a townhouse on John St. In her twenties, she had lived with her siblings in "Bloomsbury-like" accommodation in south Manchester. Now she had her own flat in Bloomsbury. The small Georgian neighbourhood in the borough of Camden surrounding the British Museum and the University of London was the epicentre of literary London in the 1920s. The neighbourhood is known as the home of the "Bloomsbury set," the bohemian, sexually unorthodox group of writers, artists, and intellectuals whose most famous members were the novelist and publisher Virginia and Leonard Woolf. The Woolfs; Virginia's sister, Vanessa, and her husband, Clive Bell; and their friends Lytton Strachey, Duncan Grant, and John Maynard Keynes formed the core of a diffuse group of men and women Strachey's wife would describe as "a marvelous combination of the highest intelligence and appreciation of literature combined with a lean humour and tremendous affection. They gave it backwards and forwards to each other like shuttlecocks, only the shuttlecocks multiplied as they flew in the air." Ellen, tongue only slightly in cheek, described them less charitably as an "exclusive . . . circle who bestowed fame on themselves by writing reviews of each others' books."[62]

Although the Bloomsbury set put the neighbourhood on the map, the picturesque squares of WC1 were also the home to a diverse group of writers, artists, feminists, and progressive intellectuals. The headquarters of the WIL were located at 55 Gower Street, and, before moving to Hampstead, Vera Brittain and Winifred Holtby lived off Mecklenburgh Square. This was literary territory, and Ellen's decision to move there says much about her self-conception as a "modern" young intellectual. She was not bereft of radical socialist neighbours, however—Frank and Winifred Horrabin lived a few blocks away.

She came to love the neighbourhood and, after a few years, moved to a slightly larger flat on Guilford Street. In November 1926, a journalist from *Lady's Companion* interviewed Ellen at home and described her as living in "a blue and orange little one roomed flat . . . —with orange cups and saucers, blue mugs and [she] had painted her chairs blue . . . it was charming." Toward the end of her life, Ellen attributed her love of colour to a spiritual revolt against the "gloomy" drabness of her Manchester childhood, where, even in the small park near her home, "the leaves were always sooty." Between long sessions in parliament, speaking engagements, trips to her constituency, and union work around the country, her flat served as a warm and cosy oasis.[63] Once she moved to Guilford Street, she became a regular hostess, throwing impromptu soirées for a motley array of international intellectuals, spies, politicians, and celebrities.

The commute from Bloomsbury to Westminster was less than two miles. But the long hours of the parliamentary session meant Ellen frequently left the House too late either to walk home or take the tube. She could, and did, travel by taxi—or hitch a ride with Lady Astor—but the distance served as an excuse for Ellen to make her most extravagant purchase: an Austin Seven motorcar, which she bought in summer 1925. During session, she used the car to scoot back and forth, but during recess she logged thousands of miles in recreational travel. She came to love the car, and her Who's Who entries list her hobbies as reading, chess, golf, and motoring. She learned to do basic repairs, a necessary skill given her frequent accidents behind the wheel. After buying the car, she in short succession collided with a motor-van and with a horse and cart. One spring weekend during the 1925–1926 session, she and Annie went motoring in Wales. On the coastal drive between Chester and Rhyl, Ellen let her older sister have a hand behind the wheel. When the two were overtaken by a speeding motorcycle, Annie instinctively swerved, and the car tumbled over the bank of the road into a stream. Ellen was knocked unconscious and badly bruised, but typically, her principal concern was for the car. As she told a journalist for the *Daily Mail,* she and the Austin Seven had survived worse and, "It is evident that I am not intended to meet my death in a motor accident."[64]

She did not often drive her car up to Middlesbrough, however. The long journey was easier by train, which allowed her to work while she travelled. She maintained a small flat in the northeast steel town, which was more a bolthole than a home.[65] Like most of her colleagues, she did not hold a regular constituency "surgery"; however, she was frequently up in Middlesbrough chairing or speaking at local party and community events and asked numerous questions in the House on behalf of her constituents, principally concerning the denial of entitlement to pension and unemployment benefits—cases that confirmed her conviction of the need for "work or maintenance" as a universal right.

Ellen's status as one of the few women MPs meant she was in high demand as a speaker and chairwoman for events around the country. Shortly after her election, she opened a beautiful baby contest in Ilford; early in 1926, she presided over the "domestic hygiene" section of the Royal Sanitary Institute's jubilee congress and headlined a demonstration held by the Labour Women's Advisory Council in Glasgow and a meeting of the Gloucester Trades Council and Labour Party the same month. There was hardly a county in Britain that could not boast of having hosted Ellen for an event.

Both her frenetic schedule and her courtship of publicity meant Ellen was a constant feature in the press columns almost from the moment of her arrival in London. She once quipped, "MPs pretend to be quite indifferent to the Press. Don't believe it. I should be prepared to wager that every member of this House subscribes to a Press-cutting agency and reads every printed word about him."[66] Ellen employed a press-cutting agency, but given the volume of articles printed about her, it is hard to think where she could have found the time to read every word herself.

While the press covered her parliamentary speeches and her extra-parliamentary political work, a fantastic amount of ink was also spilled over her sartorial choices and personal life. When, in February 1925,

Ellen decided to shingle her long red hair, the "story" received coverage not only in the national press but in provincial papers such as the *Liverpool Echo, Sheffield Telegraph,* and *Manchester Dispatch*—several of which ran photographs of "Wee Ellen's" new hairdo. When she cut her hair even shorter the following year, sporting an Eton crop, a similar bevy of press coverage followed. The interest in her hair was equalled by the interest in her clothes. Reading through her press clippings reveals that in March 1925 Miss Wilkinson appeared in the House sporting a "gipsy scarf"—a brightly coloured scarf worn under the collar of the dress and tied in a knot in front in sailor fashion; and that, in the autumn of 1926, both Wilkinson and Mabel Philipson wore Russian boots (ruched riding boots) to the House, although they changed into slippers before taking their seats. Reporters frequently asked Ellen about her "decision" to remain single, and her skills (or lack thereof) as a cook were well-known amongst readers of the popular press. When she bought her Austin Seven, her frequent accidents and less-harrowing adventures behind the wheel became a new topic of press coverage.[67]

The exceptional degree of attention devoted to Wilkinson, compared to other woman MPs, doubtless owed something to her position as the sole young unmarried woman in the House, at least until the arrival of Jennie Lee and Megan Lloyd George in 1929. Although she was thirty-three when she entered parliament, her diminutive physique made her appear younger, and in the context of the rather moribund House of Commons, she was, in fact, relatively young. Ellen was quickly branded the House's token "modern girl," and, to the delight of the press, she looked and acted the part. Her working-class background likely further encouraged reporters' tendency to view the MP as a "girl" and perhaps invited a degree of intimacy that journalists would have been more hesitant to bestow on a woman from a different social background. Yet it was not just the impertinence of the press; Ellen actively encouraged journalists to keep her in the limelight.

In 1928, Ellen told a reporter for the *Evening Standard:* "Unfortunate politicians who have a message they want to get across find the public interested in their clothes and not their ideas. I am always being asked how I spend my £400 a year, how I do my cooking, and what I eat.

It is much more difficult for a woman MP to retain any privacy than for a man."[68] Despite such complaints, Ellen collaborated with reporters keen to make "Miss Wilkinson" a household name. Nancy Astor and Jennie Lee both adopted an inconspicuous uniform while in parliament.[69] When asked about her fashion sense by an *Evening Standard* reporter, Susan Lawrence tersely replied that "the clothes an MP wore were entirely his or her own affair."[70] Ellen, in contrast, smiled for photographers who snapped her sporting a new hairstyle or a new hat and gave interviews on her inability to pull off wearing the colour red.[71] When a secret admirer sent her an Airedale puppy, she posed for photographs with the little dog before sending it north to live with her brother. She welcomed reporters into her home and answered questions about her domestic routines (she named her tea kettle Agatha after Agatha Christie), and coyly parried questions about her marriage prospects ("Nothing in the future is definite. One never knows.")[72]

Though Ellen once told a reporter that "self-advertisement does not pay in politics any more than in other things," she was an instinctive self-publicist. "Modesty," she was quoted as saying, "is not really an asset in modern politics." Over the course of her career, several detractors would cite her alleged thirst for fame against her. Conservative opponents in Middlesbrough claimed the constant attention bestowed on her by the London press was of her own invitation and "she has been using her dress and her hair-dressing for propaganda purposes."[73] Yet there was also a more pragmatic side to Ellen's courtship of the media. The celebrity she garnered by merit of the press's desire to make politics accessible to women readers gave her a platform to champion causes. This was particularly notable after the general strike of May 1926 and on her ensuing trip to the US on a fund-raising mission for the miners' families in August 1926. Her high profile in the British press meant her arguments in defence of the strikers garnered more attention than those of other backbench MPs. Although she was not as well-known in the American press, Ellen recognized that her fundraising tour would gain more publicity if she played up the "human interest" angle. In New York, she consented to answer questions about her personal life from a reporter for the *Tribune*, albeit with the protest that "she wanted any space in the newspaper she might claim to be devoted to the relief of the families of the miners." The result was a profile that combined a good deal of human interest on the "little spirited woman" with a rather thoroughgoing discussion of her views on industrial relations.[74] Talking about her personal life and fashion choices was the necessary price to pay for the column space she was determined to achieve for discussion of her politics.

7

NINE DAYS THAT (ALMOST) SHOOK THE WORLD

"The dominant factor in the present Parliament is the Tory Majority of 215 over every possible combination. Only those who have tried to work under such conditions can have any idea of their deadening effect. Nothing seems any good. Every fight is lost before it is started. Members grow indifferent. To those who come into contact with the terrible poverty in the distressed areas, our impotence is heartbreaking."[1] So wrote Ellen in January 1926, barely more than a year into her parliamentary career. As the session wore on, her sense of frustration only increased. Two months later, she was complaining of the deadening effect of "this constant fight against futility," which she saw as a "rot eating out the heart of this parliament."[2] Her own inability to affect government policy on widows' and orphans' pensions in 1925 was mirrored over and over in the failures of her colleagues to effect change to any social and economic legislation impacting the working classes. Alternatives to regressive taxation of consumer goods, amendments to factory legislation, safeguarding of government payments to friendly societies and other participants in national insurance schemes, all were proposed by the Labour opposition and rejected by the government. Often the government MPs did not even bother to listen to the arguments made by their opposition colleagues. At one point during the debates over the Unemployment Insurance Bill in March 1926, only three supporters of the government showed up for the debate. The perceived insult to the unemployed so infuriated Jack Lawson and R. C. Wallhead that they led a deputation of Labour MPs across the floor to sit on the government benches in silent rebuke of their absent opponents.[3]

Despite her feeling that there was nothing so devoid of interest as a fight with a foregone conclusion, Ellen continued to be a regular feature on the parliamentary benches and in the division lobby. Through lengthy, if futile, sittings, the elfin English firebrand took her place amongst the Scottish radicals with her feet settled upon a giant attaché case she used as a makeshift footstool. She calmed her nerves and kept herself alert by smoking countless cigarettes, although she didn't dare enter the male sanctuary of the members' smoking room, the lofty den overlooking the Thames.

After the bitter legislative defeats her party faced in June and July 1925, Ellen left Westminster behind for a brief working holiday. During the recess, she, Marion Phillips, and Lady Clare Annesley, the Labour candidate for Bristol West, travelled to Sofia, Bulgaria, to arrange for the distribution of aid raised by Labour women on behalf of the families of Socialists, Communists, and members of the Agrarian League imprisoned by the regime of Czar Boris III. On her way home, she spent a few days in Italy. The trip opened her eyes to the advances authoritarianism was making through southern Europe and she returned to Westminster in October determined to fight what she perceived to be creeping fascism at home.[4] While her emphasis continued to be on domestic politics, her rhetoric showed an awareness of the unstable international situation, as when she denounced as "completely unnecessary" a proposed bill to increase the penalties for receiving political bribes with the scathing assessment that: "The only safeguard against revolution in this country is not imprisonment and is not Bills such as this, but a real desire on the part of Members of this House to remove poverty and the causes that lead to destitution and misery and distress."[5] Despite continual bouts of ill health, she filled more column inches in Hansard and registered more votes than any of her female colleagues.[6]

The Labour opposition was too small—and in the estimation of many radicals, including Ellen, too timid—to effectively derail the "Rich Man's Government." Yet Ellen was determined to use parliament as a platform to expose what she saw to be the government's cruel irresponsibility to the working classes. Alongside James Maxton and the Red Clydesiders, the veteran Christian Socialist George Lansbury, the trade unionist Alf Purcell, and various others, Ellen became part of the self-proclaimed "Ginger Group" within the Parliamentary Labour Party, whose aim was "to use every known means of procedure to drag class issues onto the floor of the House, and when these means are exhausted, invent new ones." As she wrote on behalf of the Group: "The Treasury benches must not be allowed to shove the skeleton of unemployment back behind the draperies of official phrases and nicely selected statistics. The cry of the children must be drowned neither by the Savoy Havana Band, nor by the platitudes of Stanley Baldwin."[7]

Such parliamentary tactics depended on the willingness of the press to report the speeches of Labour MPs. In the early 1920s, however, the mainstream newspapers were more hostile to Labour than at any point since the party's creation, and opposition MPs could not be assured of gaining a hearing let alone a fair hearing in the columns of the *Daily Mail* or the *Daily Express*.[8] The best hope for a Labour MP, Ellen joked, was to pray for an election. Yet a general election would not do any good if the British people could not be awakened to the need for political reform. Ellen admitted she herself was not as "sure as some are that this Government would be smashed by its own arts through the wrath of an indignant people. Bad and insufficient food, overcrowded houses, and insecurity breed an awful apathy."[9] Rather than give in to despair, she increased her efforts to overturn such apathy through the political education of the working class.

Ellen would maintain a lifelong commitment to working-class education through her involvement with two Marxist institutions: the

Plebs League and the National Council of Labour Colleges (NCLC). Although the Plebs and the NCLC did not formally amalgamate until 1927, the two organizations had long worked in tandem, seeking to "translate the basic tenets of Marxism into English, [as] an essential prerequisite of working-class consciousness."[10] If the NCLC sought to offer intensive further education to its pupils, the Plebs League functioned as a sort of booster movement for the National Council—a vehicle for reaching a wider community that could not enrol in classes at the Central Labour College in London or one of the affiliated courses around the country. For an annual subscription, members received monthly issues of *Plebs* magazine with its reports and analyses of news of concern to the British and international left, book reviews, lengthy correspondence columns, and updates on NCLC and League activities, and Plebs/NCLC publications such as *An Outline of Economic Geography*, by Frank Horrabin, or *An Outline of Modern Imperialism,* by Thomas Ashcroft and George Hicks. They also received a badge with the signature Plebs "?," indicating a commitment to challenging the capitalist narrative. The organization was small—only around 2,000 paid-up members in 1926—but its impact was more widely felt. Members were encouraged to circulate *Plebs* amongst their friends and to sell copies at local party meetings and union events. Although the circulation never reached 10,000, its actual readership can be assumed to have been much larger.

In spring 1923, Ellen had campaigned successfully for her union to affiliate to the NCLC, and in 1924 had joined the executive committee of the Plebs League. Christine Millar, who with her husband was one of the prime movers of the NCLC movement, recalled that Ellen lectured at all seven of the earliest Plebs-NCLC "national schools," weeklong conferences held in Yorkshire. Ellen was also a regular participant at the weekend summer schools held around the country as well as at the destination conferences held in holiday towns on the continent. Despite her parliamentary duties, she contributed to nearly every issue of *Plebs* throughout 1925 and 1926, penning everything from analyses of the coal dispute to reviews of Russian literature. Her time spent at *Plebs* offices near Victoria station brought her into regular contact with Frank Horrabin, who edited the journal.

Ellen and Frank also collaborated on another propagandist journal, *Lansbury's Labour Weekly*. Already sixty-six when he founded the *Weekly,*

George Lansbury was the elder statesman of the parliamentary radicals. An early member of the Marxist Social Democratic Federation before joining the Independent Labour Party (ILP) in 1903, Lansbury had a long career championing the rights of the people of East London. In 1921, as a Poplar councillor, he had been imprisoned alongside Ellen's future boss at the Ministry of Health, Susan Lawrence, when the Poplar Council refused to pay its share of the LCC rates in protest over the administration of poor relief in London. The councillors argued that the localized system of taxation and relief provision was unjust, as it put the heaviest burden of poor relief on the boroughs least able to pay and demanded that poor relief be socialized across London boroughs. Lansbury is perhaps best remembered for his role in leading the Poplar Rates Rebellion, but his support for direct action against injustice was not limited to London politics. Before the war, he had championed the militant suffragettes. Disregarding the polite conventions of the House of Commons, he called Prime Minister Herbert Asquith "beneath contempt" for his policy of forcibly feeding imprisoned suffrage supporters on hunger strike.[11] The *Daily Herald*, the newspaper that he ran from 1912 until its takeover by the Labour Party in 1922, had supported Guild Socialism and revolutionary syndicalism and advocated directed action by the unions in protest over British intervention in the civil war in Russia.[12]

Lansbury remained involved with the *Daily Herald* as general manager of the paper until 1925. During that time, the paper's radical voice was subdued as it became the official organ of the Labour leadership. Severing his relationship with the *Herald* meant that Lansbury was able to redevote himself to the kind of crusading propaganda that had characterized the paper in its early days. The first issue of *Lansbury's Labour Weekly*, which appeared on February 28, 1925, proclaimed: "We shall stand then with the workers in Parliament or out of Parliament, in every struggle great or small, for a higher standard of life, till the day dawns when Socialism is triumphant."[13]

"We" was the editorial team behind the new paper, a group of men and women that included Ellen, author of a weekly parliamentary notes column, and Horrabin, the column's illustrator. Other regular contributors included Morgan Philips Price, the former *Manchester Guardian* correspondent Ellen had met up with in Berlin while travelling with

Harry Pollitt, who was also a frequent contributor to *Plebs*. Price wrote regularly on foreign affairs, as did his fellow pacifist journalist F. Seymour Cocks. Cocks would later join with Ellen as part of the parliamentary "Spain Lobby" that worked unsuccessfully to encourage British recognition of the Republican government during the Spanish Civil War.

Unlike *Plebs*, *Lansbury's* was not a Marxist publication. A deeply religious man, Lansbury well appreciated the causes of working-class oppression, but he was optimistic that these could be redressed and socialism achieved without resort to conflict. Like Ellen, he had travelled to Russia in the early years after the revolution and had shared her enthusiasm for the Bolsheviks. However, by 1926, he had developed reservations about the totalitarian nature of Russian Communism, bemoaning that "the check of an informed opposition . . . the greatest enemy of corruption and bureaucracy" was lacking in Russia where "democracy is little more than a name." Yet he nonetheless still felt, to paraphrase the Whig parliamentarian Charles Fox's summation of an earlier revolution, that the Russian revolution was, by far, the greatest and best event in history.[14] He was not a Communist, but he opposed the Labour Party's witch hunts against Communists and argued for their readmission to the Labour Party: "All who want Socialism must unite and work out a policy which can be followed in a spirit of comradeship and goodwill."[15] In this spirit, he embraced Ellen, Horrabin, and their *Plebs* colleagues, believing their shared intolerance for inaction in the face of class oppression united them more closely than their ideological doctrines separated them. Ellen, similarly, showed a characteristic disregard for doctrinal differences when it came to furthering the material interests of the working class.

Thus from February 28, 1925 until the paper's financial collapse two and a half years later, Ellen used her weekly pulpit in *Lansbury's* to condemn the crimes of the Baldwin government, particularly in regard to unemployment policy, or more accurately the government's lack thereof, and to call for a more radical response from the Opposition benches. Given her remit as a parliamentary diarist, she devoted little ink to the mining crisis that had begun brewing shortly after *Lansbury's* was launched, as the Miners' Federation of Great Britain (MFGB) and the mine owners both refused to back down in the face of the former's demands for a seven-and-a-half-hour workday, national wage agreements, and a promise to rationalize the increasingly unproductive industry. Yet, Ellen and her fellow "Gingerers" were united in their support for the miners and their conviction that the General Council of the Trades Union Congress should, if necessary, lead the workers in a general strike in defence of the miners' standard of living. From both a Marxist and a Christian Socialist standpoint, the greatest sin the Labour leadership could commit would be to fail to marshal the movement's full strength in defence of their comrades.

The return to the gold standard in April 1925 had overvalued the pound sterling on the international markets, increasing the price of British exports and hurting industries such as coal. In an attempt to safeguard profits, the mine owners sought to reduce the costs of production, by which they meant the costs of labour. That summer, the owners demanded wage reductions, an increase in working hours, and the termination of the existing National Wages Agreement. The Miners' Federation refused the demands, and the owners announced a lockout of union labourers on July 31, 1925.

The Miners' Federation was led by the fiery left-winger A. J. Cook. Cook was not a native of South Wales but migrated to the Rhondda Valley coalfields at the age of eighteen from the West Country. He quickly rose to prominence within both the ILP and the local union leadership. In 1911, he won a scholarship from the South Wales Miners' Federation to the Central Labour College, an experience that further radicalized the young socialist. In 1920, he had joined the Communist Party of Great Britain alongside Ellen, although he left the party a year later. But his politics retained their revolutionary hue; and in 1923, he helped launch the minority movement within the South Wales Miners' Federation, a militant Marxist faction whose support helped propel him to the general secretaryship of the MFGB the following year.

In July 1925, Cook was hailed as a hero. After refusing to negotiate with the mine owners, his union had sought support from the other principal unions. Through the mediation of the Trades Union Congress (TUC), the miners secured guarantees from the transport and railway unions that their members would not move coal if the lockout took place. This was not an agreement for a sympathetic strike. The lorry drivers, stevedores, and railwaymen would remain on the job; but if the miners were locked out, they would not load or transport either existing coal reserves or coal mined by blackleg labour. The pronouncement, and the fact that the General Council of the TUC had been authorized to make it on the unions' behalf, was an unprecedented show of industrial unity. For the first time, many within both the unions and the government began to consider that a general strike of British workers might be a real possibility. Although the possible repercussions of a general strike frightened many within the trade union leadership, Ellen was enthusiastic about the idea of the workers' showing their united strength.

In the face of such a show of trade union unity, the government—which had hitherto remained outside of the negotiations—finally intervened. On "Red Friday," July 31, the day the lockout notices were due to take effect, Stanley Baldwin announced his government's willingness to grant a subsidy to the mine owners for the next nine months, during which time a Royal Commission would be established to consider the state of the industry. What happened next, and its implications for the fate of the British Labour movement, have long been, and remain, the subject of debate.

The nine-month subsidy represented a stay of execution, but the sentence on the mining industry had in no sense been commuted. In addition to establishing a Royal Commission, under the leadership of Liberal MP Herbert Samuel, the government and the mine owners both began preparations for the next round of battle, which would come when the subsidy expired the following spring. Few in the government anticipated that the trade unions would actually overcome their differences and the risk to their own livelihoods to come out in a general strike in support of the miners. But, if they did, the government would be ready. Coal was stockpiled to ensure a stoppage would not cause a national fuel crisis. The government's Supply and Transport Committee, an interdepartmental committee chaired by Ellen's old foe, Home Secretary William Joynson-Hicks, and including representatives of the Home Office and the Service Departments, began preparations for action in the event of a strike. The committee sought to address every contingency, including the imperative to win the battle of public opinion. In April 1926, J. C. C. Davidson, who after the strike would leave government service to take up the post of Conservative party chairman, was put in charge of publicity preparations.[16] The government had already reached out to the public months before. At the end of September, the Home Secretary had established a volunteer force, the Organization for the Maintenance of Supply (OMS), to be composed of "special constables" and volunteers tasked with keeping the peace and keeping the country going in the event of a general strike.

The TUC, in contrast, made few preparations for any form of joint action should it prove impossible to reach a negotiated settlement after the expiration of the subsidy. At the same time, while deprecating the view that comprise was unreachable, the leaders of the TUC General Council allowed Cook and the Miners' Federation leadership to believe that, in the event of a conflict, the labour movement would stand behind the men. Bolstered by this belief, Cook took a hard line in the union's negotiations with the mine owners the following spring. The commission headed by Herbert Samuel reported back in March. Its recommendations, not binding on the industry, called for an eventual reorganization and rationalization and the immediate imposition of the 13 percent pay cut advocated by the owners. The commission did not recommend an extension of the working day from seven and one-half to eight hours; but the owners, cognizant that they had the support of the government, demanded lower wages, longer hours, and the end to nationally agreed wage scales once the subsidy was withdrawn. Faced with such intransigence, the Miners' Federation responded in kind. "Not a penny off the pay; not a minute on the day" became the miners' slogan. Negotiations, mediated by the government and the TUC, continued, but with little hope of success.

Given the events that followed, the union leadership's failure to prepare for the eventuality of joint industrial action appears inexplicably naive. In her novel *Clash*, Ellen had one of her characters articulate the TUC rationale for failing to prepare for the strike: "It's no use getting bitter. Our folk have a difficult problem to face. If they had started making preparations to meet the Government's activities, they would have been steamrollered by the Press. Can't you see the headlines in the *Daily Mail* or the *Morning Post*? 'General Council prepares foul blow at the Nation.'"[17] Ellen appreciated the logic, but she was unable to accept its wisdom, even three years after the fact. The novel's heroine goes on to ask her interlocutor: "But why didn't they make that a public declaration [that they would take no action to prepare for the strike] and get on with their preparations in secret?"

Ellen was even sharper in her condemnation of the General Council in the pages of *Plebs* and *Lansbury's* and in the *Workers' History of the Great Strike* which she, Horrabin, and Raymond Postgate published for *Plebs* readers in 1927. In September 1925, Ellen had written in *Plebs* of the need for preparation for a potential general strike at the expiration of the miners' subsidy. "It is emphatically the job of the General Council to find a way out for the working class," she wrote. "They cannot give a call to action without answering the question, 'And what then?'" She ended her article by exhorting all progressive left-wingers to unite in pressuring the Labour leadership to prepare for the showdown that would inevitably come.[18] In a coauthored article titled *The Plebs Point of View*, written immediately after the strike, the group reminded their readers that as early as September 1925 the magazine had advocated for a plan of action. The authors argued that "the unpreparedness which handicapped Labour during the momentous Nine Days was not only a matter of actual organization. It was mental, too—especially in the case of the 'leaders.' If they had had a glimmering of understanding of the lines of capitalist development they would have foreseen some at least of the inevitable developments of the struggle itself." They described the leadership of the General Council as "Pughsillanimous"—a reference to Arthur Pugh, head of the Iron and Steel Workers, who led the committee that negotiated with the government on the miners' behalf. To *Plebs*, "the tragedy of this strike consists in just this fact, that it was led by men who did not believe in it, who could not want it to succeed."[19] In the pages of *Lansbury's,* Ellen declared, "Men that take a righteous pride in not being ready for trouble have no right to expose other men to the risks of their own foolishness."

As women's organizer for the National Union of Distributive and Allied Workers (NUDAW), Ellen was not a delegate to the special conference of trade union executives held in London between April 29 and May 1 to discuss what, if any, action the TUC would take in the event of a failure to reach agreement between the miners and the owners. She attended the momentous congress as a spectator. After briefing the congress on Thursday, May 29, the leaders of the General Council went to

Downing Street, where they continued to carry on negotiations with the government, hopeful of at least dissuading the mine owners from implementing the lockout scheduled to go into operation the next day. All day Friday, the men (and they were nearly all men) waited in expectation for the General Council and the miners' leaders to return with news from Westminster.

In *Clash,* Ellen described the mood that Friday as seen through the eyes of her heroine, Joan Craig: "The hall was . . . suffocatingly hot and they looked down through a haze of tobacco smoke. . . . They had so much to lose. . . . [But a]t the moment, with the cheerful refusal to cross rivers till they got to them which had carried their class through the horrors of the trenches, these grown-up men were as gay as school boys." The men smoked cigarettes and cigars and sang impromptu songs, killing time until, just before midnight, the delegation returned. Pugh re-opened the conference with a review of the day's proceedings, but it was the railway leader, Jimmy Thomas, whose speech was most closely anticipated:

> When the railwaymen's leader rose there was a murmur of expectancy. His moderate views were well known. If he agreed to the strike call, then indeed there was nothing else for it. Into an atmosphere so still that every word sank like a pebble, the man who once had driven trains and now guided a great trade union said solemnly:
>
> "In all my experience—and I have conducted many negotiations—I never begged and pleaded like I begged and pleaded all day to-day . . . But we failed."
>
> The speaker paused dramatically, the audience held its breath.
>
> . . . "Those who want war must take the responsibility."
>
> That sentence shattered the self-control of the audience. This meant war. Cheer after cheer was given. "If they want it they shall have it," was yelled from every part of the hall.[20]

The next morning, May 1, the conference reassembled and the representatives voted to commit their members to a general strike, to begin at midnight on Monday, May 3. By a majority of 3,653,529 to 49,911, the men, as the transport leader Ernest Bevin put it in a moving speech, "placed your all upon the alter for this great Movement, and having placed it there, even if every penny goes, if every asset goes, history will ultimately write that it was a magnificent generation that was prepared to do it rather than see the miners driven down like slaves."[21]

Immediately after the vote, the General Council issued orders to call out the "first wave" of workers, a group that included all of the transport workers and some of the workers involved in the electrical and gas trades, and, crucially for the progress of the conflict, the printing trade, including both journalists and printers. Even after the proclamation was issued, the negotiating committee continued its talks with the government and the owners, in the desperate hope of finding a path out of the conflict. It was the government and not the unions that ultimately called off negotiations late Sunday evening. Using as a pretext the news that a group of renegade printers at the *Daily Mail* had refused to lay the type for an editorial denouncing the planned strike as an unconstitutional act of revolution, the government literally walked out on negotiations. After handing Jimmy Thomas a letter of explanation, Baldwin declared, "Good-bye; this is the end" and withdrew to his own office.[22] After reading the letter, the bewildered trade unionists walked down the stairs to the prime minister's office only to find he had turned off the lights and retired to his residence. The strike was on.

The country woke up on the morning of Tuesday, May 4 to an unaccustomed silence. Commuter trains were not running in and out of London. Early-morning lorry deliveries were not being made. Altogether, more than one and a half million men and women around the country failed to show up for work. But although they all could see how the strike affected their own community, the withdrawal of labour by the printing operatives meant that few who did not have access to a radio set could get any news of the national progress of the strike. Those newspapers that did manage to print strike editions were largely sympathetic to the government's position. Many believed the biased reports put out by these journals, which fabricated or exaggerated episodes of industrial violence and suggested that resolve was weakening in many quarters of the country. Those who did not trust available news sources were left anxious and uncertain about the progress of the conflict.

Propaganda meetings are crucial to the success of any industrial conflict, providing information and inspiration to the strike's participants. During the general strike, these meetings took on a new sense of urgency, given the lack of reliable print media. At the makeshift strike headquarters at the TUC offices in Eccleston Square, a propaganda committee "allocated speakers and organised the speaking campaign," issuing itineraries, vehicles, and fuel permits to a group of men and women, including the former MPs Margaret Bondfield and Ben Tillett, the London politician Susan Lawrence, and Ellen Wilkinson and Frank Horrabin.[23]

Ellen and Frank were by this point well embarked on their affair. Winifred Horrabin, who worked closely with Ellen at *Plebs*, was aware of their relationship, and, in an effort to escape the uncomfortable reality, had embarked on a holiday trip to Moscow with friends in April. Her daily letters to Frank from her travels reveal a passive-aggressive misery at her situation: "I want no claims, mate, except the voluntary claim of love. I never thought ever of owning," she wrote him from Riga on April 22, only to follow up with "Kissing you and belonging to you seem somehow to have been dulled by being shared" from Moscow three days later.[24] Back in England, Frank was more concerned with the strike than with his wife's anxieties, although he took the time to write her daily with updates on the conflict. His letters made little effort to disguise the fact that he and Ellen spent the nine days together, and Winifred's reply to his first letters to reach her reveals the degree to which her personal tragedy overshadowed the political situation in her thoughts: "I wish we knew how things were going and how long it's likely to last!! . . . Sorry E. is not well. I expect you went up to M'bro with the car because of the strike—I expect that was the nominal excuse—anyway! Well! Old mate ~~I'm not going to say I'm glad because I'm not glad~~ you *know* I trust you. I can only claim what *you give me* and *what isn't mine* I can't make mine again by all the tears in all the world."[25]

Frank clearly felt some compunction about the affair—his letters to his wife are filled with pleas for her to trust in his love for her. Nonetheless, a sense of propriety did not stop him from putting up Ellen's brother Harold, who was in and out of London as a dispatch rider for the General Council and, given the cramped size of his sister's apartment, often slept on the settee at 6 Mecklenburg Square. Nor, of course, did it stop him from acting as Ellen's chauffeur as the two logged over 2,000 miles so the "Fiery Particle" could address the strikers in picture palaces and market places around the country.[26]

The pair left London at lunchtime on Wednesday, travelling in Frank's car. (Ellen had likely given her Austin Seven to her brother for his use as a messenger. With most of the trains out of operation, the strike organizers needed every vehicle they could get.) The increase in motorcar commuting made for slow travel, and they reached Oxford only just before 3 p.m., where they "coyly left our car in a quiet side street, safe, as we thought, from the attention of Oxford Fascists." From there, they walked on to St. Giles, just a few blocks from Ruskin College, where they found Douglas Cole holding forth to a "huge crowd [of] Ruskin chaps." Barely a hundred meters from the medieval spire of St. John's College, Ellen and Frank preached a sermon to the strikers on the new Jerusalem in store for Britain's working class if only they held together. After the meeting, the two had tea with Cole before motoring on to Banbury, where they "had a huge meeting in the Co-operative Garage of strikers hungry for news, but prepared to stick it to the last inch." Their next stop was a sleepy railway junction, where the strikers regaled them with the story of an amateur blackleg who had smashed up his engine on the lines. The couple then moved on to Coventry, where they spent the night before continuing north. Coventry, when they arrived, appeared to Ellen to have fallen into the hands of the local soviet. At one of the largest open-air meetings at which she had ever spoken, she attempted to convince the automobile workers they should not come out until called upon to do so by the General Council, as "discipline is the main essential in a war, and that it may be harder to stay in then to come out, but that orders must be obeyed." It was an inspiring visit, yet, by the end of the strike, *Plebs* offices had confirmed reports that resolve in the great midland city had begun to weaken.[27]

On Friday the duo cut a winding path from Coventry to Crewe, addressing seven meetings, five of them in the open air. Ellen's voice started to fail her, or as Frank put it in a letter to Winifred, "yesterday I had to do the biggest whack, as E's voice had crocked rather."[28] They cut west on Saturday, speaking first at an open air meeting in Northwich, then on to a miners' gala and demonstration on the race course in Wrexham, and then to a 1,500-strong gathering in the great park in Shrewsbury. *Plebs* leaguer Alice Pratt wrote of their visit that it acted as "a real tonic" on the men and women in the crowd, and although "there was no revolutionary atmosphere in Shrewsbury . . . there was a definite advance in working-class solidarity."[29] Histories of the strike have emphasized the lack of rancour between the strikers, the public, and the representatives of the state, highlighting episodes such as the storied football match played between strikers and police at Plymouth Home Park. (The strikers won 2–1). In many narratives, such stories have been used to highlight the civilized "British" character of the conflict.[30] The co-authored *Plebs'* history Ellen wrote with Frank and Postgate indeed makes reference to such episodes. Yet in their version, the camaraderie between strikers and police owed less to a culture of civility than to the working-class solidarity Ellen and Frank witnessed in Shrewsbury. "The police are members of the working class and were loth to treat with brutality men whom they knew socially, and recognized as the reverse of criminals," she wrote. Ellen and Frank hit Hereford and Worcester on Sunday before heading back to London and arriving near 10:30 that night. Everywhere, they found the men solid, and "panting for news."

The pair had two days' respite in London before being given instructions from Eccleston Square to head up to the northeast. The strike was largely a trade union show, with comparatively little input or assistance from the nonunion members of the Labour Party leadership. That said, several national Labour organizers played key roles in the direction of transport, publicity, and propaganda. Barbara Ayrton Gould, a former suffragette and chair of the Labour Women's Committee who was, like Ellen, a member of the Women's International League (WIL), spearheaded a valiant effort "to improvise at the last moment a complicated transport service which should distribute news, intelligence, speakers, bulletins, and *British Workers* all over the country." Gould appeared in *Clash* as the thinly veiled character Beryl Gaye, whom Ellen described as "a joy to work with. Good-looking, competent, with an orderly mind trained by a scientific mother, she remained a woman, and had not become a martinet. She knew how to humanize a machine, keep overtired workers up to the mark by some odd little kindness or a joke at her own expense."

In *Clash,* Gaye/Gould is depicted as having managed a shoestring operation. She was so glad to learn that Joan knew the local Labour people in the northeast of England that she "simply handed over to her the task of getting speakers and instructions conveyed north of the Humber."[31] In reality, Ellen and Frank were given slightly more direction from TUC headquarters—but only slightly more. With the blessing of Egerton Wake, the Labour Party's national agent, the two headed first to Frank's hometown of Peterborough on Tuesday morning, where the native son had been selected as the prospective Labour candidate. At each stop, the pair received telegrams from Eccleston Square on where to go next.

As Peterborough was Frank's constituency, the duo was persuaded to speak at four meetings. Ellen reported that the local Corn Exchange was "packed, not only with strikers but with the largely conservative public of a cathedral town"—one of many testaments of the sympathy of non-Labour Party men and women that she encountered on their tour. Over the next two days, at meetings at Grantham, Newark, Retford, Worksop, and Rotherham, she reported similar shows of solidarity. Her *Plebs* history of the strike included Rotherham in the list of towns "where the response was unexpectedly and amazingly fine—where it can be stated with a fair degree of confidence that the response was nearing 100 per cent and certainly over the 90 per cent . . . towns in which the strike was immovable from the Government point of view."[32]

If the resolve of the strikers was holding firm into the second week of the conflict, the General Council's willingness to continue the strike was weakening. On Friday, May 7, day 4, Herbert Samuel, chair of the Royal Commission that had endorsed the need for cuts to the miners' wages, had approached the TUC leadership with an offer to mediate between the miners and the government. On Sunday, the General Council had approached the miners with what became known as the Samuel Memorandum, an outline of proposed terms for settlement that bore little difference to the terms suggested in the Commission report issued the previous March. The miners rejected the terms, but the trade union leadership indicated to Samuel they would be willing to make a deal to end the general strike even if the miners would not compromise with the owners.

All of this transpired unbeknownst to Ellen and Frank, who did not get word of the existence of the Samuel Memorandum until Wednesday, May 12, the day the strike was finally called off through an official pronouncement of unconditional surrender made at 12 noon by Pugh, Bevin, and Thomas to the prime minister. In calling off the strike, the General Council had thought—or at least hoped—that the terms laid out in the memorandum, which included an agreed national minimum wage in the industry and promises of a future reorganization, would be adhered to. They had also hoped that the men who came out in defence of the miners would not be victimized by their employers. Yet they had not secured guarantees to either effect; and in the days that followed, it became clear the government had no intention to offer any more than conciliatory words to those involved in the conflict. Weaker industries saw extensive victimization, particularly the engineers, whose members had only been called out on May 11 as part of a second wave of strikers. Stronger unions, such as those of the railwaymen and the transport workers, were able to avoid similar reprisals only by remaining out on strike after noon on Wednesday and refusing to return to work until guarantees of fair treatment were secured.

Ellen's personal contact with the men and her sense of what they had sacrificed spurred in her a visceral anger at the General Council. Her rage comes through in an exchange recorded by Horrabin: "when we landed Eccleston Square on Saturday, Bevin was standing outside.—E. walked up to him and said 'Well, what do you think of yourself?' B. said—'Wh-wh-why—what do you mean?' E. said 'Have you been in the country at all?' 'No' says B. 'I've been in the War Office—not the Diplomatic Service.' 'Well it's a pity you don't take a look at the country,' says E., '& you'd find out what a lot of spineless cowards people think you all are!' and left him (purple)."[33] Ellen, Frank, and Postgate denounced as "criminal" the General Council's decision to call out the engineers on May 11, when it was clear that surrender was imminent and that the callout would only bring reprisals on the already weakened union. In Clash, Ellen dramatized the plight of a young engineer in the small market town of Kelsall, who as a member of the local trades council had helped to coordinate the strike in the region. "For a week he had shown his mettle as an organizer, had risen to a great occasion. Now, if he were lucky, he would get a job as an engineer at forty-five shillings a week, and if unlucky—Joan shuddered as she thought of the hopeless tramp for work—the Labour Exchange queue."[34]

The aftermath of the general strike validated Orwell's famous quip "Who controls the past controls the future. Who controls the present controls the past." The previous decades had seen a blurring of the lines between the industrial and the political, with the trade unions exerting growing influence over the state's industrial policy.[35] Yet through fear that the general strike would spiral out of their control, the General Council allowed the government's interpretation of the conflict to dominate public discourse. In the months and years that followed, Baldwin successfully cemented his narrative of the general strike, with all of its implications for the progress of British industrial relations. In his narrative, the strike became an unconstitutional act, but one overcome largely owing to the level-headed, "English" character of both the trade union rank-and-file and the general public, and hence forgiven in the interests of national harmony.[36] This interpretation can be seen in the titles of popular histories, such as Anne Perkins's *A Very British Strike*. Although superficially conciliatory, such a reading of the strike created a rhetorical space in which harsh proscriptions on industrial action were justifiable in the public interest. The following spring Ellen would throw herself body and soul into the futile fight against the passage of the Trade Disputes and Trade Unions Act, which stripped back many of the unions' legal rights and further shifted the balance in favour of the employers. In the meantime, however, the miners remained out on strike, and Ellen turned her energies to helping the strikers and their families.

Ellen may have been a Marxist, but she was not a consistent Marxist. She never wavered from her conviction that the history of British industrial relations was a history of class conflict, and that the true emancipation of the working classes could be achieved only through the overthrow of capitalism. But, as we have seen, she gradually abandoned a commitment to violence and came to believe that the revolution could be achieved at the ballot box, if only the workers could be educated for socialism. She also believed that, in certain circumstances, charity was a necessity, even if it forestalled the moment of revolution by masking the depths of immiseration to which capitalism would allow the workers to sink. The seven-month miners' strike was one of those circumstances—yet, even as she begged for money to help the miners, she reminded her comrades that "the cry of the starving is not only a call to charity. It must be a call to action."[37]

The stockpiles of coal built up over the previous months combined with the warm weather in late spring 1926 to shield most Britons from the initial impact of the miners' strike. Many first felt the sting of the strike on Whitsuntide weekend, when curtailed railway services due to coal rationing meant many could not take advantage of the unseasonably warm weather to travel to the seaside. One paper reported that "one London firm carried more than 5,000 people to south coast resorts yesterday in a fleet of 150 motor coaches. 'Everything with a wheel' was utilised."[38] Ellen's bank holiday was not spent at Brighton or Bournemouth. Instead, she and her sister Annie spent the weekend with Frank in the village of Thaxted in Essex, where they attended Conrad Noel's Whitsun services. The Christian Socialist "Red Vicar" preached on social justice. On Monday, in the rectory garden, George Lansbury joined the London party and a group of neighbouring socialists for singing and Morris dancing.[39]

Noel's influence that weekend perhaps spurred Ellen to move from recrimination to action. Back in London the next week, she and her colleagues on the Standing Joint Committee of Industrial Women's Organizations formed the Women's Committee for the Relief of the Miners' Wives and Children. Ellen was appointed chair. Their fundraising campaign opened with a great demonstration at the Royal Albert Hall the following weekend. That week, Ellen's column in *Lansbury's* ran long, with an extra paragraph on the relief campaign that summarized her pragmatic approach to the question of socialist charity. In it, she asked her readers to "realize that £500,000 is needed *every week* to keep the miners in the bare necessities. . . . There is no room these days for the arm-chair hair-splitting Socialists. Just as the Russian revolutionists had to leave their ideals for a bit and get down to the problem of drains and sewers and transport, so in England, now that the fight has sharpened, our job is to get the miners fed."[40]

Ellen approached the job with a determination commensurate with the direness of the situation. She lobbied everyone she knew to give their utmost to help the miners and even succeeded in bringing her parliamentary colleague Nancy Astor on board to champion the committee's cause.[41] In previous strikes and lockouts, the Poor Law Boards of Guardians had at least stood between the striking families and starvation. During the miners' strike, however, Guardians in several communities refused to give assistance to the miners except "on loan," with the result that many families, already deeply in debt, went without rather than subject themselves to further indenture. In several mining communities, the schools had ceased providing free lunches to children of strikers, and in others the cost of school meals was deducted from any family relief provided by the Guardians. Although not all Boards of Guardians were equally draconian, and many resisted Ministry of Health efforts to starve out the strikers, in some areas where youths below sixteen had worked as pit boys, they were treated by the Guardians as striking miners, not as starving minors, even though they were not yet old enough to be voting members of the union. Miners' wives were granted a maximum of 12s. a week, with 4s. for their first child. Women and children in England and Wales were given food tickets. In Scotland, miners' dependents were fed in communal halls to ensure that food issued to them was not shared with their husbands and fathers. In Wales, the Welsh Board of Health received instructions from Westminster to discontinue grants of additional milk to pregnant women and nursing mothers, and in England and Scotland such provision was erratic.[42]

For Ellen, who as a child had known want but never acute hunger, the state to which the strike reduced the miners' families and the fortitude of the women in standing by their husbands during the strike proved transformational. As a union organizer, Ellen worked primarily with single women. The mothers she knew were mostly older middle-class or society women with whom she had worked on the suffrage campaigns or in the WIL. Touring the country with Frank's sister Kathleen (married to their Plebs colleague Mark Starr), Ellen came face to face with another class of women.

In *Clash,* Ellen gives Joan's impression of the lives of the women in these mining villages. Ellen's heroine, like herself, devotes herself to women's relief efforts after the general strike. "The ugliness is everywhere," Joan writes in a letter to her lover in Bloomsbury, "the things in the shops are so cheap and nasty and ugly. There is hardly a modern book in the Free Library, anything decent has long waiting lists, there's just nothing to break the awful monotonous dullness except the home-life in the over-crowded little houses, and the socials they get up among themselves at the church or chapel. I think the ugliness is worse than the poverty." Ellen herself repeatedly expressed the view that the soul-destroying bleakness of working-class neighbourhoods was one of the great tragedies of capitalism; but in the mining villages, the poverty clearly was worse than the ugliness.[43] In her novel, Ellen records Joan's horror at being brought by a local midwife into a miners' home to witness the circumstances of a recent birth: "She found that the mother had been confined in the kitchen, her four little children being taken care of by a neighbour. There was no hot water, no milk for the mother, and but for the midwife's own shawl the baby would have had no clothes at all."[44] After her tour of Somerset and Nottinghamshire with Kathleen Starr, Ellen gave an interview to *Reynold's News* in which she described "knots of people—men, women and children—standing about the street corners, too inert even to discuss the situation or to read the news. The silence is oppressive and ominous; it is the breadth of that ogre—Famine." She relayed the experience of one mother she had met whose family had had only one meal in the past two days—soup brewed from one onion and a few potatoes, which she had bought with 3d. borrowed from a neighbour. The experiences of mothers in the pit villages raised Ellen to a pitch of fury, and in her parliamentary column for *Lansbury's* she took to referring to the government as the Baby Starvers.

Another report Ellen brought back from her and Kathleen's tour gave rise to one of Ellen's most well remembered parliamentary performances. In her *Lansbury's* column, Ellen reported that in Somerset, where the seams in the mines were too narrow for pit ponies, "no less than 1,500 boys and young men" were employed to do the work of animals. "Stark naked, on all fours, with a rope round their waist, and a chain between their legs hitched on to a wagon, they pull the coal through the workings. The rope rubs off the skin, until callousites are formed. The dirt gets in, and septic wounds are the result. A doctor in the district has commented on the increase in septic sores owing to the poor nourishment of the boys. . . . The nation prosecutes if a pit pony is worked with bleeding sores and abraded skin. No one worries when it's only a lad at 9d. an hour. He is cheaper than horseflesh anyway."[45] The Somersetshire Colliery Owners Association refuted Ellen's accusations, and Conservative newspapers accused her of deliberately and unscrupulously misleading and prejudicing public opinion, and making "wild and reckless assertions."[46] In parliament, Geoffrey Peto, MP for Frome, challenged Ellen's report and claimed he had taken his wife on a tour of the pits in Somerset, and there were no conditions unfit for a lady to witness. Ellen, who had not been in the House to hear the original accusation, came prepared to defend her statements during the debate on the second reading of the Coal Mines bill, which would increase the hours miners could be continuously employed underground from seven to eight.

Ellen declared to the House that she stood by her article. To substantiate her claims, she brought photographs from the mines; testimonials from miners; and with a theatrical flourish, produced the rope and chain truss itself, pronouncing: "This is what is worn by the men. This is the rope that goes round the man's waist; this is the chain that passes between his legs, and this is the crook that is hitched on to the tub. This was worn, not 60 years ago, as stated by certain coal-owners, but on 30th April of this year by a miner."

Ellen ended her lengthy speech with a return to the question of the profit motive and the professed need of the industry to increase profitability to remain competitive with Germany and America:

> I am the chairman of the women's relief committee, which is dealing with the other side of the shield, with the wives and families, with the women who have been living on margarine and bread and tea. Whatever meat could be secured has got to be given to the man of the house, because he was working under hard physical conditions. We do not realise how much of the man's wage has got to go in food to keep him in bare efficiency to get the wages you are paying. In this staple industry men are working under conditions which in many cases are fit only for beasts, conditions which no hon. Member opposite would tolerate for half an hour if it was his children, and all you can say is, let them work longer, let them have longer hours and less wages in order that your

profits may be safeguarded. It is abominable, and those who vote for these longer hours ought not to sleep in their beds until they themselves have done what these men are doing every day in their work.[47]

Ellen's sensational speech received considerable coverage in the press, with the *Daily Chronicle* comparing her production of the truss to Edmund Burke's infamous brandishing of a dagger of the type allegedly yielded by "insidious" bloodthirsty Frenchmen in the 1792 debate over the admittance of French émigrés to Britain, or Captain Jenkins exhibiting his own severed ear to a horrified House—a theatrical move that ultimately brought Britain and Spain into the eponymously named "War of Jenkins' Ear."[48] Yet it was to no avail. Although nearly all of the Labour members remained at Westminster until 10 p.m. for the vote, the bill nonetheless passed its second reading by a majority of 192—Ellen's unorthodox efforts to garner empathy for the miners only another round in the constant fight against futility.

Given the high levels of unemployment in the community that could be most easily expected to empathize with the miners, and the extent of hostility towards the miners' cause stoked by the general strike, the Women's Committee was not unsuccessful in its fundraising efforts. It raised £5,000 in its first week, including two £500 cheques from sympathetic peeresses. After its first month, it had raised £75,000, all of which was spent on the purchase and distribution of milk and food. In total, by the end of July, around £1,000,000 had been raised for the miners and their families, including over £150,000 from the Women's Committee.[49] Yet if the men were not to be forced back to work through deprivation, greater resources would need to be found. So, with parliament set to adjourn in early August, Ellen, to quote one unsympathetic observer, "paid a visit to the United States, where, she confidently assured the world, she expected to collect at least a million dollars for the miners' funds; if the actual financial results of the tour were pitifully meagre, the fault can certainly not be imputed to any excessive restraint on Miss Wilkinson's part in carrying out her mission of blackening the institutions and the rulers of her country before audiences of foreigners."[50]

The fundraising mission was Ellen's first trip back to the United States since she and Annot Robinson had testified before the American Commission on Conditions in Ireland five years earlier. Since then, she had changed dramatically. The nervous young woman who had rambled on before Jane Addams's committee was a distant memory. The woman who boarded the Cunard flagship R. M. S. Berengaria at Southampton on July 31 was a confident public speaker, a pioneer female politician, and an internationally published journalist. She had great confidence in her ability to "put the case for the women and children" to the people of America.[51]

Ellen was a last-minute addition to the team of trade unionists that set sail for New York on July 31. Four miners representing the regional miners' unions had originally planned to travel to America with Ben Tillett, the Dockers' leader and a member of the TUC General Council, to fundraise. Two days before the group was scheduled to leave, they invited Ellen to go with them, to help fundraise amongst non-labour audiences (by which the men principally meant amongst women's groups). With such little notice, Ellen joked to a reporter at Waterloo station that she must have set a record for packing, having thrown her cases together in under an hour. Ellen was not the only woman in the party. James Robson, of the Durham miners, brought along his wife. Shortly after they landed in New York, however, the group split up, with Ellen and Tillett remaining in the New York region, while the other members addressed meetings in the mining towns of Pennsylvania, Ohio, Illinois, Indiana, West Virginia, and the great industrial centres of the Northeast and Midwest.

The day the party landed, the British prime minister gave a highly publicized interview to an American press agency in which he swore that "there is no foundation for any statements as to starvation among the mining population." The group was questioned by reporters about Baldwin's statement, first in New York and again in Washington, where they met with William Green, president of the American Federation of Labor (AFL), and the AFL's secretary Frank Morrison. The party visited the union leaders in the federation's original headquarters, which was situated closer to Congress than to the presidential mansion. In the monument built to the strength of the American labour movement, opened with a benediction from President Woodrow Wilson ten years earlier, the Americans agreed to throw the official support of U.S. labour unions behind the miners' mission. Although the AFL leaders claimed that as an administrative body, the federation could not donate money itself, Morrison agreed to act as treasurer for the funds raised by the group and to encourage the AFL's member unions to contribute. Several formal portraits, reprinted in the American press, show Ellen, her hair swelled by the intense humidity of Washington summer, looking particularly diminutive posed beside the strongly built and neatly bow-tied leaders of American labour.

As she met with union representatives around New York and New Jersey, Ellen was repeatedly impressed by the health, vigour, and prosperity of American union members. After her return home, a British journalist asked if Britain could learn anything from America. "Yes," she replied, "The wages they pay their workers."[52] The typical union branch Ellen spoke to gave generously, with individual branches not infrequently giving over $1,000. Even in the textile town of Passaic, New Jersey, where workers had been out on strike for twenty-eight weeks, the union voted to send the miners $100.[53] These men and women (as usual, her union audiences were predominantly male) were not put off from donating by the highly publicized interview Baldwin had given.

In Ellen's estimation, however, Baldwin's statement did have a significant effect on churches and wealthy individuals. Her first event in New York after her arrival was a speech at the League of Women Voters in New York. She was introduced by the league's president, the veteran suffragist Carrie Chapmann Catt, and spoke to an audience of professional and society women, including Eleanor Roosevelt. The women were extremely interested in Ellen's political career and the state of feminist politics in Britain, but her fundraising efforts at the event were not notably successful. She did manage to raise $1,250 at a meeting of the New York Civic Club, an event comprising "well-to-do businessmen and lawyers, the educated women interested in the Labour movement, who are such a feature of New York life, social workers, Labour leaders, and members of the Workers' Party." The meeting was chaired by Morris Hillquit, frequent contributor to *The Jewish Forward,* the largest circulating Yiddish-language paper. The *Forward* was a reliable supporter of the American Socialist movement, and the newspaper's editorial board voted a further $1,000 to the miners. Yet, other than such exceptional men and women, unions proved more reliable donors than individuals. Before she returned to Britain, Ellen got in touch with Nancy Astor, who was vacationing with her family in Maine. Although she might not have been successful in finding wealthy patrons for the Women's Committee, Ellen extracted a promise from Nancy to solicit her friends for money for the respectable organization Save the Children, which had established a fund to feed the miners' families.[54]

Ellen left the United States before Tillett and the miners, setting sail from New York on August 24, in order to be back in Britain in time for the Trades Union Congress in Bournemouth. Although she put an optimistic spin on the amount of money the group still hoped to raise, her dreams of raising $1,000,000 in America had been sorely dashed. In a small effort to swell the Committee's coffers, Ellen traded in her second-class ticket for a third-class passage. She spent most of the week-long journey below deck "where the work of the ship is done." A few weeks earlier, she had been lecturing to the future first lady of the United States; now, she was hanging around the lower decks of a steamship debating the meaning of the general strike with the ship's crew. It was one of the clues to Ellen's political success that she felt at home in both environments. Her growing international profile meant she could not travel in third class anonymously, and one night the first-class passengers insisted on her joining them at their after-dinner entertainment.[55] If she felt less comfortable in such opulent company, she could nonetheless enjoy the concert and the fresh air and night sky before returning to her cabin belowdecks.

The ship arrived at Southampton on August 31, and Ellen had a few days rest—or at least a few days of sleeping in her own bed back in Bloomsbury—before heading to the seaside for the Trades Union Congress. As a union MP, Ellen was a conference delegate. Frank came with her as a member of the press gang. As usual, he illustrated the reports Ellen wrote for *Lansbury's*. Nearly 700 delegates—of whom less than twenty were women—crammed into the Victorian town hall, set back in the gardens of Bournemouth's town centre. The one issue that occupied the minds of most of these men and women—as well as all the journalists present—was the conduct and consequences of the general strike. The strike, however, was not on the agenda. During the general strike, Horrabin had drawn a cartoon for *Plebs* depicting the General Council as an elephant, terrified lest it accidentally trod on the pebble of the British constitution. Now the strike itself became the elephant in the room, which the union leadership were determined to ignore.

With the strike off the table, the delegates debated—and decided against—a resolution to move toward the creation of one mass union of British workers. They also voted against arrogating further executive powers to the General Council, with the union leaders themselves arguing such changes were unnecessary, as the TUC executive already had the authority to lead the movement. At this point, Ellen interjected to demand why, "if the General Council already have the powers, they did not use the powers that they possess in order to prepare for the national strike which they knew was coming."[56] In his opening statement, Congress president Arthur Pugh had defended the constitutionality of the general strike and argued that "the weapon used by the unions last May would not be left unused, when it is sought to enforce upon any section of the workers terms which had not been made the subject of negotiation and collective agreement."[57] Yet the entire tone of the conference suggested a lack of enthusiasm on the part of the trade union leadership to use the general strike weapon again.

The closest the Congress came to an inquest on the management of the strike was the debate over a resolution denouncing the implementation of the Emergency Powers Act (EPA), which declared a state of emergency and granted the government extraordinary powers to ensure the maintenance of the peace and the provision of the essentials of life to the community. During the debate, Ellen protested that the moral authority of herself and her colleagues in parliament in fighting the continuance of the EPA had been undermined by the government's assertions that Ramsay MacDonald had been prepared to use the Act during the 1924 transport workers' strike. In her view, the Congress ought to have put forth a much stronger resolution, "calling upon the Labour Movement to make this issue a very clear and definite one and to say we will have nothing to do with this Emergency Powers Act either ourselves or through the Government, and determine that this Government shall be fought on the way it is putting our comrades in prison." She pointed to the trade unionists still imprisoned for what in normal circumstances would be protected speech and pronounced, "We have not put up anything like the fight we ought to have done, and I hope as a result of this discussion, our leaders will take much sterner measures in the future than they have done in the past."[58] Ellen's rebuke frustrated the men on the dais, who refused to entertain any more speakers who were not prepared either to argue in support of or against the principle of the bill, with the result that, as *The Times* reported, "after a desultory discussion the resolution was carried against the opposition of a small band who detested its moderation."[59]

If the tense atmosphere at the Bournemouth congress hinted at the rifts below the surface of the trade union movement, the joint TUC-Labour Party campaign against the government's Trade Disputes and Trade Unions Bill the following spring managed to unite the left, right, and centre of industrial and political labour. The bill was presented by the government as protecting the right to work. To the Labour movement, however, it was a vicious effort to push home the government's advantage after the defeat of the general strike and to cripple labour both industrially and politically. The bill declared illegal sympathetic strike action designed to "coerce the government" (an intentionally vague category). Intimidation, a category that included mass picketing, was also made illegal. Civil service unions were forbidden to affiliate to the TUC. And finally, trade union members were made to "contract in" to the political levy. Whereas previously a certain percentage of the dues of each member of a union affiliated to the Labour Party had been automatically donated to the party coffers, the bill required that individuals elect, or contract in, to making a contribution to the party. The stated intention was to protect workers from coercion. The bill's opponents believed its real intent was to cripple the party financially—and indeed, in the year after the bill was passed, contributions to the party decreased by a fifth.

Although appalled by the extent of recrimination embodied in the government bill, Ellen was heartened to find the Labour movement finally united in its fight against the government. As the debate over the bill opened, she recorded "a magnificent spirit in the party. The flinging down of a straight class issue on to the floor of the House of Commons by the Tory Party has pulled the Labour men together, forced them to sink their differences, and unite in the grim fight against Tory inso-lence." Over the past several years, she had moved away from the self-proclaimed gradualist Sidney Webb, under whom she had worked in the early days of the Fabian Research Department. Yet, in the debate to move a second reading of the bill, Ellen "almost gasped to see a hot and indignant Sidney Webb banging the table with his fist and forcing the Attorney-General to give way."[60] The radicalization of her old mentor perhaps brought the two back into closer contact. Once parliament ad-journed at the end of July, with the government's bill successfully pushed through into law, the Webbs invited Ellen and her sister Annie to recu-perate as guests at the bungalow on their property in Hampshire.[61]

Predictably, as a trade union MP and a member of the party's radical left wing, Ellen was an outspoken voice in debates over the bill. During the three months of debate, she intervened on twenty occasions, at-tacking both the principle and the specifics of the legislation in lengthy speeches that reveal her at her most impassioned and righteously indig-nant. One of her most scathing attacks was reserved for what she saw as the rebarbative defence of a freeborn Englishman's right to work put forth by Geoffrey Peto, her adversary in the battle over the alleged use of the truss in the Somersetshire mines. After an attack on Peto's ignorance of working-class experience, she charged on: "Members of the hon. gentle-man's class who are brought up with a regard for esprit de corps, whose school and colleges teach them that they have to stand by their fellows, regard what is a point of honour for themselves as a crime when it is done by the working classes of England, and they produce Clauses like this [for-bidding intimidation of blacklegs] in order to emphasize to the workers of this country that such fine sentiments are not for working people but are merely reserved for gentlemen."[62]

Ellen, of course, recognized that such acts of resistance were futile, particularly after the government introduced the guillotine motion to limit debate over amendments. As she wrote in *Lansbury's*, "The fight has become a pure farce, the banging of our heads against the giant majority of a Government boasting like Goliath in his strength." Yet she persisted in stating her objections for the record, not only as a matter of principle but also in the hope that "the country, seeing the Bill going through au-tomatically, [would not feel] that there is nothing to worry about."[63]

Although the passage of the 1927 Trade Disputes and Trade Unions Act proved a major setback for organized labour—trade union membership fell from 5.5 million before the general strike to 4.9 in 1927 and continued to plummet until 1933—it did not mark the end of trade union agitation.[64] It did however encourage a shift to a more politicized strategy that privileged high-level negotiations such as the Mond-Turner talks and political reform through the Labour Party over strike action.[65] Yet if the union leadership had practically abandoned the general strike, it had not given up on strike action as a crucial tool of industrial negotiation; and the repeal of the constraints on such action imposed by the Trade Disputes and Trade Unions Act remained a key priority of the General Council. As early as June 23, Ellen wrote that "most of the Labour MPs are giving their time to meetings in the country where the next round of this fight has got to be fought."[66] Through speeches and propaganda campaigns, the trade union leadership sought to use the Trade Disputes and Trade Unions Act to stoke anger at the government and win converts to the Labour Party. The general strike and its aftermath had underscored the need for social change, and the Labour Party's central message after 1926 was that the only way to achieve social change was through political change.

8

NO LONGER UPSETTING
THE APPLE CART

For Ellen, the general strike and ensuing political struggle over the Trade Disputes and Trade Unions Act had been a battle of class against class, in which she was a junior officer leading the troops on the front line of the economic war. Like Joan Craig, the heroine of her novel *Clash*, who is described at various points as a Joan of Arc or a Boadicea, Ellen's sex was both an attribute, which allowed her to connect with and speak out for the wives of the striking miners, and a barrier that separated her from the club of male trade unionists in parliament. These men—rightly—suspected that Ellen's loyalties would always remain divided. After the passage of the Trade Disputes Act, she redoubled her commitment to the party, throwing herself into the campaign to convert the country to Labour before the next general election.

But the class struggle was not the only fight that preoccupied Ellen in the late 1920s. Much of her time and energy were given over to the women's movement and particularly to the campaign to equalize the franchise in Britain.

Midway through her tour of the coalfields with Kathleen Starr in the late spring of 1926, Ellen abandoned her friend for two days. Leaving Kathleen behind in Nottinghamshire, she returned by train to London, quickly packed an overnight case, and hopped on a flight to Paris to petition the French premier Aristide Briand to grant women the suffrage and to broadcast a speech on the women's movement from Radio Tour Eiffel.[1] The London-Paris route was one of the first to be opened to commercial air traffic after the First World War, followed shortly thereafter by regular flights to Amsterdam, Rotterdam, and Berlin. The growing ease of air travel in the interwar years shrank both the real and imagined distance between European nations, and helped Ellen to remain in close touch with fellow activists across the continent.

The deputation to Briand was arranged by the International Women's Suffrage Alliance (IWSA), which held its tenth conference in Paris that week. The IWSA, whose president was the irrepressible British Liberal activist Margery Corbett Ashby, was an umbrella organization linking national pro-suffrage groups. Its affiliated bodies included the National Union of Societies for Equal Citizenship (NUSEC), as the National Union for Women's Suffrage Societies became known after the passage of the 1918 reform act. The Alliance's triennial conference brought together suffragists from over forty countries, including delegates from thirty-seven national auxiliaries as well as fraternal delegates from many other nations without national affiliated bodies. Women from every European country except Russia came together with women from the United States, Brazil, Peru, Egypt, India, Japan, and elsewhere to discuss the future of the women's movement. The IWSA was also increasingly concerned with the question of international peace. Although Ellen's allegiance remained with the more radical Women's International League for Peace and Freedom (WILPF), she supported the IWSA's aims and had promised Ashby months earlier that she would speak at the conference on the role of women in politics.

After a week touring the Notts and Somerset coalfields, the genteel environment of the women's conference seemed another universe. All of a sudden, Ellen "found myself in a different world. An old French duchess, a princess or two, titles galore, with eager professional women, and the gay students of the Sorbonne!"[2] Although some of her trade union colleagues may have resented her decision to leave behind her fundraising tour to give attention to the international suffrage campaign, Ellen saw the two causes as inextricably combined. In an article in the *Plebs* in 1929, she quoted a "good comrade" who had asked her, "Is there any reason why a socialist should be pleased when some woman breaks fresh ground?" and paraphrased the typical young socialist's view of women's advancement into parliament as, "What difference does it make apart from the party to which they belong?" Her response to both was to insist that "the most difficult lesson that the men have had to learn is that no class or nation can rise above the level of its women. While they are exploited and sweated, or, in a wealthier class, kept ignorant and irresponsible, the sons they raise bear the brand."[3] Although the franchise would not solve the problem of working-class poverty, if mothers and daughters in the coalfields were given a vote, their ability to influence their own lives and the lives of their families would be invaluably increased.

Ellen repeatedly reiterated her view, first expressed in her maiden speech in parliament, that franchise reform was as much a class as a gender issue. One month after the Eiffel Tower broadcast, she again drew herself away from her work on behalf of the miners to make the case for suffrage reform. On July 3, she participated in a mass demonstration in London representing forty women's organizations demanding the equalization of the franchise. Thirty-five hundred women marched with flags and banners from the Embankment to Hyde Park as the female pilot Mrs. Elliott Lynn flew her plane over the procession. At the front of the parade was a golden banner bearing the inscription "Votes for the Women Left Out." Although smaller than the mass demonstrations of the Edwardian era, the procession was in many ways reminiscent of the prewar campaigns, replete with pageantry. Ellen, walking with the Women's Election Committee on the hot summer morning, did her bit to add to the colourful spectacle, dressing in a green Amelia Earhart-style satin "jumper jacket" and green shoes.[4]

When they arrived in Hyde Park, leaders of the movement from across the generational and political divide spoke to their audience from fifteen different platforms. Both militant and constitutional suffragism were represented, in the persons of Emmeline Pankhurst and Millicent Garrett Fawcett. NUSEC president Eleanor Rathbone was there, as was the editor of *Time and Tide,* Lady Rhondda. Although the platforms were dominated by Liberals, the two Labour MPs, Margaret Bondfield and Ellen Wilkinson, both took part. Ellen hammered home the economic bias of the current legislation, reiterating that it not only disfranchised young women workers, but, due to the property qualifications, meant that a woman over thirty could not vote unless she was in possession of "a husband or some other furniture," a quip that elicited applause and laughter from the crowd.[5]

The demonstration marked the beginning of a renewed campaign for franchise equalization, under the leadership of Margaret Rhondda. Ellen and Lady Rhondda shared a strong commitment to women's rights, and the two would become increasingly close in the coming years. Margaret was the daughter of the Welsh "coal king" D. A. Thomas, and hence one of the largest mine owners in England. In 1929, Ellen would attempt a sympathetic portrayal of her in *Clash,* depicting Mary Maud Meddows, the character obviously based on the heiress, as a victim of a capitalist system larger than any one individual. In the summer of 1926, however, such perspective was impossible. Although Ellen worked with Rhondda's committee, she felt compelled to issue a public statement that she had not attended a garden party for suffrage supporters at the house of the coal heiress.[6]

Over the months and years that followed, the women's organizations kept up an intense lobbying campaign, cajoling sympathetic MPs, threatening opponents, and keeping press attention on the issue. Given the promises made by Baldwin and Joynson-Hicks, the government accepted that some form of franchise reform would have to be introduced. Yet many Conservatives, including the prime minister himself, were wary of granting the vote to what some estimated could be more than five million additional women—a move that could increase the total electorate by over a quarter. The Marquess of Titchfield, Tory MP for Newark, said in the 1925 debate over franchise extension, "I do not think a woman of 21 has either enough intelligence of the world or enough knowledge of the ins and outs of politics to be given the responsibility of the vote. . . . These ladies of 21 would be rather like a moth attracted by a candle. They would undoubtedly be attracted by [glittering] prophecies, and I am afraid, like the moth, they would fly into that candle and burn their wings very badly . . . we have at the moment enough unenlightened people who have the vote."[7] However, his belief that young women's mental capacities were inferior to those of young men was by no means universally held within his party. His view that too many uneducated people had already been granted the vote was much more widely shared.

Titchfield's proposed solution was to change the franchise for both men and women to 25. Raising the voting age from 21 to 25 had been considered several times, by successive governments, from 1911 onwards.[8] In late 1926, the Conservative Party polled its regional organizers on raising the voting age to 25. The results revealed mixed feelings. The agent for the northwest of England replied, "Proposal would be well received by our supporters if there *must* be an extension of the franchise," and the Welsh agent reported the "majority think it much better proposal than giving women votes at 21." Several other agents expressed strong reservations, arguing the party would pay a price for disfranchising young men. As the agent for Scotland wrote: "Change of age for men to 25 would provide occasion for deep criticism of the party as being reactionary, and the enfranchisement again of men at 21 would be one of the main planks of the Socialist party at the next election."[9] Ultimately, this consideration weighed heavily with Baldwin, who accepted that the 1918 franchise extension could not be undone, although he agreed that "under the shadow of the war," the government had rushed to pass franchise reform "more from sentiment than from the point of view of practicality."[10]

Thus, in March 1927, Baldwin reluctantly announced that a bill to equalize the franchise at twenty-one would be introduced, to be enacted before the next general election. On March 29, 1928, the House debated the bill. Ellen, as was to be expected, spoke in its favour, blasting the pretensions of businessman and Conservative backbencher Samuel Samuel, who feared that women were too unworldly to instruct the mighty imperial parliament. Ellen archly complimented his sensitivity to the feelings of the "Mohammedans" under Britain's imperial rule, then reminded him that even India had taken recent measures to enfranchise women.[11] Despite such anxieties, the bill passed its second reading with only Samuel and nine other backbenchers dissenting and became law on July 2, 1928. After decades of suffrage campaigning, this final triumph seemed profoundly anticlimactic. Although women were now technically equal citizens, few of their male colleagues viewed them as such.

Ellen devoted substantial attention throughout her political career to overturning such views and championing the rights of young women as wage earners and, in many cases, family breadwinners. She also championed the causes of working-class mothers, even before her experience as chairman of the Women's Committee for the Relief of the Miners' Families brought her into close personal contact with the dire reality of large families' struggle to make ends meet without even the support of the 33s. unemployment benefit. Her assiduous efforts to improve the lives of working-class women throughout her political career have won her plaudits from several historians.[12] One episode, however, stands out as an exception. In 1928, when the Labour women's conference again debated a resolution that the party's programme should include state-sponsored access to information on birth control for working-class women, Ellen sided with the party leadership in arguing that "the issues between one class and another must be planks in our programme, but this was quite another matter."[13] In doing so, she implicitly dismissed the argument—made by numerous Labour women's sections around the country—that access to contraception *was* a class issue. As one woman had said when the same resolution was (successfully) put forth at the 1924 women's conference, "We feel as working women, that working women should have the right to say how many children they are able to have.... The wealthy woman says how many children she can have ... we say that the working mother should be able to get the knowledge even though she has no money."[14]

Ellen's first biographer, Betty Vernon, attempted to excuse her reversal on this issue by arguing, "It is highly improbable that she would have trimmed her sails had she appreciated the need for disseminating information, but in the thirties the link between poverty and over-population was obscure."[15] Her statement is disingenuous on two fronts. For one thing, the link between poverty and overpopulation and their relationship to debates over birth control was by no means obscure in the interwar period. It was not by coincidence that one of the two birth control clinics for working-class women operating in London in 1921 was run by the Malthusian League.[16] For another, Ellen was firmly convinced of the value of information about contraception to working-class families. Prior to the 1928 women's conference, she had been an outspoken supporter of improving access to contraception. In 1926, she had been one of a small number of Labour MPs who had voted in favour of Ernest Thurtle's unsuccessful private member's bill to authorize local authorities to provide knowledge of birth control methods to interested married women—a rare instance when she voted in the same lobby as Geoffrey Peto, her adversary in the episode of the Somerset miners' truss.[17] She continued to sympathize with the pro-birth control lobbyists within the party in the 1930s—albeit not to the point of championing their cause on the conference floor.

Why then had Ellen "trimmed her sails" in 1928? Although the Fiery Particle was capable of great flights of idealism, at the end of the day, she was a political pragmatist, and she was also ambitious. She will go down in history as one of the more left-wing MPs to serve in government under three different prime ministers. Yet, she would never have become a junior minister, let alone the second female Labour cabinet minister, if she had not exhibited a certain degree of *nous* in knowing when to pick her battles and when to hold her fire. Years after her death, left-wing MP George Strauss would say of her, "She was a politician. . . . If it appeared to Ellen that something was not politic then she would withdraw her support."[18] Certainly, Ellen did not always put her career before principle, but here was her chance to move from the radical fringe to the centre of the party. She was not willing to expend the little political capital she had accrued fighting what she recognized to be a futile battle against the established policy of the party on birth control.

In refusing to support women's demands on birth control, the party leadership was concerned, first and foremost, about the effect of the issue on the Catholic vote, which they were actively courting in cities such as Liverpool, where the old Liberal Party was greatly weakened. More broadly, the party leaders were looking forward to the next election and were extremely reluctant to force any issues that would divide the rank and file. In the minds of the male-dominated leadership, the women were behaving selfishly by trying to advocate as an interest group instead of looking at the best interests of the entire party. Given the marginalization of women within the party organization—a marginalization Ellen had in past years attacked—this criticism rings hollow. Rather than special pleading, the women were instead making a rare united stand on behalf of an issue of great importance to them as a collective. Nonetheless, not only the leadership, but Ellen and many others were willing to sacrifice the women's interests to their hopes of finally securing a parliamentary majority. The consciousness amongst more radical MPs that they had knowingly set aside many of their long-held convictions in an effort to secure victory in the 1929 election goes a long way toward explaining the depth of resentment felt after Mac-Donald's betrayal of the party in October 1931.

Ellen clearly felt heavy guilt about her tactical decision to abandon her female comrades in 1928. When she wrote *Clash* in 1929, she included a poignant scene in which Joan discusses birth control with a group of miners' wives. Joan, a virgin, is surprised and discomfited when the women take to discussing how best to spend a £500 donation from a wealthy heiress and one woman bursts out: "Why don't we tell the truth? What the women in this place want is to know how to stop having any more babies while we're all so poor. Every one of the younger of us in this room is scared to death of conceiving another child when she hasn't food to give them." A Roman Catholic woman voices her view that babies are a gift from god, only to be silenced by the objections of the majority. The middle-class parson's wife accepts that large families are a problem in the present economic environment but then adds that "really, it all comes back to the responsibility of the individual. There is such a thing as self-control." Her comments touch off a raw fury in one of the mothers present, who retorts: "Does your class practice that? Your class who can get any advice they pay for. What do you mean by self-control, anyway? If the wages coming to my house can only feed three children, does that mean that me and my man only dare be lovers three or four times in twenty years for fear of having more than we can feed?" After listening to the women give vent to one of their favourite grievances, a fascinated and horrified Joan eventually intervenes to say that the Labour Party cannot risk offending its Catholic members by supporting the issue, only to be put in her place by one of the miners' wives, who pronounces quite matter-of-factly that Catholic women "needn't go to the clinic if they don't want."[19] For Ellen, who herself almost certainly used birth control, the argument about offending Catholic members must have seemed that much more inadequate than it did to young Joan. Unwilling to push the women's line on the NEC, she paid tribute to their suffering in her fiction.

Ellen also continued to campaign quietly for reform. In May 1930, after Labour had formed its second minority administration and Ellen had been appointed parliamentary private secretary to the Ministry of Health, she sent an encouraging report to the birth control activist Dora Russell: "There may be some news to tell you about the Ministry of Health and BC. I am working at it underground. Of course, I have to be frightfully careful about any publicity but there seems to be some movement."[20] Two months later, the Ministry of Health quietly issued a circular to local authorities stating that publicly funded clinics should be allowed to dispense birth control advice to married women if there were deemed to be a health risk to their continued child bearing. It was a comparatively conservative step, but one Ellen hoped would serve as the thin edge of the wedge.

Before Ellen could use her influence as a junior minister, Labour first had to be returned to government. The Elfin Fury was a better platform speaker than she was a committee woman, but, as the 1924 government started to grow long in the tooth, she turned her energies to all aspects of electioneering. At the party conference in Blackpool in 1927, she was elected to the National Executive Committee (NEC) for the first time, to one of four seats specially reserved for women members. Her colleagues were Agnes Dollan, Scottish suffragette and member of the Labour executive who, like Ellen, had been actively involved in the formation of the Women's International League; future Labour MP Jennie Adamson; and London-based social reformer Susan Lawrence, who had joined Ellen in parliament in April 1926, regaining the seat she had lost in the 1924 "Red Scare" election.

Shortly after her election, Ellen wrote to her friend Rajani Palme Dutt—her ex-ally in the Communist Party whom she still addressed as "Comrade" in their correspondence—"They have put me on the programme committee and the Living Wage Enquiry. The programme committee is of the first importance, but it is curiously difficult to produce a program for a Party which hasn't a philosophy."[21] Despite their philosophical differences, over the next several months, Ellen worked with her NEC colleagues to hammer out the policy priorities that would ultimately be published in July 1928 as *Labour and the Nation*. The programme, written by economist and social reformer R. H. Tawney, covered a wide range of reforms to industry, agriculture, social services, and the Empire. The published pamphlet was issued with a foreword from Ramsay MacDonald, which began: "the Labour Party, unlike other parties, is not concerned with patching the rents in a bad system, but with transforming Capitalism into Socialism." In the wake of the 1924 election catastrophe, the party leadership had shrunk from referring to Labour as a socialist party, and the prominent use of the "S word" by MacDonald doubtless heartened Ellen.

Not all of the document was equally provocative. Gone was the commitment to a "capital levy," or a one-time surtax on wealth to pay off the war debt and balance the budget, which Labour's enemies had used against them with such effectiveness in the early 1920s. In its place, the party offered a series of reforms, including the implementation of a more progressive tax system and the creation of a National Economic Council and a National Development and Employment Board—measures that reflected the growing popularity of economic planning within the party. The proposals, while radical, stopped short of the nationalization of the banking sector. Instead, the position of the banks was laid out in a separate Supplement on Banking and Currency Policy, written by Labour's former chancellor Philip Snowden. Snowden's policy would nationalize the Bank of England but not the other commercial banks. To a Marxist such as Ellen, who saw finance as key to the system of capitalist control, such an omission was unconscionable. When the issue was debated at the 1928 party conference in Birmingham, Ellen joined with James Maxton and the ILP members as well as other left-wing dissidents in opposing Snowden's policy. Socialist MPs, she argued, were not "a race of fearsome insects preying on the body politic." They were not suggesting the nationalization of the banking sector out of greed or spite, but because of political conviction, and "it was important that the views of those who believed in nationalization should find expression in the party programme."[22] Ultimately, the conference opted to replace the financial supplement with a call for a further enquiry on the issue—a compromise few found ideal, but which allowed for the passage of the party programme without controversy. Ellen, however, remained dissatisfied. Although she dutifully promoted the programme on Labour platforms, she continued to voice her discontent in left-wing publications such as the ILP's monthly, the *New Leader*. On May 3, 1929, she wrote in that journal: "It is the replacement of private Capitalism by nationally-owned resources that is the drive behind our movement. That faith is implicit in every speech we make. Why not glory in it instead of talking in our programme about 'reorganization' when what we want is nationalization?"

Labour and the Nation did make specific reference to several issues of importance to women, including the need to revise the system of widows' and orphans' pensions, which Ellen had advocated with such passion during the 1925 parliamentary session. Greater provision of maternal and child medical care was also called for, as was the implementation of a system of family allowances. The first two of these measures would be retained in the 1929 party election manifesto, also titled "Labour and the Nation." Family allowances, however, would meet the same fate as had access to birth control. Whereas a narrow majority of the party supported the measure, the majority of trade union members remained against it, for fear that cash payments to mothers would have the effect of depressing men's wages. As party secretary Arthur Henderson argued at the Birmingham conference: "We have enough to do to improve social services in areas agreed upon so we should leave the question of family allowances which appears to divide the labour movement into industrial and political sides."[23] Family allowances were removed from the program at conference, but equal pay never made it in the first place. Ellen recognized it wasn't a propitious moment to push the issue on the NEC, but she made her own views known on the airwaves. On the last day of the Birmingham conference, she upheld the "feminist banner" in a radio debate on the question "Should women be paid as much as men?"[24]

If Ellen was frustrated to see some of the issues she had long championed laid aside by the party for the time being, she could take solace that Labour firmly committed itself to other policies close to her heart, both domestic and foreign. *Labour and the Nation* advocated for negotiated disarmament, arbitration through the League, and the encouragement of international trade, all issues she had long championed through the Women's International League and other pacifist platforms. The party also committed itself to Indian self-government, an issue in which she had taken increased interest in recent years.

Ellen's points of entry into imperial politics shed light on the central role of personal connections in bridging the diverse progressive organizations in the interwar period. As a child in late-Victorian Manchester, she would have been conscious of the Empire, learning imperial geography and taking part in Empire pageants at school. But, unlike many Britons, her family had no personal connection to India or other imperial outposts. No uncles or cousins had served in the Indian civil service. No close family members had emigrated to Australia or Canada. Until she went off to university, Ellen's imagination of life in the Raj had likely been most strongly informed by the works of Rudyard Kipling.

After university, Ellen's Fabian and ILP connections brought her into contact with Shapurji Saklatvala, the son of a wealthy Parsi family in Bombay, with strong links to the Tata family business conglomerate. Saklatvala's parents had intended for him to enter the family business, and it was as an employee of the Tata firm that he first moved to Manchester in 1905. Yet once in England, his growing interest in both racial and socioeconomic inequality led him away from business and into radical politics. He married an English woman and moved to London in 1907, where he became a key figure in progressive and radical circles, becoming briefly involved with Sylvia Pankhurst's suffrage work in east London. Saklatvala joined the ILP a year after Ellen, seeing the party as the best hope for unity between British and Indian workers.[25] Although Ellen did not move to London until 1924, the ILP community was small, and the two knew each other long before Saklatvala joined Ellen as a member of the Communist Party in 1921.

Saklatvala did not accompany Jack Murphy, Harry Pollitt, Ellen, and the other Communist Party of Great Britain (CPGB) delegates to the third Comintern Congress in June 1921. Colonial issues were not as prominent in that year's conference as they had been in 1920, when Lenin and Manabendra Nath Roy had debated the arguments for

(Lenin) and against (Roy) temporary alliances between Communists and nationalist liberation movements in the colonies. Yet Ellen's introduction to men and women like M. N. Roy made a strong impression and broadened her understanding of the links between imperialism and the class struggle. Saklatvala remained in the CPGB after Ellen's departure and continued to represent Battersea North as a Communist from 1924–1929, after the Labour Party forced his resignation; but the two remained on good terms, and Leninist theory continued to shape her perception of imperialism.

At the same time, as a Labour radical in parliament, Ellen came into closer contact with a new group of men and women interested in colonial affairs. Veteran activist George Lansbury had long taken an interest in Indian politics, partially owing to his friendship with David Graham Pole, who encouraged him to join the Theosophical Society in 1915. The London branch of the Society, formed in 1875 to promote "the wisdom of the East" in the Western world, included many prominent members who would go on to become vocal advocates for Indian self-rule, including the society's president Annie Besant and Krishna Menon, who would lead the India League in the 1930s. Lansbury publicized colonial issues in the pages of *Lansbury's Labour Weekly* and drew attention to imperial issues in parliament.[26]

Lansbury's support for Indian and other colonial subjects made him an ideal target for the Comintern agent Willi Münzenberg. By 1926, the thirty-seven-year-old German had already established himself as a dominant figure in Western European Communist circles. The flamboyant and lavishly subsidized propaganda czar, caustically referred to as the "Red Millionaire" by his many enemies, spearheaded a wide range of publishing, fundraising, and propaganda initiatives, including Workers' International Relief, or "International Red Aid," which had contributed funds to the miners following the general strike. In 1926, Münzenberg began to publicize plans for an anticolonial congress to be held the following year—a Moscow-financed initiative he portrayed as free from Communist influence. Like many of his other ventures, the ostensibly non-party political congress sought subtly to "combin[e] a humanitarian concern for the oppressed (workers and colonial peoples) with adulation of the Soviet Union and sharp criticism of capitalism at home and abroad."[27] As Münzenberg's biographer noted, the "plan . . . was premised on his ability to lure in famous non-communist world leaders, so that their illustrious names would supplement the list of intellectual 'fellow travellers' whose often gullible apologias for Soviet actions in Western media organs lent legitimacy to the Bolshevik regime internationally."[28]

Lansbury's respected status as the conscience of the Labour Party, and his position as the vice-chairman of Labour's National Executive Committee in 1926–1927 made him a plum target for Münzenberg's scheme. Although the Christian Socialist Lansbury had never been a member of the CPGB, his attitude toward Communism and the Soviet Union closely mirrored Ellen's.[29] Neither Lansbury nor Ellen can be classed as a fellow traveller, in that neither unreservedly sought to do the work of the Kremlin in Britain, but both were idealistic radicals who preferred to see the progressive left united and were not averse to collaboration across party lines, particularly in international affairs. Women and men like Ellen and Lansbury played a central and underappreciated role in forging links among liberal, socialist, and Communist reformers in the 1920s and 1930s.

On December 2, Lansbury coordinated a meeting in the House of Commons between himself and six other MPs, including Ellen and Saklatvala; Reginald Bridgeman, an aristocratic former member of the diplomatic service who had left the Foreign Office over his objections to colonial rule; the Communist Helen Crawfurd; and several others, to discuss the appointment of a British delegation to attend the Congress. The final delegation included Lansbury, Ellen, Bridgeman, Crawfurd, Harry Pollitt, and other Communists and radical leftists. Saklatvala, who would have liked to have attended, had already committed to travel to India that winter.[30]

The Congress met in Brussels from February 10 through 15, after Münzenberg had been denied permission by the German and French governments to hold the event in either Berlin or Paris, given anxieties about Communism, on the one hand, and the possibility that the event would stoke anti-imperial unrest, on the other.[31] The environment in Brussels was heady with a sense of the possibilities afforded by transnational cooperation. There were over 200 delegates, the majority representing non-Western nations (even if the representatives themselves were émigrés living in exile in the West). Most of the speeches were made by non-Europeans, although the irrepressible Ellen could not restrain herself from contributing to the debate. Her intervention shows how her natural radicalism had already been tempered by political experience. Despite her empathy for the colonial cause, she felt compelled to explain that given unemployment in Britain, it was not feasible to have a transport strike over transportation of soldiers to China.[32]

The event brought together many men and women whom Ellen either already knew through her past internationalist work or would come to know over the years that followed. Here, in the halls of the neo-classical Palais d'Egmont, in the imperial seat that governed the Congo, Conrad's brutal heart of darkness, relationships were forged and solidified. The delegates included members of WILPF, such as Camille Drevet and the indefatigable Gabrielle Duchêne. Brussels was also where Ellen first met Ernst Töller, Henri Barbusse, and Jawaharlal Nehru. Ellen was an admirer of Töller, the German Jewish playwright whose *Transformation* (1919) offered a damning indictment of the experience of modern war. Töller's anti-colonialism had been fuelled by the British government's decision to deny him a visa to visit India in 1925 on the grounds of politics. He had attended the conference not as a member of the German delegation, but as a private citizen. He came away impressed by the spirit of solidarity expressed by the "wahre Völkerbund" (real league of nations), as he and others identified the Congress—a pointed contrast to the League of Nations in Geneva, which was perceived to have disappointed colonial aspirations.[33] In later years, Ellen and Töller would collaborate on another Münzenberg-backed initiative, the Committee for the Relief of the Victims of German Fascism.

Another writer and WWI veteran turned pacifist to attend the conference was Henri Barbusse, who had joined the French Communist party in 1923. Barbusse and Ellen would later travel to Spain together as part of an international anti-fascist campaign. Finally, Jawaharlal Nehru was the young general secretary of the Indian National Congress (INC), with whom Ellen would work in close contact during her later involvement in the India League. Nehru was travelling in Europe with his wife that winter and had worked the conference into their itinerary. The coincidence in Nehru's schedule made the anti-colonial Congress the first international body to which the INC had sent a delegate. The INC maintained a close relationship with the League Against Imperialism

(LAI), the international body established in Brussels, until the progressive incursion of Moscow into the League's operations led to Nehru's expulsion in 1930.

Nehru's involvement in the 1927 conference and his subsequent expulsion from the LAI illuminates both the possibilities and the limitations of many of the fellow-travelling organizations established by Münzenberg and others in the 1920s and 1930s. As Nehru wrote to his INC colleagues in explaining his decision to attend the Congress, the gathering was intrinsically valuable as a vehicle for "getting into touch with other countries and peoples so that we may be able to understand their viewpoint and world politics generally."[34] After the event, he recalled that he "could not but be influenced by some of the men and women he met there."[35] The Congress was remembered as a key moment in the personal histories of several interwar activists.[36] Yet the LAI's increasingly close links with the Comintern made continued association with the League problematic for many non-Communist radicals. At the Congress, Lansbury had agreed to act as international president of the newly formed League. However, he was compelled to resign the presidency four months later. He was in line to take up the chairmanship of the Labour Party that fall, and the party leadership made it clear to him that it viewed his position on the LAI as incompatible with his duties to the party. Lansbury was briefly replaced by ILP leader Fenner Brockway; but in August, the Labour and Socialist International explicitly prohibited its officers from associating with the LAI on the grounds of its Communist associations, which in turn forced Brockway's resignation from the League.[37]

Ellen continued to serve on the LAI's British executive, alongside her friend Conrad Noel. In 1927–1928, she used her parliamentary position to put forth questions in the House of Commons formulated by the LAI to raise awareness and embarrass the government over the position of Britain's colonies and "semi-colonies." However, at the end of 1928, Moscow began to pressure the British LAI to restructure itself along more militant lines, a move that enflamed the fears of the Labour Party; and Ellen too resigned from the organization.[38] Two years later, the Labour Party would include the LAI in its first official list of "proscribed organizations."[39]

Her resignation from the LAI was yet another instance in which Ellen, forced to choose between competing loyalties, put her devotion to the Labour Party before her dedication to other radical international causes. Yet, like the hydra, each time the Labour Party succeeded in hobbling one Münzenberg front organization, another appeared to take its place, and she showed little reluctance to join each new venture and remain on board until the Labour leadership forced her out. Despite her respect and sympathy for Münzenberg, Ellen's independence from the Comintern became increasingly visible after 1928, when she refused to accept the Communists' denunciation of the Labour Party as "Social Fascists" during the Comintern's "Third Period." Between 1928 and 1933, the Third International turned its back on cooperation with "Social Fascists" and demanded that those sympathetic to the revolution show their support through membership in national Communist parties. Moscow also demanded the denunciation of "bourgeois pacifist" organizations such as WILPF and of the League of Nations. In their place, the Comintern advocated a policy of "war resistance," or the commitment to defend the Soviet Union against attack from the capitalist west.[40] Although Ellen continued to defend the Soviet Union, she was unwilling to abandon either pacifism or her faith in the League of Nations. The fact that such ideological contradictions did not prevent her and other non-Communists from collaborating with Communists and fellow travellers on myriad anticolonial and anti-fascist initiatives in the late 1920s and early 1930s exposes the complexities of the "international society" that emerged in the 1920s. It is incorrect to say that two discrete forms of international cooperation emerged in Europe after the First World War, a "liberal and progressive" internationalism and "a separate, Western form of internationalism" forged from the Russian Revolution.[41] Rather, the lines between liberalism and Communism repeatedly blurred in the web of transnational reform movements that emerged in this period.

Thus, Ellen's resignation from the LAI at the end of 1928 should not be understood as a permanent reorientation away from international affairs and back toward domestic politics. In the short term, however, her disentanglement from the LAI gave her time to devote to electioneering. It had another advantage in that it freed her of the potential complication of explaining her ongoing participation in the organization to her constituents. The law required that parliament dissolve itself no later than October 1929; the logic of political campaigns dictated the prime minister would almost certainly call an election after the announcement of the budget in April. This knowledge meant that the half year following the 1928 party conference morphed into a protracted election campaign. And Ellen was in the thick of it.

At Birmingham, Ellen had been reelected to the women's section of the NEC for 1928–1929, alongside Susan Lawrence and Jennie Adamson. The chairman of the NEC that year was Herbert Morrison, another short, red-headed politician, but one whose talents, unlike Ellen's, lay in organization and strategy. The longtime leader of London Labour, Morrison would rise to become one of the dominant figures in the national party in the 1930s, principally due to the credit he was (justly) given for engineering Labour's successful takeover of the London County Council in 1934. Ellen and Morrison had met before, but they travelled in very different political and social circles. Over the next several years, they would become increasingly close, both professionally and personally.

In 1928, however, Ellen was still romantically involved with Frank Horrabin, who remained the prospective Labour candidate for Peterborough, increasingly hopeful of joining Ellen in the next parliament. Frank's victory would bring him and Ellen even closer together. Already, she spent the majority of her time outside of parliament in his company. Their relationship had been built on a professional cooperation, and, as lovers, they continued to collaborate on the *Plebs* and to tour the country together in Labour's cause, as when they lectured on foreign and domestic policy to a crowded Gaiety Theatre in Belfast in October 1928.

Frank remained a married man, an awkward reality that occasionally proved impossible to ignore. Winifred spent more and more time travelling in an effort to escape the discomfort of their situation, but although her absences offered the couple privacy in London, Frank could not behave like Ellen's partner in public. When Ellen's father died on February 26, 1929, she could not turn to Frank for comfort. Instead, she boarded a train back to Manchester alone. The Wilkinsons were a close-knit family, and Annie and her brothers reminded Ellen that the loss of her father had not left her alone in the world. Not long after, Annie decided to move south to London to be closer to Ellen; and in the 1930s, the two would buy a weekend cottage together in Buckinghamshire. Her sister's love had always been a source of strength to Ellen, but, in Manchester that weekend, it must have hurt not to have Frank by her side.

The combined strains of parliament, electioneering work, and her father's death took their toll on Ellen physically as well as emotionally. She was back in parliament the week after the funeral, but quickly succumbed to influenza. As usual, she refused to let her illness interrupt her schedule, but this time she was not able to cheat nature. The flu exacerbated her lifelong respiratory problems, and she was admitted to a nursing home on March 17 for two nights. Her illness convinced her she needed to take some time to slow down, rest, and grieve.

Winifred's presence in London meant Ellen could not take refuge at Mecklenburg Square. From her bed in the rest hospital, she wrote to one of the few people she knew with the resources and good heart to provide her the peace and quiet she needed. Nancy Astor and Ellen had never been close, but over their four years in the House together they had developed a mutual respect and a guarded affection. Now Ellen asked Nancy to help her out by lending her Rest Harrow, the holiday home she and Lord Astor owned in Sandwich. The house was rarely used; but, in a stroke of bad luck, Nancy had recently agreed to lend it out to Harold Macmillan, the future prime minister who shared a close friendship with the Astors. Rather than leave Ellen in the lurch, Nancy offered to book a room for her at a nearby hotel, where she "really would have a quiet time and get the air." Ellen was exhausted enough to accept gratefully—"I simply must go somewhere on Thursday, and feel unequal to thinking what places there are," she wrote.[42] Over the years, the two women would continue to spar over politics, but Nancy's kindness to Ellen at this particularly vulnerable point in her life went a long way toward diffusing any remaining animosity between them.

The weather on the Channel Coast was not ideal for the weary convalescent. Scattered showers throughout the weekend would have driven Ellen to spend much of her time in her hotel or a nearby café. But the sea air would have brought relief to her asthmatic lungs, and the time spent indoors a chance to relax and to engage in one of her favourite pastimes—reading. She was an avid reader of both fiction and non-fiction, including romances and Agatha Christie mysteries.[43] That weekend, however, Ellen may well have been reading the final proofs of her own novel. Billed as a "political romance," *Clash* was slated for release on April 19. Ellen had also agreed to serialize the novel in the *Daily Express*, beginning on April 17. The serialization was not only profitable—she joked that money from the novel would help cover her election expenses—it also meant the novel was accessible to readers who could not afford the seven and a half shilling price of a first edition.[44]

Ellen had decided to write a novel about life in politics the previous summer, after a conversation with an American friend had convinced her that, perhaps, British "people who are in things [should] write tales about them, as they do in America or Germany." [45] Her overactive imagination had led her to daydream stories about her political colleagues while sitting through tedious debates in the House of Commons, but until that moment she had never thought to put her reveries down on paper. That night Ellen sat down at her desk and began writing what would become *Clash*. She scribbled away until 4 a.m. and awoke the next morning committed to seeing her story through. Whereas previously she had let her mind wander during duller debates, that day she literally wandered out of a discussion on derating, snuck into a quiet corner of the House library and resumed writing. She briefly tore herself away when the division bell rang to call her to vote but returned eagerly to her perch, staying in the library until the House shut at midnight.

After that, she vowed not to skip debates for writing. Instead, she woke herself up at six and stayed up until two or three in the morning to work on the novel, finishing it over the parliamentary recess. She later described the eight weeks spent writing as amongst the happiest of her life. As a young woman, she had put socialism before marriage; and, in her thirties, she had made her peace with being the part-time lover of a married man. She would never, she accepted, be a mother. She had made the conscious decision to give her life to a cause larger than herself; but although she could give herself completely to socialism, socialism in turn could never be completely hers. On the eve of *Clash*'s publication, Ellen wrote in the *Star*: "I believe that the deepest impulse in each one of us, once the basic needs of food and shelter have been satisfied, is the impulse to create, to make something of our own."[46] *Clash* was Ellen's own creation.

Ellen returned from the Channel Coast rejuvenated and resumed her punishing schedule of work inside and outside the House of Commons. She did not substantially contribute to the budget debate, limiting herself to snide interjections about the class character of the present government, but she made sure she was in the House to vote in the opposition lobbies. Outside of parliament, she gave her energies not only to electoral politics but also to the women's peace movement, which had revived its propaganda efforts in advance of the coming election.

In the May 1929 issue of *Good Housekeeping*, Ellen wrote of her optimism that the enfranchisement of young women would lead to a more peaceful world. "Where men see power, women see the destruction of life; where men dream of the glory and prizes of war, women see the mutilated bodies of their sons. International peace will be the great gift to the world of the mother enfranchised." The fact that she was not herself a mother did not prevent Ellen from using an essentialist language of sexual difference to underpin her arguments for women's pacifism. The belief that women's pacifism was in part biologically determined was pervasive in the peace movements of the era, including the radical WILPF. Ironically, many of the women who espoused such beliefs were simultaneously amongst the most vocal advocates of an equal rights feminism that denied sexual difference as the basis for unequal citizenship.

This paradox was particularly visible in the work of both the WILPF and the IWSA in lobbying for international reform of nationality policy. In 1925, Ellen had played a prominent role in the unsuccessful campaign by backbench MPs to persuade the government to remove the double standard in British nationality law. The government at the time had fended off demands for reform with the argument that in an era when men and women born in any part of the Commonwealth were considered by law as citizens of the British Empire, any change to nationality law would require imperial consensus. But a small cadre of women (and a few men) refused to let the matter drop. Ellen continued to raise the issue of married women's nationality during ministerial questions, and in March 1929, she used the parliamentary ten-minute rule to propose a change to the existing legislation, exhorting the government not to hide behind the "screen" of imperial opposition. The issue was agreed, and Wilkinson's bill was tabled for a first reading. However, the dissolution of parliament in May meant the bill never got its hearing—an unfortunate outcome about which the government, less than anxious to take unilateral action on the issue, must have been relieved.

That Ellen would support the reform of marriage law is unsurprising, given her feminist track record. That she committed so much energy to the issue is harder to explain. Given her capacity for empathy, the most likely explanation is that she had met women in the course of her union work who were affected by the government legislation. She certainly peppered her parliamentary advocacy for reform with stories of personal hardships, although some of these appear to have been fed to her by the Nationality of Married Women Pass the Bill Committee, a pressure group run by Chrystal Macmillan out of the offices of the National Council of Women.[47] Whether Ellen's quixotic commitment to nationality reform was inspired by encounters with personal hardship or by more abstract feminist conviction, she remained committed to the cause even when the press of ministerial work weighed heavily on her after June 1929.

That August, she and her sister Annie both attended the WILPF conference in Prague as British delegates, and Ellen served on a four-member commission on the Nationality of Married Women and Heimatlose (the stateless). By late 1929, women's groups concerned with reforming nationality law were focusing their attention on the upcoming League of Nations Codification Conference on International Law, to be held in Geneva the following spring. The British women hoped Geneva would grant them what previous imperial conferences had failed to. In addition to presenting evidence to the conference, the IWSA and the International Council of Women arranged a mass demonstration at The Hague. Although Ellen was not a member of either organization, she was on friendly terms with many of the women and flew to Geneva to participate in the demonstration, speaking alongside Japanese, Danish, and Dutch women.

The spectacle highlighted many of the internal contradictions of the women's movement. Although the women claimed to have justice and reason on their side, the demonstration's appeal was at times decidedly irrational. Oscar Dowson, a legal advisor to Home Office, described the women's demonstration in a letter to a colleague:

Before the speeches began there was a sort of Ballet of 46 maidens who walked in and paraded in front of the platform. Some of them were dressed in white, seven in pink, and the rest in black. The white ones represented those progressive countries which had fully adopted the principle: the pink ones those who had gone half way in that direction: and the black ones, including the United Kingdom, those countries which were still clinging to the ideas of the dark ages. It was ingenious and amusing, but rather absurd. One thing struck me especially—these organizations which make almost a religion of sex equality, were fully alive to the propagandist advantages of selecting the more well-favoured maidens to represent the white and pink countries, leaving the less well-favoured the unenviable task of representing the black countries.[48]

It is hard to imagine that Ellen did not appreciate Dowson's arch analysis—she would have struggled not to raise an eyebrow at the performance. Dowson had more time for Ellen's speech, which he singled out as the best of the group. She protested the absurdity of a law that meant she and other unmarried female members of the government would have to resign their posts if they happened to be "minded to visit a registry office and marry an alien." Margery Corbett Ashby, the head of the IWSA, applauded Ellen's speech in the pages of the *International Women's Suffrage News*.[49] Ashby and Wilkinson were both suffragists of long standing, and despite their political differences (Ashby was the long-serving head of the Women's Liberal Association), they repeatedly cooperated on women's rights campaigns in Britain and internationally. Yet, unlike Wilkinson, Ashby was not a pacifist, and the two did not meet at the peace conferences and on the antiwar platforms where Ellen forged many of her friendships with British and international women from a wide range of political backgrounds.

Studies of the antiwar movements that emerged after 1918 have emphasized the cross-party nature of many peace organizations; and some have drawn connections between the supposed weaker political partisanship of women, their prominent role within these organizations, and the ability of peace movements to bridge partisan divides.[50] Ellen, of course, was anything but politically nonpartisan. She saw politics as an existential war between capitalism and socialism, and she stood on platforms throughout her career arguing for the direct link between domestic capitalism and militarism in foreign policy. Yet, she knew and respected individual Liberal and Conservative women who shared her views on foreign affairs, and she was not willing to forsake the hope that the two "capitalist parties" could be persuaded to support disarmament and collective security through the League of Nations. Her optimism was likely fuelled by the British government's signature of the Kellogg-Briand pact the previous summer. The pact, signed by all of the major European powers except the Soviet Union, committed the signatories to "condemn recourse to war for the solution of international controversies, and renounce it, as an instrument of national policy in their relations with one another." In this spirit, Ellen agreed to participate in the Women's Peace Crusade, launched in the run-up to the general election.

Britain had seen several such peace crusades by women's groups, with the first held in July 1915 when war fever was near its height. In 1929, the latest incarnation of the Women's Peace Crusade (WPC) claimed to represent twenty-nine women's organizations, including the Women's International League (WIL). The new WPC was chaired by the Liberal Lady Acland. The WIL's long-serving past president, Kathleen Courtney, acted as honourable secretary. The Crusade held meetings across the country, headlined by women from each of the principal political parties. They "call[ed] upon the voters of all parties to elect a Parliament of peacemakers pledged to make the renunciation of war a reality by accepting the obligations to settle all international disputes by peaceful means, and pledged to take the lead in pressing forward the progressive reduction of arms."[51] In the Manchester Town Hall, Ellen shared the stage with the Liberal Lady Horsley. The event was chaired by the wife of the Reverend Hewlett Johnson, the Dean of Manchester, who would go on to be remembered as the Red Dean of Canterbury for his vocal support of the Soviet Union after his appointment to that post in 1931. At the Central Hall in London, Ellen spoke alongside Lady Acland and the Conservative Lady Winifred Elwes, emphasizing her belief that "the mass of women of all parties would be dead against another war."[52] The WPC remained in existence until the outbreak of the

Second World War, one of the proliferating number of peace organizations that cooperated to lobby the government on disarmament in the 1930s.

Ellen believed in the aims of the WPC; but in her estimation the best chance of peace still lay with the election of a Labour government, one in which she hoped to play at least a supporting role. Going into the general election, Middlesbrough East was not considered a safe Labour seat. She would again be faced with a three-way contest, and in early 1929 there were rumours the party intended to move her to a solidly Labour district in Northumberland.[53] But Ellen stayed put; and in the end she retained the seat, not by 927 votes, as had been the case in 1924, but by 3,199. As she wrote for her union magazine, *New Dawn,* "It was the quietest election I have known. I made raids into other constituencies, but Middlesbrough East seemed to have made up its mind to vote for me."[54]

Ellen's increased popularity reflected her hard work in nursing her constituency. Before parliament reopened after its summer recess, she spent two weeks in Middlesbrough in September 1928 meeting with constituents. In addition to large outdoor meetings and smaller indoor events for women voters, she held several "cottage meetings" in the poorer parts of the town, where housewives could meet to discuss politics with their MP in advance of what for many would be their first trip to the polling station. Downtrodden men and women who met her at these meetings came away with the belief that Ellen understood their problems and meant to give her all for the constituency. She "was a real good mixer" and was "able to talk to people and unravel and breakdown problems and present issues to people so that they really understood." After her death, one local woman fondly remembered Ellen's willingness to "get her teeth into anything." Another woman, a teacher, recalled that she had "a real socialist outlook. [She] felt the tragedy of people living and dying without the chance to enjoy and appreciate the pleasant things of life—music, poetry and literature.[55]

Ellen's determination to use her time in Middlesbrough to full advantage gave her little opportunity for rest. A local journalist once recorded his amusement at finding her perusing her agent's register of constituency voters while grabbing a quick bite in a local café.[56] Her electioneering efforts were bolstered by help from family and friends. Her sister volunteered with organizational work, and her older brother gave speeches on her behalf—a favour she occasionally returned by preaching at his parish in Burnley. Not surprisingly, Ellen's occasional sermons at the Colne Road Wesleyan Church struck a revolutionary tone—shortly after her reelection she warned her brother's parishioners that "We are tending to become the slaves of machines, and, unless the value of the human soul is proclaimed above everything else, our civilization is going to crash into a darker age than the darkest ages ever known."[57] Less predictably, her brother's campaign speeches on her behalf appear to have struck an equally radical note. One constituent recalled that his impassioned oratory led to rumours he was "red."[58] Her colleague from the National Union of Distributive and Allied Workers (NUDAW), Amy Wilde, who worked under her as a women's organizer, also helped out, both in the office and on the platform. Ellen called Amy "the girl with the golden voice." Although Amy enjoyed the campaign, she could have done without the election results party. Ellen had her friend follow close behind her all evening so that enthusiastic punters were forced to slap Amy on the back and spare the candidate.[59]

There was a lot of backslapping in Labour committee headquarters late Thursday night and into the early hours of Friday, May 31. Labour did not win an absolute majority of seats in the new House of Commons, but they did do better than almost anyone—except Beatrice Webb, who had predicted a Labour plurality of 300—had anticipated.[60]

Labour did not quite live up to Beatrice's expectations, but the party did win more seats than the Tories. The final tally gave Labour 287 seats, the Conservatives 260, and the Liberals 59. The unexpectedly poor performance of the Liberal party took everyone by surprise—from the betting markets to the professional pundits to the Liberals themselves. After a steady decline in the early 1920s, the party had appeared poised to make a rebound. Following Asquith's death in 1928, the two factions of the party were (grudgingly) reunited under Lloyd George's stewardship and backed by Lloyd George's money. The party had on its side one of the greatest minds of the twentieth century, John Maynard Keynes, the brilliant iconoclast who had skewered Lloyd George in his influential critique of the Paris peace treaty, *The Economic Consequences of the Peace* (1920), then turned his venom on the current government with *The Economic Consequences of Mr. Churchill* (1925), a denunciation of the decision to bring Britain back onto the gold standard at the prewar exchange rate.

National unemployment levels were not as high as they were in Ellen's constituency, where close to twenty percent were out of work. Nonetheless, the stagnant economy was the dominant issue of the campaign, and the Liberals and Keynes had put forth a series of proposals to revive it. Keynes's magisterial *General Theory of Employment, Interest, and Money,* which would lay the foundations of what we now think of as Keynesian economics, would not be written until 1936. The economist had not yet fully worked out his ideas about the multiplier effect of stimulus spending, but he did appreciate that the lack of private-sector investment was preventing a recovery. Under his encouragement, the Liberals proposed the implementation of a deficit-funded public works program to "conquer" unemployment—a modest proposal by modern standards, but radically unorthodox by the standards of the day.[61] The feasibility of the Liberals' scheme has remained a subject of debate, but its appeal to the public proved disappointing.[62] The Labour Party, nervous that Lloyd George's progressive proposals would bleed votes from its left flank, devoted considerable energy to attacking the former prime minister for his long record of false promises and policy shifts.[63] In the end, few on the left deserted the Labour Party for the Liberals. Whatever their reservations, a large number of working men and women were convinced by the general strike and its aftermath of the need for a working-men's government to defend their class interests. If anything, it was the Conservative party that suffered from the Liberal intervention.

The election saw the return to parliament of many men and women who, unlike Ellen, had lost their seats during the 1924 "Red Scare" landslide, including Ellen's future collaborator and confidant Herbert Morrison. It also significantly increased the number of women in the House, from six to sixteen, including nine Labour members. The new party of government made a point of showing off its female membership in a brief "talkie" to be shown before feature films at the cinema. The film segment began with a dapper and coiffed MacDonald introducing his new Cabinet ministers. Then Margaret Bondfield, his minister of labour, in turn introduced the female MPs. It was Ellen's film debut.

The election of so many women meant the women's "dungeon" became awkwardly crowded. Fortunately, Ellen was soon to have a desk all her own. Ramsay MacDonald appointed two women to ministerial office: Margaret Bondfield and Susan Lawrence, who became parliamentary secretary to the Ministry of Health. Ellen, in turn, became Susan's parliamentary private secretary and acquired a desk in Lawrence's private room in the House. There the two women worked, debated, gossiped, and indulged their mutual love for cigarettes.

Ellen's relationship with Susan Lawrence would become one of the most significant of her life. Politics and trade unionism were both male-dominated worlds. Not since the death of Mary Macarthur in 1921 had Ellen had a female role model to whom she could look up. The tall, brash Susan Lawrence, with her close-cropped masculine haircut and her impeccable command of facts and figures, was like no woman Ellen had previously known. Lawrence helped her protégée learn to work within the system while still remaining true to her radical convictions. Amy Wilde remembered that Susan "had a great influence on Ellen," and Beatrice Webb wrote in her diary, "Ellen has been tamed politically by being the loyal PPS of Susan and is full of affection and admiration for her chief."[64] In a tribute to the woman she called herself "proud to serve," Ellen described Susan as "interesting, complex, wayward even, full of zest and vim, a little hard sometimes, ruthless in debate, kind to the point of utter selflessness in private life, a good brain and a warm heart."[65] Susan, for her part, returned the admiration. She would later describe Ellen as possessed of "one of the quickest and surest minds I have ever met" and commend her ability to "leap instantaneously to the heart of the problem," even when others struggled to make sense of a complicated issue.[66]

Susan was twenty years Ellen's senior, a fellow Fabian and an earnest advocate of local government reform. She came from a middle-class background and had studied mathematics at London and Newnham College, Cambridge. She had a mathematician's eye for detail and in the previous parliament had served as the effective shadow Minister of Health, regularly giving the Labour reply to Neville Chamberlain's speeches and tearing apart his facts and figures with a ruthlessness that simultaneously awed and frightened. One observer, who noted Susan possessed "unusual powers of logical reasoning and . . . an amazing capacity for detail," nonetheless found her fury in argument frighteningly feminine. He noted with obvious unease that "time and again she has attacked Mr. Chamberlain with an austere fury which is reminiscent of the sibyl or the prophetess. Her denunciations of him have not been the cheap taunting accusations of the politician, but they have been the utterances of one possessed of a primitive hate, into whose soul such a sense of wrong has burned that the man who has done the wrong is regarded as an enemy of his kind, who by his acts has deprived himself of all right to consideration or mercy."[67]

The "primeval" element to Lawrence's personality discomfited friends as well as enemies, and women as well as nervous men. Beatrice Webb, who unlike her husband did not regularly witness her old friend's performances in parliament, received a rude shock when she saw Susan speak to a crowd of dockers during the general strike. She recorded in her diary finding Susan "in a state of emotional excitement—I might almost say exaltation. . . . I walked off to lunch . . . thinking mostly of the amazing change in Susan Lawrence's mentality—from a hard-sensed lawyer-like mind and conventional manner of the 'moderate' member of the School Board whose acquaintance I had made five and twenty years ago to the somewhat wild woman of demagogic speech, addressing her constituents as 'comrades' and abasing herself and her class before the *real* wealth producers." To Beatrice, such behaviour was frankly "weird." To Ellen, who was herself prone to outbursts of passion, Susan's "joyful ferocity" was not the marker of a bluestocking maenad, but of "an enthusiastic, warm-hearted girl."[68]

Susan was technically second in command to Arthur Greenwood, the party's jovial, if alcoholic, head of research. In practice, it was she more than Greenwood who ran the department. A year earlier, her friend George Bernard Shaw affectionately parodied her in *The Apple Cart*. The play, about a fictional Labour government, includes a scene in which a Susan-esque government minister proclaims, "I love my department: I dream of nothing but its efficiency: with me it comes before every personal tie, every happiness that common women run after." Now, the flesh-and-blood Susan showed the same enthusiastic commitment as

Shaw's fictional avatar. Ellen described her as "the terror of a department which itself contains some whales for work. She will go through the clause of a complicated Bill seventy times until she is sure that no loophole can be found."[69]

The Ministry of Health's two principal achievements during the government's tenure were the passage of a new Widows', Orphans' and Old Age Pensions Bill, which addressed some of the anomalies in the 1925 legislation identified by Ellen and others, and the passage of a new Housing Bill, which increased funds for slum clearance and returned housing subsidies to their 1926 level. During the debates over both pieces of legislation, the left wing of the party sharply criticized the government for failing to go further. A Labour government had an opportunity to use social legislation to increase the purchasing power of the poor and help ameliorate working-class poverty, and the caution embodied in both pieces of legislation was a form of moral cowardice. Susan defended both bills as the best that could be achieved in a difficult financial time, as first instalments to further reform. Ellen would normally have allied herself with her friends the ILP radicals James Maxton and John Wheatley, who led the charge against the legislation in the committee stages. Now, she found herself in the novel position of defending an incremental approach.[70] Her friends on the parliamentary backbenches were quick to look to the bills' weaknesses, but Ellen, from her insider's perch, understood how hard Susan had fought to secure every politically feasible advantage.

As Susan's number two, Ellen spent more time reading white papers and less time attending debates on topics outside of her ministerial brief, which lost a bit of their liveliness for want of her impassioned oratory and sardonic interjections. For all that she respected Susan and liked ministerial work, she occasionally found it painfully "dull" to spend days with a "head . . . full of statistics about dead babies and worry as to why Blackpool had twice the infantile deathrate of West Ham."[71]

If only to keep herself sane, Ellen did occasionally attend debates and engage with ministerial questions on affairs outside her official remit. These included debates on imperial affairs, in which Ellen was taking an increased interest. When she moved to London in 1924, she had joined the national council of the Women's International League.

Over the next several years, she would increase her involvement with the national group, serving briefly on the executive committee before moving to the less time-consuming, if more high-profile, position of vice president, a largely honorary title that she shared with women like Emmeline Pethick-Lawrence, Vera Brittain, and Winifred Holtby. Although the WILPF remained primarily focused on European affairs, the British section gave considerable attention to conditions in the Empire, and particularly in India. Members of the League were also prominent in other anti-imperial organizations. Despite her position in the government, Ellen's signature appears alongside Brittain's and Holtby's on an April 1930 "Memorial on African Policy," denouncing the Labour government's failure to take any initiative "to secure the land rights of the natives, to alter the restrictive labour conditions, to revise the unjust systems of taxation, to increase the proportion of public expenditure on native areas, or to establish equal rights before the law."[72] Frank Horrabin also signed the memorial. It was in this period that Ellen and Frank— along with Ellen's sister Annie; Frank's wife, Winifred; and John Jagger— also became deeply involved with the pro-Congress India League.

It would be unfair to say that international affairs provided Ellen with a distraction after the bitter disappointment of the collapse of the second Labour government and the division of the party into rival factions in August 1931. Nonetheless, in the disillusioning days that followed the landslide victory of the Tory-dominated National Government in October 1931, Ellen threw herself back into the interlinking worlds of feminism and internationalism in which she had been so deeply enmeshed in the immediate aftermath of the war.

9

OUT OF PARLIAMENT

Two years into its administration, the second Labour government found itself in an impossible situation. Economic contraction led to falling tax revenues and a rising bill for unemployment assistance as more men and women were forced onto the dole. By the spring 1931 census, male unemployment stood at 17 percent nationally.[1] Unemployment in Middlesbrough, Ellen's constituency, had reached nearly 28 percent, one of the highest rates in the nation.[2] Yet the situation in Middlesbrough paled in comparison to that in Jarrow, the port town east of Newcastle that saw its shipbuilding plant shut down in 1931, with the result that unemployment surged to two-thirds of the male workforce. In 1932, Ellen was selected as the parliamentary candidate for Jarrow, and she vividly recalled her first visit to her new constituency. "At Middlesbrough I had thought I had known what poverty could mean. But in that town some industry was going, some people had work. Compared to Jarrow, things on Tees-side were moving. Jarrow . . . was utterly stagnant. There was no work. No one had a job, except a few railwaymen, officials, the workers in the cooperative stores, and the few clerks and craftsmen who went out of the town to their jobs each day."[3]

Nationally, the economy's ill-health discouraged investors. The domestic situation combined with an international liquidity crisis led to a drain on currency reserves. If the country were to continue to meet its external obligations, the government would have to either devalue the pound—effectively start printing money—or secure an external loan. A few prominent figures, including J. M. Keynes and, eventually, transport union leader Ernest Bevin, argued in favour of devaluation. The vast majority, including Labour's chancellor Philip Snowden, could not countenance going off the gold standard, which left borrowing money as the only alternative. By 1931, the only people left with the money to make that kind of investment were the Americans.

The government's dependence on American finance was so widely appreciated that in January 1931 Ellen decided to make the loan crisis the centre of her second novel, *The Division Bell Mystery*. The parliamentary whodunit focused on the murder of an American financier in the Palace of Westminster. Georges Oissel, the director of the American Foreign Loans Corporation, had come to London prepared to strike a hard bargain with the British, only to end up shot through the head in one of the parliamentary private dining rooms. In the end, the murder turned out to be a crime of passion. The home secretary had not, as had initially been feared, "murdered Oissel as a conscientious contribution to the settlement of the international problem."[4] The plot of *The Division Bell Mystery* was far-fetched, to say the least. But if it was fantastical to imagine the government brought down by the murder of a fat old banker, American finance ultimately did hold the key to the Labour administration's collapse.

As a parliamentary private secretary, Ellen had no direct involvement in the dramatic events that led to the government's breakup. She was not at 10 Downing Street for the tense meeting on the evening of August 23 when the prime minister informed the twenty members of his cabinet that the government would only be able to secure a new loan from the United States if it took substantial additional measures to balance its budget, including the implementation of a further £20 million of economies. Given the belt-tightening already undertaken, Prime Minister MacDonald argued that these additional cuts could be realized only through a 10 percent reduction in unemployment assistance, which he claimed would save the government over £12 million. This had been the course of action recommended by the May Committee, a tripartisan group of MPs tasked with proposing potential economies. (Notably, the two Labour members of the committee had dissented from its final report.)

The prime minister was aware of the hostility of many of his colleagues to such a measure. He, Chancellor of the Exchequer Philip Snowden, and Foreign Secretary and Secretary of the Labour Party Arthur Henderson had met with the members of the party's national executive committee and the general council of the Trades Union Congress (TUC) the previous Thursday and been left with no uncertainty about the TUC's attitude towards any proposal for further budget cuts. Nonetheless, MacDonald urged the cabinet to accept the cuts in recognition of "the calamitous nature of the consequences which would immediately and inevitably follow from a financial panic and a flight from the pound." He owned that "the proposals as a whole, represented the negation of everything that the Labour Party stood for, and yet he was absolutely satisfied that it was necessary in the national interest, to implement them if the country was to be secured." MacDonald ended with the warning that if members of the cabinet were to tender their resignations, the government would be forced to resign, and the cuts would be carried through by the opposition parties.[5]

The official cabinet minutes record only that "indications were given that, while a majority of the Cabinet favoured the inclusion in the economy proposals of the 10 per cent reduction in unemployment insurances benefit, the adoption of this as part and parcel of the scheme would involve the resignation of certain Ministers from the Government."[6] The diaries, letters, speeches, and published writings of those present at the fateful meeting contain conflicting accounts of what was said. This much, however, is clear. After a discussion lasting less than an hour, nine members of the Cabinet, including Henderson; Ellen's leader at the Ministry of Health, Arthur Greenwood; and her longtime friend and mentor, George Lansbury, refused to accept the proposed cuts. Eleven others, including Snowden; Minister of Labour Margaret Bondfield; and Herbert Morrison, then Minister of Transport, supported MacDonald. With the cabinet almost evenly split, the ministers all tendered their resignations, and MacDonald left to inform the king. The next day he would shock the cabinet and the nation by announcing his decision to lead a "national government" backed primarily by Conservative and Liberal support.

Although Ellen did not have a voice at the table, there is no doubt how she would have voted over the proposed benefit cuts. The previous month, she had defied the party whip by refusing to vote in favour of the passage of the Unemployment Insurance (No. 3) Bill. The so-called Anomalies Act effected savings to unemployment insurance by excluding seasonal workers and married women from eligibility. In abstaining, she sided with her Independent Labour Party (ILP) friends George Buchanan, James Maxton, and Jennie Lee—all of whom voted against the bill. Ellen would not go so far as to risk her official position by voting against the government, but she was an outspoken critic in debate and supported the ILP's strategy of laying down disruptive amendments in the committee stage of the bill, forcing all-night sittings that ate up parliamentary time and wore on the government's patience. Ellen's ministerial status likely protected her from official censure, but twenty-one of her colleagues in the rebellion were called before a party disciplinary committee for their obstreperous tactics.[7]

Ultimately, Ellen would refuse to side with the ILP when the group resigned its affiliation with the Labour Party in 1932. Her sympathy with the group that brought her into Labour politics did not trump her loyalty to the party. As she proved repeatedly, she was committed to working for reform within the Labour movement, not outside of it. Yet, she remained in close contact with the ILP rebels throughout her political career, cooperating with them on both domestic issues and international ones.

Ellen's support for government intervention on behalf of the unemployed was grounded in her socialist principles. In one of her first interviews as a new MP in 1925, she had made clear her belief in social redistribution, saying she wanted to see a drastic reorganization of society with "no millionaires and no paupers."[8] That belief had been considerably reinforced by her time spent in the United States earlier that year. Her two previous trips to the United States had been undertaken at someone else's behest. In 1920, she had gone over to testify before the American Commission on Conditions in Ireland. In 1926, she had made the journey with several other members of the TUC to raise funds for miners' relief. On December 30, 1930, she set sail for New York on her own initiative.

For Ellen, whose instinctive generosity left her perpetually short of cash, a paid speaking tour of the United States was an appealing prospect. Speaking tours of the United States became a popular working holiday for several British politicians in the 1930s. Winston Churchill helped pay the bills at Chartwell with the proceeds of his American tour to tout *The History of the English Speaking Peoples* in 1932.[9] Jennie Lee toured the country in February 1931, and returned most summers thereafter, delivering lectures arranged by William B. Feakins, Inc., a New York city publicity firm that also arranged Ellen's 1931 tour. (The firm's other high-profile clients included biologist Julian Huxley, who would later work closely with Ellen on the establishment of UNESCO.) Churchill transferred $10,000 from his US to his UK accounts at the end of his 1932 tour, but Ellen could not have hoped to net such an extraordinary sum. More likely she earned around $100 per speech, the average fee paid to her colleague Jennie Lee.[10] Feakins' 1932–1933 catalogue noted that Wilkinson was "known to our audiences as 'Five Feet of Pugnacity'" and that she was an "authoritative speaker, accustomed to appearing before large audiences."[11] During her 1931 tour, the firm arranged engagements on her behalf for audiences ranging from the Philadelphia Labour Forum to the Boston branch of the American WILPF, the Detroit Women's City Club, and Radcliffe College in Cambridge, Massachusetts. The dominance of her itinerary by women's groups reflected both her international reputation as a feminist politician and the stronger financial position of women's organizations as compared to labour groups in Depression-era America.

Although Ellen set off for the United States to make some much-needed money, the trip was also a chance to catch up with old friends and learn more about a country that both fascinated and bemused her. She sailed from Southampton on December 30, and was met in New York four days later by her friend Evelyn Preston, with whom she stayed for several days. The granddaughter of Standard Oil financier William Thompson, Evie had attended Barnard College and University of Wisconsin before moving to Britain in the early 1920s. In London, the tall, dimpled young woman joined the Labour Party, and worked as Ellen's secretary. By Christmas 1931, she had returned to the United States and was living in a townhouse in the West Village, the fashionable district in lower Manhattan that in the early twentieth century became the home of numerous bohemian radicals, including the Communist John Reed and artist John Sloan. In New York, Evie continued her commitment to social reform. Perhaps impressed by her experience of British adult education schemes such as Plebs and the NCLC, she helped to fund the establishment of Brookwood Labor College in Katonah, New York. In 1935, she was a founding member of the League of Women Shoppers, a national group aimed at exposing exploitative labour practices whose tactics included such flamboyant stunts as picketing nightclubs in evening gowns while carrying placards that declared "We won't be wined and dined until a union contract is signed."[12] The *New Yorker* later characterized the league as "a particularly weird communist front of the period."[13] Although not herself a Communist, Evie and the ACLU president Roger Baldwin, her longtime partner, were, like Ellen, not averse to working with Communist activists on a series of reform initiatives throughout the 1930s. The two women came from different backgrounds, but they formed a solid and lasting friendship, and Ellen relished the chance to spend a few days catching up with her friend. Evie brought her to a party in the village where Ellen was offered a glass of "bathtub gin"—the homebrewed cocktail staple of Prohibition-era New Yorkers.[14] The younger woman also took her friend around New York's big department stores, where Ellen shopped for silk "undies" for herself and her sister.[15]

Although Ellen enjoyed spending time with Evie, her experience in the United States, and in New York in particular, only reconfirmed her belief in the importance of the British government's commitment to provide unemployment assistance (the reviled dole) to the long-term unemployed. There was no federal unemployment program in place in the United States in 1931, and the eight million unemployed were largely forced to rely on charity, which too often meant standing in ubiquitous breadlines for handouts, or to find other means of subsistence.[16] In Ellen's estimation, the government's unwillingness to take action reflected Americans' misguided "he-man spirit," which was too proud to admit the need for state intervention to right the economic ship. Instead of government relief and jobs programs, Madison Avenue attempted to rally shoppers out of the depression. "Shops announced 'Prosperity Sales,' the restaurants put on 'Prosperity Specials,' I have eaten a 'Prosperity Sundae' and bought 'Prosperity undies' at 'Prosperity' bargain prices."[17] Although these sales helped Ellen save a few pennies on garters, stockings, and girdles, retail discounts were not enough to lift the city out of depression.

Nor were apples the answer to Manhattan's problems. When Ellen arrived in New York, she encountered a strange phenomenon: men and women "stamping in their thin clothes to keep warm in New York's special variety of cutting wind," bedecked with signs reading UNEMPLOYED, selling apples on street corners. From a British perspective, she found the condition of these men and women pitiable, but most New Yorkers she met—including the apple vendors—felt apple selling represented an opportunity for the unemployed to pull themselves up by their own bootstraps. In Ellen's slightly sardonic rendering, the craze for apple selling created a host of problems for New York's wealthier classes who were left wondering "what to do with all the apples they feel they ought to buy. . . . You press apples on your guest, your children and your neighbours, but every person who comes into the house brings yet more to be disposed of somehow." "Being English and crude," she was left wondering "whether it would not be simpler to give [the unemployed money], and save all that trouble." Alas, her attitude only confirmed her American hosts' belief that "the British are a nation of dole drawers."[18]

Ellen was frank in expressing her views on apple selling and other aspects of the international economic situation in a series of interviews she gave to journalists while in town, including an exclusive granted to the feminist pacifist journalist Miriam Teichner, who visited her at Evie's home.[19] She also expounded in impassioned detail on the benefits of the British system of unemployment insurance in speeches at a mass demonstration at Irving Plaza concert hall on behalf of unemployed workers and at the Civic Club on Manhattan's Lower East Side.[20]

Although New York remained her base during her five-week stay in America, Ellen made several brief forays out of the city. A week after her arrival, she made the two-hour train journey south to Philadelphia, where she spent two days lecturing and touring a local homeless shelter. At a luncheon for the Philadelphia Committee for Total Disarmament, she spoke before an audience of 500 on the need for unilateral disarmament. She was introduced by the Quaker William Hull, a history professor at nearby Swarthmore College. Hull prefaced her speech with a message from Albert Einstein, the German theoretical physicist whose international prestige would be used to give weight to many of the anti-fascist campaigns Ellen became involved with after Hitler's rise to power. Her speech at the luncheon revealed an idealistic pacifism that would be undermined by the horrors of fascism. Standing before the group with her hands thrust deep in the pockets of her tailored black suit, she answered the question, "If we disarm, suppose someone attacks us?," by positing that, "if the country is willing to take the risk of peace, there is no chance that any other country would attack her." What was needed was action, not words, and specifically a US lead on disarmament. With characteristic cheek, she dismissed the Kellogg-Briand pact and the naval disarmament treaties as not worth the paper they were printed on, alleging that "The diplomatists might as well have sat drawing on blotting paper pigs with curly tails. They build on paper bridges that would not carry a fly."[21]

The following day she lectured to the Philadelphia Labor Forum on the European labour movement which, despite its limitations, she praised for having won concrete gains for the European working classes which US unions should seek to emulate. Afterwards, she returned to spend a night in New York before travelling to Boston to reprise her speech on disarmament for the Boston branch of the WILPF. The next weekend saw her travelling even further north to Canada, speaking at several engagements in Montreal, including a talk to the city's Women's Club at the Mount Royal hotel, a beaux-arts behemoth that claimed the title of largest hotel in the British empire. The women's club was a heterodox group, and not all of its members were pacifists. (One member of Ellen's host committee was the club's treasurer, Dr. Helen Reid, a well-known social worker who had served as the director of the Montreal branch of the Canadian Patriotic Fund during the Great War and been honoured for her contribution to the war effort.[22]) Rather than offend her paying audience with her views on foreign policy, Ellen took as her theme "Life in the British parliament" and regaled her listeners with sketches of individual MPs cribbed from her recently published *Peeps at Politicians,* a compilation of pen portraits of her former parliamentary colleagues she had originally published in the *Evening Standard.* As usual, she was ready with a backhanded compliment for Winston Churchill, who she claimed "sits in his place like a large cuckoo which has gotten into the nest of much smaller birds. The House always warms to Churchill, even when disagreeing most violently with him, because he says what he thinks."[23] She may have exaggerated the universality of Churchill's appeal, but the fact that Ellen clearly respected his honesty made it easier for her to work with him in the wartime coalition nine years later.

If Ellen managed not to give offense to her hosts by steering clear of foreign policy, she was less successful when it came to domestic issues. As in New York, "the outspoken comments of Miss Wilkinson" on Canada's lack of provision for the unemployed and the social value of the dole "caused a stir" in the Canadian press, and spurred one indignant Québécois to write a lengthy letter to the *Montreal Gazette* outlining "Red Ellen's" long history of involvement with Communism.[24] Her defence of the dole became more outspoken the more time she spent in North America. After returning from Canada to New York, she made two more trips on her spoke-and-wheel tour of the country. First, she embarked on a second journey south, this time to Baltimore. She then headed west to Michigan, via upstate New York and Ohio. Her Baltimore engagement continued Ellen's tour of grand hotels of North America. She had been scheduled as the keynote speaker at an all-day conference of the Maryland Federation of Women's Clubs, hosted at the glamorous new Lord Baltimore hotel in the port city's downtown district. Although her principal memories were of the impact of unemployment on the country, she could not help but be impressed by her experience of the top end of the American hospitality sector—"Every hotel bedroom has a wireless beside the bed and, when the page boy deposits your luggage in your room, he turns on the wireless at the same time."[25]

Her talk in Baltimore was billed as "Problems of World Unemployment and the Complexes of the Modern Woman," but although she devoted some time to blaming the treaty of Versailles for the current economic mess and encouraging Maryland women to engage in politics, much of her energy was again devoted to unemployment. She deplored the ignorance of educated Americans about British unemployment policy, and claimed the dole was not a handout, but an insurance scheme to which the state, employers and employees each contributed. (Her explanation was true in terms of vested unemployment benefit. However, she conveniently elided the fact that entrenched unemployment had led the government to institute an unvested unemployment assistance scheme, which, however morally justifiable, was essentially a public handout.) As in Montreal, her speech offended certain sectors of Baltimore society, which had expected the British former suffragist would keep more closely to feminist politics.[26]

To judge by the press clippings she kept from her American trip, her fiery rhetoric appears to have gone down better in the Midwest. Talking to audiences on the east coast, Ellen could not be sure of the impact, if any, of her words. Often, it seemed, her predominantly middle-class audiences showed up to her events primarily out of curiosity, especially at women's institutes and other civic clubs where weekly speakers were a regular part of the social calendar. In America's industrial heartland, she discovered a group of men and women whom she described as plain-speaking and warm-hearted, many of whom claimed they had emigrated to the United States from towns in the northeast of England, including her own constituency of Middlesbrough.[27] In Michigan, Ellen again spoke primarily to women's groups, but these women appeared more interested in the state of world socialism and in colonial politics than had their east coast compatriots.[28] She toured the Motor City in the company of local women, and was struck by the number of cars on the roads, even in the financial downturn. It seemed to Ellen that anyone who could afford the cost of gasoline could get their hands on a motorcar in Detroit—an impressive situation to a woman who had saved up for ages for her own Austin Seven.[29]

Her last stop on the speaking tour was Cambridge, Massachusetts, where she spoke at a school of politics (a lecture series open to the public) hosted at Radcliffe College and organized by the state's League of Women Voters. The audience—the largest ever for such an event—listened with patient attention as Ellen explained the intricacies of British unemployment policy.[30] Two days later, she sailed for Britain, departing

Manhattan at night with a beautiful view of "the impressive picture of New York lit up on a bright clear night, with the great skyscrapers as towers of light forming a background."[31] Although she had found much to like in America—from consumer goods to Americans' innate optimism, her experience had made her that much more grateful for the limited social safety net in place in Britain. But, rather than encouraging complacency about the British system, the glaring poverty of the American unemployed had only persuaded her of the need for greater social welfare provision in Britain. It was in that vein that she opposed the Anomalies Act in July. The following month she did not hesitate over whether to remain loyal to the Labour Party or to side with its renegade prime minister.

Shortly after the August 24 crisis, Ellen made her allegiances clear in an article published in Lord Beaverbrook's *Daily Express,* the largest-circulation pro-government paper in the country. Published on the morning parliament first assembled after the crisis, when backbench MPs could expect the new national government to attempt a justification of its policies, Ellen offered a cheeky prophesy of what would take place that day: "In that rich Scotch voice of his, [MacDonald] will hint of deep, dark mysteries, and horrors to make women shudder as they clasp their children to their breasts. But he will tell us precisely nothing of what we really want to know. Mr. Baldwin, with his disarming air of a plain man doing his plain duty, will somehow bring either his Aryan ancestors or the public school spirit into the discussion, but nothing so crudely up to date as the real reason why the world lost confidence in the British pound so suddenly will be allowed to mar the classic beauty of his eloquence." Her reference to the "real reason" was an allusion to the belief, circulating widely in Labour circles, that the Bank of England had engineered the financial crisis to force reform of unemployment insurance. The "bankers' ramp" theory has since been dismissed by historians, but at the time the idea was given credence by the seeming inability of the government to offer a comprehensible explanation for the crisis.[32] Even if the new ministers would not offer any real answers, Ellen made clear she was prepared to demand them. "I for one am going to Parliament this week to fight against sacrifices being offered on any secret altar to the Unknown Gods of World Finance. People have got to be told the truth. . . . The big clash this week will come first on the question whether sacrifices are necessary, and why."

Ellen was determined to remain loyal to the parliamentary opposition now led by Arthur Henderson, but she confessed she was not sure what line the party would take. "The real drama in what remains of this Parliament . . . will be the revealing of the policy of the Labour Party. The country, which is thoroughly bewildered, will await Mr. Henderson's speech with keen interest. That he will not accept the Government's proposals is taken for granted, but people will want to know what exactly are his alternatives."[33] Henderson did not immediately rise to the challenge. He initially appeared to accept MacDonald's promise, made to the members of the former Cabinet on August 24, that the new coalition government would be short-lived.[34] Yet, over the next several weeks, the heightened ill-will and recrimination between MacDonald and his "National Labour" followers and the rump Labour Party weakened lingering hopes for a quick reconciliation. The left wing, including Ellen and the ILP, had long ago rejected orthodox finance. Before August 24, they had been in a minority. That quickly changed. As one historian has concluded, "the bulk of the [Parliamentary Labour Party], including a number of ex-ministers, had been radicalized by the crisis."[35]

Even those who had voted in favour of the cuts, such as Herbert Morrison, soon fell in line with the TUC general council, which contended that the national government was overstating the gravity of the crisis, that Britain did not need to introduce severe budget cuts to prove itself a viable candidate for international investment, and that economic stability could be maintained through increased taxation and a temporary suspension of the "sinking fund" or the allocation of funds to pay down the national debt. The government's focus, they argued, should be on raising the standard of living of the working class through job creation and the protection of wages, not lowering it through benefit cuts. In formulating its critique, the TUC was heavily influenced by the head of the transport union Ernest Bevin, who from 1929 had sat on the Macmillan committee on finance and industry with Keynes. Bevin had taken on board much of Keynes's critique of financial orthodoxy, and in July 1931, when the committee issued its report, the two produced an addendum advocating a state-sponsored program of economic expansion to combat the depression. The TUC's belief that financial austerity was not the answer to depression and unemployment would gain traction in the post-WWII period when so-called Keynesian economics was in its ascendancy. In October 1931, however, Philip Snowden, now the national government chancellor, denounced Labour's policy as "Bolshevism run mad."[36]

Snowden's damning criticism was delivered over the airwaves on October 17, in one of six party election broadcasts by government supporters during the general election campaign. (The Labour opposition, in contrast, were allowed three broadcasts.) Despite MacDonald's assurances to his colleagues that the national government was a temporary expedient, on October 6, he had announced plans for a general election in which the members of the coalition would agree not to oppose one another, and, if returned, to continue to work together on a "national" basis. During the short campaign that followed, the national government representatives used every means at their disposal to discredit the Labour opposition, even suggesting that Labour, if elected, would seize the savings citizens had invested in post office savings accounts. The national government's representatives had the support of the BBC and nearly every organ of the press, except the Labour-owned *Daily Herald*. Ellen, whose own experience writing for the popular press made her particularly sensitive to the power of the media, was quick to blame the press and the BBC for Labour's poor performance.

Personally, Ellen had a friendly relationship with the Conservative press baron Lord Beaverbrook. She wrote frequently for the *Daily Express* and its sister paper, the *Evening Standard*. Both of her novels were serialized in the *Express*, and while in parliament she had published regular parliamentary sketches for the *Standard*. Max Beaverbrook, "brash, irresponsible, amoral and great fun," collected a motley crew of writers and friends over his long career.[37] Ellen was not the only left-winger to write for his papers—Nye Bevan, Jennie Lee, and Michael Foot were other notable Beaverbrook scribes. The press lord even quixotically contributed to the finances of *Tribune*, the left-wing journal Ellen helped to found in 1937.[38]

Lord Beaverbrook's loyalty to his friends meant he did not renege on his agreement to begin serializing *The Division Bell Mystery* (under the title *Crisis*) in the pages of the *Express* on October 13, even though the election campaign was then underway and the serialization would give publicity to a politician whose party's success the paper opposed. Two weeks later, friendship, an impish love of controversy, and a flair for selling papers all drove Beaverbrook to give Ellen and George Lansbury column space to vent their spleen after the national government's landslide election victory on October 27 left Labour with only 52 MPs. Lansbury had retained his seat—the only former cabinet minister to do so; but Ellen lost hers, defeated by over 6,000 votes in a heavy turnout.

Lansbury, who remained an advocate of free trade until the end of his career, devoted the bulk of his article to denouncing the policy of imperial tariffs that had been strongly supported by the Beaverbrook press and prominent members of the national government.[39] Ellen took up the same theme, but only after a strong denunciation of the role of the press, and of Beaverbrook personally, in the campaign. Her article, titled "Well, Lord Beaverbrook, What Now?," began by suggesting Beaverbrook had orchestrated a successful "wind up" of the electorate, in pursuit of his pet policy of imperial tariffs: "I canvassed one of my constituents who with her eight children lived in one room, and as far as I could see slept in one bed. She was terribly distressed about the probable fate of the pound if the Labour Party won. I talked at my street meetings to people who firmly believed that the Labour Ministers had stolen all the peoples' savings in the Post Office. . . . The electorate has been induced at this election to think that it wants tariffs because Lord Beaverbrook has "produced" tariffs, as a Hollywood film director "produces" any other piece of fiction."[40]

Ellen's disgust at Beaverbrook was genuine; but without her parliamentary income, financial exigency quickly forced her to swallow her principles and her pride. Ellen, of course, was still a salaried employee of the National Union of Distributive and Allied Workers (NUDAW); but over the past seven years she had grown accustomed to a larger income, and had taken on significant financial obligations, including not only her Bloomsbury flat and Austin Seven motorcar but also the increasing medical expenses for treating her own and her sister's recurrent respiratory ailments. Rather than trim her expenses, she sought to round out her income through journalism. Her willingness to take up her pen for the "capitalist press" drew scorn from many members of her party. Her NUDAW colleague Rhys Davies was particularly scathing about her journalistic career. When, in a debate over free trade versus protection at the 1932 NUDAW conference, Ellen argued that both were only capitalist "red herrings" meant to distract the workers from socialism, "the true solution," Rhys Davies retorted: "I want to tell Miss Wilkinson that I do not think I am quite so familiar with the capitalist system as she is." The pointed allusion to her relationship with the Beaverbrook press drew a mix of cheers and boos from the audience.[41]

Similar jibes, issued by detractors from both sides of the political spectrum, followed Ellen throughout her career and doubtless took their toll. Although she could console herself that some of her journalism drew popular attention to social and political issues close to her heart, other pieces, like the parliamentary sketches she agreed to write for the *Daily Express* in February 1932, were pure entertainment, with little to no political substance. In 1925, Ellen had been the sole Labour woman MP in the house. In February 1932, she became the first woman gallery correspondent. Her brief stint looking down on her former peers from the lofty vantage of the press gallery did not last long. Ellen was destined to be the subject, not the author, of parliamentary journalism. But her week spent penning lighthearted observations on her former colleagues did lead her to resolve to make one change when and if she were returned to parliament. She would no longer wear short skirts in the house. Ellen had long embraced higher hemlines as a liberating convenience—on a par with "the ever useful jumper"—but from an aerial vantage point, whence calves and ankles were exposed to unflattering advantage, the postwar revolution in women's fashion struck her as profoundly undignified.[42]

If Ellen was unsuited to a career as a gallery correspondent, it wasn't initially clear what she could or should be doing with herself after her election defeat. Her sense of disorientation and drift was magnified by the dissolution of her relationship with Frank Horrabin. By 1931, the pair's six-year affair had become an open secret within the Labour movement. When, in June 1931, Ellen spent a weekend at Passfield corner, Beatrice Webb's diary entry revealed that even the seventy-three-year-old had finally become aware of the two radical MPs' romance.[43] Their relationship continued through the second Labour government, likely propped up by their shared experience as MPs. They shared a personal secretary; and once, when Ellen was suffering from one of her many bouts of illness, Frank reportedly carried her in to her seat in the Commons.[44] Years later, Frank's wife Winifred would draft an embittered letter to him, recalling that "Over the years since 1925, when you told me that you loved Ellen, . . . I tried to apply my reason to the situation between us and NOT to concentrate on feeling hurt *or humiliated* but to make the best of the what I had left of the old, deep, love I still felt for you. *Gossip and rumours from parliament were either not listened to, or denied by me for years, but they did humiliate me, and make me unhappy.*"[45] During the 1931 campaign, Ellen and Frank again spoke on election platforms together, including a "crowded out" meeting at the Temperance Hall in Woodford.[46] But after both lost their seats, things fell apart.

Ellen had expressed uncertainty about the propriety of the relationship in her conversation with Beatrice Webb the previous summer, but it was Frank who ended it, having transferred his affections from Ellen to Margaret McWilliams, their shared secretary, whom he would ultimately marry in 1948. In a brutal letter written to Winifred while the two were negotiating their separation, Frank gave vent to his long-held disillusionment with their marriage: "18 years ago, . . . I fell in love with Ellen; and the fact that I 'fell out' of love with her six years later, and 'in love' with Margaret, didn't in any way alter the fact that I had, by falling in love with someone else in the first place, fallen out of love with you."[47] Frank's "falling out" of love hit Ellen like "a sudden and overwhelming bereavement which knocked me flat."[48] More than a year later, Ellen confided to her former parliamentary colleague Jennie Lee that she was still mourning Frank.[49] The former couple continued to work together on several causes and ultimately were able to remain friends. Yet in the immediate term, Ellen understandably wanted to put some distance between herself and her former lover, a situation that temporarily alienated her from many of the social and activist groups in which she might have found purpose and solace in the wake of her dual loss.

Ellen continued her organizing work for NUDAW, but the harsh economic climate and the seeming impotence of the unions in the aftermath of the 1927 Trade Disputes and Trade Unions Act mitigated against efforts at unionization. Overall union membership fell from over 5.2 million in 1926 to under 4.4 million in 1933.[50] With trade union activity failing to fill the void once occupied by parliament and love, Ellen turned her energies to the two other causes with which she had long been closely enmeshed: feminism and international social and political reform.

Ellen had never abandoned her commitment either to the improvement of women's position at home or to the international women's peace movement. Yet once out of parliament, she did give much more of her time and energy to both the Women's International League (WIL) and the feminist journal *Time and Tide*. Women's activism had a renewed appeal in the face of the national government's dominance of the political stage. As she wrote in January 1933, "*Time & Tide* has been a big thing to me this last two months or so. Politics have become so barren somehow."[51] Her involvement with both these organizations brought her into closer contact with two women who would become Ellen's close friends in the 1930s: Vera Brittain and Winifred Holtby.

The two women were Ellen's near-contemporaries—Brittain was two years her junior, and Holtby three years older. Vera Brittain is best remembered as the author of *Testament of Youth*, her moving autobiographical account published in 1933 of the effect of the Great War on a generation of British men and women. Vera's experience of war, both as a participant—she served as a nurse on the Western Front—and as a bereaved family member—she lost both her fiancé and her brother—pointed her toward what became a lifelong pacifism. She retained her pacifist commitment through the Second World War, even in the face of public censure.[52] Her commitment to the peace movement and her experiences on the front also shaped her domestic politics; and both she and her husband, political scientist George Catlin, were members of the Labour Party.

Before marrying Catlin, Vera had embarked on what would become an exceptional lifelong friendship with Winifred Holtby, her contemporary at Somerville College, Oxford. Holtby, who never married, had a prolific literary career before her early death in 1935. She was a regular contributor to, and sometimes editor for, *Time and Tide* and the author of several novels, including the anti-imperial satire *Mandoa, Mandoa!* Her posthumously published *South Riding*, a novel about love and municipal government reform with a radical redheaded heroine, was partially inspired by Ellen. After university, the young graduates briefly shared a flat around the corner from Ellen's Bloomsbury apartment. Although the three women travelled in many of the same circles in the late 1920s, they did not become friends until the following decade.

Ellen first got to know Vera and George Catlin through the Labour movement. During the second Labour government, George had been adopted as a candidate for Brentford and Chiswick, a safe Conservative seat he lost in 1931. Vera and their mutual friend Margaret Rhondda acted as intermediaries in introducing Ellen and Winifred. Shortly after the 1931 general election, Vera reported to Winifred that Ellen had told Lady Rhondda about a new drug called Hypotensyl used to treat high blood pressure, from which Winifred suffered. Winifred took the initiative and wrote to Ellen to ask about the new treatment. Ellen's reply reflected her keenness to forge a friendship with the talented author. She began formally—"Dear Miss Holtby . . . how glad I would be if I could be of use in any way." She then confessed she didn't know much about Hypotensyl other than that she had seen at "an exhibition of new products made from pigs," which she had attended at her union's behest. But she offered to ask the "wallah who took us round" for more information on the product. Her eager and chatty letter ended on a note of flattery. Referring to the series of articles she was recently commissioned to write for *Time and Tide,* she said she was "awfully glad to be helping," but feared she would not be able to live up to a standard set "by folk like you and Rebecca West and Rose Macaulay."[53]

Over the next few years, a warm friendship grew between the two women. Ellen included Winifred on her gift list when shopping for souvenirs from her India trip that autumn, bringing her back a little statuette as a Christmas present.[54] Winifred in return gave Ellen an autographed copy of her new novel *Mandoa, Mandoa!,* which Ellen declared *"great* . . . just genius"—an assessment no doubt encouraged by Holtby's fleeting reference to Ellen in the novel, which left the former MP "touched beyond words . . . I feel as tho I'd been given a medal."[55] (Early in the novel, the distracted guests at an election party respond to the news that "Ellen Wilkinson's out," by exclaiming "No, not *possible!*"[56]) The following summer, Winifred offered to arrange for Ellen and Annie to rent the rooms she normally stayed in for a holiday in Surrey—Ellen instead rented a furnished cottage, which she professed to have been a mistake—"much better to have a nice landlady like you seem to have collected and whose address I have duly noted. I'd rather cope with a crisis in the world's affairs than one mess of dishes on a cottage sink, wouldn't you? Or am I utterly depraved?"[57] The lighthearted tone of their correspondence indicates the quick intimacy that had grown between the two women, an intimacy Ellen, who did not have many close female friends, clearly cherished.

Ellen also began spending more time with two older women with whom she had frequently disagreed but who shared her passionate belief in women's rights: Margaret Rhondda and Nancy Astor. Lady Rhondda, whose garden party she had once felt it necessary to issue a public denial that she had attended, was now a close confidant, so much so that, as Ellen confided to Holtby, "I feel rather ashamed when I've left her. I feel as tho I've talked her head off. She would have made a wonderful psychoanalyst."[58] Outside of the political spotlight, it was possible for the socialist firebrand and the coal heiress to share an intimacy Ellen would have found problematic before October 1931. The same held for Ellen's friendship with Nancy Astor. After Ellen's father's death in 1929, Astor had done her a quiet kindness that the younger woman did not forget. Yet although the friendship between the two women had deepened, Ellen did not visit Cliveden, Astor's resplendent weekend home in Surrey, until after she had ceased to be an MP. It is unlikely Nancy had never before invited Ellen—the American heiress cared little for convention, and her weekend guests spanned the political and professional spectrum. For Ellen the Labour MP, accounting for such an indulgence would have been politically problematic. Yet, between January 1932 and January 1933, Ellen the private citizen stayed at the estate three times, in motley company that included Alison Neilsons, the ex-suffragette and member of the executive committee of the Women's Freedom League; Robin Barrington-Ward, the politically conservative leader writer for the *Times*; and Labour's former secretary of state for India Wedgwood Benn.[59] The January 1933 visit was to be Ellen's last until the outbreak of the war, however. From summer 1932 onwards, Ellen became an active member of the international campaign against German fascism. The Astor family, in contrast, argued for international tolerance of the Nazi regime; and their Buckinghamshire estate became known as a meeting place for the so-called Cliveden set, a group of Germanophiles including Barrington-Ward and several members of the journalistic and political establishment. Although Ellen maintained a personal affection for Nancy, her deepening commitment to the anti-fascist cause kept her away from Cliveden in the 1930s.

In her postmortem analysis of the general election written for the *Daily Express,* Ellen had prophesied that Prime Minister MacDonald was "sure to be taking an aeroplane to somewhere when it appears as though he had been at last cornered."[60] In the end, Ellen's frustration at Britain's bleak political situation and her own impotence to affect it ultimately drove her to leave—first to Germany and later to India—on journeys that would refocus her political energies outside the British Isles.

10

ON THE INTERNATIONAL STAGE

Since her election to parliament in 1924, Ellen's attention had been focused primarily on domestic affairs. Yet she had maintained contact with many of the men and women she had first met through the Comintern and international women's peace movement in the heady optimism of the immediate postwar period. She also forged new contacts that would play a key role in her life as the war against fascism took centre stage in the 1930s.

In 1929, Ellen and her sister, Annie, served as delegates to the sixth congress of the Women's International League for Peace and Freedom (WILPF), which was held in the medieval city of Prague in August. Annie was still working as secretary of the Manchester branch of the Women's International League (WIL), having returned to work in

February after a long illness and several weeks spent in a sanatorium in Holland—a treatment Nancy Astor may have helped Ellen pay for.[1] The congress, held in the modernist Center for Agricultural Education in the new neighbourhood east of the main railway station, proved a beacon of calm, level-headed debate.

The Wilkinson sisters joined twenty-five other women in the British delegation, matched in numbers by the Germans and Americans. Several of the German women present would later be forced into exile or imprisoned by the Nazis, including Magda Hoppstuck-Huth, who fled to England in 1934 and led an international campaign against the regime before returning to Germany to face imprisonment during the war. The French delegation was significantly smaller. Only six French women attended, including two who would go on to play a central role in lobbying the WILPF to take a hard line against European fascism in the 1930s, Camille Drevet and Gabrielle Duchêne.

Gabrielle Duchêne was the most controversial figure in the interwar French feminist movement. The grey-haired fifty-nine-year-old described herself as possessing "a natural, organic predisposition toward independence," which frequently undermined her efforts at cooperation with other feminists. One biographer has described her as "an enigma even to her closest associates, who at times described her as both a hero and villain, a kind, compassionate woman and an 'iron lady,' a person of great vision, and yet one blinded by her unwavering faith in Stalin and the Soviet Union."[2] Ellen and Duchêne, both involved in the Comintern-backed League Against Imperialism (LAI), each presented papers on the challenges of settling social disputes within national borders that highlighted their socialist sympathies and the broadening political remit of an association ostensibly concerned with international affairs. Duchêne took as her theme the relevance of conciliation and arbitration—the methods for resolving conflicts endorsed in the WILPF's constitution—in reference to internal disputes. She admitted she did "not entirely share the unlimited confidence of some people in conciliation and arbitration, even for international conflicts" and gave as an example the bias of most of the international community against the Soviet Union. She reminded her listeners that "the class struggle is more a fact than a doctrine, and will exist as long as society is divided into classes. . . . It is therefore somewhat out of place for those who belong to the privileged classes to talk of Social Peace." In defence of the right to strike, she demanded of her colleagues, "Have we the right to ask the victims of injustice to accept the indefinite postponement of the satisfaction of their just claims so that there may be apparent peace . . . ?"[3] If Duchêne's advanced age and middle-class circumstances helped soften the radical effect of her rhetoric, the same could not be said for Ellen, whose working-class background and comparative youth—at thirty-seven she was one of the younger women at the conference—only underscored her revolutionary message.

Ellen similarly attacked the efficacy of conciliation and arbitration, although on the broader socialist grounds that "in these days of the beginning of a world society the workers are realizing, as finance-capital has done, that they can no longer think effectively in terms of their own nation's industries. . . . Thus, with strong international trade union organization to secure international standards must go strong political movements to secure control of Governmental machinery. If both of these are inspired by Socialist ideals, by the aim of replacing capitalism by a Socialist state, then and then only can stable peace, both national and international, be hoped for." Ellen made clear how she envisaged the WILPF and the socialist movement working in concert: "Such organizations as the WIL can reach people who are quite out of touch and out of sympathy with labour, and show them the real root difficulties in the way of peace."[4] She considered herself a pacifist, but, unlike many other interwar peace activists (including her sister), for Ellen the causes of peace and socialism were inextricably intertwined. Ultimately, the conference did not endorse a resolution on international social conflict. Yet when Ellen travelled to the United States on her speaking tour in 1931, her lectures to American WILPF branches and other women's organizations included frequent references to her view that social reform was a prerequisite for peace.

In years to come, Ellen and Duchêne would meet at countless international antiwar conferences, many orchestrated by Comintern impresario Willi Münzenberg. Already they had crossed paths at the LAI conference in Brussels in 1927. Both would become intimately involved in Münzenberg's next grand international scheme, the so-called Amsterdam-Pleyel movement, which brought together an eclectic cosmopolitan group of intellectuals and activists in opposition to "imperialist war." Unlike Duchêne, Ellen did not attend the original Amsterdam congress, as she was travelling through India in August 1932 on a fact-finding tour in support of Indian independence. She was, however, at the second meeting of the group at the Salle Pleyel in Paris in June 1933, by which point the movement had shifted its focus from Asia to Europe, reorienting its pacifist campaign from imperialist war to fascist aggression.

Over the course of the 1930s, many supporters of the Amsterdam-Pleyel movement, including Ellen, Duchêne, and their frequent collaborator Romain Rolland, would move away from pacifism towards a more muscular defence of democracy.[5] Ellen's journey away from pacifism began in July 1932, when she first visited Germany. She had, of course, read reports of the rise of Nazism with mounting alarm. Her time spent in Germany electioneering on behalf of the Social Democratic Iron Front opened her eyes to the existential threat Nazism posed. Over the next decade, she would devote the full force of her extraordinary propagandist talent to raising awareness of the fascist threat.

Ellen's trip to Germany had been intended as a much-deserved holiday. In retrospect, Germany in July 1932 would strike few as an attractive vacation destination. Reichstag elections were scheduled for the end of the month, and the country was caught up in virtual civil war. On June 15, Nazi stormtroopers (SA), the paramilitary organization led by Ernst Röhm that had been banned by the government in April, had been allowed back onto the streets. The new German chancellor, Franz Von Papen, did not share his predecessor's anxieties that the organization posed a threat to government and the rule of law; and he mistakenly believed he could co-opt the SA to his own authoritarian ends. The SA and other reactionary paramilitary organizations formed a force three-quarters of a million strong.[6] Once rehabilitated, they promptly launched a series of violent attacks on suspected Communists, including women and children, and engaged in street fighting with members of the two left-wing paramilitary groups, the Social Democratic *Reichsbanner* and the Communist Red Front. One historian has described the July 1932 elections as "Germany's most frenetic and most violent election campaign yet, fought in an atmosphere even less rational and more vicious than that of two years before."[7]

Yet when Ellen made her travel plans that spring, the rapid devolution of the German political situation would have been difficult to predict. The long-serving chancellor Heinrich Brüning was still in power. Although he was governing the country largely by decree, Brüning was able to rely on support from the Social Democrats and the Catholic Centre party in the Reichstag. The British, French, and Germans were preparing to meet in Lausanne to discuss a further modification of Germany's World War I reparations payments; and the German republic, although bruised and fragile, seemed poised to survive.

Artistically avant-garde, with a vibrant theatre and cabaret culture and a much more open attitude towards sexuality and self-expression than Britain, Weimar Germany offered an alluring prospect of hedonistic escape, famously chronicled by Christopher Isherwood. Berlin was not the type of city to look askance at two unmarried lovers travelling together, and it is likely Ellen had planned for Frank to join her for at least part of her holiday. However, before she left for Germany, Frank broke the bitter news that he was leaving her for Margaret McWilliams. In her heartbreak, she lost some of her enthusiasm for the impending holiday. But her regular itinerary of public appearances seemed unendurable, and an escape to the continent appeared the lesser of two evils. So she confirmed her travel plans and began studying up on the basics of the language.[8] She also, fatefully, wrote to her friend Frederick Voigt, the *Manchester Guardian*'s Berlin correspondent, to let him know she was planning to visit the country.

The social circles of the British literary and political left were intimate and gossipy; and even if Ellen had not told Voigt of her recent breakup, it is likely he had heard about Frank's shift of affections. He suggested to Ellen that she give over part of her holiday to the German elections. Ellen claimed to find the prospect of public speaking impossible in her current "bereaved" state, but anyone who knew the fiery redhead knew that the high she invariably felt in front of an audience was a better cure than self-pity.[9]

The *Guardian* journalist, who had been in Germany since 1920, did not believe the elections would result in "fascism in the Polish or Italian sense." In his letter to Ellen, he was disparaging about the leadership on the right. He dismissed Von Papen as "a horrible creature, small and mean, an insect clogged with the dust of a dead past and swollen with accumulated rancour." Hitler he characterized as "a traveling showman with a booming voice and inwardly so paralysed by dark fears and apprehensions that he is totally incapacitated except when he can boom away. His booming has filled both himself and his hearers with a portentous bravura that carries him and them into a drunken ecstasy of sadistic revivalism." Voigt's contempt for the right did not translate into optimism about the political fortunes of the left. He was convinced that the recent formation of the Iron Front—a working coalition of the Social Democratic Party (SDP), the trade unions, and the paramilitary *Reichsbanner*—had "arrested the decline of the Socialist Party." But, despite the new organization, he emphasized the German workers felt abandoned by the international community. "Some recognition, some sign of solidarity coming from the British Labour movement would have the most heartening effect here," he wrote. "It would reach the remotest villages, and would do something to relieve the isolation so great that I can hardly understand how they endure it."

Ellen was a born propagandist, and she doubtless would have consented to speak on a few Iron Front platforms even without further prodding. What decided her to give the entire trip over to electioneering was Voigt's description of German workers, especially those living outside the major cities:

> In villages and small towns [wherever] there are perhaps one or two factories there will be a handful of workmen (mostly unemployed) in permanent danger of being beaten up, and knowing perfectly well that at any moment there may be a general armed rising in which they at least are doomed, whatever may happen in the big cities. They are like a few pioneers— pioneers of the idea, only without any glory, recognition or reward, in a hostile country and amid a malignant population. They will sometimes show you the graves of friends, relatives or comrades killed in resisting the counter-revolution of 1920, which was smashed in Berlin. This they will do with full awareness (never expressed, because taken for granted) that they themselves may be under the ground tomorrow.[10]

Voigt was sincere, but his letter self-consciously laid it on thick. Anyone who knew Ellen at all appreciated her instinctive human sympathy; she was more easily moved by personal suffering than by abstract rhetoric. Temporarily forgetting her own woes, Ellen typed out a copy of her friend's letter and sent it to Labour Party headquarters, expressing her intent to work on the German campaign and asking if the party could provide the sign of solidarity Voigt argued would do the German workers such good. The ensuing back and forth between Ellen; the head of the Labour Party's international department, William Gillies; and the SDP underscores just how isolated and abandoned the SDP felt by their British comrades. Gillies agreed to arrange for an official statement to be issued by the British movement in conjunction with Ellen's trip. The statement, signed by Walter Citrine for the trade unions, George Lathan for the National Executive Committee (NEC), and George Lansbury for the Parliamentary Labour Party, was addressed to "Our comrades of the German Social Democratic Party" and began by praising the SDP's "magnificent fight for Socialism, Freedom and Peace." It went on to assert that the SDP were "fighting not only the battle of the German workers, but our battle—the battle of Socialism the world over."[11] The SDP were pleased to have the letter, but wanted a telegraphed confirmation of its authenticity in the event someone from the British movement later attempted to repudiate it. They took the same attitude towards the proposed presentation by Ellen of a flag sewn by British Labour women declaring "Three Cheers for the Iron Front from the British Labour Party." Although Gillies assured the SDP that "there was no danger of repudiation," the Party was not prepared to allow Ellen to present the flag unless it was given official written sanction by the Labour movement.[12] The SDP's anxiety and arguable paranoia reflected the heightened stakes of the July election contest. Ellen would be the first British politician ever to speak on the German hustings.[13] The propaganda potential of such a coup was significant, but the Party could not afford the potential humiliation of the British Labour movement subsequently distancing itself from Red Ellen's sure-to-be-fiery remarks.

German electioneering propaganda was known for being more creative than its British counterpart—the Labour Party had sought advice from the SDP before the 1929 general election on the use of portable cinema trucks and gramophone records in election campaigns.[14] Although Ellen was aware of this, she was not prepared for the spectacle that awaited her when she arrived in Munich on July 16. As one historian of German propaganda has written, "The staging of identities through a war of political symbolism took the place of real debate."[15] Or as Ellen more prosaically observed, "Argument has been swept aside in this election...the contending parties conduct their campaigns with rival spectacles of magnificent pageantry."[16] The Nazis, of course, had their swastikas, brown shirts, and Heil Hitler address. The Social Democratic Iron Front, in turn, had their "three arrows," blue uniforms, and raised-fisted *Freiheit* (Freedom) salute; while the Communists boasted the hammer and sickle, red flags and costumes, and Comrade greeting. Historians have dismissed the three downward sloping arrows that formed the Iron Front insignia as "fail[ing] to capture the popular imagination," but for Ellen the ubiquity of the symbol was remarkable.[17] She marvelled at the ingenuity of the Iron Front in printing the logo on small coloured stickers to be worn on lapels or plastered over enemy posters. And she thrilled at the risk she and several young Iron Front women took one night, running through the streets of Berlin chalking the three arrows over Nazi swastikas on city walls.[18]

Ellen was immediately impressed by the political engagement of the German women compared with their British counterparts. Coming from Britain, where even during the general strike physical violence remained more a threat than a reality, she initially failed to comprehend the existential nature of the German contest. Shortly after she arrived, Ellen and a companion (likely Voigt) went as spectators to a Nazi demonstration. Thinking she was making a sporting protest against Hitler's party, Ellen set off wearing her Iron Front three arrows sticker. Her friend cautioned her to remove the badge. "'And if I don't?' 'You will probably be killed,'" he answered quietly. She removed her sticker to oblige her companion but quickly realized he was not joking. Inside the Nazi auditorium, she found herself surrounded by a group of middle-class women, impoverished by inflation and "raging at their altered status." "I thought I had seen this type at its worst when a group of fur coated women in Middlesbrough caught me alone in a quiet street during the last election campaign and hammered me with the steel frame of their handbags," she wrote. "But these women, worked up by a magnificent, revivalist speech and the chanting of the Nazi anthem . . . would have lynched me had they seen the Three Arrows."[19]

After a day in Munich, Ellen travelled by train to Berlin on Sunday, July 17, in preparation for the big rally on Tuesday at which she would present the Labour Party's message and the women's flag. She arrived in the pouring rain and was met by a group of several hundred Iron Front women and a detachment of police, dispatched to ensure the SA did not attempt to forcibly break up the event.[20] At the same time that Ellen disembarked in Berlin, less than 200 miles away in Altona, a working-class suburb of Hamburg, a violent altercation was raging between Nazi stormtroopers and Communist Red Front fighters. The street fighting was broken up by police, who, in a panic, opened fire on the civilians. The episode left eighteen dead and over one hundred wounded. Although later evidence revealed that most of the dead and wounded had been shot by police bullets, the carnage provided further ammunition in the propaganda war between the Communists and the Nazis.[21]

In the past Ellen had supported the Communists, and she would in future work with Communists in Germany and internationally in the fight against fascism. In 1932, however, her sympathies lay wholeheartedly with the SDP. The German Communists, under instructions from Moscow, were espousing the rhetoric of "Social Fascism," an ideology that viewed the constitutionalist Social Democrats as equally as, if not more, dangerous than the fascists, on the grounds that their support for the existing capitalist system threatened the spread of the revolution. The Communists' emphasis on Social Fascism drove a bitter wedge between the two working-class parties and weakened resistance to Hitler. Their mutual antipathy renders suspect the contention printed in the London *Times* (an increasingly pro-Nazi paper) that many of the men and women who attended the SDP rally on Tuesday wore "with the three arrows the badge of the 'Anti-Fascist Front,' in which the Communists are the main moving element."[22] The *Times*'s assertion was further undermined by the report of the rally in the British Communist *Daily Worker.* Inspired by the same Social Fascist policy as the German CP, the *Worker* claimed that Ellen was "adept at using 'Left' phrases as a cover for the utmost treachery," and that the SDP, like the British

Labour Party, was "making increasing use of this type of demagogue to gull the workers into the belief that they really are 'opposing' the rising capitalist offensive."[23]

With or without significant Communist attendance, the Berlin rally drew nearly 20,000 men and women. Held in a large hall in a pleasure garden south of the city, it was, Ellen claimed, "the most impressive spectacle I have seen outside of Russia."[24] She stood before the massive crowd in a cloche hat and blue blouse with a three arrows band around her left arm. Behind her, two *Reichsbanner* officials held aloft the large flag the British Labour women had made.[25] She was able to make a few opening remarks in German before switching over to English, and although few listeners understood the speech, the crowd applauded her enthusiastically, shouting *"Freiheit!"* with raised fists before breaking into the *Internationale*.[26]

The next day the chancellor used the pretext of the Altona riot to place Prussia—the dominant state in Germany, containing two-thirds of the population and the capital city of Berlin—under presidential control and declared martial law in the capital. If Ellen retained any illusions that German politics was merely a hypersaturated analog to its British counterpart, her experience in Germany over the next several days proved to her otherwise. She made speeches on SDP platforms around the country, focusing her efforts on industrial cities such as Waldenberg, centre of the coal and porcelain industries in Upper Silesia.[27] In Silesia, she met a Catholic priest and a "frankly free-thinking doctor" working to save an experiment in children's homes and special flats for consumptives against a Nazi attack on such so-called cultural Bolshevism and was left with the sense she was witnessing an existential fight "between an old way of life and a new one."[28] Writing for the *Daily Herald* the day after martial law was declared, Ellen recorded the tense atmosphere in the offices of *Vörwarts,* the SDP newspaper, as she and SDP leader Rudolf Breitscheid headed off for a workers' military demonstration at Brandenburg: "The question is being asked, 'Will Breitscheid come back alive?'"[29] (Breitscheid would emigrate to France a year later, where he was ultimately arrested by the Nazis, and would die in Buchenwald concentration camp.)

Despite the intensity of her itinerary, Ellen carved out time to relax and socialize in Berlin, which both helped her overcome her heartbreak and gave her an opportunity to forge new and lasting friendships with men and women who would form the vanguard of the anti-Fascist campaign. The social circle of Frederick Voigt and his wife, American journalist Margaret Goldsmith, consisted principally of other foreign correspondents and writers and artists based in the Berlin neighbourhood of Charlottenburg and was regularly found among the cafes on the Kurfürstendamm. It was a bohemian group—Margaret had had a brief affair with Vita Sackville-West when Vita came through Berlin a few years earlier[30]—that charmed Ellen while simultaneously impressing upon her the danger facing German society from the Nazi menace.

On one of Ellen's first nights in Berlin, a friend of the Voigts took her sailing on the Wannsee: "The night was moonless . . . quite dark but for the stars. The water was so still that the stars were beneath our boat as well as above it. The sails seemed to be carrying us . . . not on water, but through the Ultimate Peace. He sat, a silhouette at the tiller, and I huddled under wraps at the prow. . . . No word was spoken till the dawn broke; Then . . . 'Here's a bargee's cafe open. What about some boiling hot coffee?'"[31] The evening was a perfect tonic for Ellen.

Her newfound friends threw parties in the evenings to introduce her to others of their set.[32] She met Bauhaus artists and professed an admiration for the modernist austerity of their design. She befriended Jews who within the year would flee the city, many for a life of poverty and enforced idleness in émigré Paris. It may have been at one of these parties that she first met Gustav Regler, the pacifist novelist whose work she had long admired. During the day, when not on the platform, Ellen and her new friends observed the spectacle of Nazi rallies, visited caravan communes established by the unemployed, and talked politics. They schooled her in the recent history of Germany and the economic hardships that had pushed the German petit bourgeois into the arms of the Nazis. Those lessons, combined with conversations with embittered Germans, helped convince her that Nazism could just as easily come to Britain if the economic situation became sufficiently dire.

Ellen left Berlin before election day, July 31, and was not there to see the Nazis more than double their voting strength to 13.1 million, giving them 37.4 percent of the vote, and 230 seats in the Reichstag. In contrast, the SDP lost a net total of 10 seats and, with 133 deputies, was dwarfed by the Nazis. The Socialists' poor performance was brought into further relief by the Communists, who raised their representation from 77 to 89 deputies. If others around Europe needed time to fully appreciate the implications of the election result, Ellen was clear that it spelled the triumph of "nationalism [and] racism gone mad."[33]

The imminent threat of Fascism in Europe partially eclipsed the anti-imperialist campaigns of the 1920s. Yet, despite her anti-Fascist work, she maintained a commitment to the campaign for Indian self-government. By 1927, Ellen was already sufficiently concerned about the injustices of the British Empire to attend the inaugural meeting of the League Against Imperialism, and to agree to serve on the British executive committee. Marxist-Leninist theory emphasized the importance of the self-determination of nations, a key tenet of the Bolsheviks' early calls for an international workers' revolution. The LAI was founded in 1927 with this spirit in mind, although it quickly devolved into a Communist front organization that demanded its members follow Stalin's line in opposing all "Social Fascist" parties, Socialist as well as Liberal. In both Britain and India, advocates of Indian independence were forced to make a choice to support the LAI or leave the organization. Ellen's decision to resign from the League echoed her decision to distance herself from the Communist Party of Great Britain (CPGB) and to align herself with the SDP against the Communists in the 1932 Reichstag election campaign. Yet, her departure from the LAI was not merely a kneejerk repudiation of Stalinist authoritarianism. Ellen had become increasingly involved with a group of individuals and organizations that closely supported the Indian National Congress (INC). By the early 1930s, she had come to believe that the only path to Indian independence lay through the Congress movement.

The 1919 Government of India Act established a limited role for the Indian population in local government administration and called for a commission of inquiry to revisit the question of Indian government reform within a decade. By the time Stanley Baldwin's Conservative government appointed an all-party commission, known as the Simon Commission, to propose suggestions for Indian government reform in 1927, the INC had undertaken a national civil disobedience campaign demanding India be granted dominion status along the same lines as Australia and Canada. The government, in turn, responded by suspending civil liberties and introducing rule by ordinance, or direct order, in many parts of the Raj. When, in November 1930, Ramsay MacDonald's government convened what would become known as the first Round Table Conference to discuss the constitutional reforms proposed by the Simon Commission, the INC refused to participate on the grounds that the proposals did not include dominion status, and the India League supported that decision. It soon became clear that the talks could not produce a workable settlement without the participation of the INC, and, after prolonged negotiations between Gandhi and Viceroy Lord Irwin, the INC agreed to send Gandhi as its sole representative to a second Round Table Conference, convened in London in September 1931. That round of talks, as well as a third round a year later, similarly failed to reach a consensus.

The organization with the strongest influence on Ellen's thinking about Indian policy in the 1920s was the Women's International League (WIL). The WIL had long argued that the recognition of self-rule in both Ireland and India was the most important contribution the British Empire could make to international peace.[34] After publication of the American journalist Katherine Mayo's blockbuster exposé *Mother India* in 1927, which posited that practices such as child marriage illustrated India's unfitness for self-government, the WIL did not follow the lead of some British feminists in supporting calls for British intervention and reform of Indian misgovernment.[35] Instead they argued, alongside Indian female reformers, that *Mother India* highlighted the necessity for Indian women to have a say in their own government. Ellen was not a member of the WIL's India subcommittee, yet the influence of the WIL's critique is visible in a letter she wrote to fellow MP Eleanor Rathbone in September 1929, explaining her refusal to sign a proposed letter to the *Times* regarding child marriage in India: "I think the danger when you have one country governing another, such as is the case of either Ireland or India, however well-intentioned the people of the governing country and however necessary the reform may be, is that it tends to make the governed elevate the abuse into a principle to be maintained against the oppressor, as they consider it. . . . I feel that a word from Gandhi could not only do a thousand times more good than any letter in 'the Times', but such a letter could be positively harmful in so far as it seems to press a reform upon them by an alien race."[36] The letter illustrates how completely Ellen accepted the argument that Indian reforms must arise through the popular consent of the population. Although she lacked personal familiarity with India, her political analysis reflected that which she and her WIL colleagues had brought to Irish politics a decade earlier.

Although Ellen never became a member of the WIL's India subcommittee, her sister, Annie, briefly did. After their father's death, Annie moved from Manchester to London, where she continued her involvement with the WIL, serving for a year on the organization's National Executive Committee (NEC) and sitting on the NEC's India subcommittee. Although the WIL's politics were more pro-self-government than specifically pro-Congress, in practice the organization developed close ties with the Congress movement. During the second series of Round Table Conferences in 1931, the India subcommittee invited several Indian women to attend its meetings. The two most frequent guests were the family planning pioneer and wife of the Indian secretary to the Round Table Conference (RTC), Dhanvanthi Handoo Rama Rau, and Sarojini Nehru, a leader of the Women's Indian Association, an Indian suffrage movement with ties to the Congress Party. The Indian women and the WIL members worked in cooperation to raise the profile of the Indian women's movement in Britain.[37]

At the time that Annie served on the WIL's India subcommittee, she was also acting as treasurer of the more radical India League. If the WIL was the greatest influence on Ellen's thinking about India in the 1920s, it was the India League that informed her approach to Indian politics in the 1930s. At an early point in her career, her friendship with Conrad Noel and George Lansbury had brought her into contact with the Christian Socialist critique of the brutalities of the Empire.[38] Within the trade union movement, her boss and close friend, John Jagger, also took an exceptional interest in colonial affairs, having begun his career in business in India, Burma, and China. Frank Horrabin, too, was closely concerned with imperial issues. Noel, Lansbury, Jagger, and Horrabin were members of the London-based India League, which supported the INC's calls for *swaraj*, or self-rule, within the British Empire; and it was through their influence that Ellen joined the League in the early 1930s. By then, the group had thirteen branches in London and another thirteen around Britain.[39] Although a formal relationship between Congress and the League was denied by both sides, the Government of India insisted the League was heavily financed by Madan Mohan Malaviya, president of the Congress Party in 1932–1933; and one local branch chairman later referred to the League as "the Sister Organization of the Congress Party in India."[40] The Home Office would later suspect Krishna Menon, the League's charismatic secretary, of links with the Comintern, but his loyalty remained to Congress.[41] In the early 1930s, the British Communist Party denounced him as a "lackey for the Labour Party" and claimed that "the India League was not interested in furthering the Indian struggle but in smothering it."[42] After Indian independence, Menon would serve in Nehru's government first as High Commissioner to the United Kingdom and later as India's representative to the United Nations and Minister of Defence.

The India League rented offices on the Strand, a stone's throw from the offices where Ellen had once attended meetings of the Red International of Labour Unions years earlier. During the second series of Round Table Conferences in 1931, the group had entertained Gandhi and the other unofficial members of the Congress delegation. Ellen first met Gandhi at this time. At a meeting the Mahatma held with Labour MPs, Ellen proved sceptical of the policy of boycotting machine-made British cotton, asking him whether "it was not a reactionary policy to refuse to use the inventions of science" to improve Indians' standard of living.[43] Although Gandhi attempted to assuage her concerns about the aims of his homespun campaign, the policy clearly sat ill with his Mancunian interlocutor. Ellen nonetheless warmed to Gandhi during his visit, and a friendship was forged in the intimacy of the Horrabins' Bloomsbury flat, where the Congress leader spent late nights talking policy with members of the India League.[44]

While the RTC was still in session in London, the first of a series of ordinances was issued in India that together prohibited free speech and association and curtailed habeas corpus rights in most regions. In December 1931, Jawaharlal Nehru was arrested and remained imprisoned until August 1933. In January 1932, shortly after his return from London, Gandhi was arrested. In the first three months of 1932, nearly 40,000 Indians, mostly supporters of the Congress movement, were detained under the ordinances. In the context of the renewed political oppression, the

League decided to send a delegation to India to gather information and hopefully visit and report on the state of the imprisoned population.

The delegation was initially conceived by Mirabehn (Madeleine Slade), the aristocratic English woman who became one of Gandhi's closest associates.[45] After much consultation, the League settled on a delegation of two men and two women: the League's secretary, Krishna Menon; ex-Labour MP Leonard Matters; former suffragette Monica Whately; and Ellen. Ellen was eager to go not only for professional but for personal reasons—her friend and fellow MP Leah Manning later recalled she "went to Indian to try to forget [Frank Horrabin]."[46] But, unlike the other three, she had commitments at home that made a three-month journey to India problematic. Fortunately, Jagger arranged for her to take an unpaid leave of absence from her union work.[47]

Neither the Indian Government nor the India Office at home was enthusiastic about the proposed delegation. The government debated denying Matters's request to renew his passport, anxious about his "deep pink connections" and his history as a contributor to the *Moscow Daily News*. Ultimately they concluded that "he is not a personage of importance and no doubt will be under the female thumbs," and so decided to let him go.[48] It was less Whately's influence that concerned the India Office than Ellen's, as "Miss Wilkinson would presumably be the moving spirit whoever else goes!"[49] But prohibiting Ellen from making the journey would, they appreciated, be politically problematic, and all four received their visas successfully. On August 5, after a long train journey and a few days spent in Italy, the group set off on the two-week steamer voyage, embarking at Venice, passing through the Suez Canal and finally arriving at the bustling port of Bombay (modern-day Mumbai). Although Ellen and Monica travelled second class, the men made the journey in steerage to save on travel expenses.[50]

The ship reached Bombay on August 17. Over the next three months, the group would cover 12,000 miles, travelling from Bengal south to Pune and across to Madras (modern-day Chennai), up the east coast to Calcutta, north to Delhi and up through the Punjab to Simla and Lahore into the North-West Frontier Province (NWFP), through Gujarat and back down to Bombay. It was the most difficult and ambitious journey Ellen would make during her career, one where barriers of language, culture, custom, and religion posed the greatest challenges to mutual understanding. The Indian struggle for independence did not become the guiding light in Ellen's political life, but she did make a serious effort to come to grips with the challenges facing British India, to listen to and show solidarity with the Indian people, and to communicate their cause to her countrymen.

At Bombay, the group was met by Govind Malaviya, son of the Congress Party president, and three other prominent Congress leaders. They had booked rooms at the Grand Hotel, but on the second day they moved out to stay with friends of Pandit Malaviya. For the rest of their trip, they stayed in locals' homes, ranging from opulent estates to modest huts. The one attribute nearly all their hosts had in common was support for the INC, which had played a leading role in organizing the expedition. The government subsequently argued that Congress intentionally presented the delegates with a distorted view of Indian life, provoking altercations between Indians and police for the visitors' benefit and spreading lies of alleged atrocities. "The India League is merely a tool used by the Gandhi crowd," an India Office staffer would tell one newspaper editor.[51] Yet, as the director of the India Office's information bureau conceded, although the delegation's resulting report "contains more Congress propaganda than any volume seen by me . . . very many of the allegations are or may be true."[52] Certainly, Ellen was convinced by the evidence. She had arrived in India "very doubtful as to some of the atrocity stories she had heard, and she had vexed [Krishna] Menon from time to time when some particularly bad instance was alleged by saying 'English officers do not do these things.'"[53] But her sense of disillusionment was commensurate with her initial faith in her fellow citizens, and the resultant report she coauthored was an "exhaustive and cleverly compiled presentation of the anti-Government case, in its cumulative effect perhaps the ablest piece of Congress propaganda yet published."[54]

Late in the afternoon on their second day in the city, Ellen and Whately paid a visit to Commissioner Kelly, head of the Bombay police department, and attempted to obtain permission to see Mirabehn, then imprisoned at Sabarmati jail. Kelly denied their request. He also denied that whipping was frequently resorted to by colonial officials. He spent much of the rest of the interview encouraging them to keep in touch with government officials on their journeys and discouraging them from "accept[ing] everything they heard against the administration as gospel truth."[55] Although the women agreed to keep an open mind, the group spent the next three days principally in the company of Congress leaders, before departing from what E.M Forster termed "that oddest portal," Bombay's bustling Victoria Terminus, to begin their continental tour.[56] Their first Indian train journey, from Bombay to Pune, was considerably more comfortable than many of its successors. They made the trip on the Deccan Queen, the newly launched electric locomotive service originally designed to ferry Anglo-Indians to the weekend races. Yet despite the comparative luxury of their arrangements, Ellen was already feeling the effects of travelling in such a hot and humid climate. It was the monsoon season, and although temperatures did not reach the heights they would in drier months, the moisture held the heat, and it rarely dipped below twenty-five degrees Celsius during the region's sultry nights. The heat sapped Ellen's energy and the humid weather aggravated her asthma, and on arrival in Pune she took to her bed to rest.[57]

Ellen's respiratory problems were not helped by her heavy smoking, and she preferred regular medication to a regimen of healthy eating and eight hours sleep. She brought an extra suitcase to India filled with "every tropical remedy the wit of a chemist could suggest" topped off with "a variety of insecticides." Despite her open-minded attitude towards Indian civilization, she had taken on board the metropolitan assumption that Indians were ignorant of modern medication and was duly put in her place when she discovered "excellent chemist shops in every town."[58]

The group stayed at the headquarters of the Servants of India Society, an educational and social welfare organization, founded in 1905 by the early independence activist Gopal Krishna Gokhale, that established libraries and founded schools and adult education classes throughout India.[59] The leaders of the society were local Brahmins, but the delegation also met with less well-educated Hindus, as well as with Untouchables and Muslims. By Wednesday, Ellen had recovered sufficiently to attend a birthday celebration for Tatyasaheb Kelkar, the steadfast advocate of nonviolent resistance whose "logical way of thinking" appealed to her.[60] She was also able to meet with the district governor.[61] As in every city and village they visited, the local police in Pune kept close tabs on the group, employing spies within the Servants of India

Society to report on their meetings. The police ultimately took a relatively sympathetic view of the delegation's activities. Rather than dismissing them as irredeemably biased, they owned that the group appeared to be making a sincere effort "to understand the different schools of thought in the city."[62] The foursome would not receive the same benefit of the doubt in other parts of the country.

From Pune, they journeyed to Madras, escorted by a young Congress official. They were met at the station by acting Congress president Chakravarti Rajagopalachari, and Congress officials accompanied the delegates on their tour of the region. Like Menon, "Rajaji," who had recently been released from prison for his role in the salt boycotts, would later become a senior minister in Nehru's post-independence government. For part of the time, the group stayed in the house of a trade union leader, who arranged for Ellen to speak to local trade unionists. The group visited some of the poorer quarters of the city and surrounding towns, as well as a number of outlying villages, addressing the occupants through interpreters. Ellen and company were taken into peasants' homes, mud huts with floors carefully polished with cow dung with the same attention with which working-class Manchester housewives "stoned" or whitened their front stoops. Although many of the women were proud housewives, there was little they could do to combat conditions in the courtyards, where the family cooking and cleaning were done. "Taxes that should go for drainage pay for the main roads that the Europeans need and the growing army of police."[63]

Conversing with the peasant women who ran these households, Ellen was struck by the casual prejudice that several expressed against the Untouchables, even as they revered "Gandhiji," then waging a campaign on the lowest caste's behalf.[64] Despite her instinctive desire to empathize and find commonality with her Indian hosts, the caste system was something she could not properly appreciate. The next month, in a speech at Ahmedabad, she told her listeners that "they had Untouchability even in England, and that she, as a trade union official, belonged to a class of English Untouchables," a statement that provoked a journalist from the otherwise sympathetic *Times of India* to conclude: "This shows how misleading an idea Miss Wilkinson has managed to get of the facts about this country. Otherwise, the inference is that she is simply making fun of the problem. It is objectionable to compare class differences in England with the lot of India's many millions of Untouchables. Miss Wilkinson's words will have an evil effect, for they will be used to belittle a really serious problem and will materially help orthodox interests to hamper progress."[65]

Her Untouchables speech was the most public but not the only time Ellen's ignorance of Indian culture became an issue on the journey. While staying with a comparatively well-off peasant family in Madras, the red-headed foreigner expressed her determination to see the city's famed bazaars. Her hostess explained that she could not take her, as it would be unseemly for a high-caste woman to be seen in the bazaar doing her own shopping. Not to be deterred, Ellen "collect[ed] a couple of amused males, and [created] a sensation in the shopping street. An English mem-sahib does not wander round the bazaar, especially with Indians who are obviously friends but not servants." It would not be inappropriate for a woman to go shopping on Oxford Street in the company of male companions, and Ellen would not allow herself to be anything other than bemused by the impropriety of such behaviour in India. Without the guiding hand of a local woman to advise her, she bought what she fancied and came back with arms jangling with gaudy glass bangles, only to "lear[n] too late that I had rather shocked some of these gentle ladies because the brightly coloured joys I had chosen are only bought by women of the depressed classes."[66] It took all the outspoken Englishwoman's self-possession to restrain herself from giving her hostesses a lecture on the evils of class snobbery.

The speech on Untouchability in Ahmedabad was not the only instance when Ellen shared her political views with her interlocutors. Before the delegation left for India, Monica Whately had assured the India Office they had "no intention of making any speeches while in India,"[67] but Ellen was never able to resist a platform. She was in India to ask questions, not answer them, but she nonetheless shared her views with the assembled crowds, waxing "specially eloquent on the subject of poverty and housing conditions" and encouraging them to "strengthen the Indian trade union movement."[68] Many of the men and women with whom Ellen spoke showed an almost holy reverence for Gandhi. Their attitude only confirmed her view, expressed years earlier to Eleanor Rathbone in reference to child marriage, that political change in India would have to come through cooperation with Gandhi.

In Madras Province, the group finally managed to talk their way into visiting a local jail. In Cannamore jail in Malabar, Ellen accidentally offered the government a propaganda coup. The jail was composed of a series of "long low buildings, perfectly white, shining under the topical sun, masses of trees and flowers in the courtyards in sight of the prisoners' workshops," and Ellen exclaimed without thinking that conditions in Cannamore were much better than in Dartmoor prison in England! Nonetheless, she and her colleagues took exception to the number and treatment of prisoners jailed for civil disobedience. They were also horrified by the conditions in the small women's jail. While the prison was "reasonably decent for men, it was a sheer horror for the women, who were crowded together in a very small compound with a mad woman who had to be handcuffed to the grating and who screamed day and night."[69]

After touring the Madras Province, the group split into two, the men going west to Bangalore and the women travelling south. Ellen and Monica did not make ideal travel companions. Before the war, Ellen had been a constitutional suffragist, while Monica had been a militant suffragette. Although Ellen had been a founding member of the CPGB, she quickly left to hoe a reformist row through the Labour Party. Monica, in contrast, thrice failed to win endorsement as a Labour Party candidate because of her political extremism.[70] In most of the working partnerships throughout her career, Ellen was the passionate, intemperate one. Yet compared to Monica, she was a beacon of level-headed reason. Indian government officials repeatedly identified Ellen as the more moderate of the two women. In one view, while Ellen was "open to receive impressions of the situation other than those presented by Congress supporters," Monica was "a staunch advocate of the theory and principle of Government followed by the Russian Bolsheviks."[71] The observation overstates the political differences between the two women, both of whom supported Congress and denounced the Indian Communist Party for its hostility to the INC and other non-Communist labour organizations, noting that "their propaganda is of the kind which makes unity of action between them and other sections impossible."[72] But only Whately would have thought it appropriate, as the delegate of an ostensibly impartial commission, to actively participate in a Congress meeting at the Ochterlony monument in Calcutta, standing "conspicuously on the topmost step of the monument, holding aloft above the head of the Indian president of the meeting a tri-coloured Congress flag."[73]

Later in their journey, the group would divide differently, with Ellen and Menon forming one party, Monica and Leonard Matters the other. Menon, then aged thirty-six, defied categorization within London social circles. A nationalist and a socialist, he worked to organize Indian labourers within London's East End. Yet, he was also a trained barrister, with master's degrees from the LSE and UCL, who lived in Camden and worked in Bloomsbury as the editor of the Bodley Head's Twentieth Century Library series and the founding editor of Penguin's nonfiction imprint Pelican Books.[74] Ellen was certainly capable of forging intimacies outside of her own social milieu. Nonetheless, the fact that she and Menon moved in similar circles and shared a keen appreciation for literature doubtless eased their relationship as travelling companions. So too would their temperamental similarities. Menon, like Ellen, was passionately committed to social reform. But, like Ellen, he was "not inclined to circumscribe his vision by the directions of a particular discourse or a dogma," preferring a pragmatic focus on ends not means.[75] He was also an attractive and charismatic figure, whose company provided a welcome distraction from her recent heartbreak.

From Madras, the four travellers made the long journey north along the coast to Calcutta via Cuttack.[76] The commission successfully demanded to tour a local jail and was taken around the Hooghly facility. The old Dutch prison formed a sharp contrast to the one in Malabar. Ellen declared it unfit for human habitation and claimed the "kindly Englishman" who oversaw the facility "wasn't proud of his charge" and shared the "general rage" of Bengali citizenry at the recent cuts to public services in that state. Ellen could not decide on the worst aspect of the jail, the overcrowded living conditions that made solitary confinement seem like a luxury or the ever-present lice and insects, kept at bay only by strips of wet pitch tar painted on the prison walls.[77]

From the Bengali capital, the group split into two and made several side trips. Ellen and Menon went north to Narayanganj, where Ellen created a sensation by embracing the mother of a political prisoner whose condition she had witnessed in Cannamore jail.[78] In Chittagong, according to the Bengali government's spies, she and Menon were "met at the station by a number of persons including one ex-*détenu*, two civil disobedience ex-convicts, several political suspects and the Editor of an Extremist Local newspaper the 'Panchanjanya.'" Government agents claimed Ellen "spent the day listening to persons with alleged grievances against Government. She avoided meeting any of the Government's own representatives except the Superintendent of Police whom she saw at his request. She talked with different people regarding the riot which took place" after a local Hindu boy shot a Muslim police inspector the previous August. (In an acknowledgment of the power of the India League to damage the government's reputation in Britain, an official in Simla wrote in reference to Ellen's enquiry about the riots: "I am afraid we may have trouble over this, which will be a pity as the government of Bengal have got away with it so easily."[79])

Although the government resented that Ellen did not speak to officials in Chittagong, she was given significant exposure to the official viewpoint a few days later. The newly appointed governor of Bengal was Sir John Anderson, a career civil servant who had served as permanent undersecretary at the Home Office during the general strike. Ellen and Sir John had been on opposite sides during the strike, and there was no love lost between them. Yet, amongst the Anglo-Indian community, their professional acquaintance passed for friendship, and Ellen alone was invited to stay as the governor's guest at Government House in Darjeeling, the hill station 400 miles north of Calcutta to which the Bengal government retreated during the hot summer months. From the mud huts of the Bengali villagers, Ellen was transported to another world. Against a backdrop of opulent colonial-era splendour, Sir John "took care to see that the reverse side of the picture presented by Congress of the situation in this Province should be shown to her."[80] Ellen respected Anderson's position. Unlike one female member of their party who advocated attempting to palm off the Indians with no more than "high sounding phrases" and the illusion of liberty, the governor felt it was "better to give a little and be honest about it than make a parade about giving a lot and let the Indians find out that we are bluffing them."[81] Despite Anderson's sincerity, Ellen remained convinced that he and his kind had no place in the country. "India must achieve her own step to united self-government, without interference from England," she argued. "Even if India makes a mess of it, she has the right to make her own mess."[82]

After departing Bengal, the group embarked on the longest and most arduous leg of their journey, crossing back to the west coast via Patna in Bihar province. From Patna, the original itinerary had called for the group to head north to Benares, but Ellen and Menon returned south to Pune.[83] On September 16, Gandhi began an eleven-day fast that would ultimately succeed in persuading the government to alter its stance on Untouchability. Although he refused the government's offers of a temporary provisional release, the government did allow him to grant interviews during his protest, in the presence of jail officials.[84] It also let him receive audiences in the jail's inner courtyard, with the result that men and women from around the country assembled before dawn every morning for a glimpse of Gandhiji. As Ellen put it, "all rules had been relaxed by the fast,"[85] including his access to the telegraph, which he used to contact the delegation and request an interview with Ellen.

On Wednesday, September 19, the third day of the fast, Ellen and Menon were driven to Yervada jail and ushered into Gandhi's inner sanctum, accompanied by Padmaja Naidu, another political prisoner, normally held in the women's jail across the road, who was given permission to visit Gandhi during his protest.[86] During that first visit, Gandhi's spirits remained high. "This little brown figure," Ellen later wrote, "went on spinning, asking for news of friends in London, news of Parliament, eager for all the latest details. . . . Gandhi seemed a dynamo of energy, spinning hard, talking hard, stopping to laugh at some of Padmaja's jokes as we sat on the end of the bed." Yet, when the pair returned a few days later, "the difference was shocking. The gaiety and energy had gone. He could only whisper." His bodily statement of solidarity with the Untouchables helped make him, as Ellen would later tell English audiences, "the one name the villages, the Untouchables, love."[87] Although Ellen may not have fully grasped the cultural complexity of the Untouchables' position, her belief in equal human rights led her to instinctively support Gandhi's aims. The *Times of India* was correct to emphasize that there was a wide gulf between the lowest Hindu caste and the British unemployed; but Ellen saw both groups as forgotten victims in need of a champion, and she returned to Britain determined to impress upon her fellow citizens that Gandhi's "work for the Untouchables is a social revolution we hardly realize."[88] On the second trip to the jail, she had bent low over Gandhi as he whispered a statement of his aims for dissemination in the British press. She did her best to garner publicity for that statement, but in the tense political climate, she was unsuccessful in persuading any paper other than the pro-Labour *Daily Herald* to publish it.[89]

In addition to the situation of the Untouchables, Ellen and Gandhi discussed the program of economic self-reliance encouraged by the INC. Ellen had long ago abandoned her faith in free trade, but she did hold a strong faith in the power of technology to ease the burdens on the working class. She questioned the value of hand weaving, when "a Lancashire mill could turn out thousands and thousands of yards of cloth a week." Gandhi's reply was that the homespun campaign was less about crippling the British economy than about helping lift the Indian peasant out of desperate poverty. "The Indian peasants could not work except during the harvest seasons, which sometimes lasted only three months of a year, and so for the rest of the year hand weaving gave them something to do and enabled them to make something themselves that they wouldn't have to buy. The extreme poverty of the Indian peasant is the social problem of the world," he argued. "If they were only lifted up two steps, what a tremendous market they would be." After Ellen's return to Britain, she would relate Gandhi's response to an audience that included many unemployed spinners and weavers at the Victoria Methodist Church in Blackburn.[90] She may not have been able to reconcile herself completely to his cotton boycott, but, as she later claimed, "You may feel critical of his economics, or his political judgment . . . but Gandhi as a man grips one's heart."[91]

After visiting the Mahatma, Ellen and Menon travelled back north to Agra to rejoin the other two members of the group. The four made the journey further north into the Punjab, the sight of the worst altercations between the government and the native population in the period immediately following the First World War. In Amritsar, General Dyer, a career Indian Army officer, had ordered his men to open fire on an unarmed demonstration of men, women, and children in April 1919. Official reports placed the fatalities at 379. The true figures were significantly higher. The episode sparked an international controversy and reopened parliamentary and public debate in Britain over the future of India.[92] In the intervening years, the place had become a pilgrimage site for anti-Raj activists or, as one hostile official termed it, "a rendezvous of Congress undesirables."[93] A photograph from the trip shows Ellen, clad in a long-sleeved white cotton jersey and skirt and clutching her handbag under her arm, posing with a group of six Punjabi men and two young boys who had sought her out to discuss their grievances under British rule.[94] For Ellen, who was not yet in parliament when the events at Amritsar were debated, the memory of what some of her future colleagues had said in defence of Dyer's actions must have filled her with shame.

From the Punjab, Ellen and Menon continued north, taking the Bombay Express to its terminus in Peshawar. Although the four were in India on a fact-finding mission, not a tourist holiday, it would have been extraordinary if they had not taken advantage of the opportunity to see some of the great natural wonders of the Raj. For Menon, born and raised in the south, where the terrain was lush and hilly and camels a novel sight, the Himalayas and the Hindu Kush were as much must-see attractions as they were for Ellen.[95] Guided by the Northwest Frontier Province's publicity officer, who put himself and a car at their disposal, the pair visited the Khyber Pass, the mountain passage on the historic "silk road" connecting central and southern Asia. They also crossed over the much more precarious Kohat Pass, and visited the Hindu temple in Gorkhatri. Although Ellen had at this point become resolutely disillusioned with government propaganda, she and Menon "accepted this kindness gratefully. It meant seeing the sights."[96] A government intelligence agent noted cynically that Ellen had "evidently enjoyed the social and sight-seeing side of her visit, which, on the whole, has probably done more good than harm from Government's point of view."[97]

The government needed all the good will it could accrue. The political environment on the frontier was more fraught than in the other districts the delegates had visited. In April 1930, the Indian army had been called in to forcibly disperse a peaceful demonstration in the Qissa Khwani Bazaar in Peshawar, killing several hundred. Troops of the Royal Garwhal Rifles had refused to fire on the unarmed protestors, an act of military disobedience that frightened the government and fur-

ther inflamed tensions between the Anglo-Indian and native populations. Khan Abdul Ghaffar Khan, leader of the Congress-aligned Servants of God, or Red Shirts, had counselled peaceful resistance—Ellen
would later tell a British audience that had it not been for Ghaffar
Khan's restraining influence, "there would not have been an Englishman
left alive in the Frontier province when the troubles were at their height
some months ago."[98] But while the Red Shirts stopped short of armed
insurrection, the government perceived itself to be under threat. Ordinance rule was imposed in the NWFP earlier than in the rest of the
country. *Lathi,* or baton, charges were frequently used to disperse
crowds, and heavy fines were imposed on the families of political dissidents. Ellen's expressed shock "that the repression has been, and is, so
severe and bitter and passionate resentment is felt throughout the villages of this area.... Whether it be the wife in the zenana [women's
quarters] mourning over her ruined household, or the husband returning from a beating at the hands of the police, feelings are there as a
result of nine months of Ordinance rule, the depth of which the British
official well knows."[99] It was in Mardan in the NWFP that she witnessed the most aggressive acts of police brutality, and the kicking and
beating of unarmed men left a strong impression on her. She spent time
speaking, through an interpreter, to local families and "was particularly sympathetic to the women who are indirect sufferers when their
husbands and sons have to pay the penalty for breaking the law."[100]

The pair met with several government officials, who put it to them
that the British presence was necessary to ensure stability, as a British
withdrawal would doubtless "be followed by the oppression (or actual
massacre) of the Hindu minority by the Muslim majority."[101] In Peshawar, the pair stayed as guests of Mehr Chand Khanna, one of the few
Hindu political leaders in the predominantly Muslim province. Although the central role of Congress in arranging their itinerary meant
the delegation spent more time in the company of Hindus than Muslims, Ellen and Menon sought out members of Abdul Ghaffar Khan's
Red Shirt nationalist movement and interviewed representatives of
each group about relations between the Muslim, Hindu, and Sikh communities. All apparently told them that, absent the British policy of
"divide and rule," the various religious groups would "gladly" bury
their sectarian animosity.[102] The reassuring impression Ellen received

of interfaith harmony in the region was belied by the bloody fighting that took place there after independence, during which Mehr Chand Khanna was arrested and ultimately forced to flee to Delhi.

The last major stop on the delegation's tour was Gujarat. Matters and Whately had taken testimony in and around Delhi while their colleagues were up on the frontier, including a meeting with the Viceroy on October 13.[103] The fact that Menon and Wilkinson were content to leave the interview with Earl Willingdon to their colleagues suggests the low priority either accorded to official justifications by this point. The four travellers reunited in the capital on October 17 and spent two days in the city before moving on to Gujarat. The deputy commissioner of police believed that Ellen and Menon's seeming disinterest in the city reflected the fact that "Congress and its activities were at a low ebb" there.[104]

The reunited group left Delhi on the afternoon of October 19, arriving in Ahmedabad after nightfall. The bustling city was the home of Sabarmati Ashram, Gandhi's headquarters when he was not imprisoned, and a pilgrimage site for his supporters. It was also the headquarters of the Ahmedabad Labour Association, a federation of eight textile unions that claimed a membership of 25,000. Apart from the effect of ordinance rule on the country, the delegation was particularly interested to study labour conditions, and found themselves impressed by the Association, which they termed "the best organized and most successful Unions in India."[105] In Gujarat, Vallabhbhai Jhaverbhai Patel, the former Congress president imprisoned with Gandhi in the Yeravda jail, was, they found, "a household name."[106] From Ahmedabad, Ellen and Menon again split off together, visiting surrounding villages to observe the process of government "attachment" of crops as tax in kind.

In the coastal city of Surat, Ellen met with a native administrator and attempted to shame him with an injustice she had witnessed in the neighbouring village of Bardoli. A "dear old woman," she asserted, was left homeless after government officers burned down her home. Throughout Ellen's trip, government administrators, both Anglo-Indian and native Indians, had attempted to persuade her she was being sold a pup by Congress agents determined to paint the government in a bad light. She had largely dismissed these admonitions, but the tale T. T. Kothavala told Ellen for once gave her pause. Kothavala claimed that "the old woman had a smart grown-up son who had insured the house heavily before going out on [Hijra to Mecca]" during the time of great unrest in Gujarat in 1930. When he returned "after the agreement between the Viceroy and Mr. Gandhi he found that his house still stood as it was and that as the time to pay premium drew near there was an accidental fire about which the Insurance Company grew suspicious and after enquiry lodged a complaint with the police who prosecuted the son for incendiarism and cheating but was let off as the evidence was not conclusive." She confessed she had not heard that aspect of the story. Her interlocutor went on to point out "that if Government servants wanted to burn the house they could have done so easily when the villagers were away from the village and not wait till their return."[107] Ellen was momentarily floored but soon regained her composure, cleaving to the point that, even if the woman's son were an arsonist, his decision to buy insurance in the first place indicated the widespread threat posed to Indian property by government officials. The exchange, while comic, gave Ellen a personal insight into how local administrators came to believe that the perfidy of the few justified suspicion of the entire local community.

Before returning to Bombay to set sail for the return to England, Ellen and Menon made one final detour to Uttar Pradesh—if a 750-mile train journey can be termed a detour. The return to Uttar Pradesh had not been on their original itinerary, but the pair had already spent more time than anticipated in Pune, due to their unexpected visit to Gandhi the previous month, and they were interested to see the Lucknow and Rae Bareli jails. A principal part of their mission had been to investigate conditions in the Indian jails, and they were determined to see as many as possible. In the Frontier province, they had visited the Peshawar jail, but their permit to visit the new camp jail where the Red Shirts were being interred was withdrawn at the last minute. They were hopeful however, that they would be able to see these last two prisons in Uttar Pradesh, including the jail in which Nehru had his first imprisonment.

Their first stop was Allahabad, where they spoke to the province's tax collector, who noted Ellen "seemed reasonably broad-minded." They travelled north to Rae Bareli, and in the end were allowed into the notorious jail—"it was a special triumph to bag that"—but it was clear the District Commissioner "hated the job of piloting around a possible critic." At Rae Bareli, Ellen saw children as young as eight imprisoned for months on minor political charges, but the commissioner refused to engage her on the topic.[108] The Lucknow Central Prison and District Jail was less draconian, although its administration had become harsher and crowding had increased since the onset of the Congress's passive resistance campaign a decade earlier.[109] In Lucknow, the Home Member noted that he had "found Miss Ellen Wilkinson very much more moderate and reasonable in her outlook than I had expected. She assured me, and I have the impression that she was talking genuinely, that she was really anxious to ascertain the facts and that she was conscious of the possibilities of misunderstanding that arose from her Congress connections. . . . Another point that struck me in my conversation with Miss Ellen Wilkinson was that, apart from the questions of what was true and what was not true, she was prepared to make allowances for the difficulties, both of the Government and of the Police, in dealing with an unlawful movement."[110]

If the Lucknow Home Member was impressed by Ellen's sincerity, he nonetheless considered her a dupe. After the meeting, he told a colleague, "Miss Wilkinson does not know very much about India, but wants to become very popular with Indians and wishes to identify herself with Indian aspirations."[111] Such an accusation would have hurt Ellen deeply. Despite barriers of language and culture, she had done her best to get to know the "real" India, and she sincerely believed she had gained an insight into the country in her three months there. That sense of communion and commonality of purpose with the Indian people would stay with her and give passion to her advocacy on behalf of self-rule.

The group had a few final days in Bombay before setting sail back to Europe. Ellen used part of that time to buy souvenirs, including a goddess figurine she would later give to Winifred Holtby as a Christmas gift. The delegation met with industrialist G. D. Birla, whose family owned the English-language *Hindustan Times,* and entrusted him with an early draft of their conclusions for publication in the country.[112] They set sail on 7 October and landed in chilly Genoa ten days later. But even before they disembarked, bundled up in their winter coats, they were conscious they had left one world behind and entered another. As E. M. Forster observed, "Somewhere about Suez there is always a social change: the arrangements of Asia weaken and those of Europe begin to be felt."[113] After a brief stopover in Italy, they returned to London on November 20, on a typical dull, drizzly winter night. After nearly four months away from home, Ellen gratefully made the journey back to her Guilford Street flat and collapsed into sleep.

The next day, she attended a welcome home party around the corner at Frank and Winifred Horrabin's. Frank was vice-chairman of the India League executive, and Ellen knew her return would bring the two of them back into contact. Fortunately, the awkwardness of their meeting was eased by the size of the gathering, which was attended by about forty people, both India League members, including Morgan Jones, Lord Snell, C. F. Andrews, and Harold Laski, and others sympathetic to the cause, such as Eleanor Rathbone and the *Daily Herald* journalist Hannen Swaffer. Each of the four delegates gave a speech about their experiences. All denounced the effects of ordinance rule, although Ellen, according to the report of a Scotland Yard informant in attendance, was more "moderate and careful" in her criticism than were her colleagues.[114] Over the next several months, she spoke on India to meetings around the country, emphasizing that an end to ordinance rule and Gandhi's release were necessary prerequisites to any peaceful resolution of the Indian conflict. She spoke to a wide range of groups, including the executive committee and regional branches of the Women's International League.[115] Although her interest in Indian affairs had been focused through the lens of the India League, she remained involved with the WIL's efforts to raise British awareness about the political situation in the subcontinent; she became a vice-president of the WIL in 1933.

Scholars have argued that the collaborative relationship between Jawaharlal Nehru and other Congress leaders, on the one hand, and radical Labourites such as Ellen, Lansbury, and Laski, on the other, encouraged Marxist tendencies within the INC.[116] The reverse also holds true. After three months travelling through India under Congress guidance, Ellen became convinced that the future of India lay with Gandhi and the Congress party. She henceforth directed her political energies solely toward support for the INC. She showed sympathy for the prisoners in the ongoing Meerut conspiracy case, the protracted four-year detention and eventual show trial of trade unionists, many Communist Party members, who were accused of organizing a railway strike in Uttar Pradesh. But unlike Leonard Matters, Ellen kept her distance from the Comintern-led defence movement. Yet in the none-too-distant future, she, Menon, Nehru, and other British members of the India League would share platforms with British and international Communists, not in support of Indian independence, but in defence of European democracy against the growing threat of Fascism.

In April 1937, Dame Rachel Crowdy, Ellen, the Duchess of Atholl MP, and Eleanor Rathbone MP (left to right) toured Spain on behalf of National Joint Committee for Spanish Relief. Although ostensibly in Spain on a humanitarian mission, the group also compiled a secret report on German and Italian naval activity along the Iberian coast. Courtesy Daily Herald Archive/National Media Museum/Science & Society Picture Library

Ellen, Philip Noel-Baker MP, and Clement Attlee MP (second from left) travelled to Spain in December 1937 as part of an official Labour Party delegation in support of the Republican government. Courtesy Daily Herald Archive/National Media Museum/Science & Society Picture Library

Ellen surrounded by school children in Madrid, December 1937. Her fundraising efforts helped to feed thousands of children in the Spanish Republic. Courtesy Daily Herald Archive/ National Media Museum/Science & Society Picture Library

Ellen and her longtime friend and mentor, NUDAW president John Jagger, at the Southport seaside for their union's annual conference in 1938. Courtesy Daily Herald Archive/National Media Museum/Science & Society Picture Library

Ellen campaigning with a group of women in 1938. She was a fierce champion of
the rights of working women and working-class housewives. Courtesy Daily Herald Archive/
National Media Museum/Science & Society Picture Library

Ellen headlined an International Peace Campaign meeting in Trafalgar Square during the run-up to the Munich Crisis in September 1938. Before an audience of tens of thousands, she denounced Neville Chamberlain for prattling to the dictators and stealing the liberties of the people of Eastern Europe. Courtesy Daily Herald Archive/National Media Museum/Science & Society Picture Library

In 1940, the *Picture Post* ran a photo spread of Ellen, including this picture of her lounging on her bed in her Bloomsbury flat. Shortly thereafter, she was bombed out of her home. Picture Post/Courtesy of Getty Images

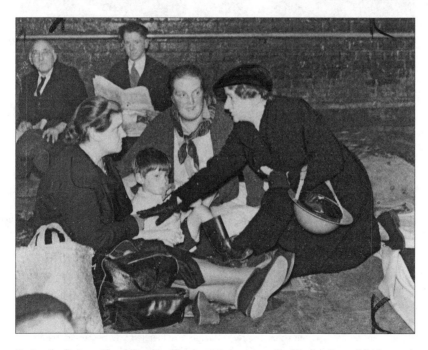

During the first months of the Blitz, Ellen became known as the "Shelter Queen" for her work improving shelter provision in the London Underground. Courtesy Daily Herald Archive/National Media Museum/Science & Society Picture Library

During the Second World War, Ellen served as undersecretary of home security alongside the Home Secretary Herbert Morrison. The two diminutive redheaded MPs became romantically involved during the war. Courtesy Daily Herald Archive/National Media Museum/Science & Society Picture Library

Ellen Wilkinson, Eleanor Roosevelt, and Minerva Bernardino of the Dominican Republic were amongst the small cadre of female delegates to the 1945 UN conference in San Francisco. Ellen resented the thought that she was chosen as a delegate because of her gender. Courtesy Keystone/Hulton Archive Getty Images

As Minister of Education, Ellen was the only woman in Attlee's 1945 Cabinet. Courtesy People's History Museum

In October 1945, the new Minister of Education toured schools in British-occupied Germany. Ellen was optimistic that reeducation and denazification programs could turn former Hitler Youth like the boys pictured into model democratic citizens. Courtesy Daily Herald Archive/ National Media Museum/Science & Society Picture Library

Ellen and U.S. representative Archibald Macleish sign the founding charter of the United Nations Educational Social and Cultural Organization on 16 November 1945. Ellen played a formative role in crafting the charter. Courtesy Daily Herald Archive/National Media Museum/ Science & Society Picture Library

Ellen's last formal portrait, taken in her office at the Ministry of Education shortly before her death, shows her looking tired and frail. Courtesy Daily Herald Archive/National Media Museum/ Science & Society Picture Library

Just days before her death, Ellen braved subfreezing temperatures to join the directors of the Old Vic theatre, including actor Laurence Olivier, for the ceremonial reopening of the theatre school. Courtesy Daily Herald Archive/National Media Museum/Science & Society Picture Library

11

A FIGHT FOR HUMANITY ITSELF

Ellen, Menon, Leonard Matters, and Monica Whately
had returned from India on November 20, 1932. They had prepared detailed notes as they travelled and in the ensuing months worked quickly
to produce *The Condition of India*, a 554-page denunciation of British rule
on the subcontinent. Although the India Office had exerted pressure on
several publishers not to contract the volume, a small press called Essential Publishers ultimately released it in March 1934.[1] Ellen also contracted with George G. Harrap Publishers to produce a more accessible
account of her travels under the title *Indian Parade*.[2] However, not for
the first time, the overextended politician-cum-author pulled out of a
contract with the publisher, likely as a consequence of her growing commitments to the anti-fascist movement.[3] The government banned *The*

Condition of India on the subcontinent but could not enforce the same level of censorship within Britain. Even in India, the proscription could not entirely silence discussion of the report. Pro-Congress papers of course gave it publicity, and even some organs of the pro-government Anglo-Indian press, such as the Lucknow *Pioneer,* questioned the government's decision to censor the report and disobeyed instructions not to discuss it in their columns. One article in the *Pioneer* prompted a member of the Home Department to write a telling letter to the paper's editor justifying the government's actions. Although the report "is remarkably unfair and one-sided," he argued, the "exhaustive and cleverly compiled presentation of the anti-government case" was, "in its cumulative effect perhaps the ablest piece of Congress propaganda yet published." It was for that reason, and in recognition of the fact that "public opinion, owing mainly to the extremely low standard of literacy and education, is a very different thing in India than in England; and in consequence the right to freedom of speech and freedom of publication can be far more dangerously abused here than there," that the government had had no choice but to censor the report for the good of the Empire.[4] It would be difficult to imagine a higher compliment for the delegation's work.

At home, the British government breathed a sigh of relief when *The Condition of India* failed to attract the anticipated media attention. As their counterparts in the subcontinent had done, the India Office used its contacts within the conservative press to ensure that the publication was either ignored or poorly reviewed. Even outlets inclined to be sympathetic to the report, such as the *Manchester Guardian,* conceded, "The propagandist distortion, the willingness to keep ears wide open for anything to the government's discredit, is all too evident." Yet, despite the report's evident prejudice, the *Guardian* accepted it as a "formidable indictment" of "things . . . done under the Ordinances which Britain might well wish to forget."[5] Over the next several months, Ellen wrote numerous articles on her experiences in India, principally in the Labour-owned *Daily Herald* and the London evening *Star.* She also spoke about her experiences on India League and Women's International League (WIL) platforms around the country and briefed members of the WIL's India subcommittee.

In May 1932, Ellen had been selected as the prospective candidate for Jarrow, an industrial constituency in County Durham whose economy would soon be blighted by the shuttering of Palmers' shipyard in 1934. The writing was on the wall for the Jarrow shipyard well before its closure. Yet while the residents of Jarrow could not be blamed for being more concerned with domestic than international affairs, in January 1933 they turned out at the Felling Labour Hall to hear Ellen speak on her experiences in India—impassioned tales of imperial injustice combined with stories of riding on the back of an elephant.[6]

Ellen's absorption in Indian affairs did not mean she ceased to be concerned by the impact of the 1932 Reichstag elections on German political and social life. In the spring of 1933, Ellen divided her attention between Indian and German politics, occasionally combining the two, as at a lecture to the Manchester branch of the Women's International League on April 24. However, from the night of the Reichstag fire, on February 27, 1933, the situation in Germany took clear precedence over the campaign for Indian independence.

At 9 o'clock on the evening of February 27, 1933, the German Reichstag went up in flames. The fire spread with awesome speed. Within an hour, the main chamber, with its domed glass roof, was entirely destroyed. The flames were visible for miles around, drawing crowds of onlookers. Many of those assembled caught a glimpse of Hermann Goering, president of the Reichstag and Nazi commissioner for the Prussian Ministry of the Interior, who was the first Nazi high official to arrive on the scene.

By the time Hitler arrived at 1:20 p.m. to view the charred main chamber, the police had made their first arrest. A Dutchman, Marinus van der Lubbe, was found in the building, clad only in his trousers, covered in sweat, and seemingly bemused by all the commotion. The police issued a statement that a member of the Dutch Communist Party had been apprehended on the scene, though van der Lubbe had resigned his party membership in April 1931.[7] The *Manchester Guardian* reported "wild rumours" circulating in the city, from the story that van der Lubbe was only one member of a broader Communist conspiracy to the story that renegade Nazi stormtroopers had started the blaze.[8] Buoyed by the police's seemingly genuine conviction that the fire was an act of conspiracy, Goering publicly declared it to be a Communist plot and vowed to hold those responsible to account. Before sunrise on the following day, he had already ordered mass arrests of Communists.

When the cabinet met the next morning, the Nazis secured support for the passage of an emergency decree that abrogated civil liberties across Germany, suspending freedom of speech, freedom of association, and freedom of the press; legalizing unwarranted surveillance; and transferring executive powers from the states to the central government. On January 30, President Paul von Hindenburg named Hitler chancellor. The emergency decree fanned an atmosphere of fear and intimidation in the run-up to the Reichstag elections held on March 5. With Nazi stormtroopers roaming the streets, many of the leading Communists and Social Democrats in prison, and the press reporting the fire as a Communist conspiracy, the Nazi vote soared to nearly 44 percent.

Even before the elections, the Nazis had taken action to frame the legal case against the alleged Reichstag fire conspirators. Their principal targets were the leader of the Communist party in the Reichstag, Ernst Torgler, and his colleague Wilhelm Koenen, despite the fact that both had a clear alibi. The two men were arrested, and while Koenen was released and emigrated shortly thereafter, Torgler was put on trial alongside four alleged co-conspirators: van der Lubbe and three Bulgarians, including Georgi Dimitrov, head of the Central European section of the Comintern. Although the evidence connecting the Bulgarians to the fire was at best suspect, their arrest gave credence to the Nazi theory that the fire was an international Communist conspiracy.

Once the Reichstag reassembled, Hitler forced through the passage of the Enabling Act, which granted exclusive legislative power to the chancellor and his ministers, bypassing the president and the Reichstag. By summer 1933, the Nazis had used their unchecked power to ban all other political parties and trade unions and to terrorize, arrest, and send to concentration camps more than 100,000 Communists, Social Democrats, trade unionists, Jews, and other perceived enemies of the regime.[9] The German press was silenced from reporting anything contrary to the government's official version of events, but several foreign correspondents who remained in the country painted an unsettling picture. Amongst the most vocal of them was Ellen's friend Frederick Voigt, whose reports ultimately got him expelled from Germany.

Alarmed by what she heard from Voigt and others, Ellen determined to undertake her own investigation of what was happening in Germany. She flew to Berlin five days after the fire and was in the country when the delegates passed the Enabling Act.[10] On her return to Britain, she reported on what she had seen and heard, including the treatment of Wilhelm Sollmann, a Social Democratic Reichstag minister and former minister of the interior who was seized from his home in Cologne by stormtroopers and taken to a makeshift torture centre alongside his colleague Herr Efferoth, his assistant at the local trade union newspaper. The two men were extensively beaten for hours and forced to drink castor oil, before being taken into "protective arrest" by the local police and removed to the prison infirmary.[11] Ellen also wrote of an artist friend who had been tortured in front of his lover on the night of the fire, suffering severe facial injuries and losing an eye. She wrote of Jewish doctors who had been rounded up and tortured, with their noses broken as a "symbolic act" inflicted with such brutality that many suffered vision damage. She denounced the widespread use of the *Totschläger* (literally the "knock 'em dead'"), a lead ball on a steel spring with a leather handle designed to inflict internal injuries without breaking bones. A colleague would later obtain a *Totschläger* for Ellen, who displayed it to great effect on platforms for the Relief Committee for Victims of German Fascism, just as she had earlier shocked parliamentary colleagues with the painful and dehumanizing truss worn by half-naked Somerset miners.

Ellen the fiery feminist was appalled by the speed with which the Nazis had undone the progress toward women's liberation that had taken place in the Weimar republic. In an article excoriating German attitudes toward women, she cited with revulsion Goering's assertion: "woman, her place is in the home, her duty the recreation of the tired warrior."[12] The Nazi policy of addressing the unemployment problem appeared to be to move women and Jews out of the workforce and give their jobs to loyal men of the Reich. She detailed the Nazi policy of removing women from civil service posts, usually not on the grounds of gender but of their alleged Jewish origins or Communist sympathies. She reported an alleged instance in which a Nazi officer came into a university during final exams for a law degree "to enforce the decree that Jews and Socialists must put down their pens and leave at once. 'And the women may as well go, too,' added the commandant. 'Law exams won't help them to bear better children.'" She decried the hounding out of Germany of the leaders of the German branch of the Women's International League for Peace and Freedom (WILPF), Anita Augsburg, Lida Gustava Heymann, and Gertrud Baer, and noted with fear, "While the cases of Nazi violence against women are as yet fewer than the number of their male victims, the horrible torture of Frau Marie Jankowski, the chairman of the Copenick relief municipal committee, shows that women are not immune from the sickening Nazi savagery."[13] (Jankowski would later die of her wounds.)

Ellen ended her first published report on her trip to Germany by underscoring the importance of international publicity.[14] Press censorship, she believed, was keeping the average German ignorant of the extent of the terror. She witnessed a torchlight procession of the Nazi stormtroopers (SA) through the streets of Berlin and suspected that few of the bystanders appreciated what these *"exaltés"* had done.[15] Foreign correspondents could not truthfully report all they had seen and heard without risking expulsion from the Reich. It was the responsibility of those who witnessed what was happening to ensure that the international public did not remain as blind to the Nazi terror as the Germans themselves. Ellen went to Geneva after her visit to Germany to report on the progress of the Disarmament Conference for the British press. In March 1933, she still professed faith in the peace efforts of those assembled in Switzerland.[16] Gradually, however, she would come to the conclusion that defeating Hitler was worth the risk of war.

Ellen did not return to Britain at the end of March with any coherent plan for how to combat fascism. Her friends in Germany had asked her to tell the world what she had seen, and she did her best, leaning on her connections both at the Labour-run *Daily Herald* and in the "capitalist press" to publicize the horrors she had witnessed as well as the harrowing stories she had heard. As she had done after her return from India, she used her scheduled public events in Jarrow to raise her constituents' awareness about events in Germany.[17] As a regular speaker for feminist organizations, such as the Six Point Group, Ellen increasingly oriented her lectures toward the threat of fascism to women.[18] Although she maintained a feminist critique of fascism throughout the 1930s, she came to acknowledge, along with many other feminists, that "the very real threat to the lives of European opponents of Fascism and their children meant that the specific threat of Fascism to *women* assumed secondary importance."[19] She felt, however, that one-off speeches could not constitute a coherent campaign against the fascist threat. Inspired as she had never been before by an overwhelming desire to take action, Ellen sought out other ways to help. She ultimately found an outlet for her energy in the work of the World Committee for the Relief of the Victims of German Fascism.

The World Committee's epicentre was Paris, where Willi Münzenberg, the Comintern agent and mastermind behind many Comintern-funded publicity schemes, ran the international organization with the aid of a group of Communist exiles from Eastern Europe, including novelist Gustav Regler, Czech journalist Egon Kisch, and Otto Katz, the international spy Ellen referred to cryptically as "The Man Who Knew Everyone."[20] Münzenberg fled Germany on the night of the Reichstag fire after hearing the Nazis had issued a warrant for his arrest. Kisch was not so lucky. He was arrested, tortured, and released before following Willi to the border. Katz, in contrast, had come to Paris via Moscow, where he had spent the past several years heading up Münzenberg's film enterprise Mezhrabpomfilm and receiving training as a Russian spy.

Arthur Koestler, who remained personally devoted to Münzenberg even after losing faith in Communism in 1938, wrote an exceptional pen portrait of the master propagandist.[21] Willi in his mid-forties was "a short, square, squat, heavy-boned man with powerful shoulders, who gave the impression that bumping against him would be like colliding with a stream-roller. His face had the forceful simplicity of a woodcut, but there was a basic friendliness about it. His broad, cosy Thuringian dialect, and his simple, direct manner further softened the powerful impact of his personality." His collaborators, a group that from 1933 included both Koestler and Wilkinson, were, the novelist wrote, "devoted to him."[22]

In building support for his newly formed committee, this incomparable impresario turned first to those men and women with whom he had worked on previous ventures, from Workers' International Relief, his first fundraising front, to the League Against Imperialism and the Amsterdam-Pleyel peace movement. As Münzenberg was too well-known to travel safely outside of Paris, it was Otto Katz who made the journey to London to lay the groundwork for a British Relief Committee. Gustav Regler described Katz as Münzenberg's "second-in-command": "a considerable linguist, age forty-three, with a thin-lipped hard-bitten face, lined with suffering, that had hitherto been known only to the higher agents of the Comintern."[23] Katz's face was lined not only with suffering but with a duelling scar obtained in his twenties. Koestler, who had a tempestuous relationship with Katz, described him as "a smooth and slick operator": "Otto was dark and handsome, with a somewhat seedy charm. He was the type of person who, when lighting a cigarette, always closes one eye.... In spite of all his seediness, Otto was, paradoxically, a very likeable human being.... He was the invisible Willy's roving ambassador.... He had political contacts everywhere; he was attractive to women, particularly to the middle-aged, well-intentioned, politically active type, and used them adroitly to smooth his path."[24] He was, in short, perfectly suited to the task of attracting allies to the Münzenberg crusade.

On the morning of Tuesday, March 28, 1933, Otto travelled by ferry from Normandy under the alias Rudolf Katz, landing in Folkestone, where immigration officers took immediate notice of the suspicious foreigner and alerted the Home Office. MI5 were quickly placed on his tail; and, according to their reports, Otto/Rudolf met first with R. S. Shube, who alongside Reginald Bridgeman and John Strachey had been one of the original founders of the British Anti-War Council (an outgrowth of the 1932 Amsterdam conference). He then went to see Isabel Brown, who had succeeded Ellen's old friend Helen Crawfurd as national secretary of the British branch of Workers' International Relief (WIR). Brown would thenceforth combine her work as secretary of the WIR with her position as secretary to the newly formed British Relief Committee. Before Katz left Britain, he met with Bridgeman, Leslie and Carmel Haden Guest, and Lord Marley, all regular names in the anti-imperial and anti-war conference scene. He hoped to make contact with George Lansbury, whose involvement with the 1927 League Against Imperialism (LAI) conference had done so much to counter accusations that the LAI was a Communist front. Although Lansbury kept his distance from the Czech spy, Ellen proved more than willing to do her bit in the fight against fascism.

Alongside Helen Crawfurd, Carmel Haden Guest, sexologist Havelock Ellis, Jewish novelist Louis Golding, physicist Hyman Levy, novelist Ethel Manin, socialist journalist Henry Nevinson, former suffragette Sylvia Pankhurst, general-secretary of the Communist Party Harry Pollitt, and former Communist MP Shapurgi Saklatvala, Ellen attended the founding meeting of the British Relief Committee at the Conway Hall in London on March 29, along with several men and women she had known and worked with on different campaigns on and off for years.[25] Their presence in the Bloomsbury lecture room must have reassured Ellen that this would be a serious and respectable committee. Her own participation, in turn, would help to bring other men and women on board.

Katz took the stage and explained the committee's remit, which was to publicize the atrocities occurring inside Germany and to raise funds for the relocation of refugees, principally in the Saar region and in France. The meeting raised £50, and the assembled group pledged to raise at least £1000 more for the cause.[26] The following Sunday, Ellen spoke at the new organization's first public demonstration in Hyde Park alongside a motley crew of Communists, non-Communists, and Jews.[27] Before his arrival in London, Katz had travelled to Switzerland, Holland, Belgium, and Czechoslovakia to establish relief committees in those countries.[28] These and the British committee worked alongside the French *Comité d'aide aux victimes du fascisme Hitlérien,* led by Barbusse and artist Francois Jourdain, and the American committee, led by novelist Theodore Dreiser. Significantly, several members of the French branch of the WILPF were involved with the *Comité,* and this group of feminists would later collaborate with Ellen on another anti-fascist venture: the Women's Committee against War and Fascism.

For some, the long history of cooperation of many of the committee members and the overlapping networks that connected the League Against Imperialism, Workers' International Relief, and the new organization were evidence the Relief Committee was no more than another link in a great Comintern conspiracy. This view was laid out in graphic detail by the international secretary of the Labour Party in a 1933 pamphlet entitled *The Communist Solar System.* The truth was more complex. To call the assembled group puppets of the Comintern discounts the sincerity of many non-Communist activists whose commitment to fighting fascism overrode any residual reservations about collaborating with Communists. It also, arguably, overplays the extent to which Willi Münzenberg functioned as a Comintern factotum. In a collection of essays published in 1995, François Furet described him as a faithful executor, just like any other militant in Moscow's vast Jesuitical bureaucracy.[29] Yet, both Willi's contemporaries and subsequent scholars have offered alternative readings that emphasize the German's independence from Moscow, the sincerity of his commitment to the fight against fascism, and the awareness and agency of the "innocents" who collaborated with him. Both Koestler and Regler perceived Willi's anti-fascist activism as akin to a crusade, untainted by the cynical manoeuvrings of Moscow foreign policy.[30]

Koestler was being more than slightly facetious when he claimed that the "highly respectable people" who supported the World Committee "had never heard of the name Münzenberg and thought that the Comintern was a bogey invented by Dr. Goebbels," yet he clearly believed in the naiveté of Münzenberg's collaborators.[31] In fact, however, many of these men and women were conscious of the role they were playing. Some actively embraced Stalinism, but for others, including Ellen, the decision to work with Stalinists in the fight against Hitler required significant rationalization and moral compromise.

Ellen's relationship toward Communism, the Comintern, and the Soviet Union in this period was complex and, both at the time and subsequently, subject to considerable misconstruction. As we have seen, she was profoundly impressed by the Soviet Union's efforts at social, economic, and gender reform during her visit to the country in 1921. In 1930, she wrote a preface to the pamphlet *Anti-Soviet Lies Nailed*, which defended Stalin's Soviet Union against alleged libel in the capitalist press. She continued to support the Soviets' progress toward gender equality into the 1930s, linking Russian women's social position to the overthrow of capitalism.[32] Nonetheless, by 1934, her uncritical appreciation for Stalinism had already begun to fray. As we have seen, she rejected Stalin's attack on Socialist parties as "bourgeois fascists" in the period before 1933. She was equally put off by Stalin's persecution, arrest, and show trials of former party leaders.

Ellen had first met Leon Trotsky on her 1921 visit to Russia and had reencountered him at various international economic congresses while a member of the Red International of Labour Unions. Despite occasional disagreements about policy, she respected the sincerity of his politics and his central role in securing the success of the Bolshevik revolution. When Stalin forced him first into internal exile and then into exile abroad, Ellen pled in the Commons for the Labour government of which she was a junior minister to grant the former commissar a British visa.[33] At the time he was living on Büyükada, a small bucolic island off the port of Istanbul, and Ellen sent him copies of *Hansard* and British parliamentary papers. The two kept up an occasional correspondence; and although she claimed "not to know enough facts to pronounce an opinion" on the charges Stalin laid against him, she held little faith in the "hot stream of vilification that the Third International can turn on when it really tries," and felt a piteous contempt for the "Bright Young Things who on the strength of three weeks membership of the Communist party . . . denounce him by bell, book and thesis."[34]

Ellen likely held a similar contempt for those members of the Communist Party of Great Britain (CPGB) who had been willing to swallow the party's frequent denunciations of her own alleged crimes against socialism in the 1920s and early 1930s. Nonetheless, she had maintained personal relationships with several members of the party, including Dutt and Crawfurd, and did not believe that all British Communists should be written off on account of the occasional misguided excesses of their leadership. And when the Labour Party sought to proscribe membership in the Relief Committee for the Victims of German Fascism because of its Communist associations, Ellen retorted "I wonder which member of the Labour Party executive or the General Council of the Trades Union Congress, if they have to deal with a man bleeding from Fascist whips, would have to ask him before they helped him whether he belonged to the second or third International."[35] Fighting fascism was more important than infighting within the left.

The principal weapons with which Münzenberg and the World Committee waged the battle against Nazism in 1933 were the *Brown Book of*

Hitler Terror and the Reichstag Fire Counter-Trial, held in London in October 1933, at the same time the Germans were trying van der Lubbe and the four Communists in Leipzig. Both the *Brown Book* and the Counter-Trial generated enormous publicity for the anti-fascist cause and were instrumental in securing the acquittal of Torgler and his alleged Bulgarian co-conspirators.

Münzenberg and Koestler worked at high speed and in great secrecy in their cramped office in the Rue du Faubourg Saint-Honoré to collate smuggled documents, witness testimony, and a not inconsiderable amount of exaggeration and outright fabrication into what became the *Brown Book*. Their resulting masterpiece, which purported to prove that the Nazis had set fire to the Reichstag building and then framed the Communists for their crime, was published simultaneously in London and Paris in August 1933 and would ultimately be translated into twenty-four languages and published in more than fifty-five editions.[36]

If one is looking for evidence that the Nazis themselves started the fire, the *Brown Book* is not a great place to start. Leaving aside its innuendo that van der Lubbe was a homosexual prostitute who may have had a physical relationship with the SA leader Ernst Roehm, the *Brown Book's* "smoking gun" was the so-called Oberfohren memorandum in which the leader of the German Nationalist faction in the Reichstag allegedly confessed that the Nazis had forewarned him of their intention to start the fire and expressed uneasiness about the extent of Nazi repression of the Communists and Social Democrats in the aftermath of the conflagration. By the time the *Brown Book* was published, Ernst Oberfohren had been found dead, allegedly by his own hand, and could not refute the legitimacy of the letter. If Münzenberg knew at the time the memorandum was a forgery, and he almost certainly did, he kept the information to himself. To Willi, lies and forgeries were fair game in the fight against fascism. As one historian has written, "The *Brown Book* was a work of enormous ingenuity which brilliantly matched fabrication with fabrication, conspiracy with conspiracy, and combined mendacity and imagination, invention and plausibility."[37]

Willi's fast and loose attitude toward the truth ultimately led to Ellen's memorable encounter with Albert Einstein in October 1933. Ellen had agreed to act as the *Brown Book's* publicist in London and had been instrumental in arranging for the English edition to carry an endorsement from Einstein, after Katz assured her the physicist had authorized the use of his name.[38] She felt personally mortified when Einstein issued a public denial to the Jewish Telegraphic Agency, stating he had no involvement with the *Brown Book* and lodging a formal protest against the press's use of his name.[39] Privately, Einstein wrote to a colleague explaining his rationale: "It is critical that only foreign non-Jews express themselves, that is to say, only bystanders who are not personally involved. If I appear publically as a prosecutor of the German government, it will have terrifying consequences for the German Jews."[40] Publicly, however, his statement caused temporary embarrassment for the World Committee and anxiety for Ellen.

When she next flew over to Paris to check in with the World Committee headquarters, Ellen arranged to visit Einstein in his rented villa in the seaside village Le Coq sur Mer on the Belgian coast. The villa was guarded by the Belgian police against a possible assassination attempt by Nazi agents or sympathizers. Inside, Ellen found the fifty-four year-old physicist dressed in "a pair of old trousers and a well worn pull over." His face was tired but to Ellen seemed illuminated by his "simple dignity." (In an article for the *Daily Express* in September 1933, Ellen would write, "I have been privileged, almost by accident, to talk informally with Lenin, with Gandhi, and with Einstein. Each of the three had this baffling quality. One knew one was in the presence of greatness."[41])

Abashed by his public disavowal of any association with the *Brown Book,* and assuming he feared the personal retribution a link with the publication might invite, Ellen asked him whether he would prefer, for his own safety, to renounce his honorary presidency of the World Committee. She was earnest in her willingness to sacrifice the publicity brought by Einstein's support rather than risk his safety, although Münzenberg and Katz more likely than not sent Ellen as their emissary in the hopes her evident sincerity would dissuade Einstein from taking further steps to distance himself from their campaigns. With his wife at his side, the older man listened to the bright-eyed woman seated opposite him, before responding, "They shall not force me to do that. The work your committee has done is good." Shortly thereafter, Einstein and his wife fled the continent for England, in the wake of rumours that the Nazis had offered a reward of £1,000 for the "silencing" of

Einstein, believing he had been instrumental in the publication of the *Brown Book*. Faced with this new threat to his safety, Einstein issued a public statement that while he "did not write anything in it," he was "on the committee which authorized the publication of the book" and "agreed with its contents."[42]

Ellen and Einstein sincerely believed the Nazis had themselves burned down the Reichstag, as, most likely, did Münzenberg and Katz. The initial reports had all pointed to multiple conspirators; and once the Nazis had determined to try the Communists for the crime, they suppressed any indication the fire might have been the work of a lone anarchist Dutchman. In the 1960s, two West German scholars produced what have become widely accepted studies showing that van der Lubbe did in fact commit the crime himself and that the Nazis merely capitalized on a happy coincidence. Yet so ingrained was the belief in the Nazi conspiracy that many refused to believe the Nazis were not involved, despite the preponderance of evidence compiled by Tobias and Mommsen. Recent scholarship has once again reopened the debate over Nazi involvement in the fire.[43]

Ellen's belief in the righteousness of the anti-fascist cause likely discouraged Ellen from questioning the authenticity of the claims made in the *Brown Book* too closely. Certainly, the otherwise law-abiding ex-MP proved willing to bend other rules in the name of the cause. During Katz's many clandestine trips to the United Kingdom, Ellen frequently acted as his chauffeur. Her little Austin Seven became his getaway car, and she clearly thrilled at the challenge of evading MI5. After a meeting with Frederick Voigt and Katz in her flat, Ellen once tried to shake off a police tail by winding through the streets of Bloomsbury to Regents Park, where they "circled the inner circle twice and the outer circle twice before making their way back east to Guilford Street."[44] It must have been a harrowing experience for Otto—another friend recalled his own journeys in the passenger seat of Ellen's little vehicle, trying desperately to keep his feet "from going through the frail floor" and praying the motor would hold up after the fraught process of warming up the car.[45]

Such cloak-and-dagger antics were arguably innocent fun, but Ellen's devotion to the cause pushed her toward recklessness. So too did her growing intimacy with Katz. As his visits to the UK were fleeting, and always shadowed by the threat of imminent arrest and deportation, he invariably made the most of every minute. On one visit, he and Ellen closed down the Little Hungary restaurant on Wardour Street at midnight on Saturday night, then were forced out of the bar of the Grosvenor Hotel in Victoria the next evening, only to move on for another several hours at the Corner House, Lyons's flagship café-cum-restaurant-cum-delicatessen off the Strand, which stayed open twenty-four hours.[46] On another of his visits, Katz introduced Ellen to a new friend: László Lowenstein, better known by his stage name, Peter Lorre. Lorre had made his name in Weimar Germany for his star turn as a child murderer in the Fritz Lang thriller *M*. The actor was one of countless Jewish artists who had fled Germany after the March terror, heading first for Paris and ultimately for London. Katz and Wilkinson dragged him on their usual tour of Soho and Bloomsbury's late-night establishments, including Chez Viani on Charlotte Street, Martinez Spanish restaurant on Swallow Street, and Bogey's Bar on Woburn Place. Few British filmgoers were familiar with Lorre's work in 1933; but Ellen, a dedicated foreign film buff, would almost certainly have seen *M*, and, while meeting Lorre could not have been as thrilling as her introduction to Charlie Chaplin two years earlier, it must have sent chills up her spine.[47] Seven years later, the actor, by then established in Hollywood, would become indelibly associated with another Bogey's bar, as the shifty-eyed con artist who arranged for Ilsa and Victor's exit visas in *Casablanca*. Lorre and other refugees, including Charlie Chaplin and Fritz Lang, provided important financial and influential assistance to Katz (then travelling under the name Rudolf Breda) when he visited California in 1936 to establish what would become the Hollywood Anti-Nazi League. The dashing Czech spy charmed his way through Los Angeles and allegedly served as the prototype for Victor Laszlo, the Czech leader of the anti-Nazi underground in *Casablanca*.[48]

Katz travelled to Hollywood with his wife, Ilse, to whom he was by all evidence happily married. Yet, his status as a married man did not stop him from spending several nights in Ellen's small one-bedroom flat on Guilford Street or later from taking a few days' holiday with her on the French Riviera on their way back from Spain.[49] Even before the release of the *Brown Book*, rumours were flying around London that Ellen and Katz were having an affair. Koestler, in relating a memory of

Otto's finesse at bargaining with a fishwife, notably described him as "displaying the same earnest charm that I have seen directed on other occasions at Miss Ellen Wilkinson."[50]

Ellen affected not taking the rumour too personally, claiming, "I have had so much of this sort of talk to put up with during the last ten years, that I am afraid I should normally just shrug my shoulders." However, she did protest to one friend that "it is so very wide of the mark," as her attentions were in fact otherwise directed.[51] Her letters to Katz intercepted by MI5 are peppered with lines such as "All my loving wishes to Ilse. She will be glad to be back with you," which do not exactly suggest an affair.[52] Yet given that her personal papers have not survived, it is impossible to know for certain whether the two were romantically involved. As her relationship with Horrabin and a later prolonged affair with Labour leader Herbert Morrison proved, she certainly was not above entering into a relationship with a married man.

Whatever her relationship with Katz, no one who knew her would have suggested her devotion to the fight against fascism was anything but sincere. In fact, her principal anxiety about the rumours surrounding her and Katz was that those who did not know her might suspect "the work I have done . . . was motivated by my personal interest in [Otto]."[53] And the work she did was prodigious. In addition to her publicity efforts on behalf of the *Brown Book,* she raised funds for the World Committee's refugee home for children in the Saar, another Münzenberg operation, which ran until shortly before the plebiscite held on January 15, 1935 reunited the border land with Germany and forced the refugees to flee further west. (As the outcome of the plebiscite shaped up to be a Nazi-landslide, Ellen, Katz, and Isabel Brown travelled to the Saar to personally smuggle several schoolchildren across the border into France.[54]) She published several pamphlets and longer exposés of the fascist threat, including *The Terror in Germany,* a clinical catalogue of Nazi crimes, and *Why Fascism?*—a book-length tract coauthored by émigré Edward Conze that argued that the Nazis' rise could be attributed in part to the failure of both the Social Democratic and the Communist left to capture the imagination of the working class. As yet further evidence of the enmeshed relationships of anti-imperial and anti-fascist activists in this period, *Why Fascism?* was published in Selwyn & Blount's "Topical Books" series, whose editor was none other than Krishna Menon.

If *Why Fascism?* was a cri de coeur to Europe's fractured left to rise to the fascist threat, Ellen's shorter works, published by the *Relief Committee,* were intended to appeal to the public conscience and raise money for the relief fund. Willi was keenly aware of the utility of images in influencing conscious and subconscious opinion. The English edition of the *Brown Book* included seventeen photographs of Nazi abuse, including a particularly harrowing image of Marie Jankowski's mutilated body, taken days before her death. The photograph of Jankowski was reproduced in *The Terror in Germany.* Ellen's other pamphlet for the World Committee, *Feed the Children,* showcased images of innocent children forced into exile in the Saar.

Ellen's skills as a propagandist made her an excellent asset to the anti-fascist movement. As German audiences discovered during her first visit to that country, even when her words could not be understood, her passion and commitment came across clearly on the platform. Thus, Katz enlisted Ellen to travel to Spain with Lord Marley, the president of the British committee, and Henri Barbusse to establish a Spanish branch of the World Committee. She had recently fallen down a flight of stairs and broken bones in her hand, and her arm was in a sling—yet another example of the accident-prone MP's inveterate clumsiness. Nonetheless, she made the journey to central Spain, where the group headlined a meeting at the Madrid Athenaeum Club on Monday, July 10, 1933.[55]

The Spanish Republic was a relatively new creation, dating back just two years to the collapse of the dictatorship of Primo de Rivera and the subsequent overthrow of the Bourbon monarchy. The centre-left government that had come to power in the 1931 elections was increasingly under threat from conservative, royalist, and proto-fascist forces. Ellen saw in the Spanish situation an eerie echo of Weimar Germany in the 1920s. Although she emphasized it was of the utmost importance to preserve the Republic at all costs, she warned her new friends against making concessions to the apparently democratic conservatives in an effort to outmanoeuvre the extreme right. It was, she argued, imperative to start preparing Spanish workers for the ultimate acquisition of power and not to allow the working class to rely on the professional classes to save the Republic.[56] This was fighting talk, and her colleagues worried that her radicalism, combined with the World Committee's reputation as a Münzenberg front, would undermine the delegation's credibility. In a separate interview with the Partido Socialista Obrero Español (PSOE) newspaper *El Socialista,* Henri Barbusse explicitly, if somewhat disingenuously, denied the World Committee was controlled by the Communists, disowned responsibility for the attacks made by individual committee members on Social Democrats, and emphasized the participation of prominent non-Communist individuals in the committee's efforts.[57] Despite Ellen's revolutionary rhetoric, the fact that she and Marley had both been junior ministers in the former Labour government was intended as a signal of the delegation's respectability. But although Ellen would still have classed herself as a parliamentarian, it was clear the renewed collaboration with Communists had rekindled her fire for the class struggle.

As she had in India, the petite porcelain-skinned activist, with *"las mechas cobrizas rebeldes"* (rebellious, coppery strands of hair) constantly flying loose across her brow in the humidity, stood out in Madrid. Yet Ellen felt immediately at home in Spain, which was much more relaxed and easygoing than Britain. She, Marley, and Barbusse enjoyed sitting out on their host's balcony overlooking the Sierra de Guadarrama north of the city, as the late-afternoon breeze took the sting out of the Madrid summer.[58]

Their mission was a success, and the World Committee secured an outpost in the Iberian Peninsula. It was, for Ellen, the beginning of a long and intimate connection with the country. She made at least eight visits to Spain in the 1930s, mostly in aid of the Republican government during the 1936–1939 civil war, a conflict she and many others on the British and international left viewed as a proxy battle against European fascism. Even before the outbreak of the civil war, Ellen would return to Spain, painfully anxious that the Spanish Republic might be headed the way of its German predecessor. In November 1934, she travelled with Otto Katz and another Labour peer, Lord Listowel, to the Republic under the auspices of the Society of Friends of the New Spain (another Münzenberg-front group), to investigate the government's repression of an uprising by miners in the industrial region of the Asturias, and to arrange for the distribution of funds and the planned arrival of a supply ship to relieve those whose husbands and fathers had been imprisoned by the government.[59] The group was the first delegation of foreigners to attempt a visit to the region.

When Ellen had last set foot in Spain, a centre-left government had been in power, under the leadership of Manuel Azaña. Shortly after she left the country, the PSOE had pulled out of the coalition, arguing that their Radical partners had not gone far enough on the path toward economic and social reform. For many in the country, particularly in the traditional south, however, the 1931–1933 government had already gone too far. The November 19, 1933 elections had returned a majority for the centrist and conservative parties, and a new government had been formed under the leadership of the Radical Alejandro Lerroux. His government quickly moved to halt or reverse many of the reforms put through by the previous administration, particularly in regard to workers' rights and land tenure. In the months after the election, strikes broke out in both agricultural and industrial regions of the country, particularly in Catalonia in the east, which resented the new government's efforts to assert central control. The Asturian miners did not, however, take up arms until the following October, after the prime minister invited three members of Gil Robles's Confederación Española de Derechas Autónomas (CEDA), a fascistic party which had refused to swear allegiance to the Republican constitution, to join his cabinet. The miners organized into workers' militias, and successfully took control of the city of Oviedo, armed with seized munitions and miners' tools of axes, picks and dynamite.

When the regular army proved incapable of suppressing the rebellion (many soldiers actually joined the rebels), the government sent in North African troops and members of the Foreign Legion, and bombed the city of Oviedo and surrounding mountains. After ten days of fighting, the miners surrendered, at which point government forces moved in and exacted violent revenge against the men and their families. Both the Asturian and the Republican governments publicly denied accusations of brutality and reprisals by the armed forces and claimed the miners themselves had been principally responsible for the destruction of private property. Ellen and her two companions had come to Spain to publicize the "truth" about the conflict.

The delegation was also an opportunity to strengthen Spain's anti-fascist networks and bring them into closer cooperation with Münzenberg's Paris-based operation. The conservative victory in Spain had coincided with an official shift in Comintern policy in favour of "unity" between Communists and Social Democrats. During their visit, Otto and the two British politicians were able to make contact with many former government ministers, several of whom, in an eerie echo of the March terror, had been imprisoned in the hysteria following the Asturias uprising. It was on this trip that Ellen first met Largo Caballero and Giner de los Rios, both then in prison.[60] She maintained those relationships after returning to Britain, keeping closely informed of the events leading up to the Royalist uprising in July 1936. In addition to making contact with Socialists, the two Labour politicians leveraged their official position as former ministers of His Majesty's Government to secure interviews with government ministers and access to the Asturias region, which had been declared off-limits to all but sympathetic reporters.

Upon their arrival in Madrid, Ellen and Listowel met with the British ambassador, Sir George Grahame. Grahame apparently "advised them to drop their role of self-appointed foreign inquisitors in this country and return to England."[61] Instead, after two days in the capital, the group secured an interview with Lerroux. "This elderly, testy ex-journalist," as Ellen described him, grudgingly gave them a letter of introduction to Major Doval, Military Acting Governor of the province of Asturias. The travellers made their way to Asturias that evening on the sleeper. What happened next was subject to dispute. According to the *New York Times* correspondent, who was presumably briefed by the government, "Major Doval politely escorted Miss Wilkinson, Lord Listowel, and Mr. Katz through the battle-ravaged streets of Oviedo." Thereafter, "a polite hint that there was no need for the investigators to prolong their stay . . . was accepted with alacrity by Lord Listowel," and one of Doval's lieutenants drove the group to Santander, whence they departed by ferry for France.

According to Ellen, things proceeded slightly less politely. In her version, the group was ushered into the Town Hall by "the sort of Spaniard you see on posters, magnificent, rather suitable for opera." While they were kept waiting to see Doval, their new "Operatic Tenor friend" did his best to round up a menacing crowd outside the hall. The commander finally arrived, and Ellen could not help but be impressed by how attractive he was. His "sensitive eyes," however, belied a hardnosed determination. Using the crowd assembled outside as a pretext, he cancelled their promised tour of the city and ushered them into a car that drove them through the mountains to the border. Although they heard numerous secondhand stories of intimidation and hostage-taking of civilians, they did not have a chance to interview a single inhabitant of the city.[62]

As a fact-finding mission, the trip was a failure; but as a propaganda exercise, it garnered immense international publicity in both the European and American press. Alvarez del Vayo, foreign minister during the civil war, would later claim the publicity surrounding the visit helped pave the way for wider international sympathy for the Republicans during the civil war.[63] Ellen's reports of her expedition in the feminist weekly *Time and Tide* instigated what was most likely the lengthiest exchange of letters in the magazine's history. Her article first appeared on November 24, six days after her return to Britain. She condemned the Spanish for sending in "coloured troops, Arabs and Moroccans, against the miners in the Asturias." She took a relatively lenient view of Prime Minister Alejandro Lerroux, whom she presented as a decent man unable to control the young right-wing rebels within his ministry. Her most biting criticism was reserved for the young CEDA leader Gil Robles. "If Gil Robles would only realize that politically he is not a man, but a limited company, in which the shares are held by the military, the Jesuits and the big banks, things would be easier for Lerroux," she mused—a fierce attack on a man who saw himself as a leader, not a puppet. The exchange of letters on Ellen's column continued until her final reply was published on March 24, 1935. After her letter, yet one more defence of the miners' innocence and the government's culpability, the magazine's editors printed simply: "This correspondence must now cease." The letters pounced on several alleged falsehoods and libels in her reporting, including her disparaging characterizations of the Jesuits and the civil guards. What no one commented on was her blatantly racist emphasis on the blackness of the African soldiers sent in to quell the uprising in the Asturias. Despite her ability to make empathic connections across racial, ethnic, and linguist barriers in her career, she does not appear to have questioned the appropriateness of playing to Britons' racial anxieties to stir up outrage against the Spanish government.

In addition to her work as publicist for the *Brown Book* and her travels to Spain and elsewhere on behalf of the World Committee, Ellen acted as secretary or treasurer to other Münzenberg anti-fascist endeavours, such as the Reichstag Counter-Trial, and, once the accused were acquitted, committees for the defence of other Germans imprisoned by the regime, including the leading Communists Ernst Thaelmann and Ernst Torgler. The Counter-Trial was the kind of publicity stunt Ellen loved. Officially known as the Reichstag Fire Enquiry, the five-day hearings were not technically a trial itself but an effort to bring influence to bear on another trial about to commence 1,000 kilometres away.

The trial of the Reichstag conspirators was scheduled to open in Leipzig on September 21, 1933. In the interval between the arrests and the opening of the trial, Münzenberg and his group had rushed through production of the *Brown Book,* which appeared in France, Britain, and America in August. Its accusations were taken seriously not only in the Communist and Social Democratic Press but also in such conservative publications as the London *Times,* whose reviewer wrote, "Much of the material is clearly drawn from Communist sources, and equally clearly some of its sections have been written by Communists. This does not invalidate the indictment. The record of outrages, always brutal and sometimes bestial as well, make appalling reading."[64] The majority of Conservative politicians were embarrassed by the *Brown Book* and quietly hoped the Reichstag controversy would melt away. Some, however, such as the Duchess of Atholl, promised their support to Münzenberg's crusade.[65] Like Ellen, Katharine Atholl was quick to recognize the threat fascism posed, not just to socialism but to parliamentary democracy more broadly.

While copies of the *Brown Book* were banned in Germany, five illegal German editions were printed, and "various 'camouflaged' and 'miniature' copies hidden in Schiller's *Wallenstein* and Goethe's *Hermann und Dorothea* were smuggled into Germany by a well-coordinated system of underground couriers that even the Gestapo admitted 'functioned very well.'"[66] The book frightened the regime as, although the Nazis could largely control information within Germany, they remained concerned about public opinion outside its borders. The Reichstag Counter-Trial was an effort to capitalize on the success of the *Brown Book* and turn up the international pressure on the Nazis to acquit the Communist defendants. It was headed by Ellen's future colleague on the National Executive Committee of the Labour Party, barrister D. N. Pritt, and included jurists from across Europe and the United States, including Arthur Garfield-Hays, general counsel for the American Civil Liberties Union, founded by Ellen's old friend Roger Baldwin. The jurists held hearings in the courtroom of the Law Society in Carey Street, and the surroundings gave the private event an air of formality. Ellen played a key role in arranging the venue and sorting out other practicalities. The week before the trial saw her "haring about . . . without sleep for ninety-six hours."[67] Over twenty witnesses were called, some of whom were in hiding and had to be smuggled into the courtroom at the risk of their lives, and hundreds of documents were examined, before the lawyers released their conclusions that the evidence exculpated the accused and that the fire "must have been the work of the Nazis."[68] The results of the enquiry were released on the evening before the Leipzig trial commenced and had a profound effect on its conduct. Goebbels appreciated the impact of the *Brown Book* and the London Counter-Trial on public perceptions of the prosecution and went so far as to call the *Brown Book* "the sixth defendant" at Leipzig.[69]

The work of the World Committee was international in its scope, and, in the immediate context of the *Brown Book* campaign and the Reichstag Fire Enquiry, was specifically concerned with using international public opinion to influence policy *within* Germany. But the rising spectre of fascism on the continent had also alerted Ellen to the need for action within Britain's borders, both to unify the forces of the left against a potential fascist threat in Britain and to coordinate and strengthen efforts to influence the British government's stance in diplomatic negotiations with its neighbour across the North Sea. To that end, Ellen became an early supporter of the Unity Campaign, which aimed to bring the Labour Party, the Independent Labour Party (the ILP had formally split from the Labour Party in 1932), and the Communist Party together in a united front against fascism.

Ellen also became more aggressive in her support for positive action to counter the orthodoxies of liberal political economy. In the run-up to the 1929 general election, Ellen, as a junior member of the party's National Executive Committee, had grudgingly accepted her colleagues' view that radical economic proposals would lose the party crucial votes. After the collapse of the Labour government, she, like many on the left, came to the conclusion that Labour's future lay in promulgating concrete socialist alternatives to capitalism. Yet, perhaps unsurprisingly given her past attraction to radical economic programmes such as that of the National Guilds League, the alternatives she envisaged were considerably more audacious than most. Unlike the Communists, with whom she increasingly collaborated on both anti-fascist and anti-colonial campaigns from 1933, she did not go so far as to reject the constitutional path to socialism. She wanted "something different, in which we shall keep something of our private initiative and our characteristic discipline. I think it better that we shall have agreed planning rather than enforced planning."[70] But, in order to build a constituency around "agreed planning," Labour could not be constrained by the "Victorian" ideas that had hamstrung MacDonald and Snowden.

The reciprocal impact of Ellen's experiences in Europe on her domestic politics are most clearly visible in *Why Fascism?* The book seeks to explain how both Communism and democratic socialism have failed to counter the fascist advance on the continent, and, in so doing, to offer a cautionary tale to the Labour Party. If Labour continues on its current vacillating and timid path, Ellen and Conze argue, Britain could face the same fate as Germany. The authors denounce the German Communists for being helplessly beholden to Moscow and claim that, while "the heroic illegal work of the Communists since Hitler came to power has tended to silence criticism," it is shortsighted to make excuses for men and women who "could not stand up to Moscow when they had the resources of an immense party." But although they see little to praise in the conduct of the German Communists before March 1933, they place equal if not more blame on the party Ellen had campaigned to bring to power in July 1932. "Accustomed to regard themselves as a permanent minority, the Social Democratic leaders had never thought very concretely about how they would introduce Socialism if ever they got the chance," with the result that, when they did come to power in 1918, they essentially abdicated control to the capitalists. To avoid a similar fate, the British Labour Party should come up with a concrete set of proposals to implement when and if they were returned to government.[71]

Asked in April 1932 what she would do, if she were made chancellor, Ellen audaciously answered: "All cuts in doles and salaries would be abolished, State salaries increased, and a substantial allowance to families with an income of less than £1,000 a year would be paid on the condition that they did not save a penny of it." When asked how she would pay for such a scheme, she did not bother to talk in terms of capital levies or emergency bond issues. Instead, she said, she would "make it. And I mean *make* it; not earn it, or tax for it, but just make it. . . . The blunt fact . . . [i]s that money is a creatable commodity based on public confidence. We are suffering because the money it has been agreed to have will not stretch to cover the goods and services we are producing."[72] Such a proposal presupposed direct government control over the Bank of England and the regional joint-stock banks, something Ellen had advocated in 1928 in debates over the content of the party election manifesto, *Labour and the Nation*. The Socialist League, a new ginger-group formed in October 1932 under the leadership of Ellen's past and future collaborators, including Douglas Cole, Frank Horrabin, Clement Attlee, and Attlee's future chancellor Sir Stafford Cripps, had also come out in favour of nationalization. Given the overlap between their ideas at the time, and Ellen's later involvement with the organization, scholars have glossed over her initial scepticism about the group.[73] In fact, Ellen initially felt the Socialist Leaguers did not go far enough. It was all well and good to propose the nationalization of the banks, but what was needed was a plan for how to use that power once it had been seized. She defended Cripps's controversial assertion that Labour, if elected as a majority government by a majority of British electors, should use this mandate to pass an emergency powers act that would allow it to immediately implement reforms by decree.[74] Yet in

January 1933, Ellen publicly chided the League for being too intent on winning votes and insufficiently interested in "looking at the realities of our social muddle" and coming up with "something fresher than the old slogans" to offer as a solution to Britain's social ills.[75]

After two and a half years toeing the line as a junior minister, Ellen was back in crusading mode, a self-fashioned Socialist Joan of Arc. At the ministry of health, she had accepted her responsibility to carry out the government's program, overcautious as she felt it to be. With Labour out of power, she threw her energy into advocating for a stronger, more robust socialist platform, with a clear roadmap for government, if and when Labour was again placed in the driver's seat. Her commitment to her convictions, regarding both domestic and international policy, put her in frequent conflict with the party leadership. Ellen and Lord Marley were taken to task for their involvement with Münzenberg's Relief Committee, and the party issued a formal denial that the visit to Asturias had any endorsement from the party.[76] Repeatedly in the mid-1930s, she used the party's annual conference as a forum to publicly air her differences with the leadership.

The National Union of Distributive and Allied Workers' (NUDAW) highest-profile delegate arrived in Hastings on October 3, 1933 amid calls for Ellen and Marley to be expelled for "coquetting with communism."[77] Never one to remain on the defensive, Ellen put forth a rousing defence of the need for cooperation between all parties of the left, in which she specifically attacked Herbert Morrison, a member of the executive and coauthor of the party's pamphlet *The Communist Solar System*. The spirited exchange between the two politicians gave few indications of the close relationship that would grow up between them in a few years' time. Ellen began with an appeal to her own authority, reminding the conference of her personal experience of events in Germany, both in 1932 and during the March terror. She went on, directing her appeal "particularly to the platform" and to Morrison, who the day before had stated the case for the NEC:

> Today, many of the German leaders are sitting in concentration camps very largely as a result of the deep divisions in the working class of Germany. Let us say quite frankly that both sides are equally to blame. But . . . I want to ask

Mr. Morrison why he is going on the defensive? If democracy is going to win through this crisis, democracy must have teeth and claws; democracy cannot afford to have divisions in its own ranks.

Herbert patiently waited Ellen out, then rose from the platform to rebut her attack, cutting her down to size with backhanded compliments. His colleague, he argued, "is possessed of energy and drive—I say that in all sincerity—but I sometimes think that her energy and drive go into wrong channels and sometimes she is a bit of a nuisance to us. But may I put it to Miss Wilkinson, with the greatest respect, that . . . she, instead of running straight over and starting an unofficial organization in association with people whom she knows she ought not, in loyalty to the Party, to associate with, instead of criticizing the Executive for lack of energy and drive, would be better occupied by concentrating her undoubted energy and drive on the forward work of the party."[78]

Ellen must have appreciated the irony. At the same time that Morrison and the executive were chastising her as a "nuisance," they continued to rely on her "energy and drive." She did not hesitate to give her time to the party. Immediately after the conference, she travelled up to Kilmarnock at the leadership's behest to campaign for James Barr in the by-election to replace the National Labour MP Craigie Aitchison, who had been appointed Lord Justice Clerk of Scotland. She wore herself out in Scotland, and, not for the first time, returned from campaigning with a severe cold that developed into laryngitis and bronchitis. She was laid up for the better part of the week, leaving Annie to respond to her unwelcome correspondence from Labour Head Office further attacking the activities of the Relief Committee.[79]

Given a packed itinerary of travel, conferences, and platform meetings, the months flew by quickly, and before Ellen realized it, it was conference season again. After last year's conference on the Channel coast, in 1934 the party chose a venue farther north, at Southport. It was an inconvenient location for Ellen, as Annie was very ill and had only recently regained enough strength to travel back to London from the country cottage the two sisters had bought together in Penn in Buckinghamshire.[80] But it was imperative that Ellen make the journey to the northwest. The previous year Ellen had faced private calls for her expulsion; she now had to contend with an executive motion to add the Relief Committee to the official list of "Communist front" organizations ineligible for party membership. The *Manchester Guardian* (whose own Frederick Voigt was intimately involved with the Relief Committee's work) unequivocally condemned the proposed action. Conceding that the Relief Committee "may not be all that it seems," they nonetheless argued, "The party seems to be in danger of establishing the illiberal principle that its members must support only such organizations as its Executive approves."[81]

Nonetheless, the following day the conference overwhelmingly endorsed the Executive's decision, despite an impassioned defence of the committee's work by Harold Laski. Marley also took the platform in the committee's defence. Officially, Ellen refrained from speaking, but she carried out an "energetic protest" on the committee's behalf amongst her fellow delegates.[82] Following the vote, the *Guardian*'s Labour correspondent cynically declared, "It may be taken as certain that the Labour members of the committee will resign from it and not allow themselves to be expelled from the party."[83] From all evidence, Ellen did resign from the Relief Committee, as there is no further record of her appearing on its platforms, and, at least temporarily, there is no further correspondence between her and Katz in the MI5 files. However, as Herbert Morrison fully appreciated, Münzenberg's network was a hydra-like beast. Ellen's name soon resurfaced at the head of other British and international anti-fascist organizations run by the German émigré.

One such organization was the Women's Committee against War and Fascism. Ellen's central role in its foundation highlights her persistent links with feminist internationalism in this period. In January 1934, she and ten other women issued an appeal "for the defense of women against fascism." Of the ten, three were members of the Comintern, while six of the remaining seven were prominent figures within the Women's International League for Peace and Freedom, from Denmark, France, Ireland, Sweden, and Switzerland.[84] The WILPF women were part of the substantial left-wing of the movement, which, while continuing to subscribe to pacifism, believed that "State-Fascism is our worse enemy and we cannot possibly stand for a programme which claims justice if we do not take a clear position on this question and declare ourselves to be with those who are exploited, oppressed and murdered by fascism." For these women, it was "more important to work for a new social order [than] for disarmament." As a consequence, they were "prepared to be more indulgent with violent action if resorted to by the oppressed than if by the oppressors."[85]

Ellen's relationship with the Women's Committee over the next several years exposed both the growing tensions within her pacifism, and the growing strains in her relationship with the Comintern. When the Women's Committee was formed, both its WILPF supporters and its Communist members united behind its critique of capitalist militarism and call to join the "millions . . . organizing to end war." "We must," the first British appeal argued, "unite with women like ourselves to forge links of comradeship—solidarity which the capitalist, with all his power of the press, cinema and control of wealth will be unable to break."[86] The pragmatics of how this feminist solidarity would work to defeat fascism were unclear. Ellen had played a role in the successful publicity campaign which forced the Nazis to acquit the accused Communists of conspiracy in the Reichstag fire, and perhaps she genuinely believed the united power of world opinion could compel the Nazis to reform their own regime. Or perhaps she hoped a mass display of international solidarity would encourage the German people to rise up against the Nazis, despite the pervasive censorship she knew to exist within Germany and the government's virtual monopoly on the use of force. Ellen was, at this point, committed to a United Front policy of collaboration between all leftwing political and industrial organizations for the peaceful overthrow of capitalism. The United Front policy sought influence through extra-parliamentary as well as formal political channels. Strike action, as much as the ballot box, should be the workers' tool in throwing off the capitalist yoke. Supporters of a United Front did not realistically envisage left-wing coalitions winning parliamentary majorities across Europe, and focused less on winning elections than on mobilizing public opinion.

While Stalin had orchestrated the Comintern's shift away from the doctrine of "Social Fascism" toward support for a United Front of all leftwing parties, he had little faith that such a policy would bear fruit. In May 1935, the Soviet government accepted that fascism was only likely to be defeated on the international battlefield, and negotiated a military alliance with the conservative government then in power in

France. To Ellen, the Franco-Soviet treaty seemed a betrayal of the campaign for leftwing unity, and she did not hesitate to denounce the Soviet Union in her capacity as a founder of Women against War and Fascism.[87] Over the months and years that followed, however, she and her fellow radical pacifists would be forced to grapple with the question of how and whether fascism could be defeated without resort to an alliance with "capitalism" and international war. Ultimately, Ellen would come to support the Popular Front policy unveiled by the Comintern in 1935, and to accept that fascism would need to be defeated on the battlefield. That she took the time to work through and come to this position on her own underscores her autonomy from Moscow, even as she collaborated with individual Communists on shared goals.

Ellen's unwillingness to accept the party line—either Communist or Labour—was equally evident in her approach to domestic politics. At the 1934 Labour Party conference at Southport, Ellen spoke out against her party's domestic policy with as much fervour as she attacked its position on the Relief Committee. The morning after the conference voted to exclude Relief Committee members, the Fiery Particle took the platform to spur the party to more concrete action in support of the growing ranks of unemployed. She urged the Executive to consider how the party "could get into closer touch with the human problem of the mass of the unemployed themselves." While their resolutions condemning the government's inaction were laudable, she felt the party had missed a trick in not getting behind the National Unemployed Workers' Movement's (NUWM) hunger march in protest against the inadequacy of the Unemployment Bill earlier that year. Although she was not involved with the planning of the march, Ellen had spoken before the crowd of marchers and other supporters that assembled in Hyde Park on February 25—a crowd that, by one estimate, neared 50,000, including several thousand police and special constables. The NUWM was a Communist movement, but she and her old friend the ILP leader James Maxton stood together on a small platform at one corner of the mass demonstration and, according to one observer, said, "the worst things of the Unemployment Bill, but such was the enthusiasm of the compact body of disciples near the tumbril that, above their applause, little could be heard."

Following the demonstration, she agreed to act as delegate to take the men's grievances to the prime minister.[88] The NUWM march was, she conceded, merely a publicity stunt, but such publicity might serve to awaken government and public sympathy to the plight of the unemployed in a way the official statistics had failed to do.

Speaking at Southport, she also suggested the executive come up with some modest schemes "to give immediate succor to those devastated areas," which included her own hard-hit constituency of Jarrow. While this could only be "ambulance work," "we should not keep our eyes focused too much on things 25 years hence, but on the men, women and children who are starving now in these areas and have been for ten years."[89] Her advocacy of immediate, if modest, palliatives, recalled her work on the Manchester Council and the various Trades Boards in the early 1920s. It also foreshadowed her strategy for the Jarrow Crusade in 1936.

Ellen capped off her visit to Southport with a lecture on India at Cambridge Hall, hosted by the local Labour Party. The discussion of international affairs at conference had been dominated by the spectre of fascism, and it was an opportunity for Ellen to remind her audience that human rights were in peril in parts of the British Empire as well as within the borders of Hitler's Reich.[90] Shortly after the Southport conference broke up, Ellen and Listowel made their abortive visit to investigate the situation in the Asturias. A month later, she set sail for America, where her agents had arranged for her to spend two months lecturing in cities in the northeast and midwest. The itinerary of lectures gave her an opportunity to clarify her thinking on the relationship between pacifism, anti-fascism and anti-capitalism. At the same time, her experience of labour struggles in the United States inspired new ideas about how to approach the social crisis in Britain.

12

PURSUING SOCIAL JUSTICE IN
BRITAIN AND BEYOND

As Ellen looked ahead in her diary toward 1935, she was confronted with a comparatively uncluttered itinerary. The *Brown Book* campaign had ended, and the Comintern's adoption of a popular-front strategy had led to a temporary cooling off between Ellen and her Communist allies in the anti-fascist crusade. She was still out of parliament, and there was little prospect of a general election. She remained the National Union of Distributive and Allied Workers (NUDAW) national women's organizer, but high levels of unemployment combined with stable real wages meant there were no major strikes to organize. Throughout her career, Ellen's critics argued that her foreign travel detracted from her domestic responsibilities. In January 1935, however, there were few immediate calls on her attention to prevent her from making another visit to the United States.

Ellen set sail from Southampton on the penultimate day of 1934, one of only 216 passengers to embark from the Channel port on the SS Washington, a mammoth new ocean liner that could accommodate over 1,000 travellers. Notably, on the manifest she listed her profession as "writer," not union organizer. Although she continued to draw a salary from her union, it was increasingly her journalism and speaking engagements that covered her expenses. Writing and lecturing would remain her dominant source of income after her return to parliament in November 1935. As she declared in one of her many well-paid articles for the London evening *Star* in 1937, it was almost impossible for an MP to make ends meet on a £400 salary unless he or she had the benefit of either "unearned income, or the professions of law, journalism, or something 'consultant' which can be fitted in to suit."[1]

Ellen landed in New York on January 6, on a cloudy evening with the temperature an unseasonably mild 50 degrees.[2] When she had last visited, Franklin Roosevelt was the state's governor. Now he was the country's thirty-second president. In 1932, he had run on a platform of progressive change, promising to use the power of the state to return jobs and prosperity to the American people.[3] Roosevelt's emphasis on state-funded schemes to boost employment and his willingness to intervene in the banking sector to return liquidity to the U.S. economy echoed Ellen's prescriptions to address Britain's economic woes in the early 1930s. Some of Ellen's American friends who shared her social outlook were enthusiastic about the New Deal, including Arthur Hays, who had worked with Ellen on the Reichstag Fire Counter-Trial. Others, such as Hays's colleague at the ACLU Roger Baldwin, remained sceptical. Baldwin had pessimistically prophesied that the outcome of the 1932 election would not "make much difference to the cause of civil liberties" and was hostile toward the institution Roosevelt claimed as one of the chief successes of his first one hundred days, the National Recovery Administration. The NRA suspended existing antitrust laws and facilitated collaborative agreements between business and labour in the interests of creating employment. Baldwin saw the program as the product of the president's close ties to business interests. He denounced the NRA as a "violation of . . . the workers' right to organize and strike—their only resources of power and liberty" and likened it to Italian or German policy.[4]

While visiting New York, Ellen normally stayed with her good friend Evie Preston, Baldwin's longtime mistress and soon-to-be wife, and she likely discussed the NRA with Roger during her visit. His analysis is evident in her writing on the New Deal after her return from America, as well as in her comments on the lecture circuit after New York. In Baltimore, Ellen told an audience that fascism was likely to come to America before it gained purchase in Britain and pointed to the NRA as "a strong movement towards the corporate state." Writing in *Time and Tide,* she argued that Mr. Roosevelt "had never yet tried" to fight "Big Business monopolies" and that the enforcement of the pro-worker terms of the NRA "has been left to where the unions were strong enough to get the [advantages] anyway."[5] This analysis of U.S. politics aligned with her increasing conviction that corporatist ventures in her own country, such as the introduction of the Agricultural Marketing Act, the creation of the government-supported cartel National Shipbuilding Securities Ltd, and other instances of "planning with the consent of the capitalist at the expense of the consumer," were evidence of fascistic tendencies within British society.[6]

If Baldwin's analysis of New Deal corporatism helped sour Ellen's impression of Roosevelt, the omnipresent evidence of persistent unemployment and slump despite the president's efforts to inject money into the economy underscored the inadequacy of the New Deal's stimulus schemes. In the early 1930s, Ellen's prescription for the British economy had been to address the Hobsonian crisis of underconsumption by increasing consumers' purchasing power.[7] The New Deal had tried to do exactly that; but the results, from Ellen's perspective, appeared to be little more than rising corporate profits and a widening gulf between purchasing and productive power.[8] She denounced the continued high levels of poverty in the United States, the stagnant real wages of those who remained in employment, and the overall inadequacy of the New Deal to redress the nation's ills.[9] The problem, as Ellen saw it, was that industrial control remained in the hands of capitalists, even where the capitalists had become salaried employees of the state. She compared the situation in New Deal America to that in Spain under the centre-left coalition that came to power in 1933. In Spain, "Socialists were among the members of the cabinet. But they were content to obtain higher wages for the workers and similar improvements rather than insist on an entire reorganization. . . . It is so much better not to worry about advanced ideas unless you mean it."[10] Half measures, it became increasingly clear, were not enough. The only long-term solution was the abolition of private capital combined with the introduction of economic planning. Over the next several years, Ellen began to spell out a recipe for social justice that rested on those dual pillars.

In Washington, DC, she spoke at the National Public Housing Conference, opened by Eleanor Roosevelt and headlined by Secretary of the Interior Harold Ickes. The event was held in the glamorous Willard Hotel, a few blocks from the White House. Ickes used the opportunity to unveil government proposals for slum clearance and the construction of low-cost rental housing, and Ellen followed his speech with her own testimonial to the success of such schemes in Britain and Europe. It was a sign of her popularity in the United States that ABC News broadcast Ellen's speech.[11] It wasn't the only syndicated broadcast during her visit. Two and a half weeks later, listeners from New York to Los Angeles tuned in to hear her talk about the political situation in Europe and the fascist threat.[12]

As with her previous tour of the United States in 1931, Ellen was booked to speak to women's and socialist organizations in almost equal measure. She made many repeat appearances before groups she had lectured to four years earlier. These included several local branches of the Women's International League for Peace and Freedom (WILPF), such as the Syracuse, New York, branch, whose members she addressed on "The Struggle for Peace." It was an exhausting schedule of speaking and travelling. By the time Ellen boarded ship on Wednesday morning, February 27, to return to Britain, she was in need of rest. The seven days of enforced confinement gave her a much-needed opportunity to recuperate before her return to politics as usual.

Within days of her return, Ellen was chairing an India League meeting in the library of the Memorial Hall in Farringdon that, despite its small attendance (250 British and Indians), merited the attention of the Metropolitan police, who planted a spy in the audience.[13] The following week saw her travelling to the southwest, where she spoke at a regional NUDAW rally in Bridgewater and addressed a local Labour

Party meeting.[14] She had just begun to settle back in when she was violently jolted out of her routine on the night of April 4. She was home when detectives called to interview her about the suspicious death of two German exile friends of hers, Dora Fabian and Mathilde Wrum, in their rented flat a few blocks away. The deaths, officially declared a double suicide after a cursory and arguably prejudiced police investigation, remain one of the great unsolved murder mysteries of 1930s London.[15] To Ellen, and to many of the women's friends in the Relief Committee for Victims of German Fascism, the Women's International League (WIL), and the Independent Labour Party (ILP), the deaths were the clear work of Nazi agents operating in Britain. Just days after Ellen's return from America, the anti-fascist community had been shocked by the news that the German Jewish journalist Berthold Jacob had been kidnapped from Basel by Nazi agents and forcibly repatriated to prison in Germany. The man responsible for the kidnapping was Hans Wesemann, a Nazi agent who had effectively infiltrated the anti-Nazi exile community in London.

Ellen and her friends became convinced the two women had been murdered to prevent their revealing information about Nazi spies at work in London. The police, they believed, were aware of the Nazi involvement in the women's deaths and covered up evidence to avoid an international incident.[16] As well as being a personal loss for Ellen, her friends' deaths and the alleged cover-up underscored the imperative need to replace the sitting government with an administration more committed to standing up to the Nazi threat. The audacity of the Nazis in carrying out an assassination on British soil was yet further evidence that the regime was unlikely to be stopped by means short of war and contributed to Ellen's gradual conversion to support for a broad-based anti-fascist military alliance.

If the Fabian-Wurm murders were an ominous sign of the extending reach of Nazi aggression, the principal threat to international peace in 1935 came not from Germany but from Italy. In December 1934, a minor skirmish between Abyssinian forces and Italian and Somali troops garrisoned at Walwal on the disputed border between Italian Somaliland and Abyssinia proved the catalyst for an international crisis.

Abyssinian emperor Haile Selassie insisted on bringing the incident before the League of Nations for arbitration, arguing that the Italian garrison stood on Abyssinian territory. The Italians denied the charge and began massing troops on the southern border of their African colony. As tensions rose during the summer of 1935, the world looked to the League to see what, if any, action it would take to defend Abyssinian sovereignty. The League, anxious not to offend Mussolini, sought to diffuse the situation and, after some prevarication, issued a ruling that neither side had been at fault. Britain and France attempted to localize the conflict by declaring an embargo on the sale of arms to either side, but Selassie continued to press for League intervention. Sensing that neither France nor Britain would push the League to act, Mussolini invaded Abyssinia on October 3, 1935.

The invasion took place on the penultimate day of the Labour Party conference at Brighton, in the wake of an acrimonious debate over the party's position on the conflict. That summer the League of Nations Union, a popular organization committed to the principles of international understanding and collective security through the League, organized a massive "peace ballot" in which over 11 million Britons volunteered responses that underscored the strength of pacifist sentiment in Britain.[17] As Baldwin would say in his election broadcast on October 25, there were "no two opinions in the country today as to what must be the main objective of all Parties in the State. It is peace—peace for us here at home, peace in Europe, and peace throughout the world."[18] Yet there were deep divisions within each party over how best to secure peace. At the Labour conference, those divisions hinged on the question of whether the policy of collective security through the League of Nations, including the enforcement of economic and military sanctions against aggressor states, was inconsistent with the party's commitment to avoid imperialist war. The entire party was united in its opposition to the government's rearmament proposals, but there agreement ended. The majority of the leadership supported the right of the League to impose sanctions, including, if necessary, military sanctions. Hugh Dalton put the position for the executive: Sanctions might (but did "not necessarily") mean war; however, "the scrapping of sanctions certainly means war, and a more terrible war than that between Italy and Abyssinia, with many more people coming in."[19]

The executive's view was challenged from two directions—the anti-capitalist and the absolute pacifist. William Mellor and Stafford Cripps put forward the view of the Socialist League that the League of Nations was merely "a new cover" for capitalist imperialism, and that the Labour Party should not sacrifice its men and women to the "capitalist military machine." Speaking as a lifelong pacifist, the party leader, George Lansbury, claimed he personally felt the party was "making a terrible mistake," declaring to considerable applause that he "could see no difference between mass murder organized by the League of Nations and mass murder organized between individual nations." Recognizing the position this put him in, Lansbury told the party he would be willing to resign the leadership, a suggestion trade union leader Ernest Bevin accepted with relish. The party leader, Bevin argued, should follow the course his conscience directed him toward and not go "hawking your conscience round from body to body asking to be told what to do with it." Given the need for unity, Bevin was undoubtedly right, but the cruelty of his delivery left a bitter taste in the mouths of many of "GL's" friends and supporters.[20] The vote taken the next day resulted in an overwhelming endorsement of the executive's policy—2,163,000 to 102,000. Ellen's union had delivered its bloc vote for the platform, but her own sympathies, despite her hatred of fascism, lay with Mellor, Cripps, and the Socialist League. As a protest against the decision, she withdrew her name from consideration for a seat on the National Executive Committee, underscoring her unwillingness to actively carry out a policy she could not endorse. Through this period, Ellen had been vocal in her support for a United Front peace policy, but this was the first time her convictions came into direct conflict with her political ambition. For someone as ambitious as Ellen, it was a difficult decision to make.

In the Conservative view, the Labour Party had committed itself to the worst of both worlds: a bellicose position toward Italy and a crippling commitment to disarmament. With apologies to Lewis Carroll, the Conservative *Daily Express* quipped:

> We are told, Father Labour, the young man said,
> To disarm, and trust to the right;
> But now you persistently stand on your head—
> And ask us, with no arms, to fight!

Yet, Labour's opponents were faced with their own internal divisions. Few in either the British or the French governments wanted to get involved in the Abyssinian crisis, but the two leading powers in the League felt compelled to back at least a policy of minor economic sanctions against Italy. Baldwin claimed to want peace, but his government was committed to a policy of rearmament, or military "modernization," particularly of the navy. A modern navy, he argued, would be a necessity if, heaven forbid, the government's obligations to the League led to Britain taking part in a naval blockade. Meanwhile, the isolationists within his party, backed by the press barons Lord Beaverbrook and Lord Rothermere and their mass circulation dailies the *Mail* and the *Express,* also supported the modernization of the armed forces but did not want Britain to become involved in Abyssinia or any other conflict where the British Empire's interests were not directly involved.

Into this environment of confusion and international anxiety, Baldwin decided to introduce a general election campaign. Politically it was an astute move in that it took advantage of the divisions within the left—Baldwin called the election only three days after the comparatively unknown Clement Attlee had been selected to replace the disgraced Lansbury as Labour leader—and preyed on electors' unwillingness to change leaders in the midst of an international crisis. To Ellen, the surprise election was a disaster. Her party was committed to a foreign policy she did not believe in, and one that seemed unlikely to win broad support given the Conservatives' determination to present Labour as the war-mongering party. Its domestic program was, she felt, woefully ill thought through and lacking in the bold solutions she believed necessary to combat unemployment effectively.

Ellen had made her own views on Labour's program clear in an essay, "Labour and the Middle Classes," published shortly before the party conference. Part of a volume entitled *New Trends in Socialism*, edited by her friend and fellow Labour candidate George Catlin, the essay argued that the party's current strategy of appealing to the middle classes in terms of security of wages and pensions was misguided. Although this might help the party win votes from clerks and administrative workers, it had limited appeal to "the most socially valuable section Socialists must wish to attract," namely "the inventors, the organizers, the technicians who are indispensable to any planning of the machine age."

The party needed to offer something beyond economic security, or even beyond schemes of nationalization that in practice meant little more than "inviting whatever Capitalist is already doing the job to go on doing it, at a salary instead of a profit." A truly revolutionary appeal to the middle classes would, Ellen argued, focus on uniting the interests of the technicians and the workers against "the superfluous parasites on the economic system. . . . The new wave of socialist thought which is to organize the actual transition from Capitalism to Socialism must arise out of the experience of the workers, manual, technical and administrative, deliberately and carefully encouraged to meet together and discuss problems on the basis of coming power, on the lines of 'taking over.'"[21] It was a radical plea that harkened back to the syndicalist thinking of her days as a Guild Socialist, but it bore little practical resemblance to current Labour policy.

The other contributors to *New Trends* were not her fellow Socialist Leaguers but rather political moderates, many of whom were acolytes of Hugh Dalton, including Evan Durbin, Hugh Gaitskell, and Douglas Jay. Of the fifteen contributors, Ellen was the only woman, and the only one to have been officially reprimanded by the party leadership. Her views, especially on the optimal direction of state-owned industries, were opposed to those of her fellow contributors, but her participation in the volume indicated her desire to open a dialogue with the young men increasingly seen as the architects of Labour's blueprint for a future planned economy. She remained conflicted about the extent of her willingness to compromise with the party leadership, but she had not given up hope of productive collaboration between the party's radical and moderate wings.

Ellen went into the 1935 general election determined to campaign hard for the party, despite her conviction they would lose. In an article in the *Daily Herald* published immediately after the election was called, she exhorted her fellow candidates and party activists around the country to focus on the question of poverty in Britain rather than on the no-win issue of the Abyssinian crisis. Campaigning in Jarrow, she did her best to heed her own advice. It was not difficult. Vera Brittain, whose husband, George Catlin, was the candidate for Sunderland, gave an unvarnished account in her diary of the depth of poverty she encountered while campaigning in that city's slums, so similar to those in Ellen's constituency less than ten miles away: "Afternoon, spent most of time in damp and dark East End, canvassing in houses with pitch-dark stairs worn and broken in many places; tin baths & buckets on landing; walls felt shiny and damp to touch. Habitations more fit for monkeys than human beings; wondered how many bugs I was picking up." Vera's heart was in the right place, but her instinctive revulsion in the face of northern poverty likely wounded the pride of many voters she encountered on the campaign trail. Ellen appreciated her friend's willingness to speak for her at two campaign events on the Tuesday before the election. Yet despite Vera's national profile as a committed pacifist, her husband undoubtedly got the better end of the deal when Ellen returned the favour by speaking for Catlin at the Sunderland Gaiety Theatre and at the Roker baths. Even though the fiery redhead "had a sore throat and was obviously much tired," her instinctive ability to connect with her audience made her an asset on any Labour platform.[22] Although she herself felt strongly about events in Abyssinia, in her Gaiety Theatre address she quickly shut down discussion of foreign policy as a "red herring" intended to distract voters from the real issue of unemployment. "Here as in Jarrow," she argued, "we have got great areas whose misery, suffering, poverty and unemployment are due directly and indirectly to the rotten capitalist system." She levelled her criticism firmly at the Means Test to qualify for unemployment benefit, which she described as "incredible in its meanness." It was a typical Ellen performance: She addressed big political issues, but in a folksy, straightforward manner that conveyed her empathy for and understanding of constituents' concerns.[23]

Ellen did not make campaign promises she was unlikely to be able to keep. She did not promise socialism, but merely to do her best to provide employment and protect the standard of living until such as time as socialism could take hold. Her campaign made little mention of either foreign policy or of the party's nebulous domestic program, instead focusing on a critique of "the so-called 'national' government" for its legacy of rate hikes and benefit and wage cuts.[24] Essentially, Ellen asked her electors to believe in her sincerity and her determination to fight for their rights to the best of her ability. Her appeal succeeded, and she was returned with 20,324 votes, giving her a majority of 2,350 over the sitting Conservative MP William Pearson. An article she wrote shortly after the election encapsulates the essence of her 1935 campaign: "A wakening social conscience demands a greater sense of responsibility to the unfortunate. The claims of the vast army of unemployed call for attention . . . *Whatever else we may have promised, this at least we have vowed, that we will work for those who are suffering so much.*"[25]

Events over the next twelve months would force Ellen to rethink how best to achieve reform both at home and abroad and to redefine her political priorities and strategy. Some onlookers interpreted her political reversals and reorientations in this period as signs either of insincerity or careerism. The truth was more complex. The *Guardian* commentator Jonathan Freedland recently observed of Karl Marx, "[He] was not a body of ideas, but a human being responding to events. . . . Accordingly, much of what scholars have tried to brand as Marxist philosophy was instead contemporary commentary, reactive and therefore full of contradiction."[26] Ellen, who identified as a Marxist throughout her life, was a Marxist in just such an undoctrinaire sense. Her political philosophy, such as it was, was grounded in a materialist analysis; but her strategy and priorities evolved with the shifting domestic and international landscape.

As the last polling results came in on the morning of November 15, the political landscape did not look auspicious for the Labour Party. Although Ellen regained Jarrow for Labour (albeit on the comparatively narrow margin of six percent), the party performed below expectations. The previous election had been the largest landslide in British history, with national government candidates winning a whopping 554 out of 615 seats, giving them an absolute majority of 493. Almost no one had expected a Labour victory in 1935; but politicians, pollsters, and pundits had all assumed the party would regain considerably more territory than it ultimately did. The Conservative party strategist Sir Joseph Ball confessed his anxiety on the eve of the election, noting, "It is not easy to frighten the electorate twice running."[27] Yet, when all the results were tallied, the national government maintained a majority of 243, while Labour's representation rose from 52 to a comparatively modest 154 MPs.

Looking at the dispiriting result, Ellen drew four key conclusions. First, Labour should not have endorsed a policy of League sanctions, which only allowed the government to paint them as warmongers. As she said to her union's annual conference in April 1936, "Those who raised this anti-sanctions policy [last year], surely have been proved right?"[28] Second, under current conditions, Labour politicians could best serve their constituents by "ambulance" measures that would provide immediate, practical improvement to the working classes under the existing capitalist system. Third, if Labour wanted to win a majority at the next election, they would need to articulate clearly what socialism was and how, practically, they would implement it. Finally, Clement Attlee was not the best man to lead the Labour Party. Over the next several years, Ellen would abandon the first of these conclusions, as the war in Spain impressed upon her the urgency of defending democracy at any cost. The other three would remain central tenants of her politics through the Second World War.

History has been kind to Clement Attlee, the diminutive former settlement worker and major in the First World War who was elected to replace Lansbury as party leader just weeks before the 1935 general election was called. A 2004 poll of political scientists and historians ranked Attlee the twentieth century's most successful prime minister, the majority of respondents noting the Attlee government's welfare state reforms and the creation of the NHS as the century's principal domestic policy achievements.[29] Yet, in 1935, Ellen and many others had their doubts about him. When Attlee's election as party leader was announced, Dalton famously recorded in his diary: "A wretched, disheartening result. And a little mouse shall lead them!"[30] Several years on, Attlee had still failed to impress the two other renowned diarists, Harold Nicolson and Beatrice Webb, who alongside Dalton provide an inordinate amount of the humorous and salacious material on interwar politics. After lunch with Attlee in 1938, Nicolson, who hoped Attlee might lead the revolt against the government's appeasement policy, wrote of the Labour leader that he was a "delightful man . . . but not a pilot in a hurricane." Two years later, after listening to Attlee speak on war aims at the London School of Economics, Webb recorded: "To realize that this little nonentity is the Parliamentary Leader of the Labour Party, the representative of Her Majesty's Opposition at £2000 per year, and presumably the future prime minister, is humiliating."[31]

The week after the general election, Dalton held a small dinner party, ostensibly to introduce the visiting League of Nations official and Labour supporter Konni Zilliacus to key members of the party. In fact, "Zilly's" visit was a cover for the first of Dalton's many schemes to unseat Attlee. According to Dalton's diary entry, "Of course, the Leadership came up, and we were nearly all for Morrison. [Fred] Bellenger talked disconnected rot in a tiresome way, but did not commit himself.... Ellen pretended not to be keen. She wrote to me afterwards that she was very keen on Morrison, but feared Bellenger blabbing. She turned out to be right. He is a wretched little tyke.... A heavy evening. Rather tired and discouraged."[32] In fact, Dalton had initially suspected Ellen, whose radical convictions made her an unlikely supporter of Morrison, whatever her views of Attlee, of "blabbing."[33] Yet, for all their personal disagreements, Ellen had always respected Morrison, placing him in the same category as Winston Churchill, whose brilliance she never questioned.[34] Morrison's successful direction of Labour's victory in the 1934 London County Council elections was a sharp counterpoint to Attlee's leadership of the general election campaign. And, although Ellen disagreed with Morrison on policy, she never doubted his socialist convictions. Within the party, they had long run in different circles. However, in a few months, the outbreak of the Spanish Civil War would bring them together in support for the Republican cause and form the basis for a close working and personal partnership.[35] Her faith in his potential never wavered. She would become his most reliable sidekick in his numerous attempts to replace Attlee with Morrison.

With her party stuck with a mouse for a leader and less than a quarter of seats in parliament, Ellen ploughed ahead with her own agenda of extra-parliamentary activism. She hired a new private secretary, Diana Hopkinson, whom she paid out of her own income. Hopkinson was the daughter of Eva Hubback, who, like Ellen, had been a suffrage activist before the war and who remained active in the National Union of Societies for Equal Citizenship (NUSEC) in the interwar period. In a testament of the overlapping personal and political connections that bound together so many politically active women in the period, Hubback co-owned a cottage in Cornwall with Mary Moorhouse, Ellen's old friend from the Manchester Guilds League with whom she had attended the founding conference of the Communist Party in 1920. It was likely as a result of these connections that Diana got the job, despite her appalling shorthand. Diana soon felt herself overwhelmed by the task, later recalling that Ellen's "energy was tremendous but it was most variously dispersed. . . . She was not easy to work for because she had so many strings in her bow. I found it difficult to sort them out. In addition to her parliamentary work there was her representation of NUDAW, her involvement with the India League, with a Left Wing theatre project, and with journalism. She was then writing notes for *Time and Tide*—the Sapphic Graphic. Sometimes she used to dictate while she was in the bath shouting to me as I sat in the sitting room."[36]

Diana's reference to the India League reflects Ellen's renewed engagement with the League and the Indian National Congress (INC) in this period. This was partly the result of the passage of the Government of India Act in August 1935, which many advocates of *swaraj* feared would shut down discussion over further reform. It also reflected Ellen's growing friendship with the young Congress leader Jawaharlal Nehru, who made several trips to London in the late 1930s as an informal ambassador for the INC.

Nehru and his wife Kamala travelled to Europe in 1935 so she could receive treatment for tuberculosis in Lausanne, Switzerland. Nehru first visited London shortly after their arrival, in November 1935, and returned in January 1936. Ellen and Nehru became fast friends during his 1936 visit, as her letters to him show.[37] During that visit, Diana Hopkinson made the arrangements for his stay. At her suggestion, Sheila Grant Duff, a young journalist who would later make a name for herself writing exposés of fascism in Eastern Europe, acted as Nehru's guide.[38] Ellen hosted a private reception for him to meet with politicians and journalists interested in Indian affairs. She also arranged for Nehru to meet some of the members of her *Time and Tide* set. Shortly before his arrival, she wrote to Lady Rhondda with the hasty, irreverent tone she saved for her close friends: "You know Jawaharlal Nehru . . . (Harrow, Trinity, London's pet . . . goes back to North India, turns ascetic, Gandhi's spiritual son . . . but with clothes . . . and next leader after the old man). That biography may sound formidable, but actually he is a real person and the sweetest sort of character." Nehru, she told Rhondda, wanted to meet people who were "doing things." To that end, could she host a small dinner for him on Sunday? "Theodora [Bosanquet] would like him, and I know you would . . . something very informal at home . . . is the thing he would love, and he is worthwhile."[39] Hopefully, Nehru did not share Edward Conze's estimation that the *Time and Tider*s were a "raffish lot" of sexual deviants.[40] Conze took an equally scathing view of Nehru. His assessment of Nehru as "either a Pukka sahib, only slightly off-white, or . . . the typical WOG, the Worthy Oriental Gentleman who had swallowed the values of his white masters hook line and sinker," did little to heal the growing rift between Ellen and the German émigré.[41] In addition to these informal gatherings, Ellen chaired several events at which Nehru was the featured speaker. On February 3, 1936, for example, she presided over a meeting at Caxton Hall at which Nehru spoke out against the imperialist behaviour of the British government, and its hypocrisy in condemning aerial bombardment of the Abyssinians by Italy while using similar tactics against Indians in the Northwest Frontier province. Ellen had repeatedly denounced the "fascist" practices of the British in the northwest frontier, drawing upon events she had witnessed in the region. Following his return to India in March 1936, Nehru took up the rotating presidency of the Congress party.

The comparative quiet on the Hitler front in 1935–1936 meant that the behaviour of German fascists attracted less public and political attention in Britain than the allegedly fascistic behaviour of British officials in India. Yet Ellen remained acutely alert to the Nazi threat. In February 1936, she accepted an invitation from the *Sunday Referee* to travel to Germany and report on conditions. The paper promoted her story with a photo captioned: "Ellen Wilkinson, red-headed, pocket-sized Labour MP for Jarrow, took her life in her hands when, stopping only to cast her vote in a House of Commons division, she flew to Germany on a Special mission of investigation for the 'Sunday Referee.' She is an expert investigator of foreign conditions. Was forbidden entry into Germany for speaking truth about the Nazi regime—defied the ban to go into Germany for the 'Sunday Referee.'" It was a dramatic, if slightly exaggerated, introduction. Although it was almost certainly true that "from the moment she crosses its frontier her every move is watched," she flew into Germany and cleared immigration legally. Hitler and

Goebbels may have hated her. They may have attempted to discredit her reports by denouncing her, preposterously, as a "Jew of the Jews."[42] But they recognized that they could not ban a British MP, and particularly a female MP, from entering the country. As Ellen had written to Nancy Astor after an earlier visit, "It is rather safer for me to go than the men, only, as Herr Hitler's intelligence officers may have read the articles I have been writing about his doings I am keeping my visit quiet—until I return."[43]

Ellen's 1936 trip resulted in one of the biggest foreign policy scoops of the year—arguably of the decade. Her article was printed on the *Referee*'s front page under the giant headline "Hitler Prepares to March on Rhine: 'WE CAN MOBILISE IN 24 HOURS.'" Through an old contact in the German Social Democratic student movement who had become a member of the Nazi administration, Ellen learned the Nazis were making preparations to reoccupy the Rhineland. Recognizing that if she were caught passing on such information not even her status as a British MP would protect her, she hid under the bedcovers in her hotel as she phoned the story into her editor so her voice would not be overheard by any potential Gestapo agents in the adjacent rooms. As soon as the story was relayed, she packed her bags and left for the airport, returning home just before the paper hit the newsstands.[44] Vera Brittain described the article in her diary as "like a prewar Blatchford article"—a reference to the ten-part series published by socialist Robert Blatchford in the *Daily Mail* in December 1909 that warned of German preparations for war.[45] Blatchford's articles had a tremendous impact. They were republished as a pamphlet and sold 1.5 million copies, caused a diplomatic incident between Britain and Germany, and helped frighten voters into sticking with the incumbent government in the January 1910 election.[46] Ellen's own report did not produce a similar effect. Although the government did question the German ambassador Leopold von Hoesch about the accusations, Hitler had not brought him into the loop and he sincerely denied any knowledge of the Führer's plans. The British government was thus taken by surprise when, three weeks later, the German army marched into the Rhine.[47]

Ellen's personal connections abroad kept her similarly well-informed of events in Spain. She was instinctively loyal and kept in touch with Largo Caballero and the other Socialists with whom she had made contact on her 1934 visit. Despite her continued reservations about the Popular Front strategy, she would have been heartened when, following the 16 February 1936 elections for the Cortes, the centrist Radicals refused to form a coalition with the right-wing parties and instead entered a coalition with the left. Manuel Azaña's centre-left government soon antagonized the nationalist and agrarian forces by freeing political prisoners; reintroducing land reforms reversed by the previous administration (more land was redistributed between May and July 1936 than in all previous years of the Republic combined); granting a degree of regional autonomy in the northeast; and removing hardline conservative military leaders to imperial outposts. If the capitalist and landowning forces were angered by the official actions of the Azaña government, they were terrified by the wave of strike action that swept through the country as workers, no longer fearing industrial action would lead to imprisonment, reacted against years of falling real wages and rising unemployment. In order to keep control of the situation and withstand rising right-wing opposition, the left-wing parties needed to remain unified. Unfortunately, they could not. Caballero opposed his colleague Indalecio Prieto's attempts to bring the Socialist party into an administration he viewed as insufficiently revolutionary. Spanish historian Francisco J. Romero Salvadó is scathing in his assessment of Caballero and his followers' behaviour: "The *Caballeristas*, poised in a personal vendetta against the executive of their own party, ignored the danger presented by the rightest enemy. . . . [Their] stance involved the worst of two worlds. Their verbal rhetoric had the effect of terrorizing the middle classes and speeding up preparations for an armed insurrection. However, by vetoing Socialist participation in the cabinet, they impeded the formation of a strong government that might have averted armed insurrection."[48]

In the chaos of spring 1936, however, Ellen was unsure how to interpret the reports coming from the Iberian peninsula. Driven by her journalist's instinct and by her sympathy for Caballero, she made two trips to Spain, in May and June 1936, to see what was going on. In May, she crossed the Channel by ferry and drove through France into Spain with Edward Conze, to help with research for his book *Spain Today*. The pair first went to Madrid and then headed back north to the Asturias. Everywhere they went, they witnessed strikes, some organized by Caballero's *Unión General de Trabajadores* (UGT), and some by the anarchist *Confederación Nacional del Trabajo* (CNT).[49] The civil guards closed the CNT offices in Madrid during their visit, and the anarchists responded by throwing a bomb through the window of the Café Madrid while Ellen and Conze were dining nearby. It was Ellen's first time seeing a bomb—a sight with which she would become all too familiar over the next five years—and her response was not to flee for cover but to run into the melee and investigate. Conze was not sure whether to admire her bravery or question her sanity.[50] On her visit in June, Ellen stayed with Caballero and through interpreters and in broken Spanglish and French spoke to strikers and to representatives of the various parties in the Popular Front. Exhibiting her trademark empathy, she was able to understand the motives of all sides, from Prieto, who felt the Socialists had a responsibility to work with the government they had put in power, to Caballero, who did not want to compromise his Socialist principles in coalition, to the anarchists who had known such terrible poverty for so long that they "cannot afford to wait" for legislation to improve their lot. It was a chaotic situation, but Ellen was optimistic the Popular Front forces would be able to sort it out.[51]

Ellen's experience of revolutionary fervour in Spain was compounded by her visit to Paris during the sit-in strikes of June 1936.[52] From Spain, she drove north across the border and made her way slowly to the French capital. As she approached the city, she recalled seeing red flags flying alongside the *Tricolour*. Like Madrid, Paris was convulsed by strikes, following the victory of the Popular Front candidates in that spring's elections to the Chamber of Deputies; but of most interest to Ellen were the occupations of the *grands magasins*—Galleries Lafayette, Printemps, and the now-defunct Samaritaine, Trois Quartiers, and the Louvre. (At Bon Marché, the owners had locked the staff out on full pay rather than risk them occupying the shop.) In the early 1920s, Ellen had bemoaned her difficulties organizing men and women in Harrods, Whiteleys, and Selfridges. Here the French workers, few of them even union members, had proved it could indeed be done. It was, she claimed, her "weirdest" experience in a long history of union organizing. In one store she visited, the young women had never before been to a political meeting or even heard a woman make a speech. So Ellen stepped up— literally. "I just got up on a chair and told them how all [my NUDAW colleagues] were watching their fight, and hoped they would win it. Fortunately they were very kind about my accent!" Both the Spanish and the French strikes reinforced her faith in the potential strength of ordinary working people.[53]

This faith is evident in Conze's book *Spain Today,* in which he unequivocally backs the trade unionists as the key to the country's future. Ellen's conviction that the workers could bring about their own liberation without recourse to violence explains her public recommitment to pacifism in this period. Shortly after her return from Spain and France, she agreed to support Canon Dick Shepperd's proposal to form a Peace Pledge Union (PPU), whose aim would be to gather a million signatures from men and women committed to renouncing war. She signed her name to the initial PPU appeal, alongside her friends George Lansbury and novelist Storm Jameson and physicist Aldous Huxley.[54] Vera Brittain, who later joined the movement, recalled that Ellen only "[came] over to it . . . after a long struggle with herself."[55] Unlike Vera, she was not an absolute pacifist, but recent events had bolstered her conviction that the workers, after all, might be able to liberate themselves without recourse to violence. Franco's invasion of the Spanish mainland two weeks later shattered that illusion.

Ellen's actions during the early weeks of the Spanish conflict remain something of a mystery. A clue can be found in the memoirs of Leah Manning. Leah started her career as a teacher, and she and Ellen were both involved with the National Council of Labour Colleges. She had briefly served in parliament with Ellen as the member for Islington East. After the fall of the Labour government, she had been selected as candidate for Sunderland, and thus she and Ellen occasionally met on shared platforms as part of the group of Labour candidates in the northeast. Leah shared Ellen's early interest in Spanish politics. In January 1935, she had made her own visit to Madrid and Oviedo to investigate the Asturian atrocities. She produced an account of her visit, *What I Saw in Spain,* in which she shared Ellen's misplaced optimism that the forces of the left could defeat the fascist CEDA without resort to armed conflict. If the two were not friends, they were at least friendly and shared a committed anti-fascism.[56]

In early August 1936, Leah travelled to the Soviet Union with D. N. Pritt and his wife. Pritt remained to observe the August 19–24 show trial of Grigori Zinoviev for conspiracy against the state and famously staked his legal reputation on the trial's legitimacy. The three travellers crossed the North Sea on the same steamship as a NUDAW delegation led by John Jagger. J. J.'s lengthy report of his visit to Russia makes no mention of Ellen's presence, and she does not appear in any photographs from the trip.[57] However, she almost certainly was in the party, as Leah recalled in her memoir, "I was in the Soviet Union in 1937 [sic], with Johnny [D. N.] Pritt, when the storm broke. Ellen was there with a delegation from her union. I rushed round to her hotel to ask her if she would fly back to London with me the next day if I could make the arrangements: I had already seen Intourist about them. . . . Ellen, always impetuous, had already set out by boat, which meant I would be in England many days ahead of her."[58] As the Spanish coup had already been launched by the time the women set sail for Leningrad, the "storm" Leah referred to was most likely the capture of Badajoz and the orgy of terror and reprisals unleashed by both sides in its aftermath. If Ellen left by boat, it would have been impossible for her to get to London in time for the founding meeting of Spanish Medical Aid (SMA) on August 8. However, she must have cabled her willingness to become involved to the men and women who convened at the National Trade Union Club that afternoon. The group agreed to form the SMA "to send a Medical Unit or Units to relieve the suffering caused in Spain, and to assist the Spanish Democrats against Spanish aggression" and elected Ellen a member of their executive committee.[59]

The Spanish Civil War triggered a crisis in Ellen's understanding of the international political situation. Up to then, she had maintained a belief in the idea that the workers of the world, if sufficiently united, had the strength to throw off the yoke of fascism without resort to another world war. Her understanding of world politics followed a largely Marxist analysis, which saw current events as the product of a heightened stage of capitalist development, which would soon be followed by the collapse of that system and the rise of the workers' state. Inside Germany, censorship and police terror meant the working classes were cowed from taking the kind of industrial or political action that could cripple the Nazi regime. Yet, Ellen's anti-fascist publicity efforts over the past several years had focused on uniting the forces of the left outside Germany in the hope that the workers would use strike action and, where feasible, the power of the ballot box to stop the spread of fascism and cripple the economic strength of the fascist states. Once fascism was marginalized and ultimately defeated, the workers, conscious now of their own power, would set about implementing true socialism.

The election results in November 1935 had underscored the distance the British working classes still needed to travel before they would be willing to use either direct or political action to put an end to capitalist aggression at home or abroad. It was a sharp disappointment that temporarily put Ellen's ambitions for revolutionary reform in Britain into cold storage. In such circumstances, the best work she could do was to use her parliamentary position to achieve practical if modest improvements to working-class conditions while continuing to educate her fellow Britons about the horrors of the "fascist stage of capitalism" and underscoring the threat to their own welfare and to international security of another "imperialist war."

Industrial developments in France and Spain, in contrast, had seemed to show a rising consciousness amongst the European working classes and to give hope to the view that the workers could throw off their chains. The speed and force with which Franco's troops made their way north from Seville shattered any hope that the Spanish people were on the verge of establishing a socialist state. In place of her previous optimism, Ellen was confronted with the reality that Azaña's "bourgeois" government might soon be replaced with a Hitlerite satellite state. And whatever the faults of bourgeois democracy, Ellen had no illusions that fascism was not much worse. If, in 1935, she had believed that a Popular Front strategy discounted the potential of the workers to secure their own liberation, she now embraced the defence of bourgeois democracy with all the zeal of the convert. As homage to her commitment, friends dubbed her the "Pocket *Pasionaria*," a reference to Dolores Ibárruri, the Communist firebrand known as *La Pasionaria*, who famously declared of the Royalists in a national radio broadcast, "*¡No Pasarán!*" (They shall not pass!) The American Socialist journalist Louis Fischer, who briefly fought with the international brigade before becoming a publicist for the Republican cause, characterized Wilkinson as "the heart and fire of the pro-Loyalist movement in England." He termed her "indefatigable." She "wrote articles, organized committees, called committee meetings, travelled up and down the country, and shot stinging questions at complacent ministers in the House of Commons."[60] At one point, after a tetchy response from Anthony Eden to a question on the evacuation of foreign nationals from Spain, Ellen shot back with biting sarcasm: "In view of the present situation, does the right hon. Gentleman not think that the time has arrived to evacuate all the Spaniards and leave the other countries to fight it out?"[61]

On the SMA committee, Ellen worked alongside not only Communists like Isabel Brown but also pacifists like George Lansbury.[62] "GL" could support the dispatch of medical supplies or food ships to Spain, or the acceptance of refugees from Spain on British soil, but he and other pacifists could not accept the sale of weapons to the Spanish government or the recruitment of volunteers to serve in the Republican International Brigades. Unlike Lansbury, Ellen had never questioned the right of workers to defend themselves against aggression, but she had maintained that "capitalist" institutions such as the national government or the council of the League of Nations could not be trusted to use military force. Yet when confronted with the choice, she did want her government, however much she distrusted its leaders, to provide arms for Spain.

After her return from Leningrad in August, Ellen lost no time in making herself a key player in the discussions over the British and international labour movements' response to Franco. On Wednesday, October 13, she attended a lunch at the Spanish Embassy with Julio Álvarez del Vayo, the multilingual former student of Beatrice and Sidney Webb who would soon become Spain's foreign minister once Caballero took over as prime minister in September. Del Vayo was in the country to ask the Mineworkers Federation whether they could arrange for a delegation from the International Federation of Mineworkers to visit the Spanish mining town of Gijón. He hoped the presence of international observers would serve as a check on Franco's forces if they captured the town and that they would not massacre civilians with the same fervour as they had recently applied in Badajoz. The guest list gave an early glimpse into the future leadership of the Aid Spain movement within the British left. Besides Attlee and Citrine, then head of the International Federation of Trade Unions (IFTU) as well as the general secretary of the Trades Union Congress (TUC), the guest list included diplomat Philip Noel-Baker, who had recently been returned to parliament; Lieutenant-Commander Reginald Fletcher, MP for Nuneaton; Ellen's companion on her 1934 visit to the Asturias, Lord Listowel; and publisher Victor Gollancz.[63]

After the lunch concluded, Del Vayo, Ellen, Listowel, and Viscount Churchill (Winston's distant cousin, a Labour peer, and a member of SMA) flew to Paris. There they took part in a Special European Conference on Spain, ostensibly organized by the leaders of the IFTU and the French trade unions but in reality another Münzenberg-front organization.[64] According to one report, "The meeting recognized that the French Government had 'completely done its duty and could not be expected to do anything more than take up its attitude of neutrality'. This forced it to place all the onus on the British labour movement to change its own government's policy—a point strongly supported at the meeting by Ellen Wilkinson."[65] The government's policy was "nonintervention," or the policy of refusing material aid, including the sale of arms by private manufacturers, to either side. On her return to Britain, Ellen rang Citrine and harangued him with the need for the TUC to take action to persuade the government to abandon nonintervention and support the elected government of Spain.[66]

Ellen soon became convinced nonintervention was a sham on two fronts. On the one hand, it was unjust to pretend that the Republican government should be held to the same standards as the Royalist insurgents. On the other, all reports indicated the Germans and Italians were not, as they claimed, abiding by a policy of nonintervention themselves. Never one to trust to secondhand reports, Ellen returned to Iberia in August. Afterward, she revealed to a meeting of the Peace Pledge Union in Bradford: "In Lisbon . . . I saw three great German ships flying the Swastika and two ships flying the Italian flag. They were unloading all day. . . . As to the destination of the munitions—well, it was obvious. There was no war in Portugal." According to the *Manchester Guardian,* "She criticized the British government for luke-warmness towards nonintervention. If Portugal had believed that the British government meant what it said no arms would have passed through that country to rebels."[67] Nonintervention, in this reading, could not be a passive act. It must not only mean withholding arms from combatants but also ensuring that the other powers did not supply such material. Despite lip service to such a commitment, the British navy did little to prevent fascist cargo from reaching Franco.

As the summer wore on, the Pocket *Pasionaria* became increasingly estranged from her pacifist friends. At a meeting of the Sunderland District Peace Council on 14 September, she let her frustration show. "I am determined not to indulge in that facile talk of peace that does not face facts," she declared. "That does not get us anywhere. The horrors of war—and we have had a few object lessons lately—are well enough known. Horrors have never stopped a war yet."[68] She had by that point begun to consider leaving Shepperd's Peace Pledge Union. She officially resigned in March 1937, writing to Shepperd, "I feel in view of the Spanish situation that 100% pacifism is for me impossible . . . I am sorry to have failed you . . . and I know you are right."[69] At the Labour Party conference in October 1936, she expressed contempt for the party's timid resolution demanding an investigation into the accusations that the nonintervention agreement was not being observed in good faith. "How many hours" would the party waste on this sham exercise, she wanted to know. Everyone knew the Germans and the Italians were arming Franco; the question was how Britain should respond.[70] But, despite protests from Ellen, Noel-Baker, Manning, and others, the NEC was not prepared to go beyond the call for an investigation.

Failing to find support within her own party, Ellen increasingly turned to those on the Liberal and Conservative benches in Westminster who shared her views. From the autumn of 1936, a small group of MPs began a strategy of barraging the government with pointed questions and supplementaries about the enforcement of the nonintervention agreement and the legality of placing an elected government on the same basis as an insurgent army. The group of MPs who made up what came to be referred to as the "Spain Lobby" included Independent Liberal MP Eleanor Rathbone, the long-standing head of the National Union of Societies for Equal Citizenship. Among others in the lobby were the Duchess of Atholl, the reliably socially Conservative member for Kinross and West Perthshire whose committed anti-fascism and collaboration with Willi Münzenberg earned her the sobriquet "the Red Duchess"; the Liberal MPs Richard Acland and Wilfrid Roberts, who became their party's fiercest advocates of a Popular Front strategy; Communist Willie Gallacher; and several of Ellen's colleagues on the Labour benches, including Noel-Baker, Fletcher, Will Thorne, David Grenfell, Seymour Cocks, and Arthur Henderson, son of the late Labour foreign secretary. As the civil war wore on, the group expanded to include several more members. Although Herbert Morrison never became a key member of the Spain Lobby, he supported the Republicans and spoke at Aid Spain rallies—a stance that further raised him in Ellen's estimation.[71]

Ellen's close cooperation with Eleanor Rathbone over Spain represented an evolution in the two women's relationship. As Susan Pedersen has noted, "cross-party cooperation [between women MPs] was the exception" in the interwar period. "For the most part, women hoped that loyalty to party would wash out the stain of sex."[72] Nonetheless, Ellen and Eleanor had a long history of cooperation on feminist issues by the time the Spanish Civil War broke out. In 1936, both women had committed to members of the women's movement that they would put forward a resolution to equalize civil service pay, if given the opportunity. Ellen's name was selected to put forth a private member's resolution, and she duly won the support of the House for her proposal to equalize pay grades between men and women in the upper levels of the civil service. Civil servants were in a less precarious position within the capitalist system than the unaffiliated midwives, factory-shift workers, and female clerks working in moldy subbasements whose causes Ellen also championed in parliament in 1936. Yet, as she pointed out, single middle-class women were often handicapped by the obligation to care for dependents. The "caveman" mentality within the Treasury (and the country more broadly) held to the conceit "that most men have wives and families to keep . . . whereas the single woman wage-earner has no one but herself to keep." In truth, "It is a fact that to-day a very large number of salaried women . . . have others dependent on their salaries."[73] Ellen spoke from experience. In addition to Annie, whose medical bills largely fell to her younger sister, she was, as she once explained to Nancy Astor, committed to "my various pensioners whom I help."[74] The argument in favour of equal pay for equal work was self-evident from a women's rights perspective, but Ellen argued it was also imperative to ensure the welfare of postal workers' spinster aunts. Had Rathbone or another member won the lottery to put forth a resolution, the argument for reform might have cleaved more tightly to an equal rights argument. But, for Ellen, the case for women's equality was inextricably tied up with economics, and her arguments in favour of women's rights always incorporated an analysis of the economic injustice that accompanied gender inequality.

Ellen's increased involvement with international affairs after 1935 did not distract her attention from the ongoing impact of unemployment on many regions of Britain, including, especially, her own constituency of Jarrow, where adult male unemployment hovered around two-thirds of the population. For Ellen, the human tragedy of Jarrow was indistinct from the scourge of fascism or the brutality of the Spanish Civil War. All were products of a corrupt capitalist system that pitted owners of capital against wage labourers and drove men to disown their common humanity in the name of profit and greed.

By 1936, Britain had turned the corner and was slowly rebounding from the Great Depression. After peaking in 1932 at 17 percent of the workforce, national unemployment had fallen to just over 10 percent by 1936.[75] But the national recovery marked significant regional variations. Although automotive and other industries created new jobs in the Midlands and the Southeast, unemployment in parts of Wales, Scotland, and the Northeast remained devastatingly high. For men and women in what became known as the Special Areas, unemployment seemed to have become a permanent fact of life. By the time Ellen became MP for Jarrow, the majority of the adult male population of the constituency had been out of work for over two years. Diana Hopkinson wrote to a friend about the endless constituents' letters her boss received in 1936 and their "pathetic faith" that somehow Ellen could solve their problems: "Sometimes their accumulated misery depresses me unbearably. Letters about their starving children, faithless husbands, bad landlords, unemployment and every form of cruelty and injustice and hardship."[76] Despite her growing absorption in the Spanish conflict, Ellen remained acutely conscious of her constituents' plight and of her own impotence to make good their faith in her.

Ellen's frustration made her eager to lend her support to the proposal for a town-led "hunger march" from Jarrow to London to gain publicity for the situation in the town and petition the government to bring industry back to Jarrow. The idea for the march originated with the town's mayor, Alderman William "Billy" Thompson, and David Riley, Labour chairman of the Jarrow council, who served as the march's marshal. Plans for the march were first mooted at the council in July, while Ellen was out of the country. By the end of the summer, it was decided that a group of 200 men, selected for their fitness to withstand the 300-mile slog, would depart from Jarrow on October 5, winding south through Durham and Darlington, through posh Ripon and Harrogate and bustling Leeds, through the Yorkshire cities Wakefield and Sheffield onto Nottingham, through the Midlands to Market Harborough and Northampton, through Bedfordshire and Hertfordshire, then finally approaching London from the north and entering Hyde Park through Marble Arch, where a mass open-air demonstration was planned to precede the final procession to parliament. Ellen was soon brought in on the planning, and her organizing skills, connections, and public profile made her an indispensable asset to the campaign. She helped sort out the hire of a bus to carry the men's kit from town to town; the equipment of each man with a waterproof sheet; the feeding and accommodation of the marchers in school halls, churches, and, civic buildings; and medical assistance from the Society of Socialist Medical Students (here, her connections with the Socialist Medical Association through Spanish Medical Aid came in handy).

It was likely Ellen's idea to march alongside the men. By doing so, she would show a bodily solidarity with her constituents that might make up for her inability to do more on their behalf. And she appreciated the publicity her elfin presence on the march path would draw. In the event, hardly a day went by without a photo on the picture page of at least one of the popular dailies showing her on the march trail, or sitting amongst the marchers with a mug of warm tea, or cigarette in mouth, being taught to play the drums by a group of her fellow crusaders. Her high profile in the United States meant the march received coverage in American papers such as the *Chicago Tribune*, which ran a story under the headline: "Ellen Wilkinson leads 'Jarrow Crusade' 300 miles to London to draw attention to unemployed plight."[77] It even made the radar of the Gold Coast daily the *African Morning Post,* then edited by the young Nigerian nationalist and future president Nnamdi Azikiwe, who wrote, "We see in the Jarrow Marchers lessons of importance to the African. Unless a person proves that his condition is desperate, no one will be convinced."[78]

The largely sympathetic coverage of the Jarrow Crusade in the British press owed much to Ellen, and not just because her celebrity status rendered the Crusade newsworthy. She understood the popular press well enough to know what kind of hunger march the papers' editors could be persuaded to support. When the Jarrow city council began contemplating its own march, Wal Hannington and the National Unemployed Workers' Movement (NUWM) were already planning a sixth national march in protest against revisions to the regulations of the Unemployment Assistance Board (UAB) that would stiffen the already punitive means test on benefit. Ellen respected Hannington and she personally leant her support to the NUWM march.[79] However, she was conscious of the NUWM's connections to the Communist party and the way in which the taint of Communism poisoned any instinct for sympathy with the marchers in the eyes of Britain's major broadsheets and evening papers. Thus, although she sought Hannington's advice on the logistics of managing a hunger march in preparation for the Jarrow Crusade, Ellen made a point of distancing Jarrow's march from the NUWM event.[80] She also used her influence to keep the text of the men's petition as devoid of class-based language as possible. The brief petition she ultimately brought to the bar of the House of Commons struck a simple, humanitarian cord: "During the past fifteen years Jarrow has passed through a period of industrial depression without parallel in the town's history. Its shipyards closed. Its steelworks have been denied the right to reopen. Where formerly 8,000 people, many of them skilled workers, were employed, only 100 are now at work on a temporary scheme. The town cannot be left derelict and therefore your petitioners humbly pray that His Majesty's Government and this honourable House should realise the urgent need that work should be provided for the town, without further delay."[81]

Ellen's efforts to emphasize the "apolitical" nature of Jarrow's crusade reflected, in part, her appreciation of the lessons of 1926. Then, opponents of the general strike had focused on the alleged unconstitutionality of extra-parliamentary mass action intended to influence government policy.[82] In 1936, the government again trotted out the rhetoric of constitutionality in an effort to delegitimize the Jarrow Crusaders. Two weeks into the march, the Cabinet issued a statement: "In this country governed by a parliamentary system, where every adult has a vote and every area has its representative in the House of Commons to put forward grievances and suggest remedies, processions to London cannot claim to have any constitutional influence on policy."[83] The Bishop of Durham, who condemned the march, claimed, "It substitutes for the provisions of the constitution the method of organised mob pressure."[84]

Ellen rejected this analysis, but she appreciated the sway it held over members of her own party as well as over national government MPs. In her speeches along the march's path and in her journalism, she made a point to emphasize the constitutionality of the marchers' actions. In *Time and Tide,* she reminded her readers that the march had "the backing of all parties on the Council [which] meant an office in the town hall, the official stamp and all that that implies in constitutional England."[85] She tied efforts to delegitimize the march to the determination of the fascist powers to quash free speech: "To stigmatise as 'revolutionary' the quiet exercise of our constitutional right to offer a petition to parliament is dangerous in these days. When constitutional rights are threatened on every side, democrats should watch vigilantly rights that have been struggled for and won through centuries of British history."[86]

Ellen became the public face of the crusade, but she did not march the full 300 miles. This was not because, as critics claimed, her vanity led her to skip out on the march to have her hair set in the mornings, although it is telling that Diana Hopkinson believed the story and argued it was a wise decision, as "her hair was a symbol of fiery determination which illuminated the march all the way to London."[87] Ellen simply had neither the health nor the stamina to tramp upwards of 10 miles a day alongside six-foot-tall shipwrights for weeks on end. A journalist who approached her in Leeds, after the party had marched 15.5 miles, scored a particularly tetchy quote from the tired MP: "It isn't any use my pretending I am enjoying it. I should like to be able to say that

I am having the time of my life, but it wouldn't be true, because I'm not."[88] Her hectic itinerary of domestic and international travel in the mid-1930s took a toll on her, and she was perpetually overextended and exhausted. Ellen became an even heavier smoker in this period and in February 1936 had been chastised by the chair for lighting up a cigarette in a Commons standing committee.[89] When asked to prepare her own "ten health commandments" for a feature in the *Daily Express,* she owned to living on a diet of chocolates ("lots of them, they are excellent energy producers"), coffee, and China tea.[90] After yet another all-night sitting in the Commons in February 1936, she again put her stamina down to "plenty of coffee."[91] Had she committed to go the entire length of the march, she likely would have collapsed before reaching Sheffield.

Even if Ellen had had a stronger constitution, it would have been counterproductive for her to march the whole route. As it was, she cancelled nineteen engagements to spend as much time with the marchers as she could.[92] One engagement she could not miss was the Labour Party conference, which opened in Edinburgh the same day the marchers set off from the Jarrow town hall, with their wives, children, friends, and a local brass band accompanying them to the borough border. Ellen and Jarrow's Labour councillors had hoped to take up a collection for the marchers at the party conference and win a powerful endorsement for their cause. Instead, their requests to raise a collection were denied—as Ellen disgustedly quipped, "because if it went to Jarrow it would have to go to the whole lot and there might be some Communists in the whole lot."[93] The Labour leadership's narrow-minded obsession with combatting Communism reduced her to tears of anger and frustration. It was not the first time she had cried on a public platform, but her emotionality was a sign both of her anger and of the high level of stress under which she was operating that autumn.[94]

Not only did the leadership discount Ellen and her colleagues' earnest efforts to distance the march from the Communists, they publicly admonished the march's leaders for their tactics. Lucy Middleton, wife of the long-standing party secretary Jim Middleton and candidate for Lady Astor's seat of Plymouth Sutton, stood up on the dais and attacked the march's leaders. "Miss Wilkinson, together with others comrades from the distressed areas," should "send out their best men and women into the country to tell the story, on a non-Party basis, of what is happening in the areas, and I suggest it would be infinitely more important, infinitely more influential than sending hungry ill-clad men on a march to London."[95] Lucy's statement caused Ellen to jump to her feet and protest in white rage at the imputation that she and her Jarrow colleagues were ill-using the marchers. If they were ill-used by anyone, it was the party, which should stand behind them. As in 1933, she saved her most acute venom for Labour's arch anti-Communist, Walter Citrine. (It was perhaps a sign of her growing friendship with the London County Council leader that Herbert Morrison escaped similar censure this time around.)

> What has the National Council done? It has disapproved of it. What has gone out from our General Council? Letters to the local areas in fact saying, in the politest language, 'Do not help these men.' We have had to appeal to the Local Authorities. Why? Because some of these marchers might be Communists. I hope when Sir Walter Citrine gets to the pearly gates, St. Peter will be able to assure him there is no Communist inside.... I tell the Executive that they are missing the most marvelous opportunity in a generation. You have no conception of the depth of indignation there is, far outside our Party ranks.... If you had seen that march from Jarrow you would have realized that it was a great folk movement.... What propaganda speech in your life was equal to that vast object lesson of what had been done in that town which has been murdered in the interests of the Stock Exchange and of rationalization.[96]

The Town That Was Murdered became the title for Ellen's most famous book, detailing the closure of Palmers' shipyard and the unsuccessful efforts to bring industry back to the region in the long years before accelerated rearmament finally brought a return of near full employment. Although ultimate responsibility for inaction lay with the government, the Labour leadership were accessories before the fact for their failure to give the Crusade the full weight of their moral support. Ellen's disappointment in her party was overwhelming. Margaret Bondfield would long recall seeing her "sobbing broken-heartedly" in the middle of Princes Street the evening after the debate.[97] Four of the march leaders were so vocal in their anger at the party leadership that they were expelled within weeks of returning to Jarrow.[98]

From Edinburgh, Ellen returned to the march trail, rejoining the Crusade en route to Harrogate. Over the next several weeks she alternated marching with advocacy work on behalf of German refugees, a brief appearance in the House of Commons, and one luxurious Sunday back in her own attic flat in Bloomsbury. On Friday, October 30, Ellen, Thompson, Riley, and other members of the town council held an open-air meeting in Hyde Park to discuss the march and the petition Ellen would present to parliament. The next day, the marchers covered the last leg of their journey, originally intended to take them from Hendon to Hyde Park for an open-air picnic. Labour's opponents on the Jarrow council, feeling that the "best woman marcher in England" had done too much to associate the march with her own party, sent one of their own women down to London to march the final leg of the journey so that, for the first time since the march set off from Jarrow, Ellen was not the only woman in the ranks. Unfortunately for the new arrival, it was Halloween weather, with a howling northwesterly wind bringing driving rain before it, and the marchers were met by a dispiritingly apathetic reception. According to one of the many "embedded" journalists who tramped along for sections with the marchers: "It was cold and horrible, and no day for standing out on the pavement. Groups here and there stood in the doorways of shops and blocks of flats, but hardly a word was said as the marchers went by. On the faces of the few onlookers, most of them elderly, one could read pity; on others what seemed an expression of bitterness that such things should be; but most of the Londoners on the pavements just gazed at the Jarrow men with a long intent look, guarded and inscrutable."[99] It was an anticlimactic ending for the marchers, who went on from Hyde Park to the East End, where they stayed the weekend to await the presentation of their petition to parliament.

On Tuesday morning, Ellen showed her constituents around the House of Commons—they were the first large deputation of working men ever to tour the Palace of Westminster. She then left them in the tearoom as she traversed the corridors to the debating chamber to present their petition. As she brought the document to the bar of the House, she was once again overcome with emotion. It was a dramatic moment. If her tears were spontaneous, they were further evidence of the strain she was operating under. If they were theatrics, she must have realized she was walking a fine line. Her sobs could be interpreted as a testament to the hardship faced by her constituents, and a symbol of her identification with the men and women she served in parliament. Alternatively, they could be taken as evidence of her hysterical femininity and, by extension, her irrationality and unfitness to govern.[100] In the event, the sympathetic press overlooked her emotionalism, while the Conservative papers drew pointed attention to her outburst. The *Daily Mail*'s headline read: "Miss Ellen Wilkinson in tears in Commons." Its report began: "Miss Ellen Wilkinson, highly strung socialist MP for Jarrow, laid her copper-coloured hair on the rails at the bank of the speaker's high chair in the House of Commons tonight and wept. It seemed the smallest and slightest of MPs was praying. When she looked up, though, praying or not, there were tears in her eyes." The *Yorkshire Telegraph* reported that "after her petition had been presented Miss Wilkinson burst into tears and almost collapsed. A member caught her in his arms and comforted her."[101]

Ellen's performance was a dramatic climax, but the denouement was considerably less hopeful. The men were denied an audience with the prime minister. After a tense moment during which they contemplated a sit-in strike in the Palace of Westminster, they boarded a train back to Jarrow. They arrived home to find their wives faint with hunger.[102] The local Unemployment Assistance Board had used their month-long absence as a pretext to deny assistance to their families, on the grounds that the men did not meet the criterion of availability for work. Faced with the grim reality that the government had no intention of taking action to address the proposals made in the men's petition, Ellen was reduced to lobbying the House to intercede with the UAB to win payment of the men's allowances, arguing that they had remained in touch with the council and each man had been prepared to return to Jarrow if work became available.[103]

Ironically, the men's case was arguably undermined by an ill-timed offer of assistance. The day before the presentation of the petition, John Jarvis, a Surrey businessman and Conservative MP who had taken an interest in Jarrow, had announced plans to open a new steel tube works on the site of the old shipyard, a plan he had not previously shared with the town's politicians. Ellen's response was sceptical at best. She emphasized that Jarrow had had promises come to nothing before, and she did not want Jarvis to give them false hope, before continuing, "We have got the Government cornered and on no account must this latest offer enable it to avoid its responsibilities."[104] Government ministers did point to Jarvis's scheme as evidence that there was no need for state intervention. His tube works benefited from government-subsidized loans; but when it opened in December 1937, it only employed 200 people, a fraction of the around 2,000 long-term unemployed in the region.[105]

The Jarrow crusade was a bitter lesson for Ellen on the perils of trusting to appeals to the personal conscience of the "capitalist class" to redress social ills. As she would make clear in a 1940 speech on social justice, capitalist men and women were not "villains," but the system propelled them to privilege profits over social welfare.[106] The only way to achieve social justice would be to do away with the profit motive, and this could only be done by a socialist government. Ellen was thus presented with a wrenching moral choice. She could either focus her energies on building support for a Labour victory in the next general election, which was unlikely to be held until 1940, or she could try to build a coalition within the existing House of Commons committed to replacing the current government with one more committed to combatting fascism abroad. The latter strategy would almost certainly mean the postponement of meaningful social reform until after fascism had been defeated; but, faced with the need to choose, Ellen placed the defence of basic human rights for men and women outside of Britain's borders above the improvement of social conditions at home.

Yet even as Ellen seemingly gave up hope for reforming European capitalism before fascism was defeated on the continent, she was heartened by the news that American autoworkers were making a stand for higher wages in the United States.[107] Her decision to visit the United States during the January 1937 parliamentary recess was, like so much of her international travel, impetuously taken. A trade unionist had written to her of the strikes taking place in the U.S. auto industry, and she had decided to go see things for herself. "Hastily I collected enough lecture engagements to pay my expenses comfortably—and dashed over for the Christmas recess," she wrote.[108] In an instance of her feminism subsidizing her socialism, speeches at venues such as the Cook County League of Women Voters and the Chicago Women's Club underwrote her visits to striking factories in Cleveland, Detroit, and Flint, Michigan.[109] In Cleveland, Ellen described a scene of well-dressed men, in "heavy cloth overcoats, good shoes and soft hats," picketing in the "cold sleet-rain." The men, many of them immigrants, were amongst the highest-paid group of American workers, earning wages of between sixty cents and one dollar an hour. So too were their counterparts in Michigan, who were holding stay-in strikes in the plants. In both Detroit and Flint, she spent the night in the factories with the strikers—in Flint, climbing in through a window in defiance of a police cordon. The young strikers in the Flint factory had, she claimed, barraged her "with a fire of questions from all sides—about England, and Hitler, Spain and Leon Blum," but their minds were focused on their present economic circumstances.[110]

After years of industrial depression, there were fewer and fewer strikes in 1930s Britain. (The previous year had seen less than 2,000,000 total days lost to industrial action across the country—a precipitous drop from nearly 35,000,000 in 1919.[111]) The American autoworkers might be comparatively well-off, but Ellen, the incurable film buff, claimed that their monotonous working conditions made Charlie Chaplin's *Modern Times* seem like an understatement.[112] It was heartening to see them taking a stand against their exploitation—and heartening to witness the support they received from the president. Ellen left America in February 1937 much more fondly disposed to President Roosevelt than she had been after her last visit.

Ellen had travelled to the United States principally to get over her disappointment at the outcome of the Jarrow Crusade and to seek comfort and inspiration in the strength of the U.S. labour movement. Yet on her return to Britain, she justified her trip on the grounds that "the shadow of war was coming nearer . . . and it was important to know what the attitude of the USA would be." However, when asked, she was forced to concede that America, at this juncture, did not seem interested in getting involved.[113] Although the autoworkers showed a keen interest in events in Spain, the middle-class audiences at her speaking engagements were more concerned to hear her take on Edward VIII's recent decision to abdicate and marry the American divorcée Wallis Simpson. "In lectures on which I was advertised to speak on the war situation in Europe, women would seize my hands before the lecture. 'If you don't say something about "Wally" we'll just die.' "[114] When Edward VIII's affair became public, the British working class had largely supported the prime minister, who had urged the king to abdicate to maintain the honour of the monarchy. Attlee had supported Baldwin's position and persuaded the Labour Party and the *Daily Herald* to back the government line in parliament and in the press.[115] If Ellen saw the political logic behind Attlee's decision, she personally thought that the whole crisis was puritanical and misogynist. As a republican, she did not think that there should be either a king or a queen; but, as a feminist, she thought the idea of a morganatic marriage even more reprehensible. "The American Poppa and Momma of Middle Age" were doubtless slightly scandalized by her view that "in saying that a lady is fit to be his wife but not fit to be queen, the monarch holds the chosen woman as an inferior, and deprives her children of their rights and status. This is a retrograde step that affects the whole status of women and the equal moral standard which they have fought for and won in this country."[116] Ellen liked good gossip as much as the next person, but America's comparative obsession with the abdication crisis and indifference to the brewing international conflict filled her with dread for the future.

13

THE ANTI-FASCIST TRIBUNE

No sooner had Ellen disembarked at Southampton on February 12 than she was reabsorbed into the campaign on behalf of the Spanish Republic. In the weeks immediately following the outbreak of hostilities, Ellen had characterized the conflict as "a class struggle, pure and naked."[1] Four months later, she was still referring to the war as "a class issue."[2] Recently, however, she had begun following the lead of Liberal and Communist party colleagues who claimed "to take no account of the political complexion of the Spanish government, nor of the political causes and rights and wrongs of the struggle," but merely to support a democratic government against the rebels who sought its overthrow.[3] Speaking in a Commons debate over the proposed ban on the export of arms to Spain in December 1936, she had opened her speech by accusing the government of "tak[ing] a lead in organizing a blockade by democratic governments of the democratic Government of Spain." In a ten-minute bitter oration, she charged, "this Bill is . . . completing the British blockade of democracy in Spain."[4] A few days earlier, she had spoken on Spain at a local "men's parliament" in the west London suburbs and admonished her comfortable audience to "think of those men who are fighting with their backs to the wall, knowing that either death or torture is their lot, [and] realise that their fight is a fight to save democracy, not only for themselves, but for us as well."[5] The emphasis on defending democracy was intended to make it more difficult for the Republic's would-be supporters to remain on the sidelines. Gradually, over the course of 1937, Ellen and her fellow advocates of intervention in Spain gained traction amongst the Labour Party leadership.

At the October 1937 party conference in Bournemouth, Labour unequivocally repudiated nonintervention, and Ellen was elected to the National Executive Committee (NEC) and named secretary of the executive's newly appointed Spain Campaign Committee (SCC). Under her direction, the SCC's literature continued to cleave to a pro-democracy message. Their first circular announced, "This Campaign has been devised to give a new stimulus to the Party action for Food, Freedom and Justice for Democratic Spain at what may prove to be a decisive moment for the Spanish Working-class and Democracy in Europe."[6] On the second anniversary of the outbreak of the war, the SCC issued a manifesto, most likely written by Ellen, which claimed, "The Democratic States are willing that Republican Spain should fight for Democratic Right, but refuse to allow the purchase of arms for Democracy's defence. The nations forming the League of Nations have declined to act, and by this weakness the Cause of Democratic Government is assailed throughout the world. . . . We honour the courage of the Spaniards and their comrades who have fallen in the defence of Democracy."[7]

Did Ellen, alone in her attic flat in the wee hours of the night, truly believe her own rhetoric about the fight to defend democracy? If so, how much had her perception of democracy changed as a consequence of the Spanish conflict? Historian Tom Buchanan has argued that "the rise of fascism forced the left to reassess its relationship to this 'bourgeois' democracy and to consider under what conditions it could work within it." The majority of Communists, he claims, came to view parliamentary democracy in instrumentalist terms, as, to quote Stalin, providing "a great many rights" that could be "used by the working class in its struggle against its oppressors." Both the Soviets and the Spanish government over which they exercised increasing influence deployed "a powerful and seductive language of liberty, democracy and democratic rights which asserted that theirs was a cause worth fighting for precisely because it represented a defence of democracy (and not some ulterior motive)," yet they readily practiced dictatorial methods. Buchanan contrasts the attitude of French Socialist Leon Blum, who "appears to have fundamentally believed the Popular Front could actually reinvigorate democratic institutions by proving that 'Parliamentary Government is capable of action.'"[8] Was Ellen's public support for Spanish democracy an example of Stalinist cynicism or the optimism of Leon Blum? Edward Conze, whose relationship with Ellen deteriorated over the Spanish conflict (he supported the anarchists and abhorred the Soviet influence over the Spanish government) thought she had been duped by the Comintern into believing the Communists were truly on the side of democratic liberty. He harshly accused her of having a "fairly negligible . . . blotting paper mind" on which "the last impression always showed," and claimed, incredibly, that she was "a helpless victim of the English class structure [who] adored northing so much as the aristocracy," on account of her collaboration with the fellow-travelling Lords Marley and Listowel in the anti-fascist cause.[9] George Orwell was the most famous, but by no means the only, socialist to denounce Soviet intervention in the Spanish conflict, and specifically Moscow's role in crushing the *Partido Obrero de Unificación Marxista* (POUM, the Workers Party of Marxist Unification) and the anarchists within the Republic coalition; and Conze's comments are a testament to the lasting tears the Soviet involvement in the Spanish Civil War rent through the left.[10] But if the hostility that animated Conze was sincere, his analysis was wide of the mark. Ellen's quiet acceptance of Soviet behaviour in Spain was evidence not of her naiveté or suggestibility but of a growing conviction that the defeat of fascism took precedence over (and in fact was a prerequisite for) the realization of socialism.

Although Ellen was not willing to condemn openly the actions of Juan Negrín's administration, she increasingly publicly criticized the Soviet Union's dictatorial methods in the late 1930s. In June 1937, for example, she wrote a rather disparaging review of the Communist Hilary Newitt's *Women Must Choose*. Newitt had argued that totalitarian regimes offered opportunities for women to serve the state in ways democracy did not and reserved special praise for what she saw as the socioeconomic liberation of women in the Soviet Union. Ellen's review lauded the Soviet attitude toward women as workers and citizens over the repressive policies of the Nazi state. However, she concluded that dictatorship, even a dictatorship of the proletariat, was bad for women. Adopting the rarely used voice of the old-guard feminist, she condemned Newitt's disdain for democracy and enthusiasm for the Soviet Union. "The women who won the vote thought that at least they had done a bit of good work. They had firmly debunked the legend of the big male bow-wow," she wrote. She went on to assert: "I want to rally women to fight as hotly as ever they did for the democratic rights we are in danger of losing. . . . To maintain these rights, I am willing to sacrifice a lot of the benefits Miss Newitt sees in the dictatorships, even [the Soviet Union]."[11]

Her response to Conservative arguments that "Franco was driving Russian influence from Spain" betrayed her ambivalence toward the role of Russian influence within the republic: "Has not the net result of the British policy been to hand over the leadership of the small nations to Russia, even in those small nations whose present rulers hate Russia as hard as any London financier? Russia came to the aid of Spain with arms, with the result that the Communist Party—weak and foreign before the Officers' Rebellion—is now regarded as the friend of the people."[12] She supported Cripps' Unity Campaign for a united front of Labour, the Independent Labour Party (ILP), and the Communists because she supported the defeat of fascism; but she appreciated that the Soviets over the past few years had rather queered the pitch for themselves. Her writing in *Tide and Tide* was always much more ironically forthright about the tensions within the socialist movement than was her journalism for the left press. Writing in that journal on the fortunes of the United Front, she opined:

> For the lack of warmth about Russia at the moment, . . . really what else could the Russian Government expect? They can't have the argument both ways. Too many of us

here knew personally some of the men who have recently been shot or jailed. If all the charges brought against Radek and Sokolnikov were true—and for all I know they may be—then what is the internal atmosphere that produces that effect on such tested men? . . . The British workers [can] admire the achievement [of the Soviet revolution] without necessarily wanting to copy the political conditions existing there just now.

Somehow I doubt whether this is the moment when the Labour Party, and still more the trade unions, are likely to be persuaded to accept Russia's current policies. And that in essence is what the United Front, on which Sir Stafford Cripps has staked his whole parliamentary future, means—if it means anything more than an emotional gesture.[13]

The remarkably self-aware admission helps explain Ellen's at-best-lukewarm support for the Unity Campaign after 1936.[14] Only once did she come close to similar frankness in her analysis of the moral compromises made by the Republican government during the conflict. Returning from a visit to Spain with Clement Attlee and Philip Noel-Baker in November 1937, she wrote a scathing précis of the political situation in that country over the previous few years. In a reversal of her previous views, she denounced the *Caballeristas* as obsessed with the niceties of parliamentary democracy while the growing Communist party showed "an iron determination that this war must be won." The priority was to defeat fascism. If a temporary suspension of civil liberties and democratic practice was the cost of victory, it was a cost she was willing to countenance—a conviction she would reiterate five years later as a minister in Churchill's wartime government.

Diana Hopkinson, Ellen's private secretary in 1935 to 1936, recalled, "There was perhaps something a bit slap-dash about Ellen's political attack, but no one could doubt her sincerity. Her energy was tremendous but it was most variously dispersed."[15] Although the late 1930s witnessed Ellen's developing commitment to prioritize the defeat of fascism over either the pursuit of social justice at home or the end of imperialism abroad, she remained committed to both causes. Wherever practicable, she pursued her long-held social goals in harness with her anti-fascist campaigns. When her domestic or imperial agenda came into conflict with her determination to form a broad-based anti-fascist coalition, however, she repeatedly privileged the latter. Nowhere was this clearer than in her on-again, off-again relationship with her parliamentary colleague and fellow beacon of the radical left, Sir Stafford Cripps.

Cripps was a difficult man. He inspired intense loyalty in some and a visceral dislike in others—most notably Hugh Dalton. Like Dalton, he came from an affluent, politically conservative background. (While young Stafford was at Winchester, Hugh studied at Eton.) He was the nephew of Beatrice Webb and ultimately followed her into Labour politics. But if his aunt had become by the 1930s an elder stateswoman of the movement, her nephew was an iconoclast—in, but not of, the party and unencumbered by the lifelong party man's instinct toward loyalty. After Frank Wise's death in November 1933, Cripps took over as chairman of the Socialist League and acted as a spearhead for almost every left-wing challenge to the party leadership between 1933 and 1938. Historian Ben Pimlott assigned Cripps significant personal responsibility for the ineffectiveness of the left in the 1930s.[16] Ellen's own attitude was more ambivalent. She ultimately joined the League and was involved in several of Cripps's other ventures; but, as Kenneth O. Morgan has written, "she would not undermine the party by blind adherence to the cause of Cripps."[17]

It is tempting to view Ellen as an enthusiast who jumped on every far-left bandwagon. From the vantage of the early 1930s, such a view isn't wide of the mark. After 1936, however, her focus on defeating fascism made her more selective about the crusades she was willing to support. She championed the Socialist League's domestic agenda but gave more thought than many of her League colleagues to making its proposals palatable to the party. As a career trade unionist, Ellen steered clear of the so-called constituency campaign to increase the influence of individual members over party policy. After the 1937 party conference, she argued that the trade unions' willingness to accede to grassroots requests for the direct election of constituency representatives to the NEC was a sign of the unions' magnanimity.[18] Although she refused to condemn Cripps's Unity Campaign, she had already become convinced that effective resistance to fascism would require a broader agreement encompassing, at the very least, the Liberals. She was unwilling to waste too much time on the vexed question of cooperation with the Communist Party of Great Britain (CPGB). Rather than being simply an enthusiast, Ellen developed a "realism and tough-mindedness" in the late 1930s that formed a sharp counterpoint to Cripps's "uncompromising idealism."[19]

If Cripps's idealism sent him up a series of blind allies, it did produce one lasting impact in the form of the radical journal *Tribune*. Cripps left the 1936 Labour Party conference, at which the party had refused to support the Jarrow Crusaders and parried the issue of nonintervention in Spain, as frustrated and angry as Ellen with the party leadership. He founded *Tribune* as a journalistic call to action—the most enduring of a long line of similar publications, including the original *Daily Herald, Lansbury's Labour Weekly,* and the *New Leader.* The paper brought together a new generation of activists, including Ellen's neighbours Aneurin Bevan and Jennie Lee, recent Oxford graduate Barbara Betts (later Barbara Castle), and rising journalist Michael Foot. Ellen, at forty-five, was one of the oldest members of the editorial team and must have felt she was passing the radical baton.

Tribune's official remit was "to fight Capitalism, Imperialism and Fascism on every front; to make resolutions of support for Spain and China living realities in action; to defend democratic rights by using them to end economic dictation; and to support to the full the great Soviet Union, the citadel of the workers in a world of desperate capitalism."[20] In terms of practical policy, the paper advocated both for a United Front of progressive parties within British politics and for an international peace alliance with the Soviet Union. The cover of the inaugural issue of January 1, 1937 struck a provocative tone. It featured a tamed lion, dressed as a British working man, sitting docile as a capitalist raised his whip hand and gazed out over his industrial empire, a copy of *Mein Kampf* hidden behind his back. Ellen's article in that issue, "Depression has half of Britain in its harsh grasp," both gave vent to her bitter anger at the plight of the unemployed and pointed to her new determination to work with and through the Labour Party to achieve her ends.

Just three months earlier, Ellen had condemned the party's preference for enquiries over action, asking sarcastically whether there remained "a pore in the body of an unemployed man that has not been card-indexed?"[21] Now she noted, "The Labour Commission of Enquiry under Dr. Dalton's skilled and experienced direction, is not restricting itself to a picture of what is, but endeavouring to lay down a basis for future action. Their report may well be one of the most important documents of 1937." At the party conference in Bournemouth, Ellen would publicly apologize for her scepticism about the proposed commission, praising the report as "one of the finest and most direct pieces of work that the Labour Party has undertaken."[22] A few months later, she offered a show of good faith to Walter Citrine and her trade union colleagues. In a *Tribune* article titled, "Who wants a means test on wages?" she publicly denounced her long-held sympathy for family allowances, or government-paid stipends to mothers, arguing that "as a feminist, I have a certain sympathy," but, as a trade unionist, she could not support any scheme that might serve as a pretext to cut working men's wages.[23] It was a public symbol of her willingness to give ground—even at the expense of her colleague in the parliamentary Spain Lobby, Eleanor Rathbone, a lifelong champion of the scheme. She hoped, in turn, her sacrifice would encourage a greater open-mindedness from her colleagues on international issues.[24] While other *Tribune* journalists took a more bellicose tone toward the leadership, Ellen consistently used her columns to showcase her loyalty and to underscore the fact that she had the party's best interests at heart. Having failed to catch flies with vinegar, she was doing her best to lure them with honey.

Ellen's hopes of winning the leadership around to a more robust anti-fascism were boosted by the shift within the NEC during 1936–1937. Dalton had been elected to chair the executive that year and was determined to turn the chairmanship into a position of power. Although he did not share Ellen's commitment to the Spanish Republicans, he wanted the party to make clear to Hitler that they were committed to defending the British Empire's interests against any sign of Nazi aggression. Ellen was no imperialist—in fact, she claimed she "was not prepared to go to war" if Hitler tried to reclaim Tanganyika or any of its other former colonial possessions, arguing cynically that, for Britain's colonial subjects, life under Nazi rule might be better "than anything we are giving them."[25] Although Ellen's detractors could and did accuse her of holding colonial life at a discount, her time in the North-West Frontier Province had convinced her that the British could be as barbaric as the Nazis. "I am not one of those who say that the present Government is Fascist at home. That's talking nonsense.... But I say, with all seriousness, that the British government abroad is Fascist. If you don't believe me, take a holiday in India," she told a meeting of the Staffordshire Labour Party in September 1937.[26] If unwilling to fight for the Empire, she was unequivocally committed to the defence of Europe's democratic nation states against fascist aggression, and she recognized this could not be achieved without, at the very least, a credible military threat.

Although she did not participate in the debate over rearmament at the 1936 party conference, Ellen appreciated the difficult truth Dalton put forth: "The time has come when we must say to the Fascist States . . . [t]here is a limit," and Britain must rearm. There was growing support for rearmament, especially within the trade unions, but that support was tempered by serious reservations about the trustworthiness of the national government to carry out such a policy—reservations Ellen shared. Ultimately, Attlee wound up the debate by dodging the issue of rearmament: "We are not prepared to support a Government that has betrayed the League, that is not, I believe, in earnest, and that has not related its arms policy to any intelligible foreign policy . . . and we shall therefore continue to oppose this government on its foreign policy and its arms policy, and endeavour to get rid of it at the earliest possible moment."[27] The *Manchester Guardian* took a dim view of the debate, arguing that "the confusion of opinion" on show during the lengthy and acrimonious discussion exposed the party as "an enfeebled political force. . . . After five and a half hours of speeches no one knows whether Labour will vote for the Service Estimates or not."[28]

Four months later, the question could no longer be dodged. In February 1937, the party faced the decision of how to respond to the government's bill authorizing the borrowing of £150,000,000 now and up to £400,000,000 over five years to finance rearmament. After a special meeting of the Parliamentary Labour Party, the Labour MPs determined to react with outrage, denouncing the government's willingness to mortgage the country's future on an arms race when they had repeatedly denounced more modest borrowing schemes to address unemployment as dangerously unorthodox.[29] Although some, including Ellen, had reservations about the decision, the Labour membership voted en bloc against the loan; and Attlee, Morrison, Ellen, and others made hay of the government's hypocrisy and financial imprudence during a bitter by-election campaign fought in the snow and sleet of February in Manchester.[30] Ellen's topical column in *Time and Tide* offers an insight into her indecision in the run-up to the vote. In it, she described leaving the Palace of Westminster on February 12, having rushed back to the House from Southampton after her tour of the United States. Jetlagged and overwhelmed, "she drove out of Palace Yard with every nerve tense, my very scalp tight with worry and anxiety," and made her way out of the city to Twixtlands, the cottage in Buckinghamshire she owned with her sister, for a night of rest before heading north for the Gorton by-election campaign. There, "sleep in that utter silence relaxed nerves and muscles. In the early morning I started on a pre-breakfast walk determined to get to some conclusion with regard to the armaments votes I must give these coming weeks." The morning spent in peace and nature gave her the strength to face both the vote and her schedule of twelve election meetings over the next forty-eight hours. Yet, her need to weigh up the issue in the first place suggests how far she had come from her conviction that the national government could under no circumstances be trusted with rearmament.

That autumn, Ellen would support the party leadership's decision to reverse its long-held policy of voting against the defence estimates. As she told a crowd of local Labour supporters shortly before the 1937 party conference: "If you want peace, be a realist, don't let us disarm this country—that's nonsense.... Today Labour is faced with a new menace—Fascism ... it is utterly impossible to leave our own country defenceless. I am not one of those who will agree to that."[31] In supporting rearmament, Ellen broke with Stafford Cripps, Aneurin Bevan, and other members of the *Tribune* group.[32] Although she agreed with Cripps on many aspects of social policy, she could never embrace the view he articulated to a Stockport audience in November 1936 that "it would [not] be a bad thing for the British working class if Germany defeated us. It would be a disaster for the profit-makers and capitalists, but not necessarily for the working class."[33]

Given that America in 1937 was not prepared to throw its weight against Hitler, it was that much more important for Britain to take a firm stand. Ideally, this would mean a firm stand through the League of Nations. In 1935, Ellen had joined with Cripps in denouncing the League as a capitalist front. Now she argued, "The only way to remove the tension causing war was . . . to get together to make the League of Nations something real."[34] Labour, she told a party meeting in September 1937, "stands . . . for collective security through the League of Nations and for the development of an international conscience. . . . If you want peace start actively to remove the causes of war."[35] One of the principal causes of war, as Ellen saw it, was Neville Chamberlain's determination to appease fascism at the expense of European democracy. Thus, the first priority was to remove Chamberlain from power. Ellen started to build bridges with the Liberal party in parliament and the country, believing their support would be crucial to any effort to unseat the national government. In the winter of 1936–1937, she began speaking on platforms for the League of Nations Union, a Liberal-dominated mass organization she had previously dismissed as middle class.[36] In October 1937, she successfully stood for a seat on the NEC. On the executive, she, D. N. Pritt, Harold Laski, and Cripps repeatedly lobbied for a special party conference to discuss the merits of a Popular Front of Labour, ILP, Communists, and Liberals.[37] In April 1938, she spoke at an all-party National Emergency Conference on Spain at the Queen's Hall in London that championed itself as "the first meeting of the Popular Front in England." Her co-speakers included the Duchess of Atholl; Liberals Gilbert Murray and Wilfrid Roberts; her Labour colleagues Cripps, Noel-Baker, and James Griffiths; and Left Book Club publisher Victor Gollancz. The conference, notably, had support from Lord Meston, president of the Liberal Party Organization, and from the Durham Miners' Association.[38] In May 1938, Ellen championed a Popular Front resolution at the National Union of Distributive and Allied Workers (NUDAW) annual meeting, which passed in the face of the party's recent condemnations of Popular Front activity. Although some fellow union delegates, including her long-time nemesis Wright Robinson, expressed concerns about an alliance with the Communist Party, she focused on the electoral benefits of an alliance with the Liberals. "Let us get together and win the next election," she told the conference. "We may not be able to get all we want after we have won it, but we shall get a great deal more both at home and abroad than if we in disunity and three-cornered fights go down and leave the Chamberlain Government in power."[39] She supported Vernon Bartlett's Popular Front candidacy in Bridgewater in November 1938 and in December called on the Labour voters of West Perth to vote for the Duchess of Atholl, "who has put the cause of humanity and democracy against Fascism before the claims of party and class."[40] Ellen also endorsed the controversial Popular Front candidacy of Alexander Lindsay at Oxford, alongside Harold Macmillan, Megan Lloyd George, Violet Bonham Carter, Archibald Sinclair, Isaac and Dingle Foot, William Beveridge, Richard Acland, J. B. S. Haldane, and Randolph Churchill.[41]

Lindsay's supporters included many men and women with whom Ellen had collaborated as part of the Parliamentary Committee for Spain in the House of Commons. In July 1938, Ellen and fourteen other MPs established the committee "with the primary object of letting the public know the facts" about the Spanish situation, and dispelling "tendentious and incorrect statements" spread by "the friends of General Franco in this country," as "propaganda no less than the bombing aeroplane and the blockade is a method of modern warfare."[42] The group was made up of a near-equal number of Liberal and Labour MPs, as well as the Conservative Duchess of Atholl and the Independent Eleanor Rathbone. Their primary aim was the dissemination of information on Spain written from a pro-Republican perspective. The committee made its position clear: "The outcome of the Spanish war has become an issue which may ultimately determine the fate of democracy in Western Europe."[43] Martin Pugh's work on Liberal supporters of the Popular Front makes little mention of the early involvement of many pro-Popular Front Liberals in cross-party campaigns on behalf of the Spanish Republic.[44] However, for many Liberals, as for Ellen, Spain was a key catalyst in converting them to a Popular Front strategy.

Although Ellen's election onto the NEC in 1937 increasingly drew her into party work, she continued to give time and energy to the Aid Spain campaign. Given the obduracy of the national government in banning military support for the Republicans, much of Ellen's work on behalf of the Republic was perforce humanitarian. Throughout her career, she remained adamant that the state, not private charity, should redress social injustice, yet she never took the doctrinaire position that charity only propped up the capitalist system. In the early 1930s, in addition to her political work in Britain and internationally, Ellen led fundraising campaigns to aid German refugees and devoted considerable personal energy to finding homes for displaced Germans in Britain.[45] Later, through Spanish Medical Aid and as a representative of the National Joint Committee for Spanish Relief, she worked to raise funds for food and medical supplies and to find homes for child refugees. In 1937, she spearheaded a campaign by the Labour and Co-operative movements to purchase milk for Spanish school children. In an article in *Tribune*, she gave short shrift to critics who denounced such humanitarian activities: "I have heard some of our own people sneer at the Milk Token Fund as mere charity. That's damnable nonsense."[46]

The National Joint Committee for Spanish Relief had been established over Christmas 1936 to act as a coordinating body and administrative centre for various charities, including Spanish Medical Aid, "with the object of preventing over-lapping in appeals, of facilitating the allocation of funds and of effecting economies in the dispatch of goods."[47] In 1937, the Committee sent a delegation of four women to Spain to assess the operation of relief organizations and the condition of refugees. On Tuesday, April 13, Ellen, Katharine Atholl, Eleanor Rathbone and Dame Rachel Crowdy, former head of the League of Nations Social Section, made their way to the Republican stronghold of Valencia. The mission's remit was ostensibly solely humanitarian, yet Rathbone's biographer has described it as an act of solidarity with the Republican government, underscoring the women's meetings with prime minster Largo Caballero and president Azaña.[48] (The women also met with the Catalan regional president Lluis Companys and cabinet ministers Indalecio Prieto, Julio Alvarez del Vayo, Jesus Hernandez, and Garcia Oliver.[49]) Ellen's own response to the question "What good did your visit do?" likewise stressed its symbolism, although, characteristically, she highlighted the women's show of solidarity with the Spanish people, not with their leaders. Writing in *Time and Tide*, she painted "the picture of three English women, standing on the ruins [of a recently shelled Madrid street], Eleanor Rathbone like an embattled

Britannia in her indignation, the tall sweetness of Rachel Crowdy, and the frail Duchess in her courage and sympathy, while the simple working women gathered round to tell of the homes buried in those ruins. Here were women from that England that they had always been told believed in freedom and democracy. It comforted them so much that someone had come from that outside safe world to understand and help."[50] This was Ellen at her propagandistic best, playing on her readers' sense of pity and self-righteousness.

The women visited prisons in Valencia, officer training schools, hospitals, orphanages, and even front-line trenches in Madrid. (Ellen had insisted on visiting the trenches, despite warnings from their guides.) The danger was not, however, limited to the front. While the women dined at a hotel on the Gran Via in Madrid, shells began falling nearby. As Ellen described the scene, "Shells from rebel six-inch guns, smashing in the street outside, tearing through the roof of a theatre opposite, blew mangled bodies of women and children through the doorway of the Gran Via Hotel. . . . Outside mangled bodies lay on the ground. There were splashes of blood everywhere."[51] The next day, as the Duchess drove out of Madrid to return to Valencia, a shell fell within sixty yards of the car. The same day, Ellen's car was struck by shrapnel as she drove to University City, one of the scenes of intense fighting in the ongoing battle for Madrid. Two of the militiamen escorting her were rushed to the hospital.[52]

In Madrid, they stayed in the infamous Hotel Florida, the base for many of the English, French, and American correspondents covering the conflict. They collected news from sources including Claude Cockburn, the editor of the Communist newspaper *The Week,* who published reports on the conflict under the pen name Frank Pitcairn; Philip Jordan of the *News Chronicle;* Mathieu Corman of *Ce Soir;* and none other than Otto Katz, now going under the alias André Simon and acting as an editor for the Comintern-funded, Paris-based news agency *Agence Espagne.*[53] When the other women had gone to bed, Katz roused Ellen and invited her to meet with a group of young Republican officers in his room—he knew Ellen would not be kept from spending an evening in a hotel room in the company of six foreign men by any outworn sense of propriety.[54] At the Florida, they also ran into the Communist MP Willie Gallacher, with whom Ellen had remained friends after her departure from the CPGB. He and the Conservative Atholl seemed remarkably pleased to see each other—a phenomenon their bemused observers didn't know whether to put down to their shared commitment to the Republic or joy at encountering a fellow Scot in the besieged city.[55]

After their return to Britain, the women published the official *Report of a Short Visit to Valencia and Madrid in April 1937,* focused on the humanitarian crisis. They also produced an unofficial report, *Notes on the Scheme of Spanish Frontiers Observation.* This second, secret report compiled evidence from government ministers and foreign journalists on the ways in which the German and Italian navy were already abetting Franco and the possibilities for further pro-Franco intervention if, as proposed, the fascists were given official authority by the nonintervention committee to police shipping and border crossings. As the report emphasized, "In the coast zones operated by German or Italian naval observers, the system might result in nothing short of a blockade of the loyalist coast."[56] The women circulated the secret report to sympathetic allies, including Winston Churchill, to use as talking points in attacks on the national government. In a letter to Churchill, Katharine Atholl revealed that Otto Katz/André Simon was the principal source of information for the report.[57]

If Atholl served as one bridge with Churchill and other Conservative backbenchers, Lloyd George served as another. Lloyd George's relationship both to his party and to international politics in this period was somewhat tortured and contradictory. In 1935, the Welsh Wizard had founded the Council of Action for Peace and Reconstruction (COA), funded from his own pockets with the aim of promoting a Roosevelt-style New Deal policy. The COA was an ostensibly nonparty body; and such disparate figures as Rathbone, Harold Macmillan, Ernest Bevin, and George Lansbury all cooperated with the COA at various points.[58] After a brief split with the Liberal party, Lloyd George officially rejoined the Liberal ranks after the 1935 general election but kept the COA in operation as a personal fiefdom. In September 1936, he and his two children, the MPs Megan and Gwilym, visited Hitler in Berchtesgaden, and Lloyd George proclaimed him a "great man." He was, on the other hand, implacably hostile to Mussolini and opposed nonintervention in the Spanish Civil War.[59] His daughter Megan took a less equivocal anti-appeasement line. She was a member of the

Parliamentary Committee for Spain and an early supporter of the Popular Front, and she may have been partially responsible for her father's hardening against Hitler after the Munich crisis. Churchill may have been another influence. In any event, the former prime minister and Ellen were able to find common cause in opposition to Chamberlain. She visited him at his country house in Churt to discuss foreign policy and even arranged for him to meet with Katz/Simon to discuss developments in Spain.[60] These relationships outside the party would fortify her conviction that Labour could work productively with Liberal and even Conservative politicians.

That conviction was further stiffened by Ellen's experience piloting her private member's bill on hire purchase practices through to law in 1937–1938. The practice of buying on instalments, or "on the never-never," had become increasingly popular in the interwar period, particularly in working-class households. Ellen, who was congenitally incapable of saving money, admitted to frequently buying on hire purchase herself.[61] Whereas Ellen could always write a few lucrative articles in the *Express* or the *Star,* working-class hire purchasers were frequently left in the lurch due to layoffs and reductions in wages. Under the system in place before Ellen's bill, if a purchaser fell behind on payments on a new radio set or dining table, the sellers could repossess the item and sue the purchaser for arrears, even if 75 percent of the purchase price had already been paid off and the goods were in suitable condition to resell. In the current political climate, Ellen held out no hope of overthrowing the capitalist system and ushering in socialism in its place. Here, however, was an example of capitalism's egregious overreach within her power to correct. As she said with a bitter dose of realism when given an opportunity to bring forth her bill in 1937, "When a private Member has the good fortune to win a place in the Ballot, it is possible to use that good fortune in two ways. Either one can bring in a Bill which will reform the entire country and make it a decent place to live in, in which case there will be a good field day during the whole of the Friday sitting, but alas, one's efforts will be finished at four o'clock; or one can bring in some small measure of social reform."[62] Ellen had had enough of symbolic field days. She wanted her small measure.

Ellen had first attempted to introduce legislation to curb hire purchase abuses in 1930, after a local solicitor in her constituency of Middlesbrough had written to her about a case where a constituent had bought £80 worth of goods on hire purchase, paid off £60, and then lost his job and fallen £10 into arrears. "Not only did the hire purchase company come in and take the whole of the goods, but they were able to prosecute for the £10 of arrears—the poor person not only did not get a penny, but had to pay the costs as well," she told the House.[63] The bill was allotted a second reading in February 1931; but, like so much worthy legislation, it got crowded out of the parliamentary schedule and died with the fall of the second Labour government that October. When Ellen's 1937 bill was assigned for a second reading on Friday, December 10, she could rest assured that the national government would keep to its parliamentary schedule; and so she set about courting special interests and supporters on both sides of the aisle to ensure the bill would pass.

Between winning the ballot for a first reading and introducing her bill, Ellen had gone over the wording of the proposed legislation with the Hire Purchase Trade Association (HPTA) and the Wireless Retailers' Association in an effort to achieve "the greatest common measure of agreement." In a deft display of lobbying acumen, she had persuaded the HPTA to send a letter to every member of parliament expressing support for the bill. Typically, this was all arranged while she was simultaneously juggling ten other campaigns; and she made plans to return from a weeklong visit to Spain the day before her bill was presented. On her way back from Spain, flying from Paris to London "through snow and sleet squalls in dense black clouds," her plane had been struck by lightening, causing "a deafening noise like an explosion" and a "blue-white flash" that lit up the windows of the forty-two-seater jet. It was enough to unsettle even the most seasoned flier, but Ellen kept her cool. She landed, spent three hours with the International Brigade Dependents and Wounded Aid Committee, grabbed a few hours of sleep, and was in the House the next morning to introduce the bill with a self-mocking joke about her "known impartiality" on matters affecting social welfare.[64] It was a feat of bravery and endurance Attlee would commemorate in the House of Commons after her death.[65]

The bill that went forward into committee on December 10 provided that retailers state the cash value of hire purchase goods up front so that it was clear to buyers how much interest they would pay; gave increased power to county court judges to modify the terms of repossessions; and mandated that sellers clearly state the terms under which the contract could be terminated and the goods returned without penalty. In committee, Ellen worked with Donald Somervell, the long-serving attorney general, to amend the bill. Amendments included the introduction of provisions governing the hire purchase of livestock, an issue of particular interest to MPs in rural areas such as Robin Turton, the Conservative MP for Thirsk and Malton, whose constituency Ellen had marched through on the Jarrow Crusade the previous year. Ellen showed an uncharacteristic "tact and assiduity" in piloting the bill through committee and surprised her Conservative colleagues with a willingness to compromise rather than to "die in the last ditch" over minor amendments. When the bill passed through its third reading and was sent across the hall to the Lords, MPs from both sides lavishly complimented her negotiating skills, with one Conservative MP noting tellingly that "she formed a Popular Front Government in this country and completely enslaved the Attorney-General and the whole of the Government Departments concerned."[66] Shortly after the bill was sent across to the Lords, the newsreel series *March of Time* included a short film on hire purchase abuses starring a group of Labour MPs. In a move reminiscent of her theatrics at Fabian summer schools in the 1920s, Ellen, the Scottish MP J. J. Mallon, George Lansbury, and Lord Amrulee as the country court judge, enacted a family's successful use of the new bill to fight a seller's unlawful "snatch back." The idea perhaps originated with producer Ivor Montagu, with whom Ellen was then working on the selection committee of the Forum Cinema in Soho as well as on anti-fascist work.[67] Given the wide circulation of the *March of Time* in cinemas, it was a brilliant way to publicize the new consumer rights introduced by the bill and a huge thrill for the tiny film buff who starred in the show.

As tempting as it was to sneak into the cinema and catch a glimpse of herself in the newsreels, Ellen barely had a spare moment in spring and summer 1938. During her tenure as parliamentary secretary to the minister of health between 1929 and 1931, she had repeatedly overworked herself to the point of ill-health. In 1938, her parliamentary scheduled combined with her work for the India League and the Aid Spain movement again led to illness. In July, she was ordered to bed rest. Ellen being Ellen, she attended parliament despite doctors' orders, with the result that she became acutely ill. That weekend, her sister brought her out to their cottage in Buckinghamshire and forced her to recuperate properly. Ellen stayed in Penn for several days, pulling out of an engagement to speak at an Aid Spain rally in Trafalgar Square and cancelling a planned visit to Spain.[68]

In conjunction with her Spanish work, Ellen was again spending a lot of time in the company of Otto Katz, now known as André Simon, who had become a ubiquitous figure in the pro-Republican movement, even supplying background information to the Duchess of Atholl for her best-selling *Searchlight on Spain*.[69] If Ellen was ever involved with the Czech spy, it was likely in this period, when the two travelled regularly together, including on holiday. Certainly, Special Branch, who followed Otto's every move in Britain, were convinced Ellen was "infatuated" with him.[70] On June 26, 1938, Otto arrived at Heston airport and stated his intention in entering the country was to visit Ellen. Jawaharlal Nehru had also recently arrived in Britain, on his third trip in three years. As on his earlier visits, he spent several late evenings in conversation at informal parties in Ellen's Bloomsbury flat in 1938. Throughout her career, Ellen was responsible for bringing together men and women from wildly different walks of life, but the meeting she almost certainly facilitated between Katz and Nehru must have been one of the strangest.

By the time of his 1938 visit, Nehru's international profile had risen considerably. The trip was sparked by a concern over the spread of fascism, and he spent five days in Barcelona before returning to Britain. Stopping in Paris en route from Spain, he championed the Spanish Republicans in language intentionally susceptible to a double reading. In a radio broadcast from the French capital, he expressed his conviction that "the spirit of the indomitable Spanish people can never be crushed, and that Spain cannot be subjugated by foreign armies, however long the struggle lasts."[71] From Nehru's arrival in Britain on June 23, Ellen again acted as his host through the auspices of the India League. She organized a conference at the House of Commons at which Nehru made clear his objections to both the program of federation laid down in the 1935 India Act and the foreign policy of the British government. The two friends spoke on a series of India League and Aid Spain platforms, where Nehru expressed his own conviction—shared by Ellen—that the cause of anti-colonialism should be understood as inherently in sympathy with anti-fascism. The two spoke at a "Peace and Empire" rally over July 15–16, alongside Stafford Cripps, the African-American actor Paul Robeson, the Liberal MP Wilfred Roberts, and others, as well as at India League and Left Book Club events.[72] They had intended to share a platform at a July 17 rally for Republican Spain in Trafalgar Square, but Ellen had to pull out due to ill health. The following week, they attended the World Conference for Action on the bombardment of open towns in Paris. The event was organized by the British liberal pacifist Lord Cecil, under the auspices of the International Peace Campaign, and Nehru made clear his disdain for Cecil's imperialist assumptions.[73] Nonetheless, they both then rationalized that the severity of the European crisis merited cooperation with less-progressive men and women as long as they took a similar attitude toward fascism.

After leaving for a tour of the continent in July, Nehru returned to Britain in the autumn, and became increasingly vocal in his criticism of British foreign policy, with an analysis that again echoed Ellen's own. Writing in the *Manchester Guardian* on the eve of the Munich crisis, he contended that the British government "pursues even more intensely its policy of encouraging aggression and giving support to General Franco and the Fascist and Nazi powers. No doubt it will carry on in this way, if allowed to do so, till it puts an end to itself as well as the British empire, for overriding every other consideration are its own class sympathies and leanings towards Fascism. . . . I would be the last person to object to an ending of Imperialism. But I am deeply concerned with the prospect of World War, and it distresses me exceedingly to realize how British foreign policy is directly leading to war."[74] Following Chamberlain's return from Munich, both Ellen and Nehru would denounce "The Shame of England."[75] Like Ellen, Nehru also recognized that charitable aid to the Spanish Republicans could serve both practical and propagandist ends. After his visit to Spain with Krishna Menon and his daughter Indira in 1938, Nehru launched a campaign to send an Indian Ambulance Unit to the country, as well as campaigning for Indians to send foodstuffs and medical aid. Nehru made clear his call for aid was not mere humanitarianism: "We seek [this help] in order to throw our weight, such as it is, on the right side in a vital conflict which is of tremendous significance to us and the world . . . [and] to dissociate ourselves publicly and through action from the policy of the British government."[76]

Nehru's tour of Europe had also included a visit to Czechoslovakia, where conflict between pro-Nazi separatists in the majority German Sudetenland and the Czechoslovak government under Edvard Beneš was reaching fever pitch. The British and French governments had a defence treaty with Czechoslovakia, and fear began to mount that a second world war was going to begin. That fear increased when Hitler, speaking at the close of the Nazi Party's annual rally at Nuremberg on September 12, accused Beneš of bullying and asserted that the Germans would not stand by and watch their fellow nationals be mistreated. On September 15, Chamberlain flew to Hitler's residence at Berchtesgaden to discuss the situation, returning a day later with promises to consult with his cabinet and return to Germany. Many feared the British government would agree to force Czechoslovakia to hold a plebiscite over the future of the territory, an outcome that in the current climate of antagonism and intimidation would almost certainly give Hitler a mandate to take forcible control of the region, just as he had taken control of Austria in March. The International Peace Campaign, on whose platform Ellen and Nehru had spoken in Paris in July, quickly organized a mass demonstration in Trafalgar Square for September 18 under the banner "STAND BY CZECHOSLOVAKIA—NO PLEBISCITE." The demonstration attracted a massive crowd of over 30,000, who filled out the square for the speeches and then marched up and down Whitehall and finally to the Czech Legation at Grosvenor Place. The crowd was so large the police were forced to close Whitehall to pedestrian traffic for the first time in years. The principal speakers were Ellen, Eleanor Rathbone, Ramsay Muir, and Lord Meston. Ellen was the lone Labour Party speaker. Attlee also spoke out against the plebiscite that night, but on a separate platform in his constituency of Limehouse. Ellen's decision to wage her protest in solidarity with the Liberals was a stark statement about the need for a Popular Front.

Ellen's speech was captured on newsreel footage, which offers a rare chance to see and hear the famous platform orator in action. Dressed in a black pencil skirt, a buttoned-down white blouse, and a dark cardigan, with strands of hair flying loose around her face, she stands out from the crowd of men in lounge suits who surround her on the platform. Her voice is strong, with long rolling vowels that lend her an almost Celtic cadence. She speaks with her whole body, balling her hands into fists, then squaring them defiantly against her hips, then shaking a finger in the air as she chastises Chamberlain. Her speech, shouted into the microphone, rings with outrage and contempt for the premier. "This man," Ellen declares, "He has sold the liberties of the people of every country.... We say to Neville Chamberlain, 'We do not trust you. We believe that you went to Germany to fix up the sale of the liberties of Czechoslovakia.'" She goes on to demand that parliament be recalled, claiming, to roars of applause, that "Britain and the liberties of the people of all the world fighting for peace are too big to be managed by one Birmingham family."[77]

Chamberlain had no intention of recalling parliament. Four days later, he returned to Munich and offered Hitler the outright cessation of the Sudetenland to Germany. Hitler pressed his luck even further, demanding the immediate evacuation of Czech troops from the border; and for a few tense days, it appeared as if war might break out. In France, Prime Minister Edouard Daladier ordered a partial mobilization of the army; on September 27, the order was given to mobilize the British navy. On the home front, the government accelerated the preparations of the Air Raid Precautions [ARP] volunteers, including the digging of trenches and bomb shelters and the fitting of civilian gas masks. September 25 was declared "gas mask Sunday"; and a London couple purportedly got married in one room of the registry office then walked down the hall to queue up for their gas mask fitting—the enactment of their vows to stay together for better or for worse.[78] Ultimately, however, Chamberlain made it clear to Beneš that the Czechs could either accede to Hitler's demands or fight the Nazis on their own, and the Czech president backed down. Having achieved his objective, the prime minister flew home and claimed he had saved "peace in our time." Foreign Minister Antony Eden and the First Lord of the Admiralty Duff Cooper resigned from the government over the issue. Yet, the majority of the country almost certainly felt, as the prime minister claimed, a "joy and thankfulness that the prayers of millions have been answered, and a cloud of anxiety has been lifted from our hearts." In the debate over the prime minister's handling of the crisis, Ellen argued that key Conservatives had undermined the prime minister's negotiating position by making it clear to the Nazis "that in no circumstances would Great Britain fight for these people," leaving him in a position where "only by some dramatic improvisation in the last five minutes, and by throwing away practically everything for which this country cared and stood, could he rescue us from the results of his own policy." The only hope of avoiding war, if war could indeed be avoided at this point, was, she insisted, a guarantee of collective security through the League of Nations, backed by Britain, France, and Russia.[79]

In the immediate aftermath of Munich, it looked like there might finally be an opportunity to forge the kind of parliamentary Popular Front to unseat Chamberlain toward which Ellen had long been working. The key overtures took place between Dalton and Attlee on one side, and Churchill and Harold Macmillan on the other. There was sympathy all around for some kind of "1931 in reverse," or the formation of a government of Labour, Liberals, and Tory rebels. But agreement could not be reached. On the Tory side, Eden was not out for blood to the same extent as Churchill, Macmillan, and others; and on the Labour side, the leadership were concerned that the rank and file, and particularly the trade unions, would revolt at the idea of another coalition. Ellen was not part of the talks. Despite her place on the international subcommittee of the NEC, she was not close enough to the inner circle to be taken into confidence. If she did hear rumours of what was afoot, she would have realized that the tentative moves toward a coalition had fallen flat by mid-October. Rather than let the ball drop, Ellen put together her own proposal for an all-party coalition in December and began circulating it to a group of Labour MPs with whom she had cooperated on Spanish issues.

The coalition proposal was a new venture for Ellen and highlighted the length of her journey from backbench radical and extra-parliamentary crusader to political insider. Over the previous year, she had religiously attended the meetings of the full NEC, and the international, Spanish, publicity, and campaign subcommittees of which she was a member. Increasingly, she felt herself a part of the party leadership, capable of making decisions about high-level strategy. The text of her proposal does not appear to have survived, but the papers of Ellen's old friend Rajani Palme Dutt contain a lengthy critique by Ernest Bevin's close confidant Arthur Creech Jones, as well as notes from a meeting of several MPs active in the Parliamentary Spain Lobby at which her memorandum was apparently discussed. Creech Jones, for his part, was hostile to the idea of a coalition. "Your programme sacrifices any economic change toward Socialism, moreover to pacify Liberals, and hopes that communists can convince the public of their disinterested service to the maintenance of democratic rights," he told her. He went on to state that "I have no room for co-operation with the Democratic Tories," and concluded: "I would not, on grounds of tactics, make an election a contest between 'pro' and 'anti' fascist principles and principals." Ellen's proposals received a slightly warmer welcome from others. Most sceptical was Jim Griffiths, who warned that "every political alliance with the right ends in triumph of Right, e.g. triumph of Daladier over Blum," and went on to muse whether the "glamorous" Eden would perforce be appointed prime minister if such a coalition were to triumph. Yet, whereas Creech Jones had questioned Ellen's view that "the Labour case . . . looks sectional or that the basis of the Party is too narrow," Garro Jones agreed that there was "something wrong with Labour Party's appeal to country." D. N. Pritt concurred and underscored that "home programmes become matters of academic or even historical interest if differences have to be argued out in concentration camps." Cripps agreed with Pritt. Frank Bellenger shared Ellen's concerns about the inability of Labour to secure an independent majority, but said "definitely" that he was "against any alliance that included Communists." A few, however, objected to a coalition on any grounds. Chuter Ede contended that it was "better to be a strong united opposition of the one party, than a weak coalition which always tended to break up when pressure removed or at moments of difficulty," a view largely shared by Frederick Pethick-Lawrence. John Morgan proposed a continuation of what he contended was the emergent status quo of "coming to a de facto understanding regarding seats it was not possible to fight, and see how that situation developed. Though attempts to get anything more would lead to even that much understanding being smashed by bloc votes."[80] Her colleagues' hesitancy must have convinced Ellen the time was not ripe to push ahead, as there is no further record of her proposal in the archive.

After Ellen let her own memorandum quietly die, Cripps took up the cudgels in her place. On January 9, 1939, he sent a letter to the NEC outlining the urgent need for an electoral alliance between all progressive parties to defeat fascism. He emphasized the suggestibility of the electorate, particularly the younger voters, and the need for Labour to offer a lead to them before they fell under the sway either of fascist forces or of a "reformed" National Government promising to lead the country into an imperialist war against Germany. The attached memorandum clearly stated the reality that Labour could not win an election on its own and that any effort to unseat the national government would require the party to come to an agreement with the Liberals. This, he accepted, would mean putting socialism on hold; but he believed the two parties could come together around a shared foreign policy and a domestic agenda of moderate progressive reforms, including raising workers' wages and increasing the school leaving age. The suggested platform Cripps laid out was constructed to be potentially attractive to ILP and Communist supporters as well as Liberals, while its insistence on the abolition of the Means Test and other reforms de facto ruled out the participation of dissident Tories. Cripps's proposals were thus both more and less ambitious than Ellen's the previous month. In place of a grand coalition to defeat fascism, Cripps proposed only a coalition of the left; but, unlike Ellen, he appeared optimistic such a coalition could succeed in enacting a progressive domestic program.[81]

Cripps's decision to exclude the Tories from his proposed coalition, despite his support for Ellen's memorandum the previous month and his involvement in the schemes to cooperate with dissident Tories in October, remains something of a mystery. Ben Pimlott dismissed the reversal with the simple explanation that Cripps was "not a man of fixed opinions." Hugh Dalton, writing in his diary at the time, carped that Cripps had "the political judgment of a flea."[82] If this latest flip-flop, combined with the explicit invitation to the Communist party, was enough to discredit the proposal in the eyes of Attlee, Dalton, and Morrison, Cripps's high-handed presentation of his ideas signed their early death warrant. In a letter to party secretary Jim Middleton, he had stated, "I desire to put on record that in the event of [the NEC] not seeing their way to accept the principles of this memorandum or to take any definite action in the direction indicated I shall claim the right to circulate it . . . with the object of gaining support within the Movement for the views therein expressed."[83]

After an acrimonious special meeting of the NEC lasting over two hours, only Cripps himself, Pritt, and Ellen voted in favour of the memorandum's adoption. Like Ellen, Pritt would have preferred a broad Popular Front coalition to a more narrow combination of the left, but any action to unseat Chamberlain was better than no action. In preparation for the meeting, Middleton had prepared several documents on the state of public opinion within the party, including a list of affiliated organizations that had sent in resolutions requesting a special party conference to discuss the international situation. These included four trade unions, one of which was NUDAW; three socialist societies, including the Socialist Medical Association instrumental in founding Spanish Medical Aid; four federations of Labour parties, including the Durham County federation; and 236 Constituency and Central Labour Parties, including Jarrow. The myriad organizations with which Ellen was associated clearly shared her desire to break through the deadlock and propose a more robust response to Chamberlain's policy.

The fallout from the Cripps affair was ugly. Someone on the NEC leaked the substance of the January 13 meeting to the *Daily Herald,* which published Ellen's name as one of the three to vote in favour, painting her as a traitor to the party. Cripps responded to the leak by immediately printing and circulating the memorandum. Thrown by the speed of this betrayal, the NEC met on the January 18 and again five days later to decide Cripps's fate. At the second meeting, they formally proposed his expulsion both on the grounds of his present action and in light of his long history of attempting "to weaken the unity of the Party and to give aid and comfort to its opponents."[84] With Harold Laski and D. N. Pritt not in attendance, only Ellen voted against, and Cripps duly picked up his things and walked out of Transport House, not to return until 1945. Over the next several months, Ellen would do her best to repair the damage done by the affair, insisting that media attempts to present "a difference of opinion in a democratic party as a party split" were ill-informed and childish.[85] Yet in March 1939, she resigned her position as an editor of *Tribune.* George Strauss and Anuerin

Bevan had left the party with Cripps: and, despite her sympathy for their ideas, Ellen believed the international situation was too precarious to risk losing her influence within the leadership.

Ellen continued her agitation inside and outside parliament as the international situation went from bad to worse. On March 15, German troops marched across the border of the Sudetenland into Czechoslovakia. On March 16, Hitler proclaimed the country the German protectorate of Bohemia and Moravia. The next day, Chamberlain broadcast from Birmingham, in a speech relayed to the Empire and the United States, and admitted appeasement had failed. Ellen, listening on her radio in her flat, was bowled over by the premier's reversal. Knowing that her friend Louis Fischer did not have a radio in his hotel room, she phoned him and placed her telephone up to her radio speaker so he could listen to the broadcast.[86] Despite her relief, she remained convinced Chamberlain needed to go. As the *News Chronicle* wrote on Saturday morning, "His recantation is welcome, but it has yet to be proved that the Premier who has led this country into such humiliation and democracy into such danger is the man to lead it with energy and determination along an entirely new path." Or as the *Daily Herald* less equivocally put it, "His resignation is essential if national and international cooperation in the bold policy which the times demand is to be secured."

The fourteen months between Hitler's takeover of Czechoslovakia and Chamberlain's resignation saw Ellen in a state of limbo. The so-called Phoney War did not begin until Britain and France's declaration of war on Germany on September 3, 1939, two days after Hitler invaded Poland. Nevertheless, from Chamberlain's broadcast on March 17, Britain moved onto a war footing. The next month, the government introduced a limited military training bill for men between the ages of twenty and twenty-one. Ellen recognized the necessity of the bill but opposed the high-handed manner in which the government presented it without opportunity for amendment. As she complained to the House, "They put before us something which goes a certain way along the road we wish, but they fail to meet important objections. Then we are told that we must have that or reject it."[87] She viewed the handling of the bill (which the Labour Party, with considerable misgivings, voted against) as emblematic of broader problems with the Chamberlain administration. Even while ostensibly pursuing the same goals as Labour, it invariably gave the appearance, if not the reality, of being at cross-purposes with the opposition. Ellen was relieved the government was now committed to a policy of collective security but anxious Britain had left things too long to come to a workable agreement with the Soviet Union. She was angry that they remained unwilling to do anything for the victims of the Spanish Civil War. (The last Republican troops had surrendered to Franco on April 1, 1939.) She supported war preparation but wanted to ensure that it was pursued equitably and that the working classes were not asked to shoulder an unfair share of the burden. Unable to influence policy directly, she spent an unhealthy amount of time lobbying for Attlee's replacement by Morrison and Chamberlain's replacement by Churchill, two personnel changes she perceived as crucial to the prosecution of the war.

Personally, Ellen had nothing against Attlee. The two had travelled to Spain together in November 1937, and she respected both his politics and his personal courage. But she did not see him as a leader capable of navigating the Parliamentary Labour Party (PLP) through war. In 1930, she had written: "In a world of pushful politicians no man could be less self-assertive than Major Attlee. . . . Charming, amusing, sympathetic, too fastidious for intrigue, too modest for over-much ambition, and yet with a mind that makes it worth while for a Prime Minister to discuss problems with him—the ideal minister without portfolio."[88] A decade later, she held to her initial assessment. In 1935, she had schemed for his replacement by Morrison. In 1939, she resumed her scheming on Morrison's behalf—much to the London leader's ultimate embarrassment. Attlee fell ill that summer, and required multiple operations on his prostate, which removed him from active work until the late autumn. As a consequence, he was absent for most of the 1939 Labour Party conference, held in Southport over the Whitsuntide recess (due to the Czechoslovakian crisis, the party had not held a conference in October 1938). The weekend after the conference, Ellen published an article in the *Sunday Referee* that purported to be a profile of Cripps. However, she ended the piece by emphasizing the need for decisive, courageous, and inspiring leadership in the party and mused that were

Morrison to replace Attlee, the Chamberlain government would likely fall under the weight of Labour's skillful opposition. On the June 10, a second article appeared, this time in *Time and Tide*. It was published not under Ellen's name but in the magazine's occasional unsigned column "Four Winds." Here, Ellen wrote that although the delegates had felt personal sympathy for Attlee, "his absence from conference made not the slightest difference to anybody." She went on to boost Morrison— not for the first time. In December 1938, she had written in Four Winds that "the star of Herbert Morrison has risen so appreciably in this Parliament that the socialists have a really good alternative if they decide that they would like a change."[89] There was not, however, enough traction to move against Attlee while he was ill, and those who did want a change of leadership were divided over whether Morrison or deputy leader Arthur Greenwood would make the better replacement. Greenwood remained loyal to Attlee and called a meeting of the PLP for June 14 to discuss the incident.

For a few days, it looked as if Ellen might do something drastic. On June 12, she, Dalton, and Morrison held a secret meeting to discuss strategy. She told the two men that Greenwood had drunkenly threatened her with a vote of censure. Dalton urged her to attack Greenwood at the PLP meeting. J. J. Jagger had apparently also urged her to fight. Only Morrison wanted the whole issue to disappear. When the PLP assembled, Ellen was taken aback by the extent of the "fury" directed at her and ultimately did not "counter-attack." A vote of confidence in Attlee was taken, and passed *nem. con.* with only Ellen abstaining. James Walker proposed a vote of "severe condemnation" on Ellen, which was ultimately withdrawn after Jagger made an effective speech in her defence and Morrison made clear that although he had had nothing to do with Ellen's articles, he would not support her censure. It was, as Dalton confided to his diary, "an unfortunate and miscalculated affair."[90]

Ellen's reasons for becoming embroiled in such a scheme remain a mystery. She had long been a champion of Morrison, even when the two disagreed, as they often did. At some point during the war, the two embarked on an affair; but, given Morrison's apparent belief that Ellen's move was ill-timed and almost certain to backfire, it is highly unlikely that the articles were a lovers' plot. Attlee, for his part, did not believe Morrison was involved.[91] Most likely, Ellen's plotting reflected genuine anxiety that Chamberlain was mishandling war preparations and that Attlee was proving ineffective in putting pressure on the government. In the summer of 1939, her principal concern was the government's failure to conclude a security alliance with the Soviet Union. When, on August 23, 1939, Germany and the Soviet Union announced they had signed a non-aggression treaty, she blamed Chamberlain for the missed opportunity. "This week has seen what is everywhere regarded as a serious defeat for that joint foreign policy that Mr. Chamberlain has personally conducted," Ellen wrote on August 26, in reference to the premier's efforts to keep Russia onside without actually committing the country to a mutual assistance treaty.[92] When the Molotov-Ribbentrop Pact proved, a few weeks later, to have been not only a nonaggression treaty but a secret agreement to divide Poland, her hatred of Chamberlain reached fever pitch. The only silver lining to the debacle of the invasion of Poland was that it brought Churchill back into the Cabinet as First Lord of the Admiralty. As she wrote shortly after his appointment, "The House welcomed Mr. Churchill as a Minister, so obviously feeling that things might have been very different if he had been in the Cabinet these last two years."[93]

Having accepted the failure of her efforts to replaced Attlee with Morrison, Ellen now swung her energies into drumming up support for Churchill to replace Chamberlain. After his first major speech in the House, Ellen wrote enthusiastically in the press: "Buoyant yet fighting, cheery yet not over-optimistic, Churchill gave the impression . . . of a Minister who was conscious of the tremendous resources he had behind him in a struggle in which he personally believed." In her view, there was a desperation "for someone in the Premiership who will either give the impression of resolution in the war, and/or has the imaginative drive to take the initiative in the diplomatic struggle that is being waged across Europe and Asia during these critical days." Churchill was that man.[94] As the "Phoney War" raged on and the Scandinavian countries began to fall to the Nazis, Ellen predicted Churchill would soon be given his day. "The House just doesn't want to be bossed right now—not till the bombs begin to drop anyway. . . . But if the earthquake of war disaster were to come, and with it inevitably a drawing together of the whole House to face the danger, I opine (to use his own pet word) that

Mr. Churchill will be forced into the Premiership whatever the Whips' Office and the Carlton Club say."[95]

Ellen's enthusiasm for Churchill withstood even her deep-rooted disagreement with his imperial agenda. Throughout the 1930s, Churchill had managed to alienate even the members of his own party with his die-hard opposition to proposals for Indian constitutional reform. Although his memoirs present him as a political martyr to the anti-appeasement cause, his exile from the government front benches in the decade before the war owed as much to his imperial as to his foreign policy. As Richard Toye has shown, Churchill continued to take a high-handed view of the Empire's obligations to the metropole during the Second World War, a stance that frequently caused conflict not only between Churchill and Gandhi but also between the British premier and leaders of the Commonwealth, especially Canadian Prime Minister Mackenzie King.[96] Although the First Lord of the Admiralty did not take part in the April 18, 1940 Commons debate over the continuation in force of the proclamations issued shortly after the war that temporarily abrogated representative government in the provinces of Madras, Bombay, the United Provinces, the Central Provinces, Bihar, Orissa, and the North-West Frontier, he strongly backed the government's position. Gandhi and other leaders of the Congress movement had expressed their unwillingness to support the British war effort unless the government agreed to grant full dominion status. The British government, unwilling to risk the strategic and financial implications of allowing India the freedom to decide its own foreign policy, had responded by sidestepping Congress-dominated legislatures. In light of the national security situation, few of even the government's most ardent critics were willing to question this decision, and it was clear when the House met in April 1940 that the proclamations would be extended.

Only two MPs—Reginald Sorensen and Ellen, took the opportunity to criticize the government's policy. Sorensen was a Unitarian minister and parliamentary secretary to the India League and shared Ellen's commitment to Indian self-rule. In 1933, he had told the Labour Party conference, "The operation of Imperialism in India is in essence no different from the operations of Hitlerism.... We are appalled by what is happening to the Jews in Germany, but what has been happening in India is just as bad."[97] In his speech, he again drew the parallel, justifying Congress's opposition by saying: "Denmark, Norway, Finland, Poland and Czecho-Slovakia . . . have been dominated by an alien will and have been told that they must accept the position for their own good, or because it is a natural necessity of the situation. Those countries resent that. The Indians are in the same position. They say that whatever the English may feel about the matter and whatever plausible or genuine explanations the English may advance, the fact remains that the Indians are under an alien will, and the British are determined that they shall remain under it."[98] Yet even as he condemned Britain's subjection of India, he ended by suggesting Britain should "at least make it quite clear that as soon as this tragic episode in the life of man has come to an end, we shall be prepared to implement to the full the demand India makes, . . . Then, however lamentable as it may now be to continue these Proclamations and impose this autocratic Government on India, I am sure the people in India will realize that we have turned away from the old conception of Imperialist domination, and that we are sincere in our claim for free co-operation between nations."[99]

At the end of the day, Sorensen was willing to accept the temporary proclamations, even if he found them disrespectful. Ellen, in contrast, despite her ardent support for the war effort, upheld the right of the Indian people to refuse their support to the British. She began her speech by emphasizing she was speaking not only to her colleagues in the House but to the people of India. She went on, as was her wont in debates over India, to establish her credibility as a voice on Indian affairs, calling Nehru "one of my personal friends," and name-checking many of the other Congress leaders. She then listed the reasons why any right-thinking Indian would doubt Britain's claims to be the defender of democracy, emphasizing not only her country's record in India but also its recent foreign policy: "For one who went through the Spanish campaign, sympathizing ardently for the cause of democracy in Spain, and came back and saw how often we condoned Nazi and Fascist intervention, it is clear that you cannot expect the Indians to accept all we say about this war for democracy on its face value." It was, for that matter, difficult to convince even British citizens that "a Government like this can fight for democracy, . . . At meetings of my own trade union members I am often asked whether I believe that these men are fighting for democracy when they say they are, when the Government has done so much to back up the leaders of Fascism and Nazism. We have had to tell the great industrial areas to forget the Government and to think about the country and realise we are fighting for our very lives and the lives of a great many others too. . . . If we find it difficult to explain to our own people these facts, imagine how difficult it is to get it across to the Indians." She went on to suggest that if the government wanted India's support, it should court it with "deeds not words. If I were an Indian, I would not believe one word of what the Prime Minister or the Government said about India. I would ask them, 'What are you going to do about it? If you do something about it we will at least examine it.'" She then exhorted her colleagues to accept the reality that their ill-advised decision to implement the proclamations the previous autumn and to renew them would likely result in civil disobedience, and to direct the Government of India to respond to that disobedience with restraint. She warned, "If we get civil disobedience we must remember what will be the effect in America of every *lathi* charge against the civil disobedience people. . . . every blow that goes on a defenceless Indian's head is echoed in America and it will not lose anything by telling. I lectured in America after the civil disobedience movement of 1929–1932, and I know what the Indian propagandists will make of everything we do. I appeal to the Under-Secretary [of State for India, Sir Hugh O'Neill] for his own British interests to realise that that sort of thing simply cannot happen again." She ended by arguing that the best solution to the problem of British-Indian relations was also the solution to the problem of domestic British governance: a change of leadership. "I know that in this House one is always supposed to turn up with a constructive proposal," she began. "We get round that by saying that we have a constructive proposal and then indulge in generalities about the British Empire. I do not wish to indulge in generalities, but I would rather have . . . somebody with some sensitiveness—anybody except the present Under-Secretary and the present Viceroy and the present Secretary of State—to deal with Mr. Nehru at the present time. That is the only constructive solution for the present difficulties which I can offer at the moment."[100]

Her hopes for a constructive solution to the stand-off in India were not realized. However Ellen did get her wish for a change of administration less than a month later. Once Norway joined the list of Scandinavian countries to surrender to Hitler, the Labour leadership and the backbench Tories finally made their move. May 7 saw the opening of the infamous debate on the conduct of the Norwegian campaign in which Leo Amery quoted Cromwell's admonition to the Long Parliament: "You have sat too long here for any good you have been doing. Depart, I say, and let us have done with you. In the name of God, go."[101] Finally, after 10 p.m. on the evening of May 8, the House divided on what was effectively a motion of confidence. The government majority fell from its normal ±240 to 81, with 43 government supporters in the opposition lobbies and another 70 abstaining. The premier technically retained a majority, but it was immediately clear to everyone but Chamberlain himself that he would have to go.

Ellen's only contribution to the debate had been one sarcastic interjection, but her relief was palpable. A few days earlier, as news of the Norway debacle filtered in across the ticker tape, she had knocked out what would prove to be her last article in *Time and Tide*. She exhorted her party to come together at their upcoming conference at Bournemouth and take the difficult decisions necessary to save the country: "Big decisions will have to be faced. For this country and France and all they stand for in the world must be saved at whatever the cost, even the sacrifice of ancient premiers or still more old-established prejudices."[102]

The party rose to the occasion. On Friday, May 10, Ellen and the other members of the NEC met in a basement room in Bournemouth's Highcliff Hotel and, in short order, determined that the party should agree to come into coalition under a new prime minister. Attlee communicated as much to Chamberlain by phone, and, by the time he and Greenwood returned to London, Chamberlain had resigned and the King had called on Churchill to form a premiership. Up until the last minute, Churchill had not known whether he or Lord Halifax would be asked to replace Chamberlain. Had Halifax been selected, both Ellen's career and history more broadly might have taken a very different course. As a member of the Lords, and an outsider to the anti-fascist campaigns of the 1930s, Halifax had had little contact with Ellen. Churchill, in contrast, knew and respected her. When he sat down with Attlee to discuss the allotment of ministerial positions to Labour MPs, Churchill made clear he was "very keen" on having Ellen in the government. Attlee, to his credit, concurred, and so Red Ellen became one of two female ministers. She was not given a cabinet post, and as a consequence, her appointment was not announced until several days after the coalition was formed. In the meantime, she continued as usual. She wrote a series of pen portraits of the newly announced ministers for *Tribune,* now edited by her old friend Raymond Postgate, and she spoke at public meetings in Bournemouth, championing the party's decision to join the government. After hearing her speak to a mass meeting in Bournemouth, Vera Brittain concluded, "Ellen's brilliant speech, fiery as her flaming hair, makes doubly certain her chance of being included amongst those invited to serve."[103] A few days later, Ellen was indeed invited to serve as parliamentary secretary to the ministry of pensions, making her one end of a coalition spectrum that, as Churchill bragged with satisfaction, stretched from "Lord Lloyd of Dolobran on the extreme right of the Conservative Party to Miss Ellen Wilkinson [on the far left]."[104]

14

ELLEN IS NOW A MINISTER

" 'Ellen' is now a minister," ran a headline in the *Daily Mail* on May 18, 1940. Her appointment to the Ministry of Pensions had a certain ironic symmetry. In December 1924, the sole female Labour MP had made her maiden speech in the House of Commons on pensions policy, arguing for more attention to social justice in the administration of widows' pensions. A quarter of a century later, the sole female Labour minister in the wartime coalition was appointed parliamentary private secretary to the Ministry of Pensions and put in charge of overseeing the administration of war service grants—special ad hoc payments offered to the families of conscripted soldiers on the grounds of social justice. During her five-month tenure at the ministry, Ellen did her best to prove her ardour for the issue had not dimmed.

In the June 25 debates over Ministry of Pensions estimates, Ellen stood beside the despatch box and laid out the case for war service grants. (She was too short to deliver her speeches from behind the box, like the rest of her colleagues.[1]) She spoke with pride of the "very big social experiment... being made in war service grants."[2] As she explained to the House, the sudden introduction of conscription in May 1939 had had a destabilizing effect on family economies. Many servicemen had obligations, such as mortgages, hire purchase contracts, school fees, and the care of large families, that they could not cover on their service salary. The state appreciated that it had some obligation to keep such men from running into debt as a consequence of their national service. With war service grants, conscripted soldiers could petition for additional aid to meet financial obligations.

The challenge for the government was to determine which of these petitions, in the interests of social justice, it behoved the state to meet. Say, for example, that two men were conscripted, each with a mortgage on one side of a semidetached. One man was an engineer who had purchased a home within his means and kept up with his payments. Another was a seasonal labourer who had taken possession of the house on his father's death but had been unable to keep up payments and was facing the likelihood of repossession when he was called up for service. Did both men deserve equal grants to meet their mortgage obligations? Was there a different moral imperative at play for a working-class family whose son had won a place at a grammar school, but who needed to find money for the associated fees than for a middle-class family who had elected to send their child to private school? Did the patriotic man who had volunteered in 1939 have the same right to grants-in-aid as the reluctant conscript?

Ellen and her departmental staff did their best to streamline the process and create a system of rules and precedents. At ministerial questions, Ellen emphasized that her department processed most claims within forty-eight hours. However, the opaque process of the review panels, and the fact that difficult or exceptional circumstances could often take weeks or months to resolve, led to MPs bombarding her with countless questions from constituents about their individual circumstances—questions that ate up much of her already overstretched time. It is not surprising that she occasionally lost her temper with her colleagues.[3]

Underscoring Ellen's national profile, her old friend Kingsley Martin offered a portrait of the minister in *Picture Post*, with photographs of the new minister at work and at play. Ellen emerged as a natural leader who had made a career out of championing the cause of the oppressed both domestically and internationally. Her career was, he argued, an illuminating "commentary on the social system in England, where born revolutionaries have the scope to express themselves and get something useful done for the workers." Her reputation as an advocate for the oppressed made her a wise choice to head a socially sensitive venture such as the war service grants scheme. Ellen had "brought off the difficult feat" of rising through the ranks of the Labour movement "without ever being seriously accused of getting out of touch with the working class electorate which trusted her."[4] In government, she drew on that reserve of trust to ask the British working class to be patient as the ministry ironed out the kinks in the service grant system.

Although Ellen threw herself into her appointed work, she was only at her desk for less than two months before first illness and then military necessity ended her career at the Ministry of Pensions. In her first months as a minister, she worked herself to near exhaustion. Yet, when she was rushed to St. Mary's hospital in Paddington on July 26, 1940, it was not for her usual respiratory infection, but for appendicitis. She had once joked that her Bloomsbury friends gossiped about lesbian affairs with the same nonchalance they used for discussing appendectomies. Now, at least, she would experience one of the two.[5] Her convalescence was interrupted by the escalation of the Battle of Britain, which had begun on July 10 and would continue to rage through October. On August 13, when Ellen, minus a vestigial organ, returned to her desk at the Ministry of Pensions, the Germans launched their largest air attack on Britain to date, sending nearly 2,000 aircraft against the country. More high explosive was dropped and more civilian casualties incurred during the week of August 14–21 than during the preceding month.[6]

The August bombardment proved to be a foretaste of things to come. Early on Saturday evening, September 7, over 300 bombers, supported by a 600-strong fleet of fighters, flew up the Thames and bombed the Woolwich Arsenal, the West Ham power station, docks, gasworks in the East End, and large areas of the City, Westminster, and Kensington. The initial sortie was followed by a prolonged bombardment that lasted until 4:30 a.m. on Sunday. The resulting destruction disrupted railway lines and caused 430 deaths and over 1,600 casualties. The following night saw attacks on a similar scale, resulting in 412 civilian deaths. The capital was bombed every night between September 7 and November 2. During the night of September 18, the Germans dropped more bombs on London than they had during the entirety of the First World War.[7] The "Big Blitz" would continue—with occasional shifts of emphasis from London to the industrial Midlands to the provincial port cities—until the end of May 1941. Surviving the Blitz would require the mobilization of Britain's civilian population on an unprecedented scale. Just as Churchill had brought the tough-minded transport leader Ernest Bevin into the government as Minister of Labour to mobilize his fellow trade unionists in May, he now looked to the charismatic leader of the London County Council, Herbert Morrison, to mobilize not only his fellow Londoners but the entire British nation for civil defence. In putting together his team at the Ministry of Home Security (MHS), Morrison, in turn, looked to Ellen.

As they worked together over the next five years, Herbert and Ellen would develop an extremely close relationship. One friend recalls a story of Ellen bursting into Morrison's office at 1 a.m. with a bouquet she had been given at a Hackney oil works that evening. She interrupted a meeting between the minister and a group of discomfited civil servants, but Herbert simply burst out laughing at her dishevelled appearance.[8] Morrison's official biographers have dismissed the idea of an affair, but at least for a time they were almost certainly physically intimate. When Ellen lived in a ninth-floor flat in Hood House in Pimlico's Dolphin Square, the naval officer and journalist Stephen King-Hall lived on the floor below and recorded in his diary that he often saw Morrison in the lifts. Terry Gourvish notes Ellen rented the flat under the assumed name "Nellie N. K. Wilson," and attributes the deception to her desire to keep her relationship with the married Morrison discreet.[9] It is just as likely, however, that she wanted to keep her address hidden from the Germans in the event of invasion, as she ranked high on their "most wanted" list. Nonetheless, Secretary of State for War P. J.

Grigg claimed the two of them were essentially "living together" and noted he had "met them once broken down in Morrison's car coming back from a weekend with all their luggage in a ditch."[10] Either Ellen had been driving, or the partially blind Morrison was as accident-prone a motorist as she was. Barbara Castle believed they were intimate, and rumours circulated through the party of how they danced too closely at the annual conference.[11] Although it would have been taboo for the press to comment on their private lives, suspicions of an inappropriate relationship between the minister and deputy circulated in the wider public. The opinion organization Mass-Observation noted a rumour making the rounds in November 1943 that Herbert paid for Ellen's clothes.[12]

Ellen split the role of parliamentary secretary to the Ministry of Home Security with William Mabane, a National Liberal MP who had previously held the position alone. The appointment of a second parliamentary secretary to the department reflected the growing role of civil defence during the Blitz. The ministerial offices in Whitehall became the nerve centre coordinating the nation's emergency responders. Mabane was put in charge of overseeing air raid precautions while Ellen initially oversaw shelter policy. It was a stiff remit, as the provision and maintenance of shelters was one of the largest and most complicated tasks facing local and national government in 1940–1941.

In May 1924, the Committee on Imperial Defence had appointed a subcommittee on aerial defence known as the Air Raid Precautions (ARP) committee. It was originally headed by Sir John Anderson, the civil service stalwart who defended the constitution against the strikers in 1926 and was appointed governor of Bengal in 1932. He returned to Britain in 1937, was made Lord Privy Seal in October 1938, and a year later became Home Secretary and Minister for Home Security. It was an appointment Ellen approved of. Although she confessed to hating his name and all he had stood for in the 1920s, she had developed a respect for his courage and integrity during her time in India and was convinced he was the "strong man" the country needed to prepare it for war.[13]

From October 1938, Anderson began tackling the long-overdue task of arranging for civilian shelter in the event of air raids. In January 1939, he authorized an initial issue of 400,000 family-sized shelters made of corrugated steel that homeowners were meant to assemble and partially bury in their backyards.[14] These shelters—which came to be known as Andersons in honour of both the minister and David Anderson, the civil engineer who designed them—were intended as short-term refuges. The communal shelters the government encouraged local authorities to build in urban areas were similarly designed as temporary accommodation, with chairs instead of bunks. These urban shelters were, for the most part, above ground. During First World War air raids, Londoners had sheltered in the tubes; and, as early as 1929, the ARP committee interviewed Frank Pick, director of London Underground, about the possibility of again using the tubes as bomb shelters. Pick, however, had strongly condemned the idea, and proposals for "deep shelter" in the Underground were ultimately abandoned.[15]

With the onslaught of the Blitz, however, the government was forced to overhaul its shelter policy. The week Ellen took office, the War Cabinet discussed "Civil Defence Report No. 22," covering the period since the start of the Blitz. It made clear certain changes in shelter policy would be necessary, as "night raiding has become regular and the civil population in the Metropolitan area have adopted as a matter of routine the practice of going at dusk, irrespective of warnings, to shelters, there to remain until dawn."[16] Both disused tube tunnels and operative subway platforms quickly became de facto sleeping berths for tens of thousands of Londoners.[17] This presented a range of logistical challenges for the government. For one thing, people's desire for dormitory shelter rendered the Anderson shelters increasingly unappealing options, and many of the shelters were found to be in disuse by the end of 1940. For another, the use of both surface and deep communal shelters as dormitories put a severe strain on space as people took up more room lying down than sitting up. Finally, the shelters had not been designed as dormitories and lacked amenities, such as sleeping berths, water closets, or other sanitary or first aid facilities. The government needed, in Ellen's words, to "plan for something like a home life under cave conditions."[18] And they needed to do it quickly.

Just as she took up her post as Britain's new "shelter queen," Ellen found herself in need of shelter. In October, 18 Guilford Street was bombed. The Georgian building survived, but her top-floor flat was rendered uninhabitable. Ellen loved the small apartment where she had lived for nearly a decade, surrounded by shelves packed with novels, tracts on socialist economics, and foreign literature, with zebra-print upholstery in the sitting room and a framed portrait of herself drawn by Helen Kapp for a 1932 issue of *Time and Tide*. The flat, and her neighbourhood, had been crucial pieces of her self-identity as a Blooms-bury bohemian. After she was bombed out, she briefly stayed with friends before they too were bombed in November.[19] She then moved to a flat in Hood House in Dolphin Square, the newly built apartment complex just west of Pimlico station. She would remain at Dolphin Square until her death; although, after the war, she moved into an-other flat in the complex—a two-bedroom apartment with space for Annie, who returned to London to help take care of her increasingly sickly sister.[20]

Ellen's displaced, itinerant position in the autumn of 1940 helped her empathize with the men, women, and children she visited in shel-ters across London and around the country. She was appointed to the MHS on Tuesday, October 8. Thursday night she was out touring sur-face and tube shelters in the East End. In her first months in office, she conducted several inspections of shelters and civil defence posts in London, most during the evenings when raids were ongoing. Journalist Ian Mackay recalled her sinking a pint with firemen while they waited to be called out again.[21] Another journalist recalled a story about Ellen refusing official counsel to stay in a shelter she had been inspecting during an air raid until the all clear signal was given: " 'But,' she said, 'I'm due at So-and-so in ten minutes and they'll worry if I'm late. I'd better go on!' And go on she did, driving her own car because she did not think it 'right' that the official driver should be exposed to undue danger."[22] In cartoonist Vicky Thompson's retelling of the same story, it was one of the rare occasions Ellen made it to an appointment on time.[23] Like so many others, Vicky was in awe of his friend's bravery.

From November, the Germans began attacking cities outside of London in earnest, increasingly concentrating, from January 1941, on key port cities. As bomb damage became a national problem, Ellen made a tour of provincial shelters. In December, she visited Merseyside and Manchester.[24] In January, she went north to inspect shelters in Not-tingham, Sheffield, and Leeds.[25] In February, she toured Scotland.[26] In March, she made several trips to Wales, the southwest and the Channel ports, visiting Swansea, Gloucester, Plymouth, and Dover.[27] In April, she was in Hull, viewing the results of recent bombing in that city.[28] Ellen's visits were a sign to the local population that the government was taking a genuine interest in their welfare.[29]

For her first three months at the ministry, Ellen's department was faced with the dual task of improving existing shelters *and* building new shelters and bringing delinquent ones up to code. Either, alone, would have been a daunting task. As the government's official historian wrote, "The flood of problems which arose when shelters became dormitories had almost submerged the Ministry of Home Security's headquarters, and many of the new tasks were quite outside their previous experience."[30] Ultimately, the cabinet decided the MHS could not handle both tasks, and transferred shelter welfare to the Ministry of Health in 1941. Before the transfer took place, however, Ellen made significant strides in improving living conditions in the shelters. Her emphasis was on how to provide what she termed the three "S's" of shelters: safety, sanitation, and sleep.[31] At her suggestion, the larger shelters began issuing tickets so shelterers would not need to queue up for hours to ensure a bed. Bunks were ordered and installed, including fold-up bunk beds that could be fixed against the walls of tube platforms during the day. By early December, 150,000 beds were ordered for installation. Provision was made for the supply of chemical toilets. In the tubes, which were below sewer level, the disposal of chemical toilet waste proved a tricky challenge, which was ultimately overcome through pneumatic tubes that transported the waste up and into the sewers. In December, Ellen announced that the Ministry had placed an order for coal stoves for distribution to brick shelters during the winter months.[32] The same month, the MHS passed a regulation that allowed members of the Wardens' Service to police the shelters to prevent theft, sexual misconduct, and the spread of communicable disease. First-aid stations were set up, and public baths were encouraged to open early to accommodate those who either could not make it home in time before work or no longer had homes in which to bathe.[33] Ellen told Harold Nicolson, then at the Ministry of Information, that she found her job much more gratifying than his; while he dealt in ideas, "and one can never see how an idea works out," she dealt in water closets and you could always see whether a WC worked or not.[34]

If rendering existing shelters safe and sanitary was a herculean task, meeting the demand for new shelters seemed a challenge of god-like proportions. During the early months of the war, the government maintained schemes for the evacuation of vulnerable populations from London, Birmingham, and numerous coastal towns. Children, expectant mothers, and the aged and infirm were offered relocation, but resistance to evacuation steadily hardened in 1940 as families expressed a preference to remain united and in their homes, which placed an increased burden on shelter capacity.[35] Technically, shelter provision was still managed by local authorities; but in October 1940, the MHS committed to reimburse local authorities for shelter construction and to do its best to make scarce construction materials, most notably cement, available.

In addition to requisitioning materials, the MHS set guidelines for shelter construction and mass-produced in-home shelters for dispatch to local authorities. From the outbreak of the war, the government had shown a wariness about deep-shelter provision. One the one hand, Britain's damp climate meant waterproofing these shelters would be an extremely costly process; on the other, as Ellen explained to local government officials in Bootle, "Many underground shelters give only an illusory security. They can stand up to a 50lb bomb, but not to one of 250lb."[36] Yet the popularity of the London Underground for shelterers and their excellent safety record—the largest number of fatalities in the tube shelters during the war came not from bombs, but from a tragic stampede at Bethnal Green tube on March 3, 1943, which killed 173 people, mostly women and children—created a growing public and political pressure on the government to extend the network of underground shelters. In November 1940, the ministry announced a partial reversal of its policy, declaring it would extend tunnelling in the London Underground and a few other provincial locations. Ellen was clearly thrown by the reversal, which was driven in part by pressure from the Communist press, and her parliamentary statements on the new policy were more than usually testy. When her old colleague in the Spain Lobby Philip Noel-Baker asked her whether she and Morrison had personally looked into the possibilities for expanding underground shelters outside of London, she retorted with exasperation, "That is hardly a job for myself or my right hon. Friend," before responding that ministry experts were looking into the issue.[37] Finally, the ministry introduced a new form of personal shelter in late 1940 to replace the backyard Andersons, whose popularity continued to wane. The new steel-framed "Morrison shelters," which doubled as kitchen tables, were available from February 1940 at no cost to those earning less than £350 p.a. and for £7 for those earning above the threshold. Although shelter provision continued to be a significant issue throughout 1943, by the spring of 1941, Ellen, Herbert, and the MHS felt they had a workable plan in hand to tackle the challenge.

Once shelter policy had been more or less ironed out, Ellen was given a new remit: fire watching. At no time during her political career was she as unpopular as when she was charged with implementing the government's compulsory fire-watching scheme. The reasons lay both with the inherent unsavoriness of her task—forcing citizens to perform hazardous and poorly remunerated civil defence work on top of their normal work—and the particular way in which she used the remit to enforce her own social agenda of shared sacrifice and equal citizenship. Her approach to fire-watching policy and adherence to her principles in the face of public opprobrium are evidence of a deep-rooted belief that the war could serve as an effective engine for social change.

To meet the unanticipated challenge of incendiary bombs, the Home Office restructured the organization of the fire-fighting forces in August 1941 from a decentralized web of local services to a pyramid structure under the direction of the Home Office and the Scottish Home Department. A national Fire Service College and regional and area training schools were formed to systematize training, and women were heavily recruited into the administrative grades of the service. The new nationalized structure was viewed as a success and remained in place after the war. The management of the reorganization was made the particular remit of William Mabane. Ellen was placed in charge of creating a civilian fire-watching detail, which would identify and tackle small fires before they became conflagrations and liaise with the new National Fire Service (NFS) to ensure that firefighters were promptly dispatched to the scene when fire watchers could not manage fires on the spot.

In September 1940, the MHS had passed a regulation requiring all premises employing more than thirty persons and all large warehouses and timber yards to maintain fire watchers on the premises around the clock.[38] Following the large-scale firebombing of London on December 29, Morrison broadcast an appeal for volunteer fire guards and simultaneously announced plans for the introduction of compulsory fire watching in the new year. On January 18, 1941, he announced the Civil Defence Duties (Compulsory Enrolment) Order, which required all men between sixteen and sixty to register with their local authority as eligible to perform up to forty-eight hours of fire watching per month. Although women were not initially conscripted, they were encouraged to volunteer. In August 1942, the HMS announced that the compulsory enrolment order would be extended to women up to age forty-five. The decision almost certainly originated with Ellen. It accorded with her oft-stated conviction that women had a civic duty to contribute to the war effort alongside men; and in the years that followed, she defended the decision in the face of its near-universal unpopularity, despite mounting evidence that the attempt to dragoon women was not worth the effort. (In autumn 1942, a reported two-thirds to four-fifths of women in London had filed a petition for exemption from fire watching. Figures of nearly 80 percent claiming exemption were reported in Sheffield and Manchester. "Dealing with these claims involved endless clerical labour at a time when every form of manpower was scarce."[39])

From its inception, fire watching was resented as tedious work that taxed those already working long shifts in vital industries. Political cartoons often depicted fire watchers wiling away the night playing games of patience. Yet in certain areas, fire watching was dangerous work. Fire guards needed to remain above ground in sight of potential targets. They were expected to act as first responders and were trained to use stirrup pumps to fight small fires. During the "Little Blitz" in London in February 1944, fire guards extinguished 75 percent of the fires caused by incendiary bombs without assistance from the NFS.[40] Fire watchers in certain high target areas such as Hull were said to say a final goodbye to their families before leaving for duty at night.[41] The high risk was frequently cited by those who opposed the conscription of women for such duties.[42]

Yet for Ellen the conscription of women was a matter of principle. During the Spanish Civil War, she had praised the bravery and patriotism of the "Marching Amazons" who fought alongside their fathers and brothers.[43] In August 1939, she had written a piece for the *Sunday Star and Referee* entitled "Militia Girls—and why not?" which detailed the myriad ways in which women could serve the war effort, ending with an exhortation to give blood.[44] In the months and years that followed, she lost no opportunity to publicly state her view that women as equal citizens had equal obligations to the state. In June 1940, Ellen had broadcast a radio appeal to women not eligible for conscription to volunteer their services in other capacities. That August, she was invited by Lever Brothers to form one of a group of "eminent modern thinkers" contributing "helpful talks" aimed at "sustaining good spirits at a time when the men and women of this country are bearing extra burdens of responsibility and care."[45] Her first essay, "The Marthas and the Marys," which ran several times in journals including the *Daily Express* and the *Daily Mail,* was a modern-day parable in which the country was divided into two types of women. On one hand, the Marthas were "the really valuable women in war time . . . who will put up with any discomfort or sacrifice that is necessary; and then try to get as good a life as is possible within these limits, first for others, then for themselves." The "Marys . . . wallow in war worries, and expect to be commended for enduring quite unnecessary privation." Marys, she wrote with venom, "are a public nuisance who deserve slapping rather than sympathy."[46] In 1942–1943, Ellen would be heckled and booed for her insistence that women perform fire-watching work alongside men. She supported the conscription of women into the services and war industries the following year. In April 1942, in another broadcast directed at working mothers, she emphasized, "Between the conflicting claims of home and factory, the factory just has to come first."[47] Given that Ellen did not have young children at home to look after, many listeners must have found her exhortations a bit rich. Nonetheless, they were consistent with a longstanding commitment to the ideal of equal sacrifice.

Throughout the conflict, the government looked to Ellen and Florence Horsburgh, Conservative parliamentary secretary to the ministry of health, to reach out to women and shore up their support for the war effort. After Ellen's appointment to oversee the fire watchers service, she gave a candid interview with the *Daily Mail* in which she explained that Morrison had hoped she, as a woman, would be best positioned to recruit women into the service and, as a trade unionist, would be able to quell protests from men who resisted risking their lives to defend capitalist property.[48] Neither proved an easy task; Ellen took unprecedented abuse for the fire-watching scheme from both women and trade unionists, but the women proved to be the fiercer critics. Shortly after compulsory fire watching for women was instituted, Ellen lashed out to a reporter about the extent of opposition to the scheme. Opposition, she claimed, with more than a hint of her old class animus, came not from good citizens, but "from certain young painted-nailed ladies who have married officers and think that their lives' work is done." A woman was "a citizen and a human being," with all the obligations that entailed. In a nod to the Russian women whose emancipation she had long respected, she contrasted the "bleatings" of some British women to the bravery "of the women of Stalingrad who are on the front line with their husbands, manning the barricades. . . . The enemy is at their gates and women equally with men are resisting. Our women will have to do the same."[49]

Not long after the new regulations were announced, Ellen was in her most serious auto accident to date. At the beginning of August, she collided with a heavy transport lorry and totalled the Austin Seven. Some nasty bruises and a busted shoulder aside, she did not appear to be seriously injured, and she showed up in the House the next day to answer critical questions about the revised fire watching regulations. Despite mounting headaches, she continued with her ministerial work for another ten days before finally going into hospital to discover that she had fractured her skull.[50] She grudgingly consented to a week's bed rest, but was then back up and about, jostling over bumpy roads to tour bombed cities and meet with trade unions and civil defence authorities. Her frenetic schedule undermined the healing process; and by late October, Hugh Dalton noted she appeared to be self-medicating her "excruciating headaches" with "more than one small glass of sherry."[51]

Even if her status as a government minister had not exempted her from mandatory fire watching, her injury could almost certainly have earned her an exemption—"there were so many means of obtaining exemption that it was said 'that anyone not a congenital idiot could easily evade fire guard duty, and in any case a congenital idiot was entitled to exemption.'"[52] Nonetheless, both to avoid accusations of hypocrisy and because she believed in practicing what she preached, Ellen continued to carry out fire-watching duties at Dolphin Square.[53] In early October, she spoke with a group of 1,000 women in Coventry about the new regulations, fielding angry questions with retorts that the government had not "introduce[d] compulsion for women for fun." After nearly two hours on her feet before the hostile crowd, she was forced to sit down, later confiding to a reporter she was still suffering the effects of the car crash.[54] The next day, she had a tense confrontation with women in Liverpool, which left local authorities relieved that "the threatened scrap did not come off."[55] It was followed by a meeting at Picton Hall, where Ellen proved her worth to the government. Although her talk was repeatedly interrupted by "hoots, catcalls and wisecracks," and, at one point, she taunted an interlocutor with, "If it comes to a shouting match, I can do as well as you," she ultimately won over many in the crowd with impassioned promises that the government would root out male shirkers and that women would not be asked to do more than their fair share. Nonetheless, the crowd was so raucous the police had to provide her with an escort to her car and "she drove away, dishevelled but still undaunted, with jeers and cheers behind her."[56]

One group Ellen should have been able to turn to for support were the equal rights feminists of the Six Point Group and other allied organizations. Throughout the 1920s and 1930s, such women had gone further than Ellen in arguing for total equality between the sexes, even to the extent of opposing health and safety legislation in factories meant to protect women and child labourers (legislation Ellen and her trade union colleagues supported). However, the government hurt itself with this group by refusing equal compensation to male and female fire guards as inconsistent with its policy in other departments. It must have been a painful moment for Ellen when she was forced to respond to questions from colleagues Edith Summerskill and Mavis Tate about the rates of injury compensation for male and female fire guards by reading out the official government line, "The rates of compensation payable to fire-guards for war service injuries are governed by the Personal Injuries (Civilians) Scheme, and it would not be equitable or practicable to give more advantageous terms to fire-guards than to other classes covered by that scheme."[57] Tate and Summerskill, in fact, objected to the entirety of the 1939 Personal Injuries (Civilians) Act, which allowed men more compensation than women for all civilian war-related injuries; and five months later, they brought the issue to a vote. Walking into the lobby minutes before the division, Ellen endured the shame of her National Union of Distributive and Allied Workers (NUDAW) colleague Evelyn Walkden pointing out to the House that he and Ellen "are paid the same rate of pay. In our trade union we are not concerned with sex. We pay for the job and not the person."[58] She sat silently through the vote, then went into the government lobby alongside Horsburgh, while Eleanor Rathbone, Megan Lloyd George, Irene Ward and ninety-two others voted for equal pay. It was not the only bitter pill she would swallow in the interest of unity and winning the war.

Ellen also earned opprobrium from her fellow trade unionists for her willingness to back government proscriptions on strike action and to countenance what many saw to be the exploitation of working-class labour by the wartime government. In August 1941, on a visit to the northeast, she broke up a strike in a Tyneside dockyard by telling the men, "If you want to fight, fight Hitler."[59] But although she was clear that her priority was winning the war—as she told an American audience in a broadcast over NBC radio, "We daren't let ourselves think too much about the postwar world . . . we must first win this war against the fascist"—she remained acutely conscious that the war had transformed Britain from a free-market society into a largely socialized and controlled economy.[60]

Nonetheless, both contemporary observers and subsequent historians accused Ellen of veering to the right in her politics during the war. Her own union, which contained several outspoken Communists, fellow travellers, and pacifists, took a dim view of her newfound commitment to coalition government. On January 21, 1941, the Home Office had banned publication of the Communist publications the *Daily Worker* and the *Week* on the grounds that they had been spreading disinformation to stir up agitation amongst service and munitions workers. At NUDAW's annual conference in Edinburgh in May 1942, both Ellen and John Jagger, who had served as Morrison's parliamentary private secretary since the formation of the coalition, spoke in favour of the ban but were massively outvoted. A few months later, Jagger died in a road accident while driving back to London from Ellen's cottage in

Penn. It was a terrible personal loss for Ellen, who had looked to Jagger as both friend and father figure. Jagger's death left her even more exposed to criticism from her union, which continued to denounce what it perceived as her right-wing tendencies.

In November 1943, the Home Office released British Fascist leader Oswald Mosley on the grounds of ill health, which invoked loud protest from the political left. As expected, Ellen vocally supported her chief, justifying the position with an appeal to the conscience and self-interest of the left: "If Labour demanded that people should be gaoled because they were unpopular or hated, it would be a bad precedent if the time came when their own views were unpopular. . . . Labour had to fight for the principle that men and women should not be imprisoned for the opinions they held."[61] It was an ironic reversal. The previous year she had supported the suppression of Communists' freedom of speech; now she argued that Labour needed to stand up for liberty of opinion, even for Fascists. Although Ellen's posture revealed a hypocritical, if pragmatic, approach, her union took an equally contrarian line. Before, they had condemned the government for suppressing liberties. At the 1944 party conference in Blackpool, delegates sought to have Ellen fired from her union post for supporting Mosley's release, an act one delegate described as "amongst the greatest crimes ever perpetuated by an individual against the working-class." At the time, Ellen was in a nursing home recuperating from yet another respiratory infection, and the conference proved unwilling to fire her in absentia; but it was clear many felt she was no longer acting as a true representative of the working classes.[62]

If Ellen's NUDAW colleagues believed she had abandoned her radical credentials to play yes-man for a Conservative-dominated coalition, others have argued that her return to government saw a rejection of revolutionary commitments in favour of Fabian gradualism. Ironically, one was the arch-Fabian Beatrice Webb, who claimed Ellen's chapter on social justice in Harold Laski's *Programme for Victory* was "vague reformist journalese without her customary fervor but with the caution of a parliamentary under-secretary."[63] Kingsley Martin claimed Ellen "moved to the Right . . . under the spell of Mr. Churchill."[64] More recently, one scholar has argued that "as the war became more challenging and she abandoned many of the principles that she once held inviolate, her reputation as a fiery socialist diminished."[65] Such characterizations both exaggerate the extent of Ellen's domestic radicalism in the 1930s and downplay the degree to which she remained committed to a radical political agenda during and after the war. As we have seen, her prewar analysis of fiscal and monetary policy was already a vague blend of Hobson and Keynes, and both the Jarrow Crusade and her hire purchase bill can be viewed as efforts to achieve moderate reforms within the existing capitalist framework. Her conversion to the public corporation model of nationalisation mirrored that of every major member of the Labour movement and was largely a practical response to the realities of wartime nationalisation. It was, after all, the arch Socialist Leaguer Stafford Cripps who, as president of the Board of Trade and later chancellor of the exchequer, oversaw the implementation of Labour's economic policy after the war. And her foreign policy remained more radical than such assessments allow. Most importantly, as she said in the debate over the war service grants scheme, Ellen viewed the extraordinary circumstances of the Second World War as an opportunity to put into practice a giant social experiment that would redefine not only the nature of public and private capital but also the rights and obligations of citizenship in Britain.

The war drove the final nail into the coffin of Ellen's tortured romance with the Soviet Union, but from her viewpoint it was the Comintern that had abandoned the working class. She had long criticized the Communist Party of Great Britain's (CPGB) slavish adherence to the Moscow line. In 1935, she had written a contemptuous piece in *Plebs* entitled "The Whiskers of the Soviet Cat," in which she denounced "those theoreticians whom the Germans expressively called 'ink coolies' who have to watch carefully which way the Soviet cat washes its whiskers each morning, in order to keep up with the swift changes of policy in Moscow."[66] At the time, she agreed with Soviet foreign policy but even then was not blind to Stalinism's self-serving nature. Still, she never suspected the Soviet Union would actively sell out the Eastern European working class to the fascists. Asked in April 1942 why she had turned on the Communists, Ellen replied with white-hot rage: "I not only worked with the Communists, but I risked my political career because of them. I did this because I saw what Hitler did in Germany in 1933 and I was burning with a desire to make people understand the horrors of this beastly thing called fascism. . . . If anybody had told me then that the British Communist party and the *Daily Worker* would ever describe this as a 'capitalistic war' and that it would do everything for a solid year to weaken the war against fascism, I would not have believed them."[67] After the Soviet Union delivered Eastern Europe's workers to Hitler to buy itself time, the anti-fascist CPGB had "change[d] its mind about a vital issue because it receive[d] a telegram from somebody 1,000s of miles away."[68] Even after the Nazis invaded the Soviet Union and Britain and the Soviets became reluctant allies, Ellen could not get over a sense of betrayal by her erstwhile colleagues in the anti-fascist campaign. Invited to speak at a "Rally for Russia" in Trafalgar Square in October 1941, she lost her temper in the face of Communist demands for a second front and shouted at her hecklers that "we were fighting Germany whilst Russia did nothing." A few years later, she again used her own history of cooperation with the CPGB to lend weight to criticisms of the party, warning a Labour meeting in Jarrow: "I put people on guard against them. I have worked very closely with the Communist Party and know what I am talking about."[69] Her sense of personal betrayal ran deep.

Yet despite her contempt for Stalin and the national party apparatchiks who slavishly followed his lead, Ellen continued to consider herself a Marxist and to admire the Soviet Union's achievements in the social sphere. In a lecture to the Fabian Society commemorating the anniversary of the Russian Revolution in November 1934, she had underscored feminist advances in the Soviet Union. Eight years later, she again spoke at a Fabian Society event on the anniversary of the revolution. Despite her disillusionment with the Comintern and Soviet foreign policy, she could still tell her audience, "Everyone who believed in the necessity of subordinating profit motive to public interest, and of replacing the anarchy of free competition by an ordered planning, owed a debt of gratitude to the Soviet Union for having given the world an example to show" that such a world was "no mere Utopian dream, but a perfectly practicable proposition."[70] Yet her admiration for the Soviet Union's accomplishments no longer extended to a toleration for Communist party tactics, and she sided with the members of Labour's National Executive Committee who were determined to keep Communists out of the party.

Ellen had been reelected to the National Executive Committee (NEC) in 1937 and remained a member of the executive until her death.

She was not naturally a committee woman. Kingsley Martin described her as "a better leader than a follower."[71] The talking-shop aspect of committee work bored her, and the minutes of the Manchester Women's International League (WIL), the Fabian Society, and countless other organizations are littered with records of her absences. The NEC was the exception that proved the rule. The NEC was the nucleus of power and decision-making authority within the Labour movement, and Ellen wanted a seat at the table. Excepting her (not infrequent) absences due to illnesses or injury, she rarely missed a meeting of the NEC or of the various subcommittees on which she served. Her NEC voting record shows her hardened opposition to the CPGB after the Soviet invasion of Poland. On January 27, 1943, she broke with Harold Laski and other left-wingers in voting to deny a Communist application to affiliate to the Labour Party and continued to oppose Communist requests for "left unity."[72]

The day after the vote on Communist affiliation, Ellen and a small group of MPs including William Mabane went up in a military glider for an aerial view of the effects of bombardment. As the group was lofting over the south of England, Lieutenant-General Frederick Browning whispered to her, "Don't tell anybody, but we're going to crash."[73] Forty seconds later, they hit the ground. Ellen, with her typical bad luck, was the only one seriously injured, hurled through the fuselage as the machine crashed nose first. When the crew pulled her out of the wreckage, she wearily shrugged her shoulders, smiled, and in a nod to Frank Sinatra, crooned, "Everything happens to me."[74] Even in the face of death, she kept her sense of humour. She suffered a compound fracture to her leg that required multiple operations and was forced to remain immobilized in hospital. For the better part of a month, Ellen's bed became a makeshift office; and visitors were confronted with a chaotic mess of flowers, cards, despatch boxes, and detective novels strewn around the tiny room.[75] Shortly after she was released from hospital, she tripped in the House of Commons and reinjured her leg, earning her yet another entry in the Palace's accident books.[76] Nonetheless, she hobbled back to parliament the next day and shortly thereafter had lunch with Dalton and let him know she "would like more show at the next Labour Party Conference," and she had ambitions to become the next vice-chairman of the NEC.[77] In this, as in most things she set her mind to, Ellen was successful, winning election as vice-chairman, with trade unionist George Ridley as chairman. Ridley had been ill when elected, and his unexpected death in January 1944 meant Ellen acceded to the chairmanship earlier than anticipated. She became one of the longest-serving chairmen of the NEC, leading the executive through the May 1945 conference. She sat on both the policy and publicity sub-committees in 1944; and, during the crucial 1945 election year, served as chairman of the party organization subcommittee and as a member of the policy, campaign, international, and finance committees. Two se-rious respiratory infections requiring hospitalization took Ellen out of commission for nearly two months in spring 1944 and for another two months from November 1944 through January 1945, with the result that she missed the December 1944 party conference. She returned to parliamentary and party work in 1945 as the Rt. Hon. Ellen Wilkinson, having been made a privy councillor alongside Florence Horsburgh in the King's New Year's honours list. It was a high honour, if one Ellen wore lightly—at the time of the appointment, Margaret Bondfield was the only other female privy councillor. Despite her illnesses, she re-mained engaged with party activity and played a key role in discussions over when and whether to leave the coalition and how to run the 1945 election campaign.

On July 26, 1944, the executive discussed postwar plans and decided, in the face of some reservations, that when the next election was called, Labour would "fight as an independent party, aiming at an indepen-dent majority." The decision was shaped by a recognition of the growing impatience within the party for the continuation of the coalition. In the end, it was another two months before the party formerly declared it would go it alone at the next election.[78] By this point, however, the executive had already decided to launch a nationwide membership campaign. Between February and March 1945, a series of leaflets and pamphlets were issued for distribution by local party workers. A cir-cular to local councillors was sent out under Ellen's signature, asking these loyal men and women to do their utmost to help bring "more alive and keen young people in[to] the Party."[79] The circular's stilted, official style suggests it was not written by Ellen personally, but the sentiments were very much hers. The previous year, she had confided her anxieties about youth and politics to her old friend Margaret Goldsmith:

> We have had three years of war, during which political education has ceased.... Consequently, women have lacked three years of intensive political education which in the normal course of events would have included a general election, which is the best political school of all.... I find that younger women are rather bewildered about the world in which they are living. Each new event tends to seem to them a bolt from the blue, and their general tendency is, 'Well, I don't really take much interest in politics,' coupled with a resentment that some political idiots (unnamed) should have smashed the best period of their lives with a second world war.[80]

Ellen had supported the decision to call an electoral "truce" for the duration of the war and continued to support it in the face of calls within the party to resume contested elections in 1944, but she remained conscious of the opportunity the war offered to convert young men and women to the merits of state planning.[81] In highlighting the benefits of "war socialism," she frequently pointed to government programs that benefitted children and young families. At a meeting of Durham miners in October 1943, she emphasized the nutritional benefits to school children of the National Milk Scheme and the National Vitamins Scheme, as well as the provision of school meals to two million children.[82] She praised the coalition government's provision of "excellent" nursery schools, although she cautioned that the development of a culture in which women felt comfortable leaving their young children at nursery while they went off to work would take time—"this is after all a new experiment."[83] Throughout the war, Ellen repeatedly used the term "experiment" to refer to shifts both in gender relations and social welfare introduced by the war, just as she and her colleagues on the left had spoken optimistically of the "Soviet experiment" in the aftermath of the Russian revolution. She was convinced a Labour government, if given the opportunity, could prove the experiment successful.

For the previous four years, Ellen's departmental remit had meant her attention was focused almost exclusively on domestic affairs. Her ascension to the party chairmanship increasingly brought her back into the international orbit within which she had moved so seamlessly in the 1930s. In September 1944, she chaired a conference of Dominion Labour parties held in Westminster. She also participated in meetings of the "inter-allied consultative committee" of socialist organizations, which included the Belgian politicians Camille Huysmans and Louis de Brouckère and representatives of the various Socialist parties in exile in London. While the Belgians were keen to reconstitute the interwar Labour and Socialist International, Ellen and her British colleagues were concerned that an organization composed primarily of officials appointed by the small exile parties would lack the requisite accountability amongst the European working class, and did not want to be tied to the decisions of such a body.[84] Nonetheless, the reopening of dialogue between European socialists symbolized a shift from a wartime mentality to a focus on postwar reconstruction.

However much Ellen hoped for a socialist landslide on an international scale after the war, she was conscious that the postwar world would not be run by a conclave of socialist ministers. At the end of the First World War, Ellen and her colleagues on the WILPF had looked with optimism to the League of Nations as a vehicle for international social change and a mechanism to end international conflict. By the 1920s, she had grown disenchanted with the organization, which increasingly appeared to be little more than a smoke screen for vested interests intent on safeguarding the status quo. She and many on the British left had rediscovered the League after 1936, viewing it not so much as a vehicle for peaceful change but as a military deterrent that offered the last best hope of containing the dictators. The League had failed both as a vehicle for social change and as a basic guarantor of peace and stability. Nonetheless, Ellen was not alone in believing that the new international institution envisaged by Franklin Roosevelt might be able to succeed where the League had failed.

Ellen's inclusion in the British delegation to the April 1945 United Nations conference in San Francisco was the beginning of a productive involvement with the UN that would continue until her death. Yet despite her participation on the preamble purposes and principles committee and the economic and social cooperation committee, her role at San Francisco has been remembered principally for her outspoken rejection of a "women's agenda" at the conference.[85] Her refusal to act as an advocate for women at San Francisco is ironic. Although the official minutes of the May 19, 1945 cabinet meeting at which the composition of the British delegation was first discussed do not name any names, the cabinet secretary's notes indicate that all agreed "our two women privy councilors" should be included.[86] Thus, Ellen and Florence Horsburgh were sent to America not as an indication of Britain's concern for home security or health but so the British government could appear as a progressive power that included women in its decision-making processes. As an indication of their token status, they were made assistant delegates. Ellen's inclusion in the delegation meant she was privy to the government's meetings with other dominion powers to discuss strategy going in to the conference.[87] Yet, when it came to plans for participation in the conference itself, it soon became clear the government intended Ellen and Florence to focus their attention on "women's issues" that Ellen found, if not unimportant, comparatively marginal to the broader goals of the conference.

Ellen had not abandoned her feminism by 1945, but her own privileged position during the war had led her to discount the degree to which the vast majority of women were still socially and politically marginalized. She is alleged to have said at the conference that her position proved women had arrived and no further special treatment was needed, to which Brazilian politician Bertha Lutz aptly retorted, "I'm afraid not, it only means that you have arrived."[88] When a journalist from the *San Francisco Chronicle* asked Ellen why there were not more women delegates, she snapped, "We are here as political figures in our own right. . . . We are members of Parliament, we are ministers. The fact that there are fewer women delegates is doubtless because there are fewer women than men in public office."[89] She offered no comment on why and how the social and political systems in most countries colluded to exclude women from reaching public office. While Lutz and Australian representative Jessie Street lobbied for the creation of a separate commission on the status of women within the UN, the two British delegates distanced themselves from the campaign.

Ellen's standoffish attitude toward her fellow female delegates in San Francisco sits awkwardly with her long record as a feminist, her refusal to support equal pay during the war notwithstanding. A charitable assessment would argue that she overestimated the extent to which women's involvement in war work had transformed gender dynamics within Britain and abroad. An alternate reading could suggest that she was aware of her token role at San Francisco and resented her colleagues' cynicism in sending her and Horsburgh, and that, ironically, it was the feminist delegates who bore the brunt of her frustration for having pointed out the emperor was not wearing any clothes.

If Ellen was angry with Churchill, she found an outlet for her irritation. At the beginning of the war, she had expressed reservations about the orders suspending democratic government in India during the conflict. Although there is no record of her views on the issue, she almost certainly disapproved of the government's insistence on vetting Indian delegates to San Francisco and prohibiting Congress participation. In response to the British government's actions, the American pro-Congress groups the India League of America and the National Committee for India's Freedom had invited Vijaya Lakshmi Pandit, Nehru's sister and the former minister of local government and public health in India, to travel to San Francisco. Pandit embarrassed the British government by putting the Congress case in a speech before the fifty-one original UN member states. Philip Noel-Baker described the speech as "a glorious oratorical success," which "convinced those delegates who had been doubtful that, if India could produce such women, India could herself most assuredly control her national affairs."[90] Although the Conservative foreign secretary Anthony Eden kept his distance from Pandit, Ellen conspicuously dined out in Chinatown with Pandit and Vera Brittain's husband George Catlin. The meal was the beginning of a long and close relationship between George, Vera, and Vijaya—yet another incongruous friendship forged by Ellen's desire to bring together people she liked and respected.[91] Her public act of solidarity with Pandit sent a message to her Conservative male colleagues that she was a serious international actor with views on the postwar imperial landscape that should not be discounted.

Meanwhile, preparations were gearing up for the Labour Party conference, scheduled to open in Blackpool on May 21. The NEC chairman would normally be closely involved in the preparations for the event, but Ellen was holed up in a hotel room in San Francisco. She never missed an opportunity to travel, and she must have enjoyed the opportunity both to make the transatlantic journey by air for the first time and to dip her toes in the Pacific Ocean. She experienced the luxury of shopping without ration coupons, although war requisitioning meant she was not able to stock up on silk underthings as she usually did when visiting the United States. (In a moment of ill judgment, Ellen griped to a British journalist, "One of the tragedies of San Francisco was that no one could buy any silk stockings."[92])

If San Francisco was a footnote, the 1945 party conference would prove a capstone in Ellen's political career. The D-Day landings had led to the postponement of the 1944 party conference to December. Ellen had missed the last conference due to ill health, but she was determined to chair the 1945 event. At 9:30 a.m. on Monday May 21, more than 1,100 delegates assembled in the Empress Ballroom at the Winter Gardens were called to order. On the motion of new party secretary Morgan Phillips, Ellen was formally elected conference chairman. After a brief welcome from Blackpool's civic and Labour dignitaries, she took the dais and with characteristic bravado delivered a speech she had finished writing only that morning. The result was an oratorical tour de force many listeners likened to the most impassioned speeches of her youth.[93]

For five years, Ellen had worked loyally alongside Churchill and the other members of the Conservative government. She had supported controversial policies that flew in the face of her own long-held values and drew opprobrium from many colleagues in the Labour movement. Now she took a fierce stand on the imperative for Labour to leave the coalition and appeal to the electorate for a mandate to rebuild postwar Britain along socialist lines—to create a New Jerusalem on the rubble of Britain's bombed-out cities. Three days earlier, Churchill had written to Attlee ruling out the Labour Party's suggestion of an autumn election, on the grounds it would create a protracted campaign atmosphere that would undermine the government's ability to prosecute the war. Churchill's decision, in effect, pushed Attlee and his party into a corner: They could either agree to remain in coalition for an indefinite period until the conclusion of the war with Japan, or they could leave the government and force an immediate election. In his appeal to Attlee,

Churchill had argued that he was acting in the country's best interests. Ellen was not buying it. Her speech was a rallying cry to the party faithful, but it was also a shot across the bow at her wartime colleagues, intended as much for the journalists in the gallery as for the men and women on the conference floor.

Although Ellen made clear her personal respect for Churchill, she suggested to the conference, "The people who have been urging a quick July election on the Prime Minister no doubt hope to snatch a party advantage out of the transient passions of the moment of victory, as they did in 1918." The Coalition government elected in 1918—which had promised new homes and failed to deliver and which had ushered in an era of high inflation and rising unemployment—had been led by Lloyd George, but the Conservatives had arguably been the real source of power behind the premier. If the people voted for Churchill in gratitude for his war service, they would again be buying a hardline Conservative ministry wrapped up in the shine of a popular national figure. It was a dirty "trick" that would not deceive "the electorate which has been hardened in the bitter fires of unemployment and depression for which the policies of those who won in 1918 were largely responsible."

Having drawn a link between the current Conservative party and the Conservatives who dominated the 1918–1922 ministry, Ellen reminded her audience that the Conservatives were also the architects of appeasement, the "Guilty Men" of Munich. The Conservative-dominated interwar governments had treated the "democratic political heads of the Weimar Republic who had replaced the Kaiser's government as though they were war criminals, which is a sharp contrast to the way the Chamberlain Government treated the Nazis. . . . The danger of having a government in this country run by the upper social crust is that quite naturally it tends to think that the corresponding upper crust in Germany are the 'right people' in Germany. From the British point of view, apart from any party consideration, those upper-crust people in Germany—or for that matter in Greece or Italy—are the wrong people." For the last five years, Red Ellen had largely subordinated her class-based politics to national unity. Now she raised the banner of class struggle aloft and denounced the Tories as a party for "rich people" and "Big Business." Continuing the attack, she gave vent to a long-suppressed desire to hold her Conservative colleagues to account for past actions. She did not go into the details of Labour's programme—she would leave that to her NEC colleagues—but she emphasized it was crafted for the benefit of the true representatives of the nation, not the parasitic "six percent of the people [who] own eighty per cent of the property." She ended her speech with a promise to "fight for power: power for those who fought and worked and bled, power for the workers in the widest sense, for those who work with hand or brain, for the inventors and the technicians, yes, and for the managers too who do not want to see the fine work they have done in planning for the public interest thrown back into the scramble for private profit.... [I]n this programme which we are putting forward lies the one hope of building in Britain, this beloved island of ours, the type of civilization which we so passionately desire."[94] The London evening *Star* reported the great cheers that followed her speech and described it as a personal triumph. It was, Ellen claimed, the proudest moment of her life.[95]

Tuesday morning, the results of the ballot for next year's NEC saw Ellen comfortably top of the women's section.[96] Over the next several days, the party debated the policies laid out in the election programme, "Let Us Face the Future." The programme had been written principally by Michael Young, the newly recruited head of the party's research department; but Ellen, Herbert Morrison, and Patrick Gordon Walker had all contributed sections.[97] It emphasized price controls, house building, nationalization of key industries in the context of a mixed economy, and the state provision of social welfare. Richard Toye and others have underscored the limitations of the program's reformist ambitions, arguing that "the grand promises to plan in reality masked a rather more modest program of state intervention."[98] It is possible that given the national mood in 1945, the Labour Party could have put forth an even more radical scheme of social reorganization. Yet neither Ellen nor most of her colleagues on the NEC were willing to risk their reach exceeding their grasp. Without losing sight of her ultimate political aim, Ellen had consistently prioritized pragmatism over principle at every general election contest. As she said at the end of her opening speech, the party had "before them today a great chance which may not come again for a lifetime if it is missed this time."[99] Ellen would give her full energy to ensuring Labour did not miss that chance.

15

REFORMING EDUCATION

Ellen invigorated the 1945 party conference with a sense of optimism and commitment. According to Philip Noel-Barker, she was convinced the party would win: "In her little person, [she] was the very spirit of coming victory for all to see."[1] The victory was more spectacular than even Ellen could have imagined. The 1945 general election was Labour's greatest landslide. The party would win more seats in 1997, but the magnitude of the swing from the Conservatives to Labour in the 1945 election has never been matched. Labour gained nearly 250 seats, swelling their ranks to 393 MPs, including 21 women.

Historians have spilled a lot of ink debating the causes of the 1945 Labour victory.[2] Although the balance of factors remains contested, the Labour leadership should be given credit for directing a sophisticated national campaign. Labour's election committee—of which both Ellen and Morrison were members—worked with artists, journalists, and consultants to craft a multimedia campaign that made effective use of the popular press, poster art, film, and the BBC to deliver the party's message. The war had given an enormous boost to the BBC's prestige, and the radio had become the principal source of news for a majority of Britons. The 1945 election saw an unprecedented number of party election broadcasts, and Labour leaders made the most of their access to the airwaves. Each speaker was given a specific remit to focus on one aspect of Labour's plan. Ellen's broadcast, on June 14, dealt with the need for economic planning after the war.

Despite having studied economics at university, Ellen was never one of her party's leading economic theorists, and she did not pretend to be. Her strength had always lain in her ability to translate fiscal and monetary policy into language average men and women could understand. Broadcasting just before the dissolution of parliament, Ellen did her best to convince the electorate that the Conservatives' promises about the potential of private enterprise to restore prosperity were "the wildest pipe dream of the lot." She reminded listeners of the mad scramble that took place when controls were removed after the First World War, likening it the "biggest gamblers' clean-up in history," resulting in rampant inflation that turned families' "nest eggs" into "scrambled eggs." The postwar government would need to ensure that scarce foreign currency reserves were earmarked for the importation of foodstuffs and the purchase of building materials for reconstruction. If instead currency were allowed to trade freely, "some people may get luxuries—motor cars, expensive furs and jewellery—and we might very well find ourselves, as a nation, without money to pay for essential food and raw materials."

The implication was clear. Control and central planning would benefit the nation as a whole. Free markets would benefit the elite few at the expense of those who had already sacrificed so much over the previous five years. Although some found Ellen's style patronizing and abrasive, her straightforward defence of the planned economy succeeded in impressing even those who identified themselves as Conservatives. A housewife in her fifties told the survey organization Mass-Observation: "I *do* think Wilkinson—Miss Wilkinson, you know—was really very good. She spoke in the way a housewife could understand"; and a wine butler in his thirties reported, "Mrs.—who is it now?—Mrs. Wilkinson, I think they call her. She was very good. She put everything so clearly . . . there was nothing in her speech that anyone couldn't understand. Churchill, on the other hand, was the other way about. I was surprised. His was more the Hyde Park style. It was a lot of whitewash really." A twenty-one-year-old civil servant told the *Hartlepool Mail* she "had intended to vote for Mr. Churchill, but Miss Wilkinson's speech won me over." A seventy-year-old retired nurse recorded in her diary that she "could imagine Churchill, whom she attacked, listening with interest and murmuring 'Go to it, Ellen,' and wishing she was with his party, or he with hers."[3]

Ellen's was not the only Labour broadcast to win plaudits from listeners; men and women up and down the country agreed that Labour put its case clearly and well. Nonetheless, as in 1929, politicians, pollsters, and pundits continued to underestimate Labour's strength in the country. Churchill told King George VI that he anticipated a Conservative majority of between thirty and eighty. After the first day of polling, the *Daily Express* predicted a sixty-seat majority for the Tories. On the Labour side, Hugh Dalton predicted either "a Tory majority or a deadlock." Attlee believed Labour was unlikely to win more than 290 seats, and Morrison feared another hung parliament, as in 1923 and 1929. Delays in receiving overseas ballots meant that the results were not announced until two weeks after the polls had closed in most constituencies. During the interval, press and politicians alike remained chary of making prophecies. James Chuter Ede recorded in his diary that "G. R. Strauss has foretold an absolute majority for Labour, basing his forecast, apparently, on news he gathers as proprietor of the *Tribune*, but I know of no one else who takes so optimistic a view." Ede was the MP for South Shields, the constituency immediately adjacent to Jarrow, and his election agent reported to him, "it was thought in Jarrow that Ellen Wilkinson had won by 4,000 which was certainly a larger majority than anyone was expecting during the campaign."[4] She did much, much better than that.

On the morning of Tuesday, July 26, Jarrow announced its final results: Holmes—11,649; Wilkinson—22,656. Ellen had secured nearly

66 percent of the vote. At 3 p.m., the BBC reported that on the current tally the Labour Party had 364 seats, more than enough to give it a clear majority in the House of Commons.[5] Within hours Churchill had tendered his resignation, and the king called on Clement Attlee to form a government. Attlee's six key appointments were announced on Saturday. Morrison would become Lord President; Arthur Greenwood would become Lord Privy Seal; Ernest Bevin would go to the Foreign Office; Dalton would become Chancellor of the Exchequer; Cripps would head the Board of Trade; and Jowitt would be Lord Chancellor. Attlee's remaining appointments were made early the next week. Unlike Churchill's war cabinet, which had operated as a small command nucleus, Attlee's peacetime cabinet included twenty ministers. The sole woman was Ellen, whom he invited to serve as minister of education.

Ellen accepted with alacrity, although she had hitherto shown little interest in education policy. (Rumours that she had her heart set on the ministry are almost certainly apocryphal.[6]) Allegedly, she raced straight from Number 10 to the Ministry of Education's temporary headquarters in Belgrave Square to meet her new team. Her appointment says much about both her and Attlee. As a cabinet minister, Ellen would claim to respect her boss's style of leadership, telling sceptics he was "a team leader and a team worker. . . . He is always willing to listen to any case that is put to him; in fact, it is much easier to get him to listen than to speak. This is a great asset and a rare one among men of high positions."[7] Yet at the 1945 party conference, she had again done her best to drum up support for Attlee's removal as party leader. Morrison had written to Attlee that he was prepared to stand against him for the party leadership. The gambit fell flat in the face of stiff opposition from Bevin and a lack of enthusiasm amongst the rank-and-file of the Parliamentary Labour Party (PLP).[8] But the new prime minister did not hold a grudge. Or, if he did, he did not let it cloud his judgment about either Morrison's or Ellen's political value. Nonetheless, Attlee later recalled that Ellen "looked a little surprised" when he offered her a cabinet post— "she had not expected such magnanimity from one against whom she had been campaigning so actively."[9]

As a member of the war cabinet, Attlee had appreciated that sending Ellen and Florence Horsbrugh to San Francisco would send a message to the rest of the world that Britain valued women's political contribution.

Appointing a woman to his cabinet would send a similar message that British Labour was a modern, progressive party. Certainly, he wanted his cabinet to be representative of different sectors of the population. In deciding on his appointments, he first divided the party's MPs into categories, including Lawyers, Teachers, Dockers, Women, and Young Men.[10] If Attlee did want to appoint a "token" woman, Ellen was the obvious choice. She was indisputably the preeminent female British politician of her day in any party. Her ministerial and party experience, her national recognition, and her international contacts were without rival. Yet, she was not merely a symbolic appointment. Had Ellen been a man, her claims to a cabinet post would have been nearly equally strong. She had been present at the creation of the party as a national force in the 1920s, risen through its ranks, served as a junior minister from 1929 to 1931 and 1940 to 1945, and earned the right to a seat at the table alongside the men with whom she had worked tirelessly for two decades.

Attlee's decision to send Ellen to the Ministry of Education has been attributed to "the Labour Party's gendered assumptions";[11] but education, although a social issue, was by no means seen as a feminine sphere in the 1940s. It had been widely assumed the ministry would go to Chuter Ede, who had been parliamentary secretary to the Board of Education during the war, but whom Attlee ultimately placed in the Home Office. Women may have been prominent on the local education authorities that administered the schools, but nationally, education policy had remained a masculine preserve. So too, notably, had health, the ministry to which Attlee had originally considered appointing Ellen, but which he ultimately gave to a young man: Aneurin Bevan.[12] Given her personal interests and her past experience as deputy to Susan Lawrence in the 1929–1931 government, Ellen would probably have preferred health. Nonetheless, "she set herself, with guts that were . . . characteristic, to learn a quite new role."[13] How well she succeeded at her task has been a subject of much debate. Ellen would have argued that she succeeded in ensuring that the principal promises of the 1944 Education Act were fulfilled, despite the pressure of competing legislative priorities.

The men and women who served their country during the Second World War were largely the product of an education system put in place by the

1902 and 1918 Education Acts. In 1870, the British government had passed its first law requiring the universal provision of primary education, but it was not until 1880 that school attendance was made compulsory until the age of ten. By 1899, the age of compulsory attendance was raised to twelve. By the turn of the century, at least in theory, all British children were receiving an elementary education, either in schools maintained by the local authority; in religious schools; or, in the case of a select few, in private preparatory schools or in "public" boarding schools. Only a very small and elite cadre of children were educated at these last two classes of school, and few children outside them continued their education beyond the age of twelve.

When the bill that led to the 1902 Education Act was debated in parliament, the MPs' principal focus was on the controversial proposal to give state aid to church schools, thereby encouraging a dual system of state-funded education, with some schools run by the local authority and "voluntary" schools run by the Church of England and Catholic dioceses. The settlement over state funding for church schools has remained controversial to this day; however, the act's most far-reaching proposals dealt with secondary education. In 1902, for the first time, the state explicitly encouraged local authorities to make public provision for secondary education. The 1902 act required neither that all willing children be offered an opportunity to remain at school after age twelve nor that secondary education provided by the local authority be free of charge, although authorities were encouraged to provide free places for meritorious children. As a result of the act, the government began funding some grammar schools directly—henceforth known as "direct grant schools." By the time Ellen became minister of education, there were 232 direct grant schools operating in Britain.[14] Additionally, most councils began offering grants to local grammar schools to cover the cost of tuition for a select number of students, usually no more than 25 percent of the student intake. Many local authorities also erected their own selective secondary schools, which offered a combination of free and fee-paying places. These new local authority-run grammar schools included the Stretford Road girl's secondary school in Manchester, which Ellen attended. For students, like Ellen, whose school stopped at age sixteen, institutions such as the teacher training college on Princess Street provided an alternative route to higher education—albeit a route closed off to all but a select few. When Ellen entered Manchester University on the eve of the First World War, there were roughly 30,000 students enrolled in universities across Great Britain. By 1937–1938, that figure had risen to just under 50,000—a significant increase, but one that still left Britain with the worst ratio of inhabitants to university students in northern Europe.[15] In addition to state-run grammar schools, a small number of councils, mostly in the north of England, established junior technical schools, specialized secondary schools from which students with the means and qualifications could secure a place in technical colleges. By the 1930s, 4 percent of British secondary school children were educated in such schools, including, most likely, Ellen's younger brother Harold, who went on to become a radio engineer.[16]

In 1918, the school leaving age was raised to fourteen, and the exchequer took on part of the burden of funding education, which had previously been borne entirely from local taxation. In response to the latest raising of the school leaving age, many local councils built new "senior schools" to educate children between the ages of eleven and fourteen, allowing teachers to focus on more specialized tuition for mature students, while younger students received an elementary education in separate "junior schools." Yet despite government support for such schemes, by 1938 less than half of the nation's children attended these differentiated schools, while the majority were still taught in unreorganized, all-age elementary schools.

The state of the British educational system became a renewed topic of debate during the Second World War, which saw the system attacked on three distinct but related fronts. First, it was argued that the stranglehold of the "old school tie" over politics, finance, and the civil service had led the country into war. The country was run by a tiny fraction of university graduates, most of whom had been privately educated, who may have been well versed in Latin and Greek, but who were otherwise ill prepared to govern. Second, the rudimentary state of technical education in Britain meant that both the army and civil defence faced an alarming shortage of trained chemists and engineers. Third, and most fundamental, it was thought that men and women might justly question how a state that could not be bothered to educate them much beyond the basics of reading, writing, and arithmetic could ask them to die on its behalf.[17]

Under increasing pressure from both the public and the armed forces, the wartime coalition government took up postwar education reform. A draft bill was debated in the House on January 19 and 20, 1944. The House met repeatedly in committee on the bill that March, and numerous amendments were debated. (Ellen, preoccupied with responsibilities at the Ministry of Home Security, did not contribute a word to these debates and was frequently absent from the division lobbies.) The bill that ultimately passed into law on August 3, 1944 was notable both for the changes it made and for the aspects of the previous system it kept in place. The crucial innovation was the introduction of secondary education for all British children. The bill mandated the school leaving age be raised to fifteen no later than April 1, 1947 and raised again to sixteen as soon as practicable. (An amendment to specify a date for the second rise was rejected in committee. Ellen, feeling other priorities had higher claim on the exchequer, voted against the amendment.[18]) Although the act did not spell out the details of the proposed new system, it was widely assumed that once the act went into effect, children aged eleven to fifteen would receive a secondary education on either a grammar, technical or "modern" curriculum. A small percentage—less than 25 percent of children, it was assumed—would be chosen for either grammar or technical tuition, with the majority attending new secondary modern schools. This had been the policy recommended by the Consultative Committee to the Board of Education in 1938 in their report on secondary education (the Spens Report), and rejected by the Chamberlain government. Remarkably, there was no substantive debate in parliament over whether or not it was practicable to make determinations about students' aptitude at age eleven, or whether social factors might adversely impact poorer students' aptitude and lead to their being underrepresented in grammar and technical schools. In the years to come, sociologists would increasingly question the objectivity of the selection process, arguing that material prosperity and parental attitudes had a significant impact, and the 11-plus exam, previously defended as an objective metric of intelligence, would become a prime target of educational reformers.[19] In 1944, however, the principle of selection was almost universally accepted, even by critics of the bill.

In addition to the introduction of secondary education for all, the bill promised a substantial expansion of social service provision through the schools. Herbert Asquith's pre–World War I government had taken the first steps towards the limited provision of meals, milk, and medical care to school children on a means-tested basis. During the Second World War, such provision had increased dramatically, and social surveys had shown the increased provision had had measurable impact on the health of poorer students.[20] Labour members in particular were keen that this provision should be expanded after the war and strongly supported the provisions in the 1944 act that guaranteed medical care for all school children and gave the minister of education authority to make regulations regarding the provision of milk and meals in schools.[21] The issues that did provoke criticism from Labour members were the continued state support of religious education and the failure of the bill to take on the continued existence of direct grant and independent schools. The Labour Party had always had a strong nonconformist contingent, and these members vociferously objected to the autonomy and funding granted to Catholic and Church of England schools. Nonetheless, Chuter Ede recorded in his diary in January 1944, "I have found in conversation that Members generally are exasperated at the monopoly of the time by the religious issue."[22] In any event, the portion of the bill dealing with religious schools was translated into law without substantive amendment and implemented with limited controversy by Attlee's successive ministers of education. The continued state funding of direct grant grammar schools and the failure to bring the independent "public" schools under state control, in contrast, remained divisive issues within the party for decades. Critics felt strongly that the existence of these schools had done more than anything to perpetuate a two-tiered system in British society. A speech by John Parker, who ironically had been educated at Marlborough College and St. John's College, Oxford, effectively laid out the Labour Party's attitude to this portion of the bill, arguing that it "will still keep a particular form of education available to a section of the people because of their ability to find the money to pay for it. That is what we object to."[23]

When the bill went into committee stage, the Labour members forced a division on an amendment to abolish fees for direct grant schools and for young people's colleges (such as the pupil teacher training college that Ellen attended from 1908 to 1910). Ninety-three Labour members voted for the amendment, including Arthur Greenwood, deputy leader of the Labour Party and its principal spokesman on social policy. Ellen, not for the first time during the committee debates, did not appear in the division lobby. The perpetuation of fee-paying schools remained a sore point with Labour members, but they did not feel that the failure to attack the independent school system merited opposition to the bill. On May 12, 1944, the amended bill was sent up to the Lords.

In the meantime, the debate over independent schools masked the extent of ambiguity in the proposals for the state-funded secondary system. Although the bill laid down the overall principles of the new scheme, crucial details were left unresolved, including the aims and scope of a secondary modern curriculum and the proposed physical organization of the secondary education system. The ambiguities remained in the final act. Both of these questions would come back to haunt the postwar minister of education.

The passage of the Education Act during wartime was both an opportunity and a constraint for Ellen. When she moved into her office in Belgrave Square, she had a plan of action already drawn up and waiting on her desk. Unlike Nye Bevan, the new minister of health, who spent months in brutal negotiations with the British Medical Association over the terms of the future National Health Service, Ellen avoided much (but certainly not all) of the horse-trading with educationalists and other vested interests over the direction of reform. This freed up time to focus on implementation, but it also meant she was stuck with the bargains others had negotiated at a time when political realities had made Labour politicians much more inclined to compromise than they might have been after 1945. Those concerned to defend Ellen's reputation could point to her peculiar position as the executor of the coalition's trust; but, in fairness to her critics, Ellen had given no evidence during the 1944 debates that she strongly opposed any aspect of the coalition bill.

Having few coherent views on how or whether the bill could be improved upon, Ellen set out as minister to ensure its promises were implemented. Steps had been taken to bring schoolteachers home from military service; but there remained a massive shortage of teachers, notwithstanding the additional numbers that would be required to carry out the raising of the school leaving age to fifteen (known within the department as ROSLA) and to see through the government's proposals to lower teacher-student ratios. In January 1942, Ede noted that the Blitz had resulted in the destruction of 1,000 schools and the serious damage of another 2,000.[24] Continued bombardment over the next three years would add to the casualty figures. Some decrepit Victorian schools were in such need of modernization that it would arguably have been better if they had been levelled by the Luftwaffe. In areas where the schools had escaped undamaged, and where local authorities had already built separate institutions to educate older children, schools previously designated as "senior schools," "higher elementaries," or "central schools" could be repurposed as secondary moderns. In the majority of areas, new secondary school facilities would have to be built from scratch. These new schools would require desks, chairs, chalkboards, and other amenities, as well as new up-to-date textbooks. And, finally, if the school meal proposals were to be carried out, the schools would require facilities to prepare and serve the food. Confronted with the choice between the concrete challenge of building and manning an expanding school system and the uncertainty of experiments in new models of educational organization and instruction, Ellen made a predictable choice.

Attlee's cabinet convened for the first time on Tuesday, August 7, 1945, the day after the United States dropped the atomic bomb on Hiroshima. Before then, Ellen had participated in exactly two cabinet meetings in her career, in August and September 1944.[25] In both instances, she had been brought in to give the views of the Ministry of Home Security on one agenda item and then been quietly ushered out. Now she had a proper seat at the table as, at least in theory, one amongst twenty equals. Yet, as she quickly discovered, being the head of a ministry did not mean she could do as she pleased, especially in an environment where money was short and everyone was in a hurry to carry through as much as possible before the government was voted out of power. In Ellen's party election broadcast, she had made an impassioned defence of the necessity for national planning. Now she was confronted with the reality that planning meant rationing scarce resources, not only in the sense of privileging government expenditure over private consumption but also in terms of privileging the needs of one ministerial department over the needs of another. During her eighteen months in government, she proved remarkably capable of standing her own ground, cooperating with, cajoling, and occasionally bullying her colleagues into supporting her agenda.

Perhaps unexpectedly, but nonetheless painfully, one of Ellen's stiffest adversaries in cabinet was none other than Herbert Morrison, now Lord President of the Council. It is unlikely their intimate relationship survived long into the new government. Ellen did not have the time or energy to seek out a relationship outside the workplace. She liked and admired Herbert in the 1930s, but she likely became involved with him during the war because he was there. For his part, Morrison, still hopeful of eventually securing the party leadership, likely saw the end of their working relationship as an opportunity to break off a politically ill-advised extramarital affair.

As chairman of the committee that oversaw government expenditure, Morrison had a key role in determining the share of national resources that went to education. The other minister with a crucial voice in such decisions was Chancellor Hugh Dalton. Neither shared Ellen's sense of urgency about the importance of implementing either ROLSA or the sections of the education act governing social welfare provision. Her achievement of both came in the face of fierce opposition from her old friends. From her arrival at the ministry, Ellen focused on preparing the school system for the implementation of ROSLA at the earliest possible date. At her first meeting with her staff, the men (women were still barred from the higher grades of the civil service) emphasized the difficulties of pushing through ROSLA before the deadline of April 1, 1947 laid down in the act. It looked likely, they argued, that the minister would have to seek an amended order to push back the start date. Ellen refused to budge. She conferred with Joe Westwood, secretary of state for Scotland, and the two immediately prepared memoranda stating their intent to stand by the April 1947 deadline. For her part, Ellen was convinced it would be possible, although it would necessitate finding an additional 13,000 teachers above and beyond the thousands needed to replace retirees, and "although this will necessitate some over-crowding of classes in some areas and the use of [temporary] school ac-commodation (huts, prefabricated buildings, &c.)."[26] In cabinet, Ellen pressed hard, condemning the history of "procrastination" by local ed-ucation authorities (LEAs) and arguing that the LEAs would "not move unless it's made clear that we *shall* do it in 1947." Her hostile assessment of local government dated back to her time at the Ministry of Home Security, when she had fought bitterly with local authorities over remu-neration for the construction of air raid shelters. Westwood backed her up, and Attlee seemed receptive, but Morrison was quick to play devil's advocate. The cabinet, he pressed, needed to consider the potential political fallout of raising the leaving age too soon: "Overcrowding, deficiencies of teachers, lower quality of education—may lead to worse criticism than delaying the date. [I] don't like announcing before we know we can do it." Ellen's response was testy and hinted at a sense of betrayal. "If we stick to it we can do it," she insisted. "If you *first* ask whether it can be done the answer will probably be no."

The altercation between Herbert and Ellen opened up a floodgate of debate. Ede, now Home Office secretary, backed up Ellen's view that without a firm deadline, "in some backward areas you will get *no* progress. . . . If we postpone [the] date, progressive LEAs will be dis-heartened and the reactionary authorities will assume it will never be raised at all." Bevan, eager for the raw materials he needed to fulfil the party's election promises on house building, argued for postponement, only for Ellen to snap back that "you can't build houses without schools." After a heated debate, the prime minister punted the question to the Lord President's Committee for further consideration, but within a month Ellen had her way.[27] On September 28, she and Westwood for-mally announced ROSLA would be implemented on April 1, 1947.

If the announcement committed the government, there was still much work to be done. First the ministry needed to address the shortage of schoolteachers. During the war, the government and the national union of teachers had agreed to suspend the normal retirement age as well as the rule that female teachers must retire upon marriage. The ministry reached out to these teachers to stay on to help fill the gap as their colleagues were demobilized and new trainees brought in. (Although women continued to fight for the removal of the so-called marriage bar in other branches of the civil service, the 1944 act quietly removed the prohibition on the continuation in post of married teachers.[28]) Ellen coordinated with George Isaacs, now minister of labour and national service, to have the remaining teachers still serving in the forces quickly repatriated and returned to their posts. The ministry initiated an emergency training scheme, whereby willing young men and women could enrol on a one-year teacher-training crash course. Available sites around the country were converted into temporary colleges, including Alnwick Castle in Northumberland. During the war, Alnwick had served as the temporary home for a Newcastle girls' school and hence possessed most of the needed equipment. Other training colleges were opened in less auspicious surroundings, such as a former munitions works outside Wednesbury. Here Ellen, having found the site, went begging to the Ministry of Works for help with "somehow or other finding things to push into the colleges."[29] By March 1946, twelve emergency training colleges across Britain were up and running, educating 2,400 pupils, in addition to the 7,000 or so students enrolled each year at the traditional two-year pupil-teacher colleges.[30] By May the figure was up to 3,250, and the ministry predicted that 12,600 men and women would be admitted on training courses by December.[31] Although the system did not produce enough new recruits to fulfil Ellen's hopes of bringing down class sizes, there were enough to bring off ROSLA without overly swamping classrooms in most localities.

The race to train teachers was matched by the race to build new schools. Ellen recognized that the only hope of creating capacity was to go for uniformity and mass production. The long-term goal of building sustainable modern schoolhouses would have to be sacrificed to short-term expedients. The ministry brought together architects, educators, accountants, and industrialists, "and discovered by experiment how all the requirements could best be reconciled at the least cost in time and money."[32] Again working in close cooperation with George Tomlinson and his staff at the Ministry of Works, Ellen arranged for the mass distribution of "huts" and prefabricated classrooms to local authorities across the country. At the Labour Party conference in May 1946, she reported that the government had approved the supply of 4,400 huts for use as classrooms and practical rooms.[33] The prefab units came under criticism from both parents and teachers, but Ellen had little time for such whinging.[34] The scale of the construction crisis was almost insurmountable. In her view, the huts weren't pretty, but they did the trick.

The struggle to create a national system of secondary schools capable of accommodating an expanded intake of children to the age of fifteen was exhausting. Ellen knew it could have been done better, but by January 1947, she was convinced she had pulled it off. At that point, however, Dalton, Morrison, and Cripps took one last shot at derailing the ministry's proposals. By 1947, the government had become concerned about both a growing shortage of manpower and wage inflation, and the removal of a key source of cheap labour struck the three men as potentially destabilizing. The Economic Survey for 1947 and the accompanying report from the ministerial committee on economic planning, chaired by Morrison, laid out arguments in favour of postponing ROSLA. The survey estimated that when ROSLA was implemented, it would "halt the customary flow of juveniles for 12–18 months thereafter, and ultimately reduce the working population by upwards of 370,000 persons." This diminution, it continued, "will remove for a time an important source of recruitment to certain industries, e.g., coal and textiles, which it is urgent to maintain, and, in general, throw upon older workers jobs which have hitherto been done more economically by fourteen-year-olds."[35] Morrison's accompanying report recommended pushing back ROSLA from April to September, arguing the move was justified on the grounds that "a postponement for five months will mean that an additional 160,000 boys and girls will be available for employment in the latter half of 1947 in what will be a period of great man-power stringency."[36]

It was a deeply cynical manoeuvre, and Ellen was livid. She dashed off a memorandum detailing the arguments against postponement. She insisted the proposed benefits of the postponement were "largely illusory" and "certainly not worth the odium and disillusionment that would be entailed." She went on to break down the likely contribution of manpower to individual industries as a consequence of the delay and to underscore that most young men and women would not end up as miners or weavers, but poorly paid part-time labourers in "blind alley professions." She closed by stating that education had too often "been the first casualty of an economic blizzard. A Labour government should be the very last to seek protection—and a very meagre protection at that—from a fallible forecast of economic trouble by the enlistment of child labour."[37] In cabinet, she pushed home her case. The response of the majority of her colleagues shows how successful she had been in standing up to her former paramour. Attlee declared himself "horrified" by the proposal and compared it to the kind of thing that appeared in the 1931 May Report, a proposal that "hits a suffering group for little benefit." Bevan, who in the past had argued for postponing ROSLA, sided with Ellen, as did Arthur Greenwood, who declared himself "shocked" the recommendation had even been put forward. Ultimately Dalton accepted that it was "clear cabinet don't like this," and agreed to withdraw.[38] Ellen called Undersecretary John Maud (later Lord Redcliffe-Maud) at home and announced "We've won!"[39]

Ellen's anger was that much greater because it was not the first time her colleagues had sought to undercut her. She was not so self-absorbed that she could believe Morrison had sought to deprive 150,000 children of a year's education to spite her personally. At the same time, she must have remembered the number of times she had sided with him during the war, even in the face of fierce opposition within the party. Morrison did continue to advocate for Ellen—in November 1946, as her health deteriorated, a journalist close to the government told a friend at the National Association of Labour Teachers that Ellen could not be moved from her post "as long as Herbert supports her."[40] At the same time, he seemed determined to target her department for savings, despite education's comparatively small share of the national budget. (Education spending only just topped £100 million in 1946, out of a total budget of £5.5 billion.[41])

In addition to preparing to implement ROSLA, Ellen's department had prioritized the provision of social services in the schools. Although universal state-sponsored provision of milk and meals was not mandated, universal provision had been made a quid pro quo in negotiations to lower the cash payments through the 1945 Family Allowances Act. In 1942, the Beveridge Report had recommended family allowances payable at 8s. per child. In line with the long British political tradition of mistrusting the economic sensibilities of working-class families, politicians on both sides of the aisle had advocated that a portion of the payments be made in kind.[42] Ultimately, it was agreed to lower the cash payments to 5s. per child, on the understanding that the remaining 3s. should be retained in kind through the expansion of social service provision in schools. Ellen was determined to see the government make good on its commitments.

Ellen was all too aware of the impact of hunger and poverty on working-class children's ability to learn. As the chair of the Women's Committee for the Relief of Miners' Wives and Children, she had pleaded for money to keep children in pit villages from "clemming," or starving. During the Spanish Civil War, she had campaigned for donations to feed malnourished children.[43] The children of the unemployed in Britain were not quite living on the cup of powdered milk and a single biscuit a day that sustained many boys and girls in war-torn Spain; yet in 1938, nearly 70 percent of the British population was unable to afford more than 6d. per head per meal on food. "This deep grinding health-destroying poverty" manifested itself not only in malnourishment, but in perilous overcrowding. Writing in *John Bull* before the war, Ellen had shared with readers a recent visit to a house not far from her Bloomsbury flat in London where a family of seven was sharing two rooms. "These were intelligent people—interested in politics. The boy was studying for a technical scholarship. In those crowded rooms he had to study and compete with lads who went home to a private room in comfortable houses."[44]

The department of education could not do anything to address the slum conditions, but it could ensure that all schoolchildren received at least one hot meal and a glass of milk a day. In February 1946, Ellen and Westwood produced a joint memorandum for Morrison's Lord President's Committee recommending that school milk be made free to all children when family allowances went into effect in August 1946, that the government should also announce that school dinners would be made universally free as soon as all local authorities had completed the necessary arrangements for their provision, and that 100 percent of the cost should be met by the exchequer. Although the committee accepted the recommendation on school milk, it referred the decision on meals to the full cabinet. But there Ellen, Dalton, and Morrison came to loggerheads. In theory, Ellen couldn't care less whether children were fed out of local authority funds or from the exchequer, but she felt sure that without the promise of the 100 percent exchequer grant, local authorities would drag their heels on providing meals. If they wanted school dinners, the government would have to agree to pay for them.

Dalton, in turn, prophesied that capitulation would lead the authorities to go "ca'canny," or shirk, on other fronts as well, and that the exchequer would end up carrying the whole of local government. Morrison emphasized that as head of the London County Council he had never assumed the bill for any local services would be fully footed by the exchequer, nor should he have. This was a "slippery slope," he claimed, and it was Ellen's job as a minister to push back against public pressure on this front. "What is the Ministry of Education for," he asked, if it can't even succeed in putting the screws on local authorities? After an acrimonious debate, Ellen persuaded her colleagues to reconsider full reimbursement for the cost of food; but wages for dinner staff, they agreed, should come out of local taxation. Ellen, in despair, cried out: "But reluctant LAs will then use the teachers!"[45] Here, she proved prescient. By the end of the month, her ministry and local authority representatives (LAs) had set up a working party to deal with, inter alia, the question of teachers' supervision of school meals.[46] It was, nonetheless, a significant victory.

The following month, parliament passed the 1946 Education Act, an amending bill intended to clarify the terms of the 1944 act. The majority of the clauses in this relatively uncontroversial piece of legislation dealt with the upkeep of "voluntary controlled schools," or religious schools that had agreed to submit to a greater degree of secular oversight in exchange for full financial maintenance by the state. Clause 9 in the bill reflects Ellen's commitment to using the education budget to secure the physical as well as intellectual welfare of Britain's children. The 1944 act had stipulated that where a local education authority (LEA) deemed it necessary, they could provide a poor pupil "with such clothing as, in the opinion of the authority, is necessary for the purpose of ensuring that he is sufficiently clad while he remains a pupil at the school."[47] Ellen's amending legislation included a further provision clarifying that LEAs should have authority to provide clothing to needy pupils at nursery and boarding schools as well as to day school students.[48] She also acted quickly to ensure that medical care was provided to all students in schools as promised in the 1944 act. Although the details of the National Health Service bill were still being debated in parliament, Ellen announced that her ministry had negotiated a settlement with the British Hospital Association, the British Medical Association, and the LEAs to cover the cost of medical provision in schools and the treatment of school children in voluntary hospitals.[49] At the end of the year, she made one final, unsuccessful bid to expand her ministry's remit for the social care of Britain's children. The Curtis Report on children in care, published in autumn 1946, exposed significant abuse and neglect of children in foster and institutional care in Britain. In the wake of the report's revelations, a public campaign emerged in favour of the Ministry of Education taking over control of such children's welfare from the Home Office.[50] Ellen pushed hard in the Lord President's Committee for the transfer of the "deprived child" to the care of her ministry but again bumped up against opposition from Morrison.[51] Departmental jealousies and the feeling there should remain "a division between the child at home and the child at school" favoured the status quo, and Ellen did not pursue the matter.[52] Nonetheless, her impetus to bring the care of deprived children under her ministerial umbrella underscores her vision of her ministry as responsible for child welfare provision extending well beyond the walls of the classroom.

Despite the time and energy Ellen gave to domestic concerns, the Ministry of Education was not exclusively a home department, at least not under her watch. The British government had occupied parts of Germany and Austria at the end of the war, and the domestic ministries were drawn in to the administration of the occupied territories. At the first cabinet meeting, on August 7, 1945, Ernest Bevin, the new foreign secretary, gave his view that it would be invaluable for the ministers of education, health and labour to "visit Germany and discuss on the spot with British members of the Control Council what assistance could be given to our forces in carrying out their tasks. The great need at the moment was for a relatively small number of technical experts and administrators. Experienced Borough Engineers and Medical Officers of Health, and persons experienced in the administrative side of education, would be able to give invaluable help."[53] Ellen, characteristically, proved eager to make the trip—her first to Germany since 1936.

By next month everything was arranged for her to spend four days in West Germany, inspecting schools in Berlin, Hamburg and Dusseldorf and meeting with the education branch of the British control commission in Bünde. On October 2 she and two members of her civil service staff flew to Bückeberg to begin the tour of a country she had once known so intimately, but which now was transformed almost beyond recognition by the war.

The trip to Germany reinvigorated Ellen's commitment to internationalism. The war had artificially boxed her in. She was not by nature single-minded, nor was she particularly nationally minded. In the interests of winning the war, she had forced herself to focus all her energies on the domestic tasks at hand. The victory in Europe and the consequent break-up of the coalition released her from her self-imposed straightjacket. She never regretted her time as a minister in Churchill's wartime government. When parliament reconvened after the 1945 general election, she was said to have been the sole Labour member to have cheered the former prime minister as he took his seat on the opposition front bench.[54] Now that the war was over, however, Ellen was no longer willing to sacrifice her lifelong interest in international affairs, and Attlee, to his credit, did not ask her to do so. In addition to her ministerial responsibilities, he appointed her one of six members of the cabinet's India and Burma Committee, to discuss plans for constitutional reform in the subcontinent. He also gave her free rein to spearhead the establishment of the United Nations Educational, Scientific and Cultural Organization (UNESCO), and to act as a cultural ambassador to Britain's European and imperial allies. As with Ellen's earlier international travel, these trips drew censure from critics who complained that affairs in Malta or Czechoslovakia fell outside her ministerial remit. Yet for Ellen, British children were not intrinsically more important than children from outside the country's borders. Britain's comparatively privileged position after the war meant the country had an obligation to help those less fortunate. In was in this spirit that she embraced the early UNESCO proposal to create world maps without national borders and prepare textbooks that taught world as opposed to national history.[55]

Although Ellen travelled to Germany ostensibly to offer guidance to the education branch of the control commission, both she and Bevin appreciated that her preexisting relationships with Germans from the

Social Democratic and Communist parties would put her in a privileged position to gather intelligence on reconstruction and denazification. After her return, she prepared a long memorandum on her trip for Bevin, which was circulated through the Foreign Office and sent to the Criminal Investigation Detachment (CID), charged with investigating war crimes.[56] The memorandum detailed her experience touring schools across the country, many of which lacked windows, portions of exterior walls, or other weatherproofing. Despite the lack of facilities, Ellen reported that most children were being educated, albeit in overcrowded conditions, and, in some instances, for half the day or on a shift rotation. Denazification had led to the removal of between 20 and 40 percent of teachers in most regions, but she reported, "On the whole, the teachers that we saw at work made a favorable impression, though the discipline seems to me unnecessarily strict for small children." Most teachers were operating without textbooks, as "there are extremely few in any subject that have not got some undesirable taint." As one British teacher who worked for the control commission recalled, "Even the textbooks for mathematics contained problems which spread the insidious gospel: 'If it takes 50,000 members of the *Wehrmacht* 3 days to conquer Holland [area of the country stated], how many days will it take 80,000 men to conquer England [area of the country stated]?'"[57] Given both the labour involved and the paper shortage across Europe, it was unrealistic to envisage producing new textbooks anytime soon, but Ellen instructed her department to look into the feasibility of producing broadcasts and films on some educational topics along the lines of those produced for the Army Bureau of Current Affairs, the continuing education arm of the military during the war.[58] She also intervened with the control commission to ensure that part of the children's daily ration was provided to them directly in schools. As the aforementioned British teacher recalled, "it was through Miss Wilkinson's intervention that a modest school meal was introduced. It was no more than a plate of milk soup but it was a beginning." She also recalled Ellen "haranguing" her and her colleagues about the importance of their work—an entirely believable characterization of Ellen's conversational style.[59]

The control commission appreciated Ellen's input, but the Foreign Office was most interested in her views on the political situation. In reference to both schoolteachers and administrators and other German officials, Ellen noted that the general impression she received from firsthand encounters and from discussion with members of the occupying forces was that the men and women were "passive." "The greatest shortcoming among the Germans appears to be their inability to think for themselves," she reported. "This is perhaps not surprising given their history, but it is certainly accentuated by the fact that, when the Nazis were in power they removed and, indeed, killed many of the most able administrators of the Weimar Republic and that we have now removed, or are in the process of removing, the most able and prominent Nazi administrators." Yet despite the brain drain, Ellen "was by no means certain that the purges of officials had gone far enough." She had spoken with, among others, old colleagues in the German branch of the Women's International League for Peace and Freedom and understood that many collaborators were still in positions of power.

After meeting with members of the Social Democratic Party of Germany (SPD), the Communist Party of Germany (KPD), and the trade unions, Ellen remained cautiously optimistic about the eventual revival of party politics in Germany. One of the most notable aspects of her report is suspicion of the KPD, many of whose former members had been key allies in the 1930s anti-fascist struggle. Now she met with the KPD only as a "courtesy" and made clear to Bevin and his colleagues that the party was a tool of the Russians. Ellen was heartened by the fact that new trade unions seemed to be emerging to replace the prewar unions that had, essentially, been arms of the rival political parties. Yet, she underscored the importance of "get[ting] the issue clear to the young German workers that the problem is not that of a Red authoritarianism replacing the Brown in a struggle against 'western plutocrats.'" Her suggestions included providing trade union leaders with materials on the establishment and operation of a democratic union and encouraging cooperation between the further education division and political advisors within the control commission and the German trade unionists. The former founding member of the Communist Party of Great Britain (CPGB) was now concerned with forging a political consensus in Germany that left no room for Communist authoritarianism. It was a daunting task, and she left the country conscious of the magnitude of the struggle ahead.

If Ellen's views of German Communism had changed dramatically over the previous decade, her attitude towards Indian politics remained remarkably consistent; and she used her position on the India and Burma committee to champion a post-racial vision of a democratic socialist India. The six-member committee was, not surprisingly, dominated by Attlee, Cripps, and Frederick Pethick-Lawrence, secretary of state for India and Burma. Between 1927 and 1930, Attlee had served on the Simon Commission, tasked with advising on revisions to the Indian constitution. The experience had made him wary of a too-rapid transfer of power from Britain to the native population, not least because of religious tensions; but after the close of the war with Japan, he rapidly swung around to support the swift granting of independence. Stafford Cripps had headed an official mission to India in March 1942, during which he sought, unsuccessfully, to negotiate a settlement with Hindu and Muslim leaders, offering extended self-government and dominion status in exchange for support for the British war effort. Like Attlee, Cripps had become discouraged about reconciling communal differences. The committee's official minutes record only a few interventions by Ellen, but these underscore her continued optimism that India could break free from both its imperial legacy and the ties of religion and caste that kept its people divided. In November 1945, the committee presented to cabinet its recommendations that a delegation be sent to India to make clear the government's commitment to a speedy transition towards self-rule. Ellen impressed upon her colleagues the necessity of "ensuring that any delegation from this country made contact with all classes and shades of opinion in India and was not confined to an officially conducted tour. Opportunities should be given," she argued, for members "to visit the homes of Congress and Moslem League supporters and to address public meetings." Indian officials, she feared, would stress the communal arguments against self-rule, but if the committee could meet with "real" Indians, they would likely return more confident that India could in fact govern itself as a united nation.[60] The escalation of sectarian rhetoric and violence ultimately led her to concede that "it might be necessary to make an offer of Pakistan based on a re-definition of provincial boundaries." Nonetheless, Ellen remained hopeful that "the practical difficulties of establishing Pakistan might well be found so great that Indian political leaders would themselves drop the idea. It having been found to be impracticable they might then come to a settlement amongst themselves on some all-India scheme."[61] Redcliffe-Maud recorded in his memoirs, "Her instinct was always to say what she thought, whether in Cabinet or in public and whether or not the question (say about India) was primarily her business."[62] Like her friend Nehru, Ellen believed deeply that were India only given its freedom, national unity could trump sectarianism. She did not live long enough to witness Partition and the India-Pakistan war; it would have broken her heart to see the subcontinent's two main communal groups brutally turn on each other.

Ellen ultimately had little sway over Britain's India policy. She was, however, instrumental in shaping the direction of the new United Nations Educational, Scientific and Cultural Organization (UNESCO). During the war, R.A. "Rab" Butler had headed up the Conference of Allied Ministers of Education, a group of education ministers and ministers-in-exile who met in London between 1942 and 1945 to "promote closer collaboration between Allied nations, to assist in cultural rehabilitation of Allied nations and to lay the ground work for organization of [a] permanent international Secretariat or Bureau of Education."[63] As plans developed for the creation of a permanent United Nations organization after the war, the decision was made to bring the proposed international secretariat under the UN umbrella. On November 1, 1945, an international conference for the establishment of an educational and cultural organization of the United Nations opened at the institute of civil engineers at the corner of St. James Park. Every major nation except the Soviet Union sent delegates to the conference. Leon Blum, former prime minister of France's Popular Front government and Ellen's old colleague in the anti-fascist front, headed the French delegation. At his instigation, Ellen was elected as the conference president. In her opening speech, she put forward a resolution that would profoundly shape the future direction of the organization: to include the word "science" in the new organization's title. She argued, "In these days, when we are all wondering, perhaps apprehensively, what the scientists will do to us next, it is important that they should be linked closely with the humanities and should feel that they have a responsibility to mankind for the result of their labours. I do not believe that any scientists will have survived the world catastrophe, who will still say that they are utterly uninterested in the social implications of their discoveries."[64] Ellen put forth the resolution after consultation between the British and American governments and with representatives of the scientific community, but it was a resolution she backed with all sincerity. The conference opened less than three months after the atomic bombs were dropped on Hiroshima and Nagasaki, and she was painfully aware that the United Nations could not hope to educate world citizens for peace without bringing science within its remit. Over the next several months, Ellen would play an instrumental role in securing the appointment of the zoologist Julian Huxley (her old colleague on Spanish Medical Aid) to head UNESCO's preparatory committee. His position as a scientist, she hoped, would ensure that the British and American ambitions to put scientific cooperation at the forefront of the UNESCO agenda were realized. Huxley was a reluctant recruit. He claimed to be "flabbergasted" by the request and later recalled Ellen's hard sell made him feel "like one of those early Christians who were kidnapped and compelled to become bishops," but he ultimately proved an effective steward of the fledgling organization.[65]

Ellen's ability to secure a British representative as the head of the preparatory commission reflected the British government's leading role in founding UNESCO, but it was also the product of some successful horse-trading with the French delegation. The French had come to the conference keen that the new organization be grafted onto the existing Institute of Intellectual Cooperation, based in Paris. Although the British opposed the French proposals, they ultimately consented to the establishment of the UNESCO headquarters in Paris; and the French, in turn, supported the selection of a British director-general.[66] Ellen's decades of experience as a union negotiator came in handy as she managed the competing national agendas at the conference. In her opening speech, she asserted: "Our international organization, intended to be a bridge between nations, must rest firmly on foundations dug deeply into the national life and tradition of the member states. International fellowship and national personality are not incompatible."[67] Over the next two weeks, as the nearly 300 delegates worked to hammer out a constitution for the new organization, she must have been repeatedly reminded of those opening words.

After all the hard work with the preparatory stages of UNESCO, Ellen looked forward to playing a key role at the first general conference of the new organization that opened in Paris in November 1946. However, by the end of that year her health had deteriorated to the degree where, to her bitter disappointment, she was not able to travel.[68] Redcliffe-Maud later claimed that when Ellen was appointed, "she knew that she was not well, but no one else was allowed to know it."[69] In her early months at the ministry, she did her best to safeguard her failing health. Although she worked long hours during the week, she regularly escaped to Twixtlands with Annie on the weekends. She would bring along her despatch case and work on Sunday mornings, but she tried to get plenty of sleep and fresh air and was frequently seen pottering around the little garden in "comfortable slacks and a woolen pullover."[70] Britain's damp winters, however, took an increasing toll on Ellen's lungs. Her decision to undertake a visit of inspection to schools in Gibraltar and Malta in January 1946 was in fact an attempt to tack some useful work on the back of a restorative holiday to sunny Morocco with Margaret Rhondda. Rhondda, like Ellen, then lived in Dolphin Square, and the two remained fast friends, despite Ellen's departure from *Time and Tide*'s journalistic roster.[71] On New Year's Day, the two women flew via Gibraltar to Tangier, where they stayed as guests of the consul-general.[72] After a week's holiday, Rhondda returned to Bloomsbury and Ellen undertook an inspection of schools in the two British outposts before flying home. It was a well-meaning venture on her part, but her colleagues clearly doubted whether it was worth the expense. In the weeks after her return, the Ministry of Education and the admiralty got into an unpleasant wrangle over who should pay for her flight home.[73]

The trip to the Mediterranean helped restore Ellen's health in advance of the opening of the UN general assembly meeting in London on January 14, 1946, where she sat alongside Bevin as a representative of the United Kingdom. However, it wasn't long before she fell ill again. For too long, Ellen had lived on a diet of cigarettes, caffeine, and little sleep; and there was only so much that fresh air and sunshine could do for her worsening chronic respiratory condition. Increasingly, she turned to medication—a combination of stimulants and sleeping pills—

to keep her functional, but these further strained an already overtaxed immune system. In late February, she caught bronchitis, allegedly as a consequence of driving in a snowstorm.[74] At the end of April, she flew to a sanatorium in Switzerland for a fortnight to recuperate from what her doctors had diagnosed as tonsillitis.[75] In July she was ill again and forced to cancel her public engagements.[76] Her health had become so precarious that she was no longer fit to look after herself. She remained in Dolphin Square but moved into a larger flat, and Annie returned to care for her sister, just as she had when they were girls.[77]

Ellen did her best to hide her illness, carving out time for weekly trips to the Elizabeth Arden Salon to keep her hair and skin looking their best.[78] Yet, by September the press was reporting rumours that she might soon be transferred to a "less exacting post" or even leave the government altogether as a consequence of her deteriorating health.[79] Attlee did not attempt to move her out of Education, but Ellen must have feared she was in danger of losing her job. Nonetheless, in September she had to confess that she was not fit to make a planned second trip to West Germany to follow up on the progress of the British education authorities.[80] She was determined, however, to go ahead with a scheduled trip to Czechoslovakia at the end of the month. On September 27 she flew to Prague, where she had been invited to open a British film festival that evening. As she stepped uneasily from her car onto the pavement, the waiting theatre staff feared she was too ill to go through with the engagement, but she insisted on being given a shot of adrenaline and soldiering on. The Associated Press reported that she "appeared on the point off collapse" as she took the stage. "She spoke briefly, expressing appreciation of Czechoslovakia's war effort, and then, clinging to the microphone stand, apologized for not feeling well enough to continue."[81] The next day, the British government reported she had had an asthma attack and would remain in the Czechoslovak capital until she was well enough to travel.[82] It was the last time that she left Britain.

Well-meaning supporters have pointed to Ellen's deteriorating health in defence against accusations that she was a failure at the Ministry of Education.[83] It is certainly true that her health took an increasing toll. However, blaming her physical constitution for her performance implies that were she in better health, she would have pursued different priorities or made different decisions about departmental policy. Yet there are few, if any, indications this would have been the case. The principal charges against Ellen as minister are that she made little to no effort to attack either private schools or the grammar school system, two institutions that, critics have claimed, have done more than almost any others to reify social divisions in British life. Although the two forms of elite education bore many similarities, including a near monopoly on access to higher education, especially in the 1940s and 1950s, the controversies surrounding their relationship to the Ministry of Education and to the British social system more broadly differed in keys ways and deserve to be addressed in turn. A holistic evaluation of the circumstances surrounding Ellen's decisions and their subsequent interpretation by politicians and historians can shed some light on how an avowedly radical politician who devoted her career to social justice came to be viewed as such a failure by reformers concerned with using the education system as a tool to transform the British class structure.

In 1944, Labour supported the education bill despite losing votes on amendments to nationalize the public schools and to abolish direct grant schools. However, there remained a clear unity of opinion within the party that the perpetuation of these two forms of institution was detrimental to the breakdown of class barriers and the creation of a meritocratic society.[84] In 1976, a Labour government would abolish the direct grant list and force the remaining direct grant schools to choose between absorption into the state system or privatization. The 1945 Labour government had a much larger majority and an equal if not greater will to end a system that limited educational access to a wealthy elite. Yet Ellen did not seize the opportunity to revisit the fate of the direct grant schools while in office. She did trim down the direct grant list, decreasing the number of eligible schools from 232 to 166, with, in the words of her parliamentary private secretary Billy Hughes, "as much fuss as if the whole system had been abolished."[85] She also made a greater effort than any of her successors from either side of the House to open up access to the "public" schools for working-class children through locally funded scholarships facilitated by her ministry.[86] Although cost constraints limited such schemes, her efforts reflected a desire to open the private system up to wider participation. Ellen was not blind to the inequities inherent in the continued existence of the private educational sector. However, it is true that she did not prioritize the overturn of the 1944 settlement. Put simply, she believed there were bigger battles to fight. It was more important to deliver on the bill's promise of "secondary education for all" than to waste legislative and ministerial time renegotiating the 1944 act. As she told her staff in a 1946 memorandum, "the problem [of equality in secondary education] would be much easier of solution if the decision had been taken to abolish fees in all grant aided secondary schools. Though the moment for that reform has for the time being passed, the contradictions of trying to deal with the secondary problem may force us on to that solution, but not yet."[87] At the moment, she told the 1946 Labour Party conference, her aim was "to make the schools provided by the state so good and so varied that it will just seem to be quite absurd not to send the children to the schools."[88] Her concern was not to tear down the private sector, but to "level up" the state sector.

The problem with Ellen's argument about levelling up the state system is that the construction of a tripartite system of grammar, technical, and modern schools seemed to indicate that not all state school children would receive an equally rigorous education. Only those children attending grammar schools might be able to claim an education comparable to that provided in the private sector; whereas students in the modern schools would receive something different and, presumably, inferior. Here we come to the second, and more damning, indictment of Ellen's tenure as minister: She not only failed to attack but also actively promoted a state system that instantiated inequality and privilege. Her actions on this count cannot be excused or explained by saying she was simply enacting legislation already on her desk when she arrived at Belgrave Square. The 1944 act pointedly avoided any reference to a three-schools model of educational provision. Secondary students were to receive one of three types of education: grammar, technical, or modern, but it was not stipulated how such education should be provided. In theory, local authorities had a choice whether to build separate grammar, technical, and modern secondary schools or to construct bilateral or multilateral schools that would provide two or three types of secondary education. In practice, the LEAs were required to submit proposals for the reorganization of secondary education to the

Ministry of Education for approval. Given their desire to have their proposals approved quickly, the LEAs naturally looked to the ministry for guidance. And here, it is argued, Ellen acted as a brake on change. Rather than encouraging the development of multilateral schools, the official policy endorsed by the Labour Party at the 1945 party conference, she and her ministry gave a strong lead to the LEAs to put forth proposals for a three-school model.

Two decades after Ellen left office, Anthony Crosland, then Harold Wilson's education secretary, allegedly vowed: "If it's the last thing I do, I'm going to destroy every fucking grammar school in England. And Wales and Northern Ireland."[89] Crosland never succeeded in his ambition; but a decade later, another female minister of education, Shirley Williams, went further in this direction than any of her predecessors. Williams's actions, it has been argued, would not have been necessary had Ellen and her successor George Tomlinson taken a firmer stand in favour of multilateral education thirty years earlier. David Rubenstein has put the indictment of Ellen most strongly. "Early plans indicated that a considerable measure of support for comprehensive education existed in England and Wales," he argued, "and this sentiment would have been greatly strengthened by a strong lead from the Minister. Instead, she led the troops in an entirely different direction, insisting that it would be 'folly to injure' the grammar schools, which were the 'outstanding achievement' of the state educational system, and contributing to the 'trend away from multilateralism' which soon became discernible."[90]

If Rubenstein arguably overstates the enthusiasm for multilateral (*not* fully comprehensive) schools in the immediate postwar period, his contention that Ellen preferred tripartite to multilateral schemes holds water.[91] Here her background clearly played a role. She was one of three members of Attlee's cabinet to have had a grammar school education. The other two were Chuter Ede and Arthur Greenwood, neither of whom supported the abolition of the grammar school system. Like Ellen, the two men went on from grammar school to higher education, Ede at Christ's College, Cambridge, and Greenwood at Yorkshire College (later the University of Leeds). For those few men (and even fewer women) for whom the system worked successfully, grammar schools offered a pathway to social mobility. When Ellen sat down at the cabinet table alongside her privately educated colleagues such as Attlee, or Dalton or Cripps, she did not feel she had had an inferior training simply because her family had not paid for her tuition. Seven months into her tenure at the ministry, she told a group of head teachers in Lancashire that grammar schools "were amongst our finest achievements, and no one wished to degrade them."[92]

Yet for all that Ellen valued her own grammar school education, she was not an advocate of creating "grammar schools for all," as Harold Wilson famously promised. Put simply, she did not believe that all children were suited to or could benefit from a grammar school education. Some children had an inherently academic bent, whereas others "are interested in practical things and could be appealed to by the life that is around them."[93] Here, Ellen was essentially a product of her time. Hitler's Germany had shown the dangers of eugenics taken to its extreme, but eugenic thinking was widespread throughout the Western world in the first half of the twentieth century.[94] During her career, Ellen had taken a firm stand against racism; but, although she rejected the notion that any one race was naturally superior to any other, she nonetheless accepted that natural, measurable gradations of intelligence existed within races. This did not mean the "lower IQ" child should receive a merely utilitarian or vocational education. Ellen was adamant that the secondary moderns should not be "dumping grounds." Instead, she called the secondary modern an "exciting new thing" that would "be on the edge of a real revolution in the whole concept of secondary education." In place of the dull rote curricula she had abhorred as a student and teacher, the new schools would strive to make abstract subjects accessible through practical education. If teachers could "arouse an interest and teach them through that . . . there will be an unrecognizable change."[95] Ellen accepted that secondary modern schools were more likely to educate children destined for manual labour, whereas grammar and technical schools would educate students bound for university and skilled professions; but, she argued, that didn't mean the secondary moderns should be viewed as inferior. As she said in a major policy speech in 1946: "Not everyone wants an academic education. After all, coal has to be mined and fields ploughed, and it is a fantastic idea that we have allowed, so to speak, to be cemented into our body politic that you are in a higher social class if you add up figures in a book than if you plough the fields and scatter the good seed on the land."[96]

In retrospect, it has proved impossible to shift cultural convictions that an academic education is more prestigious than a practical education, or to reverse the belief that a desk job carries a higher status than a manual profession, even if a plumber might earn double the salary of a civil servant. At the time, however, neither Ellen nor many on the political left viewed such an ambition as "fatuous."[97] That is not to say she was unaware of the difficulties inherent in defining the aims and curricula of the new secondary modern schools. During the winter and spring of 1946, Ellen and her staff wrangled extensively over the drafting and redrafting of *The New Secondary School,* a pamphlet intended for distribution to LEAs as guidance in writing curricula for new secondary moderns. Ellen's response to the first draft (then titled *The Modern School*) shows she was both conscious of and shared in many of the reservations about the tripartite system held by the Labour left. Channelling her inner radical, Ellen drafted a rabble-rousing speech she would have made in denunciation of the draft pamphlet if she were still a backbencher. The comically hyperbolic mock-speech was a clever way for her to soften the blow to civil servants she trusted had children's best interests at heart, while simultaneously venting her own frustrations with the current draft. It began: "I wondered why when I gave this pamphlet a first quick reading I felt so deep-down angry. Having read it again, I know why." She went on: "This pamphlet is fundamentally 'phoney.' Phoney because everything suggested in it subconsciously (and I am quite sure 'sub' if not 'un') is to dispel the real question that the authors feel has to be answered, i.e. 'What shall we do to get miners and agricultural workers if 100% of the children able to profit by it are offered real secondary education?'" Through searing invective, Ellen underscored that the authors would need to remove any references to modern schools "foster[ing] the qualities which employers want to find." Although she herself would say publicly that some children are interested only in practical things, she urged her staff to tone down the references to making arts and sciences relevant through practical studies:

Can't these precious few years of secondary school education be at least a relief [from the lives of practical drudgery
for which many were destined]? Can't Shakespeare mean
more than the scrubbing brush? Can't science be taught free
from immediate practical application, and at least enough
of a foreign language to open the windows on the world a bit
wider. . . . Let me be fair. By the time we reach section D, these
lyrics to practicality give way to a passing nod to the desirability of educational development. Even so the first two
paragraphs are taken up with the desirability of physical
training and improvement and "the general development of
bodily skill"—quite unexceptional of course, but still keeping
mere intellect firmly in its proper place for our 75% how-
dow's (translation [provided by Ellen for her middle-class
civil servants]: hewers of wood and drawers of water).

Ellen was insulted by the initial draft but recognized it would be
less than helpful to criticize her staff without offering constructive suggestions for revision. In two additional memoranda, she shifted tone
and laid out the practical problems as she perceived them and the options moving forward. Notably, she began by asking her staff whether
they were all in fact "committed to the three types," suggesting that she
still retained some uncertainty about the wisdom of the tripartite
system. She went on to detail the difficulties of implementing the tripartite system, which she underscored could not be done "peacefully":
"It is going to hit the most articulate section of the middle class, and
they will scream. . . . Because . . . some children with appalling accents
and worse clothes and no manners at all, but with a passion for getting on and out—than which neither love nor war provides a greater
stimulus—will gaily pass into Grammar and/or Technical while the son
of (to take an actual e.g.) an ex-Conservative minister of the crown will
have to go to Modern school because even the direct grammar have to
award their places on merit."[98] It would be not only the middle classes,
however, who balked at the reform. Working-class parents who "had
been promised free secondary education for their children" were also
likely to feel betrayed: "To each of these categories 'secondary' is synony-
mous with 'grammar' school. They are now being told of a mystery—in

many places not yet heard or seen—called a Secondary Modern School, which they are assured, not very convincingly, will provide an education much more suited to their children's interest or capacity than the grammar school." If the country's parents were ever going to accept the new scheme, they "must be convinced that we mean what we say about the 'secondary' character of the modern school. . . . Equally important, they must be convinced that a grammar school is now a specialized type of secondary school, and not the *real* thing, any others being substitutes."[99]

Ellen proposed two possible solutions to address this sense of perceived inequality. The first was the establishment of multilateral schools—the very policy the Labour Party had endorsed at its 1945 conference. Notably, however, she did not push for this solution, and her comments above make it clear that she did not seriously consider doing away with grammar schools. The second option would be to reform the current system: making the "creamery less drastic" by further opening the late-transfer window into grammar or technical schools for children whose aptitude became apparent only after age eleven; abolishing the proposal not to have external examinations in the modern school while retaining them in the other two types; removing the references to wheelbarrows and housewifery from their circulars to the LEAs; and stressing certain cultural subjects, "especially art and music both practice and appreciation, and I would like to add French. These have always been high school subjects. Their inclusion would both consider and encourage parents." Finally, "special stress" should be placed on the importance of English, not only reading, but writing and speech, and a nod should be made to the advisability of students remaining in school until age sixteen, even before the school leaving age was officially raised again.[100]

Some of Ellen's views involving curricula were taken on board by the LEAs; however, by the time of her death neither the proposal to open the technical and grammar schools to late bloomers nor her advice to retain external examinations for the modern school were adopted. Although the implementation of these proposals may have lessened the vitriol of some of Ellen's critics, her steadfast support for the retention of the grammar school (and, to a lesser extent, the technical school) has remained the principal point of contention in discussions of her administration. The Labour Party's official policy during Ellen's tenure remained multilateral schools, in which students would have the opportunity to socialize and pursue nonacademic studies jointly and, crucially, where students whose aptitude became apparent at a later age could more easily switch from a modern to a grammar or technical curriculum. However, Ellen's most vocal contemporary critics wanted her to go even further in establishing a universal "comprehensive" curriculum.[101] This view was put most clearly at the 1946 party conference by Scottish MP Peggy Herbison, who, like Ellen, had worked as a lecturer for the National Council of Labour Colleges, and W. G. Cove of the left-wing National Association of Labour Teachers. Herbison argued, "The only way of really ensuring that our children will have equality of opportunity . . . is by sending every child to the common secondary school. If we do not want to have any differentiation, and if we do not want to have vocational training, we must make it possible for every child until he or she is 15, and I hope very soon until he or she is 16, to have the most liberal education that he or she can possibly get." She ended with a warning: "The old system perpetuated a class distinction on financial grounds, but if we are to approve the policy of the Government we will have a class distinction on intelligence, or on brains. That is ever so much worse than even the previous class distinction."[102] At the end of the debate, the conference voted with Herbison and Cove to censure Ellen, but it is by no means clear that everyone voting for censure endorsed their analysis in its entirety. No one (including, in fairness, Ellen) wanted the secondary moderns to offer vocational training, but many on the left saw a place for the state-funded grammar school as a guarantor that the most talented working-class students could have access to an academic education and the opportunity to continue on to university. For these men and women, social justice did mean the replacement of a financial hierarchy with an intellectual one.

In the 1950s and 1960s, however, sociologists began to argue that the grammar school system did not so much replace a hierarchy of wealth with one of brains as perpetuate the existing hierarchy of wealth. A growing body of data showed that the 11-plus exam, pioneered under Ellen's tenure at the ministry, did not accurately capture intelligence. Rather, it reflected a combination of aptitude and social opportunity.

All other things being equal, middle-class children with educated parents were likely to score better on the secondary school exam than children from poorer homes whose parents neither had nor valued a higher education.[103]

This insight has become so obvious as to seem intuitive; yet prior to the 1960s, evidence of educational wastage had not been systematically collected, and criticisms from this corner are ahistorical. There is reason, however, to argue Ellen should have had some sensitivity to such questions. She was acutely conscious that inequalities of opportunity could lead to differential performance in the classroom. Her determination to provide milk, meals, and other material benefits to school children reflected her desire to level the playing field so that the cleverest working-class children would have a fair chance to compete with their middle-class peers. At the university level, she was determined to increase grants and bursaries so that working-class children would not have to "scramble" for grants to make ends meet.[104] Yet having taken parental support for granted as a child, she clearly underestimated the importance of informed, supportive, and engaged parents to a child's development. In this, she was by no means alone. A minute by one of her civil servants, which Ellen singled out for praise, claimed—seemingly uncontroversially: "Now that . . . admission or allocation is determined by qualification and not by ability to pay, no question of class distinction arises."[105] In retrospect, her optimism that a level playing field could be achieved appears misplaced and naïve. Her attitude was, however, consistent with her essentially materialist analysis of Britain's woes. As she said in a speech to the Fabian Society on social justice in 1940: "Do we by social justice mean equality of income? As an ultimate ideal, I should say clearly Yes."[106] It is fitting that her last substantive contribution to cabinet debate before her death was a biting retort to Bevan's suggestion that the government needed to enforce a ceiling on wages to keep down inflation. "Then on profits also," she quipped.[107]

Throughout her career, Ellen believed the path to social reform, be it in gender, race, or international relations, lay in economic transformation. It was in this sense that she continued to consider herself a Marxist, long after she abandoned Communism. Her commitment to viewing the world through an economic lens occasionally alienated her from feminists, who saw her support for protective legislation for women and children as inimical to an equal rights agenda. It also kept her from appreciating the centrality of Hitler's anti-Semitism in the early 1930s, as her attention focused naturally on the persecution of trade unionists and the economic undercurrents of fascism. And, as minister of education, this view blinded her to noneconomic arguments against what one of her civil servants termed the "socio-political considerations" against the grammar school system.[108] But if Ellen's Marxism imposed limitations, it also acted as a spur to her politics. Her advocacy on behalf of women workers, her involvement in the international peace movement, the Jarrow Crusade, her commitment to the Indian National Congress, her work as Britain's "shelter queen" during the Second World War, and her determination to finance the pledges undertaken in the 1944 education act were all fuelled by a belief that if the world's economic system could be reformed, peace and social justice would follow.

16

DEATH OF A GOOD COMRADE

On the morning of January 27, 1947, Ellen attended her final cabinet meeting. To reach 10 Downing Street, she had to brave the frosty cold, wind, and snow of the worst winter in modern British history. The meeting included only three agenda items, all about foreign policy; but Ellen, tired and ill, is not recorded as having taken part in the debate.[1] Three days earlier, she had attended the ceremonial reopening of the Old Vic Theatre School alongside Laurence Olivier, the theatre's new director. It was at this, her final public event, that she made her famous remark about Britain becoming a "Third Programme nation," a reference to the new BBC national radio network that went on air the previous September. The Third Programme, which has since become Radio 3, began its life broadcasting classical music, theatre, and intellectual talks and debates, and was from its inception criticized for its elitism. Yet Ellen, for all her blithe acceptance that three-quarters of the population could be classed as unfit for a classically academic secondary education, remained hopeful that the BBC could bring high culture to the masses and make the love and appreciation of fine art and music a central component of working-class as well as elite culture.[2]

The Old Vic had been badly damaged in the Blitz, and the ceremony took place in the drafty and unheated theatre. The high temperature for the day was 1 degree Celsius. Ellen stuck it out, wrapped in her trusty fur coat, but a few days later came down with acute bronchitis. Her doctor, Robert Gilchrist, paid a house call and prescribed penicillin. The drug, the first patented antibiotic, had only been commercially available for little more than a year but had already worked wonders in easing bacterial infections such as bronchitis. By the time Gilchrist checked back in with his patient, her temperature had returned to normal and the penicillin appeared to have improved her cough. Yet she was still suffering from asthma, the chronic condition that had plagued both her and her sister Annie since childhood.

Between January 22 and March 17, it snowed over part or all of the island nation every day. The *Times* reported people skiing in the streets in Surrey.[3] For an asthmatic, the cold, damp air was much more treacherous than the ice that slicked the London pavement. When Gilchrist looked in on Ellen on January 30, he gave her a prescription for three theamine tablets a day, and a combined theamine and amital tablet for the nights. Theamine was a potent bronchodilator, whose chemical composition closely resembled caffeine, which Ellen already consumed in excess. (Coffee, she once told members of the Anglo-Brazil Society, was her "one vice."[4]) Although the drug helped open her airways, its stimulant effects led to its regular combination with the sedative amital, especially for nighttime use. On Monday night, February 3, Ellen phoned her doctor to say she was "restless," and he suggested she take another theamine tablet. It is likely she had already taken more than the prescribed dose of theamine by the time she phoned Gilchrist. An acute asthma attack produces an effect similar to drowning or being smothered, the victim literally gasping for breath. No matter how many warnings they receive from their doctors, most asthmatics in the grip of an attack will take more than the recommended dose of medication in hopes of regaining control of their breathing. Over the years, Ellen had likely become accustomed to taking higher than recommended doses of the drug. Reports that she was a compulsive fidget certainly indicate she may have been addicted to stimulants.[5] If the restlessness was the result of her excessive stimulant consumption, taking more theamine would only have made her more highly wrought.

In addition to the amital prescribed by Gilchrist, Ellen had a stash of medinal, an over-the-counter sleeping aid taken off the market in the 1950s. For years, she had been taking the pills to counteract the effects of theamine, caffeine, nicotine, and stress.[6] That February night, she overdosed on medinal and fell into a coma. Annie was apparently down in Penn, as it was Ellen's housekeeper who phoned Gilchrist to come over that evening. He found her breathing regularly, though unconscious, and gave her yet more stimulants to rouse her from the coma. She came around long enough for the doctor to ask what had happened, and Gilchrist decided it was safe to leave her in the care of the housekeeper. He returned the next morning with a Harley Street consultant, William Brooks, and the two decided to admit her to St. Mary's Hospital on February 4. Over the next forty-eight hours, she swam in and out of a coma but never regained sufficient consciousness to answer her doctors' questions about what drugs she had ingested. She died two days later, in the early morning of February 6, 1947. The diagnosis recorded on her death certificate was heart failure following an attack of bronchitis.

Despite the lack of evidence of foul play, an autopsy was carried out by the hospital that pointed to a "gross overdose" of barbituric acid as the cause of death. In other words, she had overdosed on sleeping pills. The Home Office pathologist, G. Roche Lynch, confirmed the diagnosis; and as a consequence, a formal inquest was held. The inquest ended with the coroner's verdict that "there is no shred of evidence that these [the lethal overdose of drugs] were taken deliberately by Miss Wilkinson." Brooks with his experience of the drugs and Lynch with his extensive pathological experience were in agreement that, "persons who take these drugs may inadvertently take an overdose."[7] Despite the verdict, rumours have persisted that Ellen's death was an intentional suicide. Certainly, the volume of amital and medinal she would have had to ingest to overdose is suggestive. It is clear from his guarded testimony to the coroner that her younger brother Harold was anxious about the possibility. Although he made clear to the coroner that he could not imagine his sister committing suicide, and that she had been "lively and healthy" over the Christmas holiday, he admitted that "she appeared to be suffering from the strain caused by her responsible position."[8]

Whatever Harold's misgivings in the coroner's witness box, he and Ellen's other relatives were later adamant that her death was accidental, as were the friends and acquaintances interviewed by either her first biographer, Betty Vernon, or by David Reid, who had conducted extensive research into her life.[9] Given the limitations of the evidence, it is impossible to rule out suicide entirely, but it is almost incredible that Ellen took her own life.[10] The single most repeated word used by friends and colleagues to describe her in contemporary and retrospective interviews, obituaries and posthumous memoirs was "courage." It would have been entirely out of character for her to seek an easy escape. Most likely, she unwittingly took what proved to be a lethal dose of sedatives in an effort to offset the effect of excessive stimulants and catch a few desperately needed hours of sleep.

News of Ellen's death reached Clement Attlee as he was preparing for the Commons debate on the management of the agricultural sector that afternoon. The Speaker was instructed to inform the House of their colleague's passing, and Attlee opened debate with a moving eulogy to his late minister of education. Ellen, he said, "had a great courage and a burning sympathy for all those who suffered which extended beyond the bounds of this country." Embracing the socialist language Ellen never abandoned, he called her a "good comrade, a proud and brave spirit." Liberal leader Clement Davies agreed that her most remarkable quality was "her deep human sympathy with those who were in distress and suffering, and her desire to relieve it." Speaking for the Conservative opposition, Winston Churchill added a note of patriotism to these tributes to Ellen's humanist sympathies. "She had a very warm sympathy for social causes of all kinds, and was fearless and vital in giving expression to them. But she also had a great pride in our country and in its flag. . . . She always wished to see this Island great and famous, and capable of offering a decent home to all its people."[11]

The three politicians' testaments to Ellen's passion and commitment were echoed in newspaper headlines across the globe and in personal tributes that flooded in from foreign leaders and private individuals.[12] In the United States, the *New York Times* ran a long obituary that granted her "a unique place in contemporary British history for her fiery courage and untiring lifelong battle for the underdog." Paris's *Le Monde* described her as a fierce orator and praised her "boundless energy and a hatred of oppression in all its forms."[13] In Melbourne, the *Argus* noted her "uncompromising championship of women's rights." In contrast, the *Sydney Morning Herald*'s colourful obituary focused on her fervent socialism. Their staff correspondent, who had seen Ellen in action, recalled, "when she spoke you sat transfixed at the sound of the searing, scorching words that poured from her lips in a torrent of dynamic oratory. For she had a biting tongue and emotions difficult to control, and her forthright speech matched the fiery copper-red of her hair." To her more commonly used sobriquets "Wee Ellen" and "the Mighty Atom," the *Herald* added "the Pocket Dreadnought of the Socialist Party." The *Manchester Guardian* ran three separate articles on the MP's passing, memorializing her career in terms that made clear the paper's affection for the local girl who had become one of the key voices of the international radical movement.[14]

Ellen was buried in the churchyard of Holy Trinity Church in Penn, near her beloved Twixtlands, on February 10. Annie, suffering from bronchitis, arranged the simple, intimate ceremony. (Two decades later, Annie would be buried in a plot next to her.) In addition to Ellen's three siblings, and her nephew Richard and his wife, the guests included only her closest colleagues from the ministry, her election agent, her old friend J. J. Jagger's son and his wife, and a few others. Wreaths were sent by Attlee and Churchill as well as other members of the cabinet and a few foreign leaders. The following Thursday, a memorial service was held at St. Margaret's Westminster, attended by the prime minister and hundreds of MPs, civil servants, union colleagues, and foreign dignitaries. Ellen's brothers were present, but Annie was too ill to make the trip into the city. Another notable absence was Herbert Morrison, in hospital for a blood clot. His long-serving personal secretary, Ethel Donald, feared that if not broken gently, the news of Ellen's death "could kill Herbert." Such was the concern that she contacted the BBC and arranged for them to hold off broadcasting the news until Morrison's doctor could tell him personally. Hearing the news, "Morrison did not say anything, but he suddenly looked years older."[15]

In addition to members of parliament, a long list of lords and ladies, including Ellen's good friends Nancy Astor and Margaret Rhondda, attended the service at St. Margaret's, testaments to her ability to forge personal friendships across social barriers despite her commitment to the class struggle. Amongst the foreign dignitaries in attendance was one whose presence would have particularly touched Ellen. Pablo de Azcárate had been the Spanish government's ambassador to London during the civil war and had worked closely with Ellen on behalf of the Republican cause. The wide range of feminist, trade union, socialist, and international publications that ran obituaries of Red Ellen are a testament to the range of her impact on domestic and international affairs. Her life is remarkable for its exceptionalism, but it is also a measure of the scope for action and engagement that ordinary men and women could realize in the early twentieth century. Ellen's career took her from a working-class street in south Manchester first to university, then to Russia, America, and continental Europe, and on to parliament and a political career that spanned decades and continents in pursuit of social justice. The advances in travel and communication and the emergence of new international networks of socialist, feminist, and peace activism in the first decades of the twentieth century paved the way for the emergence of a new type of political actor, one who was committed to realizing social and political reform on an international scale. After Ellen's death, Harold Laski, her successor as chairman of the National Executive Committee (NEC), wrote that she had throughout her life taken "the whole world of people in pain or sorrow to her heart. For Ellen fundamentally was a crusader and she took great causes for her crusades."[16] Her old friend the miners' MP Jack Lawson voiced a similar sentiment: "The driving power of Ellen was neither ambition nor her desire for power. It was the urge of great compassion for mankind, and a vision of the world 'that might be.'"[17]

It is difficult to categorize neatly Ellen Wilkinson's career. Her first biographer set out to present her as a Labour worthy, one of the founding pillars of the party who, although an early radical, ultimately curbed her left-wing tendencies and helped steer the party towards the 1945 victory. Yet her radicalism remained a crucial part of her political identity throughout her career. She occasionally "trimmed her sails" when she thought it politically necessary or expedient, and her instinct for survival and political advancement led to her appointment as the sole female member of Attlee's cabinet, despite her outspoken and ill-judged criticism of the party leader from 1935 on. Yet, Ellen repeatedly risked her career to stand behind individuals and ideas in which she firmly believed, as when she refused to disassociate herself from Willi Münzenberg's anti-fascist networks in the early 1930s, or when she stood by Stafford Cripps after he threw down the gauntlet against the party leadership in 1939. More recently, she has been presented as a feminist icon; but her feminism, although a consistent part of her identity throughout her career, was never the guiding principal behind her politics.[18] Her colleague Eleanor Rathbone came into politics to advance a women's rights agenda and became a vocal champion for human rights.[19] Wilkinson in contrast entered politics to advance the class struggle, and her championship of women's rights was most often framed within the context of the advancement of the working class. Finally, although her internationalism has been long appreciated, it is too often treated as a discreet aspect of her career.[20] Wilkinson was a British politician, but a British politician who came of age in the decades following the First World War, a period when even staunch isolationists conceded that the old system of nation states and empires would have to make way for some form of new, more internationalized global order.[21] Her career is best conceived as a sustained effort to come to terms with the changing social, economic, and geostrategic realities of the post–World War I world and the possibilities and barriers for reform they created. Nearly three-quarters of a century on, politicians and activists in Britain and across the globe continue to struggle with how best to secure individual liberty and social welfare in an increasingly globalized world. Although Ellen Wilkinson did not have all the answers, her career is a testament to the importance of questioning the existing system and striving to create a more peaceful, prosperous, and equitable future for the generations to come.

NOTES

INTRODUCTION

1. Telephone interview with Ellen's niece Julia Wilkinson, July 19, 2015.
2. To cite only a few examples: Susan Pennybacker, *From Scottsboro to Munich: Race and Political Culture in 1930s Britain* (Princeton, NJ: Princeton University Press, 2009); Daniel Gorman, *The Emergence of International Society in the 1920s* (Cambridge, UK: Cambridge University Press, 2012); Susan Pedersen, *The Guardians: The League of Nations and the Crisis of Empire* (Oxford: Oxford University Press, 2015); Udi Greenberg, *The Weimar Century: German Émigrés and the Ideological Foundations of the Cold War* (Princeton, NJ: Princeton University Press, 2015).
3. *Manchester Guardian,* Feb. 7, 1947; Ellen Wilkinson, "Social Justice," in *Programme for Victory: A Collection of Essays Prepared for the Fabian Society,* ed. Harold Laski (London: G. Routledge and Sons, 1941); Kenneth O. Morgan, *Labour People: Leaders and Lieutenants, Hardie to Kinnock* (Oxford: Oxford University Press, 1992), 105.

1. THE ONLY GIRL WHO TALKS IN SCHOOL DEBATES

1. Ellen Wilkinson, "Notes on the Way," *Time and Tide,* Apr. 23, 1932.
2. C. Stella Davies, *North Country Bred: A Working-Class Family Chronicle* (London: Routledge & Kegan Paul), 224.
3. Ellen Wilkinson, "Ellen Wilkinson," in *Myself When Young,* ed. Margot Asquith (London: F. Muller, 1938), 400.
4. Frederich Engels, *The Condition of the Working-Class in England in 1844,* trans. Florence Kelley Wischnewetzky (London: George Allen, 1892), 46, 60.
5. Clare Hartwell, *Manchester* (New Haven, CT: Yale University Press, 2001), 305.

6. Betty Vernon, Interview with Ross Waller, Sept./Oct. 1978, Vernon papers, Hull History Centre. At the time I conducted the research for this book, Vernon's papers had not yet been catalogued, and hence no detailed file information is provided. According to the 1911 census, the Wallers lived at 29 Everton Road.

7. The 1891 census gives the family address as 41 Coral Street, and the address of Elizabeth Wood and sons as 31 Coral Street. The 1901 census lists the Wilkinsons at 35 Everton Road, and the 1911 census puts them at 40 Everton Road. In 1915, Ellen gave her temporary address as 107 Plymouth Grove in a letter to Labour Party headquarters. LP/WNC/32/3/66–67, Feb. 18, 1915, Labour Party Archive, People's History Museum, Manchester.

8. *Manchester Guardian,* Nov. 24, 1937.

9. Robert Roberts, *The Classic Slum* (Manchester: Manchester University Press, 1971), 17.

10. Ibid., 25.

11. Ellen Wilkinson, "Born and Bred in Lancashire," *Listener,* Nov. 29, 1945, 617–618.

12. Wilkinson, "Ellen Wilkinson," 400.

13. Ellen Wilkinson, "Notes on the Way," *Time and Tide,* Dec. 28, 1935.

14. Vernon, Waller interview.

15. Wilkinson, "Born and Bred."

16. Ibid.

17. Wilkinson, "Ellen Wilkinson," 400.

18. Vernon, Waller interview.

19. Letter sent by R. H. Wilkinson to Betty Vernon, Dec. 10, 1978, with information from his mother.

20. Wilkinson, "Ellen Wilkinson," 400.

21. *Manchester Guardian,* July 31, 1905. The 1901 census lists Richard A. Wilkinson as an apprentice cabinetmaker.

22. Vernon, Waller interview. Harold began work for the BBC on Apr. 19, 1927 and worked with the company until his retirement in 1958. Staff records, BBC Written Archives Centre, Caversham Park, Reading.

23. Davies, *North Country Bred,* 224–225.

24. Ibid., 223.

25. Betty Vernon interview with Fred Meadowcroft, n.d. 1978.

26. Betty Vernon interview with Arthur Logan Petch, June 1978.

27. Roberts, *The Classic Slum,* 44.

28. Vernon, Waller interview.

29. Wilkinson, "Ellen Wilkinson," 410, 401.

30. Wilkinson, "Born and Bred."

31. Ibid.

32. Davies, *North Country Bred,* 224.

33. Wilkinson, "Ellen Wilkinson," 404.

34. Ibid., 409, 403.

35. Davies, *North Country Bred,* 223.

36. *Manchester Guardian,* Nov. 19, 1941.

37. Anne Summers, "British Women and cultures of internationalism, c. 1815–1914," in *Structures and Transformations in Modern British History,* ed. David Feldman and Jon Lawrence (Cambridge: Cambridge University Press, 2011), 187–209. There have been several studies of nineteenth century female internationalists, many of them Quaker.

38. See Andrew Thorpe's forthcoming biography of Arthur Henderson.

39. Betty Vernon, *Ellen Wilkinson, 1891–1947* (London: Croom Helm, 1982), 17. Wilkinson, "Ellen Wilkinson," 411.

40. On the League of Nations Union's encouragement of such children's costume pageants, see Helen McCarthy, *The British People and the League of Nations: Democracy, Citizenship and Internationalism, c.1918–45* (Manchester: Manchester University Press, 2012), chap. 4.

41. Vernon, Meadowcroft interview.

42. Wilkinson, "Ellen Wilkinson," 411.

43. Davies, *North Country Bred,* 222.

44. Betty Vernon, *Ellen Wilkinson,* questions whether Ellen attended Stretford Road. However, the school is listed in her *Who's Who* entry (*Who's Who, Men and Women of the Time* [London: A. & C. Black, 1926], 3108).

45. *Daily Herald,* Mar. 2, 1946.

46. *Manchester Guardian,* Nov. 19, 1941

47. Wilkinson, "Ellen Wilkinson," 404, 405.

48. Ibid., 405.

49. *News of the World,* Dec. 15, 1946.

50. Wilkinson, "Ellen Wilkinson," 408.

51. Davies, *North Country Bred,* 224.

52. Ellen Wilkinson, "Organising and Political Work" in *The Road to Success: Frank Talks on Women's Careers,* ed. Margaret Cole (London: Methuen, 1936), 65.

53. Wilkinson, "Ellen Wilkinson," 47.

54. ED 136/788: Secondary Modern Schools: Minute by Minister, n.d. 1946. The National Archives, London.

55. *Manchester Guardian,* Feb. 7, 1947.

56. *Time and Tide,* Apr. 2, 1932.

57. Wilkinson, "Ellen Wilkinson," 401.

58. *Time and Tide,* Apr. 9, 1932.

59. Wilkinson, "Ellen Wilkinson," 411–412.

60. Ibid., 406.

61. Ibid., 410, 406–407.

62. Vernon, Waller interview.

63. Kate Rigby, "Annot Robinson: A Forgotten Suffragette," *Manchester Region History Review* 1, no. 1 (1987): 11–20, at 12.

64. Wilkinson, "Ellen Wilkinson," 412.

65. Peter d'Alroy Jones, *Christian Socialist Revival, 1877–1914,* (Princeton, NJ: Princeton University Press, 2015), 270.

66. Arthur Burns, "Beyond the 'Red Vicar': Community and Christian Socialism in Thaxted, Essex, 1910–84," *History Workshop Journal* 75 (Spring 2013):101–124.

67. *Manchester Guardian,* Feb. 4, 1909.

68. Wilkinson, "Ellen Wilkinson," 414.

69. Betty Vernon interview with Muriel Nichol, née Wallhead, Nov. 1978.

70. Michael Harrison, "Burnage Garden Village: An Ideal for Life in Manchester," *Town Planning Review* 47 (1976). Cited in Alison Ronan, "'A Small, Vital Flame': Anti-war Women's Networks in Manchester 1914–1918," (PhD thesis, Keele University, 2009), chap. 3.

71. George Orwell, *The Road to Wigan Pier* (London: Gollancz, 1937), chap. 11.

72. For Nichol's work with the EFF, see Janet E. Grenier, "Nichol, Muriel Edith (1893–1983)," in *Oxford Dictionary of National Biography,* ed. H. C. G. Matthew and Brian Harrison (Oxford: Oxford University Press, 2004; online ed., Jan. 2011), http://www.oxforddnb.com/view/article/70447 (accessed May 22, 2014).

73. Wilkinson, "Organising and Political Work," 73.

74. Wilkinson, "Ellen Wilkinson," 416.

75. *Northampton Evening Telegraph,* Mar. 21, 1931.

76. Wilkinson, "Ellen Wilkinson," 411.

77. Ibid., 415.

78. Mabel Tylecote, *The Education of Women at Manchester University, 1883–1933* (Manchester: Manchester University Press, 1941), 53.

79. Ibid., 61–62. Email to author from James Peters, University Archivist, University of Manchester Library, Jan. 16, 2014.

80. *Manchester University Magazine,* May and Dec. 1912.

81. Tylecote, *Education of Women,* 66.

82. Ibid., 69.

83. Sandra Holton, *Feminism and Democracy: Women's Suffrage and Reform Politics in Britain 1900–1918* (Cambridge: Cambridge University Press, 1986).

84. Betty Vernon manuscript notes on MCWS.

85. T. A. Lockett, *Three Lives: Samuel Bamford, Alfred Darbyshire, Ellen Wilkinson* (London: University of London Press, 1968), 48.

86. David Howell, *British Workers and the Independent Labour Party 1888–1906* (Manchester: Manchester University Press, 1984).

87. Ellen Wilkinson, *Clash* (Nottingham: Nottingham Trent, 2004 [1929]), 183.

88. Philip Graham, *Susan Isaacs: A Life Freeing the Minds of Children* (London: Karnac Books, 2009).

89. Ronan, "'A Small, Vital Flame,'" chap. 3; Obituary: Miss Mary Quaile: Women's trade union pioneer," *Manchester Guardian,* Dec. 17, 1958.

90. University Socialist Federation, *1st Annual Report* (1913); Betty Vernon interview with Robert Page Arnot, 1978.

91. J. Walton Newbold, Unpublished draft autobiography, John Rylands Library, University of Manchester.

92. Vernon, *Ellen Wilkinson,* 30.

93. "The Montessori System: Parents Taught to Think," *Times,* Jan. 6, 1928.

94. CP/IND/DUTT/06/03: Wilkinson to Dutt, June 25, 1924, Communist Party Archive, People's History Museum, Manchester.

95. Christine Millar, *Plebs,* Mar. 1947.

2. ELLEN'S GREAT WAR

1. Ellen Wilkinson, "Organising and Political Work," in *The Road to Success: Twenty Essays on the Choice of a Career for Women,* ed. Margaret Cole (London: Methuen, 1936) 62–73, at 65.

2. Wilkinson to James Middleton, Feb. 1915, WNC 32/3/66, Labour Party Archive, People's History Museum, Manchester, gives her address pro tem as 107 Plymouth Grove.

3. Betty Vernon interview with John Parker, Jan. 7, 1978, Hull History Centre. Wilkinson, "Organising and Political Work," 69.

4. *Time and Tide,* Jan. 21, 1933.

5. *Action,* Sept. 18, 1937, quoted in Matt Perry, *'Red Ellen' Wilkinson: Her ideas, Movements and World* (Manchester: Manchester University Press, 2014), 98.

6. C. Stella Davies, *North Country Bred: A Working-Class Family Chronicle* (London: Routledge & Kegan Paul), 223. Interview with Helen Wilson, quoted in Alison Ronan, "'A Small, Vital Flame': Anti-war Women's Networks in Manchester 1914–1918," (PhD thesis, Keele University, Dec. 2009), chap. 3.

7. Davies, *North Country,* 225; Margery Corbett Ashby, quoted in Betty Vernon, *Ellen Wilkinson, 1891–1947* (London: Croom Helm, 1982), 41. *Manchester Guardian,* Oct. 27, 1913, lists her as the speaker at an "at home" to be held in Parker's Restaurant in St. Ann's Square that evening.

8. National Women's Labour League leaflet, n.d., available at http://www.co-op.ac.uk/politicalwomen/cs4.html (accessed June 10, 2014).

9. Christine Collette, *For Labour and for Women: The Women's Labour League, 1906–1918,* (Manchester: Manchester University Press, 1989), 86. On Annot Robinson's work for the WLL, see ibid., 88–90.

10. Paula Bartley, *Ellen Wilkinson: From Red Suffragist to Government Minister* (London: Pluto, 2014), 7.

11. Collette, *For Labour,* 88; Kate Rigby, "Annot Robinson: A Forgotten Suffragette," *Manchester Region History Review* 1, no. 1 (1987): 11–20.

12. Johanna Alberti, *Beyond Suffrage: Feminists in War and Peace, 1914–1918* (New York: St Martin's, 1989), 64–69; Ronan, "'A Small Vital Flame,'" 114.

13. R. Page Arnot, *History of the Labour Research Department* (London: Labour Research Department, 1926), 9.

14. Walton Newbold, Unpublished draft autobiography, John Rylands Library, Manchester University.

15. Wilkinson to James Middleton, Feb. 1915, WNC 32/3/66, Labour Party Archive.

16. Alison Ronan, "The Work of the Women's War Interest Committee in Manchester (1915–1917)" (paper presented at War and Gender conference, Newcastle University, Mar. 12, 2011), 5.

17. Two letters to the *Manchester Guardian,* dated Dec. 11, 1914 and Jan. 14, 1915, identify her as secretary of the Women's Registration Office.

18. *Manchester Guardian,* Aug. 11, 1915.

19. AUCE Executive Committee minutes, Mar. 28 and July 18, 1915, USDAW library, Manchester.

20. Vernon, *Ellen Wilkinson,* 46; Bartley, *Ellen Wilkinson,* 10.

21. See reports in *Co-Operative Employee,* July 1916, 8, 16–17; Oct. 1916, 74; Nov. 1916, 101–104.

22. *Co-Operative Employee,* Aug. 1916, 40.

23. Wilkinson, "Organizing and Political Work," 62.

24. *Co-Operative Employee,* Sept. 1916, 62.

25. *New Dawn,* Mar. 5, 1921, 17.

26. Ellen Wilkinson, "The Women's Guild Congress," *Co-Operative Employee,* Aug. 1916, 31.

27. Ellen Wilkinson, "After the Battle at Plymouth," *Co-Operative Employee,* Jan. 1917, 133.

28. "End of the Plymouth Strike," *Co-Operative Employee,* Dec. 1916, 120, 118.

29. See, for example, the NAUSA and AUCE wage demands for male and female Co-Operative workers printed in the *Co-Operative News,* Feb. 28, 1920, and reprinted in Sidney and Beatrice Webb, *The Consumers Co-Operative Movement* (London: Longmans, Green & Co., 1921), 205.

30. For discussions of AUCE publicity, see E. C. Wilkinson and J. S. Simpson, "The Bairns O'Falkirk," *Co-Operative Employee,* Feb. 1917, 175; E. C. Wilkinson, "Perth and Its Paltry Pay-Sheet," *Co-Operative Employee,* Mar. 1917, 186.

31. Margaret Bondfield, *A Life's Work* (London: Hutchinson & Co., 1948), 54.

32. *New Dawn,* Mar. 5, 1921.

33. "Judge Shocked: Silk Stockings not Necessaries," *Newcastle Journal,* Nov. 17, 1927.

34. E. C. Wilkinson, "Reconstruction: Women Trade Unionists Confer," *A.U.C.E. Journal,* Sept. 1917, 60.

35. *Labour Woman,* Mar./Apr. 1947.

36. *New Dawn,* Mar. 5, 1921.

37. Krista Cowman, "The Political Autobiographies of Early Women MPs c.1918–1964," in *The Aftermath of Suffrage: Women, Gender and Politics in Britain, 1918–1945,* ed. Julie Gottlieb and Richard Toye (Basingstoke, UK: Palgrave, 2013).

38. Wilkinson, "Organising and Political Work" 68.

39. See Wright Robinson's description of Jagger in Vernon, *Ellen Wilkinson,* 124; and J. Hallsworth's memorial in *New Dawn,* Aug. 1, 1942, 247.

40. Vernon, *Ellen Wilkinson,* 125.

41. Margaret Cole, *Growing Up into Revolution* (London: Longmans, Green and Co, 1949), 70.

42. *Co-Operative Employee,* July 1916, 8, 16.

43. *AUCE Journal,* July 1918.

44. "Plymouth Society's 'War on Poverty,'" *Co-Operative Employee,* Sept. 1916, 50.

45. "Organisers' Reports," *Co-Operative Employee,* Sept. 1916, 58.

46. "Trade Unions Congress," *Manchester Guardian,* Sept. 4, 1918, 4.

47. "Co-Operative Strike: The Award," *Manchester Guardian,* Oct. 3, 1918, 4.

48. Bartley, *Ellen Wilkinson,* 13.

49. University Socialist Federation, *The Organization of a University Socialist Society* (London: USF, March, 1915), 22.

50. Edward R. Pease, *The History of the Fabian Society* (Project Gutenberg, 2004 [1916]), chap. 8, http://www.gutenberg.org/files/13715/13715-h/13715-h .htm (accessed April 27, 2016).

51. "The Fabians and I," written and narrated by Gertrude Hutchinson, produced for the BBC by Terence Tiller (aired Wednesday, 31 Dec. 31, 1955), from Glasgow Caledonian Sound Archive: Spoken Word Service.

52. Margaret Cole, "Guild Socialism and the Labour Research Department," in *Essays in Labour History, 1886–1923,* ed. Asa Briggs and John Saville (Hamden, CT: Archon Books, 1971), 271; Margaret Cole, *The Story of Fabian Socialism* (Palo Alto, CA: Stanford University Press, 1963 [1961]), 181.

53. On Slesser's role in the group, see Wilkinson, HC Deb, June 21, 1927, vol. 207, cc. 1693–1694.

54. Beatrice Webb diary, Mar. 8, 1914.

55. Wilkinson, HC Deb, June 21, 1927, vol. 207, cc. 1694.

56. Cole, "Guild Socialism and the Labour Research Department," 271.

57. David Blaazer, "Guild Socialism and the Historians," *Australian Journal of Politics and History* 44, no. 1 (1998): 1–15.

58. A. J. Penty, *The Restoration of the Guild System* (London: Swan Sonnenschein, 1906); S. G. Hobson, *National Guilds: An Inquiry into the Wage System and the Way Out* (London: G. Bell, 1914).

59. James Hinton, *The First Shop Stewards Movement* (London: Allen & Unwin, 1973).

60. Vernon, *Ellen Wilkinson*, 49–53.

61. Cole, *Story of Fabian Socialism*, 166.

62. Sidney Webb, *The Basis & Policy of Socialism* (London: A. C. Fifield, 1908).

63. Beatrice Webb, manuscript diary, May 15, 1915. Available at http://digital
.library.lse.ac.uk/objects/lse:mod807hoq?page=127 (accessed Apr. 7, 2016).

64. Cole, *Growing Up*, 72.

65. Vernon, *Ellen Wilkinson*, 58.

66. Cole, "Guild Socialism and the Labour Research Department," 261.

67. See "Women in a Guild Socialist State," in the Storrington Document, produced by the Guild Socialists Dec. 1914 and reproduced in Briggs and Saville, *Essays in Labour History*, 347–8.

68. Davies, *North Country Bred*, 224.

69. Betty Vernon interview with R. Page Arnot, January 1978.

70. Hutchinson, "The Fabians and I."

71. Ibid.

72. Cole, *Growing Up*, 67.

73. Ellen's contemporary as a University Socialist, the Oxford undergraduate C. E. M. Joad went on earn a doctorate in philosophy and attained popular fame as a regular panelist on the BBC program *The Brains Trust*.

74. Cole, *Growing Up*, 71.

75. Arthur Penty, *Guilds and the Social Crisis* (London: Allen and Unwin, 1919), 78.

76. Pease, *Fabian Society*, chap. 10. Beatrice Webb typescript diaries, Sept. 28, 1913, available at http://digital.library.lse.ac.uk/objects/lse:six767gol (accessed June 5, 2014).

77. Betty Vernon interview with Fenner Brockway, 1978.

78. For the weather and other details of the conference, see The Fabian Society, *Thirty-first annual report of the executive committee* (May 1914), 12.

79. *Time and Tide,* Apr. 28, 1932.

80. Taped interview Stella Davies recorded Oct 1970, National Sound Archive Clitheroe, quoted in Ronan, "'A Small, Vital Flame,'" chap. 3.

81. Davies, *North Country*, 223.

82. WILPF/2011/1: Manchester branch minutes, 1915–1919. British WIL archives, Women's Library, London School of Economics and Political Science Archive.

1. When, two years later, Ellen and Annot travelled to Washington, DC, Annie Wilkinson and their friend Mary Welch watched the girls until school let out and they joined their aunt in Glasgow for Christmas. See Annot Robinson to her sister, Dec. 8, 1920, Annot Robinson papers, Manchester Central Archive.

2. Beatrice Webb, typescript diaries, addendum, May 1918, http://digital .library.lse.ac.uk/objects/lse:vat325giy/read#page/30/mode/2up.

3. "Labour and the Women's Votes," *Times,* Oct. 14, 1918.

4. *Manchester Guardian,* Oct. 17, 1918; Ellen Wilkinson, "Labour Party Women's Conference," *AUCE Journal,* Nov. 1918, 73.

5. *AUCE Journal,* Nov. 1918, 73.

6. Ellen Wilkinson, "The Washington Labour Conference: Another Broken Pledge," *New Dawn,* Mar. 19, 1921.

7. Margaret Macmillan, *Peacemakers Six Months That Changed the World: The Paris Peace Conference of 1919 and Its Attempt to End War,* 2nd ed. (London: John Murray, 2003), 2.

8. Erez Manela, "Imagining Woodrow Wilson in Asia: Dreams of East-West Harmony and the Revolt Against Empire in 1919," *American Historical Review* 111, no. 5 (Dec. 2006): 1327–1351, at 1327.

9. Laura Beers, "Is This Man an Anarchist? Industrial Action and the Battle for Public Opinion in Interwar Britain," *Journal of Modern History* 82, no. 1 (2010): 30–60.

10. Ellen Wilkinson, "The Lisburn Shop Strike: We Asked! We Waited!! We Struck!!!," *AUCE Journal,* Aug. 1919, 39–40.

11. For this view, see "Records and Recollections of Alexander Boyd & Co. Ltd," at http://www.lisburn.com/books/boyds/alexander_boyds2.html (accessed June 25, 2014).

12. E. C. Wilkinson, "Café Girls Strike at Leeds," *AUCE Journal,* Aug. 1919, 38–39; Ellen Wilkinson, "The Problem of the Food Server," *AUCE Journal,* Dec. 1920, 6–7.

13. *Illustrated London News,* Nov. 8, 1924, 866, contains photographs of Ellen's Fallowfield flat.

14. E. C. Wilkinson, "A Woman's Impression of Congress," *New Dawn,* Sept. 27, 1924, 26.

15. *Daily Express,* Mar. 1, 1928, "Women MPs 'Slighted,' Not Wanted in a Glee Party."

16. GB127.M284: diaries. Wright Robinson papers, Manchester Central Archive, entries from 1922–1923.

17. "Steam and Starvation," *New Dawn,* July 22, 1922, 9.

18. Pamela Cox's recent three-part series "Shopgirl" for BBC Two does an even-handed job of treating the simultaneous exploitation and excitement of shop life (first aired June 24, 2014).

19. Ellen Wilkinson, "Canvassing in London: Tragedy and Pathos in Shop Life," *AUCE Journal,* Apr. 1920, 12.

20. Ibid. For "organizing the angels," see "Miss E. C. Wilkinson," *New Dawn,* Apr. 28, 1923, 5.

21. *Manchester Guardian,* Feb. 22, 1916.

22. Report of AUCE meeting, *AUCE Journal,* May 1920, 18–19.

23. Gertrude Bussey and Margaret Tims, *Pioneers for Peace: Women's International League for Peace and Freedom 1915–1965* (London: Allen & Unwin, 1980), 27. Johanna Alberti, *Beyond Suffrage: Feminists in War and Peace, 1914–28* (New York: St. Martin's Press, 1989), 55. *Report of the International Congress of Women: Zurich, May 12–17, 1919* (Geneva: WILPF, 1919), 423.

24. WILPF/2011/1: Manchester branch minutes, 1915–1919, Women's Library, London School of Economics and Political Science Archive.

25. 11/4291/4192 [Box 572]: May 11, 1920: Resolution of Manchester Branch re: Polish Invasion of Russia, League of Nations Archive, UNOG, Geneva.

26. *Manchester Guardian,* May 14, 1920.

27. The women did hold "several international meetings of an informal and partial character" during the war including "one among the Scandinavian Sections at Stockholm in 1916 and one at Berne in 1918." See *Report of the International Congress of Women* (Geneva: WILFP, 1919), II.

28. CP/IND/MISC/10/1: Helen Crawford, Typescript Autobiography, f. 153. Communist Party Archives, People's History Museum, Manchester.

29. On Addams, see her *Twenty Years at Hull House: with Autobiographical Notes* (New York: Macmillan, 1912 [1910]), 70–71. On the class background of most women internationalists, see Leila Rupp, "Constructing Internationalism: The Case of Transnational Women's Organizations, 1888–1945," *American Historical Review* 99, no. 5 (Dec. 1994): 1571–1600.

30. *Report of the 1919 Congress,* 63–64.

31. Bussey and Tims, *Pioneers for Peace,* 33.

32. CP/IND/MISC/10/1: Crawfurd autobiography, f. 154.

33. *Report of the 1919 Congress,* 78, 92, 138.

34. Kevin Morgan, *Labour Legends and Russian Gold: Bolshevism and the British Left: Part One* (London: Lawrence & Wishart, 2006), 207.

35. John Callaghan, *Rajani Palme Dutt: A Study in British Stalinism* (London: Lawrence and Wishart, 1993), 34.

36. John Reed, *Ten Days That Shook the World* (New York: Penguin, 1990 [1919]), chap. 10.

37. Arthur MacManus, "The Third Anniversary," *Communist,* Aug. 5, 1920, 7.

38. Ibid., 6.

39. *Official Report of the Communist Unity Convention, London, July 31st and August 1st, 1920* (London: Communist Party of Great Britain, 1920), 24.

4. FROM IRELAND TO RUSSIA

1. WILPF/BRAN/1: Manchester WIL Executive Committee, Feb. 10, 1920, London School of Economics and Political Science Archive.
2. Susan Bruley, "Socialism and Feminism in the Communist Party of Great Britain, 1920–1939" (PhD thesis, London School of Economics and Political Science, 1980), 138.
3. June Hannam and Karen Hunt, *Socialist Women: Britain, 1880s to 1920s* (London: Routledge, 2002), chap. 7; Pamela Graves, *Labour Women: Women in British Working-Class Politics, 1918–1939* (Cambridge: Cambridge University Press, 1994). See also Richard J. Evans, *Comrades and Sisters: Feminism, Socialism and Pacifism in Europe, 1870–1945* (Wilmslow, UK: Wheatsheaf, 1987); and Leila Rupp, *Worlds of Women: The Making of an International Women's Movement* (Princeton, NJ: Princeton University Press, 1997), 34, 36.
4. *Time and Tide,* Apr. 16, 1932.
5. *Manchester Guardian,* Oct. 19, 1920.
6. Jane Addams papers, microfilm, reel 13: Helena Swanwick, *A "Sort of War" in Ireland* (London: Women's International League, 1920).
7. Jane Addams papers, microfilm, reel 13: Helena Swanwick to Jane Addams, Dec. 22, 1920.
8. "Labour Women: The Manchester Conference," *Manchester Guardian,* Apr. 12, 1921, 10.
9. Swanwick to Addams, Dec. 22, 1920; Gertrude Bussey and Margaret Tims, *Pioneers for Peace: Women's International League for Peace and Freedom 1915–1965* (London: Allen & Unwin, 1980), 40.
10. Albert Coyle, ed., *Evidence on Conditions in Ireland Comprising the Complete Testimony, Affidavits and Exhibits Presented before the American Commission on Conditions in Ireland* (Washington, DC: Bliss Building, 1921), III; Finding aid, L. Hollingsworth Wood papers, Haverford University archive, Haverford, PA. Available at: http://www.haverford.edu/library/special/aids/wood/acci.php.
11. Swanwick to Addams, Dec. 22, 1920.
12. Annot Robinson to Nellie Wilkie, Dec. 7, 1920, Annot Robinson Papers, Manchester Central Library.
13. Annot to Nellie, Dec. 8, 1920.
14. Coyle, *Evidence on Conditions in Ireland,* 535.
15. Annot to Nellie, Dec. 8, 1920.
16. Annot to Nellie, n.d., Dec. 10 or 11, 1920.
17. Coyle, *Evidence on Conditions in Ireland,* 562, 555.
18. Ibid., 585.

19. Ibid., 591.
20. Annot to Nellie, Jan. 11, 1921.
21. "Miss Wilkinson's Rest," *Daily Sketch,* Dec. 19, 1930.
22. Jane Addams papers, microfilm, reel 13: Ellen Wilkinson to Jane Addams, Jan. 24, 1921.
23. U DAR.x2/2/27: Red International of Labour Unions, July 1978, transcript of taped interview with R. Page Arnot, Arnot Papers, Hull Archives Centre.
24. Ellen Wilkinson, "The 'Red T. U.,'" *Communist,* June 4, 1921.
25. CAB/24/129: Report on Foreign Support of the Communist Agitators in the United Kingdom, Oct. 15, 1921, the National Archives, London.
26. CAB/24/125: Report on Revolutionary Organizations in the United Kingdom, June 9, 1921.
27. U DAR/2/x2/21: Transcript of taped interview with R. Page Arnot: Red Trade Union International Congress, Aug. 1978.
28. Ellen Wilkinson, "The Women's Movement in Soviet Russia," *Communist Review,* Nov. 1921.
29. Ibid.
30. H. G. Wells, *Russia in the Shadows* (Sydney: Project Gutenberg of Australia, 2006 [1920]); *Manchester Guardian,* Aug. 10, 1921.
31. Quoted in Patrick Wright, *Iron Curtain: From Stage to Cold War* (Oxford: Oxford University Press, 2007), 205, 206, and reprinted in Appendix II, 392.
32. Wilkinson, "The Women's Movement in Soviet Russia," 26–27.
33. *Manchester Guardian,* Nov. 6, 1922; Ellen Wilkinson, *Communist,* Aug. 27, 1921.
34. *Manchester Guardian,* Aug. 10, 1921.
35. Margaret Cole's characterization of the appeal of Communism, quoted in Betty Vernon, *Ellen Wilkinson, 1891–1947* (London: Croom Helm, 1982), 61.
36. "Aspects of Adventure: First meeting of the under-twenty club," *Listener,* Oct. 13, 1938, 761; *Manchester Guardian,* Nov. 6, 1922, 11; *Communist,* Aug. 27, 1921; *Communist Review,* Nov. 1921, 28.
37. Wilkinson, "The Women's Movement in Soviet Russia."
38. Helen McCarthy, *Women of the World: The Rise of the Woman Diplomat* (London: Bloomsbury, 2013), chap. 4.
39. Wilkinson, "The Women's Movement in Soviet Russia," 29.
40. Ibid.
41. J. T. Murphy, *The "Reds" in Congress: Preliminary Report of the First World Congress of the Red International of Trade and Industrial Unions* (London: British Bureau, RILU, 1921). From Marxists Internet Archive, www.marxists.org (accessed Dec. 29, 2015).
42. Wilkinson, "The Red Trade Union Congress," *Communist,* Sept. 17, 1921.
43. Wilkinson, *Communist,* Aug. 27, 1921.
44. Kingsley Martin, "Ellen Wilkinson," *New Statesman and Nation,* Feb. 17, 1947, 130.

45. Maurice Reckitt, *As It Happened* (London: J. M. Dent, 1941), 79. Ironically, the revolution would ultimately turn on Cohen, who was executed for treason after moving to the Soviet Union in the 1930s.

46. *Manchester Guardian,* Aug. 10, 1921.

47. MI5's surveillance of his correspondence turned up no actual evidence of either role. See KV2/567, National Archives, London.

48. Harry Pollitt, *Serving My Time: An Apprenticeship to Politics* (London: Lawrence and Wishart Ltd, 1961), 142; John Mahon, *Harry Pollitt* (London: Lawrence and Wishart Ltd, 1976), 90.

5. A WOMAN CANDIDATE WITH COMMUNISTIC VIEWS

The chapter title comes from *Manchester Guardian,* Dec. 3, 1923.

1. Matt Worley, *Class against Class: Communist Party in Britain between the Wars* (London: I. B. Tauris, 2001), 200.

2. Quoted in Betty Vernon, *Ellen Wilkinson, 1891–1947* (London: Croom Helm, 1982), 28.

3. *Plebs,* June 1926.

4. *New Dawn,* Apr. 14, 1923.

5. *New Dawn,* May 10, 1924; *New Dawn,* Aug. 30, 1924.

6. *Plebs,* Mar. 1947.

7. *New Dawn,* May 28, 1921.

8. Ibid.

9. *New Dawn,* Oct. 1, 1921.

10. Ian Bullock, *Romancing the Revolution: The Myth of Soviet Democracy and the British Left* (Edmonton, AB: Athabasca University Press, 2011), 341.

11. G. D. H. and Margaret Cole, eds., *The Bolo Book* (London: Labour Publishing Co.: Allen & Unwin, 1921).

12. Maurice Reckitt, *As It Happened: An Autobiography* (London: J.M. Dent and Sons, 1941), 79.

13. *Communist Review,* Nov. 1921.

14. CAB/24/120: Report on Revolutionary Organizations in the United Kingdom, Feb. 17, 1921, The National Archives, London.

15. *All Power,* Jan. 1922.

16. *All Power,* Aug. 1922.

17. CAB 24/159/51: Report on revolutionary organizations in the United Kingdom, Mar. 15, 1923, 1–3.

18. CAB 24/158/26: Report on revolutionary organizations in the United Kingdom; Jan. 18, 1923, 4.

19. Monthly Record of the London and Home Counties District Council of the CPGB, Mar. 1922, in R. Page Arnot papers, Hull History Centre, U DAR/x1/6/1.

20. CAB/24/159, Report on Revolutionary Activity, Feb. 15, 1923.

21. CAB/24/136, Report on Revolutionary Activity, Apr. 1922.
22. Sue Bruley, *Leninism, Stalinism and the Women's Movement in Britain* (New York: Garland Pub., 1986), 102.
23. CAB/24/164, Report on Revolutionary Activity, Jan. 10, 1924.
24. Monthly Record of the London and Home Counties District Council of the CPGB, Mar. 1922.
25. Bruley, *Leninism, Stalinism and the Women's Movement*, 103.
26. *All Power,* Mar. 1923.
27. *New Dawn,* Jan. 7, 1922, 7–8.
28. GB127.M284: diaries. Wright Robinson papers, Manchester Central Archive, entries from December 1921.
29. *New Dawn,* Jan. 7, 1922, 7–8.
30. Ibid.
31. Vernon, *Ellen Wilkinson,* 51.
32. Report of the Committee of Enquiry into the Working and Effects of the Trade Boards Acts Cmd. 1645. (HMSO, 1922), 45.
33. WILPF/2011/1: Manchester branch minutes, 1915–1919, British WIL archives, Women's Library, London School of Economics and Political Science Archive.
34. Ibid.
35. Declan McHugh, "A 'Mass' Party Frustrated? The Development of the Labour Party in Manchester, 1918–31," (PhD diss., University of Salford, 2001), 115.
36. WILPF/2011/1: Manchester WIL executive committee minutes, Oct. 21, 1924.
37. Ms 1416/1/2/62, Ellen Wilkinson to Nancy Astor, Jan. 28, 1929 and n.d. [likely Feb. 3, 1929], Astor papers, University of Reading.
38. Annot Robinson to Nellie Wilkie, June 10 or 11 [illegible], 1920, notes that "The Misses Wilkinson are not back from holidays yet," Annot Robinson papers, Manchester Central Archive.
39. *Manchester Guardian,* Mar. 15, 1920.
40. *Manchester Guardian,* May 14, 1920.
41. ILO Convention C003; date of adoption Nov. 28, 1919; date of coming into force June 13, 1921.
42. See HC Deb, Apr. 7, 1921, vol. 140 cc436; HC Deb, June 22, 1921, vol. 143 cc1359. The Labour women's conference unanimously passed a motion condemning the government's inaction at its 1921 conference. See report in *Labour Woman,* June 1, 1921, 87–88.
43. Irene Stoehr, "Housework and Motherhood: debates and policies in the women's movement in Imperial Germany and the Weimar Republic," in *Maternity and Gender Policies: Women and the Rise of the European Welfare States, 1880s-1950s,* ed. Gisela Bock and Patricia Thane, (London: Routledge, 1991), 228.

44. *Woman's Leader,* Nov. 6, 1925.

45. Declan McHugh, "A 'Mass' Party Frustrated?," 109–110.

46. Ibid., 115.

47. *Party Organisation* (London: The Labour Party, 1957), 29.

48. *Labour Woman,* June 1922.

49. McHugh, "A 'Mass' Party Frustrated?," 115.

50. GB127.M284: diaries, Wright Robinson, Oct. 1923.

51. C. Stella Davies, *North Country Bred: A Working-Class Family Chronicle* (London: Routledge & Kegan Paul, 1963), 222.

52. *Manchester Guardian,* Nov. 2, 1923.

53. GB127.M284: diaries, Wright Robinson, Nov. 1923, Manchester Central Archive.

54. *Manchester Guardian,* Nov. 17, 1923.

55. Davies, *North Country,* 226.

56. *New Dawn,* Dec. 22, 1923, 16.

57. GB127.M284: diaries, Wright Robinson, Dec. 1923.

58. *Manchester Guardian,* Dec. 3, 1923.

59. GB127.M284: diaries, Wright Robinson, Nov. 1923; *Manchester Guardian* photo, Nov. 26, 1923, 8.

60. *Manchester Guardian,* Dec. 4, 1923.

61. *New Dawn,* Dec. 22, 1923, 16.

62. GB127.M284: diaries, Wright Robinson, Feb. 1924.

63. *Manchester Guardian,* Feb. 7, 1924.

64. Betty Vernon interview with Mabel Tylecote, née Pythian, July 1978, Betty Vernon papers, Hull History Centre.

65. Betty Vernon interview with Fred Meadowcroft, June 1978.

66. *Manchester Guardian,* Feb. 29, 1924, 4.

67. *Manchester Guardian,* May 8, 1924, 18.

68. Kevin Morgan, *Labour Legends and Russian Gold: Bolshevism and the British Left: Part One* (London: Lawrence & Wishart, 2006), 115.

69. Walton Newbold, unpublished manuscript memoir, John Rylands Library, Manchester.

70. See interview with Harold Wilkinson quoted in Matt Perry, *'Red Ellen' Wilkinson: Her Ideas, Movements and World* (Manchester: Manchester University Press, 2014), 39.

71. *New Dawn,* Oct. 25, 1924.

72. Betty Vernon interview with Mrs. Godfrey, longtime Middlesbrough resident, Feb. 21–22, 1978.

73. Betty Vernon interview with Mrs Turner, retired Middlesbrough school teacher, n.d., 1978.

74. Vernon interview with Godfrey.

1. Laura Beers, "Punting on the Thames: Electoral Betting in Interwar Britain," *Journal of Contemporary History* 45, no. 2 (2010): 282–314.
2. *Daily Mail,* Oct. 15, 1924.
3. James Johnston, *A Hundred Commoners* (London: H. Joseph, 1931), 112.
4. Martin Pugh, "Astor, Nancy Witcher, Viscountess Astor (1879–1964)," in *Oxford Dictionary of National Biography,* ed. H. C. G. Matthew and Brian Harrison (Oxford: Oxford University Press, 2004; online ed., Jan. 2011); Ellen Wilkinson, *Peeps at Politicians* (London: Philip Allan & Co., 1930), 103; Ellen Wilkinson, *The Division Bell Mystery* (London: Garland Publishing, 1976 [1931]), 175; *Daily Graphic,* Nov. 13, 1924.
5. Duncan Sutherland, "Philipson Mabel (1887–1951)," in Matthew and Harrison, *Oxford Dictionary of National Biography;* HC/SA/SJ/10/25 f. 308: Police Report, Dec. 15, 1927, Parliamentary Archives, London.
6. Wilkinson, *Peeps at Politicians,* 34, 36; Johnston, *A Hundred Commoners,* 116.
7. Wilkinson, *Peeps at Politicians,* 2; *Daily Graphic,* Nov. 13, 1924.
8. *Daily Graphic,* Nov. 13, 1924; *Northern Echo,* Dec. 22, 1924; HC/SA/SJ/10/15–19: Police & Custodians reports, including accidents, plans, disturbances, petty crime.
9. *Punch,* Dec. 10, 1924, 662; HC Deb, 5th series, Dec. 2, 1924, vol. 179, cols. 7–8.
10. Wilkinson, *Division Bell Mystery,* 9; *Yorkshire Evening News,* Dec. 10, 1924.
11. Nicholas Owen, "MacDonald's Parties: The Labour Party and the 'Aristocratic Embrace,' 1922–31," *Twentieth Century British History* 18, no. 1 (2007): 9–10.
12. HL Deb, Dec. 9, 1924, vol. 60, col. 7.
13. *Yorkshire Evening News,* Dec. 10, 1924.
14. *Evening Standard,* Dec. 10, 1924.
15. *Western Mail,* Dec. 11, 1924; *Birmingham Evening Despatch,* Dec. 10, 1924.
16. *Daily Mirror,* Dec. 10, 1924; *Cork Examiner,* Dec. 11, 1924.
17. *Labour Woman,* Jan. 1, 1925, 5; *Daily Sketch,* Dec. 11, 1924.
18. *Labour Woman,* Jan. 1, 1925.
19. *Methodist Times,* Feb. 26, 1925.
20. Sandra Stanley Holton, *Feminism and Democracy: Women's Suffrage and Reform Politics in Britain,* 1900–1918 (Cambridge: Cambridge University Press, 1986), 53–54.
21. June Hannam and Karent Hunt, *Socialist Women: Britain, 1880s to 1920s* (London: Routledge, 2002), 44.
22. *Clarion,* Dec. 12, 24.
23. *Northern Echo,* June 12, 1933.
24. *Manchester Guardian,* Oct. 14, 1926.
25. *Westminster Gazette,* Mar. 10, 1925.

26. Betty Vernon, *Ellen Wilkinson, 1891–1947* (London: Croom Helm, 1982), 37.

27. Margaret Cole, "Frank Horrabin," *Tribune*, Mar. 9, 1962, 3; Margaret Cole, "Horrabin, James Francis (1884–1962)," rev. Amanda L. Capern, in Matthew and Harrison, *Oxford Dictionary of National Biography*.

28. *Northern Echo*, Dec. 22, 1924.

29. *Liverpool Express*, Jan. 7, 1925; *Manchester Dispatch*, Mar. 21, 1925; *Daily Mail*, Mar. 31, 1925; *Lancashire Post*, Mar. 31, 1925.

30. *Report of the Trades Union Congress* (1925), 379, 421–422.

31. HC Deb, Mar. 18, 1926, vol. 193, col.575.

32. Quoted in, inter alia, *Daily Express*, Dec. 11, 1924.

33. Beatrice Webb, diary entry, Aug. 17, 1927, in *Typescript Diaries: October 1924–19 May 1929*, 391–392. Available from: http://digital.library.lse.ac.uk/objects/lse:ret529jev.

34. Brian Harrison, *Prudent Revolutionaries: Portraits of British Feminists between the Wars* (Oxford: Oxford University Press, 1987), 131, 145.

35. Although MacDonald, as a member of the ILP, technically supported women's suffrage, he was personally sceptical of women's political rationality. See Stuart MacIntyre, "British Labour, Marxism and Working-Class Apathy in the Nineteen Twenties," *Historical Journal* 20, no. 2 (June 1977): 485; Holton, *Feminism and Democracy*, 55–56.

36. "M. P.s' Good Looks: Woman Member Reassures Them," *Liverpool Courier*, Feb. 20, 1925; "Women and the Franchise," *Times*, Feb. 21, 1925.

37. Laura Beers, *Your Britain: Media and the Making of the Labour Party* (Cambridge, MA: Harvard University Press, 2010), 73.

38. *South Wales News*, Mar. 19, 1925.

39. Ronald Blythe, *The Age of Illusion: England in the Twenties and Thirties, 1919–1940* (London: Faber, 1963), 42.

40. See reports in, e.g., *Vote*, Jan. 22, 1926; and *Daily Dispatch*, Feb. 27, 1926.

41. Harold Smith, "British Feminism and the Equal Pay Issue in the 1930s," *Women's History Review* 5, no. 1 (1996): 97–110, at 104.

42. Pamela Graves, *Labour Women: Women in British Working-Class Politics, 1918–1939* (Cambridge: Cambridge University Press, 1994), 134.

43. *Manchester Guardian*, Dec. 17, 1924.

44. Maude Royden, quoted in Susan Pedersen, "The Failure of Feminism in the Making of the British Welfare State," *Radical History Review* 43 (1989): 86–110, at 91.

45. Quoted in ibid., 97–98.

46. HC Deb, May 18, 1925, vol. 184, cols. 182–183.

47. HC Deb, June 30, 1925, vol. 185, col. 2255–2256.

48. Johnston, *A Hundred Commoners*, 112–113.

49. *Birmingham Post*, July 2, 1925.

50. HC Deb, June 30, 1925, vol. 185, col. 2478.

51. HC Deb, July 1, 1925, vol. 185, col. 2557.

52. HC Deb, July 1, 1925, vol. 185, col. 2627.
53. *Sketch,* July 2, 1925.
54. *Newcastle Journal,* Nov. 17, 1927.
55. John Kenneth Galbraith, *Money: Whence It Came, Where It Went* (New York: Houghton Mifflin, 1995 [1975]), 170.
56. *Manchester Dispatch,* June 12, 1925.
57. Joni Lovenduski, *Feminizing Politics* (London: Polity, 2005), 172.
58. 22 Mich. J. Int'l L. 523 (2000–2001). Remembering Chrystal Macmillan: Women's Equality and Nationality in International Law; Knop, Karen; Chinklin, Christine.
59. Dorothy Page, "'A Married Woman, or a Minor, Lunatic or Idiot': The Struggle of British Women against Disability in Nationality, 1914–1933" (master's thesis, University of Otago, October 1984), 35–36.
60. Ibid., 170.
61. HC Deb, Oct. 31, 1930, vol. 244, col. 341.
62. David Boyd Haycock, *A Crisis of Brilliance: Five Young British Artists and the Great War* (London: Old Street, 2009), 83. Ellen Wilkinson, *Clash* (London: Virago, 1989 [1929]), 17.
63. *Lady's Companion,* Nov. 1926. Ellen Wilkinson, "Born and Bred in Lancashire," Home Service Broadcast printed in *Listener,* Nov. 29, 1945, 617–618.
64. *Daily Mail,* Mar. 19, 1926.
65. *Daily Graphic,* Nov. 13, 1924.
66. *Weekly Dispatch,* Mar. 1, 1925.
67. Laura Beers, "A Model MP? Ellen Wilkinson, gender, politics and celebrity culture in interwar Britain," *Journal of Cultural and Social History* 10, no. 2 (June 2013): 231–250.
68. *Evening Standard,* Mar. 11, 1927.
69. Patricia Hollis, *Jennie Lee: A Life* (Oxford: Oxford University Press, 1997), 41–42.
70. *Evening Standard,* Dec. 5, 1928.
71. See, e.g., *Evening Standard,* May 6, 1925; *Morning Post,* July 3, 1925; and *Sketch,* June 20, 1925.
72. *Labour Party People,* Apr. 12, 1925; *Newcastle Evening Chronicle,* June 3, 1929; *Liverpool Echo,* Jan. 13, 1927.
73. *Daily Herald,* Mar. 14, 1927; *Northampton Daily Echo,* Sept. 21, 1929; *Evening Standard,* Feb. 26, 1925.
74. *New York Tribune,* Aug. 29, 1926.

7. NINE DAYS THAT (ALMOST) SHOOK THE WORLD

1. *Plebs,* Jan. 1926.
2. *Lansbury's Labour Weekly,* Feb. 27, and Mar. 27, 1926.

3. *Lansbury's Labour Weekly,* Mar. 27, 1926.

4. *Western Daily Press,* Sep. 22, 1925; *Nation,* Nov. 4, 1925. Southern and central Europe's authoritarian regimes were not by definition fascist. Although some were royalist and backward looking, others showed to-talizing fascist tendencies. For a discussion of interwar European au-thoritarianism, see Mark Mazower, *The Dark Continent: Europe's Twentieth Century* (New York: Knopf, 1999), 27ff.

5. HC Deb, Dec. 2, 1925, vol. 188, cc2243.

6. *Evening Standard,* Jan. 28, 1926.

7. *Plebs,* Jan. 1926.

8. Laura Beers, *Your Britain: Media and the Making of the Labour Party* (Cambridge, MA: Harvard University Press, 2010), chap. 3.

9. *Lansbury's Labour Weekly,* Mar. 27, and Dec. 18, 1926.

10. Andy Miles, "Workers' Education: The Communist Party and the Plebs League in the 1920s," *History Workshop Journal* 18, no. 2 (1984): 102–114.

11. John Shepherd, *George Lansbury: At the Heart of Old Labour* (New York: Oxford University Press, 2002), 112.

12. Alastair Hatchett, "The Role of the Daily Herald with Particular Reference to Direct Action, 1919–1921" (master's thesis, University of Warwick, 1971).

13. Quoted in Shepherd, *George Lansbury,* 227.

14. *Lansbury's Labour Weekly,* Nov. 6, 1926.

15. *Lansbury's Labour Weekly,* Aug. 21, 1926.

16. HO45/12431: J. C. C. Davidson, "Government News Service, Report of the Deputy Chief Civil Commissioner," June 24, 1926, The National Archive, London. (This document was exempted from the 30-year rule and re-mained sealed until 1977.)

17. Ellen Wilkinson, *Clash,* ed. Ian Haywood and Maroula Joannou (Nottingham, UK: Trent, 2004 [1929]), 71.

18. *Plebs,* Sept. 1925, 338–341.

19. *Plebs,* June 1925, 205.

20. Wilkinson, *Clash,* 27.

21. Quoted in Raymond Postgate, Ellen Wilkinson; J. F. Horrabin, *A Workers' History of the Great Strike* (London: Plebs League, 1927), 17.

22. HC Deb, May 5, 1926, vol. 195, col. 420.

23. "General Strike 1926: Report of the Propaganda Committee," n.d., G. C. 14/4, 1925–26, TUC Library, London Metropolitan University.

24. U DWH/3/31: Winifred to Frank Horrabin, Apr. 25, 1926, Horrabin pa-pers, Hull History Centre.

25. U DWH/3/31: Winifred to Frank Horrabin, May 7, 1926. Stricken text and emphasis in original.

26. Unless otherwise noted, details of Ellen and Frank's 2,000-mile propa-ganda journey are from *Lansbury's Labour Weekly,* May 22, 1926, 8–9.

27. Postgate, Wilkinson, and Horrabin, *Workers' History*, 30.
28. U DWH/3/26: Frank to Winifred Horrabin, May 8, 1926.
29. *Plebs,* Aug. 1926, 281.
30. Anne Perkins, *A Very British Strike* (London: Macmillan, 2007).
31. Wilkinson, *Clash,* 70.
32. Postgate, Wilkinson, and Horrabin, *Workers' History*, 27.
33. U DWH/3/26: Frank to Winifred Horrabin, May 19, 1926.
34. Postgate, Wilkinson, and Horrabin, *Workers' History*, 37; Wilkinson, *Clash,* 89.
35. Keith Middlemas, *Politics in Industrial Society, Part I*; David Howell, *Trade Unions and the State,* chaps. 1–3.
36. Perkins, *Very British Strike,* 244, 249–50; Peter Mandler, *The English National Character* (New Haven, CT: Yale University Press, 2006), 150–151.
37. *Plebs,* July 1926, 245.
38. *Sydney Morning Herald,* May 24, 1926.
39. *Lansbury's Labour Weekly,* May 29, 1926. U DWH /3/26: Frank to Winifred Horrabin, May 20, 1926.
40. *Lansbury's Labour Weekly,* May 29, 1926.
41. *Morning Advertiser,* June 9, 1926.
42. *Lansbury's Labour Weekly,* June 5, 12 and 19, 1926.
43. *Listener,* Nov. 29, 1945, 617.
44. Wilkinson, *Clash,* 151–52.
45. *Lansbury's Labour Weekly,* June 5, 1926, 7.
46. *Hull Daily Mail,* June 6, 1926; *Morning Advertiser,* June 9, 1926; *Western Daily Mail,* June 9, 1926; *Shrewsbury Chronicle,* June 25, 1926.
47. HC Deb, June 29, 1926, vol. 197, col. 1027.
48. *Daily Chronicle,* July 3, 1926.
49. *Daily Herald,* May 28, 1926; *Lansbury's Labour Weekly,* June 26, 1926. *New York Evening Post,* Aug. 7, 1926.
50. Janitor [John Gilbert Lockhart and Mary Lyttelton], *The Feet of the Young Men: Some Candid Comments on the Rising Generation* (London: Duckworth, 1928), 72.
51. *Birmingham Evening Despatch,* July 31, 1926.
52. *Western Mail,* Sept. 1, 1926.
53. Ibid.; *Passaic New Journal,* Aug. 21, 1926.
54. *New York Telegraph,* Aug. 11, 1926; *Washington Times,* Aug. 21, 1926; *Chicago Workers,* 27 Aug 1926; *Daily Mail,* Sept. 1, 1926; *Lansbury's Labour Weekly,* Sept. 4, 1926, 5.
55. *New York Sun,* Aug. 24, 1926; *Western Mail,* Sept. 1, 1926.
56. *Report of the Trades of the Union Congress [TUC]* (1926), 372.
57. Reported in *Times,* Sept. 7, 1926, 7.

58. *Report of the TUC*, 348.

59. *Times,* Sept. 8, 1926.

60. *Lansbury's Labour Weekly,* May 7, 1927.

61. Beatrice Webb diaries, typescript edition, Aug. 17, 1927, London School of Economic and Political Science Archives.

62. HC Deb, June 22, 1927, vol. 207, col. 1887.

63. *Lansbury's Labour Weekly,* June 4, 1927, 7, and June 18, 1927, 14.

64. Henry Pelling, *A History of British Trade Unionism* (London: Macmillan, 1987), 208–209.

65. Cronin, *Industrial Conflict,* 129.

66. *Lansbury's Labour Weekly,* June 23, 1927, 7.

8. NO LONGER UPSETTING THE APPLE CART

1. *Liverpool Post,* June 3, 1926.

2. *Lansbury's Labour Weekly,* June 12, 1926, 6.

3. *Plebs,* Aug. 1929, 172.

4. *Leeds Mercury,* July 5, 1926; *Westminster Gazette,* July 5, 1926. On the spectacle of Edwardian suffrage processions, see Lisa Tickner, *The Spectacle of Women: Image of the Suffrage Campaign, 1907–1914* (Chicago, IL: University of Chicago Press, 1988).

5. Johanna Alberti, *Beyond Suffrage: Feminists in War and Peace, 1914–28* (New York: St. Martins, 1989), 186; Johanna Alberti, "'A Symbol and a Key': the Suffrage Movement in Britain, 1918–1928," in *Votes for Women,* ed. June Purvis and Sandra Holton (London: Routledge, 2000), 283; *Times,* July 5, 1926; *Daily Herald,* July 5, 1926.

6. *Lansbury's Labour Weekly,* June 26, 1926, 13.

7. HC Deb, Feb. 20, 1925, vol. 180, col. 1539–40.

8. See letter from Herbert Samuel to J. A. Pease, Dec. 18, 1911, re: "the memorandum which you circulated on the Franchise Laws Amendment Bill," Gainford papers, 141, Item 11, Nuffield College, Oxford.

9. Undated memorandum containing agents' responses to queries on franchise reform. Stanley Baldwin papers, vol. 52, fols. 138ff., Cambridge University Library.

10. Baldwin to George V, Mar. 30, 1928, in Baldwin papers, vol. 63: King's Letters, carbon copies of daily reports to the Sovereign on proceedings in the Commons, Feb. 8, 1928–May 11, 1929.

11. HC Deb, Mar. 29, 1928, vol. 70 cols. 1402–03.

12. Brian Harrison, *Prudent Revolutionaries: Portraits of British Feminists between the Wars* (New York: Oxford University Press, 1987); Martin Pugh, *Women and the Women's Movement in Britain 1914–1999* (Basingstoke, UK: Palgrave, 2000).

13. *Report of the National Conference of Labour Women, Portsmouth, May 16 and 17, 1928,* 26–27.

14. Quoted in Stephen Brooke, *Sexual Politics: Sexuality, Family Planning, and the British Left from the 1880s to the Present Day* (New York: Oxford University Press, 2012), 50–51.

15. Betty Vernon, *Ellen Wilkinson, 1891–1947* (London: Croom Helm, 1982), 98.

16. Brooke, *Sexual Politics,* 47.

17. HC Deb, Feb. 9, 1926, vol. 191, cc857.

18. Betty Vernon interview with George Strauss, Aug. 1979, Vernon papers, Hull History Centre.

19. Ellen Wilkinson, *Clash* (Trent Editions, 2004 [1929]), 152–153.

20. Wilkinson to Russell, May 26, 1930, quoted in Brooke, *Sexual Politics,* 63.

21. CP/IND/DUTT/6/3: Wilkinson to Dutt, Nov. 12, 1927, Communist Party Archive, People's History Museum, Manchester.

22. *Times,* Oct. 5, 1928, 7.

23. Quoted in Pamela Graves, *Labour Women: Women in British Working-Class Politics, 1918–1939* (Cambridge: Cambridge University Press, 1994), 106.

24. *Radio Times,* Oct. 5, 1928.

25. Susan Pennybacker, *From Scottsboro to Munich: Race and Political Culture in 1930s Britain* (Princeton, NJ: Princeton University Press, 2009), 151–3.

26. George Shepherd, *George Lansbury: At the Heart of Old Labour* (Oxford: Oxford University Press, 2002), 219–20, 247; Emil Lengyel, *Krishna Menon* (New York: Walker & Co., 1962), 37ff.

27. Helmet Gruber, "Willi Münzenberg's German Communist Propaganda Empire 1921-1933," *Journal of Modern History* 38, no. 3 (Sept. 1966): 278–97, at 288.

28. Sean McMeekin, *The Red Millionaire: A Political Biography of Willi Münzenberg* (New Haven, CT: Yale University Press, 2004), 196.

29. In his "Why aren't you a communist?," *Lansbury's Labour Weekly,* Aug. 31, 1926, 3–4, Lansbury argued that "We . . . must also do whatever is possible to secure the admission of Communists to the Labour Party. All who want Socialism must unite and work out a policy which can be followed in a spirit of comradeship and goodwill."—a sentiment that Ellen would have endorsed.

30. Jean Jones, "The League Against Imperialism," *The Socialist History Society Occasional Papers Series,* no. 4 (1996); Appendix One: The Official List of Officers Elected and Delegates in Attendance at the Brussels Congress.

31. Vijay Prashad, *The Darker Nations: A People's History of the Third World* (New York: The New Press, 2007), 19.

32. *The Living Age,* Apr. 15, 1927.

33. Richard Dove, "Fenner Brockway and Ernest Toller: document and drama in Berlin—Letze Ausgabe!," *German Life and Letters* 38, no. 1 (1984): 45–56, at 48.

34. Jones, "League against Imperialism," 6.

35. Quoted in Shepherd, *Lansbury*, 247.

36. See opening remarks of General Sukarno at the Afro-Asian Conference in Bandung, Indonesia, 1955. Quoted in Prashad, *The Darker Nations*, 30.

37. Jones, "League against Imperialism," 12.

38. Ibid., 18–19.

39. LP/ID/CI/8/22i: Organizations Ineligible for Affiliation to the Labour Party, n.d., Labour Party Archive, People's History Museum, Manchester.

40. Martin Cedael, "The First Communist 'Peace Society': The British Anti-War Movement 1932–1935," *Twentieth Century British History* 1, no. 1 (1990): 58–86.

41. Daniel Gorman, *The Emergence of International Society in the 1920s* (Cambridge: Cambridge University Press, 2012), 3, 7.

42. Wilkinson to Astor, Mar. 17, 1929; Miss Irvine (Astor's secretary) to Wilkinson, Mar. 18, 1929; Wilkinson to Irvine, Mar. 19, 1929. In Ms 1416/1/2/62, Nancy Astor papers, University of Reading.

43. "Diligent Girl," *Newcastle Evening Chronicle,* June 3, 1929.

44. *North-Eastern Daily Gazette,* May 18, 1929.

45. *Star,* Apr. 12, 1929.

46. Ibid.

47. Dorothy Page, "'A Married Woman, or a Minor, Lunatic or Idiot': the Struggle of British Women against Disability in Nationality, 1914–1933" (master's thesis, University of Otago, October 1984), 238–239.

48. Page, "A Married Woman," 222–223.

49. Ibid.

50. See especially Helen McCarthy, *The British People and the League of Nations: Democracy, Citizenship and Internationalism, c.1918–1945* (Manchester: Manchester University Press, 2011), chap. 7.

51. Resolution reprinted in *Manchester Guardian,* May 10, 1929.

52. Ibid.

53. *Northern Evening Dispatch,* Feb. 20, 1929.

54. Quoted in Vernon, *Ellen Wilkinson,* 101.

55. Betty Vernon's interviews with Jack Feeney, Railwayman and Middlesbrough Communist Party member; Mrs. Godfrey, occupation unidentified; and Mrs. Turner, teacher, conducted Feb. 21–22, 1978.

56. *North-Eastern Daily Gazette,* Sept. 24, 25, and 28, 1928.

57. *Burnley Express and Advertiser,* Nov. 26, 1930.

58. Vernon interview with Mrs. Godfrey.

59. Vernon interview with Amy Wilde, Oct. 1978.

60. Tom Jones, *Whitehall Diary, vol. 2,* ed. Keith Middlemas (Oxford: Oxford University Press, 1970), 185.

61. The Liberal Party, *We Can Conquer Unemployment* (1929).

62. For a defence of the Liberal proposals, see Robert Skidelsky, *Politicians and the Slump: The Labour Government of 1929–1931* (London: Macmillan, 1967), 52ff. Ross McKibbin has remained one of Skidelsky's most vocal critics, from his "The economic policy of the Second Labour Government," *Past & Present* 68 (1975): 95–123, to his most recent reiteration of his views in *Parties and the People, 1914–1951* (Oxford: Oxford University Press, 2010).

63. Laura Beers, *Your Britain: Media and the Making of the Labour Party* (Cambridge, MA: Harvard University Press, 2010), 127–128.

64. Vernon interview with Wilde, Oct. 1978; Beatrice Webb typescript diary, June 28, 1931. London School of Economic and Political Science Archive. Available at http://digital.library.lse.ac.uk/objects/lse:qux395wip?page =426 (accessed Apr. 11, 2016).

65. Ellen Wilkinson, "Susan," *Labour Magazine*, Nov. 8, 1929.

66. Susan Lawrence, *Fabian Quarterly,* Mar. 1947.

67. James Johnston, *A Hundred Commoners* (London: Herbert Joseph, 1931), 138–139.

68. Beatrice Webb typescript diary, May 14, 1926. Available at http://digital .library.lse.ac.uk/objects/lse:ret529jev?page=180 (accessed Apr. 11, 2016); Wilkinson, "Susan."

69. Ellen Wilkinson, "'My Chief': Miss Susan Lawrence," in her *Peeps at Politicians* (London: Philip Allan, 1930), 27.

70. Neil Riddell, *Labour in Crisis: The Second Labour Government 1929–1931* (Manchester: Manchester University Press, 1999), 145–146.

71. Wilkinson, "Susan."

72. L WH/4/4.28/04b: Memorial on African Policy, Apr. 15, 1930, Winifred Holtby papers, Hull History Centre.

9. OUT OF PARLIAMENT

1. Timothy J. Hatton, "Unemployment and the Labour Market, 1870– 1939," in *The Cambridge Economic History of Modern Britain, Vol. II,* ed. Roderick Floud and Paul Johnson (Cambridge: Cambridge University Press, 2003), 348.

2. GB Historical GIS/University of Portsmouth, Middlesbrough UA through time | Historical Statistics on Work & Poverty for the District/Unitary Authority | Rate: Male Unemployment, A Vision of Britain through Time. Available at: http://www.visionofbritain.org.uk/unit/10056986 /rate/CENSUS_MALE_UNEM (accessed May 20, 2013).

3. Ellen Wilkinson, *The Town that Was Murdered* (London: Gollancz, 1939), 191–192.

4. Ellen Wilkinson, *The Division Bell Mystery* (New York: Garland, 1976 [1931]), 183.

5. CAB 46(31): Conclusions of Cabinet meeting, Aug. 23, 1931, the National Archives, London.

6. Ibid.

7. For a list of the disciplined MPs, see *Times,* July 22, 1931, 13. Notably, Frank Horrabin voted against the government but was not censured.

8. *Methodist Times,* Feb. 26, 1925.

9. Peter Clarke, *Mr. Churchill's Profession: The Statesman as Author and the Book that Defined the "Special Relationship"* (London: Bloomsbury, 2012), 147.

10. Patricia Hollis, *Jennie Lee: A Life* (Oxford: Oxford University Press, 1997), 74.

11. Attractions—Season 1932–1933, William B. Feakins, Inc.

12. Meg Jacobs, *Pocketbook Politics: Economic Citizenship in Twentieth-Century America* (Princeton, NJ: Princeton University Press, 2007), 157.

13. *New Yorker,* July 18, 1953, 29.

14. *Los Angeles Times,* Mar. 1, 1931.

15. *New York Evening World,* Jan. 9, 1931.

16. The official figure for U.S. unemployment in 1931 was 8,020,000. By 1933, the height of the Depression, that number had reached 12,830,000. U.S. Bureau of the Census, *Historical Statistics of the United States, Colonial Times to 1956* (Washington, DC: U.S. Deptment of Commerce, 1960), 70.

17. Interview reprinted in *Western Star and Roma Advertiser* (Queensland), Mar. 18, 1931.

18. Ibid.

19. Miriam Teichner, "Woman Labourite, Defending Dole, Hits Apple Selling," *Sun* (Hanover, PA), Jan. 14, 1931. Teichner wrote occasionally for the *New Yorker* and served as a rotating editor of the Women's Peace Party journal *Four Lights,* alongside Baldwin's first wife Madeleine Doty. She likely knew Evie Preston socially. Erika Kuhlman, "Four Lights," in *Women's Periodicals and the United States: Social and Political Issues,* ed. Kathleen Endres and Therese Lueck (Westport, CT: Greenwood Press, 1996), 114.

20. *New Leader* (New York), Jan. 10, 1931; *Standard Union* (Brooklyn), Jan. 21, 1931.

21. *Evening Ledger* (Philadelphia), Jan. 10, 1931; *Public Ledger,* Jan. 11, 1931.

22. Ellen is mentioned in Reid's obituary as one of the many internationally renowned guests whom the social worker entertained at her home on Sherbrooke Street. *Montreal Gazette,* June 9, 1941.

23. *Montreal Gazette,* Jan. 20, 1931.

24. *Montreal Gazette,* Feb. 5, 1931.

25. *Los Angeles Times,* Mar. 2, 1931.

26. *The Sun,* Jan. 24, 1931, 3; *News* (Baltimore), Jan. 26, 1931.

27. *Northeast Daily Gazette,* Feb. 16, 1931.

28. *Detroit Free Press,* Jan. 28, 1931; *Detroit News,* Jan. 28, 1931.

29. *Newcastle Sunday Sun,* Feb. 8, 1931.

30. *Boston Globe,* Jan. 29, 1931; *Boston Herald,* Jan. 29, 1931.

31. *Glasgow Bulletin,* Feb. 13, 1931.

32. Philip Williamson, "A 'Bankers' Ramp"? Financiers and the British political crisis of August 1931," *English Historical Review* 99, no. 393 (Oct. 1984): 770–806.

33. *Daily Express,* Sept. 7, 1931.

34. CAB 47(31): Conclusions of Cabinet Meeting, Aug. 24, 1931.

35. Neil Riddell, *Labour in Crisis: The Second Labour Government, 1929–1931* (Manchester: Manchester University Press, 1999), 209.

36. Quoted in Philip Williamson, *National Crisis and National Government: British Politics, the Economy and Empire, 1926–1932* (Cambridge: Cambridge University Press, 1992), 453.

37. Patricia Hollis, *Jennie Lee: A Life* (New York: Oxford University Press, 1997), 93.

38. Kenneth O. Morgan, *Michael Foot: A Life* (London: Harper Collins UK, 2007), 68.

39. *Daily Express,* Oct. 29, 1931.

40. Ibid.

41. *Bolton Evening News,* Mar. 28, 1932.

42. *Daily Express,* Feb. 16, 1932. On short skirts and jumpers, see *The Worker* (Brisbane), Feb. 11, 1931, 18.

43. Beatrice Webb typescript diary, June 28, 1931, London School of Economics and Political Science archive. Available at http://digital.library.lse .ac.uk/objects/lse:qux395wip/read/single#page/426/mode/2up. (accessed Apr. 11, 2016).

44. Betty Vernon, *Ellen Wilkinson, 1891–1947* (London: Croom Helm, 1982), 126.

45. U DWH/3/31: Draft letter Winifred to Frank. Italicized sections handwritten, 1942? [n.d.], Horrabin papers, Hull History Centre.

46. *Northampton Evening Telegraph,* Oct. 23, 1931.

47. U DWH/3/2: Frank to Winifred: Nov. 14, 1943.

48. Vernon interview with Margaret Cole, quoted in Vernon, *Ellen Wilkinson,* 126.

49. Hollis, *Jennie Lee,* 81.

50. Henry Pelling, *A History of British Trade Unionism* (New York: Macmillan, 1963), Appendix, 319.

51. L WH/3/3.27/03h: Wilkinson to Holtby, Jan. 30, 1933. Holtby papers, Hull History Centre.

52. Richard Overy, "Pacifism and the Blitz, 1940-1941," *Past and Present* 219, no. 1 (2013): 201-236.

53. L WH/5/5.21/06/01K: Wilkinson to Holtby, Mar. [n.d.], 1932.

54. L WH/6/6.1/13/09e: Holtby to Brittain, Dec. 27, 1932.

55. L WH/3/3.27/03h: Wilkinson to Holtby, Jan. 30, 1933.

56. Winifred Holtby, *Mandoa, Mandoa!* (New York: Macmillan, 1933), 32.

57. L WH/5/5.21/06/01L: Wilkinson to Holtby, [n.d.] summer 1933.

58. L WH/3/3.27/03h: Wilkinson to Holtby, Jan. 30, 1933.

59. Cliveden guest books, Lady Astor papers, University of Reading archive.

60. *Daily Express,* Oct. 29, 1931.

10. ON THE INTERNATIONAL STAGE

1. MS 1416/1/2/62: Wilkinson to Astor, n.d., postmarked Jan. 28, 1929, Astor papers, University of Reading archive.

2. Lorraine Coons, "Gabrielle Duchêne: Feminist, Pacifist, Reluctant Bourgeoise," *Peace & Change* 24, no. 2 (1999): 121–147, at 122.

3. *Report of the Sixth Congress of the Women's International League for Peace and Freedom, Prague, August 24th to 28th, 1929* (Geneva: WILPF, 1929), 67–69.

4. Ibid., 80–81.

5. D. J. Fisher, *Romain Rolland and the Politics of Intellectual Engagement* (New York: Transaction, 2003), 158; Emmanuelle Carle, "Women, Anti-Fascism and Peace in Interwar France: Gabrielle Duchêne's Itinerary," *French History* 18, no. 3 (2004): 291–314.

6. Richard J. Evans, *The Coming of the Third Reich* (London: Penguin, 2004), 286.

7. Ibid., 289.

8. *Northern Daily Mail,* June 30, 1932.

9. *Time and Tide,* Dec. 21, 1935.

10. LP/ID/GERM/7/11: Copy of Frederick Voigt to Ellen Wilkinson, n.d, Labour Party Archive, People's History Museum, Manchester.

11. LP/ID/GER/7/10: To Our Comrades of the German Social Democratic Party.

12. LP/ID/GER/7/12/21: Correspondence re: flag ceremony and greetings from SJCIWO for Wilkinson's visit, with Wilkinson, Crispien, and Mary Sutherland.

13. *Northern Daily Mail,* June 30, 1932.

14. Minutes of National Executive Committee research and publicity subcommittee, June 25, 1928, filed in NEC minutes, Labour Party Archive.

15. Julia Sneeringer, *Winning Women's Votes: Propaganda and Politics in Weimar Germany* (Chapel Hill: University of North Carolina Press, 2001), 220.

16. *Daily Herald,* July 25, 1932.

17. Sneeringer, *Winning Women's Votes,* 228.

18. *Daily Herald,* July 22, 1932.

19. Ibid.

20. Ibid.; *Manchester Guardian,* July 18, 1932.

21. Evans, *Third Reich,* 285.

22. *Times,* July 20, 1932.

23. *Daily Worker,* July 21, 1932.

24. *Daily Herald,* July 25, 1932.

25. *Daily Herald,* July 22, 1932.

26. *Daily Herald,* July 25, 1932; *Times,* July 20, 1932.

27. *Star,* Aug. 2, 1932.

28. *Star,* Aug. 23, 1932.

29. *Daily Herald,* July 22, 1932

30. Mary Ann Caws, ed., foreword to *Vita Sackville-West: Selected Writings* (Basingstoke, UK: Palgrave, 2002), 6.

31. *Time and Tide,* Dec. 21, 1935.

32. *Star,* Aug. 23, 1932.

33. *Manchester Guardian,* May 19, 1933.

34. WILPF 4/2: Resolution passed by the British WILPF governing council, Oct. 30, 1919, British WIL papers, Women's Library, London School of Economic and Political Science Archive.

35. Mrinalini Sinha, *Specters of Mother India: The Global Restructuring of an Empire* (Durham, NC: Duke University Press, 2006), 106 and 149.

36. 7ELR/03/05: Wilkinson to Rathbone, n.d. [Sept. 1929]: Eleanor Rathbone papers, Women's Library, LSE.

37. WILPF 4/2: Oct. 31, 1930, Nov. 8, 1930, May 28, 1931; Sinha, *Spectres,* 207.

38. Arthur Burns, "Beyond the 'Red Vicar': Community and Christian Socialism in Thaxted, Essex, 1910–84," *History Workshop Journal* 75, no. 1 (2013): 101–124.

39. Nicholas Owen, *The British Left and India: Metropolitan Anti-Imperialism, 1885–1947* (New York: Oxford University Press, 2007), 203–209; Rehana Ahmed and Sumita Mukherjee, *South Asian Resistances in Britain, 1958–1947* (New York: Continuum, 2012), xiii.

40. L/PJ/12/488: Telegram from Government of India, Home Dept to S/S, from Simla, July 22, 1932; L/I/1/50: Stephens to MacGregor, Nov. 13, 1932, Memorandum on the India League Delegation, India Office Records, British Library, London; Julius Silverman, "The India League," in *A Centenary History of the Indian National Congress,* vol. 3, 1935–1947, ed. B. N. Pande (New Delhi: All India Congress Committee/Vikas Publishing, 1985), 844.

41. See Scotland Yard reports on Menon in KV/2/2509, the National Archives, London.

42. *Daily Worker,* July 14, 1932.

43. Owen, *British Left and India,* 188.

44. *Daily Herald,* Dec. 7, 1932.

45. Suhash Chakravarty, *Crusader Extraordinary: Krishna Menon and the India League 1932–1936* (Delhi: India Research Press, 2006), 3.

46. Betty Vernon, *Ellen Wilkinson, 1891–1947* (London: Croom Helm, 1982), 126.

47. Ibid. 9.

48. L/PJ/12/448: Peel to Maurice Hallett, Aug. 5, 1932.

49. L/PJ/12/448: Handwritten note by Clauson, July 22, 1932.
50. Chakravarty, *Crusader Extraordinary*, 52.
51. L/I/1/50: MacGregor to Douglas Crawford, Mar. 31, 1934.
52. Quoted in Partha Sarathi Gupta, *Power, Politics and the People: Studies in British Imperialism and Indian Nationalism* (London: Anthem Press, 2002), 396.
53. L/I/1/50: Unsigned report, Nov. 24, 1932, "The India League: Welcome to Delegation," Notes on meeting of India League supporters at home of Frank and Winfred Horrabin, Nov. 21, 1932.
54. L/I/1/50: MacGregor to Crawford, Mar. 31, 1934.
55. L/PJ/12/448: PA Kelly to C. B. B. Clee, Aug. 18, 1932.
56. E. M. Forster, *A Passage to India* (New York: Penguin, 2005 [1924]), 63.
57. *Times of India*, Aug. 22, 1932, 13.
58. Wilkinson, "Mr. Gandhi's Friends at Home," *Star*, Nov. 25, 1932.
59. Carey A. Watt, "Education for National Efficiency: Constructive Nationalism in North India, 1909–1916," in *Modern Asian Studies* 31, no. 2 (May 1997): 341–342, 355.
60. L/PJ/12/448: Poona Police Intelligence Report, Aug. 26, 1932.
61. *Times of India*, Aug. 23, 1932, 13.
62. L/PJ/12/448: Poona Police Intelligence Report, Aug. 26. 1932.
63. Article by Ellen in the *Star*, quoted in IOR/L/I/1/50: Stephens to MacGregor, Dec. 19, 1932.
64. Ibid.
65. *Daily Mail*, Oct. 29, 1932.
66. Wilkinson, "Mr. Gandhi's Friends at Home," *Star*, Nov. 25, 1932.
67. L/PJ/12/448: Whately to Lord Lothian, July 19, 1932.
68. L/PJ/12/448: Extract from the Weekly Confidential Diary of the Asst. Superintendent of Police, Patna City, dated Sept. 23, 1932.
69. *Daily Herald*, Feb.15, 1933; L/PJ/12/448: Copy of a note on the activities of the India League Delegation in the Madras Presidency, n.d., anon.
70. Linda Walker, "Whately, (Mary) Monica (1889–1960)," in *Oxford Dictionary of National Biography*, ed. H. C. G. Matthew and Brian Harrison (Oxford: Oxford University Press, 2004; online ed., Jan. 2011).
71. L/PJ/12/448: note on the activities of the India League Delegation in the Madras.
72. Suhash Chakravarty et al., *Condition of India: Being the Report of the Delegation Sent to India by The India League in 1932* (Delhi: Delhi Konark Publ. Pvt Ltd, 1999 [1934]), 437.
73. L/I/1/50: Memorandum, Stephens to MacGregor, Nov. 13, 1932.
74. Rehana Ahmed, "Networks of Resistance: Krishna Menon and Working-Class South Asians in Inter-War Britain," in Ahmed and Mukherjee, *South Asian Resistances*, 71.
75. Chakravarty, *Crusader Extraordinary*, 44.

76. Chakravarty, preface to Chakravarty et al., *Condition of India,* xxxviii.
77. *Daily Herald,* Feb. 15, 1933.
78. L/PJ/12/488: Extract from a Secret Report dated Sept. 21, 1932.
79. L/PJ/12/488: Copy of Oct. 17, 1932 report from Government of Bengal to Government of India, home dept.
80. Ibid.
81. Wilkinson, "A Palace of pretty words," *Daily Herald,* Mar. 20, 1933.
82. L/I/1/50: Private Report of India League Conference: Nov. 26, 1932, Kingsway Hall, London.
83. L/PJ/12/448: Weekly Report of the DIB, Home Department, Simla, Aug. 25, 1932, appendix: dates of the delegation's provisional tour programme.
84. *Manchester Guardian,* Sept. 21, 1932.
85. *Daily Herald,* Dec. 7, 1932. All details of the visit come from this article, unless otherwise noted.
86. The *Manchester Guardian* article of Sept. 21, 1932, cited as its source two "friends" who visited Gandhi on Sept. 19. Given her connections to the journal, this likely referred to Ellen and Menon.
87. L/I/1/50: India League Conference, Nov. 26, 1932.
88. Ibid.
89. Statement reprinted in Pyarelal, *The Epic Fast* (Ahmedabad, India: M.M. Bhatt, 1932), 136–137. See also Tim Pratt and James Vernon, "'Appeal from this fiery bed . . .': The Colonial Politics of Gandhi's Fasts and Their Metropolitan Reception," *Journal of British Studies* 44, no. 1 (Jan. 2005): 92–114.
90. *Northern Daily Telegraph,* Oct. 10, 1934.
91. *Daily Herald,* Dec. 7, 1932.
92. Derek Sayer, "British reaction to the Amritsar massacre 1919–1920," *Past and Present* 131, no. 1, (May 1991): 130–164.
93. L/PJ/12/488: Copy of letter from Government of Punjab to Sec to the Government of India, Home Dept, Nov. 16, 1932.
94. *Daily Herald,* Jan. 3, 1933.
95. On Menon's exoticism to the Punjabis, see L/PJ/12/488: Chief Secretary of the Government of the NWFP to the Secretary of the Government of India, n.d.
96. *Tribune,* Dec. 28, 1932.
97. L/PJ/12/488: Criminal Investigation Department Report, NWFP.
98. L/I/1/50: Report dated 24/11/32, "The India League: Welcome to Delegation."
99. Chakravarty et al., *Condition of India,* 430.
100. L/PJ/12/488: Criminal Investigation Department Report, NWFP
101. Chakravarty et al., *Condition of India,* 430.
102. Ibid.
103. Chakravarty, preface, *Condition of India,* lxxvi.

104. L/PJ/12/488: Confidential note from the Deputy Commissioner of Police A. H. Layard.
105. Chakravarty et al., *Condition of India*, 439.
106. Ibid., 96.
107. L/PJ/12/488: Report from T. T. Kothavala, to Clee, Oct. 25, 1932.
108. *Daily Herald*, Feb. 15, 1933.
109. Jawaharlal Nehru, *Jawaharlal Nehru, an Autobiography* (London: John Lane, 1942) 92.
110. L/PJ/12/448: Note from the Hon. Home Member, Oct. 31, 1932.
111. L/PJ/12/448: Report from Government of the United Provinces to Government of India, Home Dept, Nov. 3, 1932.
112. L/I/1/50: Clipping from *Hindustan Times*, Dec. 1, 1932, and accompanying letter Stephens to MacGregor, Dec. 12, 1932.
113. Forster, *A Passage to India*, 285.
114. L/I/1/50: Unsigned report, Nov. 24, 1932, with covering note, MacGregor to RAB Butler and CM Patrick.
115. WILPF 1/8: Ellen Wilkinson's report on her trip to India, to special meeting of Executive Committee WIL, Nov. 30, 1932; *Brighton World*, Feb 11, 1933.
116. Gupta, *Power, Politics and the People*, 400.

11. A FIGHT FOR HUMANITY ITSELF

1. L/I/1/50: Draft letter from Macgregor to Davies, Oct. 18, 1933; L/PJ/12/449: Clauson to Hallett, Mar. 9, 1934; Scotland Yard report on Essential News, Apr. 25, 1934. India Office Records, British Library, London.
2. *Times Literary Supplement*, Feb. 2, 1933.
3. Ellen also pulled out of a 1932 contract to write a draft memoir on her time in parliament. Information courtesy of Naomi Farmer, Chambers Harrap Ltd, via email Feb. 13, 2009.
4. L/I/1/50: Stephens to Young, Apr. 11, 1934.
5. *Manchester Guardian*, Apr. 17, 1934.
6. *Woodford Times*, Jan. 6, 1933.
7. World Committee for the Victims of German Fascism, *The Brown Book of Hitler Terror and the Burning of the Reichstag* (London: Victor Gollancz Ltd, 1933), 54.
8. *Manchester Guardian*, Feb. 28, 1933.
9. Richard J. Evans, "The Conspiracists," review of *Burning the Reichstag: An Investigation into the Third Reich's Enduring Mystery*, by Benjamin Carter Hett, *London Review of Books* 36, no. 9 (2014): 3–9.
10. *Report of the Labour Party Annual Conference* (1933), 220.
11. *Daily Herald*, Mar. 27, 1933. On the treatment of Sollmann and others, see Richard J. Evans, *The Coming of the Third Reich* (London: Penguin Press, 2003), 340ff.

12. *Daily Herald,* Apr. 6, 1933.

13. *Daily Mirror,* May 22, 1933. See also, *Daily Herald,* Apr. 6, 1933.

14. *Daily Herald,* Mar. 27, 1933.

15. *Daily Express,* Apr. 10, 1933.

16. *Star,* Apr. 19, 1933.

17. *Newcastle Journal,* Mar. 31, 1933.

18. *Manchester Guardian,* May 19, 1933; *New York Times,* Dec. 16, 1934.

19. Johanna Alberti, "British Feminist and Anti-Fascism in the 1930s," in *This Working-Day World: Women's Lives and Cultures in Britain, 1914–1945,* ed. Sybil Oldfield (London: Taylor & Francis 1994), 118.

20. *Daily Herald,* Apr. 29, 1937.

21. On Koestler's departure from the Communist party, see Michael Scammell, *Koestler: The Indispensable Intellectual* (London: Faber, 2011) 161ff.

22. Arthur Koestler, *The Invisible Writing: The Second Volume of an Autobiography: 1932–40* (London: Hutchinson, 1954), 205.

23. Gustav Regler, *The Owl of Minerva: The Autobiography of Gustav Regler* (London: R. Hart Davis, 1959), 162.

24. Koestler, *Invisible Writing,* 209–210.

25. Susan Pennybacker, *From Scottsboro to Munich: Race and Political Culture in 1930s Britain* (Princeton, NJ: Princeton University Press, 2009), 200–201.

26. KV2/1382: Intercepted telegram, Isabel Brown to S.O.I. Boulevard de la Villette 114, Paris, Mar. 30, 1933, The National Archives, London.

27. *Times,* Apr. 3, 1933.

28. KV2/1382: MI5 memorandum "regarding international delegate from the WIR," Mar. 31, 1933.

29. Francois Furet, *Le passe d'une illusion: essai sure l'idee communiste au XXe siècle* (Paris: Laffont, 1995), 254.

30. Koestler, *Invisible Writing,* 188; Regler, *Owl,* 163; Bibliothèque Municipale Méjanes, *Willi Münzenberg: Un homme contre, 1889–1940* (Paris: le Temps des cerises, 1993). The essays, especially Stephane Courtois's "Willi Münzenberg ou l'antifascisme entre revolution et démocratie," largely accept Münzenberg's early fidelity to Moscow and emphasize the gradual process of his estrangement from Stalin, instigated by the purges begun in 1934.

31. Koestler, *Invisible Writing,* 198. Contrast this to Manès Sperber's assertion that these "compagnons de route" "n'attendaient qu'un signe de lui pour se metre en route; it choisissaint aussi la direction." Quoted in Furet, *Le passe d'une illusion,* 255.

32. Ellen Wilkinson, "A Feminist Looks at Women's Status," *New York Times,* Dec. 16, 1934.

33. HC Deb, July 3, 1930, vol. 240, cc2131–2132.

34. *Clarion,* May 26, 1934.

35. *Manchester Guardian,* May 28, 1933.

36. Anson Rabinbach, "Staging Antifascism: The Brown Book of the Reichstag Fire and Hitler Terror," *New German Critique,* no. 103 (Winter, 2008): 97–126, at 101.

37. Anson Rabinbach, "Otto Katz: Man on Ice," in *Jüdische Geschichte als allgemeine Geschichte: Festschrift für Dan Diner zum 60 Geburtstag,* ed. Raphael Gross, Yfaat Weiss (Göttingen: Vandenhoeck & Ruprecht, 2006), 325–354, at 334.

38. KV2/1392: Intercepted letter, Ellen Wilkinson to Otto Katz, June 27, 1933. MI5.

39. Bulletin, *Jewish Telegraphy Agency,* July 9, 1933. Available at: http://www.jta.org/1933/07/09/archive/prof-einstein-to-take-position-in-university#ixzz3OuWz4kFG (accessed Feb. 2, 2015).

40. Translation of Albert Einstein to Lionel Ettinger, July 20, 1933. Letter held in Shapell Manuscript Foundation. Available at: http://www.shapell.org/einstein-and-hitler-1933.aspx (accessed Feb. 2, 2015).

41. "Ellen Wilkinson meets a great man," *Daily Express,* Sept. 12, 1933.

42. *Times,* Sept. 11, 1933.

43. Benjamin Carter Hett, *Burning the Reichstag: An Investigation into the Third Reich's Enduring Mystery* (New York: Oxford University Press, 2014). Hett's thesis has received short shrift from Richard J. Evans in *London Review of Books* 36, no. 9 (May 8, 2014).

44. KV2/1382: Police report, Aug. 5, 1933.

45. Louis Fischer, *Men and Politics* (New York: Duell, Sloan and Pearce, 1941), 533, 536.

46. KV2/1382: Police report, July 4, 1933.

47. Stephen D. Youngkin, *The Lost One: A Life of Peter Lorre* (Lexington, KY: University Press of Kentucky, 2005), 89–90.

48. Jonathan Miles, *The Dangerous Otto Katz: The Many Lives of a Soviet Spy* (London: Bloomsbury, 2010), 155.

49. Fischer, *Men and Politics,* 521.

50. Koestler, *Invisible Writing,* 211.

51. KV2/1382: Wilkinson to I. Brown, Sep. 9, 1933.

52. KV2/1382: Wilkinson to Katz, n.d. [late Apr./early May 1933].

53. KV2/1382: Wilkinson to Brown, Sept. 9, 1933.

54. Miles, in *The Dangerous Otto Katz,* identifies this trip as taking place "days before the vote" (142); however, Ellen was in the USA from Dec. 30.

55. *Times,* July 12, 1933; *El Socialista,* July 11, 1933.

56. *El Socialista,* July 13, 1933.

57. Ibid., July 11, 1933.

58. Ibid., July 13, 1933.

59. *Daily Worker,* Nov. 8, 1934, appeal from Ellen Wilkinson and Leah Manning on behalf of the Relief Committee for Victims of German Fascism, Nov. 10, 1934, and other documents filed in LP/ID/CI/28/2–10, Labour Party Archives, People's History Museum, Manchester.

60. Matt Perry, 'Red Ellen' Wilkinson: Her ideas, Movements and World (Manchester: Manchester University Press, 2014), 304.

61. New York Times, Nov. 16, 1934.

62. Time and Tide, Nov. 24, 1934.

63. Matt Perry, "In Search of Red Ellen Wilkinson beyond Frontiers and Beyond the Nation State," International Review of Social History 58, no. 2 (August 2013): 219–246, at 232.

64. Times, Sept. 1, 1933.

65. Regler, Owl, 163.

66. Rabinbach, "Staging Antifascism," 101.

67. L Wh.5/5.24/04/05a: Winifrid Holtby to Lady Rhondda, Sep. 6, 1933. Winifred Holtby papers, Hull History Centre.

68. D. N. Pritt, The Autobiography of D. N. Pritt: Part One, from Right to Left (London: Lawrence & Wishart, 1965), 64; "The Burning of the Reichstag: Official findings of the legal commission of enquiry," (London: Relief Committee, Sep. 21, 1933), filed in LP/ID/CI/13/10.

69. Rabinbach, "Staging Antifascism," 101–102.

70. Nottingham Evening Post, Sep. 14, 1934.

71. Ellen Cicely Wilkinson and Edward Conze, Why Fascism? (London: Selwin & Blount, 1934), 205, 193.

72. Daily Express, Apr. 18, 1932.

73. Paul Corthorn, In the Shadow of the Dictators: The British Left in the 1930s (London: I. B. Tauris, 2006), 2.

74. Stafford Cripps, Can Socialism Come by Constitutional Methods? (London: Forum Lecture, 1933); Time and Tide, Oct. 7, 1933.

75. Time and Tide, Jan. 28, 1933.

76. Labour Party Archives, LP/WG/SPA/56–63. "Ellen Wilkinson Censured," Sunday Chronicle, Dec. 16, 1934.

77. Daily Express, Oct. 3, 1933.

78. Report of the Labour Party Conference (1933), 220–221.

79. LP/ID/CI/27/3: Annie Wilkinson to J. Middleton, Oct. 17, 1933.

80. KV2/1383: Wilkinson to Katz, Sept. [n.d.], 1934.

81. Manchester Guardian, Oct. 1, 1934.

82. Daily Herald, Sep, 22, 1934.

83. Manchester Guardian, Oct. 2, 1934.

84. The signatories were: Lilla Fenner Brockway (Great Britain); Charlotte Despard (Ireland); Rosa Dimitrova (Bulgaria); Gabrielle Duchêne (France); Anna Lindhagen (Swedish); Karen Michaëlis (Denmark); Marguerite de Saint-Prix (France); Elena Stassova (USSR); Mme Sun Yat Sen (China); Ellen Wilkinson (Great Britain); Dr. Gertrud Woker (Switzerland). Cf. Emmanuelle Carle, "Gabrielle Duchêne et la recherche d'une autre route: entre le pacifisme féministe et l'antifascisme" (PhD diss., McGill University, Apr. 2005), 265.

85. Gertrud Baer and Clara Ragaz at 1934 International Congress of Women in Zurich, Typescript report, 4, 15.

86. LP/ID/CI/17/1: Appeal from British Women's Organizing Committee, Women's International Congress Against War and Fascism.

87. *Daily Worker,* May 20, 1935.

88. *International Labour News,* Mar. 3, 1934; *Yorkshire Post,* Feb. 26, 1934.

89. *Report of the Labour Party Annual Conference Report* (1934), 221.

90. *Bolton Journal,* Oct. 5, 1934.

12. PURSUING SOCIAL JUSTICE IN BRITAIN AND BEYOND

1. *Star,* Apr. 9, 1937.

2. *New York Times,* Jan. 7, 1937.

3. David M. Kennedy, *Freedom from Fear: The American People in Depression and War* (New York: Oxford University Press, 1999), 98–103.

4. Samuel Walker, *In Defense of American Liberties: A History of the ACLU* (New York: Oxford University Press, 1990), 96.

5. *Baltimore Sun,* Jan. 21, 1935; *Time and Tide,* Mar. 28, 1935.

6. Edward Conze and Ellen Wilkinson, *Why Fascism?* (London: Gollancz, 1934), 65–66.

7. "If I Were Chancellor Tomorrow," *Daily Express,* Apr. 18, 1932.

8. *Time and Tide,* Mar. 28, 1935.

9. See, for example, *North Mail,* Mar. 25 and 26, 1935; and *Birmingham Town Crier,* Apr. 12, 1935.

10. *Baltimore Sun,* Jan. 21, 1935.

11. *Washington Post,* Jan. 18 and 19, 1935; *New York Times,* Jan. 19 and 20, 1935.

12. *Los Angeles Times,* Feb. 7, 1935; *New York Times,* Feb. 7, 1935.

13. L/PJ/12/450: India League: reports on members and activities, 1935, India Office Records, British Library, London.

14. *Taunton Courier,* Mar. 27, 1935.

15. The mystery featured in the historical thriller by Anna Funder, *All That I Am* (London: Penguin, 2012).

16. Charmain Brinson, "The Strange Case of Fabian and Wrum," *German Life & Letters* 45, no. 4 (1992): 323–344.

17. Martin Ceadel, "The first British referendum: the Peace Ballot, 1934–1935," *English Historical Review* 95, no. 377 (1980): 810–839.

18. *Listener,* Oct. 30, 1935.

19. *Manchester Guardian,* Oct. 2, 1936.

20. The official conference report and most press reports attempted to tone down Bevin's cruelty by intentionally misquoting "hawking" as "taking." John Shepherd, *George Lansbury: At the Heart of Old Labour* (Oxford: Oxford University Press, 2002), 325.

21. Ellen Wilkinson, "Labour and the Middle Classes," in *New Trends in Socialism*, ed. George Catlin (London: Dickson & Thompson Ltd, 1935), 213, 215.

22. Vera Brittain, *Chronicle of Friendship: Diary of the Thirties, 1932–1939*, edited by Alan Bishop (London: Gollancz, 1986), Nov. 8 and 12, 1935, 232, 234.

23. *Sunderland Echo*, Nov. 8, 1935.

24. Ellen Wilkinson, Jarrow election leaflet, 1935.

25. *Daily Mail*, Nov. 22, 1935. Emphasis in original.

26. Jonathan Freedland, *New York Times Book Review*, Mar. 26, 2013.

27. Laura Beers, "Polling public opinion before opinion polling: election prediction between the wars," in *Numbers, Norms and the People: Statistics and the Public Sphere in Modern Britain, c. 1750–2000*, ed. Tom Crook and Glen O'Hara (London: Routledge, 2011), 244–263.

28. NUDAW, "Report of the proceedings of the 15th annual delegate meeting, 12–13 April 1936," 39, published in *New Dawn*.

29. See "Rating British Prime Ministers," Ipsos MORI, http://www.ipsos-mori.com/researchpublications/researcharchive/661/Rating-British-Prime-Ministers.aspx (accessed June 4, 2015).

30. Nicklaus Thomas-Symonds, *Attlee: A Life in Politics* (London: I. B. Tauris, 2010), 77.

31. Ibid., 205, 92.

32. Hugh Dalton, Nov. 20, 1935 diary entry in *The Political Diary of Hugh Dalton, 1918–1940*, ed. Ben Pimlott (London: Jonathan Cape, 1987), 194.

33. Dalton, Wednesday, Apr. 6, 1938 diary entry in ibid., 224.

34. Louis Fischer, *Men and Politics: An Autobiography* (London: Jonathan Cape, 1941), 506; *Time and Tide*, Apr. 16, 1932.

35. Bernard Donoughue and G. W. Jones, *Herbert Morrison: Portrait of a Politician* (London: Weidenfeld and Nicolson, 1973), 250, 258.

36. Diana Hopkinson, *The Incense Tree: An Autobiography* (London: Routledge & Kegan Paul, 1968), 149, 153, 151.

37. Jawaharlal Nehru, *A Bunch of Old Letters: Being Mostly Written to Jawaharlal Nehru and Some Written by Him* (New Delhi: Viking, 2005 [1960]), letters of Feb. 17 and Mar. 22, 1936, 173, 178.

38. Hopkinson, *Incense Tree*, 152.

39. Printed in *Time and Tide*, May 17, 1941.

40. Edward Conze, *The Memoirs of a Modern Gnostic*, Part I (Golden, CO: Samizdat Publishing Group, 1979), 17.

41. Ibid., 25.

42. *Daily Herald*, May 4, 1933, quoting *Völkischer Beobachter*.

43. Ms 1416/1/2/63: Wilkinson to Astor, n.d. [1933], Nancy Astor papers, University of Reading.

44. Profile by Victor ("Vicky") Thompson, *Daily Herald*, Nov. 1, 1945.

45. Vera Brittain, *Chronicle of Friendship,* Sunday, Feb. 16, 1936, 252.

46. A. J. A. Morris, *The Scaremongers: The Advocacy of War and Rearmament 1896–1914* (London: Routledge, 1984), 213-214.

47. Zara Steiner, *The Triumph of the Dark: European International History, 1933–1939* (New York: Oxford University Press, 2011), 142-143.

48. Francisco J Romero Salvadó, *The Spanish Civil War* (Basingstoke: Palgrave, 2005), 57-58.

49. *Daily Herald,* June 22, 1936.

50. Edward Conze, *Modern Gnostic.*

51. *Daily Herald,* July 18, 1936.

52. On the strikes, see H. W. Ehrmann, *French Labour from Popular Front to Liberation* (New York: Oxford University Press, 1947), 38ff.

53. *New Dawn,* June 27, 1936.

54. *Manchester Guardian,* July 1, 1936, Letters to the Editor. On the Peace Pledge Union, see Richard Overy, *The Morbid Age: Britain and the Crisis of Civilisation, 1919–1939* (London: Allen Lane, 2009), 245-255.

55. Vera Brittain, *Testament of Experience* (London: Gollancz, 1957), 166.

56. Leah Manning, *Life for Education* (London: Gollancz, 1970), 90.

57. Jagger published a series of illustrated essays on the trip in *New Dawn,* between Nov. 28, 1936 and Mar. 20, 1937.

58. Manning, *Life for Education,* 113.

59. Mss 15/3/8/225: The Spanish Medical Aid Committee: Report of the Committee, August n.d., 1936, Publications from the Archive of Henry Sara and Frank Maitland, Modern Records Centre, University of Warwick.

60. Fischer, *Men and Politics,* 439.

61. HC Deb, Nov. 30, 1936, vol. 318, col. 824.

62. For Lansbury's involvement see *Manchester Guardian,* Aug. 14 and 15, 1936. On the extent to which the SMA was a truly apolitical organization, see Tom Buchanan, *The Impact of the Spanish Civil War on Britain: War, Loss and Memory* (Brighton, UK: Sussex Academic Press, 2007), chap. 3.

63. Mss TUC 292/946/16b/50: W. Citrine, memorandum of interview, Oct. 13, 1937, Trade Union Congress Archives, MRC.

64. On the origins of the meeting, see note in file KV2/774, The National Archives, London: "The comite d'aide a l'Espagne republicaine is the outcome of an international united front conference which was held in Paris on 13.8.36. All shade of left opinion were represented, but the initiative was largely that of WM and the communist group in Paris."

65. Tom Buchanan, *The Spanish Civil War and the British Labour Movement* (Cambridge: Cambridge University Press, 1991), 49.

66. Mss 292/946/41/185: Citrine to Schevenels, Aug. 15, 1936.

67. Mss 292/946/180/63: Harry Pollitt, "Spain and the TUC," n.d.; *Manchester Guardian,* Sep. 7, 1936.

68. Lewis Mates "The United Front and the Popular Front in the North-east of England, 1936–1939," (PhD thesis, University of Newcastle, 2002), 36, 38, fn. 84.

69. Overy, *Morbid Age,* 340.

70. *Report of the Labour Party Annual Conference* (1936), 259.

71. Donoughue and Jones, *Herbert Morrison,* 259.

72. Susan Pedersen, *Eleanor Rathbone and the Politics of Conscience* (New Haven, CT: Yale University Press, 2004), 223.

73. HC Deb, Apr. 1, 1936, vol. 310, cc2018–2021.

74. Ms 1416/1/2/62: Wilkinson to Astor, n.d. [autumn 1931], Nancy Astor papers.

75. W. R. Garside, *British Unemployment 1919–1939: A Study in Public Policy* (Cambridge, Cambridge University Press, 1990), 5.

76. Hopkinson, *Incense Tree,* 152.

77. *Chicago Tribune,* Oct. 31, 1936.

78. *African Morning Post,* Nov. 5, 1936.

79. Matt Perry, *The Jarrow Crusade: Protest and Legend* (Sunderland, UK: University of Sunderland Press, Kindle Edition, 2012), Kindle Locations 23912–23956.

80. Wal Hannington, *Unemployed Struggles 1919–1936: My Life and Struggles amongst the Unemployed* (London: Lawrence and Wishart 1977 [1936]). 314.

81. HC Deb, Nov. 4, 1936, vol. 317, col. 75.

82. On the language of constitutionalism, see Laura Beers, " 'Is This Man an Anarchist?' Industrial Action, Publicity and Public Opinion in Britain, 1919–1926," *Journal of Modern History* 82, no. 1 (Mar. 2010): 30–60.

83. CAB 24/264/31: Appendix II to cabinet memorandum, Oct. 12, 1936, The National Archives, London.

84. Perry, *Jarrow Crusade,* Kindle Locations 27641–27651.

85. *Time and Tide,* Oct. 31, 1936.

86. Perry, *Jarrow Crusade,* Kindle Locations 27713–27746.

87. Hopkinson, *Incense Tree,* 150.

88. *Manchester Guardian,* Oct. 15, 1936.

89. *South Wales Echo,* Feb. 21, 1936.

90. *Daily Express,* July 26, 1933.

91. *Daily Mail,* Feb. 29, 1936.

92. *Manchester Guardian,* Oct. 6, 1936.

93. *Report of the Labour Party Annual Conference* (1936), 228.

94. *Western Daily Mail,* Oct. 9, 1936.

95. *Report of the Labour Party Annual Conference* (1936), 230.

96. Ibid., 228.

97. *Labour Woman,* Mar./Apr. 1947.

98. Paddy Scullion, David Riley, Joe Symonds, and Jock Hanlon. See Perry, *The Jarrow Crusade,* Kindle Locations 9552–9567.

99. *Manchester Guardian,* Nov. 2, 1936.
100. On the affective deployment of emotion, see Martin Francis, "Tears, Tantrums, and Bared Teeth: The Emotional Economy of Three Conservative Prime Ministers, 1951–1963," *Journal of British Studies* 41, no. 3 (2002): 354–387.
101. *Yorkshire Telegraph,* incorrectly dated in Ellen Wilkinson scrapbooks as Nov. 3, 1936.
102. *Daily Herald,* Nov. 6, 1936.
103. HC Deb, Nov. 19, 1936, vol. 317, cc1895–1896.
104. *Hartlepool Northern Daily Mail,* Nov. 4, 1936.
105. Perry, *The Jarrow Crusade,* Kindle Location 37978.
106. Ellen Wilkinson, "Social Justice," in *Programme for Victory,* ed. Harold Laski (London: Fabian Society, 1940).
107. Sidney Fine, *Sit-down: The General Motors Strike of 1936–1937* (Ann Arbor: University of Michigan Press, 1969), 206, notes the propaganda value of Ellen's visit to the strikers.
108. *New Dawn,* Mar. 20, 1937.
109. *Chicago Tribune,* Jan. 17, 1937.
110. *New Dawn,* Mar. 20, 1937; *Time and Tide,* Feb. 20, 1937
111. Keith Laybourn, *Modern Britain since 1906: A Reader* (London: I. B. Tauris, 1999), 158.
112. *New Dawn,* Apr. 3, 1937.
113. *New Dawn,* Apr. 3, 1937.
114. *Time and Tide,* Feb. 13, 1937.
115. Kenneth Harris, *Attlee: A Life* (London: Weidenfeld and Nicolson, 1982), 132–134. On the *Herald,* see Martin Pugh, "The *Daily Mirror* and the Revival of Labour, 1935–1945," *Twentieth Century British History* 9, no. 3 (1998): 420–38, at 431.
116. *Time and Tide,* Dec. 12, 1936 and Feb. 20, 1937.

13. THE ANTI-FASCIST TRIBUNE

1. *Manchester Guardian,* July 21, 1936.
2. *Manchester Guardian,* Nov. 15, 1937.
3. Liberal ex-MP Philip Oliver on platform with Wilkinson, reported in *Manchester Guardian,* Sep. 7, 1936.
4. HC Deb, Dec. 1, 1936, vol. 318, cc1114–17.
5. *Manchester Advertiser,* Nov. 27, 1936.
6. Mss 292/946/16b/18(i), Nov. 1937, Trades Union Congress archives, Modern Records Centre, University of Warwick
7. *Report of the Labour Party Annual Conference* (1938), 35.
8. Tom Buchanan, "Anti-fascism and Democracy in the 1930s," *European History Quarterly* 32, no. 1 (2002): 39–57, at 41, 46, 53.

9. Edward Conze, *The Memoirs of a Modern Gnostic, Part I* (Manchester: Samizdat, 1979), 15.

10. Another noted American example was John Dos Passos, whose friend José Robles was murdered by the NKVD in Spain.

11. *Daily Herald,* June 10, 1936.

12. *Time and Tide,* June 18, 1938.

13. *Time and Tide,* Feb. 27, 1937.

14. Lewis Mates attributes the failure of the Unity Campaign in the north-east in part to its lack of support from left-wingers such as Ellen and Ruth Dodds. See Mates, "The United Front and the Popular Front in the North-east of England, 1936-1939," (PhD thesis, University of Newcastle, 2002), 120, 150.

15. Diana Hopkinson, *The Incense Tree: An Autobiography* (London: Routledge & Kegan Paul, 1968), 153.

16. Ben Pimlott's *Labour and the Left in the 1930s* (Cambridge: Cambridge University Press, 1977) is essentially an indictment of the Socialist League.

17. Kenneth O. Morgan, *Labour People: Leaders and Lieutenants, Hardie to Kinnock* (Oxford: Oxford University Press, 1992), 104.

18. *Southern Daily Echo,* Oct. 6, 1936. On the constituency campaign, see Matthew Worley, *Labour Inside the Gate: A History of the British Labour Party Between the Wars* (London: I. B. Tauris, 2005), 187-192.

19. Morgan, *Labour People,* 104.

20. *Tribune,* July 8, 1938.

21. *Report of the Labour Party Annual Conference* [LPAC] (1936), 228.

22. *Report of the LPAC* (1937), 188.

23. *Tribune,* July 8, 1938.

24. See Eleanor Rathbone's reply in *Tribune,* July 22, 1938.

25. *Time and Tide,* Mar. 6, 1937.

26. *Walsall Observer,* Sep. 25, 1937.

27. Kenneth Harris, *Attlee: A Life* (London: Weidenfeld and Nicolson, 1982), 127.

28. *Manchester Guardian,* Oct. 6, 1936.

29. Richard Toye. "The Labour Party and the Economics of Rearmament, 1935-39," *Twentieth Century British History* 12, no. 3 (2001): 303-326.

30. *Time and Tide,* Mar. 6, 1937.

31. *Walsall Observer,* Sep. 25, 1937

32. *Manchester Guardian,* Oct. 8, 1937.

33. Quoted in Pimlott, *Labour and the Left,* 102.

34. *Daily Herald,* July 8, 1937.

35. *Walsall Observer,* Sep. 25, 1937.

36. *Rugby Observer,* Dec. 5, 1936.

37. Pimlott, *Labour and the Left,* 153.
38. *Manchester Guardian,* Apr. 21 and 25, 1938.
39. *Manchester Guardian,* May 3, 1938.
40. *Manchester Guardian,* Nov. 11, 1938; Mates, "The United Front," 172; *Forward,* Dec. 10, 1938.
41. Roger Eatwell, "Munich, Public Opinion, and Popular Front," *Journal of Contemporary History* 6, no. 4 (1971): 122–139, at 128.
42. Mss 292/946/30/37: Parliamentary Committee for Spain circular, n.d. [1938]; Mss 292/946/17b/6: Parliamentary Committee for Spain circular, Apr. 14, 1939. See also, Hugo Garcia, *The Truth About Spain! Mobilizing British Public Opinion, 1936–1939* (Brighton, UK: Sussex Academic Press, 2010), 97.
43. Mss 292/946/12a/27: "Food and Freedom for Spain Conference" circular, Nov. 1938.
44. Martin Pugh, "The Liberal Party and the Popular Front," *The English Historical Review* 121, no. 494 (Dec. 2006): 1327–1350.
45. See, for example, Ms 1416/1/2/63: Wilkinson to Nancy Astor, Apr. 11, 1933, Nancy Astor papers, University of Reading.
46. *Tribune,* Dec. 17, 1937.
47. Mss 292/946/186/26: National Joint Committee for Spanish Relief (Feb. 1937).
48. Susan Pedersen, *Eleanor Rathbone and the Politics of Conscience* (New Haven, CT: Yale University Press, 2004), 285.
49. *Time and Tide,* May 1, 1937; *Agence Espagne*: Número 97, Apr. 19, 1937.
50. *Time and Tide,* May 1, 1937.
51. *Sunday Referee,* Apr. 18, 1937.
52. *Manchester Guardian,* Apr. 19, 1937.
53. CHAR 2/314: Atholl to Churchill, May 7, 1937, Churchill papers, Churchill College, Cambridge.
54. *Daily Herald,* Apr. 29, 1937.
55. Ibid.
56. Atholl, Wilkinson, Rathbone and Crowdy, "Notes on the scheme of Spanish frontiers observation," Private, Apr. 1937. The collection at Blair Castle, Perthshire, Box 44, file 10.
57. CHAR 2/314: Report appended to Atholl to Churchill, May 7, 1937.
58. Pugh, "The Liberal Party," 1332.
59. Richard Grayson: *Liberals, International Relations and Appeasement* (London: Routledge, 2013), 133–34.
60. Louis Fischer, *Men and Politics: An Autobiography* (London: Jonathan Cape, 1941), 502–506; KV2/1384: Copy of letter from Wilkinson to Katz, 19 June 1938, The National Archives, London.
61. HC Deb, Dec. 2, 1930, vol. 245, c1989.

62. HC Deb, Dec. 10, 1937, vol. 330, c729.

63. HC Deb, Dec. 2, 1930 vol. 245, c1989.

64. *Daily Express,* Dec. 10, 1937; *Daily Herald,* Dec. 10, 1937; HC Deb, Dec. 10, 1937, vol. 330, cc729.

65. HC Deb, Feb. 6, 1947, vol. 432, cc1983.

66. HC Deb, May 6, 1938, vol. 335, cc1208–1211.

67. In Spring 1938, the two travelled to Paris with Katz on World Committee business. See KV2/1384: Note on Katz's arrival at Croydon, Apr. 22, 1937, signed P. C. Ronald Golding.

68. She was scheduled to speak at an Aid Spain rally on July 17 and then to fly to Spain on July 18. *Continental Daily Mail,* July 18; *Hull Daily Mail,* July 19, 1938.

69. KV2/1384: Special Brach report, Feb. 22, 1938

70. KV2/1384: Special Branch report, June 24, 1938.

71. *Manchester Guardian,* June 21, 1938.

72. Partha Sarathi Gupta, *Power, Politics and the people: Studies in British Imperialism and Indian Nationalism* (London: Anthem Press, 2002), 422, fn 264; Susan Pennybacker, *From Scottsboro to Munich: Race and Imperial Culture in 1930s Britain* (Princeton, NJ: Princeton University Press, 2009), 196.

73. Fischer, *Men and Politics,* 507–508.

74. *Manchester Guardian,* Sept. 12, 1938.

75. Ibid., Oct. 5, 1938.

76. *Manchester Guardian,* Dec. 19, 1938.

77. *Manchester Guardian,* Sept. 19, 1938; newsreel footage available at http://www.criticalpast.com/video/65675053793_Ellen-Wilkinson_Peace -Campaign_British-flag_sculpture-of-a-lion (accessed, Mar. 13, 2015).

78. Susan R. Grayzel, *At Home and Under Fire: Air Raids and Culture in Britain from the Great War to the Blitz* (Cambridge: Cambridge University Press, 2012), 253ff.

79. HC Deb, Oct. 6, 1938, vol. 339, cc524–528.

80. Copy of Creech Jones to Wilkinson, Dec. 14, 1938, and notes on undated discussion, in CP/IND/DUTT/31/3, Palme Dutt papers, Communist Party Archive, People's History Museum, Manchester.

81. Memorandum and covering letter to J. Middleton, Jan. 9, 1939, filed in NEC minutes, Labour Party Archive, People's History Museum, Manchester.

82. Ben Pimlott, *Hugh Dalton* (London: J. Cape, 1985), 261, 262.

83. NEC minutes, Jan. 18, 1939.

84. NEC minutes, Jan. 23, 1939.

85. *Manchester Guardian,* Feb. 21, 1939.

86. Fischer, *Men and Politics,* 554.

87. HC Deb, May 15, 1939, vol. 347, cc1147.

88. Ellen Wilkinson, *Peeps at Politicians* (London: Philip Allan, 1930), 96.

89. Hugh Dalton, *The Fateful Years: Memoirs 1931–1945* (London: Frederick Muller Ltd., 1957), 222–223; Betty Vernon, *Ellen Wilkinson, 1891–1947* (London: Croom Helm, 1982), 178.

90. Dalton diaries, vol. 20, June 14, 1939, typescript pages 64–67, London School of Economics and Political Science archive.

91. Kenneth Harris, *Attlee: A Life* (London: Weidenfeld and Nicolson, 1982), 165.

92. *Time and Tide,* Aug. 26, 1939.

93. *Time and Tide,* Sep. 9, 1939, filed in CHAR 2/389A, Churchill College Archives.

94. *Time and Tide,* Sep. 30, 1939.

95. *Time and Tide,* Mar. 2, 1940.

96. Richard Toye, *Churchill's Empire: The World that Made Him and the World He Made* (New York: Macmillan, 2010), part III.

97. *Yorkshire Post,* Oct. 7, 1933.

98. HC Deb, Apr. 18, 1940, vol. 359, c1212.

99. HC Deb, Apr. 18, 1940, vol. 359, c1215.

100. HC Deb, Apr. 18, 1940, vol. 359, c1216–1222.

101. HC Deb, May 7, 1940 vol. 360, cc1150.

102. *Time and Tide,* May 4, 1940.

103. Vera Brittain, *England's Hour: An Autobiography, 1939–1941* (London: Continuum, 2005 [1941]), 28–29.

104. Nigel Fischer, *Harold Macmillan, A Biography* (London: Weidenfeld and Nicolson, 1982), 72.

14. ELLEN IS NOW A MINISTER

1. Jack Lawson, *Methodist Magazine,* Apr. 1947.

2. HC Deb, June 25, 1940, vol. 362, col. 397.

3. See, for example, Ellen's exchange with George Griffiths, HC Deb, June 25, 1940, vol. 362, cc403–404.

4. *Picture Post,* June 22, 1940.

5. *Time and Tide,* Jan. 21, 1933.

6. Terence H. O'Brien, "Civil Defence" in *The History of the Second World War,* ed. Sir Keith Hancock (London: HMSO, 1955), 384.

7. Ibid., 388–390.

8. Tom Driberg, *Leader,* Mar. 3, 1945.

9. Terry Gourvish, *Dolphin Square: The History of a Unique Building* (London: Bloomsbury, 2014), 78.

10. STKH 1/7: King-Hall diary, July 31, 1945, Churchill College, Cambridge.

11. Anne Perkins, *Red Queen: The Authorized Biography of Barbara Castle* (New York: Macmillan, 2003), 74.

12. Mass-Observation file report 1961, November 1943, 6, University of Sussex Archive, available online through Adams Matthew Digital Ltd.
13. *Sunday Referee,* Oct. 30, 1938.
14. Susan Grayzel, *At Home and under Fire: Air Raids and Culture in Britain from the Great War to the Blitz* (Cambridge: Cambridge University Press, 2012), 270.
15. Ibid., 146.
16. CAB/68/7/16: WP(R)(40)196: Civil Defense Report No. 22, Oct. 10, 1940, The National Archives, London.
17. O'Brien, "Civil Defence," 508.
18. *Daily Express,* Oct. 11, 1940.
19. *Daily Mail,* Nov. 18, 1940.
20. Gourvish, *Dolphin Square,* 114.
21. *News Chronicle,* [date illegible], Folio 245 of Ellen Wilkinson scrapbook, Labour Party Archive, People's History Museum, Manchester.
22. *Observer,* May 20, 1945.
23. *Daily Herald,* Feb. 7, 1947.
24. *News Chronicle,* Dec. 4, 1940; *Manchester Guardian,* Dec. 4, 1940.
25. *Yorkshire Post and Leeds Intelligencer,* Jan. 6 and 17, 1941; *Western Daily News,* Jan. 16, 1941; *Nottingham Evening Post,* Jan. 16, 1941.
26. *Scotsman,* Feb. 19, 1941; *Dundee Courier,* Feb. 20 and 21, 1941.
27. *Western Daily Press,* Mar. 15, 1941; *Gloucester Citizen,* Mar. 15, 16, and 17, 1941; *Western Times,* Mar. 14, 1941; *Dover Express,* Mar. 7, 1941.
28. *Hull Daily Mail,* Apr. 7, 1940.
29. Appreciations for these local tours appeared after her death in, inter alia, *Aberdeen Press & Journal,* Feb. 7, 1947; *Gloucester Citizen,* Feb. 7, 1947.
30. O'Brien, "Civil Defence," 514.
31. *Daily Express,* Oct. 11, 1940.
32. *Daily Telegraph,* Dec. 6, 1940.
33. *Daily Herald,* Nov. 27, 1940; O'Brien, "Civil Defence," 512–522.
34. Harold Nicolson, *Diaries and Letters: Vol II, the War Years* (London: Atheneum, 1966), 128.
35. O'Brien, "Civil Defence," 397. See also CAB/68/7/16: WP(R)(40)196: Civil Defense Report No. 22, Oct. 10, 1940; Evacuation policy is discussed in detail in R. M. Titmuss, *Problems of Social Policy,* part of the series *History of the Second World War,* ed. Keith Hancock, (London: HMSO, 1950), chap. 18.
36. *Manchester Guardian,* Dec. 4, 1940.
37. HC Deb, Feb. 4, 1941, vol. 368, cc791.
38. CAB/68/7/16: WP(R)(40)196: Civil Defense Report No. 22, Oct. 10, 1940.
39. O'Brien, "Civil Defence," 600; *Daily Mail,* Oct. 6, 1942.
40. O'Brien, "Civil Defence," 607.
41. Ibid., 595.
42. *Daily Mail,* Oct. 7, 1942.
43. *John Bull,* Aug. 8, 1936.

44. *Sunday Referee,* Aug. 6, 1939.
45. David Clampin, "The British Advertising Industry at War, 1939-1945," (paper presented at the Conference on Historical Analysis and Research in Marketing, Long Beach, CA, April 2005), 75-76.
46. *Daily Mail,* Aug. 23, 1940.
47. *Daily Express,* Apr. 16, 1942.
48. *Daily Mail,* May 15, 1941.
49. *Star,* Sept. 29, 1942.
50. *Glasgow Evening Times,* Aug. 14, 1942.
51. Dalton's diary of Oct. 28, 1942.
52. O'Brien, "Civil Defence," 597-8.
53. *Daily Express,* Oct. 5, 1942.
54. Ibid.; *Daily Mail,* Oct. 5, 1942.
55. *Daily Mail,* Oct. 6, 1942.
56. *Daily Mail,* Oct. 7, 1942.
57. HC Deb, June 25, 1942, vol. 380, cc2133-4.
58. HC Deb, Nov. 25, 1942, vol. 385, c813.
59. *Daily Mail,* Aug. 18, 1941; *Daily Express,* Aug. 18, 1941.
60. *Manchester Guardian,* Aug. 25, 1941.
61. *Daily Mail,* Nov. 29, 1943.
62. *Manchester Guardian,* Apr. 18, 1944.
63. Beatrice Webb typescript diary, Jan. 17, 1941. Available at http:digital.library.lse.ac.uk/collections/webb.
64. *New Statesman,* Feb. 1947.
65. Paula Bartley, *Ellen Wilkinson: from Red Suffragist to Government Minister* (London: Pluto, 2014), 101-102.
66. *Plebs,* Jan. 1935, 7.
67. *Llandudno Advertiser,* April. 25, 1942.
68. *Daily Mail,* Feb. 22, 1940.
69. *Shields Evening News,* May 17, 1943.
70. *Times,* Nov. 7, 1942.
71. *Picture Post,* June 22, 1940.
72. Dalton diary, Jan. 27, 1943.
73. Tom Driberg, *Leader,* Mar. 3, 1945.
74. *Observer,* May 20, 1945.
75. *Newcastle Evening Chronicle,* Jan. 29, 1943; *Manchester Guardian,* Feb. 1, 1943.
76. *Daily Mail,* Nov. 5, 1943.
77. Dalton diary, Friday, Apr. 9, 1943.
78. Hugh Dalton and Ben Pimlott, *The Second World War diary of Hugh Dalton 1940-45* (London: Cape, 1986), 772-773, 779 (Wed., July 26 and Wed., Aug. 16, 1944).
79. Circular to members of Labour groups on local authorities, March 1944, filed in NEC minutes, Apr. 26, 1944.

80. Margaret Goldsmith, *Women at War* (London: L. Drummond, 1943), 188.

81. For her views on youth, see her speech to Oxford Labour Party rally, *Oxford Times,* Nov. 5, 1943.

82. *Sunday Chronicle,* Oct. 10, 1943. See also, Ina Zweiniger-Bargielowska, *Austerity in Britain: Rationing, Controls, and Consumption, 1939–1955* (Oxford: Oxford University Press, 2000), 130ff.

83. Goldsmith, *Women at War,* 190.

84. Minutes of the International subcommittee of the NEC, Sep. 1 and 8, 1944, filed in NEC minutes, Labour Party Archive.

85. Glenda Sluga, "'Spectacular Feminism': The International History of Women, World Citizenship and Human Rights," in *Women's Activism: Global Perspectives from the 1890s to the Present,* ed. Francisca de Haan et al (London: Routledge, 2012), 43–58.

86. CAB 65/49/33: Cabinet conclusions Mar. 19, 1945; CAB/195/3: Cabinet Secretary's notebooks, Mar. 19, 1945.

87. Dalton and Pimlott, *The Second World War Diary,* 851, (Wed., Apr. 18, 1945).

88. Sluga, "'Spectacular Feminism,'" 48.

89. Ibid., 47.

90. Quoted in Avy Mallik, "Women Presidents of the UN General Assembly." Available at http://www.wunrn.com/news/2007/03_07/03_05_07/031107 _women.htm (accessed Apr. 30, 2015).

91. Vera Brittain, *Testament of Experience* (London: Virago, 1981), 355.

92. *Daily Mail,* May 18, 1945.

93. *Star,* May 21, 1924.

94. *Report of the Labour Party Annual Conference* (1945), 78–81.

95. *Star,* May 21, 1945; *Report of the LPAC* (1945).

96. *Report of the Labour Party Annual Conference* (1945), 89.

97. Richard Toye, *The Labour Party and the Planned Economy, 1931–1951* (Woodbridge, UK: Boydell Press for the Royal Historical Society, 2003), 154.

98. Ibid., 155.

99. *Report of the Labour Party Annual Conference* (1945), 81.

15. REFORMING EDUCATION

1. *Report of the Labour Party Annual Conference* (1947), 108, 30.

2. See discussion in Laura Beers, *Your Britain: Media and the Making of the Labour Party* (Cambridge, MA: Harvard University Press, 2010), chap. 10.

3. Mass-Observation file report 2268: A Report on the General Election, June–July 1945, University of Sussex archive, Brighton; *Hartlepool Mail,* June 28, 1945.

4. James Chuter Ede, *Labour and the Wartime Coalition: From the Diary of James Chuter Ede, 1941–1945,* ed. Kevin Jefferys (London: The Historians' Press, 1987), 226.

5. Ibid.
6. Betty Vernon, *Ellen Wilkinson, 1891–1947* (London: Croom Helm, 1982), 201. Although Attlee claimed in his memoirs (*As It Happened* [London: Heinemann, 1954], 153) that he "knew she was an enthusiast for education," there is little in Ellen's history to suggest that this was the case.
7. *Calcutta Statesman,* Oct. 7, 1945.
8. Hugh Dalton, *The Fateful Years: Memoirs 1931–1945* (London: Frederick Muller Ltd., 1957), 467.
9. Francis Williams, *A Prime Minister Remembers* (London: Heinemann, 1960), 8.
10. Nicklaus Thomas-Symonds, *Attlee: A Life in Politics* (London: I. B. Tauris, 2010), 138.
11. Matt Perry, *'Red Ellen' Wilkinson: Her Ideas, Movements and World* (Manchester: Manchester University Press, 2014), 368.
12. Thomas-Symonds, *Attlee,* 139.
13. John Redcliffe-Maud, *Experiences of an Optimist* (London: Hamish Hamilton, 1981), 51.
14. Olive Banks, *Parity and Prestige in English Secondary Education: A Study in Educational Sociology* (London: Routledge, 2013), 232.
15. Brian Simon, *Education and the Social Order, 1940–1990* (London: Lawrence & Wishart, 1991), 30.
16. William Richardson and Susanne Wiborg, "English Technical and Vocational Education in Historical and Comparative Perspective: Considerations for University Technical Colleges," (London: Baker Dearing Educational Trust, 2010).
17. Simon, *Education,* chap. 1.
18. Chuter Ede, *Labour,* 176.
19. J. E. Floud, A. H. Halsey, and F. M. Martin, *Social Class and Educational Opportunity* (London: William Heinemann, 1956); J. W. B. Douglas, *The Home and the School: A Study of Ability and Attainment in the Primary School* (London: Macgibbon and Kee, 1964).
20. Ina Zweiniger-Bargielowska, *Austerity in Britain: Rationing, Controls, and Consumption, 1939–1955* (Oxford: Oxford University Press, 2000), 134–137.
21. Education Act 1944 (1944 c. 31), sections 48 and 49.
22. Chuter Ede, *Labour,* 164.
23. HC Deb, Jan. 19, 1944, vol. 396, cc233–234.
24. Bill Bailey, "James Chuter Ede and the 1944 Education Act," *History of Education* 24, no. 3 (1995): 209–220, at 213.
25. CAB/65/43/22; CAB/65/43/45, The National Archives, London.
26. CAB/129/1: "Raising the School Leaving Age," memorandum by the minister of education, Aug. 16, 1945.

27. CAB/195/3: Secretary's minutes, Cabinet meeting, Aug. 23, 1945. Abbreviations in handwritten minutes have been written out in full in this and all subsequent quotations.

28. Education Act 1944 c. 31, Part II, section 24 (3). Significantly, the act did not introduce equal pay for male and female teachers, despite the House voting to support an amendment to that effect in the committee stage. Ellen, conveniently, absented herself from the debate rather than be put in the awkward position of choosing between the government and her feminist principles. HC Deb, Mar. 28, 1944, vol. 398, cc1389–1391. The amendment was easily overturned on a vote of confidence two days later, when Ellen did vote with the government.

29. *Report of the Labour Party Annual Conference* (1946), 189, 191.

30. Ibid., 190; *Times*, Mar. 4, 1946.

31. Simon, *Education*, 100.

32. Redcliffe-Maud, *Experiences*, 53.

33. *Report of the Labour Party Annual Conference* (1946), 190.

34. Steven Cowan, Gary McCulloch and Tom Woodin, "From HORSA Huts to ROSLA Blocks: the School Leaving Age and the School Building Programme in England, 1943–1972," *History of Education* 41, no. 3 (2012): 361–380.

35. CAB/129/16/19: Economic Survey for 1947, Jan. 7, 1947.

36. CAB/129/16/25: Economic Survey for 1947: Report of the ministerial committee on economic planning, Jan. 10, 1947.

37. CAB/129/16/29: Economic Survey for 1947: Proposed postponement of the raising of the school leaving age, Jan. 14, 1947.

38. CAB/195/5: Cabinet secretary's notebook, cabinet meeting, Jan. 16, 1947.

39. Redcliffe-Maud 7/7: Notes on the minister of education. Redcliffe-Maud papers, London School of Economic and Political Science Archive.

40. D. W. Dean, "Planning for a postwar generation: Ellen Wilkinson and George Tomlinson at the Ministry of Education, 1945–51," *History of Education* 15 no. 2 (1986): 95–117, at 97.

41. Billy Hughes, "In Defence of Ellen Wilkinson," *History Workshop Journal* 7 (Spring, 1979): 157–160, 157. For size of 1946 budget, see http://www.ukpublicspending.co.uk/uk_down1946_0.html (accessed June 4, 2015).

42. CAB/129/7: "Benefits in kind for school children," joint memorandum by the minister of education and secretary of state for Scotland," Feb. 21, 1946.

43. See, for example, her appeal in *Warrington District Labour News,* Jan. 8, 1938.

44. *John Bull,* Jan. 1, 1938. The 70 percent statistic is given by Ellen in this article.

45. CAB/105/4: Cabinet secretary's notebook: cabinet meeting, Feb. 28, 1946.

46. HC Deb, Feb. 21, 1946, vol. 419, c296W.

47. Education Act 1944 c. 31: Part II: Ancillary Services: Section 51.

48. Education Act 1946 c. 50: Section 9.

49. *Times,* May 11, 1946.

50. HC Deb, Oct. 31, 1946, vol. 428, cc775–778.

51. Redcliffe-Maud 7/7: Notes.

52. HC Deb, Oct. 31, 1946, vol. 428, cc775–778; Dean, "Planning," 105.

53. CAB/128/1: Cabinet minutes, Aug. 7, 1947.

54. Brian Harrison, "Wilkinson, Ellen Cicely (1891–1947)," in *Oxford Dictionary of National Biography,* ed. H. C. G. Matthew and Brian Harrison (Oxford: Oxford University Press, 2004; online ed., Jan. 2011), http://www.oxforddnb.com/view/article/36902 (accessed May 7, 2015).

55. *Daily Herald,* Feb. 23, 1946.

56. FO 371/46935: Covering note on "Visit to Germany, 2nd to 6th October 1945," report by the minister of education. The National Archives, London.

57. Edith Davies, "British Policy and the Schools," in *The British in Germany: Educational Reconstruction after 1945,* ed. Arthur Hearnden (London: Hamish Hamilton, 1978).

58. FO 371/46935: "Visit to Germany, 2nd to 6th October 1945," report by the minister of education.

59. Ibid., 99.

60. Nicholas Mansergh, ed., *The Transfer of Power, 1942–7: constitutional relations between Britain and India: Vol. VI* (London: HMSO, 1976), 549.

61. Ibid., 663.

62. Redcliffe-Maud, *Experiences,* 51.

63. Telegram from Ambassador in the United Kingdom (Winant) to the US Secretary of State, Sept. 4, 1943, available at: http://images.library.wisc.edu/FRUS/EFacs/1943v01/reference/frus.frus1943v01.i0028.pdf (accessed May 15, 2015).

64. ECO/CONF/29: Report of the Conference for the Establishment of the United Nations Educational, Scientific and Cultural Organisation (UNESCO), held at the Institute of Civil Engineers, London, from the 1st to the 16th November, 1945, 24. Available at: http://unesdoc.unesco.org/images/0011/001176/117626e.pdf (accessed, Apr. 14, 2016).

65. Julian Huxley, *Memories II* (London: Harper & Row, 1973), 14; John and Richard Toye, "One World, Two Cultures? Alfred Zimmern, Julian Huxley and the Ideological Origins of UNESCO," *History* 95 no. 319 (2010): 308–331.

66. H. H. Krill de Capello, "The Creation of the United Nations Educational, Scientific and Cultural Organization," *International Organization* 24 no. 1 (1970): 1–3, gives a clear sense of the horse trading with the French.

67. Report of the Conference for the Establishment of UNESCO, 24.

68. R. A. Butler tribute in *Times,* Feb. 7, 1947.

69. Redcliffe-Maud, *Experiences,* 51.

70. Trevor Evans for *New York Times,* Sept. 2, 1945.

71. Angela John, *Turning the Tide: The Life of Lady Rhondda* (London: Parthian Books, 2014), 488.
72. *Times,* Jan. 5, 1946.
73. ED 136/764: Visit of Ellen Wilkinson to Gibraltar and Malta, Jan. 1–14, 1946, the National Archives, London.
74. LP/GS/NEC 38: Ellen Wilkinson to Morgan Phillips, Feb. 26, 1946, Labour Party Archives, People's History Museum, Manchester.
75. *Yorkshire Post,* May 11, 1942; *Hartlepool Mail,* Apr. 27, 1946; *Dundee Courier,* Apr. 30, 1946.
76. *Times Educational Supplement,* Aug. 3, 1946.
77. She moved from Hood House apt. 902 to apt. 607. Terry Gourvish, *Dolphin Square: The History of a Unique Building* (London: Bloomsbury, 2014), 114, fn. 31.
78. STKH 1/7: King-Hall diary notes, July 31, 1945. Churchill College Archives Centre, Cambridge University.
79. *Daily Express,* Sept. 25, 1946.
80. *Times,* Sept. 21 and 23, 1946.
81. *Yorkshire Post,* Sept. 28, 1946.
82. *Yorkshire Evening Post,* Sept. 30, 1946.
83. Jean Mann, *Woman in Parliament* (London: Odhams, 1962), 39; Paula Bartley, *Ellen Wilkinson: From Red Suffragist to Government Minister* (London: Pluto, 2014), 123; Perry, *'Red Ellen' Wilkinson,* 384.
84. See discussion in *Report of the Labour Party Annual Conference* (1946), 192–5.
85. Hughes, "In Defence of Ellen Wilkinson," 158.
86. Nicholas Hillman, "Public schools and the Fleming report of 1944: shunting the first-class carriage on to an immense siding?" *History of Education* 41, no 2 (2012): 235–255.
87. ED 136/788: "Secondary modern schools: part II of minute by the minister," n.d., 1946.
88. *Report of the Labour Party Annual Conference* (1946), 189.
89. Quoted in Kevin Jeffreys, *Anthony Crosland* (London: Richard Cohen, 1999), 103.
90. David Rubenstein, "Ellen Wilkinson Re-considered," *History Workshop Journal,* no. 7 (Spring 1979): 161–169, 165.
91. Simon, *Education,* 129–130.
92. *Manchester Guardian,* Mar. 4, 1946. Her characterization of grammar schools as an "outstanding achievement" that it would be a "folly to injure" was made to the Fabian Society in October 1945. See *Yorkshire Post,* Oct. 27, 1945.
93. *Report of the Labour Party Annual Conference* (1946), 189.
94. Mark Mazower, *The Dark Continent* (London: Penguin, 1998), chap. 3.
95. *Star,* Sep. 23, 1946.
96. Quoted in Rubenstein, "Ellen Wilkinson Re-Considered," 167.

97. As David Rubenstein later dismissed it. See ibid., 167.
98. ED 136/788: Secondary Modern Schools: Part II of minute by the minister, n.d., 1946.
99. ED 136/788: Minister's view on the modern pamphlet, August 1946 draft.
100. ED 136/788: Secondary Modern Schools: Part II of minute by the minister, n.d., 1946
101. Banks, *Parity*, 134–135.
102. *Report of the Labour Party Annual Conference* (1946), 192.
103. This view is outlined in Floud et al., *Social Class and Educational Opportunity*; and Douglas, *The Home and the School*.
104. *Report of the Labour Party Annual Conference* (1946), 196.
105. ED 136/787: Minute by Sir Robert Wood on problems of secondary education, Apr. 15, 1946.
106. Ellen Wilkinson, "Social Justice," in *Programme for Victory: A Collection of Essays Prepared for the Fabian Society*, ed. Harold Laski (London: Routledge, 1941), 133.
107. CAB/195/5/9: Cabinet secretary's notes, Jan. 17, 1947.
108. ED 136/787: Minute by Sir Robert Wood.

16. DEATH OF A GOOD COMRADE

1. CAB 128/9/12: Cabinet minutes, Jan. 27, 1947, the National Archives, London.
2. *Times,* Jan. 25, 1947.
3. *Times,* Jan. 27, 1947.
4. *Daily Telegraph,* Nov. 16, 1945.
5. *News of the World,* Dec. 15, 1946.
6. Betty Vernon conducted interviews with Ellen's staff that highlight the extent of her pill addiction (*Ellen Wilkinson, 1891–1947* [London: Croom Helm, 1982], 234–235).
7. *Citizen,* Feb. 28, 1947.
8. Ibid.
9. This view was confirmed by Ellen's niece Julia Wilkinson in a telephone interview on June 19, 2015. See also Vernon, *Ellen Wilkinson*, 234–235, and her interview notes deposited at Hull History Centre. Matt Perry's *'Red Ellen' Wilkinson: Her Ideas, Movements and World* (Manchester: Manchester University Press, 2014) makes extensive use of Reid's interviews. Although not yet available to researchers, these have been deposited in the University of Newcastle special collections.
10. While Perry raises the spectre of suicide in his *'Red Ellen' Wilkinson* (387–389), the evidence brought to bear in support of this is largely speculative.

11. HC Deb, Feb. 6, 1947, vol. 432, cc1982–1984.

12. Diplomatic and other letters of condolence are filed in FO 370/1447, the National Archives, London.

13. *Le Monde,* Feb. 7, 1947.

14. *Manchester Guardian,* Feb. 7, 1947.

15. Bernard Donoughue and G. W. Jones, *Herbert Morrison: Portrait of a Politician* (London: Weidenfeld and Nicolson, 1973), 392.

16. *Reynolds News,* Feb. 9, 1947.

17. *The Methodist Magazine,* Apr. 1947.

18. Paula Bartley, *Ellen Wilkinson: from Red Suffragist to Government Minister* (London: Pluto, 2014).

19. Susan Pedersen, *Eleanor Rathbone and the Politics of Conscience* (New Haven, CT: Yale University Press, 2004).

20. Perry's *'Red Ellen' Wilkinson* endeavours to recentre her international work.

21. On the contested and contradictory emergence of a new international order in the interwar period, see Glenda Sluga, *Internationalism in the Age of Nationalism* (Philadelphia: University of Pennsylvania Press, 2013) and Mark Mazower, *Governing the World: The History of an Idea* (London: Allen Lane, 2012).

ACKNOWLEDGEMENTS

The idea for this book dates back to my discovery in 2008 of the complete microfilm collection of Ellen Wilkinson's press clippings at the British Library. Thanks to a small research grant from the British Academy, I was able to photocopy the approximately 2000 pages of the collection; and as I read through the press articles, I became convinced that Ellen's wide-ranging career deserved to be the subject of a new biography that took full account of her domestic and international work. My then-colleagues at the University of Cambridge were supportive in reading and commenting on my early research on Ellen and celebrity journalism, which was ultimately published as an article in *Cultural and Social History*. I owe Peter Mandler, in particular, a debt of gratitude for his feedback on both this early work and my later writing on Ellen and the Ministry of Education. My thinking on Ellen's attitude towards gender and sexuality was further developed in an article published in 2011 in *Parliamentary Affairs*.

In 2009, I left England to return to the United States to teach at American University in Washington, DC. I am extremely grateful to all my colleagues at American for their feedback and to the university administration, which supported my research through two Mellon Foundation grants as well as generous departmental and college funding. Two American University students, Jacob Sullivan and India Pasiuk, worked as research assistants on the project, sifting through back issues of *Time and Tide* and the *Daily Mail*, and the reports of the Labour Party annual conference and the Labour Women's Conference. Both were dedicated and meticulous researchers, and this book is much richer for their valuable contributions. In 2011–2012, I received a Leverhulme Trust fellowship to spend the year as a visiting fellow at the University of Exeter, which provided an invaluable opportunity to carry out research in the United Kingdom and to workshop parts of the project at the Universities of Exeter and Bristol. Richard Toye, Andrew Thorpe, David Thackeray, and Tim Rees, as well as others, offered valuable comments on early drafts of the chapters on Ellen's international activism.

In 2013, the American Historical Association awarded me a grant that allowed me to carry out research in the MI5 files at the National Archives. The first draft of the book was completed at the University of Birmingham in 2015, and I owe a huge debt to the Birmingham Fellowship scheme, which granted me the time and resources to keep to schedule. In 2014 and 2015, I gave seminar papers on Ellen and social justice at the Institute of Historical Research and the University of York and received valuable feedback at each. Finally, I am extremely grateful to Kathleen McDermott for her willingness to believe in *Red Ellen* and for her care and devotion in editing the manuscript.

I owe countless other debts to friends and colleagues. Kevin Morgan was unfailingly responsive to my numerous queries about the Communist Party of Great Britain and the Comintern. Anson Rabinbach generously advised me on Willi Münzenberg and Otto Katz. Susan Pedersen, Susan Pennybacker, and two other anonymous reviewers read the manuscript in full, and the final product is stronger for their feedback. Shortly before she passed away in September 2015, I had the pleasure to speak with Julia Wilkinson, Ellen's great-niece, and her stories about the family history have enriched the book. This book could not have been produced without the support of my own family, who have been incredibly patient in living with Ellen over the past eight years. When he was in the womb, my son Gabriel was toted around while I gave seminar papers on Ellen. As an infant, he suffered the abandonment of his mother sneaking off on archive trips to Hull, Manchester, and Paris. As a toddler, he endured the boredom of countless Ellen-centric dinner table conversations. Through it all, he has been impressively tolerant of his mother's other baby. This book is dedicated to him.

INDEX

Astor, Nancy Witcher, 155–156, 160, 184, 326, 335; Cliveden group of Germanophiles, 245; in Parliament, 2, 43, 134–136, 148, 163, 340; Six Point Group, 151; Wilkinson, personal relationship with, 117, 190, 213, 245, 248, 454

Atholl, Duchess of, "the Red Duchess." *See* Stewart-Murray, Katharine Marjory

Attlee, Clement Richard, 318, 346, 363, 380–381, 437, 440–441; Aid Spain movement, 332, 351; Czech plebiscite, 367; debate on rearmament, 355–356; India and Burma committee, 430, 433; Labour leader, 303, 322–323; Popular Front to unseat Chamberlain, 369, 371–372; post WWII elections, 407; Prime Minister, 413–414, 421, 423, 426, 455; Wilkinson, travel to Spain (1937) with, 351; Wilkinson in War Cabinet, 414–415; Wilkinson push to replace with Morrison, 323, 374–376, 414

AUCE. *See* Amalgamated Union of Cooperative Employees (AUCE)

A Very British Strike (Perkins), 182

Azaña, Manuel, 297, 327, 331, 359

Baker, Philip John Noel-, 333–335, 351, 357, 391, 406, 411

Baldwin, Roger Nash, 232, 301, 312–313

Baldwin, Stanley, 123, 136, 138, 316, 317–318, 346; British pound issue, 237; comments of Ginger Group about, 167, 170; franchise reform promise, 199; and mine worker strike, 172, 176, 182, 188–189; resignation, 126; Simon Commission, 258

Balfour, Arthur James, 21

Bamber, Mary, 68, 110

Band of Hope, 17

Barbusse, Henri, 209, 287, 295, 296

Barton, Nellie, 42

BBC, "Third Programme nation," 449

Beaverbrook, Lord. *See* Aitken, William M. "Max"

Beneš, Edvard, 367, 368

Bentinck, William Henry Cavendish, 198–199

Bevin, Ernest, 228, 238, 317, 370, 491n20; Council of Action for Peace and Reconstruction (COA), 361; foreign office, 414, 429–432; general strike, 176, 181; Minister of labour, 386; United Nations, 436

"Big Blitz," 385–386

Birth control, issue of: Catholic vote and, 202–203; and Labour Party, 200–202; Ministry of Health to local authorities, 203

Blair, Eric Arthur. *See* Orwell, George

Blatchford, Robert Peel Glanville, 21–23, 326

Blum, Leon, 345, 349, 370, 434

Bolshevism, 80–81; British opinion of, 96–97; Wilkinson, complex relationship with, 288; Wilkinson, support for, 79–80; Wilkinson, views on treatment of women in Russia, 97

Bondfield, Margaret Grace, 45–46, 84, 128, 198, 230, 341; in Parliament, 132, 222; privy councillor, 404; TUC General Council, 146–147, 177

Bosanquet, Theodora, 324

Breitscheid, Rudolf, 256

Briand, Aristide, 196

Britain for the British (Blatchford), 21

British Nationality Act of 1948, 157

British Committee for the Relief of the Victims of German Fascism. *See* World Committee for the Relief of the Victims of German Fascism

Brittain, Vera Mary, 243–244, 319–320, 326, 329, 381; Mecklenburgh Square, 160; Women's International League, 225

Brown Book of Hitler Terror, 289–290, 300; Einstein denies involvement, 291–292; Oberfohren memorandum, 289–291

Brüning, Heinrich, 251

Buchanan, George, 139, 230

Committee of Inquiry into the Working and Effects of the Trade Boards Acts, 113–114

Communist International. *See* Comintern

Communist Party of Great Britain (CPGB), 1, 52; creation of, 64; "dictatorship of the proletariat," 56, 80; lack of women's organization, 110; new Communist Women's Conference, 112, 113; ordered to form women's groups, 112; tension with Labour party, 129; Wilkinson, denunciation of, 289; Wilkinson, disappointment in trade union movement, 73; Wilkinson, final split during WWII, 399–400; Wilkinson, rejection of orders from Moscow, 112–113; Wilkinson, quits, 130–131; Wilkinson, support for, 80–82, 106; Wilkinson, vote to deny affiliation with Labour Party, 401; women's organizations vilified, 84

The Communist Solar System (pamphlet), 287, 304

Communist Women's Committee, 106

The Condition of India, 279–280

Conscientious objector. *See* World War I

Consultative Committee to the Board of Education report (1938) (Spens Report), 418

Conze, Edward, 294, 302, 324–325, 327–329, 349

Cook, Arthur J., 171, 173

The Cooperative Employee, 48

Council of Action for Peace and Reconstruction (COA), 361

Courtney, Kathleen D'Olier, 218

CPGB. *See* Communist Party of Great Britain (CPGB)

Crawfurd, (née Jack) Helen, 75, 84, 112, 208, 286–287, 289; in Paris, 77, 80

Cripps, (Richard) Stafford, 352–353, 374, 399, 455; Board of Trade, 414; Chancellor of the Exchequer, 303; Cripps memorandum and expulsion

from Labour Party, 371–373; Wilkinson, disagreements with, 356–357, 370; on education, 425, 441; India and Burma committee, 433; "Peace and Empire" rally, 366; Unity Campaign, 350–351, 353; view on League of Nations, 317, 357; wartime national government, 370–372

Crosland, (Charles) Anthony Raven, 440

Crowdy, Rachel Eleanor, 359–360

CSL. *See* Church Socialist League (CSL)

Curtis Report on children in care (1946), 429

Czechoslovakia. *See* Munich Crisis (1938)

Daily Express (newspaper), 237, 239; Lansbury and Wilkinson articles after Labour defeat, 240

Daily Express, "The Marthas and the Marys," 394

Daily Herald, 169

Daily Mail, Wilkinson's emotion in Parliament, 343

Dalton, (Edward) Hugh Neale, 316, 322–323, 352, 369, 375, 425–428; Chancellor of the Exchequer, 414, 422; on Cripps, Stafford, 371; on education, 441; election prediction, 413; Labour Commission of Enquiry report, 354–355; *New Trends*, 319; Wilkinson's health, 395, 401

Davies, Clement, 452

Davies, Rhys (Rees Vivian), 69, 152; NUDAW, 240–241

Davies, Stella, 12, 14, 56, 59, 122, 124

Defence of the Realm Act (1914), 158

Dickens, Charles John Huffam, 19

The Division Bell Mystery (Wilkinson), 137, 228; serialized in *Daily Express*, 239–240

Dollan (née Moir), Agnes Johnston, 85, 203

Dowson, Oscar, 216–217

Doyle, Arthur, 34

Duchêne, Gabrielle, 77, 209, 248–250

Duff, Sheila Grant, 324
Dutt, Rajani Palme, 33, 82, 203, 289, 370; University Socialist Federation (USF), 79–80; Women's International League (WIL) speaker, 84

The Economic Consequences of Mr. Churchill (Keynes), 221
The Economic Consequences of the Peace (Keynes), 221
Ede, James Chuter, 370, 413, 419, 421; Home Office, 415, 423, 440
Eden, Anthony, 332, 368, 369, 370, 406
Education: British educational system prior to WWII, 416–417; church schools funding issue, 416, 419; curricular reform and class distinctions, 439–445; Curtis Report on children in care, 429; direct grant schools, 416, 419–420, 438; emergency training colleges for teacher education, 424; grammar schools, abolition or continuation of, 440–441, 444–446; need for additional teachers, 422–424; need for new schools, 424–425; poverty, hunger and, 427–428
Education Act (1944), 415–416, 420–421; equal pay provision voted down, 504n28; Labour support, 438; social service provision in, 419, 426–427; universal secondary education, 418–419
Education Act (1946), clothing, medical provision for children, 428–429
Edward VIII, King, 346
EFF. *See* Election Fighting Fund (EFF)
Einstein, Albert, 234, 290–292
Election Fighting Fund (EFF), 26, 31, 39–40
Elliott, W. E., 20
Emergency Powers Act (EPA), 191
Employment and unemployment: apple selling, 233, 481n19; concern for unemployed in Jarrow, 336; situation in 1931 United States, 232–233, 481n16; Wilkinson,

speeches on unemployment insurance, 235–236; Unemployment Insurance Act (1924), 140; Unemployment Insurance Bill (1926), 166; Unemployment Insurance (No. 3) Bill (Anomalies Act, 1931), 230, 237
Engels, Friedrich, Little Ireland, 8–9
Equal pay advocacy, 41–42, 45–46, 48; equal compensation denied during WWII, 396–397; Wilkinson, support in Parliament, 150–151, 335–336
The Jewish Forward, donation to striking miners, 189

Fabian, Dora, 315
Fabian Colonial Bureau, "Memorial on African Policy," 225
Fabian Research Department (FRD), 49–51, 55; fun, games and songs in, 56–57. *See also* Labour Research Department (LRD)
Fabian Society, 25; Control of Industry Committee, 51; Glasgow, Oxford and Cambridge branches, 33; summer school at Barrow House, 57; summer school revue mocking political violence, 102–103, 169n15.
Fairhurst, Susie, 29, 34
Fascism, Wilkinson's fight against: concern after trip through Italy, 166, 475n4; International Peace Campaign rally for Czechoslovakia, 367–368; Nazi involvement in Reichstag fire, 292; observations in Germany, 283–285; "Peace and Empire" rally with Nehru (1938), 366; publications on threat of fascism, 294; support for League of Nations, 357; work with Labour Party on, 353; World Conference for Action with Nehru, 366. *See also* Women's Committee against War and Fascism
Fascism and anti-fascism: Amsterdam-Pleyel movement against, 249–250; anti German fascism campaign, 245, 248; Cliveden group of Germanophiles, 245; Communists in Germany, 255;

Parliamentary Labour Party (PLP), 375

Guild Socialism, 53–55; early idealism of, 81; and feminism, 55–56. *See also* National Guilds League (NGL)

Hallsworth, Joe, 69, 73
Hardie, (James) Keir, 23
Hare, William Francis, 296, 298
Haverfield, Eveline, 41
Henderson, Arthur, 64, 109, 205, 229, 238, 335; Labour Foreign Secretary, 16
Herbison, Margaret McCrorie (Peggy), 445
Hire-Purchase Bill (1937), 362–364; *March of Time* newsreel on, 364
Hire Purchase Trade Association (HPTA), 363
History of British Trade Unionism (Webbs), 50
Hitler, Adolph, 361; and anti-Semitism, 447; and Communists, 400; foreign policy of, 33, 326; and Lloyd George, 361; and Munich Crisis, 367–368, named Chancellor, 282; Nazi party, 254–255, 325; and Poland, 373, 380; Reichstag fire and Communist conspiracy, 281; Voigt's opinion of, 251–252; Wilkinson, desire to defeat, 284, 288; Wilkinson, opinion of, 354, 357, 362, 399, 441
Hobson, John Atkinson, 33, 399
Hobson, S.J., 52
Hollywood Anti- Nazi League, 293
Holtby, Winifred, 150, 243–245, 276
Hopkinson, Diana, 323–324, 336, 339, 351
Horrabin (née Batho), Winifred, 177–178, 212, 225, 242, 277; Communist women's committee, 112; in London, 160; in Moscow, 144
Horrabin, James Francis (Frank), 168, 177, 181; cartoonist, 57, 190; illustrator for *Lansbury's Labour*

Weekly, 169; and imperial issues, 260; LRD executive committee, 110; and memorial on Africa policy, 225; *Plebs* (journal), 143–144, 168–170, 174; and Socialist League, 303; and Wilkinson, 168–169, 177, 212, 241, 262, 294
Horsburgh, Florence, 394, 397, 402, 405–406
Housing Bill (1930), slum clearance and housing subsidies, 224
Hull, William Winstanley, 234
Hutchinson, Gertrude, 56–57
Huxley, Aldous Leonard, 329
Huxley, Julian Sorell, 18–19, 231; UNESCO preparatory committee, 435
Huxley, Thomas Henry, 19, 131

Ickes, Harold, 314
IFTU. *See* International Federation of Trade Unions (IFTU)
ILP. *See* Independent Labour Party (ILP)
Imperialism (Hobson), 32–33
INC. *See* Indian National Congress (INC)
Independent Labour Party (ILP), 22–24, 31–32; Wilkinson, membership in, 26, 205. *See also* Glasier, Katherine Bruce
India League, 3, 225, 260; Wilkinson, hosting Nehru, 365–366; Wilkinson, sisters' role in, 260–261; Wilkinson, Untouchables speech, 264–265
India League, fact-finding mission (1931), 262–276; Ahmedabad and labour conditions, 274; British army and Ordinance rule, 271–273, 277; *The Condition of India*, 279–280; Hindu Muslim discord, 273–274; peasants' homespun and poverty, 271; prison conditions, Cannamore jail, 267; prison conditions, Hooghly facility, 268; prison conditions, Lucknow and Rae Bareli jails, 275–276; visit with Gandhi during his fast, 270–271; welcome home party, 277; Wilkinson, Untouchables speech, 266

India League of America, 406
Indian National Congress (INC), 2,
    261; call for self-rule, 260; national
    civil disobedience campaign,
    258–259; seeking full dominion
    status for support in war effort,
    377–378; Wilkinson, support for,
    277–278, 280. *See also* Second Round
    Table Conference (RTC, 1931)
Indian Parade (Wilkinson), 279
India self-government, 4, 206, 207;
    India and Burma Committee and
    religious divisions, 433–434; Simon
    Commission, 258–259; Untouch-
    ables, prejudice against, 265;
    Wilkinson, support for, 378–379;
    Wilkinson on women's rights in,
    259–260. *See also* Second Round
    Table Conference (RTC, 1931)
The Industrial System (Hobson), 33
Inter-allied consultative committee
    of socialist organizations, 404
International Committee of Women
    for Permanent Peace (ICWPP), 58.
    See also Women's International
    League for Peace and Freedom
    (WILPF)
International Federation of Trade
    Unions (IFTU), 332; Special
    European Conference on Spain, 333;
    trade union organization reform,
    92–93
International Peace Campaign, 366;
    support for Czechoslovakia, 367
International Women's Suffrage
    Alliance (IWSA), 196; issue of
    nationality after marriage to
    foreign nationals, 215; Paris
    conference, 196
Ireland: loyalist nationalist conflict
    in local affairs, 66–67; Wilkinson
    and WIL mission, 85–86. *See also*
    American Commission on Condi-
    tions in Ireland
Iron Front: official Labour Party
    statement, 253; Wilkinson, Berlin
    event, 255–256; Wilkinson, speeches
    on behalf of, 250, 252

Isherwood, Christopher William
    Bradshaw, 251
Italy, invasion of Abyssinia, 315–316
IWSA. *See* International Women's
    Suffrage Alliance (IWSA)

Jacobs, Aletta, 75
Jagger, John, 69–70; AUCE president,
    45–47; Lisburn shopworkers' strike,
    67; Morrison's parliamentary
    private secretary, 397–398; NUDAW
    delegation to Soviet Union, 330;
    pro-India and colonial affairs, 225,
    260; Wilkinson, support for, 94,
    122–123, 127, 262, 375, 397–398;
    WIL speaker, 74, 118
Jameson, Margaret Ethel (Storm), 329
Jankowski, Marie, 284, 295
Jarrow, Wilkinson parliamentary
    candidate, 227, 281, 383
Jarrow Crusade, 3–4, 337–344; Labour
    Party rejection of, 340–341;
    monetary crisis, 228; Unemploy-
    ment Assistance Board during, 343
Jarvis, (Joseph) John, 343–344
Jewish refugees and victims of Nazism,
    4, 283, 287, 293, 315
Joad, Cyril Edwin Mitchinson, 57,
    464n73
Joint Committee on Women in the
    Civil Service, 150–151
Jowett, Frederick William, 24–25
Joynson-Hicks, William, Home
    Secretary, 21, 146, 149, 172, 198

Katz, Otto, 285–287, 291–296, 298,
    306, 360–362, 365
Keynes, John Maynard, 159, 220–221,
    228, 238–239, 399
Koestler, Arthur, 285–286, 288, 290,
    293
Kollontai, Alexandra, People's
    Commissar for Social Welfare,
    99–100
Krupskaya, Nadezhda, 100

Labour and the Nation (1929 party
    manifesto), 204, 303; disarmament

and international trade in, 206;
India self-government, 206;
women's issues in, 205
Labour Leader, 42
Labour Party: 1934 Southport
conference, 305–306, 308, 309;
1935 Brighton conference and
Italy-Abyssinia crisis, 315–317; 1935
election loss, lessons from, 322;
1936 Edinburgh conference,
rejection of aid to Jarrow Crusade,
340; 1937 Bournemouth conference, Labour Commission of
Enquiry report, 354; 1937 Bournemouth conference, rejection of
nonintervention in Spain, 348;
1939 Southport conference, 374;
1945 Blackpool conference,
independent party post WWII,
406–409; 1945 Blackpool conference, programme of socialist goals,
409; Attlee Prime Minister, 414;
bellicose toward Italy, commitment to disarmament, 317–318; *The
Communist Solar System* (pamphlet),
287, 304; disassociation with LAI,
210–211; disavowal by party of visit
to Asturias, 304; Geneva conference
of socialist students, 79–80; and
(German) Social Democratic Party,
253; membership in women's
organizations discouraged, 84;
NUWSS support, 40; Phillips, Chief
Woman Officer, 62; policy priorities
in *Labour and the Nation* (Tawney,
pamphlet), 204, 303; Popular Front
coalition against fascism, efforts
for, 369–372; Popular Front of
Labour against fascism, 357; post
WWI support for organized labour,
65; rearmament debate, 355–356;
Relief Committee addition to list
of Communist front organizations,
306; Socialist League in, 303, 317,
352; Spain Campaign Committee
(SCC), 348; Supplement on Banking
and Currency Policy, 204–205;
Westminster dominion Labour
parties conference, 404; Wilkinson,
efforts to replace Attlee with
Morrison, 374–376; Wilkinson, BBC
broadcast on planned economy
post WWII, 412–414
Labour Party, National Executive
Committee (NEC), 119–120,
203–204, 212; agreement on
coalition under Churchill, 380;
Cripps memorandum, 371–372;
Wilkinson, elected vice-chairman,
then chairman, 401–402; independent party post-WWII, 402;
Wilkinson, views on economics,
302–304; Wilkinson, vote to deny
CPGB affiliation, 401
Labour Party, women's issues in:
annual women members meeting,
61–63, 119–120; female representatives to National Executive Committee (NEC), 119–120; Labour
representation for women, 39;
Manchester Labour Women's
Advisory Council (MLWAC),
119–120; National Executive
Committee (NEC) seats in, 203;
party platform in 1929, 205;
Standing Joint Committee of
Industrial Women's Organizations
(SJCIWO), 120–121; Wilkinson
and Annot Robinson role in,
119, 470n42; and women's suffrage,
31
Labour Publishing Company (LPC),
108; *Bolo Book*, 109–110; *Defense of
Terrorism* (Trotsky), 108–109
Labour Research Department (LRD),
55, 106, 108–109; Wilkinson, ties to,
143. *See also* Fabian Research
Department (FRD)
LAI. *See* League Against Imperialism
(LAI)
Lansbury, George, 183, 240, 317, 329;
Christian Socialist, 96, 108, 208;
League Against Imperialism
president, 210; pro-Indian self
government, 207–208, 260. *See also
Lansbury's Labour Weekly*

Front resolution against fascism, 357; support for trade boards before Cave Committee, 114–116; support for Wilkinson for MP, 124, 131–132; Wilkinson, career-long work in, 144, 242; Wilkinson, criticized during WWII, 397–398. *See also* Amalgamated Union of Cooperative Employees (AUCE)

National Union of Societies for Equal Citizenship (NUSEC), 147; formerly National Union of Women's Suffrage Societies (NUWSS), 196

National Union of Women's Suffrage Societies (NUWSS), 26–27; "Conciliation Bill" and Labour candidates, 39; electoral organization, 38; support for Labour candidates, 31; "Women's War Interest Committee" (WWIC), 41, 48

NCLC. *See* National Council of Labour Colleges (NCLC)

NEC. *See* Labour Party, National Executive Committee (NEC)

Nehru, Jawaharlal, 261, 265, 275, 378–379, 434; Czechoslovakia visit to Sudetenland, 367; India League, 277–278; Indian National Congress (INC), 209–210, 289; visit to Britain, 4, 324–325, 365–367

Nehru, Sarojini, 260

Newbold, (John Turner) Walton, 32–33, 41; in Manchester, 49; Manchester University Fabian Society, 33 35; support for Wilkinson for MP, 132; Wilkinson, continued contact with, 105, 123, 143–144; Wilkinson, engagement to, 37–38, 57–58

Newbold, Marjorie, 84

Newitt, Hilary, 350

New Leader, Wilkinson article on bank nationalization, 205

New Statesman, 50

New Trends in Socialism, Wilkinson essay, "Labour and the Middle Classes," 318–319

NGL. *See* National Guilds League (NGL)

Noel, Conrad Le Despenser Roden, 183, 210, 260; "Red Vicar," 24–25

NUDAW. *See* National Union of Distributive and Allied Workers (NUDAW)

NUSEC. *See* National Union of Societies for Equal Citizenship (NUSEC)

NUWSS. *See* National Union of Women's Suffrage Societies (NUWSS)

Oberfohren, Ernst, 290

Old Vic Theatre School, 449–450

Orage, Alfred R., 52

Orwell, George, 26, 182, 349

Owens College. *See* University of Manchester

Pacifism. *See* antiwar movement

Pandit, Vijaya Lakshmi, 406

Pankhurst, (née Goulden) Emmeline and Christabel Harriette, 30, 198; militant suffragist movement, 40

Pankhurst, Sylvia, 62, 134, 206, 287

Parliament, 2; "Ginger Group" in Parliamentary Labour Party, 167, 303; Jarrow petition, 342–343; King's Speech, 137, 138–139, 140; Labour Party, increase in women MP's, 221–222; Parliamentary Committee for Spain, 358; "Spain Lobby," 334–335; vote of no confidence for Chamberlain's government, 380

Parliamentary elections: 1924 "Red Scare" campaign, 133, 221; 1924 Zinoviev Letter affair, 146; 1929 election, 220–221; 1931 Labour loss, 225, 240; 1935 national government majority, 321, 331; 1945 election, 411–413

Parliamentary Labour Party (PLP), "Ginger Group," 167, 303

Peace Pledge Union (PPU), 329; Wilkinson, report on German and Italian role in Spain, 333; Wilkinson, resignation from, 334

Social and Political Union member, 40; "Women's War Interest Committee" (WWIC) secretary, 41

Robinson, Wright, 69–70, 114–115, 124, 125, 128, 357; Manchester City Council, 121–122, 127

Roosevelt, Eleanor, 189, 314

Roosevelt, Franklin Delano, 312–313, 345; United Nations plan, 404

ROSLA, raising of the school leaving age to fifteen, 421–426

Roy, Manabendra Nath, 143, 206–207

Rubenstein, David, 440

Russell (née Black), Dora Winifred, 203

Russia, condition after the revolution, 95–96, 97–98

Saklatvala, Shapurji, 123, 206–208, 287

Samuel, Herbert Louis, 172, 173, 180–181

Samuel, Samuel, 199, 200

Searchlight on Spain (Atholl), 365

Second Round Table Conference (RTC, 1931), 259–261

Servants of India Society, 264

Shaw, George Bernard, 50, 51, 134, 223

Sheppard, Richard Herbert, 329, 334

Simon, André. *See* Katz, Otto

Six Point Group: equal compensation denied during WWII, 396; threat of fascism to women, 284; "white list" for women's rights, 151

SJCIWO. *See* Standing Joint Committee of Industrial Women's Organizations (SJCIWO)

Slade, Madeleine (Mirabehn), 262, 263

Snowden, Ethel, 78, 84, 96, 109

Snowden, Philip, 109, 137, 204, 228–230, 239, 302

Sollmann, Wilhelm, Social Democratic Reichstag Minister, 283

Sorensen, Reginald William, 377–378

A "Sort of War" in Ireland (pamphlet), 86–87

South Riding (Holtby), inspired by Wilkinson, 243–244

Soviet Communism: A New Civilization (Webbs), 50

Soviet Union, Wilkinson critical of dictatorial methods, 349–350

Spain: Aid Spain movement, 332, 358; British blockade of democracy, 347–348; Civil War and impact on international politics, 330–331; defeat of fascism priority over Socialism, 349, 351; Indian Ambulance Unit and foodstuffs sent, 366–367; Manuel Azaña's centre-left government, 327, 331, 359; miners' uprising, Asturias, 297–298; nonintervention by Britain and France, 333–334; political situation (1933), 295–298; Republican cause, 4, 299, 331–332. *See also* World Committee for the Relief of the Victims of German Fascism

Spain Today (Conze), 327, 329

Spanish Medical Aid (SMA), Wilkinson on executive committee, 330, 332

Spencer, Victor (Peter), 333

Spens Report. *See* Consultative Committee to the Board of Education report (1938) (Spens Report)

Stalin, Joseph, 97, 258, 307, 349; Wilkinson, opinion of, 248, 288–289, 399–400

Standing Joint Committee of Industrial Women's Organizations (SJCIWO), 45, 62, 120–121, 145, 183

Starr, Ellen, 92

Starr, Kathleen, 184, 185, 196

Starr, Mark, 107, 184

Stewart-Murray, Katharine Marjory, 134, 135–136, 300–301, 334, 359

Strauss, George Russell, 201, 372, 413

Suffrage and Labour Club, Ancoats, 39

Sunday Referee, "Hitler Prepares to March on Rhine," 326

socialist students, 79–80; strike of female sweated labourers, 35; Wilkinson, degree conferred, 36, 37; Wilkinson, examination in political economy, 32–33; Wilkinson on executive committee, 49; Wilkinson, study of international affairs, 33

Women's International League for
Peace and Freedom (WILPF) *(continued)*
    issue of nationality after marriage
    to foreign nationals, 159, 215–216;
    mixed views on Versailles peace
    terms, 77; new name of International
    Committee of Women for Permanent
    Peace, 76–77; Prague conference
    (1929), 216; Prague conference, Annie
    and Ellen delegates to, 247–248;
    Wilkinson's radical role, Zurich
    congress and, 75–78; Wilkinson,
    speech against conciliation and
    arbitration, 249; Zurich congress and
    Wilkinson radical role, 75–78
Women's issues: equal rights or
    protective legislation split, 150;
    nationality after marriage to foreign
    nationals, 21–22, 156–159, 215–217;
    silk tax (silk stockings), 156–157;
    state pensions for women, 152–155;
    Wilkinson, rejection of "women's
    agenda" at UN conference, 405–406
Women's Peace Crusade (WPC),
    218–219
Women's peace movement, 26, 83;
    Wilkinson article on international
    peace, 215; WIL mission to Ireland
    (1920), 86–87. *See also* Women's
    International League for Peace and
    Freedom (WILPF)
Women's Social and Political Union
    (WSPU), 30, 40
Women's suffrage, 31; class as well as
    gender issue, 196; "Conciliation Bill"
    defeat, 39; equalization of franchise,
    196, 197–200; Wilkinson, in France
    for IWSA, 196; vote to women over
    30, 61–63; Wilkinson, support in
    Parliament, 140, 147–150, 473n35;
    Wilkinson's strong support for, 40.

See also Manchester Society for
    Women's Suffrage (MSWS); National
    Union of Women's Suffrage Societies
    (NUWSS)
Wood, Eliza, 9, 10
Wood, George, 11
Wood, L. Hollingsworth, 90
Workers' Weekly, lawsuit against, 129
World Committee for the Relief of the
    Victims of German Fascism, 209,
    285–286, 289–291, 306–307,
    490n84; British Relief Committee,
    question of Comintern conspiracy,
    286–288; Spanish branch, 295–296;
    Wilkinson, fundraising for, 294
World War I, 40–41; No Conscription
    Fellowship, 41; NUWSS equal pay
    for women push, 41–42; post war
    monetary impact, 65–66; Versailles
    settlement disappointments, 64;
    Wilkinson, concern for impact on
    women, 41, 63
World War II: *Daily Worker* banned
    by government, 397; proscription
    on strike actions, 397; Wilkinson,
    view of women's role, 393–396;
    Wilkinson accused of moving to the
    right, 399; Wilkinson, personal
    fire-watching at Dolphin Square,
    396; Wilkinson praises "war
    socialism," 403. *See also* Civil
    defence
WPC. *See* Women's Peace Crusade
    (WPC)
Wrum, Mathilde, 315
WSPU. *See* Women's Social and
    Political Union (WSPU)

Zetkin, Clara, 111
Zilliacus, Konni, 323
Zinoviev, Grigori, 101, 146, 330